European Distance and E-Learning Network Annual Conference (EDEN 2021)

Lessons from a Pandemic for the Future of the Education

Short Papers

Madrid, Spain
21-24 June 2021

Volume 1 of 2

Editors:

Sandra Kucina Softic
András Szucs
Judit Komuves
Gabor Roman

ISBN: 978-1-7138-3702-2

Printed from e-media with permission by:

Curran Associates, Inc.
57 Morehouse Lane
Red Hook, NY 12571

Some format issues inherent in the e-media version may also appear in this print version.

European Distance and E-Learning Network (EDEN)
Budapest University of Technology & Economics
H-1111 Budapest, Egry J. u.1.
Hungary

Phone: +36 1 463 1628
Fax: +36 1 463 1858

secretariat@eden-online.org

Additional copies of this publication are available from:

Curran Associates, Inc.
57 Morehouse Lane
Red Hook, NY 12571 USA
Phone: 845-758-0400
Fax: 845-758-2633
Email: curran@proceedings.com
Web: www.proceedings.com

SHORT PAPER BOOK

European Distance and E-Learning Network (EDEN)

Lessons from a Pandemic for the Future of the Education

EDEN 2021 Online Annual Conference

hosted by

Universidad Nacional de Education a Distancia (UNED), Madrid, Spain

21-24 June 2021

Edited by

Sandra Kucina Softic, András Szucs
on behalf of the European Distance and E-Learning Network

European Distance and E-Learning Network, 2021

Lessons from a Pandemic for the Future of the Education
Short Paper Book
2021 Annual Conference | Madrid, 21-24 June, 2021

Published by the European Distance and E-Learning Network

Editors:
Sandra Kucina Softic
András Szucs

Editorial co-ordination:
Judit Komuves
Gabor Roman

EDEN Secretariat, c/o Budapest University of Technology and Economics
H-1111 Budapest, Egry J. u. 1, Hungary
Tel: (36) 1 463 1628, 463 2537
E-mail: secretariat@eden-online.org
http://www.eden-online.org

The European Distance and E-Learning Network is co-operating with EDEN Digital Learning Europe MTÜ (Estonia), in order to sustain the legacy of the EDEN Association brand after the United Kingdom having left the EU, to ensure continuity of services and activities for the benefit of the European academic and professional community in open, distance and online learning.

Supported by the Erasmus+ Programme of the European Union
The publication reflects the authors' view, the EACEA and the European Commission are not responsible for any use that may be made of the information it contains.

Introduction

For the EDEN association and its members, the EDEN Annual Conference is the biggest and most The gradual transition from traditional classroom-based education to online teaching and learning has been accelerated by the global crisis caused by the COVID-19 pandemic. Since it started, our way of life, work, and education have been irrevocably changed. When we look back upon this extraordinary period in our history, we see that this crisis has forced educators to reappraise their roles, professional practices, and beliefs. As a consequence, teachers and students have been forced online, highlighting a range of skills and knowledge that were sorely in demand. There has been an inevitable need for educational institutions to make key strategic decisions on how to provide both access to relevant tools, support in their use, and training for both educators and learners, so that teaching staff can engage online with their students in a meaningful way.

EDEN has a long history of supporting educators in online and distance education, providing a forum for discussion, learning, and refinement of best practices in this area. This pandemic has been no exception. Since the first national lockdowns started in European countries back in early 2020, a series of initiatives have been launched to support EDEN members during this crisis. The interest shown by members for these initiatives has been very high, with large numbers of participants and a clear desire to share and reach consensus.

This year's conference is, therefore, intended as a continuation of the efforts of EDEN to support educators by providing a space to explore the issues and insights that have emerged during the COVID-19 pandemic. It is intended to enable educators to share their experiences and best practices related to a range of topics relevant to this situation. These topics furthermore include issues such as:

- learner-centeredness in education;
- the continued evolution of online and distance learning;
- transitioning from emergency remote teaching to online learning;
- digital preparedness, digital literacy, and digital citizenship;
- the continued adoption of Artificial Intelligence;
- methodological advances;
- potentiating health and wellness in online education;
- and non-traditional assessment solutions.

Not only does this conference provide attendees with the perfect opportunity to explore this range of topics, but it also provides us with a space to reflect upon the role that online and distance education will have after the pandemic. As noted in our webinar series #covid19 #onlinetogether Education in a time of a pandemic, fully online education on a global scale is unprecedented in the history of education. Today we are talking about the "new normal" and "future normal". What will this future look like? How can EDEN members help to shape it and bring their insights to bear?

Andras Szucs	Timothy Read	Sandra Kucina Softic
EDEN Secretary General	National Distance Education University (UNED), Spain	EDEN President

Acknowledgement and thanks are given to the

Chairs

Sandra Kucina Softic, EDEN President, University of Zagreb, Croatia
Timothy Read, EDEN Vice President, UNED, Madrid, Spain

Scientific Program Committee

Alberto Andújar, University of Almería (UAL), Spain
Alfredo Soeiro, University of Porto, Portugal
Ana Ibañez, National Distance Education University (UNED), Spain
Andras Szucs, EDEN, United Kingdom
Antonio Pareja, University of Almería (UAH), Spain
Beatriz Sedano, National Distance Education University (UNED), Spain
Blanca García Riaza, Universidad de Salamanca (USAL), Spain
Covadonga Rodrigo, National Distance Education University (UNED), Spain
Cristina Calle, Complutense University of Madrid (UCM), Spain
Denise Whitelock, The Open University, United Kingdom
Diana Andone, Politehnica University of Timisoara (UPT), Romania
Don Olcott, Jr., Global Consultant, Romania
Ebba Ossiannilsson, Swedish Association of Distance Education, Sweden
Elena Barcena, National Distance Education University (UNED), Spain
Elena Caldirola, University of Pavia, Italy
Elena Martín-Monje, National Distance Education University (UNED), Spain
Ferenc Tatrai, EDEN, United Kingdom
Francisco Iniesto, The Open University (OUUK), United Kingdom
Helga Dorner, Eötvös Loránd University, Hungary
Ines Gil Jaurena, National Distance Education University (UNED), Spain
Jesús Garcia Laborda, University of Alcalá de Henares, Spain
Jorge Arús, Complutense University of Madrid (UCM), Spain
José Luis Delgado, National Distance Education University (UNED), Spain
Josep Maria Duart, Open University of Catalonia (UOC), Spain
Lisa Marie Blaschke, Learnlife, Barcelona, Spain
María Dolores Castrillo, National Distance Education University (UNED), Spain
María Jordano, National Distance Education University (UNED), Spain
Mark Brown, National Institute for Digital Learning, Dublin City University (DCU), Ireland
Mercedes Sanz, Jaume I University (UJI), Spain
Rebecca Galley, The Open University (OUUK), United Kingdom
Ulf-Daniel Ehlers, Co-Operative State University Baden-Wurttemberg (DHBW), Germany
Vlad Mihaescu, Politehnica University of Timisoara (UPT), Romania
Wim Van Petegem, Katholieke Universiteit Leuven (KUL), Belgium

TABLE OF CONTENTS

PROJECTS PRESENTED IN THE SYNERGY SESSION

Lessons from a Pandemic for the Future of Education
Short Paper Book of the European Distance and E-Learning Network (EDEN)
2021 Annual Conference | Madrid, 21-24 June, 2021
ISBN 978-615-5511-31-8

DIGITAL COMPETENCE FOR CITIZENS: UPDATING AND VALIDATION OF THE ACTIC FRAMEWORK TO THE NEW DIGITAL CONTEXT

Miquel Àngel Prats, FPCEE Blanquerna, Teresa Romeu, Universitat Oberta de Catalunya, Montse Guitert, Universitat Oberta de Catalunya, Elena Sofia Ojando, FPCEE Blanquerna, Jordi Simón, FPCEE Blanquerna, Spain

Abstract

The Catalan Accreditation of Competences in Information and Communication Technologies, ACTIC (2009) takes the guidelines of the European Union and the OECD on learning by competencies and was the prelude to the future definition of DigComp. The aim of the article is to present the new version of the ACTIC (2020) developed by researchers from the Universitat Oberta de Catalunya and the Fundació Blanquerna of the Universitat Ramon Llull, at the initiative of the Department of Digital Policies and Policies and Public Administration of the Generalitat de Catalunya.

The research process has been carried out by a group of experts who have validated the new framework. Through a mixed method structured in 3 phases, the results of the study present the updated version of the ACTIC aligned with Digcomp that is specified in the definition of 5 competence areas, 19 competencies, 3 levels of achievement and a total of 233 indicators.

These results allow us to conclude that three key dimensions have emerged that facilitate awareness and empowerment of citizens on digital issues and that will allow their accreditation and recognition in the work environment: (a) the identity dimension, focused on participatory issues, social, ethical and civic; (b) the dimension of citizen competence learning and, (c) the dimension of technological evolution and digital autonomy of citizens.

Introduction

The Digital Revolution has left us immersed in the Information Era at a speed and a globality that breaks the sequence of paradigm shifts described by Khun (1962). On this occasion, the Third Industrial Revolution shakes the period of transition between paradigms. Information and communication technologies are extended everywhere at all levels of social relationship, and the science involved in their understanding seeks to anchor the new paradigm. It is in the liquid and hyper-connected society described by Bauman (2003) and Castells (2006) respectively, where we now have to learn to live. And that implies exercising a citizenship with the competences to understand and manage the implications of our access to technology.

The definition of digital competence for citizens includes skills such as the incorporation of technologies in different personal spheres, incorporating attitudes such as the critical and responsible use of digital technologies, or promoting privacy and respect for the community:

> *"Digital Competence is the set of knowledge, skills, attitudes, abilities, strategies, and awareness that are required when using ICT and digital media to perform tasks; solve problems; communicate; manage information; collaborate; create and share content; and build knowledge effectively, efficiently, appropriately, critically, creatively, autonomously, flexibly, ethically, reflectively for work, leisure, participation, learning, and socialising" (Ferrari, 2012; p.30).*

Before this definition, the Catalan Accreditation of Competences in Information and Communication Technologies (ACTIC) was born in 2009, which is based on the guidelines of the European Union and the OECD on learning by competences and is a prelude to the future definition of DigComp (Ferrari et al., 2013), the common European framework on Digital Competition. This framework referred to as DigComp was updated in 2016 with the DigComp 2.0 version (Vuoraki et al., 2016).

The project to update and validate the ACTIC framework is supported by DigComp and is an initiative of the Department of Digital Policies and Policies and Public Administration of the Generalitat de Catalunya developed jointly by the Universitat Oberta de Catalunya (UOC) and the Fundació Blanquerna of the Ramon Llull University.

Since its origins, the contents and indicators of the ACTIC have been periodically reviewed and updated to improve the clarity and updating of its contents. Its objectives have always been: (a) to promote the digital training of citizens to achieve an inclusive, dynamic and competitive knowledge society; (b) contribute to the promotion of competences training in the use of ICT; and (c) officially certify digital competence to facilitate job access, professional promotion, access to virtual learning platforms, among others in the Catalan context.

The high speed of ICT development and its global implementation requires its profound updating and transformation. It is from this perspective that the update of the ACTIC begins to better meet the needs of digital citizenship in today's society. Based on the literature review, the following key elements are defined on which to base the update of the ACTIC:

1. Transversal vocation.
2. Digcomp alignment.
3. More competence and less instrumental evaluation.
4. Reinforcement of attitudinal, ethical, well-being and safety issues.
5. Enhancement of citizen participation in the transformation of the digital society.
6. Incorporation of digital autonomy.
7. Inclusion of data analysis, exploitation and visualization with digital tools.

Based on these elements, the research focuses on the following questions: what competence areas, competences, indicators and levels of achievement do the citizens of Catalonia require to be digitally competent? And more specifically: what are those digital competences that favour citizen participation?

In this way, the main objective of the project has been to develop a new accreditation framework for digital competence in Catalonia based on the key elements indicated. In this research, the process of generation and validation of the new ACTIC version is presented through the participation of a group of experts, who have configured the new framework in 5 competence areas that group 19 competences, for whose evaluation 233 indicators have been defined.

Methodology

To carry out the process of validation and updating of the new version, ACTIC is committed to a mixed method (Creswell et al., 2010) that is structured in 3 phases: (a) Definition of competence areas, competences and achievement indicators that It includes a previous documentary research work that bases the definition of the new framework for the development of competence areas, competences and indicators and levels of achievement; (b) Validation by judges of the competence areas, competences and indicators and levels (c) Updated version of the ACTIC. Each of them are described below:

Phase 1 – Definition of competence areas, competences, indicators and levels of achievement

The criteria adopted to analyse the selected frameworks have been: (a) identify the main competences developed as a whole, (b) assess the coherence of vision and competences developed within each framework, (c) establish the substantial differences and key similarities between the selected frames and (d) identification of missing elements, if applicable. Once the competence areas and competencies have been established, the group of Researchers formulates a set of indicators. Following the definition of Roegiers (2005) an indicator is a concrete indication, a precise index, both qualitative and quantitative that specifies and makes operational an evaluation criterion. In the case of ACTIC, between three and six qualitative and complementary indicators are formulated by level of acquisition for each of the 19 competences.

Phase 2 – Validation of the competence areas, competences, indicators and levels of achievement

Once the proposal of competence areas, competences and indicators has been generated, the validation process is carried out at two levels, as shown in Table 1. On the one hand, the transversal validation focused on the competence areas, competences, keywords and level proposal. On the other hand, a specific validation, where different members of the group of experts in a corresponding area are classified by areas. Validation is carried out through six validation questionnaires (one for each of the five areas and one for the cross-sectional evaluation) that are accompanied by an explanatory video of the proposal and a PDF document that incorporates all of the indicators, ordered by areas of competence and competences.

For cross-sectional validation, the questionnaire asks to evaluate the competence areas, competences and levels based on three factors: (a) from the point of view of the formulation: if the wording of the areas and competences is clear, concrete and with a language adequate, (b) from the point of view of coherence: if the competences are consistent with the corresponding area, and (c) from the point of view of applicability: if the competence is important and applicable to citizens.

For the specific validation, the questionnaires ask to evaluate each set of indicators based on three factors: (a) from the point of view of the formulation: if the wording of the indicators is clear, concrete and with an appropriate language, (b) from the point of view of coherence: if the indicators are coherent within each level of each competence, and (c) from the point of view of evaluability: if the indicators are easily evaluable.

The answers of the experts consulted by professional profile of each one of the areas, as well as the cross-sectional validation, obtaining a 66.7% participation.

Phase 3 – Final validation of the ACTIC

Finally, the ACTIC Advisory Commission as a regulatory body for the accreditation of ICT competencies and which is established based on Decree 89/2009 DOGC, carried out a final validation. This committee is made up of 19 members responsible for different areas of the Administration, the business and trade union world, as well as other professionals with an outstanding knowledge of ICT and their participation and involvement in the digital society.

Conclusions

The result of this project is materialized in the definition of digital competence for the citizens of Catalonia based on 5 competence areas, 19 competences, 3 levels and their corresponding indicators that answer the research question.

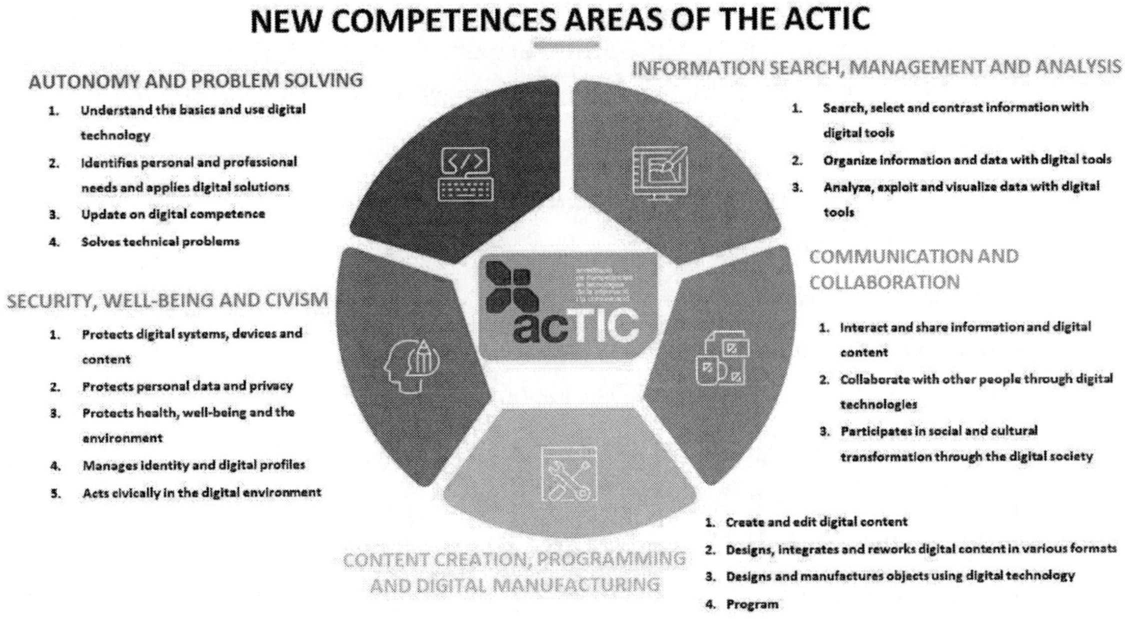

Figure 1. Map of competence areas and competencies of ACTIC

Finally, it is found that this study is key in the current context, accelerated even if possible by the pandemic and the digitization needs of citizens to offer an accreditation framework and to reduce the digital divide.

References

Area Moreira, M. (2014). La alfabetización digital y la formación de la ciudadanía del siglo XXI. *Revista Integra Educativa, 7*(3), 21-33. Retrieved February 24, 2021, from http://www.scielo.org.bo/scielo.php?script=sci_arttext&pid=S1997-40432014000300002&lng=es&tlng=es

Area, M., & Pessoa, T. (2012). De lo sólido a lo líquido: Las nuevas alfabetizaciones ante los cambios culturales de la Web 2.0. *Comunicar, XIX*(38), 13-20. http://dx.doi.org/10.3916/C38-2011-02-01

Bacigalupo, M., Kampylis, P., Punie, Y., & van den Brande, G. (2016). *EntreComp: The Entrepreneurship Competence Framework.* Luxembourg: Publication Office of the European Union. EUR 27939 EN. doi:10.2791/5938844

Bauman, Z. (2003). *Modernidad Líquida.* Fondo de cultura económica.

Castells, M. (ed.) (2006). *La sociedad red: una visión global.* Alianza Editorial.

Creswell, J. W., Plano Clark, V. L., Gutmann, M. L., & Hanson, W. E. (2010). Advanced mixed methods research designs. In A. Tashakkori & C. Teddlie (Eds.), *Sage handbook of mixed methods in social & behavioral research* (pp. 209-240). London, UK: Sage.

EC (2006). Recommendation of the European Parliament and of the Council of 18 December 2006 on key competences for lifelong learning. *Official Journal of the European Union.*

Ferrari, A. (2012). *Digital competence in practice: An analysis of frameworks.* Sevilla: JRC IPTS. doi: 10.2791/82116

Ferrari, A., Punie, Y., & Brečko, B. N. (2013). *DIGCOMP: a framework for developing and understanding digital competence in Europe.* Retrieved from http://dx.publications.europa.eu10.2788/52966

Guitert, M, Romeu, T, & Baztán, P. (2020). The digital competence framework for primary and secondary schools in Europe. *European Journal of Education, 2021*(56), 133-149. https://doi.org/10.1111/ejed.12430

Guitert, M., Romeu, T., & Colas, J.-F. (2020). Basic digital competences for unemployed citizens: conceptual framework and training model. *Cogent Education, 7*(1), 1748469. https://doi.org/10.1080/2331186X.2020.1748469

Kuhn, T. S. (2012). *The structure of scientific revolutions.* University of Chicago press.

Pozos Pérez, K., & Mas Torelló, O. (2012). The Digital Competence as a Cross-cutting Axis of Higher Education Teachers' Pedagogical Competences in the European Higher Education Area. *Procedia – Social and Behavioral Sciences, 46*, 1112-1116. ISSN 1877-0428. https://doi.org/10.1016/j.sbspro.2012.05.257

Redecker, C. (2017). European Framework for the Digital Competence of Educators: DigCompEdu (Joint Research Centre, Institute for Prospective Technological Studies, Hrsg.). Luxembourg: Publications Office of the European Union. Zugriff am, 23, 2018.

Roegiers, X. (2005). L'évaluation selon la pédagogie de l'intégration: est-il possible d'évaluer les compétences des élèves? In K. Toualbi-tha Libi & S. Tawil (Eds.), *La*

Refonte de la pédagogie en Algérie – Défis et enjeux d'une société en mutation (pp.107-124). Alger: UNESCO-ONPS.

Vuorikari, R., Punie, Y., Gomez, S. C., & van den Brande, G. (2016). *DigComp 2.0: The digital competence framework for citizens.* Update phase 1: The conceptual reference model (No. JRC101254). Joint Research Centre (Seville site).

Lessons from a Pandemic for the Future of Education
Short Paper Book of the European Distance and E-Learning Network (EDEN)
2021 Annual Conference | Madrid, 21-24 June, 2021
ISBN 978-615-5511-31-8

IMPACT OF COVID-19 PANDEMIC ON DISTANCE LEARNING PERFORMANCE: AN ANALYSIS OF APPLIED ECONOMICS' STUDENTS

Eva Pardo, Cristina Castellanos-Serrano, Gonzalo Escribano, Juan Diego Paredes-Gázquez, Enrique San Martín González, Universidad Nacional de Educación a Distancia (UNED), Spain

Abstract

This communication shows the preliminary results of an ongoing investigation on the effects of COVID-19's social derived changes on the academic performance of undergraduate distance learning students in applied economics. Specifically, the study focuses on identifying if the COVID pandemic restrictions has impacted on distance learning students' performance and, if so, is this due to mobility restrictions or to content and methodological adaptations to the COVID context carried out by the teaching teams. Results are obtained from a sample of almost 17,000 observations from 6,000 students coursing nine economic policy subjects taught in the distance education modality by the Department of Applied Economics of UNED, the first and largest Spanish distance learning university.

Introduction

In response to the serious health crisis initiated in 2020 by COVID-19, numerous measures have been taken at the international, national, regional and local levels focused on restricting population movements and promoting non-contact activities in all areas (education, labour, social, etc.). All of this coupled with a greater degree of uncertainty and an increase in domestic burdens for certain segments of the population, especially for those with dependents (children, the elderly, sick people, or those with special care needs).

In this context, many universities have been forced to change in a short time all their face-to-face activity to distance education methodologies and tools. Even distance education universities have been forced to adapt some of their activities to the new social context responding to students' greater demand for interaction. Studies such as those carried out by Aristovnik et al. (2020), Elumalai et al. (2020), Gonzalez et al. (2020), Green et al., 2020 or Kamarianos et al. (2020) show the great challenges that entails both for teachers and students adapting to that new context.

Analyses such as the one carried out by Gonzalez et al. (2020) show that those adaptations led to the improvement of students' academic performance in face-to-face universities after periods of confinement and lockdown caused by the COVID-19' crisis. Among the reasons that explain this improvement are precisely the implementation of distance learning methodologies.

However, to our knowledge there is not enough evidence by now of how COVID-19's restrictions have impacted on students' performance at distance learning universities. This research intends to fill this gap by analysing if there has been any change in the performance of applied economics' students at UNED – the Spanish first and largest distance learning university – during the COVID pandemic; and, if so, whether it is motivated by mobility restrictions or by content and methodological adaptations to the COVID context carried out by the teaching teams.

The following sections briefly show the main motivations that led to this study, the methodology used, and a summary of the main results and conclusions reached in the first phases of the analysis.

Methodology

As the basis for the analysis we considered a group of 16,888 observations from nine economic policy subjects taught in the distance education modality by the UNED's Department of Applied Economics from the 2016/17 academic year to the first term of the course 2020/21 (Table 1). These subjects are offered in different degrees: Economics, Business Administration, Tourism and Political Science. Five subjects are coursed in the first semester, and four more in the second semester. The latter were the most affected by the COVID pandemic during the 2019-20 academic year.

Comparing the results obtained by students enrolled during and after March 2020 (4,997) versus a control group constituted by the students enrolled in previous courses (11,911) allows to identify any change in students' performance due to COVID-19 pandemic. It also allows to identify any changes between the semesters most affected by COVID-19 mobility restrictions existing in Spain during the months of March to September 2020.

As Table 1 shows, the sample includes 4 subjects in which no teaching innovation were made during that period to adapt materials or examinations to COVID context and restriction and 5 subjects in which teaching innovations were implemented: in 3 of them the innovations were only focused in adapting ordinary examinations and in 2 of them both in adapting ordinary examinations and teaching materials in response to the requirements of the pandemic context. The comparison between these subgroups will allow us to assess the effect of these measures of teaching innovation on the results obtained by the students.

Table 1: Sample. Number of students per year and subject

Sem.	Subject		2016-2017	2017-2018	2018-2019	2019-2020	2020-2021	Total
1	Budget and public expenditure theory	TPGP	498	497	450	416	521	2,382
1	Budget and public spending in Spain	PGPE	282	280	257	233	277 (i)	1,329
1	Economic policy: objectives and instruments	PEOI	345	307	312	262	360 (ii)	1,586
1	Spanish and compared economic policy	PEEC	282	306	331	248	288 (ii)	1,455
1	Tourism economic policy	PET	437	372	325	283	330 (ii)	1,747
	SUB-TOTAL Semester 1		1,844	1,762	1,675	1,442	1,776	8,499
2	Public economic policies – Economy	PEP(ECO)	406	328	346	293 (iii)	-(ii)(iii)	1,373
2	Public economic policies - Business Administration & Management	PEP(ADE)	965	895	797	816 (iii)	-(ii)(iii)	3,473
2	Spanish tax system	STE	418	497	515	275 (i)	- (i)	1,705
2	Theory of public revenues	TIP	518	519	426	375	-	1,838
	SUB-TOTAL Semester 2		2,307	2,239	2,084	1,759	-	8,389
	TOTAL		4,151	4,001	3,759	3,201	1,776	16,888

(i) COVID teaching general adaptation to online test in ordinary examinations
(ii) COVID specific teaching adaptation to online test in ordinary examinations
(iii) COVID teaching innovation in materials

The academic performance of the students in each subject has been carried out through the following commonly used indicators:

- Average marks of the students;
- Evaluation rate = total students sat for examination / total students matriculated;
- Pass rate = total students passed / total students examined;
- Achievement rate = total students passed / total students matriculated.

To deep in the reasons beneath any change in students' performance due to COVID-19 pandemic, a second phase of the investigation is being carried out. This new phase is based on surveys to the students of all courses asking for socioeconomic aspects relevant to the analysis and, in the case of the students from the second semester of the 2019-2020 academic year, also on their specific socio-labour situation during the months in which there was restriction of movements derived from COVID-19.

Results and conclusions

As it can be seen in Figures 1 and 2, preliminary results evidence an increase in the total number of students sat for examination and better evaluation rates in all the subjects and terms analysed. Nevertheless, there are differences in students' performance depending on the term the subject was coursed, and on the inclusion (or non-inclusion) of teaching innovation practices.

Students coursing subjects during the months with stricter COVID lockdowns (i.e. in Spain it occurred between March and September 2021) show better performance in terms of the evaluation rate, pass rate and the average marks obtained. This improvement occurs regardless the subject or the innovation practices implemented by the teaching team. Nevertheless, results and rates have increased more in those subjects which did implemented teaching innovation practices.

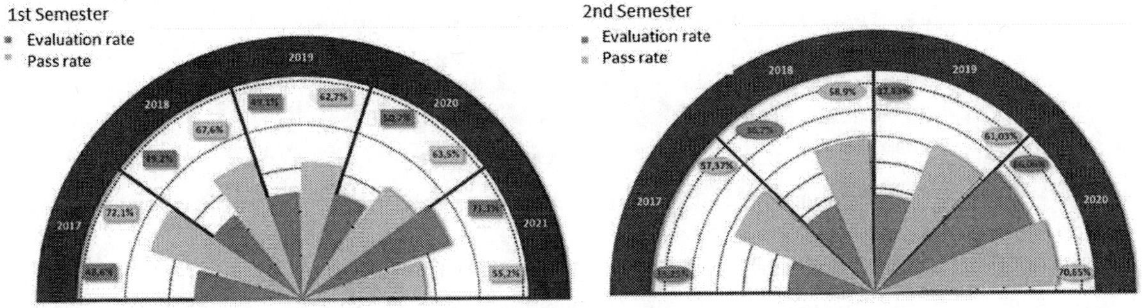

Figure 1. Evaluation and pass rates by semester.

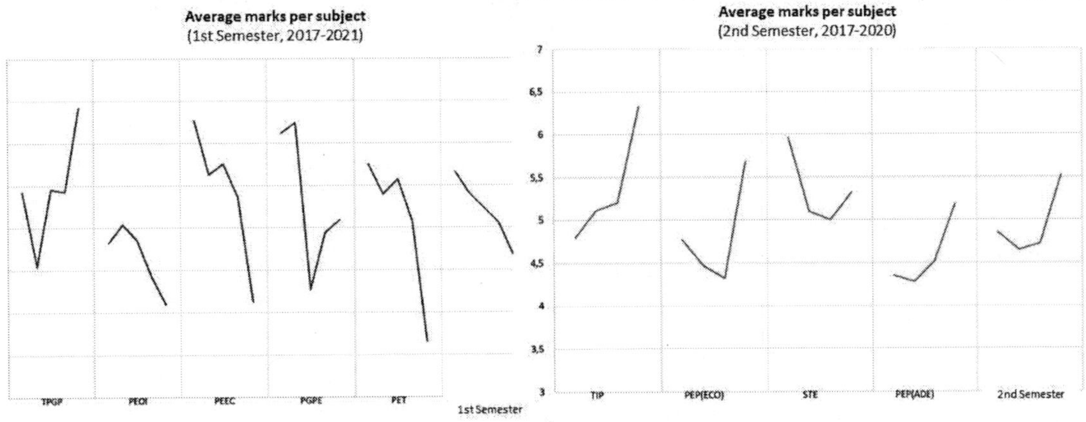

Figure 2. Students' performance. Average marks.

These results suggest that COVID-19 has impacted positively in distance learning students' performance. The next step of the research is to identify the reasons beneath this positive relationship. Thus, a first survey has been sent to the students enrolled during the first semester of the 2020-21 course asking for socioeconomic aspects relevant to the analysis and also on their specific socio-labour situation during these months, in which there were still restrictions of movements derived from COVID-19. First results of the survey show that students perceive COVID-19 pandemic have increased their workload and family obligations and negatively affected the studying of the subjects analysed (Figure 3).

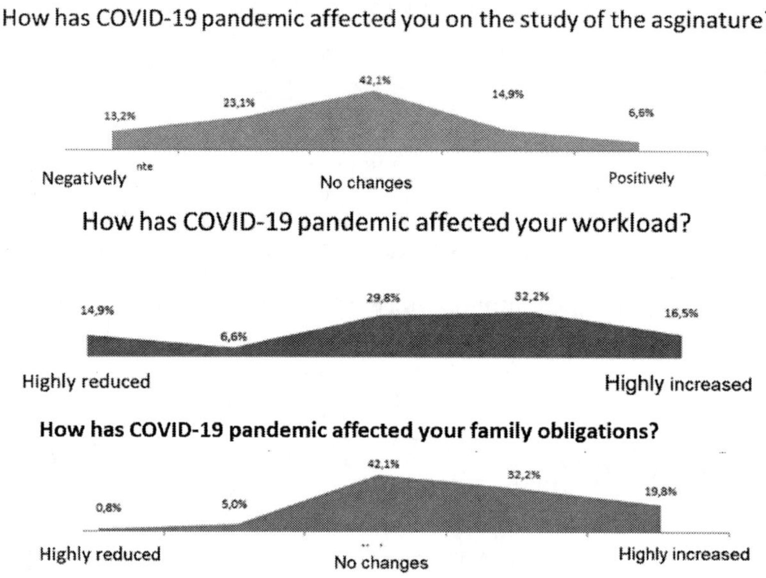

Figure 3. Students' perception of COVID-19 impact on their workload, family obligations and study

Further research is needed to confirm the preliminary conclusions outlined in this communication and determine if the better students' performance during COVID-19 pandemic can be linked to a greater study dedication due to the obligation of staying at home, teleworking and the limitations for carrying out other social activities. Another important aspect to study in depth is that associated with the possible differences in the results obtained from a gender perspective.

References

Aristovnik, A., Keržič, D., Ravšelj, D., Tomaževič, N., & Umek, L. (2020). Impacts of the COVID-19 Pandemic on Life of Higher Education Students: A Global Perspective. *Sustainability, 12*(20), 8438. https://doi.org/10.3390/su12208438

Elumalai, K. V, Sankar, J. P., John, K., Menon, J. A., Alqahtani, N., & Abumelha, M. S. N. M. A. (2020). Factors affecting the quality of e-learning during the COVID-19 pandemic from the perspective of higher education students. *Journal of Information Technology Education: Research, 19*, 731-753. https://doi.org/10.28945/4628

Gonzalez, T., de la Rubia, M. A., Hincz, K. P., Comas-Lopez, M., Subirats, L., Fort, S., & Sacha, G. M. (2020). Influence of COVID-19 confinement on students' performance in higher education. *PLOS ONE, 15*(10), e0239490. https://doi.org/10.1371/journal.pone.0239490

Green, W., Anderson, V., Tait, K., & Tran, L. T. (2020). Precarity, fear and hope: reflecting and imagining in higher education during a global pandemic. *Higher Education Research and Development, 39*(7), 1309-1312. Routledge. https://doi.org/10.1080/07294360.2020.1826029

Kamarianos, I., Adamopoulou, A., Lambropoulos, H., & Stamelos, G. (2020). Towards an understanding of university students' response in times of pandemic crisis (COVID-19). *European Journal of Education Studies, 7*(7). https://doi.org/10.46827/ejes.v7i7.3149

Lessons from a Pandemic for the Future of Education
Short Paper Book of the European Distance and E-Learning Network (EDEN)
2021 Annual Conference | Madrid, 21-24 June, 2021
ISBN 978-615-5511-31-8

IS THERE A GENDER GAP IN DISTANCE EDUCATION OUTCOMES ON APPLIED ECONOMICS? COVID-19, WORK-LIFE BALANCE AND DIGITAL GAP

Cristina Castellanos-Serrano, Gonzalo Escribano, Eva Pardo, Juan Diego Paredes-Gázquez, Enrique San Martín González, Applied Economics Dpt., Universidad Nacional de Educación a Distancia (UNED), Spain

Abstract

This poster presents the preliminary results of an ongoing research on the academic performance of undergraduate students in several applied economics' courses, considering the gender perspective and the social and labour changes resulting from the COVID-19 pandemic. Specifically, the study focuses on some applied economics subjects taught in the distance education modality at UNED, one of the largest European universities by enrolment. In this poster an exploratory analysis of the database is carried out that allows us to propose the hypotheses that will be statistically contrasted in the following phases of the investigation.

Introduction

In general, higher education is thought of as a stage in the first part of adulthood in which young people must make sense of who they are and who they will become, in addition to learning certain knowledge and competencies (Cullen & Castellanos, 2014). However, the profile of UNED students is different, with people who are usually considerably older and who may have spent periods of time out of formal learning. In addition, the increasing need and desire for lifelong learning adds profiles of students who expand and continue with their education. Moreover, the UNED has some unique characteristics in Spain. It has a vocation to ensure equal opportunities and social inclusion. In territorial terms, the UNED has campuses both in large cities and in small towns, more accessible to those living in rural areas. It also has associated centres abroad in Europe, America, and Africa. In social terms, students from penitentiary centres and people with disabilities are highly visible cases of social inclusion, but there is also a generalized profile of students who combine their studies with other responsibilities such as paid work and caring for their families.

This paper focuses on analysing whether there are gender biases in the learning outcomes of subjects in applied economics at a university where new technologies and virtual platforms are the basis of its teaching, while examination usually happens face-to-face, except over the COVID-19 period. Therefore, it may show different processes and outcomes than teaching and learning in other universities, whether face-to-face or distance. Specifically, the poster presents a gender analysis of the learning outcomes, considering the possible differential effects of measures taken against COVID-19, teaching innovations, and other sociodemographic factors of UNED students.

Gender equality in higher education

In Spain, the vast majority (81.1%) of university students are undergraduate students (both for men and women). In social and legal sciences, almost 81% were under 25 years of age and only 5% were over 30 (M. Universidades, 2020), showing a profile clearly different from that of the UNED students. The average age of male students at the UNED is 36.6 years and 34.7 in the case of female students (Moreno González, 2015b). In social sciences, the average score was 7.26 (7.37 for women and 7.07 for men). It seems that gender equality is achieved, but to confirm this objective we must look deeper, with a higher level of detail, also considering the factors behind traditional gender biases.

What do we know about academic results? Why do we analyse the results of UNED students? For several reasons. On the one hand, although the UNED is a non-face-to-face university, it has the particularity of offering face-to-face services through its associated centres to those who wish to use them. Several studies (Aristovnik et al., 2020; Elumalai et al., 2020; Green et al., 2020; Kamarianos et al., 2020) show the significant challenges for both teachers and students to continue teaching in the context generated by COVID-19 measures. However, few yet analyse academic outcomes. The question is whether the improvement in the academic performance of face-to-face universities due to the change to distance education methodologies observed (Gonzalez et al., 2020) is similar to that which occurred in universities that previously used distance education methodologies such as the UNED and if a gender bias is observed. On the other hand, 75% of UNED students have chosen this university because it gives them the possibility of combining studies with family obligations and 87.8% because it gives them the possibility of combining studies with their work activity (Moreno González, 2015a).

Our objective is to assess if there are gender gaps in the results and what factors may motivate them. To do so, we analyse teaching innovations, before and during COVID-19 periods, sociodemographic characteristics, and other factors outside the university, such as the gender gap in care, which may be affecting differentially the academic results of men and women.

Database and methodology

The general data of the UNED Statistical Portal are not disaggregated by sex. To carry out an analysis with a gender perspective, it is therefore essential to use a database made ad hoc for the study. A sample of undergraduate students has been used, specifically from various subjects of economic policy, public finance and tax system, all of them taught in the distance education modality from the Applied Economics Department of the UNED. The sample includes mainly students from the degree in Economics, but also from the degrees in Business Administration, Political Science, and Tourism. Only in this last degree, women are majority (Figure 1). Information is available for four academic years, from 2016/2017 to 2019/2020. The sample collects 15,112 registers, the academic results of 6,845 students who have taken one or more subjects, from the first and/or second term of these academic years. Less than 12% are under 25 years old. Over 50, three out of four students are men. The average age of the sample is 37 for men and 36 for women.

Degree in...	Subjects	Year	Term	Type	Academic years					%Women from total
					2016-2017	2017-2018	2018-2019	2019-2020	Total	
Economics	Economic policy: objectives and instruments	3	1	M	345	307	312	262	1.226	29,7%
	Budget and public spending in Spain	4	1	M	282	280	257	233	1.052	29,5%
	Spanish and comparative economic policy	4	1	M	282	306	331	248	1.167	39,9%
	Theory of public revenues	2	2	M	518	519	426	375*	1.838	30,1%
	Public economic policies	3	2	M	406	328	346	293*	1.373	31,3%
	Spanish tax system	4	2	M	418	497	515	275*	1.705	32,9%
Economics /Political Science	Budget and public expenditure theory	2/ 4	1	M / OP	498	497	450	416	1.861	29,4%
Business Administration	Public economic policies	3	2	M	965	895	797	816*	3.473	42,3%
Tourism	Tourism economic policy	4	1	M	437	372	325	283	1.417	67,3%
	Total (9 subjects)				4151	4001	3759	3201	15112	37,4%

Age	Men	Women	Total	% Women	% Tot.
17-25	478	271	749	36,2%	11,9%
26 - 50	3118	1828	4946	37,0%	78,3%
51-100	466	156	622	25,1%	9,8%
Total	4062	2255	6317	35,7%	100%

* Subjects taught during the period COVID-19, M: mandatory, OP: optional

Figure 1. Number of students per year and subject, and by sex and age (sample of Applied Economics subjects at UNED)

In addition, we are currently working on expanding the information for a sample for 2020-2021 year with an ad-hoc survey including key factors of the learning-teaching process, as well as socio-labour and family. From a quantitative approach, the academic results (assessment rate, success rate, and average score) are analysed, considering the sex variable systematically, and considering factors that may contribute to explain the differences observed. The variety of subjects in the sample allows us to analyse differences considering control and treatment groups, in semi-experiment conditions such as the case of movement restriction due to COVID-19. We can compare academic years without COVID-19 vs. COVID-19 year besides the first term of 2019-2020 (October 2019 – February 2020) in contrast to the second term (March – June 2020). The first term was not affected by the COVID, but the lockdown was established in the second term.

Academic results considering gender perspective and COVID-19 shock

We wanted to capture if the lockdown and the change to online exams have produced significant changes in students' results. The assessment rate (examined/enrolled) in the degree in Economics was 59.1% at UNED in 2020. In the subjects analysed, the average assessment rate over the last three previous academic years was over 40%, slightly higher for women than men. In the first term of 2020, the assessment rates kept quite stable: from 48.8% as average in three previous years to 51% among men and from 49.2% to 50.2% among women. Over the second term of 2020, when the lockdown was declared, a significant increase of the assessment rate among men and women was observed: from 34.9% to 64% among men and from 37.3% to 69.8% among women.

Using the selected sample and only ordinary exams, we analyse the evolution of the success rate. Men's success rate on average over the four years analysed is 67.3% while women's one is 60.3% (Figure 2). The success rate of men was 11.3 percentage points (p.p) higher than women, on average, in subjects of the first term of the three previous years (10.5 p.p. in 2020). However, there was a significant change in the second term, from 4.5 p.p. of difference on average to almost cero. The trend of the gap is also relevant, as in the second semester, the direction of the gap has reversed in comparison to the first term in 2019, but in 2020 the men's success rate become higher again, but just slightly.

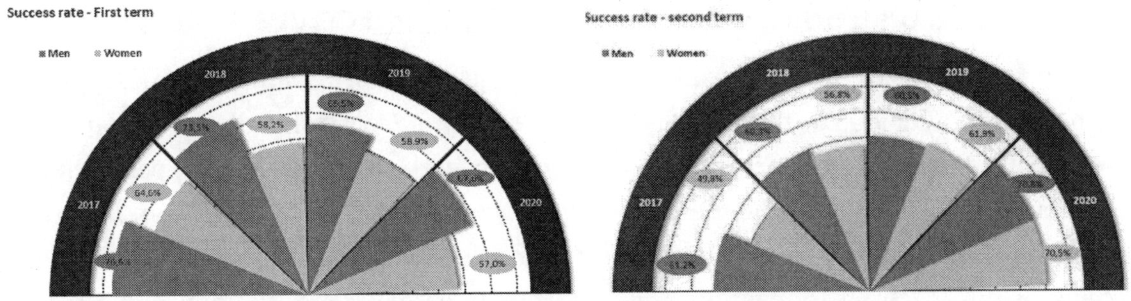

Figure 2. Success rate in ordinary exams by term and academic year (2016-2020), by sex

Regarding the mean scores, gender differences are also observed. There are statistically significant differences at 99% between men and women. It is observed that these differences exist when considering other variables such as age or subject. Considering only students who have passed the subjects, in each and all subjects and age groups, average grades are higher for men than women, this difference varies between 0.1 and 0.6 points. On average, female students obtained 5.9 and male students received 6.2. Considering all students examined, average marks keep being higher for men than women and women's overpass in 2019 second term is reversed in the term characterised by the lockdown (Figure 3). Lockdown affected differently to workload to men and women (Figure 4).

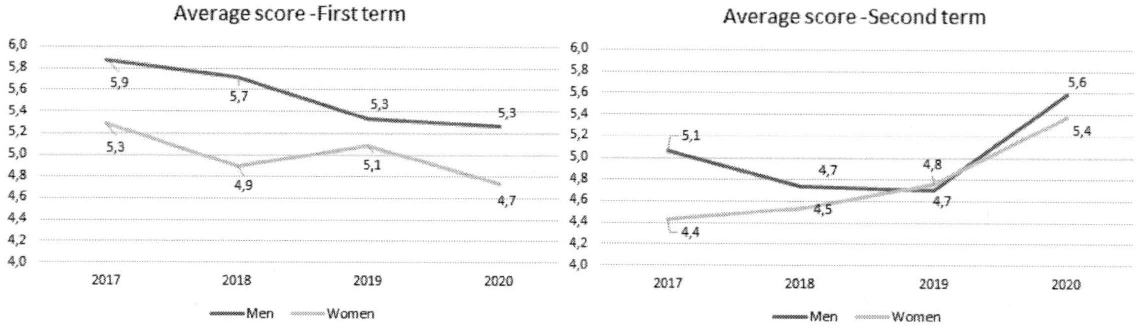

Figure 3. Average score by term and academic year (2017-2020), by sex

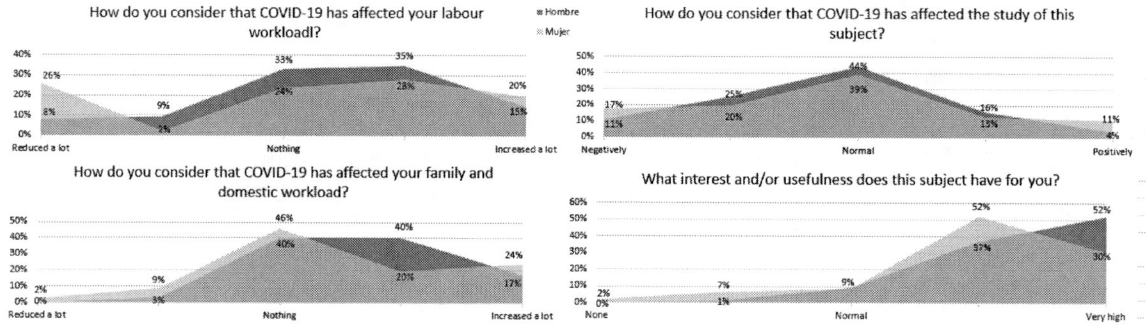

Figure 4. Effects perceived of COVID-19 on labour, family and domestic workload and study, by sex (2020)

Use of digital platforms, teaching innovation and COVID-19 lockdown

Certain gender biases are observed in the use of digital platforms, although most men and women (88% and 91.3%, respectively) perceive they have strong digital competences. Women use them less than proportionally with respect to students enrolled per subject. In addition, it is observed that the mobility restriction due to COVID-19 led to an immediate activity increase in the learning platform by men, while women follow a time lag. Both the effects of the teaching innovation and the COVID-19 converge in time, but not in all subjects, so it will be observed whether there is evidence of the success of the changes proposed in some subjects and how it affects gender bias (Figure 5).

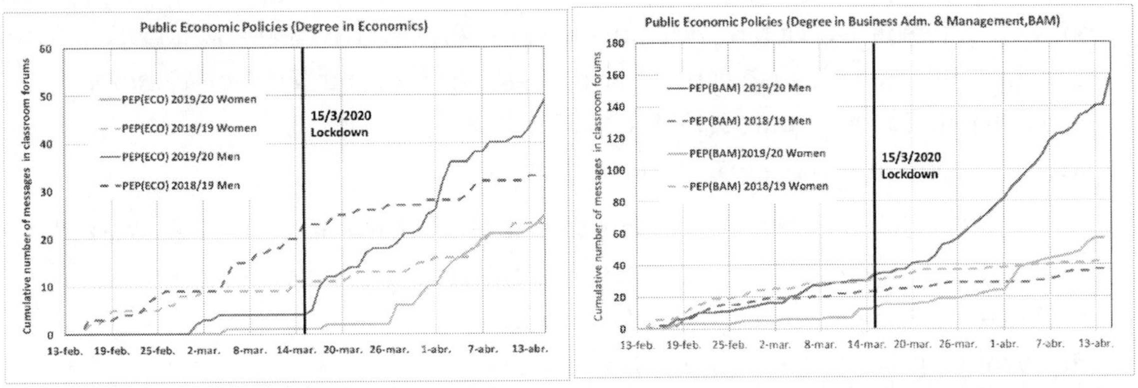

Figure 5. Cumulative number of messages by sex (Public Economic Policies in BA and Economics Degrees)

Conclusions

With this exploratory analysis we have found some preliminary results regarding gender biases in academic outcomes based on which we will try to contrast the following hypotheses:

- The academic consequences of the COVID-19 period have affected students differently by sex.
- Participation in virtual platforms has also changed differently by sex.
- Changes in the work-life balance by sex due to COVID-19 seem to have affected academic results.

References

Aristovnik, A., Keržič, D., Ravšelj, D., Tomaževič, N., & Umek, L. (2020). Impacts of the COVID-19 Pandemic on Life of Higher Education Students: A Global Perspective. *Sustainability, 12*(20), 8438. https://doi.org/10.3390/su12208438

Cullen, J., & Castellanos, C. (2014). Cloud Cuckoo Land: evidence from a study of student drop-out. *Revista Campus Virtuales, III*(01), 22-30. Retrieved from http://uajournals.com/ojs/index.php/campusvirtuales/article/view/47/46

Elumalai, K. V, Sankar, J. P., John, K., Menon, J. A., Alqahtani, N., & Abumelha, M. S. N. M. A. (2020). Factors affecting the quality of e-learning during the COVID-19 pandemic from the perspective of higher education students. *Journal of Information Technology Education: Research, 19*, 731-753. https://doi.org/10.28945/4628

Gonzalez, T., de la Rubia, M. A., Hincz, K. P., Comas-Lopez, M., Subirats, L., Fort, S., & Sacha, G. M. (2020). Influence of COVID-19 confinement on students' performance in higher education. *PLOS ONE, 15*(10), e0239490. https://doi.org/10.1371/journal.pone.0239490

Green, W., Anderson, V., Tait, K., & Tran, L. T. (2020). Precarity, fear and hope: reflecting and imagining in higher education during a global pandemic. *Higher Education Research and Development, 39*(7), 1309-1312. https://doi.org/10.1080/07294360.2020.1826029

Kamarianos, I., Adamopoulou, A., Lambropoulos, H., & Stamelos, G. (2020). Towards an understanding of university students' response in times of pandemic crisis (COVID-19). *European Journal of Education Studies, 7*(7). https://doi.org/10.46827/ejes.v7i7.3149

Ministerio de Universidades (2020). *Datos y cifras del sistema universitario español. Publicación 2019-2020.* Retrieved from https://www.educacionyfp.gob.es/dam/jcr:b9e82c7a-1174-45ab-8191-c8b7e626f5aa/informe-datos-y-cifras-del-sistema-universitario-espa-ol-2019-2020-corregido.pdf

Moreno González, E. (2015a). *Estudio descriptivo realizado con las respuestas dadas por los participantes en el formulario de matrícula.* Oficina de Tratamiento de la Información, UNED.

Moreno González, E. (2015b). *Estudio descriptivo realizado con las respuestas dadas en el formulario sobre el proceso de matriculación y sobre las características sociodemográficas de los estudiantes de la UNED.* Oficina de Tratamiento de la Información, UNED.

ISBN 978-615-5511-31-8

CHALLENGES AND SOLUTIONS: THE WEAVING WEBS OF STORIES PROJECT

Anca Colibaba, EuroEd Foundation, Romania, Irina Gheorghiu, Albert Ludwigs University Freiburg, Germany, Cristian Timofticiuc, EuroEd Foundation, Anca Constantin, Alexandra Hanu, Evelina Oancea, EuroEd School, Adrian Lucian Dinu, Al.I.Cuza University Iasi, Romania

Abstract

In the pandemic context of 2020, the EuroEd School and Foundation faced a new challenge: continuing not only its teaching processes but also developing its European projects during the lockdown. All the Erasmus+ projects the organisation is involved in include a piloting stage running in associated partner schools, where the outputs of the projects are tested and evaluated. This crucial stage in the development of the projects had always been done face-to-face in all partner schools before the pandemic. The article focuses on The Weaving Webs of Stories project, the challenges encountered and solutions provided when transferring it from the face-to-face to the online environment.

Managing changes during the pandemic

In the pandemic context of 2020, the EuroEd School and Foundation faced new challenges: continuing not only the teaching / learning processes but also developing its European projects during the lockdown. The existing pandemic context required the use of another medium: during the lockdown, the projects had to be successfully implemented online. One of the main challenges associated with this endeavour was change management. Our main objective was rebranding both digitally and pedagogically. This meant improving the organization by updating technologies, solving problems, seizing opportunities, aligning work and strategy and streamlining information flow within the organization. It also included preparing, training and supporting our staff and associated partners, establishing the necessary steps for change, and monitoring pre- and post-change activities to ensure successful implementation. To this end, we used a wide range of strategies: discussions with colleagues about the changes we wanted to implement, building the team, shaping the vision (goals, objectives and strategy), identifying the resources needed to make the change and planning the steps to communicating openly and frequently. We also empowered colleagues to engage in the change process by giving them freedom to make their own decisions and implement new ideas. We never gave up, we incorporated the change and made it part of our workplace culture. We aimed at creating learning communities which connect organizations that are eager to learn and work across boundaries for a shared goal.

Our teachers did technical and pedagogical training courses on online teaching organised and run within our institution, which enabled them to manage the online environment, live sessions and digital apps. Pedagogical training looked in detail at the online learning/teaching processes. Courses focused on how and why to use certain methods, techniques, activities or apps, how to motivate students, how to increase student participation and engagement, how to digitise their activities and how to assess in the online environment. Following the training, teachers cascaded their knowledge and new skills to parents and children, who were taught how to use the new platforms and apps.

The Weaving Webs of Stories project

We started with the Weaving Webs of Stories Erasmus+ project by addressing primary and secondary school children from 7 to 13 years old and their teachers. The associated partner was a school situated approximately 100 km away from our city, so all activities had to be carried out online. The Weaving Webs of Stories project is expected not only to improve children's literacy skills but also to develop their understanding of inclusion, diversity and equality, and enhance creativity, self-confidence and motivation to become lifelong readers.

We carefully selected a list of books according to the children's age and interests, as well as the project's main values: equality, diversity and inclusion. We chose short texts so that the children would not lose their concentration or we spread longer stories over the session and engaged children in pre-, while- and post-listening / reading tasks in between (i.e. predicting, guessing what will happen next in the story). Stories embracing diversity, equality and inclusion topics are a rich vital learning source for our children, promoting positive attitudes and behaviour towards equality and diversity and setting examples which can be followed. Stories generate discussion about bias and discrimination, challenge students' thinking and make them reflect on their attitudes and values.

Our planning considered encouraging children to both read and write stories. Reading out loud in the form of a dialogue between children and adults stimulated the children's imagination and curiosity, just like the use of pictures, online activities (word associations, synonyms, word explanations, word families, bingo), discussions (likes and dislikes, lessons learned) or drawings.

The reading stage also gave children insights into the structure of a story by drawing their attention to its main elements (setting, plot, character) (Figures 1 & 2).

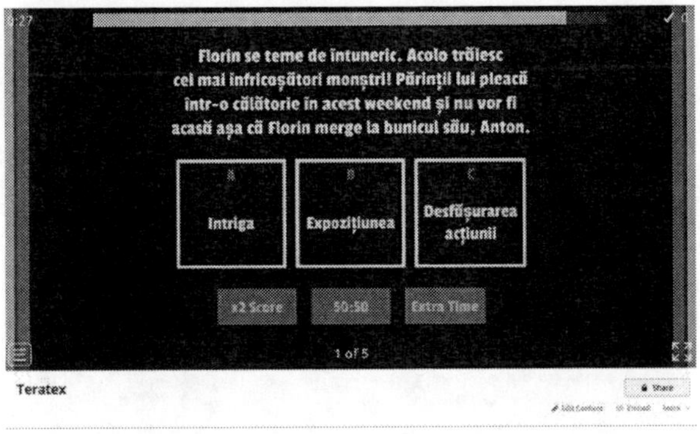

Figure 2. Main elements of a story

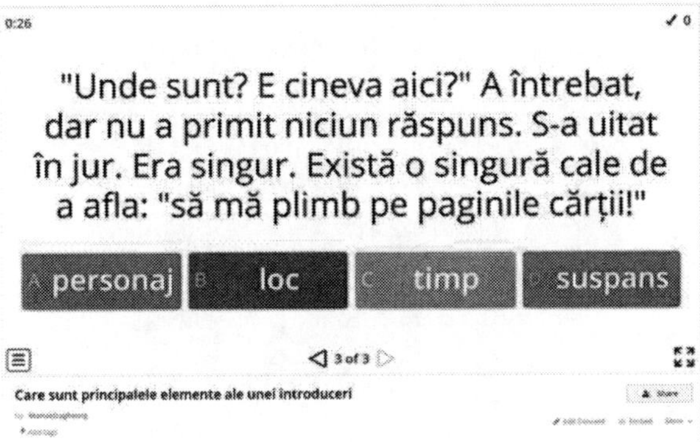

Figure 2. The introduction to a story

Technology facilitated understanding of literary concepts such as character, setting, events, problem, resolution; interactive activities worked very well with our 10-year olds throughout their reading journey (Figures 3, 4, 5).

Figure 3. The significance of the titles

Figure 4. Characters and places

Figure 5. Who is your character?

It was a gradual process which paved the way for the writing section of the project. We used effective strategies for improving writing skills, tapping into children's interests through the use of technology, implementing interactive writing techniques (asking students for ideas to complete sentences, stories, etc.) or diverse literacy practices (graphic organizers, cooperative learning, scaffolding, reading aloud or group discussions).

Preparing and planning teaching online

Zoom was the platform which accommodated all our virtual meetings. We set expectations for online participation, communication and netiquette and had clear protocols for turn-taking as well as instructions on how to use the chat box or the hand raising function. We usually planned 3 or 4 different tasks per session and used a PowerPoint presentation to support all its stages. The slides were accompanied by images, icons, tables and illustrations to support our tasks, as well as "welcome" and "thank you" screens for the beginning and ending of each session. We started off with simple brainstorming exercises having children typing their replies in the chat box, or writing them on the whiteboard or the Padlet app. Other apps and platforms such as WordWall, Cloze, Kahoot, BookWidgets or Mentimeter encouraged children to engage in quick word games to practise vocabulary.

Discussions worked well in breakout rooms too, especially when they centred round a meaningful task to which everybody had to contribute, negotiate commonly agreed upon answers and report back in plenary at the end of the activity. Such tasks with a clear goal were successfully carried out in the breakout rooms (children worked together to provide a suitable outcome for the characters by solving a mystery or finding solutions to an issue, deciding on matters of importance to their community and creating a presentation, a poster or a story in their group). Image-based activities provided the necessary scaffolding and stimulated conversation (for instance, we shared a photo of the protagonist and asked children to annotate questions addressed to the character.

Challenges and solutions

The challenges we encountered related to creating a trustworthy atmosphere with a group of children we had never met in person, how to elicit interaction and collaboration and how to develop autonomy in the online environment.

How to create a trustworthy atmosphere

Creating good relationships and a relaxing atmosphere is important in the online environment. We started each session by having five-minute informal conversations which allowed students to bring their culture and identity into the classroom. In this respect, we asked children to show us (pictures of) their pets, their little brothers and sisters or to talk about their favourite objects and books. We wanted our students to feel part of a reading community. Warm up and energising activities proved to be useful in our focus on student wellbeing as they made students open up, share and relax.

In time we succeeded in gaining children's trust. We taught them that mistakes are normal steps in the learning process and therefore failure should be considered a learning opportunity which encourages development. Sometimes we needed to engage in small talks because a child suddenly became shy or uncomfortable. Emoticons and the chat box were useful in encouraging reactions and expressing opinions. We were always present by asking children in the private chat if everything was fine or by moving through breakout rooms and monitoring activities. We asked children to give us feedback (*What are your questions? / How did you feel today?*) and gave them choices to express themselves either writing their views in the chat box or saying them out loud.

Interaction

Stories provide opportunities for children to talk and interact with their peers. We encouraged three types of interaction: student-student, teacher-student and student-content. Children were encouraged to interact with the teacher and their peers individually in the chat, in groups (in the breakout rooms) or in plenary (orally or via chat). Breakout rooms were particularly useful for pair work and group work to practise activities, share ideas, or do tasks that encouraged interaction such as problem-solving, providing a beginning or ending to a story, making up a story according to some given clues or discussing and negotiating an issue (CUP, 2018; English teaching 101, 2020). As to student-content interaction, the most successful strategy was prediction. Predicting required the children to use the clues provided by the author in the text and to rely on what they knew from their personal experience or previous knowledge (Pinterest, 2014; VSG, 2014; Top Notch Teaching, 2018). They had to combine these two aspects to make relevant and logical predictions. When looking for evidence in the text to support their assumptions, children also asked questions, reread, interpreted, drew conclusions, and, as a result, comprehended the text better. It was also a fun and engaging activity; children talked about what was happening in the story, which stimulated their motivation to listen to or read the story and check if their predictions came true or not. The title of the book, the front and back covers, illustrations, a specific passage enabled children to make connections between new information and what they already knew. The use of online discussions combined all three above-mentioned forms of interaction. Children read or watched the materials to prepare for the discussion, then shared their thoughts with peers, and ultimately received feedback from the teacher.

Each online session was accompanied by discussions with teachers about the main issues that surfaced in the live meeting. Teachers looked into and assessed each strategy, analysed the children's reactions and discussed ways of enhancing their engagement. For instance, it was unanimously agreed that prediction was worth taking into consideration as it encouraged children to think ahead and ask questions, to interact with the text and understand the story better. Predicting what was going to happen when reading a story gave children a reason to read (to find out if their predictions were right), activated language or vocabulary and also improved their comprehension.

Collaboration and communication

As collaborative learning is at the core of a successful distance learning environment, we used breakout rooms and had children work with peers on tasks, be they presentations, stories or posters. Such group interactions introduced children to the art of constructive and enjoyable conversations within teams focused on tasks; they enabled practising active listening, turn taking, negotiating, knowledge sharing, co-creation of knowledge. In time, a supportive e-learning community emerged, a sense of community and assuming an active role and responsibility for their learning.

Enhancing student autonomy

Children spend a lot of time on their own behind the screen watching videos, answering questions or doing online exercises, most of the time with no adult around. We used several ways to promote student autonomy in online discussions. Expecting them to employ decision-making skills encouraged them to think autonomously. We often provided multiple prompts to choose for tasks. Children were allowed to choose their mode of response to discussions: an online, written, audio, visual, or multimedia response. Below are several ways children accomplished their task: the creation of an e-book, an animated video, drawing and reading aloud (Figures 6, 7, 8).

Figure 6. Ebook

Figure 7 Animated video

Figure 8. Oral presentation

Children were also encouraged to take the initiative and learn new modes of presentation or video editing or use a new app and presentation software.

Conclusions

We realised that we, teachers, have to become agents of change, get out of our comfort zone and teach our colleagues and students change skills which enable them to adapt, seize opportunities and evolve. The benefits of the steps we have taken are visible in the children's progress in language and literacy learning, in understanding the value of diversity, and in promoting a positive outlook towards school, learning and peers. Technology-wise, a learning community of teachers, students and parents getting richer after all the lessons learnt during the pandemic.

References

Cambridge University Press (2018). Motivating learners with immersive speaking tasks. Retrieved from https://www.cambridge.org/us/files/5615/7488/6044/CambridgePapersInELT_ImmersiveSpeakingTasks_2018_ONLINE-2.pdf

English teaching 101 (2020). Vocabulary Workshop Activities and Game. Retrieved from https://englishteaching101.com/vocabulary-workshop/

Imagine Forest (January 21, 2020). Story cube games. Retrieved from https://www.imagineforest.com/blog/story-cubes-game/

Pinterest (2014). Four Types of Questions – factual, interpretive, evaluative, speculative. Retrieved from https://ro.pinterest.com/pin/181129216238615048/

Top Notch Teaching (2018). 3 Ways to Use Literacy Games in the Classroom. Retrieved from https://topnotchteaching.com/literacy/literacy-games/

VSG (2014). Reading with children. Retrieved from https://www.education.vic.gov.au/childhood/professionals/learning/ecliteracy/emergentliteracy/Pages/readingwithchildren.aspx

Weaving Webs of Stories (2020). Home .Retrieved from https://www.weavingwebstories.com

Lessons from a Pandemic for the Future of Education
Short Paper Book of the European Distance and E-Learning Network (EDEN)
2021 Annual Conference | Madrid, 21-24 June, 2021
ISBN 978-615-5511-31-8

PEDAGOGICAL AFFORDANCES WHEN TRANSITIONING TO HYBRID FORMS OF LEARNING

Jonas Bäckelin, M.A. Student, Faculty of Educational Sciences – Linköping University, Sweden

Abstract

This paper analyses how school leaders in City of Stockholm can participate in skills development in a flexible manner and adapt the workload to their individual capacity. There is an increasing pressure on organizations to undergo digital transformation and transitioning from emergency remote teaching to navigating what has been called 'the new normal' after the COVID-19 pandemic. The analysis is a mixed Delphi method, where our expert panel examine what happens when face-to-face Continuous Professional Development (CPD) transition to hybrid forms of learning. Predictions will be verified by the participants according to the Load Reduction Instruction Scale (LRIS). Taking an online course that present perspectives on inclusive learning environments as its case, the study reveals how participants can offload intrinsic cognitive load when applying the content in the workplace between sessions. There is also evidence that using the service design approach supports co-creation of services in the public sector.

Introduction

Continuous professional development for people working in educational settings is part of our systematic quality development work, which is described as directives and intentions in the Swedish education system. During the COVID-19 pandemic, hybrid forms of skills development tend to increase, and face-to-face seminars were often changed into webinars supported by peer interaction and guidelines (OECD, 2021). One macro-trend identified to have the highest impact on instructional design is blended and hybrid course models, due to flexible movement between remote and in-person experiences (Pelletier et al., 2021). Since organisations now are talking about the "new normal", there is a need for a more long-term strategy to retain the benefits from hybrid forms of learning.

The aim for this initiative was to design an e-learning solution for research-based Continuous Professional Development to comply with COVID-19 restrictions and regulations. Our idea was that a hybrid course design encourages participants to apply the acquired skill and knowledge in independent, novel, and creative ways (Martin & Evans, 2018). The term *hybrid* and *blended* learning strategies are often used interchangeably, but the design principle of in this study will combine researched-based content in an online course with practice situated in the workplace. This strategy has also been called Continuous Professional Development (CPD), which provide participants with the theory underlying the new instructional strategies and opportunities to practice these in their own context. This process normally also includes demonstrations and exchanging ideas with colleagues or peers (Joyce & Showers, 2002). According to the cognitive load theory participants working memory is freed up when there is sufficient opportunity for practice. This will also create enhanced fluency and automaticity, which is needed for higher-order thinking and the ability to apply skills and knowledge to new problems (Martin, 2016). Now our municipality take part in an initiative to introduce user-driven innovation in public sector. This service design approach uses step-by-step instructions with templates and films, which we believe will provide support and scaffolding when learning new skills and knowledge (Holmlid, 2009).

As we know, school leaders have an important role in the implementation of educational reform and school development (Spector et al., 2016). In this initiative the City of Stockholm has invested funds and resources to support the school leaders from approximately 300 compulsory schools to implement strategies for inclusive learning environments. Our department of research and development (FoU), supports schools in building research-based education. According to the Swedish Education Act *Education should be based on a scientific ground and proven experience* (Swedish Government, 2010). The topic of inclusion is also expressed in our school development program as "All people are unique and need different support and stimulation to learn and develop. Therefore, we compensate for background factors that research shows can otherwise affect the development of knowledge" (Skolprogram, 2018). Each school district leader will during participation make sure that peer groups are created, and the impact of transformed practice will be evaluated during the fourth quarter (Q4) of the annual systematic quality development cycle.

This study will be a part of my master's theses in adult learning at Linköping University and the theoretical perspectives for implementation of digitalization processes in educational settings was studied at Jönköping University.

Research Questions

The goal of this study is to find a long-term strategy with a balance between face-to-face seminars and hybrid forms of learning. To explore the pedagogical affordances the following research questions were addressed:

- Q1: Does hybrid forms of learning improve guided independence among participants?
- Q2: Does the e-learning solution allow opportunity for sufficient practice between sessions?
- Q3: Does the service design approach provide support and scaffolding as participants learn a topic or skill?

E-learning Solution for recorded seminars

The planning of this continuous professional development was done during spring 2021 and involved transfer of new skills and knowledge with recorded seminars. The timeframe for the hybrid e-learning solution was initiated with the formation of the expert panel and the process was then divided into planning, implementation as well as assessment and evaluation (Table 1).

Table 1: Timeframe and stages for the hybrid e-learning solution

Stage	Content	Duration
Expert panel formation	Select a panel of three experts with different competence: Pedagogy, Content and Technical	January-March 2021
Planning	Derive factors, organise and remove overlapping ones. Design the sequence of seminars and grouping the factors	March-May 2021
Implementation	Encourage the participants to assess the design. Reflect on results	May-June 2021
Assessment and Evaluation	Re-examine the factors. Verify the opinion of the expert panel with LRI-factor from participants	August-September 2021

In the beginning, our leader board of stakeholders allocated resources and formulated goals in order to start the design of the e-learning solution (i.e. backward design). The content in this educational resource was perspectives on inclusive learning environments and had school leaders from our compulsory schools as target audience. In total six seminars were recorded and divided into a sequence of three sections that each had an approximate duration of 20-25 minutes excluding peer discussions (Appendix A). The content focused on the Universal Design for Learning (UDL) framework that recently been translated to Swedish (Andersson et al., 2020) where one of our presenter Linda P. Ewe from Kristianstad University was involved. After a short introduction by our director of compulsory schools Lee Orberson, Linda introduced the research-based content of the course. The two following seminars were presented by experts from Konradsbersskolan and Rålambshovsskolan with over five years' experience in working with UDL. The last section high-lights strategies for inclusive learning environments based on experience from Enbacksskolan and Oxhagsskolan. To compliment the recorded seminar, our municipal center for accessible educational materials called Skoldatateket created strategies and guidelines for discussion.

Our e-learning platform is built with Totara Learn as learning management system (LMS) and the technical design involved uploading the recordings as interactive video (Joubel, 2013) created with open source HTML5 Package (H5P) based on JavaScripts. The effect is that the participants will experience that the media content will pause at specific times to present peer discussion activities as a pop-up screen (Appendix B). We also made the material available on the platform for downloading, if any participant needed them in a different format.

Methods

The analysis is a mixed Delphi method that is divided in two parts: (a) Predictions from three experts to create the e-learning solution (b) verification by participants of the predictions according to the Load Reduction Instruction Scale (LRIS). To gather the qualitative predictions from our group of experts we selected a panel with different competences. One was from the department of research and development (FoU), with experience from what support school leaders need to develop their school from an organisational perspective. The second expert was from the centre for accessible educational materials (Skoldatateket), with content knowledge from an inclusive perspective. Finally, my role was to participate as an e-learning specialist and acted as facilitator for the three rounds of Delphi Method (Figure 1). According to the study of Rapanta et al. (2020), the predictions of experts are seen as "crystallization points for practical insider knowledge". Each cycle involves collection and aggregation of predictions based on an initial question, which run until the announced predictions end up with a level of consensus (Turoff & Linstone, 2002). The main benefit it that the prototype for the hybrid e-learning solution could be developed relatively quick, without involving to many resources.

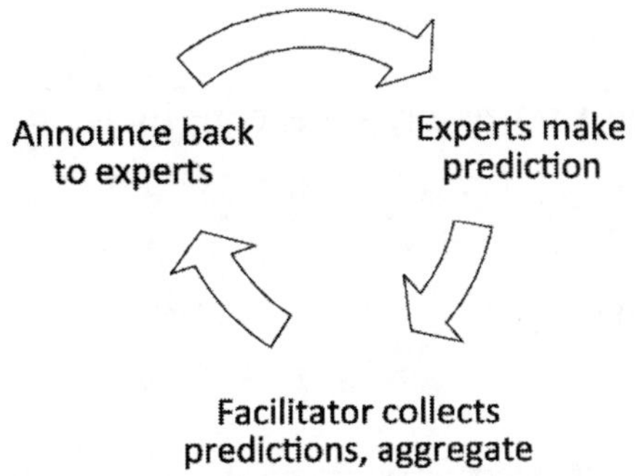

Figure 1. Three rounds of Delphi Method (Seker, 2015; p.368)

According to the "cognitive load theory", the meaning structures from experiences in the environment are stored in long-term memory. When learning new material, participants must first discover the underlaying meaning and the cognitive load is increased by distractions in the design as well as the complexity of the subject (Sweller, 1994). In the book *Advances in cognitive load theory: Rethinking teaching* (Tindall-Ford et al., 2020) this theory has been used to create the Load Reduction Instruction (LRI) framework (Figure 2).

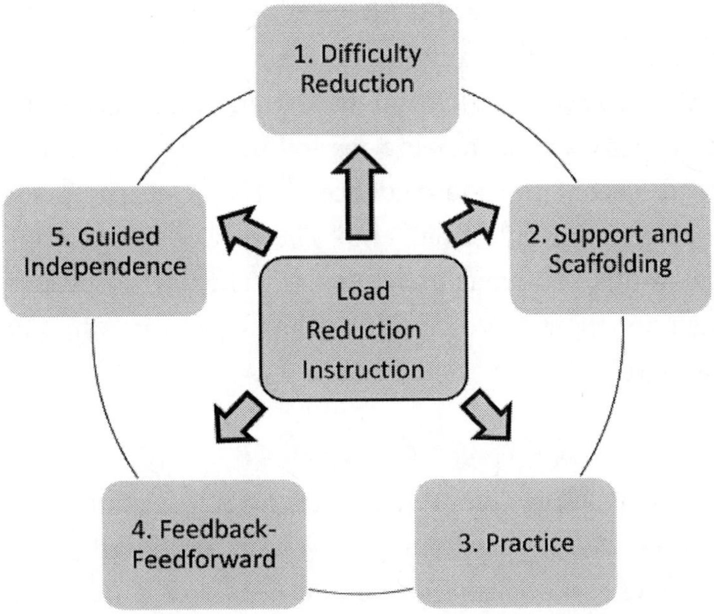

Figure 2. Load reduction instruction (LRI) framework (Tindall-Ford et al., 2019; p.35)

This framework includes instructional approaches to reduce cognitive load and use the Load Reduction Instruction Scale (LRIS) to rate teacher's instructional practice. A quantitative LRI-factor is then created from the five areas including five indicators each resulting in 25 items.

Expected results

Based on insights from expert on newly emerging topics during and after the Covid-19 crisis (Rapanta et al., 2020), this paper in progress will draw conclusions from three of the identified pedagogical affordances when transitioning to hybrid forms of learning. The preliminary results find a relation between the interventions incorporated in the e-learning solution and the Load Reducing Instruction (LRI) factors (Table 2).

Table 2: List of pedagogical affordances when transitioning to hybrid forms of learning, with Load Reducing Instruction (LRI) factors related to interventions incorporated in the e-learning solution

Pedagogical affordances	LRI-factors	Interventions
Self-regulation and autonomy	Include guided independence	Hybrid forms of learning
Pacing and reflection	Create opportunity for practice	Cognitive Load Theory
Peer collaboration and group assignments	Provide support and scaffolding	Service design Approach

The next stage is going to involve verification of the predictions from the experts with the LRI-factor perceived by the participants. To determine pedagogical affordances the group of experts will try to compare the result with traditional face-to-face seminars. Our hypothesis is that "hybrid learning increase possibilities for self-regulation and autonomy", "the Cognitive Load Theory provide evidence that an E-learning solution can have a positive effect on pacing and reflection" and "The service design approach support and scaffold peer collaboration and group assignments". The future development of this study will be to also include the factor of the LRI framework for "difficulty reduction" and "feedback-feed-forward".

References

Andersson, H., Ewe, L. P., Häggblom, P., Lüddeckens, J., & Östlund, D. (2020). *Universal Design for Learning – svensk översättning textversion.* Retreived from https://udlguidelines.cast.org/binaries/content/assets/udlguidelines/udlg-v2-2/udl-text-version-swedish.pdf

Holmlid, S. (2009). *From interaction to service. Designing services with innovative methods.*

Joubel (2013, June 10). Interactive Video. H5P [Blog post]. Retrieved from https://h5p.org/interactive-video

Joyce, B. R., & Showers, B. (2002). *Student achievement through staff development.* National College for School Leadership.

Martin, A. J. (2016). *Using Load Reduction Instruction (LRI) to boost motivation and engagement.* Leicester, UK: British Psychological Society.

Martin, A. J., & Evans, P. (2018). Load reduction instruction: Exploring a framework that assesses explicit instruction through to independent learning. *Teaching and Teacher Education, 73*, 203-214.

OECD (2021). The State of School Education – One Year into the COVID Pandemic. *Education Working Papers, 237.* Retrieved from https://doi.org/10.1787/201dde84-en

Pelletier, K., Brown, M., Brooks, D. C., McCormack, M., Reeves, J., Arbino, N., Bozkurt, A., Crawford, S., Czerniewicz, L., Gibson, R., Linder, K., Mason, J., & Mondelli, V. (2021). *2021 EDUCAUSE Horizon Report Teaching and Learning Edition.* Boulder, CO: EDU. Retrieved from https://library.educause.edu/-/media/files/library/2021/4/2021hrteachinglearning.pdf

Rapanta, C., Botturi, L., Goodyear, P., Guàrdia, L., & Koole, M. (2020). Online university teaching during and after the Covid-19 crisis: Refocusing teacher presence and learning activity. *Postdigital Science and Education, 2*(3), 923-945.

Seker, S. E. (2015). Computerized argument Delphi technique. *IEEE Access, 3*, 368-380.

Skolprogram (2018). Skolprogram för Stockholms stad. Retrieved 19 May, 2021, from https://leverantor.stockholm/globalassets/foretag-och-organisationer/leverantor-och-utforare/verksamhetsomraden/fristaende-skola/grundskola/kvalitet/skolprogram-for-stockholms-stads-forskolor-och-skolor.pdf

Spector, J. M., Ifenthaler, D., Sampson, D. G., & Isaias, P. (Eds.) (2016). *Competencies in Teaching, Learning and Educational Leadership in the Digital Age.* Papers from CELDA 2014. Cham: Springer International Publishing.

Stockholms stad – Enbacksskolan (2021). Om skolan. Retrieved from https://enbacksskolan.stockholm.se/om-skolan

Stockholms stad – Konradsbergsskolan (2021). Om skolan. Retrieved from https://konradsbergsskolan.stockholm.se/om-skolan

Stockholms stad – Oxhagsskolan (2021). Om skolan. Retrieved from https://oxhagsskolan.stockholm.se/om-skolan

Stockholms stad – Rålambshovsskolan (2021). Om skolan. Retrieved from https://ralambshovsskolan.stockholm.se/om-skolan

Swedish Government (2010). *Swedish Education Act, §5.* Retrieved May 16, 2021, from https://www.riksdagen.se/sv/dokument-lagar/dokument/svensk-forfattningssamling/skollag-2010800_sfs-2010-800

Sweller, J. (1994). Cognitive load theory, learning difficulty, and instructional design. *Learning and instruction, 4*(4), 295-312.

Tindall-Ford, S., Agostinho, S., & Sweller, J. (Eds.) (2020). *Advances in Cognitive Load Theory: Rethinking Teaching.* Routledge.

Totaralearn (2021). The adaptive learning management system (LMS) for transformational learning. Retrieved from https://www.totaralearning.com/products/learning-management-system

Turoff, M., & Linstone, H. A. (2002). *The Delphi method-techniques and applications.* Newark, NJ: New Jersey Institute of Technology.

Appendix A

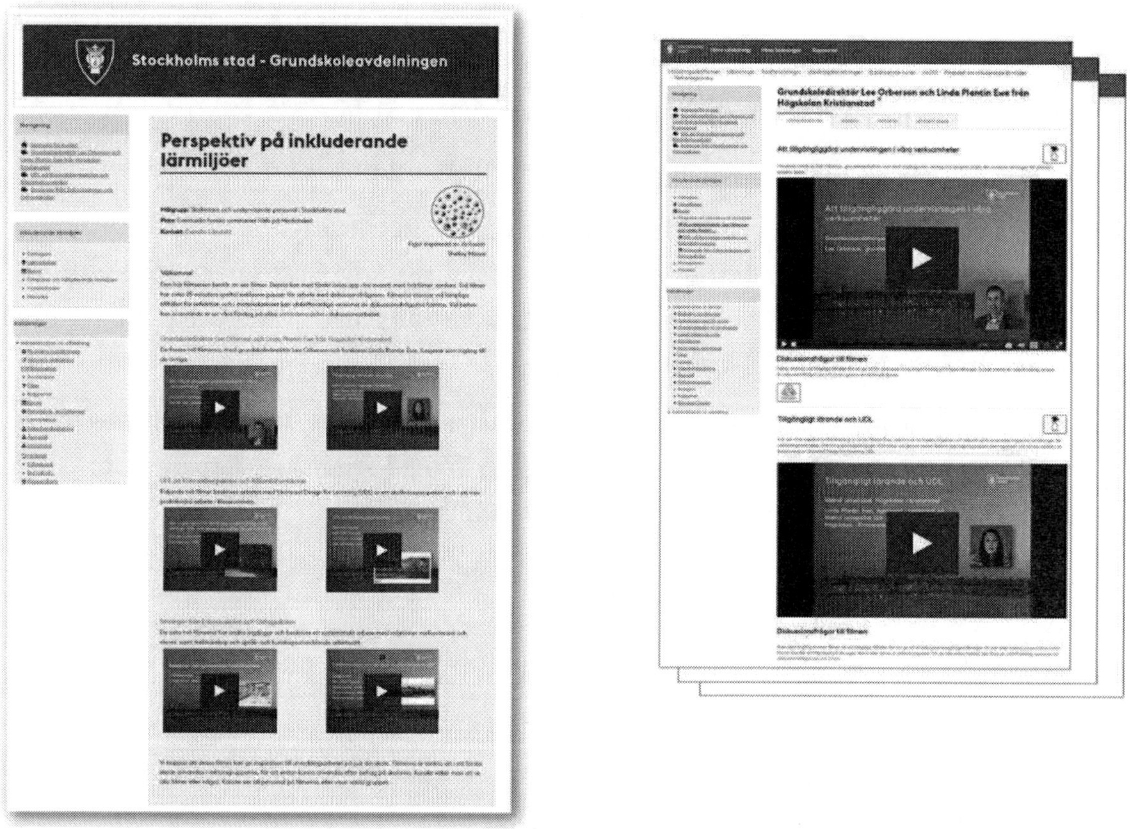

Description: Course landing page and the three sections with two videos and guidelines for peer interactions

Appendix B

Description: The first interactive video created with open source HTML5 Package (H5P) based on JavaScripts

Lessons from a Pandemic for the Future of Education
Short Paper Book of the European Distance and E-Learning Network (EDEN)
2021 Annual Conference | Madrid, 21-24 June, 2021
ISBN 978-615-5511-31-8

PROMOTING OPEN EDUCATION THROUGH GAMIFICATION – CATCH THE OPEN! A SERIOUS INTERACTIVE LEARNING GAME

Ulf-Daniel Ehlers, Tina Marie Monelyon, Baden-Wuerttemberg Cooperative State University Karlsruhe, Germany

Short Description

Come and meet Alex, a young teacher who has been tasked by the Rector of her university to *Catch the Open!* Users move through lecture halls and labs of a University-inspired web-based 2D virtual world to explore and learn about Open Educational Resources (OER) and Open Educational Practices (OEP) by engaging with students and colleagues and solving small tasks on their journey to master teaching in the open. The *Catch the Open!* game has been developed as part of the Erasmus+ funded *OpenGame* project (https://opengame-project.eu/). In order to broadly contribute to the open knowledge movement, the game was developed in English, as project Lingua Franca, and translated into German, Portuguese, Spanish and French.

The aim of the demonstration is to show participants how the individually developed 8 modules were derived based on a theoretical approach – grounded in desk research and interviews as well as a real-case-based collection of Open Practices which were systematically transformed into related knowledge and skills and further key competences comprising OER and Open pedagogies (the so-called *OpenGame Open Education Competences Framework*) – and then translated into hands-on learning activities users engage with as part of the interactive learning game. While the game and its features, such as different learning activities as well as small assessments and quizzes, will be presented live during the demonstration, participants are also given the opportunity to personally test the game and share their ideas and feedback related to the game. An additional written feedback form taking into account findings from research, such as Nielsen Norman's usability heuristics for video games (Joyce, 2019) as well as Toda et al. (2019), will round off the session.

Figure 3. "Home room" leading to different rooms corresponding with 8 modules

Figure 2. Exemplary room (Auditorium A) corresponding to Competence 1 of the OpenGame Competence Framework

Competence area	Competence	A. Attitude	B. Knowledge	C. Skills
1. OER	**1. Use open licenses**	Be ready to openly share one's work and to use the knowledge created by others and openly distributed in order to improve access, participation and quality of teaching and learning	Understand the (comparative) advantages of using open licences and know the existing open licences types	1.1. Know how to apply a CC license to teaching resources 1.2. Recognize teh respective requiremenets and restrictions of a licence and know how to determine whether a resource has one
	2. Search for OER		Know the major OER repositories and be able to identify those that are the most suited to your needs	2.1. Find OER that are relevant for own teaching 2.2. Assess materials within existing OER resources in order to use them
	3. Create, revise and remix OER		Know the different options for adaptation of an OER (translation, illustration, accessibility, contextualization, etc.)	3.1. Create an OER, taking into account the specificities of licences as well as its potential for reuse (format, language, granularity) 3.2. Revise an OER, taking into account the specificities of licences 3.3. Create an OER composed of various OERs, taking into account the specificities of licences
	4. Share OER		Know reputed OER repositories most suited for OER creators and cocreators to disseminate their creations for wider impact	4.1. Identify relevant OER repositories and publish your resource 4.2. Share your resource through social media and other means
2. Open pedagogies	**5. Design open educational experiences**		Know strategies on how to allow students participation in curriculum and learning design	5.1 Design engaging open educational experiences
	6. Guide students to learn in the open		Know about connected and network learning strategies. Be aware of the issues connected to online privacy and personal data management	6.1. Support students to learn through the open web (social networks, online communities etc.) 6.2. Provide guidancer to students about online privacy and personal data management
	7. Teach with OER		Master knowledge related to 1, 2, 3 and 4 above	7.1. Support students in searching for and using OER (either collaboratively or individually) 7.2. Support students in producing OER (either collaboratively or individually)
	8. Implement open assessment		Know the comparative advantages of open assessment and be aware of existing open assessment methods and tools	8.1. Deploy OER within an assessment (e.g. students analyse an open data set) 8.2. Guide students in doing their work in the public (e.g. blogging publicly) 8.3. Guiding students in producing OER for summative assessment

Figure 3. OpenGame Open Education Competences Framework

Project context

The OpenGame (Promoting Open Education through Gamification – Erasmus+ ref. 2019-1-ES01-KA203-065815) project consortium includes higher education institutes from across Europe, namely Universidad Internacional de la Rioja (UNIR – Project Coordinator), The University of Salamanca (USAL), University of Nantes (UNAN), Universidade Aberta (UAb), Baden-Wuerttemberg Cooperative State University Karlsruhe (DBHW Karlsruhe) and Dublin City University (DCU). Furthermore, the project consortium is completed by two important networks, the Open Education Consortium and the International Council for Open and Distance Education (ICDE), as associated partners.

- For more information on the project, please visit: https://opengame-project.eu
- Access to game's test version (please register and use English version – translations in progress): https://opengame-project.eu/play/
- Underlying Course Curriculum and Content (Intellectual Output 2 of OpenGame project, 30th September, 2020): https://opengame-project.eu/wp-content/uploads/2020/11/OpenGame-IO2-CourseCurriculumAndContent.pdf
- Handbook of Successful Open Teaching Practices (Intellectual Output 1 of OpenGame project, XX): https://opengame-project.eu/wp-content/uploads/2020/07/OpenGame-IO1-HandbookOfSuccesfulOpenPractices.pdf

References

Joyce, A. (2019, May 19). 10 Usability Heuristics Applied to Video Games. Nielsen Norman Group [Blog post]. Retrieved from https://www.nngroup.com/articles/usability-heuristics-applied-video-games/

Toda, A. M., Klock, A. C. T., Oliveira, W., Palomino, P. T., Rodrigues, L., Shi, L., Bittencourt, I., Gasparini, I., Isotani, S., & Cristea, A. I. (2019). Analysing gamification elements in educational environments using an existing Gamification taxonomy. *Smart Learning Environments, 6*, 16 (2019). https://doi.org/10.1186/s40561-019-0106-1

ISBN 978-615-5511-31-8

ACCOMPANY BOYS AND GIRLS TO ART GALLERIES IN UNCERTAIN TIMES – PROJECT OF A SUPPORT SITE

María José Lobato Suero, María del Carmen Sánchez Sánchez, CES, Cardenal Spínola CEU, Carmen Salazar-Pera, Faculty of Fine Arts, Spain

Abstract

The academic situations caused by the social distance measures as a result of the COVID-19 pandemic have also affected the projects that are supported by the scholarships awarded to students. In the case of the Accompaniment Project for children in art galleries of the Cardenal Spínola University Center, the activities that had been developed aimed at motivating families to visit art galleries had to be suspended. To alleviate the situation, without detriment to the granting of scholarships, the project is reoriented to the construction of a website that, in addition to serving to guide and train scholarship holders through the service-learning (SL) will enable online support that would allow them to maintain contact with families.

The Accompaniment Project for boys and girls in art galleries

The activity begins in the 2017-2018 academic year as an internal project of a university centre with an interdisciplinary approach integrating Pedagogy, Music, and Fine Arts teachers. Its origin is a collaborative project that involves teachers, scholarship holders, and internal students of the 3rd and 4th years of the Infant and Primary Education Degrees.

After the signing of the agreement between the university centre (attached to the University of Seville) and AGAS (Association of art galleries of Seville), on-site and systematic accompaniment is developed in the visits of families to the galleries. Each meeting is publicized through social networks, fliers, etc. A distribution list of attending families is created to communicate the events that take place on Saturday mornings.

The action of the students is framed in the modality of service-learning (SL). Its function is to support and help families, boys and girls to conquer galleries as learning spaces; awakening their curiosity and interest in culture, encouraging dialogue and communication. In coordination with the teachers, they carry out the design of activities and interact in person with the boys and girls attending.

Project redesign

From the 2017-2018 school year and subsequent years, until the pandemic broke out in 2020, the activities were carried out monthly or bi-monthly. As a result of the sanitary emergency, in the year 2019-2020, the project is redesigned, resulting in creating a support website that, although far from the face-to-face spirit of origin, aims to keep contact with families alive.

The webspace: Project boys and girls in art galleries

The website contains the basic sections to inform, and gives open proposals of activities to the specific families for each exhibition. The first interface is divided into sections: *Home*, *Who are we*, *Our project*, *Story* and *Contact*. Two side columns contain the press reviews and publications related to the project. A central mosaic gives access to the exhibitions already visited and the current ones. Each image of the mosaic gives way to a specific interface of each gallery it contains: an upper carousel with the works on display; a link to the gallery. Below, you can access the download of the documents of the activity proposals and another carousel with a sample of the presence of families in the event and the activities of the children that can be uploaded to the web through the *Contact* section (https://acompgalerias.wixsite.com/proyectogaleriasceu).

Figure 1. Home interface of the web "Project Boys and girls in art galleries". The mosaic includes each of the exhibitions.

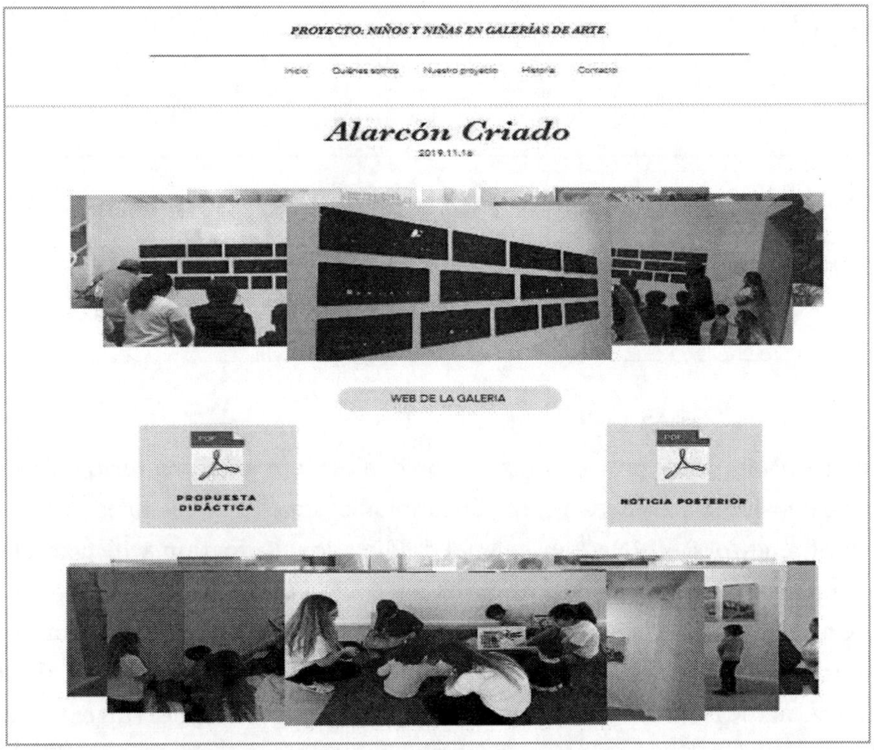

Figure 2. The specific page of each meeting in the gallery's exhibition space

Innovate through a webspace

ICTs have made it possible to create a web tool that enables continuous changes and modifications, being able to be fed according to the encounters and the needs that occur.

The potential of this practical innovation consists in the possibility of implementation in other projects with similar characteristics in educational environments; at the same time that it allows to continue the learning of the service and the expansion in other media appropriate to needs of service-learning (SL) in University students.

References

Lobato Suero, M. J., & Salazar-Pera, C. (2017). *Acción de acompañamiento cultural para niños en centros y galerias de arte.* Simposio Internacional: El desafío de Emprender en la Escuela del Siglo XXI (56-58), Sevilla, España: Universidad de Sevilla. Retrieved from https://idus.us.es/handle/11441/74094

Lobato Suero, M. J., & Salazar-Pera, C. (2019). Proyecto de acompañamiento cultural para niños. Encuentros en galerías de arte. Didacticae. *Journal of Research in Specific Didactics, 2019*(6), 57-67. Retrieved from https://revistes.ub.edu/index.php/didacticae/article/view/28136

ISBN 978-615-5511-31-8

DISTANT EDUCATION IN THE FRAMEWORK OF THE MNET PROJECT

Michael Petropoulos, Apostolos Tsirigotis, Antonios Leisos, Physics Laboratory, School of Science and Technology, Hellenic Open University, Greece

Abstract

The microNet (μNet) project aims for the deployment and long-term operation of an extensive school network of educational cosmic ray telescopes in Greece. In the framework of μNet, an extended educational program will take place, encompassing educational activities for the construction, testing and operation of μCosmics (microCosmics) detectors, as well as for the remote operation of cosmic ray detection stations and astroparticle physics experimental devices deployed at the Hellenic Open University (HOU) campus. A pilot run of the μNet project started in 2020 aiming for the deployment and operation of a small school network in western Greece. Although the original design aimed for the construction of the detection devices by students, due to the COVID-19 pandemic we redesigned our program, with greater emphasis on remote operations and the development of related tools. In the present work we present the first results and findings of this pilot run.

Introduction

Involving students in cutting-edge research activities has multiple benefits, which have been extensively presented in the international literature (Walkington, 2015; Wayment & Dickson, 2008; Straker, 2016). One of the major advantages is the increase of students' self-esteem, the development of new mental and practical skills as well as the development of cooperation in the workplace. In addition, students get to know the methodology of scientific research, the connection between theoretical knowledge and practical applications, but also the limitations imposed by the experimental procedures and the scientific instruments. The involvement in research activities also gives students the chance to explore professional employment prospects and possible alternative paths that they can follow in their professional life, i.e., basic and applied research.

Unfortunately, in the Greek educational reality, no such connection has been efficiently developed and any participation of students to research activities is often limited to that of the spectator of demonstration experiments. In addition, due to the recent COVID-19 pandemic and the mobility restrictions, any connection between the high school community and research institutes (i.e., summer schools, workshops for pupils, etc.) was reduced dramatically. Moreover, even under normal circumstances and due to the general geomorphology of Greece, a large percentage of students living in small towns, villages, and islands have sparse contact with scientific research, which is usually confined to tours at the campus of university institutions, as part of an excursion. The lack of participation of students in experimental activities is considered as one of the reasons for the low performance of Greek students in the PISA competitions, in sciences (Sofianopoulou et al., 2017; OECD, 2018).

The Physics Laboratory of the Hellenic Open University, among its other activities, has set as one of its priorities the coverage of part of this gap, long before the start of the pandemic. By designing and constructing a portable and low-cost cosmic ray telescope (μCosmics, pronounced microCosmics) along with the development of educational activities during summer schools, it created the building blocks of the μNet project which aims for the active involvement of high school students and teachers to the experimental methodology of astroparticle physics and especially to cosmic ray physics. The μNet project is expected to be in operation by the end of 2023, but very recently (June 2020) a 15-month pilot project started for the deployment of 6 educational telescopes and the development of the relevant educational and software tools. Since the remote operation of experimental devices is foreseen in the μNet project and due to the COVID-19 restrictions that maintained the schools closed for most of the 2020-2021 school period, most of the educational activities and operations were adapted to distant learning activities and operations respectively giving us an insight of how such a hybrid (both in situ and distant experimental activities) school network is expected to operate.

The μNet Project

Cosmic Rays

Primary cosmic rays are high energy protons and atomic nuclei that originate from astrophysical objects of Milky Way or other galaxies with energy spectrum orders of magnitude greater than the energy of terrestrial artificial accelerators (i.e. LHC at CERN). When these cosmic particles enter the earth's atmosphere they interact with the atmosphere and new secondary particles are produced. When the energy of the initial particle is high, millions of secondaries are produced forming a shower of particles travelling with the speed of light towards the earth's surface (Extensive Air Shower – EAS). If the shower energy is large enough, many particles reach the ground, spreading up to several thousands of square meters for very energetic showers (Figure 1, left). Among these particles, the muons (atmospheric muons) are the most numerous energetic charged particles arriving at sea level, with a flux of about 1 muon per square centimetre per minute.

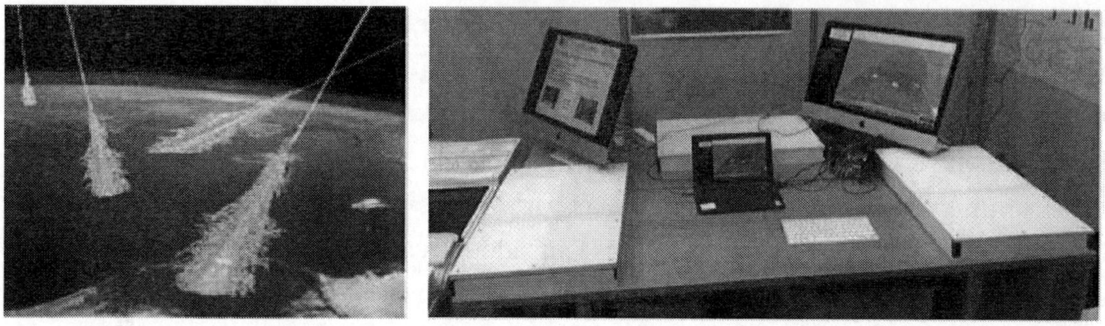

Figure 1. Left: An artistic view of extensive air showers produced in the atmosphere. Right: The μCosmics detection station. The detection units (white boxes) along with the data acquisition board and the station computer (laptop).

The μCosmics detector

Since 2014, the HOU Physics Laboratory has installed at the university campus a distributed array of air shower detection stations, consisting of scintillator detectors and Radio Frequency (RF) antennas (Avgitas et al., 2020). Based on the experience gained with the Astroneu detection system, and utilizing the latest technology, the Physics Laboratory of HOU has recently designed and built a cosmic ray telescope for educational purposes (μCosmics detector). μCosmics (Figure 1, right) is a highly portable atmospheric air shower detector that can be operated within the classroom or school lab, has low cost and does not require high voltage or potentially hazardous power supplies. In addition, the μCosmics detector can be assembled by students, while its small size and light weight allows for many educational activities to be carried out in the classroom or in a school laboratory. For a detailed presentation of the μCosmics detector and its philosophy, refer to Tsirigotis and Leisos (2019).

The μNet educational activities

The μNet project aims for the active involvement of high school students in experimental procedures of Astroparticle physics and especially in Cosmic ray physics. Specifically, the project aspires for the development and long-term operation of a Greek school network of educational cosmic ray telescopes (μCosmics detectors) that will be installed at high school laboratories in the geographical region of Peloponnese. In addition, the project includes the development of remotely operated experimental devices and the utilization of the HOU extensive air shower array (Astroneu array), in order to provide access to any high school, independently of its geographical position. The schools that will operate in situ autonomous air shower detection systems, as well as the schools that will operate remotely the Astroneu stations and the HOU experimental setups will constitute the μNet network, the 1st Greek school network of educational cosmic ray telescopes. There are many school networks of education cosmic ray telescopes around the globe. See for Leisos et al. (2018) and the references therein.

The intended training program of μNet is not just about the installation and operation of ready-to-go, and technically tested, detection systems. The main feature of the project is that it aims to actively involve the student community in the whole experimental process, which includes instrument construction, setup, testing of its operation, and finally data collection and analysis in order to draw conclusions as to the characteristics of cosmic rays. For that reason, educational activities have been designed (Petropoulos, Leisos, & Tsirigotis, 2020a) to introduce students to the modern experimental methodology of Astroparticle physics and, in particular, to cosmic rays physics (Table 1). These activities refer to the scientific studies for which the instrument is designed (e.g. measurement of the direction of cosmic rays), but also to the experimental procedures preceding the experiment (e.g. instrument construction, calibration and proper operation).

Table 1: Educational activities with the μCosmics detector, where students' tasks are described. All tasks except the 1st can also be performed remotely using experimental devices at the HOU Physics Laboratory.

1	Assembly of the μCosmics detector
2	Measurement of the detector response to muons
3	Synchronization of the detector units
4	Measurement of the atmospheric muon flux and coincidence studies
5	DAQ operation and online monitoring
6	Geometries studies and estimation of the angular resolution
7	Measurement of the cosmic ray angular distribution

All the educational activities that have been planned, with the exception of activity 1, can be performed remotely, so that one of the main objectives of the program is covered, that is, the participation of students from any part of Greece. However, the remote operation is foreseen using special experimental devices that are designed to support remote operation and will be installed at the HOU Physics Laboratory. For a detailed description of the educational project, refer to Petropoulos, Leisos, and Tsirigotis (2020a) and Petropoulos, Leisos, and Tsirigotis (2020b).

Pilot Run of the μNet Project

The pilot run of the μNet project started in June 2020 and is expected to be completed by September 2021. The original plan was to train the school teachers at the Physics Laboratory of HOU and then to deploy the detection stations at the school laboratories. There the students (under the guidance of their teachers) would accomplish the educational activities of table 1 during the whole school period. Unfortunately, the COVID-19 pandemic did not allow us to follow the original design. In order to overcome this, we adapted most of the activities to be done remotely using the μCosmics detectors (remote operations are foreseen in the μNet project using special equipment), while the training of the school teachers was completely carried out also remotely.

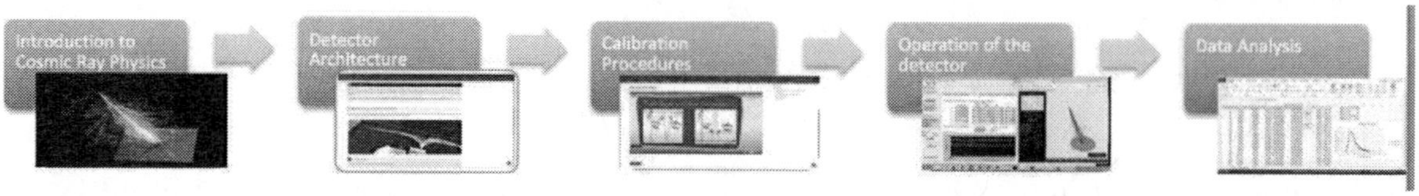

Figure 2. The workflow of trainees in the distance education program of the pilot run. Each task is supported by educational material (videos and animations) that are implemented to Moodle.

For this purpose, we developed a series of analytical, but short, videos, where the participants could study the underlying physics theory as well as the experimental procedures followed. The workflow of the trainees is sketched on Figure 2 and it was implemented to a dedicated Moodle-platform, where the trainees after watching the videos, were asked to answer comprehension questions. In case of incorrect answers, there was a rollback to the specific point in the video, where they needed to pay more attention in order to consolidate the information. The online training was performed by simultaneous self-experimentation using the experimental devices that were located at the HOU Physics Laboratory and were accessible via the https protocol (Figure 3, left). In addition, regular weekly online meetings were held through the Webex platform, where a member of the HOU Lab presented the experimental procedures, explained how to handle detectors remotely, collect data and process them (Figure 3, right).

Figure 3. Left: Five μCosmics telescopes located in one of the venues of the HOU Physics Laboratory. The telescopes are remotely operated by the corresponding school groups. Right: A snapshot of a regular weekly online meeting with the schools' teachers.

The anticipated educational program of the pilot run will be completed by the end of June 2021. Then the telescopes will be operated in shower-detection mode where the three detection units will be arranged in an almost equilateral triangle with side length of about 6 meters. The accumulation of data will last for a month and then the data analysis will follow (end of July 2021). All these procedures are designed to be performed remotely, i.e. even if the pandemic measures are withdrawn.

Feedback – First results

At the time of the writing the distant education program is ongoing and expected to be completed by July of 2021. 6 school teachers and approximately 50 pupils participate in this pilot run. Participating teachers and students are invited to evaluate the process, to submit reflections and suggestions, so that the program is as understandable and effective as possible. From the feedback we have received so far, the main feature is the enthusiasm of both students and teachers, as they consider that it is something that goes beyond the trivial, covering a significant gap in the Greek education system, as modern physics, such as and Astronomy and Astrophysics are not part of the curriculum in Secondary Education.

Students learn easily the remote control of devices and understanding the logic of the experiment is not a problem worth mentioning. The lack of knowledge regarding the physics of the experiment is covered both by the visual material we have developed and by the exchange of questions and answers during teleconferences. Although there was a phobia initially about their capability to satisfy the requirements of the program, it was quickly overcome as we avoided mathematical formalities, which are often a deterrent to students. At the same time, and for their convenience, we simplified the process of processing the data collected by the students, automating the work in spreadsheets, since Greek students are familiar with such tools being part of their curriculum.

Table 2 presents some of the questions that teachers were asked to answer, evaluating the curriculum and students' ability to meet its requirements. One of the questions we asked the teachers is from which class do they think students can adequately respond to such a research project. 75% think that the students of the 2nd Lyceum class (Grade 11) are the most suitable for such an education, while 25% think that younger students but at least from the 3rd Gymnasium class (Grade 9) may respond in a very satisfactory level. They also consider that one of the strongest points of the program is the educational videos and animations, which students definitely prefer instead of the traditional text.

Table 2: Evaluation by teachers participating in the pilot program, for the distance learning μCosmics project. (1: *Not at all satisfactory*, to 5: *Particularly satisfactory*)

Question	Answers				
	1	2	3	4	5
How interesting do you think this program is?					100%
Have you gained new knowledge from your participation?				25%	75%
The supporting material available so far, how satisfactory do you think it is?				25%	75%
How interesting do you think this program might be for students?			25%		75%
Evaluate the individual material you have studied so far.				25%	75%
How comprehensible for students can be the Physics of such a program?			25%	25%	50%
How satisfactorily do you think students can meet the laboratory and digital requirements of the program?			25%	25%	50%
Do you think that distance education can work in such research programs for students?			25%		75%

In addition, teachers consider that distance education is not a particular problem for students, since they are given the opportunity to adjust their participation to their own needs. Nevertheless, 100% consider lifelong learning to be necessary and even though that distance education is a satisfactory solution, it should be complementary to lifelong learning. Above all, however, they judge that distance learning covers the students on a more personal level, covering their personal interests and concerns. This is because it is almost impossible to allocate resources for the development of such programs, which is obviously much easier for a research institute.

Conclusions

The Physics Laboratory of the Hellenic Open University, long before the pandemic began, was interested in developing techniques and methods for distance education in cutting-edge research. The main goal was the participation of students from inaccessible areas and schools that have little or not any access to research institutions and infrastructures. The μNet project is towards this direction. It encompasses activities for high school students that can be performed by using both in situ as well as remote operated astroparticle physics devices.

A pilot run of the μNet project started in June 2020 with a duration of 15 months in order to develop tools and methods suitable both for high school teachers and students. Due to the pandemic restriction measures, the remote experimental procedures as well as the distant education tools received the main focus of the project. The school teachers participating in the pilot run evaluated our educational approach and responded positively to the methodology we applied. Their feedback was precious during the development of the videos and animations as well as to the functionality of the data analysis software.

Approximately 50 students are currently involved in the project coming from 6 high schools of western Greece. The pilot program is expected to be completed by the end of July 2021 following the distant learning methodology even if the pandemic measures are withdrawn. The feedback we receive from this pilot run, will be used to improve the remote experimental process, as in the next two years the project will be expanded in more than 50 schools in the Peloponnese. The experience to date is particularly encouraging, as students have the opportunity to participate in cutting-edge research experiments, which are not offered at school, and to satisfy their personal interests, without having to leave their place of residence. In addition, distance education, with the logic of access to knowledge not available in the standard school curriculum, seems to work more democratically, as all stakeholders have access, regardless of where they live or their financial abilities.

References

Avgitas, T., Bourlis, G., Fanourakis, G. K., Gkialas, I., Leisos, A., Manthos I., Tsirigotis, A. G., & Tzamarias, S. E. (2020). The Astroneu Extensive Air Shower Array. *JINST, 15,* T03003. doi:10.1088/1748-0221/15/03/T03003

Leisos, A., Avgitas, T., Bourlis, G., Fanourakis, G. K., Gkialas, I., Manthos, I., Stamelakis, A., Tsirigotis, A. G., & Tzamarias S. E. (2018). The Hellenic Open University Cosmic Ray Telescope: Research and Educational Activities. *EPJ Web Conferences, 182,* 02072. doi:10.1051/epjconf/201818202072

OECD (2018). *PISA – Programme for International Student Assessment, PISA 2018 results.* Retrieved from https://www.oecd.org/pisa/publications/pisa-2018-resultshtm.htm

Petropoulos, M., Leisos, A., & Tsirigotis, A. (2020a). Outreach activities with the μCosmics air shower detector. *Physics Education, 55,* 055005. doi:10.1088/1361-6552/ab921b

Petropoulos, M., Leisos, A., & Tsirigotis, A. (2020b). μNet: Towards the first array of educational air shower detectors in Greece. *International Journal of Modern Physics A, 35*(34n35), 2044022. doi:10.1142/S0217751X20440224

Sofianopoulou, Ch., Emvalotis, A., Pitsia, V., & Karakolidis, A. (2017). *Report on the Findings from the Programme for International Student Assessment (PISA) 2015 for Greece.* Athens: Institute of Educational Policy (IEP).

Straker, J. (2016). International Student Participation in Higher Education: Changing the Focus from International Students to Participation. *J. Studies Int. Education, 20,* 299-318.

Tsirigotis, A. G., & Leisos A. (2019). μCosmics: a low-cost educational cosmic ray telescope. *Universe, 5*(1), 23.

Walkington, H. (2015). *Students as Researchers: Supporting Undergraduate Research in the Disciplines in Higher Education.* The Higher Education Academy. Retrieved from https://www.heacademy.ac.uk/system/files/resources/Students%20as%20researchers_1.pdf

Wayment, H. A., & Dickson, K. L. (2008). Increasing Student Participation in Undergraduate Research Benefits Students. *Teaching of Psychology, 35*(3), 194-197. https://doi.org/10.1080/00986280802189213

Acknowledgments

This project has received funding from the Hellenic Foundation for Research and Innovation (HFRI) and the General Secretariat for Research and Technology (GSRT), under grant agreement No MIS-5050585. The authors would like to thank the μNet development group (Xiros L., Minos A., Antoniou E., Rizogiannis G., Mavromichalakis N.), as well as the high school teachers (Bakatselou K., Giannareli M., Karadimas E., Kremmydas T., Litinas A., Psinas A., Zogopoulos K.) and all the high school students that participate with great enthusiasm and eagerness in the pilot run of μNet.

ISBN 978-615-5511-31-8

PLEIADE

PLayful Environment for Inclusive leArning Design in Europe

Website: https://pleiade-project.eu

Runtime: 09.2020 – 08.2023

Supported / co-funded by: Erasmus+ Call 2020 – KA201 – Strategic Partnerships for school education – Cooperation for innovation and the exchange of good practices

Partners: National Research Council of Italy – Institute for Educational Technology, Genoa, Italy (coordinator); Sofia University St Kliment Ohridski, Bulgaria; OPEN LAB SRL, Florence, Italy; European Distance and e-learning Network (EDEN), London, UK; 144 Secondary School "Narodni Buditeli", Sofia, Bulgaria; Scuola secondaria di 1° grado "Rocca Bovio Palumbo", Trani, Italy; "S. Avgoulea-Linardatou" School, Athens, Greece; "Neapolis" Gymnasium, Limassol, Cyprus; Association for Teacher Education in Europe (ATEE), Brussels, Belgium (associated partner).

Project representative to be contacted for further info: Donatella Persico (persico@itd.cnr.it); Ferenc Tatrai (tatrai@eden-online.org); Marilina Lonigro (marilina.lonigro@gmail.com)

With sharply increasing cultural, linguistic and socio-economic diversity in Europe's school populations, there is urgency to shift towards collaborative learning practices that embrace the inclusion of all learners. The challenge is to ensure that ALL students have optimal chances of realizing their potential as individuals and future European citizens. In this scenario, PLEIADE supports its teachers to systematically integrate inclusive practices in their teaching by helping them to design, implement and share with colleagues inclusion-aware collaborative learning activities.

PLEIADE's support for teachers' capacity building comes in the form of a blended (onsite + online) playful pathway of teacher training and peer collaboration for teachers working in 4 different schools, who are facing different challenges in terms of learner diversity. The pathway features advanced game-like elements that draw on physical and digital tools designed to support teacher interaction, cooperation and, ultimately, collaboration. The pathway will entail the use of a game (the I4Ts game) and of a gamified platform developed specifically for the project. In PLEIADE, this composite learning environment will be fully developed and deployed to (a) enhance teachers' engagement in a training experience, (b) foster co-creation and sharing of inclusive activity designs, (c) support classroom enactment of those activities and (d) promote the sharing and propagation of successful inclusive practices in a teacher community.

PLEIADE engages an immediate target population of about 75 teachers at primary and secondary schools in Italy, Bulgaria, Cyprus and Greece, whose schools are consortium members. The collaborative learning activities they design and implement in their classrooms during the project are expected to benefit around 600 pupils, many of whom experience educational disadvantage due to cultural, linguistic and socio-economic diversity.

Main target groups of the project: school teachers, teacher educators, school principals and policy makers interested in fostering educational inclusion, researchers in collaborative learning, inclusive education, learning design and gamification.

PLEIADE – PLayful Environment for Inclusive leArning Design in Europe

Significant public results:

- IO1: an innovative gamified TPD pathway dedicated to inclusive education, learning design, and collaborative learning;
- IO2: a Hybrid Game (the I4Ts Game) of tangible and digital elements that supports teachers' design of collaborative, inclusion-aware learning activities based on an innovative approach called "4Ts approach";
- IO3: a gamified digital platform providing a scaffolded context for teacher interaction regarding the deployment of PLEIADE - inspired classroom activities and the exchange of related experiences;
- IO4: a collection of innovative practices generated by the PLEIADE teacher community;
- IO5: an evaluation kit for inclusive-aware collaborative learning activities;
- IO6: an impact amplification kit.

ISBN 978-615-5511-31-8

R4C

Reflecting for Change

Website: https://reflecting4change.eu

Runtime: 1 NOV 2019 - 31 OCT 2021

Supported / co-funded by: Erasmus+ KA3 Support for Policy Reform – Forward Looking Co-operation Project

Partners: Ellinogermaniki Agogi, Greece (coordinator), European School Heads Association, EU, European Distance and E-learning Network (EDEN), UK, ScienceView, EU, University of Bayreuth (UBT), Germany, Institute of Educational Policy (IEP), Greece, Fondazione Idis-Città della Scienza, Italy, NUCLIO – Núcleo Interativo de Astronomia, Portugal

Project representative to be contacted for further info: Sofoklis Sotiriou (sotiriou@ea.gr), Ferenc Tátrai (tatrai@eden-online.org)

Short description of the initiative

The Reflecting for Change (R4C) project aims at proposing an advanced support framework, as well as a set of core policy recommendations, to schools seeking to introduce a type of holistic change that will ensure a meaningful uptake of sustainable innovation, with an emphasis on achieving improved learning outcomes as set by the Europe 2020 strategy.

R4C is a Forward-Looking Cooperation Project (https://eacea.ec.europa.eu/erasmus-plus/actions/key-action-3-support-for-policy-reform/erasmus-plus-key-action-3-prospective-initiatives/forward-looking-cooperation-projects_en) that promotes the use of self-reflection tools to support innovation and systemic change in education and training institutions. These projects highlight good practice in using and, in particular, following-up results from the two self-reflection tools developed by the European Commission, namely HEInnovate (https://heinnovate.eu/en) for higher education institutions and SELFIE for schools (https://ec.europa.eu/education/schools-go-digital_en).

In R4C approach, innovation is understood in terms of a school's pathway to digital maturity (e-maturity) and its comprehensive relationship to the use of ICT, as well as a school's pathway to openness demonstrated in its relationship with external stakeholders, in parental engagement, in fostering the well-being of its community as a whole, in its ability to combine the delivering of the curriculum with a study of local challenges, in its willingness and capacity to share its achievements with other schools and in its engagement with contemporary Responsible Research Innovation (RRI) challenges.

The consortium will organize and coordinate large scale pilots with schools to evaluate the effects of, and systematically validate the proposed approach by implementing numerous activities and exploiting at the same time the opportunities offered by major ongoing initiatives and reforms, in Greece, Portugal and Italy. The project will be implemented with a bottom up approach in 300 primary and secondary schools, in urban as well as in rural areas while the sample for the validation of the proposed approach will consist of 1,500 teachers and 15,000 students.

Main target groups of the project: primary and secondary school heads, teachers, students and educational authorities. Schools in Greece, Italy, and Portugal are involved in the large scale pilot.

R4C – Reflecting for Change

Significant public results:

- School Innovation Model (https://reflecting4change.eu/wp-content/uploads/2021/02/D1.1-School-Innovation-Model.pdf)
- School Profile and Analytics Framework (https://reflecting4change.eu/wp-content/uploads/2021/02/D1.2-School-Profile-and-Analytics-Framework.pdf)
- School Innovation Profiling Tool and the School Innovation Planning Recommender System (https://reflecting4change.eu/wp-content/uploads/2021/02/D1.3-School-Innovation-Profiling-Tool-and-the-School-Innovation-Planning-Recommender-System.pdf)
- International Professional Development Course (https://esia.ea.gr/training/towards-an-open-e-mature-school/)
- Validation Tools (https://reflecting4change.eu/wp-content/uploads/2021/02/D4.2-Validation-Tools.pdf)
- School Innovation Strategies
- School Innovation Roadmap
- School Innovation Academy

Lessons from a Pandemic for the Future of Education
Short Paper Book of the European Distance and E-Learning Network (EDEN)
2021 Annual Conference | Madrid, 21-24 June, 2021
ISBN 978-615-5511-31-8

VIRTEACH

A Virtual Solution for a comprehensive and coordinated training for foreign language TEACHers in Europe

Website: http://virteachproject.eu

Runtime: 09.2018 – 08.2021

Supported / co-funded by: Erasmus+ Programme of the European Union

Partners: University of Burgos, Spain (project coordinator) – UC Leuven Limburg, Belgium – Collegium Balticum, Poland – Christian University of Bucharest, Romania – Lusofona University, Portugal

Project representative to be contacted for further info: Nele Kelchtermans (nele.kelchtermans@ucll.be)

Short description of the initiative

The increasing globalisation of contemporary societies poses great challenges to the education sector. As the Eurydice (2015) report indicates, the labour mobility of the teaching and learning collective is in continuous growth due to the constant increase in opportunities for university study abroad, and a static labour market resulting from the last years of economic crisis. Displacement in Europe is particularly evident among foreign language students and teachers, who tend to move more frequently and for longer. However, there is a lack of unified formats for teacher education at a European level, with national agencies working in each country separately.

To address these shortcomings, the VIRTEACH project seeks to find a VIRtual Solution for a comprehensive and coordinated training for foreign language TEACHers in Europe. This Erasmus+ funded project (2018-2021) has created a digital tool to improve the postgraduate certificates on Masters on Education for foreign language teachers and has provided teachers, researchers, student teachers and policy-makers with open-source tools and reports to foster convergence in the education of foreign language teachers.

Main target groups of the project: Experts, researchers, lecturers, students in the field of foreign language teacher education

Significant public results:

Interactive Toolkit: This Interactive Toolkit provides a comprehensive collection of learning materials, open education resources, methodological guidelines and examples of best practices for the construction of a foreign language teacher training model at European level. This initiative, accomplished by the participants of the VIRTEACH Erasmus+ project, hopes to be useful to lecturers, professors, teachers and researchers in the field of Higher Education. It is freely available and the VIRTEACH team encourages dissemination and implementation in educational programs.

Virtual Learning Environment: The VIRTEACH team has designed the "21st Century Foreign Language Teacher Training Course". It is a friendly and easy-to-use online course that offers innovative approaches and resources to language teacher education. This course, embedded in a Virtual Learning Environment, is a suitable tool to monitor foreign language student teachers' education. It is also a lifelong learning platform for experienced teachers of languages.

Interactive Digital Notepad: The Interactive Digital Notepad (IDN) is a practical proposal for the integration of technology into the Practicum of foreign language student teachers. It has been designed as a robust tool for mentoring and communication between student teacher, university instructor and school mentor. Thanks to this digital tool, the Practicum becomes a coherent, reflective, dynamic and enriching learning experience for all parties.

White Paper with policy recommendations for internationalisation and convergence of curricula in foreign language teacher education.

European Conference on Foreign Language Teacher Education:

As a final landmark, the VIRTEACH project team organises the Multiplier Event: I European Conference on Foreign Language Teacher Education. This 2-day conference is a meeting place and platform for researchers, teacher educators, policy makers and teachers from all over Europe. It combines inspiring keynotes, a wide variety of papers on research and practice, problems and advancements of foreign language teacher education, and active working sessions in a stimulating and friendly atmosphere. Hosted by the University of Burgos (Spain), this conference will provide a venue for the following activities:

- Presentation and discussion of the outputs of the VIRTEACH project.
- Presentations by researchers and practitioners on innovative experiences in the education of foreign language teachers.
- Discussion fora involving policy makers on convergent policy design for foreign language teacher training.
- Identification of new issues and future directions in the training of foreign language teachers in Europe.
- Practical Workshops: 21st Century Foreign Language Teacher Training Course and Interactive Digital Notepad.

ISBN 978-615-5511-31-8

Complex Trajectories

Promoting Students' Successful Trajectories in Higher Education Institutions

Website: https://web.fe.up.pt/~complext/

Runtime: 09.2020 – 08.2023

Supported / co-funded by: Erasmus+ – Key Activity 2 Strategic partnership

Partners: Fundació per a la Universitat Oberta de Catalunya (UOC) (Coordinator) – Spain, Universitat Autònoma de Barcelona (UAB) – Spain, Secretaria d'Universitats i Recerca (SUR) – Spain, Universitat de València (UV) – Spain, Universidade do Porto (UP) – Portugal, Universidade Aberta (UAB) – Portugal, Université de Bourgogne (UB) – France and The Open University (OU) – United Kingdom.

Project representative to be contacted for further info: Josep M. Duart (jduart@uoc.edu)

Short description of the initiative. The Complex Trajectories Project focuses on understanding the complex trajectories of students at university and supporting those who navigate them. In the practical domain, the project aims to contribute to establishing a system of regular monitoring of student trajectories in order to adjust the development of policies supporting these trajectories at different levels of the system and university institutions. At the conceptual level, the aim is to broaden the notion of what can be considered an inclusive university. While there has been a major movement to look at equity in access to university (known as widening access) the progress of students through the university also requires attention to achieving an inclusive university.

To do so, it is necessary to extend the concept success in progress through the university. Normally, the analysis of trajectories is done from a single degree program. This gives a restricted view of successful trajectory is, since it would only be the one that begins and ends the same degree program. The policies to be applied to promote such success are policies of student retention. Instead, we argue that the focus of the analysis should be the student. Students can shift, pause, combine their studies, move between different degree programs or different modalities (distance and face-to-face), maybe building a complex, but successful, trajectory.

To achieve the project objectives, the agents involved must be diverse, i.e., the agents working at the level of providing information and understanding the phenomenon, those making policy (at different levels), and those providing direct support to students. Given that the involvement of agents acting at various levels is required and, that the process of information gathering, trajectory analysis and policy adjustment in support of these trajectories needs to be updated, it seems clear that the best way to address the issue is through the networking of the agents involved.

To give maximum diffusion to the knowledge acquired and the materials produced, we will transform them into products of quick understanding (infographics, brochures) that can be disseminated through already existing websites (universities, student services, international education organisations, etc.) or in the student services offices. Moreover, the planned training of the partners of the consortium in all the areas of development of the project will allow us to set up Multiplier Events in four countries to carry out an extensive dissemination of the outputs and to advance in the objective of generating networks in each territory.

Significant public results: The project has three main parts, plus an area dedicated to the dissemination, which includes generating or consolidating a network in each territory of the consortium partners. The first part is focused on developing a methodology for analysing student trajectories transferable to other higher education contexts. In the second part, we will carry out a collection of good practices supporting complex trajectories by exploring policies in the HEIs that are partners in the consortium and other HEIs in their nearby territories. The deeper objective is to understand the link between the different types of good practices and the results of the trajectories analysis, trying to answer the question about which measures can benefit which trajectories and in which way. In the third part, it is planned to transform the knowledge acquired from the two previous parts into training and decision-making support material. To this end, degree program evaluation indicators will be constructed on the theme of trajectories. Two MOOCs will be designed, one aiming at learning the longitudinal analysis of student trajectories, the other for advisors on measures to support complex trajectories. A handbook for advisors and other support materials will be designed.

DISK

DISK | Digital Immigrants Survival Kit

Digital Immigrants Survival Kit

Website: https://www.disk-project.eu/web/

Runtime: Nov. 2019– April. 2022

Supported / co-funded by: The ERASMUS + program of European Union, DISK project 2019-1-PT01-KA204-060898

Partners: QOOL – Ossiannilsson Quality in Open Online Learning Consultancy, Sweden; UP – University of Porto, Portugal, co-ordinator; EFQBL – European Foundation for Quality in Blended Learning, Austria; Training 2000, Italy; EDRASE – Educational Activities Society, Greece

Project representative to be contacted for further info: Pedro Ferreira (pferreira@fpce.up.pt)

Short description of the initiative

The two-year Digital Immigrants Survival Kit (DISK, 2019-2022, 2019-1-PT01-KA204-060898) project aims to develop a Survival Kit to learn to overcome missing digital competencies of adults with a special focus on digital immigrants i.e., persons who are disadvantaged in society due to a lack of digital competences and to enable them to take an active role in the digital society. In this regard, the project team identified needs and competence profiles in potential participants and is constructing a set of 15 modules on a variety of topics related to daily life and digital competencies. The Survival Kit will use Flipped Learning 3.0 as a training approach and contribute to the development of an innovative self-evaluation tool: competence-based self-evaluation mandalas. Carefully designed transferability and implementation guides will support the flexible transfer of the results and outcomes to other European countries and its wide and open use, especially facilitated since DISK toolkit modules will be published as Open Educational Resources (OER). The results can be expressed to serve at the nano, micro, meso and macro levels.

The consortium consists of 5 partners, 3 adult education organizations, a university, and a specialist in course quality and Open Educational Resources with complementary skills, experience, and approaches to adult education. The process of creation of the profiles and modules, as of the different elements such as the self-evaluation mandalas, and its challenges, are relevant to reflect on how, under the current social circumstances in the European Union, one can act effectively on developing digital competencies with older adults.

Each developed module of the "Survival Kit" is documented in a short guide including the training material itself, all support materials (like trainees' and trainers' instructions), hints for trainers (summary of the lessons learned sessions), the ready-to-use Moodle course, the templates for the self-evaluation mandalas, and a guide of how to use the self-evaluation mandalas.

Main target groups of the project: Stakeholders involved in Adult Education, Seniors digital Competencies

Significant public results: Dissemination webpage, blogposts, Social media, Conferensies, stakeholders wbpages etc

Acknowledgements: The DISK project is co-funded by the ERASMUS + program of European Union. The authors would like to thank the ERASMUS + program which co-funds the DISK project 2019–1-PT01-KA204-060898. The authors would like to thank all the partner organizations as well as the respondents who participated in the development of the competency map and the piloting of the modules. The

DISK – Digital Immigrants Survival Kit

European Commission support for the production of this publication does not constitute an endorsement of the contents which reflects the views only of the authors, and the Commission cannot be held responsi-ble for any use which may be made of the information contained therein.

ISBN 978-615-5511-31-8

DiBiHo

Digitale Bildungsnachweise für Hochschulen
(Digital Credentials for Higher Education Institutions)

Website: https://www.dibiho.de

Runtime: 11.2020 – 12.2022

Supported by: German Federal Ministry of Education and Research, FKZ: M534800

Partners: Technical University of Munich (TUM), Germany; Hasso-Plattner-Institute (HPI), University of Potsdam, Germany; German Academic Exchange Service (DAAD), Germany

Project representative to be contacted for further info: Dr. Matthias Gottlieb, project coordinator (dibiho@tum.de)

Short description of the initiative:

Digital technologies are paving new paths of learning in higher education, which are tailored to the particular requirements of individual learners. A gradual transition from traditional classrooms to hybrid online teaching and learning formats is fundamentally changing our understanding of teaching and mobility patterns. These developments result in a need to re-examine the data associated with learners in new and old formats alike, especially with a view to how their achievements are documented. Transitioning from paper-based to digital credentials is a natural consequence of shifting education formats. While they are a necessity for online-based formats such as MOOCs, they also promise administrative efficiency, a reduction of mobility barriers, and the possibility to properly document life-long learning in all its variations.

A number of projects and initiatives have already made some strides in this area on a national, European and international level. DiBiHo is a new research project and will explore the prerequisites and technical options of an infrastructure with associated standards for interoperable digital credentials on a global scale. It therefore seeks to incorporate experiences and results from similar projects worldwide. The project will focus its development around the principle of Self-Sovereign Identity for learners to ensure transparency, interoperability and acceptance.

Project Goal: Develop a trustworthy, distributed and internationally operable infrastructure standard for issuing, storing, presenting and verifying digital academic credentials.

Actions and outputs: Core results will comprise the definition of model processes, development of Proof-Of-Concepts for several use-cases of the project partners, a specification of a reference architecture and data model, development of prototypes and a recommendation for future operator and support models.

Main target groups of the project: Higher Education Institutions, students, policy- and decision-makers

ISBN 978-615-5511-31-8

DIMELI4AC

Digital Media Literacy for Active Citizenship

Website: http://dimeli.eu/

Runtime: 01/11/2018– 31/07/2021

Supported / co-funded by: co-funded by the Erasmus+ project of the European Union/ 2018-1-DE03-KA201-047411

Partners: University of Hannover – Germany; Ellinogermaniki Agogi – Greece; Lifelong Learning Platform – Belgium; Antenna Ltd – Cyprus; Emphasys Center – Cyprus; CCS Digital Education – Greece

Project representative to be contacted for further info: Richard Heise (heise@idd.uni-hannover.de)

Short description of the initiative

Digital advances have brought new challenges for Europe's students and teachers. In recent years, the ability to read and interpret different types of media has become an increasingly essential skill to possess as most of the information we receive on a daily basis comes to us through a complex and interwoven system of media technologies. Social media and misinformation can be harmful, while data privacy has become a key concern in the digital society. EU citizens, but above all young students are vulnerable to cyberbullying and harassment, predatory behaviour or disturbing online content. In response to this, the DIMELI4AC project aims to support schools to establish their own DIGITAL MEDIA LITERACY ACTION PLAN in order:

- To empower young students to become responsible, critical, global citizens for the digitalized and connected world we live in, while creating blended learning opportunities to acquire digital and media literacy skills to safeguard democracy and common values.
- To utilise the non-working time of schools in order to set up ON-LINE AND IN-HOUSE DIGITAL MEDIA LITERACY LABS and OBSERVATORIES based on SYNERGIES to be created among teachers, parents, schools, organizations, stakeholders which will endorse the CAMPAIGN and sign the MEMORANDUM OF DIMELI4AC COMMITMENT.
- To introduce the idea of an interactive ASSESSMENT TOOL in the form of a GAME based on an AVATAR (DC-MELI) where students follow various challenges in order to be AWARDED the BADGE showing a respectful, responsible and safe use of the technology based on the digital citizenship and democratic values and critical thinking.
- To strengthen the profiles of teachers and in doing so to upgrade the quality of teaching/ earning services provided in formal schooling.
- To promote whole school approaches towards dealing with cross-sectoral issues.

Furthermore, it is worth mentioning that nowadays due to the corona virus pandemic teachers redefine teaching and learning. They are facing new challenges and are struggling to learn new techno-pedagogies needed to teach online classes. They need new resources and online tools to engage students in learning. In support to the above, during the project a variety of resources and digital tools were developed for the promotion of students' digital media literacy skills which are the following:

- The DIMELI@SCHOOL Competence Framework which contains a list of specific skills that we consider essential to become a responsible digital citizen and is based in two criteria, the benchmarks and the indicators. Benchmarks refer to specific objectives that a learner should accomplish and indicators mark the level of acquisition of a specific competence. This is the diagram of the competence framework:

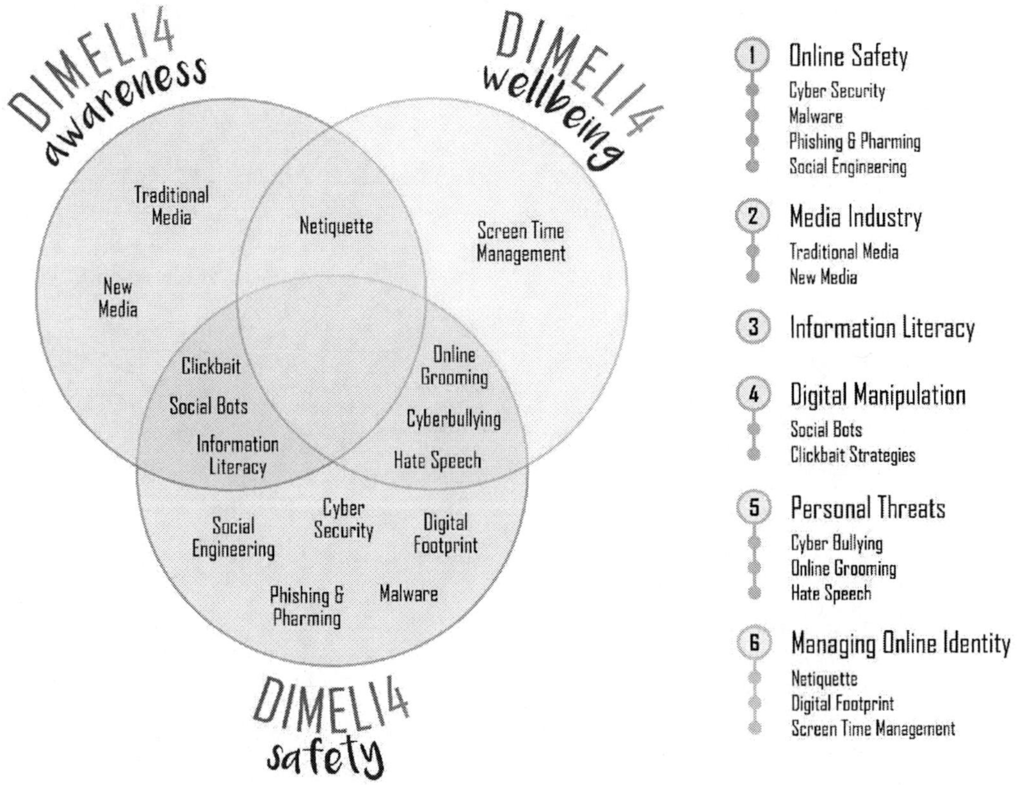

- The dynamic and interactive DIMELI Platform/ Portal which consists of a forum, a database with resources and materials, learning scenarios, quizzes and a glossary for the interpretation of difficult terms. (https://dimeli.erasmusplus.website/)
- An Assessment and Validation Tool in the form of a game with an avatar which monitors, evaluate and validate the acquisition of digital and media literacy skills.

Main target groups of the project: Teachers, Students aged 10-15 years old, Parents

Significant public results:

- A Comparative Report which offers an overview of the status quo of Digital Media Literacy in the schools of three countries: Cyprus, Germany and Greece: http://dimeli.eu/comparative-report/
- The DIMELI @SCHOOL Competence framework: http://dimeli.eu/competence-framework/
- The DIMELI@SCHOOL Learning pack: http://dimeli.eu/learning-pack/
- The DIMELI Avatar Game: http://dimeli.eu/platform-and-avatar-game/
- The DIMELI Platform: https://dimeli.erasmusplus.website/
- The A-Z DIMELI Implementation pack: http://dimeli.eu/a-zpack/
- The DIMELI@SCHOOL Digital Action Plan: http://dimeli.eu/action-plan/

AUTHOR INDEX

European Distance and E-Learning Network (EDEN)
Budapest University of Technology & Economics
H-1111 Budapest, Egry J. u.1.
Hungary

ISBN 978-1-7138-3702-2

CURRAN ASSOCIATES INC.
proceedings
.com

European Distance and E-Learning Network Annual Conference (EDEN 2021)

Lessons from a Pandemic for the Future of the Education

Long Papers

Madrid, Spain
21-24 June 2021

Volume 2 of 2

EUROPEAN DISTANCE AND E-LEARNING NETWORK

European Distance and E-Learning Network Annual Conference (EDEN 2021)

Lessons from a Pandemic for the Future of the Education

Long Papers

Madrid, Spain
21-24 June 2021

Volume 2 of 2

Editors:

Sandra Kucina Softic
András Szucs
Judit Komuves
Gabor Roman

ISBN: 978-1-7138-3702-2

Printed from e-media with permission by:

Curran Associates, Inc.
57 Morehouse Lane
Red Hook, NY 12571

Some format issues inherent in the e-media version may also appear in this print version.

Printed with permission by Curran Associates, Inc. (2021)

For permission requests, please contact European Distance and E-Learning Network (EDEN) at the address below.

European Distance and E-Learning Network (EDEN)
Budapest University of Technology & Economics
H-1111 Budapest, Egry J. u.1.
Hungary

Phone: +36 1 463 1628
Fax: +36 1 463 1858

secretariat@eden-online.org

Additional copies of this publication are available from:

Curran Associates, Inc.
57 Morehouse Lane
Red Hook, NY 12571 USA
Phone: 845-758-0400
Fax: 845-758-2633
Email: curran@proceedings.com
Web: www.proceedings.com

TABLE OF CONTENTS

NAVIGATING THE NEW NORMAL

DIGITAL SKILLS: TEACHERS PERSPECTIVE

BEST PRACTICES FOR TRANSITIONING ONLINE

ASSESSMENT AND WELLNESS

DIVERSITY & SOCIAL INCLUSION

DIGITAL SKILLS: STUDENTS PERSPECTIVE

BEST PRACTICES & CASE STUDIES

Lessons from a Pandemic for the Future of Education
European Distance and E-Learning Network (EDEN) Proceedings
2021 Annual Conference | Madrid, 21-24 June, 2021
ISSN 2707-2819
doi: 10.38069/edenconf-2021-ac0001

USING PADRISEUP AS A COLLABORATIVE WRITING TOOL IN HIGHER EDUCATION EFL CLASSES

Beyza Öz Dal, Dilek Güler, Istanbul University, Ezgi Tufan, Mentora Education Group, Ayşegül Liman Kaban, Bahçeşehir University, Turkey

Abstract

Due to the sudden outbreak of COVID-19, there has been a rapid transformation of the learning and teaching environment from face-to-face to fully online classes. Students being at home in isolated home environments challenged the language learning process profoundly which forced teachers to update and adjust their instructional strategies and activities by including collaborative learning elements. Implementing novel technologies with OCL approach might act as a considerably efficient factor if learner characteristics and the educational setting are taken into consideration seriously. Therefore, the purpose of the study is to explore an online collaborative writing tool and students' opinions towards it. The participants of the study consist of 30 students studying at a preparatory school at a state university in Istanbul. To this aim, both quantitative and qualitative methods have been benefited. According to the quantitative data, the calculated mean scores of the items revealed that the majority of students found the experience of OCW positive. As for the qualitative data, the content analysis showed that the majority of the students reported the benefits of interaction and social learning taking place in collaborative learning, and there were also some disadvantages mentioned by the participants such as disagreements, social loafing, and personality-related problems.

Introduction

The whole system of education including primary, secondary, high schools and universities have been seriously challenged during the lockdown period of the COVID-19 pandemic across the world. In fact, the circumstances all the stakeholders in education are in are unique and it is more accurate to call it crisis learning, unlike normal digital learning (Pace et al., 2020). Therefore, there has emerged a greater need for academic institutions to alter their curriculum and reconsider the utilization of novel instructional methods and strategies (Toquero, 2020). Pace et al., (2020) further state that while planning the instructional activities, it is crucial to strive for high student engagement and participation which match the lesson objectives, and the key point is providing the learners with a "choice". Messer (2020) explains that "Young adolescents thrive when given opportunities to pursue their passions and take ownership of their learning. Significant academic and social growth happen in a middle school classroom where students have a voice about their learning" (p.4). Consequently, online collaboration tools prove to be powerful tools that provide the learners choice and voice, which eventually promotes overall learning and participation online.

Online Collaborative Learning

According to the online dictionary of Lexico (n.d) collaboration is defined as "the action of working with someone to produce something". Ananiadou and Claro (2009) posit that collaboration is regarded as one of the 21st century competencies needed to cope with the fast-changing nature of the era. Collaboration is an essential component in every aspect of life, including education. Dillenbourg (1999) define collaborative learning "is that it is a situation in which two or more people learn or attempt to learn something together" (p.1). According to Johnson and Johnson (1991) Collaborative Learning (CL) is "the instructional use of small groups so that students work together to maximize their own and each other's learning". The key components of CL encompass positive interdependence, face-to-face interaction, individual accountability, and the interpersonal and small group skills (Johnson & Johnson, 1991). CL gets its roots from Vygotsky's (1978) concept of Zone of Proximal Development which posits the idea that learning through collaboration and interaction enables the person to reach a higher level of performance and knowledge compared to learning individually and without support. Along with the technological advances, especially with the invention of the World Wide Web, online education has gained momentum, and in the 21st century both teachers and students around the globe use and readjust networked collaborative learning (Harasim, 2000). Collaborativism aka Online Collaborative Learning Theory (OCL) can be defined as a type of learning where learners are motivated and assisted to work with each other to learn and produce knowledge; it is comprised of a process having three phases as "Idea Generating", "Idea Organizing" and "Intellectual Convergence" (Harasim, 2017). In OCL environments, the instructor has a crucial role as the person who is responsible for students' engagement in the particular grammar point or vocabulary along with other activities related to constructing discipline, and the learner is supposed to get involved in all three phases of collaborativist pedagogy to learn and find a solution to a problem (Harasim, 2017). Thanks to the authentic tasks that necessitate collaborative problem solving and profound involvement, learners will show improvement in terms of communication and problem-solving skills (Reeves et al., 2004).

Online collaborative writing and the use of online tools

Particularly Web 2.0 tools such as Google Docs, Wikis and blogs have attracted significant attention from researchers in the field of collaborative online writing. A reason that explains this fact is that these tools enable students to manage the whole writing process from negotiation, construction of the text, revising and editing until the final product is realized (Li, 2018). Furthermore, Web 2.0 tools, thanks to their collaborative essence, provide learners more chances to communicate and collaboratively write in the target language beyond time limitations of classrooms (Storch, 2012).

In their research, Zhou et al., (2012) have studied the effectiveness of Google Docs in an outside-class collaborative writing activity. The comparison between the experiment and control group has indicated that most students were not familiar with Google Docs before the study, the tool altered the means by which students communicated while writing collaboratively, 93% of students reported that Google Docs was a useful tool for group work, and half of the students stated they would like to use the tool in the future projects. However, the study indicated that Google Docs had no effect on students' paper grades. Another study conducted about Google Docs has demonstrated that students in the Google Docs group had significantly higher mean scores in writing than those worked in groups face-to-face. Moreover, students in Google Docs group reported positive attitudes toward collaborative writing activity, high collaboration in their groups, and ease of use (Suwantarathip & Wichadee, 2014).

As for the use of blogs, a study conducted over a four-week period has pointed out that interactive nature of weblogs established a valid peer review culture as a major part of collaborative writing. Besides, students had positive attitudes towards weblogs and wanted to carry out similar tasks in the future English classes. Another vital skill students have gained is critical thinking and the ability to judge the feedback received from peers. As the feedback was provided by peers rather than instructors, this skill required students to make good judgments on which feedback to accept or discard (Grami, 2012). Another study conducted by Aydın and Yıldız (2014) examined the use of wikis in collaborative writing projects in foreign language classrooms. The qualitative and quantitative data have demonstrated that the accuracy in grammar structures was 94%. The students also reported positive experiences using wikis in foreign language writing, and they believed that there was an improvement in their writing performance. Besides, there have been observed more peer-corrections than self-corrections in wiki pages.

Learners' attitudes in CSCL

With the increase in computer-supported learning (CSL), one of the most common fallacies has been to believe that achievement in the learning process mostly relies on technology and its effectiveness, thereby ignoring the whole system of learning environment including key constructs such as learners. That's why, with the introduction of CSL and CSCL, the research has mainly focused on the efficiency and effectiveness of the learning environment and technological tools used in this process (Zhou et al., 2012). However, without looking into learners and the affective factors impacting their views of these learning environments, the effectiveness and efficiency of these cannot be understood fully. Masgoret and Gardner (2003) state that learners' attitude toward the learning situation is one of the key variables for learning achievement, since learners cannot be separated from their perceptions, attitudes, views and emotions. Dörnyei (1994) also emphasizes the importance of learner and classroom-related factors and learners' views of these factors in his motivation studies, which proves that the studies looking into the attitude and perceptions of learners in CSCL process are quite critical. In a study by Storch (2005), it has been revealed that university students who chose to do a writing task collaboratively actually completed the task more competently compared to the ones choosing to study individually. Storch (2005) explains that collaborative work helps learners gather more ideas and get immediate feedback from their peers, a crucial part of the collaborative learning process. Another study investigating university students' perceptions of online collaborative writing demonstrates that most students saw the task co-operative instead of collaborative, and did not see online collaborative writing as an opportunity to create shared knowledge as a community, which reflects the critical guide role a teacher could play in the process (Limbu & Markauskaite, 2015). Chen and Yu (2019) also examine learners' attitudes toward collaborative writing in a longitudinal study and find that attitudes may actually show changes in time and these changes may affect group interaction and learning opportunities positively or negatively. As these studies show, in order to understand the expectations of learners and to make better instructional choices as teachers, there is a need for more research on the affective factors affecting CSCL processes.

Disaster Studies in Higher Education using The Community of Inquiry Framework

The CoI framework has three presences, each of them intersects and informs the others to support the overall educational experience, namely, cognitive, social and teaching presence (Hilliard & Stewart, 2019). In contrast, information systems students may acquire and apply knowledge and skills in relation to systems risk and recovery (Mendonca et al., 2019). As disasters present "wicked" problems that cannot be resolved from a single perspective, cognitive presence will need to support students to learn how to work in cross disciplinary teams and to understand how their specialist discipline knowledge contributes to solving transdisciplinary problems (Madrigano et al., 2017). In such contexts the CoI must also address students' need to attain "soft skills" and provide opportunities to reflect and discuss theory and practice in communication, situational awareness, coordination, decision making, negotiation, leadership, team building and stress management (Brooks et al., 2018).

During disasters, lives often depend on team cohesion, communication, coordination and cooperation (Hayes, 2015) and social presence underpins cohesive and collaborative interactions (Rourke et al., 1999). Whereas cognitive presence addresses student acquisition of hard and soft skills, social presence provides an open, trusting and lively environment to support students to develop the self-confidence to acquire them (Li, 2015). Social presence provides cohesion through establishment of not only socio-emotional presence and personal relationships but through intellectual focus, open and purposeful communication and respect. Students should feel safe to express their perspectives and views, to agree and disagree with others and yet still focus on a common goal (Hadwin et al., 2018).

This study aims to investigate EFL learners' attitudes toward online collaborative writing. With the use of the online collaborative writing tool, Padriseup, learners studying at a preparatory school at a state university have experienced online collaborative writing. With the attitude scale, we address the following research questions:

- What are students' attitudes towards using an online collaborative writing tool in pandemic EFL classes?
- What are students' experiences with using an online collaborative writing tool in pandemic EFL classes?

Methodology

Research Design

This small-scale mixed-method study, which investigates OCW with Padriseup to be able to answer the two research questions mentioned above and was conducted using an attitudinal survey along with two open-ended questions provided at the end of the online survey. In this descriptive study, a cross-sectional survey design was used. According to Creswell and Plano Clark (2011), mixed methods research focuses on gathering, analysing, and combining both quantitative and qualitative data in a single research or series of studies to gain a more in-depth understanding of research questions.

Setting

The study took place at a state university during the fall semester of 2020-2021 academic year. Education was carried out fully online due to the pandemic. In the School of Foreign Languages, a progressive system is applied, and there are three main levels such as A1, A2, and B1. At the beginning of the fall term, students first take the proficiency exam prepared by the Testing office of the school, and if they take 70, they are exempt from studying at the prep school. Upon failing, they are distributed to their levels according to the result of the placement exam prepared by the Testing Office.

Participants

The participants were students studying English at a Preparatory Department of a State University in Turkey. In order to conduct the study, a convenience sampling method was used. The total number of participants in the study was 30 (23 females and 7 males) from various departments ranging from Biology to Logistics, who consented to take part in the study. The majority of the participants (N = 19) attended online classes from Istanbul and stated that they used the internet more than six hours a day. The participants were elementary (A1:11) and pre-intermediate (A2:19) levels, which was determined by a placement test produced by the Testing Unit of the School of Foreign Languages. Finally, the participants' ages ranged between 18 and 22.

Data Collection Tool

The survey that was used to elicit participants' attitudes starts with questions regarding demographic information of the participants. As for the Online Cooperative Learning Attitude Scale (OCLAS), an online Likert scale attitudinal survey, prepared by Korkmaz (2012) was implemented in this quantitative study. The survey is comprised of 17 items with choices ranging from strongly agree to strongly disagree. Korkmaz (2012) has concluded that the Online Cooperative Learning Attitude Scale (OCLAS) has been proven to be a valid and reliable scale, and it can be utilized to determine students' attitudes towards online cooperative learning. The scale's factor and whole reliability analyses were calculated by using Cronbach's Alpha, which are as follows: Positive Attitude .899, Negative Attitude .822, and Total reliability .904 (Korkmaz, 2012). As for the qualitative data, in the last section of the survey, open-ended questions regarding the students' attitudes toward the tool have been added to gather in-depth insights.

Data Collection Procedure

Firstly, it is important to note that writing lessons of each class are four hours on the same day per week. Prior to the study, the teachers of each class gave a brief and to-the-point training session on Padriseup, also the participants were provided with a set of detailed criteria regarding the grading of their task on Padriseup.

The procedure illustrated in the table below was followed for four weeks. As a warm-up activity, brainstorming and pair discussion were carried out. Afterwards, the participants were randomly divided into groups of 3 to 5 to work collaboratively on a writing task and they were provided with writing prompts and a link to Padriseup. After completing the task as shown in Figure 1, which was writing a well-organized paragraph of an essay, the teacher and students had a whole class discussion as a post-activity. This procedure was implemented throughout the four consecutive weeks. At the end of the process, participants were asked to reflect on their online collaborative writing experience with an online Likert scale attitudinal survey prepared by Korkmaz (2012).

Table 1: Four-week Procedure of Writing Lessons Carried Out with Padriseup

Week	Warm-up	Task	Post-activity
1	Brainstorming, Pair discussion	Students write introduction paragraph of an opinion essay	Whole class discussion
2	Brainstorming, Pair discussion	Students write the 1st body paragraph of an opinion essay	Whole class discussion
3	Brainstorming, Pair discussion	Students write the 2nd body paragraph of an opinion essay	Whole class discussion
4	Brainstorming, Pair discussion	Students write the conclusion paragraph of an opinion essay	Whole class discussion

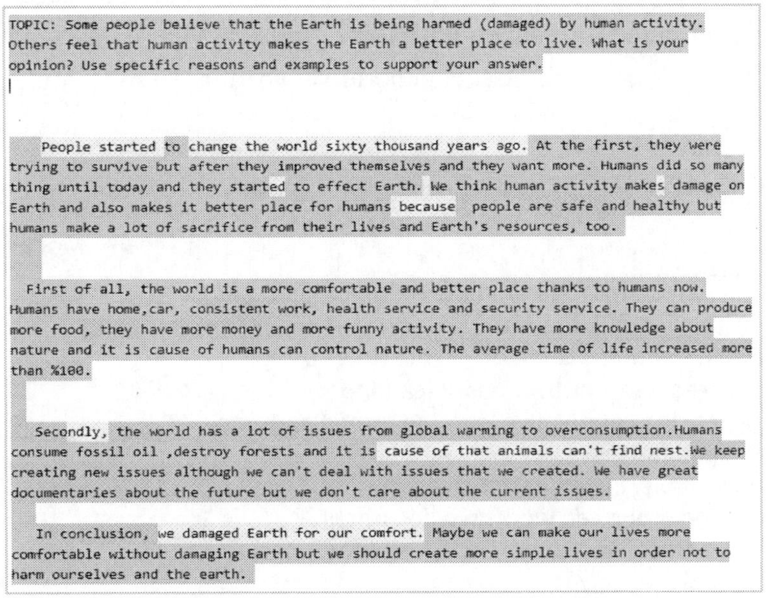
TOPIC: Some people believe that the Earth is being harmed (damaged) by human activity. Others feel that human activity makes the Earth a better place to live. What is your opinion? Use specific reasons and examples to support your answer.

People started to change the world sixty thousand years ago. At the first, they were trying to survive but after they improved themselves and they want more. Humans did so many thing until today and they started to effect Earth. We think human activity makes damage on Earth and also makes it better place for humans because people are safe and healthy but humans make a lot of sacrifice from their lives and Earth's resources, too.

First of all, the world is a more comfortable and better place thanks to humans now. Humans have home,car, consistent work, health service and security service. They can produce more food, they have more money and more funny activity. They have more knowledge about nature and it is cause of humans can control nature. The average time of life increased more than %100.

Secondly, the world has a lot of issues from global warming to overconsumption.Humans consume fossil oil ,destroy forests and it is cause of that animals can't find nest.We keep creating new issues although we can't deal with issues that we created. We have great documentaries about the future but we don't care about the current issues.

In conclusion, we damaged Earth for our comfort. Maybe we can make our lives more comfortable without damaging Earth but we should create more simple lives in order not to harm ourselves and the earth.

Figure 1 Student Essay Sample of Online Collaborative Writing with Padriseup

Data Analysis

In order to analyse the data obtained from the survey, Excel has been used to do descriptive analysis of the statistical data. The mean, mode and standard deviation of each item were calculated to better analyse the students' perceptions toward OCW. As for the analysis of the qualitative data obtained from the open-ended questions, content analysis has been conducted. This content analysis was done by taking the scale as a guide to decode the students' responses As Creswell (2009) has stated, to carry out the content analysis, students' responses were revised a couple of times and important key points from these were written and categorized to form codes. After forming the codes, categories and themes were created by taking the research questions into consideration. Therefore, the content analysis enabled us to create the relationships and meaning between the words and concepts so that they could be investigated, and inferences were made (Patton, 2002).

Findings

Students' attitudes towards using an online collaborative writing tool

To be able to answer the first research question in the study, a five-point Likert scale survey, with 17 items and the answers ranging from 1 – *Strongly Disagree* to 5 – *Strongly Agree* was administered. The survey results presented in Table 2 demonstrate the EFL students' perceptions regarding the use of an online collaborative writing tool in EFL classes. As a result of the responses to the survey, it was found out that the students in the study had a positive attitude towards using an online collaborative writing tool in EFL classes. When asked whether they enjoyed experiencing online collaborative learning via Padriseup, most of the students gave a positive answer with a mean score of 4.03. Furthermore, most of the students stated that being interactive with their group members had a positive influence on their motivation during online collaborative writing lessons and increased their creativity.

Table 2: The results of OCLAS Questionnaire

		Mean	Mode	Standard Deviation
1	I enjoy solving problems regarding the group project using Padriseup with my group members.	4.03	4.00	0.76
2	Being interactive with the other group members using Padriseup increases my motivation for learning.	4.21	5.00	0.92
3	I enjoy experiencing cooperative learning using Padriseup with my group members.	4.03	4.00	0.76
4	Online group activity increases our creativity.	4.07	4.00	0.83
5	I believe that the group can work on a document effectively with the online cooperative learning application.	4.00	4.00	0.69
6	Padriseup improves my social skills.	3.83	4.00	0.91
7	I enjoy helping others in Padriseup.	4.10	4.00	0.80
8	Padriseup is very entertaining for me.	3.66	4.00	0.88
9	Padriseup helps me feel better psychologically.	3.55	4.00	0.85
10	More ideas come up because of Padriseup.	4.10	4.00	0.84
11	I think that I have had more successful results since I work with a group in Padriseup.	3.93	4.00	0.78
12	Trying to teach something to my group members in Padriseup does not make me tired.	3.97	4.00	0.76
13	Padriseup makes sense to me.	4.52	5.00	0.77

14	I can develop my own ideas in Padriseup.	4.52	5.00	0.50
15	I like that people are depending on me in Padriseup.	3.83	3.00	0.95
16	I think that my interaction with my group members in Padriseup will contribute to me.	4.45	5.00	1.04
17	Padriseup is suitable for me.	4.34	5.00	0.88

Interestingly, 36 % of the students responded that the use of Padriseup did not influence feeling psychologically better, which is reflected in Table 2 with a mean score of 3.55 as the lowest mean score compared to the others. It is also seen that the students found Padriseup mildly entertaining despite acknowledging its benefits.

The result of the survey suggests that most of the students in the study found Padriseup useful and see the potential for its use as an online collaborative writing tool. However, the standard deviation scores also show that a small number of students remain neutral or less interested in Padriseup, which might have resulted from various factors such as technology literacy and personality.

Students' Experiences with Using an Online Collaborative Writing Tool

To gain a closer sense of the variety in the students' responses towards the use of the online collaborative writing tool, responses to the open-ended questions in the survey were analysed through a meticulous content analysis.

Categories that emerged upon the content analysis are as follow: the categories on the pros are (a) sharing of ideas, (b) social learning, (c) product and process efficiency, (d) motivation; on the other hand, the categories emerged on the cons are (e) disagreements, (f) social loafing, (g) technology and software-related problems, (h) personality-related problems.

Sharing of Ideas

The category that dominates the responses about the advantages of the online collaborative tool is sharing ideas. Most students have reported that thanks to the tool, they have benefited from the exchange of ideas, which enabled them to learn about different perspectives, be exposed to a lot of ideas and create a better work at the end of the process.

The statements below support these findings:

> *"One of the advantages of the Padriseup is that a good work is created through a process of exchange of ideas."*
>
> *"A lot of different ideas show up, which helps us to express the idea in our work in a much better way."*

Another related advantage is that students can pass their knowledge to one another. In the meantime, they can fuse their ideas together and create a better prepared work.

The statements below support these findings:

> *"The tool helps us work more productively and makes the exchange of knowledge easier."*
>
> *"When working on the task, being able to consult for ideas by using the chat box has provided an important benefit to us."*

Social Learning

Another pattern found in students' responses has indicated that the tool proved to be beneficial to learning. The responses show that students are aware of the fact that the tool has provided them a sense of learning together with an emphasis on peer-learning, peer-feedback and peer-scaffolding.

The statements below support these findings:

> *"As there are many minds involved, you can spot your mistakes faster."*
>
> *"Because it is a collaborative task, everyone can teach something to everyone."*
>
> *"Because there is a lot of team-work involved, we can help each other in terms of knowledge."*
>
> *"The things that I love most are that I am in constant interaction with my peers, working on a collaborative task together. This improves our sociality and team-work skills."*
>
> *"We can spot each other's mistakes and correct them instantly."*

Students' responses highlight that they associate the tool with a lot of interaction, more interactive lessons, communicating with peers throughout the process, and co-operative work.

The statements below support these findings:

> *"The things that I love most is that I am in constant interaction with my peers, working on a collaborative task together. This improves our sociality and team-work skills."*

Product and Process Efficiency

The findings have further indicated that students' responses included keywords such as increased efficiency and productivity both in terms of the product and process. Students mostly believe that they create a well-prepared product at the end. Also, some have reported an increased fulfilment felt towards the task and lesson.

The statements below support these findings:

> *"We achieve better productivity."*
>
> *"The tool enables us to create a better-quality task as a team."*
>
> *"Padriseup is a practical and useful tool."*
>
> *"The tool increases the efficiency of the writing lessons."*
>
> *"I believe that it increases the quality of the essay or the paragraph that we are writing."*

Motivation

Analysing students' responses, it has been also found that students get more motivated and engaged throughout the process.

The statements below support these findings:

> *"It is always more fun to work with Padriseup."*
>
> *"Together with friends, we get more motivated toward the task."*
>
> *"Working as a group, producing new ideas together, and working collaboratively is very enjoyable, and Padriseup gives us this exactly."*

Disagreements

As for the cons of the online collaborative writing tool, one of the most frequent responses was the communication-related issues. This includes conflicts among group members, conflicting ideas, not being able to reach a common ground, having disagreements, and the lack of conflict resolution.

The statements below support these findings:

> *"Sometimes there is a sentence that you want to write but cannot because this is a group work."*
>
> *"We have disagreements sometimes."*

> *"Our ideas do not seem to meet on a common ground sometimes."*

Social Loafing

The findings show that a disadvantage of the online collaborative writing tool and the task is that inactive students might increase the burden of other group members.

The statements below support these findings:

> *"Some of our friends do not participate actively in the lesson, so the other group members have to complete the majority of the writing task."*

> *"Because some peers do not simply write at all, the responsibility rests on the shoulders of the other group members."*

Technology and Software-Related Problems

Certain comments found in the findings refer to the technical issues and interface of the software itself such as the lack of necessary add-in features in the software, the bad look of different colours, problems encountered when accessing from the mobile phone.

The statements below support these findings:

> *"As I cannot access the internet from my laptop, attending the lesson online from the mobile phone is disadvantageous."*

> *"Some necessary add-in features are lacking in this tool, that's why it is limited in terms of accessibility. Also, different colours look bad sometimes." (Student here refers to the feature of the tool which enables each student to choose a colour code so that to whom a sentence belongs to is visible.)*

Personality-Related Problems

Some participants have reported that the tool may not be appropriate for introverted students.

The statements below support these findings:

> *"The tool may not be useful for students who are unsocial."*

Discussion

Discussion of Students' Attitudes towards Using an Online Collaborative Writing Tool

The results reveal that most students' experience with online collaborative writing via the web tool, Padriseup, was positive, and they conceived different benefits of it during the process. These results are in line with the research conducted by Storch (2005), whose earlier findings show that most students participating in her study regarding collaborative learning enjoyed the experience. Unlike traditional writing classes, where the teacher supports each student in their individual work, in OCW students take the responsibility of their own learning as well as their group members', being both the writer and the peer feedback provider (Chao & Lo, 2011). As it was also revealed in the survey, students understood the value of collaboration in online writing classes, which made them more willing to participate in the tasks in Padriseup. However, due to its being a new concept, it was clear that the students needed more support in the process by the teacher to be able to make the most of the online collaborative writing, which supports deeper learning and co-constructing knowledge (Limbu & Markauskaite, 2015).

Discussion of Students' Experiences with Using an Online Collaborative Writing Tool

The results have indicated that Padriseup has been beneficial in terms of sharing of ideas, social learning, product and process efficiency, interaction, motivation. In line with this study's findings regarding sharing of ideas, social learning, product and process efficiency and interaction, Limbu and Markauskaite (2015) have also pointed out in their qualitative study that OCW is regarded by students as a way to share work between participants to accomplish quality writing tasks, to blend powers together to produce a good product; as an activity which helps different ideas fuse and leads to a better understanding of content; and as a tool to gain new skills required for group work.

The rationale behind these findings lies in the fact that OCW is collaborative and social-constructivist in essence. Writers who are in collaboration are required to communicate their ideas from the very beginning. They discuss, negotiate and add on each other's' contributions, therefore, expand not only their personal knowledge, but also contribute to collective meaning-making (Dye et al., 2010). In this sense, the findings are consistent with Zhu's (2012) study which revealed that online learning platforms have the potential to enhance students' collaborative learning practices and their knowledge construction thanks to group interaction.

Furthermore, our findings are in line with the social constructivist learning framework. As Vygotsky (1978) highlighted that collaborative learning is a must for helping students develop through his or her own zone of proximal development (ZPD), which is the gap between what the student could do alone and what one could realize when cooperating with others who are more skilled or experienced. Similarly, Wells (1999) stresses that there are three major characteristics that give scaffolding its particular character: the necessity dialogic of the dialogue where knowledge is co-constructed, the importance of the type of activity where the knowledge lies and the role of tools that foster knowledge building.

Chao and Lo (2011) further states the importance of peer-scaffolding in collaborative learning and that collaborative learning is a strategy for teaching that offers opportunities for learners to be assisted by their peers; especially collaborative writing, through being exposed to various perspectives and ideas, can help decrease anxiety about experiencing a writer's block and task difficulty. As the participants in our study also indicated, online collaborative writing tools support social learning thanks to the extensive amount of interactions, exchange of novel ideas and peer-scaffolding practices as well as peer-revising, peer-feedback and peer-learning.

On the other hand, the categories that emerged on the cons are (a) disagreements, (b) social loafing, (c) software-related problems, (d) the duration, (e) personality-related problems. The findings of this study also resonate with the literature concerning the challenges in OCW. Problems with discussing the understanding of the task and sharing goals and standards for tasks might have a significant impact on regulation and task performance regardless of whether learners work on their own or collaboratively (Hadwin et al., 2018). Various studies indicate that disagreement is an inherent part of collaborative tasks (Mutwarasibo, 2013; Sharma, 2012). Mutwarasibo's (2013) research with undergraduate students in collaborative writing also revealed that profound disagreement among group members is likely to take place.

As the findings of this study have demonstrated, social loafing is another issue that has aroused during online collaborative writing processes. Hall and Buzwell (2012) reported that social loafing is one of the most important elements causing dissatisfaction among students in group projects; they tend to dislike collaborative work mostly because of the interpersonal dissension that might occur. According to the collective effort model, social loafing takes place when the team members are not able to see the value of the contribution that they make or the task itself and having quality communication helps the team members to articulate the contribution that they have made to the project (Karau & Williams, 1993).

Online education has its own requirements that need to be taken into consideration to accomplish the objectives in terms of learning. As the findings of this study revealed, the lack of technological equipment or software-related issues can be barriers that hinder this aim. Similarly, the research conducted by Assareh and Bidokht (2010) in Shahid Rajaee University in Iran indicated having access to necessary technological equipment is an essential element for online learning. According to Capra (2011) if learners are not technologically equipped for online education, this may affect both the learners and the instructor in an adverse manner.

Having a varying working pace is one of the challenges that participants of this study encountered during OCW. Barkley et al. (2005) posit that when working as a team, it is possible for some group members to work at varying speeds; some might dominate the team while others are likely to diverge from the topic of the discussion. In their study with undergraduate students on challenges in online collaboration, Hadwin et al. (2018) found out that a big number of students regarded time as the most noteworthy challenge that they experienced while working collaboratively.

Participants in the study indicated that OCL might not be suitable for introverted students. Jackson (2014) claims that introverts favour learning tasks in which they can work independently and individually; teamwork does not allocate the time they need for procession and reflection. Introverts are mainly characterized as introspective, so it creates a contrast with the spontaneous atmosphere of active learning classrooms (Condon & Ruth-Sahd, 2013).

Limitations of the study

This study has some limitations that can be considered for future studies. The very first limitation of the study is the sample size which involved 30 participants in total. The study was conducted in two preparatory classes at a state university, yet some students could not be reached because of the fully online classes without attendance taken as a result of the pandemic.

Another limitation of the study is that there were two teachers involved in the process, which may affect students' attitudes towards the online collaborative writing tool. In order to increase the number of the participants in the study, the tool was used in two different classes with different teachers; however, the teachers tried to follow the same protocol in their lesson plans.

Recommendation for future research

This study offers many possibilities for future research. First of all, the interaction patterns of the participants in chat box were not analysed in this small-scale study. In the future research, these patterns can be investigated with their relation to students' achievement and/or perceptions. How much contribution was made by each student and its relation to their level of English was not within the scope of this research, which can be considered for future research. Also, a study focusing on the longitudinal effects of using an online collaborative writing tool could reveal more insight into the area of online collaborative learning. Besides, as the tool requires each student to assign a colour to himself/herself giving the researcher to assess the individual contribution, further studies can examine the amount of individual contribution and participation in relation to other variables such as knowledge growth, motivation and sense of belonging.

Conclusion

As is clear, emergency distance education due to the pandemic has led to a higher number of attempts to incorporate OCL tools into teaching and learning. Specifically, collaborative online writing tools have been implemented in the EFL writing lessons more and more. In this regard, with the purpose of investigating the EFL students' attitudes toward an OCW tool, this mixed-method study concludes that quantitative and qualitative data analysis yielded the similar finding that the participants' attitudes towards the online collaborative writing tool were positive. The results of the questionnaire indicated that participants enjoyed using the OCW tool and reported higher levels motivation and interaction while using the tool. Similarly, the qualitative data demonstrated that the majority of students reported that advantages of the OCW tool such as social learning, motivation, interaction, sharing of ideas, product and process efficiency outweigh the disadvantages such as social loafing, disagreements, software and personality related problems. Therefore, the study might act as a valuable contributor to the literature of online collaborative learning in EFL classes.

References

Ananiadou, K., & Claro, M. (2009). *21st Century Skills and Competences for New Millennium Learners in OECD Countries.* OECD Education Working Papers. http://dx.doi.org/10.1787/218525261154

Assareh, A., & Hosseini Bidokht, M. (2011). Barriers to e-teaching and e-learning. *Procedia Computer Science, 3*, 791-795. http://doi: 10.1016/j.procs.2010.12.129

Aydin, Z., & Yildiz, S. (2014). Using Wikis to Promote Collaborative EFL Writing. *Language Learning & Technology, 18*(1), 160-180.

Barkley, E. F., Cross, K. P., & Major, C. H. (2005). *Collaborative learning techniques: A handbook for College Faculty.* Danvers: Jossey-Bass.

Capra, T. (2011). Online education: promise and problems. *Merlot Journal of Online Learning and Teaching, 7*, 288-293.

Chao, Y. C. J., & Lo, H. C. (2011). Students' perceptions of Wiki-based collaborative writing for learners of English as a foreign language. *Interactive Learning Environments, 19*(4), 395-411. doi:10.1080/10494820903298662

Chen, W., & Yu, S. (2019). A longitudinal case study of changes in students' attitudes, participation, and learning in collaborative writing. *System, 82*, 83-96. doi:10.1016/j.system.2019.03.005

Condon, M., & Ruth-Sahd, L. (2013). Responding to introverted and shy students: Best practice guidelines for educators and advisors. *Open Journal of Nursing, 3*(07), 503-515. https://doi.org/10.4236/ojn.2013.37069

Cresswell, J. W. (2009). *Research design: Qualitative and quantitative and mixed methods approaches* (3rd ed.). Thousand Oaks, CA: Sage Publications.

Creswell, J. W., & Plano Clark, V. L. (2011). *Designing and conducting mixed methods research* (2nd ed.). Thousand Oaks, CA: Sage Publications, Inc.

Dillenbourg, P. (1999). What do you mean by collaborative learning? In P. Dillenbourg (Ed.), *Collaborative learning: Cognitive and Computational Approaches (pp. 1-19). Oxford: Elsevier. hal-00190240*

Dörnyei, Z. (1994). Motivation and Motivating in the Foreign Language Classroom. *The Modern Language Journal, 78*(3), 273-284. doi:10.2307/330107

Dye, V., Herrington, M., Hughes, J., Kendall, A., Lacey, C., & Smith, R. (2010). Collaborative writing and dis-continuing professional development: challenging the rituals and rules of the education game? *Professional Development in Education, 36*(1-2), 289-306.

Grami, G. (2012). Online Collaborative Writing for ESL Learners Using Blogs and Feedback Checklists. *English Language Teaching, 5*(10), 43-48.

Hall, D., & Buzwell, S. (2012). The problem of free-riding in group projects: Looking beyond social loafing as reason for non-contribution. *Active Learning in Higher Education, 14*(1), 37-49. https://doi.org/10.1177/1469787412467123

Hadwin, A. F., Bakhtiar, A., & Miller, M. (2018). Challenges in online collaboration: effects of scripting shared task perceptions. *International Journal of Computer-Supported Collaborative Learning, 13*, 301-329. https://doi.org/10.1007/s11412-018-9279-9

Harasim, L. (2017). Connectivism as an Online Learning Theory. *Learning Theory and Online Technologies*, 80-104. doi:10.4324/9781315716831-6

Harasim, L. (2000). Shift happens: Online education as a new paradigm in learning. *The Internet and Higher Education, 3*(1-2), 41-61. doi:10.1016/s1096-7516(00)00032-4

Jackson, S. (2014). Student reflections on multimodal course content delivery. *Reference Services Review, 42*(3), 467-483. https://doi.org/10.1108/rsr-05-2014-0011

Johnson, D. W., & Johnson, R. T. (1991). Collaboration and Cognition. In A. L. Costa (Ed.), *Developing Minds: A Resource Book for Teaching* (Revised ed., Vol. 1, pp. 298-301). Alexandria, Virginia: Association for Supervision and Curriculum Development.

Karau, S. J., & Williams, K. D. (1993). Social loafing: A meta-analytic review and theoretical integration. *Journal of Personality and Social Psychology, 65*(4), 681-706. https://doi.org/10.1037/0022-3514.65.4.681

Korkmaz, Ö. (2012). A validity and reliability study of the Online Cooperative Learning Attitude Scale (OCLAS). *Computers & Education, 59*, 1162-1169. doi:10.1016/j.compedu.2012.05.021

Lexico. (n.d.). Collaboration. Lexico.com dictionary. Retrieved October 02, 2021, from https://www.lexico.com/definition/collaboration

Li, M. (2018). Computer-mediated collaborative writing in L2 contexts: an analysis of empirical research. *Computer Assisted Language Learning, 31*(8), 882-904.

Limbu, L., & Markauskaite, L. (2015). How do learners experience joint writing: University students' conceptions of online collaborative writing tasks and environments? *Computers & Education, 82*, 393-408. doi:10.1016/j.compedu.2014.11.024.

Masgoret, A. M., & Gardner, R. C. (2003). Attitudes, motivation, and second language learning: A meta-analysis of studies conducted by Gardner and Associates. *Language Learning, 53*(1), 123-163. https://doi.org/10.1111/1467-9922.00212

Mutwarasibo, F. (2013). Promoting university students' collaborative learning through instructor-guided writing groups. *International Journal of Higher Education, 2*(3). http://dx.doi.org/10.5430/ijhe.v2n3p1

Messer, J. (2020). Turning it inside out: Independent reading in the middle school classroom. *Illinois Reading Council Journal, 48*(2), 3-18.

Pace, C., Pettit, S. K., & Barker, K. S. (2020). Best practices in middle level quaranteaching: Strategies, tips and resources amidst COVID-19. *Becoming: Journal of the Georgia Association for Middle Level Education, 31*(1), 2.

Patton, M. Q. (2002). *Qualitative research and evaluation methods.* Thousand Oaks, CA: Sage Publications.

Reeves, T. C., Herrington, J., & Oliver, R. (2004). A development research agenda for online collaborative learning. *Educational Technology Research and Development, 52*(4), 53-65. doi:10.1007/bf02504718

Sharma, B. K. (2012). Conceding in disagreements during small group interactions in academic writing class. *Classroom Discourse, 3*(1), 4-28. https://doi.org/10.1080/19463014.2012.666024

Storch, N. (2005). Collaborative writing: Product, process, and students' reflections. *Journal of Second Language Writing, 14*(3), 153-173.

Storch, N. (2012). Collaborative writing as a site for L2 learning in face-to-face and online modes. *CALICO Monograph Series, 10*, 113-129.

Suwantarathip, O., & Wichadee, S. (2014). The Effects of Collaborative Writing Activity Using Google Docs on Students' Writing Abilities. *TOJET: The Turkish Online Journal of Educational Technology, 13*(2), 148-156.

Tocalli-Beller A. (2003). Cognitive conflict, disagreement and repetition in collaborative groups: affective and social dimensions from an insider's perspective. *The Canadian Modern Language Review, 60*(2), 143-71.

Toquero, C. M. (2020). Challenges and opportunities for higher education amid the COVID-19 pandemic: The Philippine context. *Pedagogical Research, 5*(4).

Trochim, W. M., & Donnelly, J. P. (2001). *Research methods knowledge base* (Vol. 2). Cincinnati, OH: Atomic Dog Publishing.

Wells, G. (1999). *Dialogic inquiry: Towards a sociocultural practice and theory of education.* New York: Cambridge University Press.

Vygotsky, L. S. (1978). *Mind in society.* Cambridge, Massachusetts: Harvard University Press.

Zhou, W., Simpson, E., & Domizi, D. (2012). Google Docs in an out-of-class collaborative writing activity. *International Journal of Teaching and Learning in Higher Education, 24*(3), 359-375.

Zhu, C. (2012). Student Satisfaction, Performance, and Knowledge Construction in Online Collaborative Learning. *Educational Technology & Society, 15*(1), 127-136.

Lessons from a Pandemic for the Future of Education
European Distance and E-Learning Network (EDEN) Proceedings
2021 Annual Conference | Madrid, 21-24 June, 2021
ISSN 2707-2819
doi: 10.38069/edenconf-2021-ac0002

AGILE APPROACH FOR E-LEARNING IN DIGITAL-LEADERSHIP TRAINING FOR SMALL AND MEDIUM ENTERPRISES

Roger Hage, Helena Lovasz-Bukvova, Matej Hopp, Marvin Hölzl, Gerhard Kormann-Hainzl, Michael Reiner, Deepak Dhungana, IMC University of Applied Sciences Krems, Austria

Abstract

Training for small and medium enterprises, especially in the context of leadership and digitalisation, has been traditionally carried out in form of presence workshops. Like other learning and training offers, this type of training needed to be carried out virtually during the COVID-19 pandemic, bringing advantages as well as disadvantages. Furthermore, the purpose of such courses is typically to convey a curriculum of preselected content and skills previously deemed useful. This paper presents the experiences from a mini-course on digital leadership carried out virtually during the pandemic that aims to incorporate SME needs in an agile manner. The presented mini-course is being developed using action research approach and aims to provide input for designing training in this context beyond the current crisis. The findings show high acceptance by the participants for the 100% virtual format and the effectiveness of the pilot run was proven to increase the digital skills of the participants. Engaging participants in order to reflect their needs has proven challenging and will be considered in the next action iteration.

Introduction

In context of training for small and medium enterprises (SME), the learning format represents an important success factor, with flexibility and informality (both supporting responsiveness to the needs of the SME trainees) playing a key role. Responsiveness in teaching has been approached from the point of view of personalisation, but also using agile methods. Finally, increased flexibility has also been connected to virtual learning (due to its time and place independence).

SME represent a heterogeneous and varied target group, with structural difference and very different needs than larger enterprises (Ates et al., 2013). They are known to struggle to adapt to innovation and market changes, possibly due to their short-term focus and reactive behaviour (Ates et al., 2013). At the same time, they play a vital role in the economy; hence additional support, e.g. training programmes, is often directed at SME. According to Johnston and Loader (2003), successful SME training must provide a suitable cost-benefit ratio, target SME-specific skills, be flexible and accommodating, have an informal setting, and be well publicised. Besides influencing the absolute participation, the format of SME training can also lead to participation biases (often self-section biases), such as favouring younger, educated, or anyway growth-oriented SME managers (Bager et al., 2015). Finally, Jones et al. (2013) also connect training format with the resulting impact (business performance). Overall, the format and structure of SME training plays an important role in the effectivity of the training – selecting and preparing the "right" content is not sufficient.

Responsiveness, adaptability, and agility have recently become prized attributes not only in educational context ("agility" has been very popular to the point of overuse). In teaching, especially in context of corporate training, the ability to respond to learners' needs and adapt the learning process is a subject of long-standing research (e.g. Li & Wong, 2019). Here too, the agile approach has been considered (e.g. Parsons & MacCallum, 2019). Unlike personalised learning, which implies adaptation to individual needs of each participant (Prain et al., 2012), the use of agile methods is focused towards identifying and responding to the needs of the current learners as a group. In SME training, responsiveness and agility can be useful to meet the needs of the heterogeneous target group.

Providing training in a virtual format was not a new topic before the pandemic, many authors having already researched the relative advantages and disadvantages of virtual learning (see Table 1). While Jones et al. (2013) deem e-learning to be acceptable and effective in SME training, traditionally, management training in Austria is delivered in a face-to-face format. In context of the pandemic, however, this option was not available.

Table 1: Advantages and disadvantages of virtual learning (Dumford & Miller, 2018; Oliveira et al., 2018; Sadeghi, 2019)

	Advantages	Disadvantages
students	flexibility, availability, low cost, time and space independent, no commuting	danger of distraction, self-discipline necessary, no immediate instructor feedback, technical difficulties
educational institutions	lower cost, no need for physical space, reuse	drop-out rates, investment costs, difficult to reach and engage students, difficult to incorporate applied activities, cultural aspects, acceptance of online qualification

Method

This paper reports the experience and findings from the iterative development and implementation of a digital leadership course for SME. In addition to the challenges of providing SME training, the course had to be delivered virtually due to the COVID-19 pandemic. The aim of our research was to systematically design the course and report the findings and identify learnings for the time after the pandemic. We studied the following research question:

- How can virtual learning be used to create a responsive learning environment in leadership training for SME?

The study was connected to the need to solve an actual practical aim. In context of this aim, the participating researchers took an active role of course designers and instructors. Given the responsive nature of the course, the participating learners also actively influenced the design. Therefore, action research was chosen as a suitable approach (Banegas & Consoli, 2020). This method allows a systematic process of inquiry where the researcher monitors and reflects on actions taken in a development or a change process using data-driven analysis to guide subsequent actions, aiming at finding effective solutions to everyday problems and improving the outcomes; the process is iterative and includes several Look-Think-Act spiral loops (Maestrini et al., 2016; Stringer, 2014).

Course in digital leadership

The course for digital leadership has been specifically developed for SME managers to support the digitalisation in SMEs in Austria. The needs of SME often differ from those of large enterprises (different context, seriously limited resources, and specific and niche markets); therefore, commonly available training might fail to provide them with actionable input. Furthermore, their size and structure vary considerably. Extensive continuing education programs in the area of digitalization, innovation or digital business transformation are available for corporate managers. However, these are either too specific, too technical, or too theoretical and require a large time investment, which is a challenge for SME managers. Many SMEs are centrally managed by their owners, so the attitude of the management is crucial for the adoption of new technologies and operating models. In order to effectively address the concerns of SME leadership regarding upskilling, the IMC FH Krems developed a new type of management mini-course in the area of continuing education as part of Digital Innovation Hub Ost project. The goal was to increase the innovation and digitization competencies of SME executives in the area of management and leadership, and to clearly stand out from conventional offerings (no frontal teaching, little theory, focus on identifying and solving problems collaboratively).

Course design principle I: Adaptive learning

Kayes (2002) addresses the role of experience in management learning and education by reviewing Kolb's experiential learning theory. In his article, Kayes recognizes four general approaches in management learning: (a) *action* (action-based learning to drive behavioural changes when solving organizational problems), (b) *cognition* (influencing thinking, e.g. memory, mental models and schemas), (c) *reflection* (encouraging reflection on assumptions and beliefs), and finally (d) *experience* (specifically experiencing positive emotions and feelings, recognizing learners as human beings who need not only to nourish their minds, but also their hearts and souls).

Our proposed education model, designated as Adaptive Lean Learning (ALL), was based on the principles of agile development and delivery as shown in Figure 1. It built on the experiential learning theory focusing on personalised, problem-based, effective and efficient learning. According to lean principles, the learners should cover only what is relevant for them, losing no time through superfluous content and generating no waste.

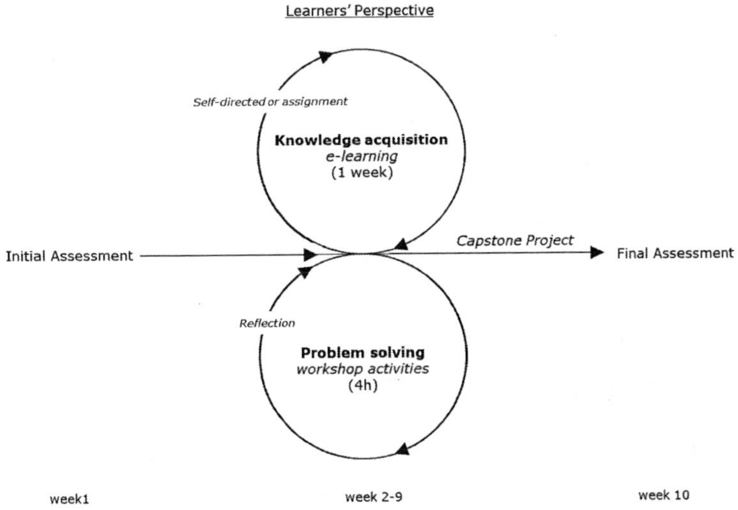

Figure 1. Adaptive Lean Learning Model: Learners' Perspective

The course consisted of 10 weekly workshops (4h each, on Tuesday afternoons), spanning a period of 3 months. Two weeks before the start, all registered participants received an online survey questionnaire concerning personal, professional and demographic information about them and their companies. Each week, the participants would attend an online workshop addressing a certain topic, contributing their own experiences and challenges. The trainers acted as a facilitators and coaches, inviting everyone to solve specific business problems. At the end of each workshop session, a reflection and discussion round were held where the participants reflected on what and how they have learned and gave feedback about the session. This corresponds to the lower loop in Figure 1 designated as "Problem solving". Between the sessions, the participants would acquire any missing knowledge or deepen their existing knowledge by either engaging in self-directed learning or fulfilling assignments given by the trainer, using an online e-learning tool for digital transformation for SMEs available on the web. This corresponds to the upper loop in Figure 1 designated "Knowledge acquisition". The process of passing through the double loop was repeated eight times during eight weeks, culminating in a capstone project presented by each participant in the last session. The last session also included a final assessment survey, as well as a 33-multiple-choice knowledge assessment quiz emulating the written exam needed for the P53 Digital Officer certification.

Course design principle II: Responsive teaching

This course targeted managing directors, business owners, or non-technical first line managers with over 10 years managerial experience working in SMEs. The pilot run was limited to 7 participants (see Table 2).

Table 2: Participants in the pilot course November 2020 to January 2021

Participant	Gender	Education	Role	Company size	Industry segment
P1	F	secondary	Manager	10-49	Food & beverage manufacturing
P2	F	tertiary	Business owner	1-9	Marketing
P3	F	tertiary	Manager	1-9	Consulting
P4	M	secondary	Manager	10-49	Conference operator
P5	M	tertiary	Business owner	50-99	Food & beverage manufacturing
P6	M	tertiary	Manager	100-250	Electrical engineering
P7	M	secondary	Business owner	1	Electrical engineering

Because little was known about the knowledge gaps and skill-needs of SME managers, we used the initial survey to assess the individual competencies and expectations as well as personal and corporate challenges of the participants. This information was used to prepare a tentative high-level curriculum and plan the first workshop.

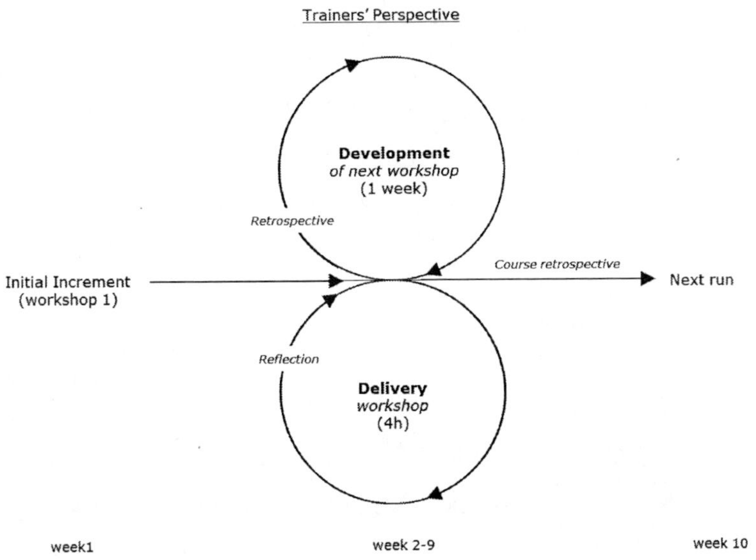

Figure 2. Adaptive Lean Learning Model: Trainers' Perspective

The course relied on a continuous, iterative process depicted in Figure 2, interweaving development and delivery along eight sprints. At the end of each *delivery sprint* or workshop, the participants gave feedback in a reflection session that would serve as an input for developing the next workshop during the subsequent *development sprint*. This double-loop (double-sprint) cycle was repeated until the last session. We did not use the exact artefact definitions of agile methods, but applied the principles as we deemed suitable for our special needs.

Learning in virtual environment

Initially, the course was to be delivered in a hybrid format, the first and the last sessions of the course being held on-site at the IMC in Krems, all remaining sessions being held virtually. Due to strict COVID-19 restrictions during November 2020, the whole course became virtual. Virtual courses are unusual in context of the target group, but in the given situation, the participants were open to the virtual format.

Course structure

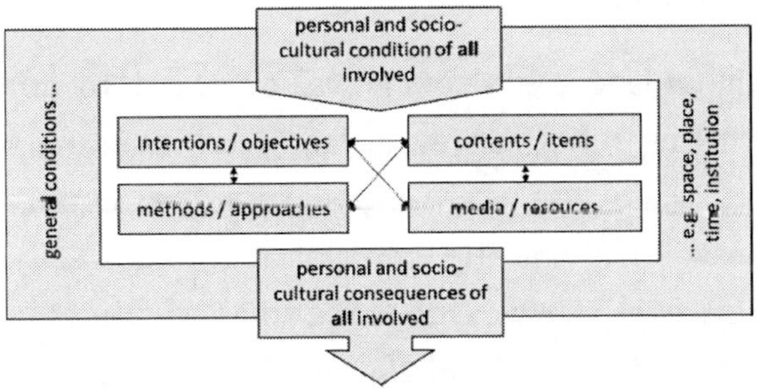

Figure 3. Didactical model of the course (based on the „Berlin Model", Heimann, 1979; Zierer et al., 2018)

The didactical model of the course was based on the Berlin Model, and alignment between the six factors was sought starting with the intentions and objectives. The primary course intentions and objectives are summarized in Table 3. The specific learning goals were to equip the participants with (a) an open *mindset* for growth including managerial ambidexterity, agility and adaptability, (b) a *skillset* comprising of the four key digital competencies, namely understanding digital trends and technologies and their application in business, business process optimization and automation, business model innovation and implementing change, and (c) a useful *toolset* comprising management models and frameworks like PESTEL, SWOT, 7S, Business Model Canvas as well as productivity-enhancing virtual communication and collaboration tools such as communication platform Microsoft Teams and the whiteboard Miro. A secondary objective was to prepare the participants for the personal competence certification of the Austrian Standards' P53 certification scheme "Digital Officer", which is carried out in accordance with the International ISO/IEC 1702 standard. The certification requirements include attending a 40-hour course covering the areas of Digital Technologies, Data & Information Security, Digital Marketing and Digital Strategies and Business Models, which also influenced the contents of the course.

Table 3: Primary course objectives (equipping participants with…)

Mindset	Skillset	Toolset
Ambidexterity	Digital Technologies	Management Frameworks
Agility	Business Processes	Collaboration Software
Adaptability	Business Models	
	Change Management	

The methods and approaches were based on the previously elaborated experiential learning theory. The media and resources were what distinguished this course from traditional courses or trainings for SME managers. These were exclusively web-based and consisted of e-learning content, virtual communication via Microsoft Teams, and a collaboration tool through Miro, defining the general conditions of the Berlin Model, namely space and place.

Findings and discussion

The pilot run of the digital leadership course was evaluated by analysing the final survey and comparing it with the initial survey using descriptive and inferential statistics. A simplified self-reported scale was used to measure the digital competency based on DigComp 2.2 AT (Swertz, 2019) and the managerial ambidexterity was measured using a scale introduced by Mom et al. (2009). Due to the small number of participants, inferences could only be made to a significance level of $\alpha = 0.08$ (see Table 4).

Table 4: Course evaluation results (n = 6) (n = 7)

Measure	Before	After	Difference	Remark
Expectation fulfilment		86%		6 out of 7 said their expectations were met
Net Promoter Score (NPS)		-29		1 promoter, 3 passives, 3 detractors
Managerial ambidexterity	2.34	2.13	-9%	Scale 1 to 7 (p = 0.77)* No significant change!
Familiarity with technology	3.81	4.57	+20%	Scale 1 to 7 (p = 0.08)*
Digital competence	2.14	2.94	+38%	Scale 1 to 4 (p = 0.06)*
Knowledge assessment		60%		3 from 5 passed the quiz (grade > 60%)
Willingness to get certified (P53)		70%		5 from 7 indicated that they will apply for P53

* a paired Student's t-test for the differences in scores after versus before was performed and the corresponding p-value is reported in the table

Among other points, the participants were asked what they liked most. More than 50% of the answers were related to the virtual character of the course, e.g. "the format despite Covid", "the e-learning and the quiz at the end", "Tools", "Tools for approaching and planning digitization projects (e.g. Miro)", which further confirmed the suitability of the online and virtual format of the course.

Conclusions

The findings show a general acceptance for the virtual format of the course. At the same time the disadvantage of such a 100% virtual course was that the on-site introduction session was skipped, which resulted in excessive efforts in training the participants to use virtual communication tools (MS Teams) for the first time, in a virtual setting (is a paradox in itself). Another disadvantage was the lack of the opportunity to build trust and rapport with the trainers, as well as socializing with peers, which normally takes place via face-to-face introductions and informal small talk. The presented Agile Lean Learning (ALL) model allowed a continuous development and delivery of the course in a responsive and adaptive manner, which was an ideal way to reduce uncertainty due to the heterogeneity of the participants as well as the unpredictability of the implications of the COVID-19 pandemic. The pilot run increased the digital competence of the participants by 38% (p = 0.06). The expectations of the participants were fulfilled, but apparently the pilot was not attractive enough to achieve a positive Net Promoter Score (NPS). The learnings from the pilot will be implemented in the next run starting April 2021, which will be carried out in a similar agile way.

References

Ates, A., Garengo, P., Cocca, P., & Bititci, U. (2013). The development of SME managerial practice for effective performance management. *Journal of Small Business and Enterprise Development, 20*(1), 28-54. https://doi.org/10.1108/14626001311298402

Bager, T. E., Jensen, K. W., Nielsen, P. S., & Larsen, T. A. (2015). Enrollment of SME managers to growth-oriented training programs. *International Journal of Entrepreneurial Behavior & Research, 21*(4), 578-599. https://doi.org/10.1108/IJEBR-12-2014-0224

Banegas, D. L., & Consoli, S. (2020). Action research in language education. In J. McKinley & H. Rose (Eds.), *The Routledge Handbook of Research Methods in Applied Linguistics* (pp. 176-187).

Dumford, A. D., & Miller, A. L. (2018). Online learning in higher education: Exploring advantages and disadvantages for engagement. *Journal of Computing in Higher Education, 30*(3), 452-465. https://doi.org/10.1007/s12528-018-9179-z

Heimann, P. 1901-1967. (1979). *Unterricht: Analyse und Planung* (10., unveränd. Aufl.). Schroedel.

Johnston, K., & Loader, K. (2003). Encouraging SME participation in training: Identifying practical approaches. *Journal of European Industrial Training, 27*(6), 273-280. https://doi.org/10.1108/03090590310479901

Jones, P., Beynon, M. J., Pickernell, D., & Packham, G. (2013). Evaluating the Impact of Different Training Methods on SME Business Performance. *Environment and Planning C: Government and Policy, 31*(1), 56-81. https://doi.org/10.1068/c12113b

Kayes, D. C. (2002). Experiential Learning and Its Critics: Preserving the Role of Experience in Management Learning and Education. *Academy of Management Learning & Education, 1*(2), 137-149. https://doi.org/10.5465/amle.2002.8509336

Li, K. C., & Wong, B. T.-M. (2019). How Learning Has Been Personalised: A Review of Literature from 2009 to 2018. In S. K. S. Cheung, L.-K. Lee, I. Simonova, T. Kozel, & L.-F. Kwok (Eds.), *Blended Learning: Educational Innovation for Personalized Learning* (pp. 72-81). Springer International Publishing. https://doi.org/10.1007/978-3-030-21562-0_6

Maestrini, V., Luzzini, D., Shani, A. B. (Rami), & Canterino, F. (2016). The action research cycle reloaded: Conducting action research across buyer-supplier relationships. *Journal of Purchasing and Supply Management, 22*(4), 289-298. https://doi.org/10.1016/j.pursup.2016.06.002

Mom, T. J. M., van den Bosch, F. A. J., & Volberda, H. W. (2009). Understanding Variation in Managers' Ambidexterity: Investigating Direct and Interaction Effects of Formal Structural and Personal Coordination Mechanisms. *Organization Science, 20*(4), 812-828. https://doi.org/10.1287/orsc.1090.0427

Oliveira, M. M. S. de, Penedo, A. S. T., & Pereira, V. S. (2018). Distance education: Advantages and disadvantages of the point of view of education and society. *Dialogia, 0*(29), 139-152. https://doi.org/10.5585/dialogia.N29.7661

Parsons, D., & MacCallum, K. (2019). Agile Education, Lean Learning. In D. Parsons & K. MacCallum (Eds.), *Agile and Lean Concepts for Teaching and Learning: Bringing Methodologies from Industry to the Classroom* (pp. 3-23). Springer. https://doi.org/10.1007/978-981-13-2751-3_1

Prain, V., Cox, P., Deed, C., Dorman, J., Edwards, D., Farrelly, C., Keeffe, M., Lovejoy, V., Mow, L., Sellings, P., Waldrip, B., & Yager, Z. (2012). Personalised learning: Lessons to be learnt. *British Educational Research Journal, 39*(4), 654-676. https://doi.org/10.1080/01411926.2012.669747

Sadeghi, M. (2019). A Shift from Classroom to Distance Learning: Advantages and Limitations. *International Journal of Research in English Education, 4*(1), 80-88. https://doi.org/10.29252/ijree.4.1.80

Stringer, E. (2014). *Action research* (4th ed.). Sage Publications.

Swertz, C. (2019). DigComp 2.2 AT.: Hintergründe und Kontexte. *Medienimpulse, 57*(1), Article 1. https://doi.org/10.21243/mi-01-19-14

Zierer, K., Matanovic, I., Werner, J., & Wernke, S. (2018). Ratings of usability of didactic models: A comparative case study in Croatia and Germany. *Journal of Curriculum Studies, 50*(4), 535–559. https://doi.org/10.1080/00220272.2018.1461933

Lessons from a Pandemic for the Future of Education
European Distance and E-Learning Network (EDEN) Proceedings
2021 Annual Conference | Madrid, 21-24 June, 2021
ISSN 2707-2819
doi: 10.38069/edenconf-2021-ac0003

LINK BETWEEN LEARNING STRATEGIES AND EDUCATIONAL GUIDANCE NEEDS – A PILOT STUDY WITH NEW STUDENTS AT UNED

Borja Guerrero Bocanegra, Universidad Nacional de Educación a Distancia (UNED), Spain

Abstract

In institutions such as the National University of Distance Education (UNED), where students must take a leading role in their own learning processes in order to be academically successful, the learning strategies, understood as a series of cognitive, metacognitive, motivational, self-regulation, emotional and support aspects, take on maximum importance. In order to establish relationships between learning strategies and the educational guidance needs of new students at the UNED, a pilot study was carried out with students of the Degree in Psychology in March 2021, who responded to the CEVEAPEU tool developed by Gargallo et al. (2009). The data shows that, at the beginning of their degree studies, students have good learning strategies. In addition to all the initial information and advice provided by the institution, it is appropriate for guidance services to provide specific guidance on a sustained basis throughout the first year, cushioning the effect of changes that may occur in learning strategies, thus helping to prevent many dropouts.

Introduction

The transition from educational concepts focused on the teacher and on the control of the student's learning process to those focused on the student and on the improvement of his or her learning process is closely related to academic guidance. Personalised attention, where the main objectives are to guide and advise students, has become increasingly important in the context of university higher education, as it is considered a key factor in enhancing retention or preventing students from dropping out.

The Distance Education, particularly those in virtual environments, is growing exponentially. With it, dropout rates also increase, especially in the first year (Sánchez-Elvira, 2014), which makes this initial stage critical. According to Carrión (2005), since the UNED was founded in 1972, dropout rates, that is to say, students who do not re-enrol, would be around 50% for those who drop out without even receiving a qualification (non-starting dropout), and around 14% for those who have actually obtained a qualification (real dropout). This data suggests that acting early, before enrolment and during the first year, is key to avoiding some of these dropouts (Luque et al, 2013). Therefore, the population of new enrolled students in Distance Education is one of the groups most susceptible to dropout, indicating that research for the prevention of it during the first year should be an institutional intervention strategy with high priority, especially with regard to issues concerning student autonomy and self-regulation of learning (Sánchez, opus cit.) and that are the direct competence of educational guidance services.

There is agreement that investment in improving the learning strategies that students deploy in order to take advantage of the resources available to them, as well as to discover what, how, and when to learn, is more academically cost-effective than improving instructional techniques or teaching materials (Gonzales & Diaz, 2007). Although the causes associated with dropout are complex and varied, and can be attributed either to the student, the teacher or the institution itself (García Aretio, 2019), investigating aspects such as lack of time, study techniques, motivation, capacity for autonomy and self-discipline, academic and social integration, etc. that are attributable to students, can provide clues to the institution on how to improve its guidance services. From this perspective, examining "the organised, conscious and intentional set of what the learner does to effectively achieve a learning objective in a given social context by integrating affective-motivational and supportive, metacognitive and cognitive elements" (Gargallo et al, 2009; p.2), in the initial stages of their university career can give us a global idea of the educational guidance needs of this group and how to optimise educational guidance services by focusing them on their real demands.

Method

Participants

The sample was selected by non-probabilistic convenience sampling, considering two criteria: first enrolment and degree, that is to say, first enrolment in the UNED in the academic year 2020-2021 and in the Degree in Psychology. Only students enrolled for the first time were encouraged to participate. However, a total of 99 students responded, of which 33 students who had already been enrolled on previous occasions were discarded. The sample consisted of 66 new students (60 women and 6 men), with an average age of 32.68 years.

Instrument

CEVEAPEU instrument developed by Gargallo et al. (2009) consists of 88 items, to be answered on a Likert-type scale with five grades. The 88 items are organised into two scales, six subscales and twenty-five strategies as shown in Table 1. Some examples of questions for the twenty-five strategies are:

- Intrinsic motivation: "What I find most satisfying is a thorough understanding of the content".
- Extrinsic motivation: "I study so I don't let my family and the people I care about down".
- Value of homework: "What I learn in some subjects I will be able to use in others and also in my future career".
- Internal attribution: "My academic performance depends on my effort".
- External attribution. "My academic performance depends on the teachers".
- Self-efficacy and expectations: "I am confident that I can understand even the most difficult content of the subjects in this course".
- Conception of intelligence as modifiable: "Intelligence is either there or it is not and cannot be improved".
- Physical and mental state: "Normally I feel good physically".
- Anxiety control: "When I take an exam, I get very nervous".
- Knowledge of the objectives and the evaluation criteria: "I know the assessment criteria by which I will be assessed by the teachers in the different subjects".
- Planning: "I plan my time to work on subjects throughout the course".
- Self-assessment: "I know what my strengths and weaknesses are when it comes to learning the subjects".
- Control / Self-regulation: "When I see that my initial plans do not achieve the expected success in my studies, I change them for more suitable ones".
- Context control: "I work and study in a suitable place – light, temperature, ventilation, noise, necessary materials at hand, etc.".
- Social interaction skills and work with fellow classmates: "I try to study or do class work with other classmates".
- Knowledge of sources and search for information: "I know where you can get the materials you need to study the subjects".
- Selection of the de information: "I am able to select the necessary information to study the subjects with guarantees".
- Knowledge building: "When I study, I integrate information from different sources: lectures, readings, practical work, etc.".

- Preparation of the information: "When I study the topics of the subjects, I do a first reading in order to get an idea of the basics".
- Organisation of the information: "I make simple graphs, diagrams or tables to organise the subject matter".
- Personalisation and creativity. Critical thinking: "I critically analyse the concepts and theories presented to me by teachers".
- Storing and mnemonics: "To memorise I use mnemonic resources such as acronyms (I make a word with the first letters of several sections I have to learn), acronyms, key words, etc.".
- Storage. Simple repetition: "To learn things, I just repeat them over and over again".
- Transfer. Use of information. "I use what I have learnt at university in everyday life situations".
- Resource management to use information effectively: "I make use of keywords that I have studied and learned, to remember the content related to them".

Procedure

The invitation to participate in this pilot was launched through unofficial channels of the institution. Specifically in WhatsApp groups of first-year Psychology subjects at the UNED, just after the February 2021 exams.

Data design and analysis

The design of the survey was type quantitative transactional. With the statistical analysis carried out with the SPSS 17.0 software, descriptive quantitative data was obtained, specifically; frequencies, percentages, means and standard deviations.

Results

The subscale "Motivational strategies" concentrates "very high" response scores in three of the strategies; "Intrinsic motivation" ($\bar{X} = 13.84$, SD = 1.61); "Value of homework" ($\bar{X} = 18.65$, SD = 1.68) and "Internal attribution" ($\bar{X} = 12.57$, SD = 2.30), "high" in other two; "Self-efficacy and expectations" ($\bar{X} = 15.96$, SD = 2.72) and "Conception of intelligence as modifiable" ($\bar{X} = 6.03$, SD = 0.89), "low" in "External attribution" ($\bar{X} = 5.12$, SD = 1.98) and "intermediate" in "Extrinsic motivation" ($\bar{X} = 4.54$, SD = 2.34). The scores, combined with the high scores obtained in the strategies that constitute the "Affective Component", "Physical and mental state" ($\bar{X} = 14.53$, SD = 3.38) and "Anxiety control" ($\bar{X} = 13.10$, SD = 2.56), show that the students in the sample are more intrinsically than extrinsically motivated, that is, they study Psychology more for satisfaction than for external incentives, they focus more on the process than on the result, they attribute their performance fundamentally to individual characteristics and traits, and they do so in a good state of mind and dominate their anxiety in the face of tasks and exams.

The subscale "Metacognitive Strategies" obtains "high" scores for all the strategies, as can be seen in Table 1, with a "very high" score for the strategy "Control / Self-regulation" ($\bar{X} = 24.25$, $SD = 3.46$), which suggest that the learners surveyed possess planning, monitoring and evaluation skills that enable them to pay adequate attention to the development of their own learning processes.

In the subscale "Strategies of contextual control, social interaction and resource management", the strategies "Context control and Social interaction skills and work with fellow classmates" shows "high" scores as referred to in Table 1. Similarly, the strategic patterns associated with "Knowledge of sources and search for information" and "Selection of the information" obtain "high" scores (see Table 1).

Finally, "Strategies for information processing and use" scored "very high" in "Preparation of the information ($\bar{X} = 16.80$, $SD = 2.53$) and "Transfer and use of information" ($\bar{X} = 12.62$, $SD = 1.90$), and "high" scores in "knowledge building" ($\bar{X} = 10.30$, $SD = 3.01$); "Organisation of the information" ($\bar{X} = 19.00$, $SD = 4.33$); "Personalisation and creativity. Critical thinking" ($\bar{X} = 18.07$, $SD = 4.02$); "Storing and mnemonics" ($\bar{X} = 11.07$, $SD = 3.11$); "Resource management to use information effectively" ($\bar{X} = 7.36$, $SD = 1.60$).

Table 1: Results of the questionnaire CEVEAPEU

Scales	Subscales	Dimension	$\bar{X}$	SD
Affective strategies of support and control (self-management)	Motivational strategies	Intrinsic motivation	13.84	1.61
		Extrinsic motivation	4.54	2.34
		Value of homework	18.65	1.68
		Internal attribution	12.57	2.30
		External attribution	5.12	1.98
		Self-efficacy and expectations	15.96	2.72
		Conception of intelligence as modifiable	6.03	0.89
	Affective components	Physical and mental state	14.53	3.38
		Anxiety control	13.10	2.56
	Metacognitive strategies	Knowledge of the objectives and the evaluation criteria	7.57	1.78
		Planning	13.21	2.23
		Self-assessment	11.21	2.16
		Control / Self-regulation	24.25	3.46
	Context management strategies, social interaction and resource management	Context control	15.28	3.69
		Social interaction skills and work with fellow classmates	19.86	4.89

Strategies related to the processing of information	Search and selection strategies and information	Knowledge of sources and search for information	14.00	3.73
		Selection of the de information	14.40	3.08
	Strategies for processing and use of information	Knowledge building	10.30	3.01
		Preparation of the information	16.80	2.53
		Organisation of the information	19.00	4.33
		Personalisation and creativity. Critical thinking	18.07	4.02
		Storing and mnemonics	11.07	3.11
		Storage. Simple repetition	5.00	2.26
		Transfer. Use of information	12.62	1.90
		Resource management to use information effectively	7.36	1.60

Discussion and conclusions

Taking the scores as a whole, we can see that the selected sample of students has an adequate strategic profile to start distance learning studies. The results obtained in the subscale "Motivational strategies", which is the one with the highest concentration of "very high" scores, suggest that the high initial motivation obtained by first degree students at the UNED may decrease at some point during the first year. Analysing the evolution of learning strategies over time during the first year can provide clues as to the critical moments when motivation begins to wane. UNED counselling services should focus on discovering how and when high starting motivation fluctuates at different points in the first year and on helping to sustain it by providing support and appropriate materials. On the other hand, monitoring students who make pessimistic or low mood comments as indicators associated with dropping out can help.

According to the results of the subscale "Metacognitive strategies", students do not seem to need special counselling in these aspects, in the same way that they report to know how to create suitable environmental conditions, to have a good control of time and space and a good management of material etc., (subscale "Strategies of context control, social interaction and resource management"), which are the direct competence of the guidance services. On the other hand, the "high" and "very high" scores obtained in the subscale "Strategies of information processing and use" except in the strategy "Storage. Simple repetition", tell us that the students have good strategies for encoding, processing, storing and organising information. Similar to the motivational aspects, it seems interesting to note when significant changes occur during the first year, because students "who do not reconfigure their styles despite needing to do so are likely to have greater difficulties in assimilating content, thus taking up more time and effort, and drop out" (Freiberg et al.,

2017; p.514). In addition to all the initial information and advice provided by the institution, it seems relevant for guidance services to provide specific guidance on a sustained basis throughout the first year, cushioning the effect of significant changes in learning strategies during the first year and helping to prevent dropout. Self-regulated learning is fundamental to success in distance learning modalities (Jansen et al., 2020). Thus, some of the actions that guidance services should insist on have to do with: better management and organisation of time, self-regulated study (teaching to set goals, orienting action in line with goals, planning, persistence, asking for help when necessary, trying other alternatives and reflecting) and realistic management of expectations. Provide courses on the technological skills needed to study in digital Distance Education, as well as help guides for the use of the different platforms.

The most striking limitations of this pilot experience are the sample; the size was not sufficient and the selection procedure was not impartial. As it is a convenience sample, which is not representative of the entire group of new undergraduate students at the UNED, the results cannot be generalised. Systematic replication on a larger scale is needed.

References

Álvarez, P. R., & López, D. (2017). Estudios sobre deserción académica y medidas orientadoras de prevención en la universidad de La Laguna (España). *Revista Paradigma, 38*(1), 48-71. Retrieved from https://goo.gl/mC5SM3.

Cabrera, L., Bethencourt, J. T., Álvarez, P., & González, M. (2006). El problema del abandono de los estudios universitarios. *RELIEVE, 1*(2). https://doi.org/10.7203/relieve.12.2.4226

Carrión, J. (2005). Una mirada crítica a la Enseñanza a Distancia (segunda parte). *Revista Iberoamericana de Educación, 36*(12), 1-13. https://doi.org/10.35362/rie36122740

Freiberg, A., Ledesma, R., & Fernández, M. (2017). Estilos y estrategias de aprendizaje en estudiantes universitarios de Buenos Aires. *Revista de Psicología, 35*(2), 511-49. https://doi.org/10.18800/psico.201702.006

García Aretio, L. (2019). El problema del abandono en estudios a distancia. Respuestas desde el Diálogo Didáctico Mediado. RIED. *Revista Iberoamericana de Educación a Distancia, 22*(1), 245-270. http://dx.doi.org/10.5944/ried.22.1.22433

Gargallo, B., Suárez-Rodríguez, J., & Pérez-Pérez, C. (2009). El cuestionario CEVEAPEU. Un instrumento para la evaluación de las estrategias de aprendizaje de los estudiantes universitarios. *RELIEVE. Revista Electrónica de Investigación y Evaluación Educativa, 15*(2), 1-31. Retrieved from https://www.redalyc.org/pdf/916/91612906006.pdf

Gargallo, B., Almerich, G., Suárez-Rodríguez, J., & García-Félix, E. (2012). Estrategias de aprendizaje en estudiantes universitarios excelentes y medios. Su evolución a lo largo del primer año de carrera. *Revista Electrónica de Investigación y Evaluación Educativa, 18*(2). https://doi.org/10.7203/relieve.18.2.2000

Gonzales, D., & Díaz, Y. (2007). La importancia de promover en el aula estrategias de aprendizaje para elevar el nivel académico en los estudiantes de Psicología. *Revista Iberoamericana de Educación, 46*(8). Retrieved from https://rieoei.org/historico/investigacion/1379Gonzalez.pdf

Jansen, R., Leeuwen, A., Janssen, J., Conijn, R., & Kester, L. (2020). Supporting learners' self-regulated learning in Massive Open Online Courses. *Computers & Education, 146.* Retrieved from https://www.sciencedirect.com/science/article/pii/S0360131519303240

Luque, E., García, F., & de Santiago, C. (2013). El abandono y egreso en la UNED. IUEDoc2. IUED. UNED. Retrieved from http://e-spacio.uned.es/fez/eserv/bibliuned:501063/Luque_et_al_Abandono_Egreso_VI_Redes_2014.pdf

Rué, J. (2014). El abandono universitario: variables, marcos de referencia y políticas de calidad. *REDU. Revista de docencia universitaria, 12*(2), 281-306. https://doi.org/10.4995/redu.2014.5649

Sánchez-Elvira, A. (2014). ¿Cómo iniciarse con éxito en el aprendizaje en línea?: La experiencia de la UNED en el entrenamiento de estudiantes autorregulados. En Los Recursos de Aprendizaje en Educación a Distancia: Nuevos Escenarios, Experiencias y Tendencias (pp. 144-173) Fidel Ramírez Prado y Claudio Rama. Retrieved from http://e-spacio.uned.es/fez/eserv/bibliuned:501049/Sanchez-Elvira_Iniciarseexito.pdf

Author

Trainee researcher at the International Doctoral School of the National University of Distance Education (UNED) in the Education Programme. Pre-doctoral contract under the UNED-Banco Santander 2019 Collaboration Agreement in the project "Detection of academic guidance needs of incoming students and proposal of a support programme" of the COIE.

Lessons from a Pandemic for the Future of Education
European Distance and E-Learning Network (EDEN) Proceedings
2021 Annual Conference | Madrid, 21-24 June, 2021
ISSN 2707-2819
doi: 10.38069/edenconf-2021-ac0004

NON-ENGLISH MAJORS' ATTITUDES TOWARDS USING YOUTUBE TO IMPROVE SPEAKING SKILLS

Nguyen Dinh Nhu Ha, University of Finance and Marketing, Vietnam

Abstract

This study aimed to explore students' attitudes towards using YouTube to improve speaking skills at the context of a Binh Duong based university. A total of one hundred and fifty students participated in the research. Both quantitative and qualitative data was obtained through two instruments, namely questionnaires and interview. For analysing the data collected, descriptive statistics and content analysis were employed. The results of the study revealed that non-English majors hade positive attitudes towards using YouTube to improve speaking skills. More interestingly, the findings revealed that they had affective attitudes towards the use of YouTube higher than the cognitive and behavioural attitudes. The study also made several suggestions for both teachers and students with the aim of contributing a small part to the teaching and learning of English speaking skills.

Introduction

It is evident that speaking is one of the most important skills for foreign language learners (Zaremba, 2006). In fact, speaking plays a major role in everyday communication. Rivers (1981) stated that speaking skill is used twice as much as writing and reading combined. According to Efrizal (2012), speaking helps people to interact and approach the world easier and more efficiently. It is obvious that humans spend much their time interacting orally with language rather than written form. More interestingly, humans are programmed to speak before they know how to read and write. In terms of English speaking skill, it is not an easy task for people to fluently communicate. In the traditional method, speaking skill is ignored by most of teachers. As a result, students become afraid of speaking English in daily life. That is why English teachers must seek for some way to facilitate their learners' speaking process.

According to Mazouzi (2013), learners' learning activities should be designed to develop the fluency and accuracy. These elements are really important in communicative approach. Therefore, classroom practice should help learners develop the competence of communicating. The main aim of English language teaching is to give learners the ability to use English language effectively in communication (Davies, 2000). English videos on YouTube, as a result, become an extremely useful source of speaking materials since it provides learners with both audio and visual input. Further than that, the subtitles in clips on YouTube can also be used to facilitate both speaking and listening activities. The controversy arises around this is whether the use YouTube can enhance learners' speaking skills. Although many studies have been conducted over this issue, the answers are still far from conclusive.

In terms of attitudes, it is known that they can totally affect people's behaviour. Hewstone and Stroebe (2004) demonstrated that the more positive attitude a person has about his level of intelligence, the more he thinks that he could solve the problems. In addition, Conner and Armitage (1998) expressed that the components of attitudes are considered a person's obvious behavioural beliefs which represent outcomes of the behaviour.

More specifically, Spooncer (1992) classifies attitudes into three components: affective, cognitive and behavioural attitudes. Remarkably, affective attitude is the responses towards an attitude object. It includes how individuals think and feel about speaking activities, how encouraged they are to practice conversation and how much they are interested in speaking activities. Besides, cognitive attitude is the belief, thoughts and attributes that individuals pay attention to. Behavioural attitude refers to the responses or reaction in doing something.

In general, based on the significance of YouTube and attitudes towards speaking skills, the objective of this study was (1) to find out the non-English majors' attitudes towards the use of YouTube in improving speaking skills. In order to achieve this objective, the following research question was formulated:

- What are non-English majors' attitudes towards the use of YouTube in improving speaking skill?

Literature Review

Definitions and components of attitudes

Attitude is an important factor that affects students' learning process and perception. According to Jung (1971), attitude is a readiness of the psyche to act or react in a certain way. Gal and Ginsburg (1994) also stated that attitude is the collection of emotions and feelings experienced during learning periods. Walley et al. (2009) stated that attitudes may be positive, negative or neutral. In the context of attitudes, three main components, including cognitive, affective and behavioural ones are mentioned.

Affective component

The affective component is the response towards an attitude object. In terms of speaking, it includes how individuals think and feel about speaking activities, how encouraged they are to take part in English conversation and how much they are interested in speaking. Eagly and Chaiken (1998) define affective factor as the "feelings, moods, emotions, and sympathetic nervous system activity that people have experienced in relation to an attitude object and subsequently associate with it" (p.272). These authors claim that affective component is mainly based on the emotional experiences and preferences. A person can show their like or dislike to an activity. The affective factor should not be judged in terms of only the beliefs because emotion works simultaneously with cognitive factor. The combination of affective component, including the evaluative judgment on beliefs are proposed as an integrated model of attitude and choice (Agarwal & Malhotra, 2005). In terms of using YouTube in speaking, affective component involves the mental process of choosing favourite clips and applying learned structures to daily conversations.

Cognitive component

Cognitive component of attitudes is the beliefs, thoughts and attributes that individuals express about the object. It refers that general knowledge of a person relates to part of attitudes. It is based on how people think about attitude objects. Schiffman and Kanuk (2004) state that cognitive factor consists of information and perceptions. These two elements can be found through the mixture of experiences of attitude objects and the information in different sources. In relation to YouTube, it is believed that when learners feel interested in learning English through YouTube, they have more positive attitudes toward it.

Behavioural component

Behavioural component refers to the listeners' responses or feedback to English clips on YouTube. According to Defleur and Westie (1963), it involves a person's response or reaction in doing something. To learners, behavioural approach helps them clearly locate the main ideas and then apply to real conversations.

YouTube and English speaking skill

YouTube was official founded by Chad Hurley, Steve Chen, and Jawed Karim in June, 2005. (Burgess, 2009). It provides a lot of videos with different categories. In terms of teaching and learning, it contains many useful videos which help to enhance the learning process (Patel, 2009). Besides that YouTube videos are limited in lengths; this helps them become appropriate for classroom's time.

YouTube has been considered an effective tool for improving English skills and help people become familiar with spoken languages. YouTube is the most popular site with lots of videos, in which English learning clips are watched by billions of people in the world (YouTube, 2013). Many users upload videos to show the real conversations which are taken place every day. Using YouTube as multimedia has been popular for people. Hence, students become familiar with different cultures, pronunciation, accents and so on (Muna, 2011). According to Prakoso (2009), YouTube helps learners find all kinds of necessary clips with different categories. In reality, students can observe how native speakers speak from videos.

Stempleski and Tomalin (1990) emphasized the role of YouTube in communication. English speaking clips on YouTube help students become more ready to communicate in the target language. Besides that the vocabulary and grammar points used in clips help to enhance learners' English competence. Watkens and Wikins (2011) proved that using YouTube lets students have exposure toward authentic English. Videos can be used for most of the students' level with the purpose of enhancing speaking skill. It is no doubt that YouTube-based videos can improve students' speaking skills and motivation (Riswandi, 2016). They can also develop students' learning autonomy and explore the target culture easily. Singhkhachorn (2014) found that students feel comfortable and enjoyable when they have the chance to learn speaking with YouTube. They also feel excited to learn and focus more in the lessons.

Previous research

In order to explore students' attitudes towards using YouTube in improve speaking skills, many researchers have recently conducted this kind of research. Researchers have proved that the movies on YouTube are effective for both teaching and learning speaking skill. As a result, many universities have implemented YouTube for teaching speaking (Arianti et al., 2018; Dorothy et al., 2013; Jia, 2019; Borko et al., 2019; Zhang et al., 2011).

There have been different studies which attempt to investigate students' attitudes towards the use of YouTube in improving speaking skills. Some noticeable studies are Buzzetto-More, 2015; Faizi et al., 2018; Balbay, 2017; Kurniawati, 2015; Kabooha, 2018; Siwi, 2008; Trang, 2017; Huong, 2014). These studies indicated that attitudes have a positive effect on students such as improving pronunciation, listening skills; expanding vocabulary and structures; and becoming confident to take part in English conversations. In a word, various studies have been detecting the learner's attitudes towards using YouTube in improving speaking skills. However, most of these investigations were pursued recently, indicating that the topic is still new to researchers. Moreover, these studies focus on the English-majors although speaking is an important skill in general English classes. That is one of the reasons why the research conducted this research to explore non-English majors' attitudes towards using YouTube to improve speaking skills.

Methodology

Research setting

This research was carried out at Thu Dau Mot University. The study was conducted in the first semester of the school year 2021–2021. The school consists of 12 departments, with the total of over 14,000 students. The students come from every part of the country. Most of them learnt English according the instruction of the seven-year or ten-year English Curriculum of Vietnamese Ministry of Education and Training through formal classes in secondary and high schools.

Participants

The participants of the present study consisted of 150 students who were the freshmen at the university. The participants' general information includes gender, time for learning English, major, time for watching clips YouTube with captions and kinds of favourite clips. The number of male and female students were 52.7% and 47.3% respectively. Students with 11 years and 7 years of learning English was 28% and 72% respectively. Most of the students taking part in this study were from Faculty of Information Technology (43%) and the others were mechanics students (30%), accounting students (28%), electronics students (29%) and business administration students (20%). In addition, time for watching movies on YouTube was divided into 4 groups. The first group with the highest frequency was 39.3%. The second group with 1-2 times per week was 34.7%. The third group with 3-4 times per week was 10%. The last group with the frequency of more than 5 times was 6.0%. Finally, the kinds of favourite clips which the participants chose to watch. More than a half of the students chose English daily conversations, accounting for 53.3%. The second choice was instruction videos for speaking and pronunciation, accounting for 43.3%. The next choice was English animated movies, accounting for 4.4%.

Instruments

The instruments employed in the study included closed-ended questionnaire and semi-structured interview. The questionnaire was designed in a multiple choice with a 5 Likert scale type ranging from 1 to 5 (1 = *strongly disagree*, 2 = *disagree*, 3 = *neutral*, 4 = *agree*, 5 = *strongly agree*). The questionnaire was divided into two parts with the total number of 25 items: personal information (6 items) and students' attitudes towards the use of YouTube (19 items). In order to avoid misunderstanding, the questionnaire was translated into Vietnamese. The Cronbach's Alpha was .953 which proved that the questionnaire was reliable. The semi-structured interview was use to evaluate the attitudes in the use of

YouTube. 20 interviewees were selected for separate interviews. The interviewees were labelled from S1 to S20.

Data collection and analysis

Regarding data collection procedure, the researcher conducted two classes and then the colleagues at the Faculty helped with three classes. The researcher and colleagues were teaching at the college. The online questionnaire and interviews were delivered to their students and an instruction how to choose the multiple choices and answer the questions in the interview was explained in detailed. For data analysis, the researcher employs SPSS 22.0 in which descriptive statistic including Mean (M), Standard Deviation (SD), Percentages (P) were processed, while content analysis was employed to deal with qualitative data.

Findings and discussion

Findings

Table 1 showed that the total mean scores of attitudes towards the use of YouTube was rather high (M = 3.63; SD = .74). It means that participants' attitudes towards the use of YouTube were relatively positive.

Table 1: Students' attitudes towards the use of YouTube

No.	Attitudes	N = 150	
		M	SD
1	Cognitive attitudes	3.55	.72
2	Affective attitudes	3.71	.69
3	Behavioural attitudes	3.63	.82
Total		3.63	.74

Note: M: mean; SD: Standard deviation

Cognitive attitudes

The questionnaire included 8 items asking respondents' cognitive attitudes towards the use of YouTube. As seen in the table 2, most of participants admitted that YouTube helped them to recognize the information (item 3: M = 3.63; SD = .862). Besides, participants realized that they could improve their pronunciation by watching YouTube (item 5: M = 3.69; SD = .781). In addition, they agreed that they can understand the contents of clips by watching subtitles and know which information is important (item 4: M = 3.68; SD = .870; item 7: M = 3.65; SD = .768). Regarding listening skills, participants said that they improved when watching subtitles in the screen (item 2: M = 3.57; SD = .785). Further to this, YouTube could help them to enhance their listening skills (item 1: M = 3.65; SD = .780). Concerning to their learning outcome, participants admitted that their learning outcomes improved thanks to practicing watching YouTube daily (item 8: M = 3.49; SD = .782). Participants also agreed that their speaking competence could improve by watching and repeating subtitles (item 6: M = 3.56; SD = .887). These findings can be interpreted that YouTube helped participants improve their speaking skills as well as learning outcomes. Participants could have more chances to practise pronunciation and ability of defining important information from clips. Furthermore, participants became more confident when they could understand the whole story of the clips.

Table 2: Students' cognitive attitudes towards the use of YouTube

No.	Cognitive Attitudes	N = 150	
		M	SD
1	I can enhance my listening skills by watching YouTube.	3.65	.780
2	I can improve my listening skills when watching subtitles on the screen.	3.57	.785
3	Daily conversations help me to receive the information.	3.63	.862
4	I can understand the whole contents of clips by watching subtitles.	3.68	.870
5	I can improve my pronunciation by listening and watching subtitles in each clip.	3.69	.781
6	I can improve my speaking competence by watching and repeat subtitles.	3.56	.887
7	I improve my ability to recognize important information.	3.65	.768
8	My learning outcomes can improve after practise watching clips on YouTube.	3.49	.782
Total		3.62	.815

Note: M: mean; SD: Standard deviation

In order to obtain more information about the usefulness of clips on YouTube, the qualitative data from the interview was collected and analysed. The participants admitted that watching YouTube was useful and important for their speaking skills. They also reported some reasons for that:

> *"Students speak more fluently and recognize many new structures." (S2)*

> *"English clips help students pronounce well." (S6)*

> *"Students can correct their mistakes in pronunciation easily." (S16)*

> *"Students can understand the cultures in communication of foreigners." (S19)*

Affective attitudes

Participants' affective attitudes towards the use of YouTube were evaluated by 6 items. Participants felt more confident to evaluate speaking skills (item 12: M = 3.92; SD = .746). Thus, participants felt excited to practise conversations (item 11: M = 3.81; SD = .817). Participants emphasized that they felt interested in engaging more in learning activities (item 10; M = 3.73; SD = .822). Thanks to clips on YouTube, they were able to correct wrong pronunciation of other members in class (item 14: M = 3.78; SD = .825). In addition, they admitted that they felt more confident to put stress and adjust their own pronunciation (item 9: M = 3.68; SD = .712). Participants also thought that they could make up the conversations on their own (item 13; M = 3.69; SD = .810). To put it briefly, participants had positive affective attitudes in using YouTube to improve their speaking skills. With the support of YouTube, they became more confident, enjoyable, engaged and interested in learning activities.

Table 3: Students' affective attitudes towards the use of YouTube

No.	Affective Attitudes	N = 150	
		M	SD
9	I feel more confident to put stress or adjust my weak pronunciation.	3.68	.712
10	I find it interesting to engage more in learning activities.	3.73	.822
11	I find it enjoyable to cooperate with my classmates in conversations.	3.81	.817
12	I find it confident to evaluate my speaking skills.	3.92	.746
13	I feel confident to make up conversations on my own.	3.69	.810
14	I find it confident to correct other students' pronunciation	3.78	.825
Total		3.77	.79

Note: M: mean; SD: Standard deviation

The qualitative data were analysed to express students' affective attitudes towards the use of YouTube. It was evident that participants had positive affective attitudes towards the use of YouTube. There were some positive comments from the interview as follows:

> *"I am confident to volunteer to join in most of speaking and pronunciation exercises." (S1)*
>
> *"I am willing to help friends to find correct their pronunciation." (S2)*
>
> *"I always volunteer to give some comments on speaking activities." (S12)*

Behavioural attitudes

Students' behavioural attitudes towards the use of YouTube were measured by 5 items in the table 5. Students always spend time watching English clips to practise pronunciation (item 15: M = 3.87; SD = .859). Participants also agreed that they often took notes of interesting words and phrases (item 16: M = 3.67; SD = .725). Furthermore, students spent several times watching the same clips (item 17: M = 6.65; SD = .740). In addition, participants also admitted that they liked to spend much time watching favourite clips (item 18: M = 3.38; SD = .854). In summary, participants expressed positive behavioural attitudes towards the use of YouTube. There were some positive behavioural attitudes such as practicing watching clips to improve pronunciation, taking notes of words and phrases and choosing favourite movies to enhance speaking skills.

Table 4: Students' behavioural attitudes towards the use of YouTube

No.	Behavioural Attitudes	N = 150	
		M	SD
15	I always find interesting clips to practise pronunciation.	3.87	.859
16	I always take notes of interesting and strange words and phrases.	3.67	.725
17	I practice watching the clips several times.	3.65	.740
18	I pay much attention to my favourite clips.	3.38	.854
19	I spend my whole free time to listen to pronunciation clips.	3.65	.774
Total		3.64	.79

Note: M: mean; SD: Standard deviation

Aligning with quantitative data, qualitative data were used to prove students' positive behavioural attitudes towards the use of YouTube. In the interview, students showed their agreement with this:

"I can improve my pronunciation by watching the clips several times." (S3)

"I always pause the clips when I recognize strange words." (S18)

"I try to listen to different accents and then practice saying like clips." (S15)

Discussion

The findings of the study have revealed some highlighted features of students' attitudes towards the use of YouTube in improving speaking skills. First of all, it is noticed that the participants showed their positive attitudes towards the use of YouTube in improving speaking skills. In terms of cognitive attitudes, the findings were corroborated with the ideas of Tarun Patel (2009), who suggested that the contents and time of clips on YouTube are suitable for conducing speaking lessons. Participants agreed that they could improve pronunciation as well as recognizing ability from English clips. Last but not least, participants admitted that they could understand the contents of clips easily. Moreover, the results also divulged that students were aware of the usefulness of YouTube to listening skills. These findings were partially supported by the previous research carried out by Manu (2011), Prakoso (2009), Heriyanto (2015) and Stempleski and Tomalin (2013), who have proved that students can expand their vocabulary, improve their pronunciation and confidence and make up English conversations effectively.

Concerning affective attitudes, the participants showed that they engaged actively in most of speaking activities. The present findings seemed to be consistent with Riswandi (2016), who has pointed out factors such as feelings, moods, emotions and sympathetic nervous system that people have experienced. The findings unfolded that students felt more confident to correct the pronunciation in classroom. The results also accorded with Singhkhachorn (2014), who have found out that students had good motivation and became more enjoyable to watch clips on YouTube. Regarding behavioural attitudes, this study produced results which were corroborated the findings of a great deal of the previous work in this field. In the same line with Dufy (2008), the finding revealed that students spent more time finding favourite clips on YouTube. Besides, students had positive attitude to their favourite clips and finding preferences to improve their speaking skills. The findings further also supported the idea of Terantino (2011), who has revealed students' positive attitudes in watching clips on YouTube. The majority of students agreed that for extra practice, they often looked for clips to practice at home.

Conclusion and implications

The results of this study shed light on students' attitudes towards the use of YouTube to improve speaking skills. One of the significant findings to emerge from this study was that students had positive attitudes towards the use of YouTube. In respect of cognitive attitudes, students agreed that their speaking skills as well as pronunciation improved a lot. Relating to affective attitudes, students believed that they felt more confident, enjoyable to engage in speaking activities. In terms of behavioural attitudes, students agreed that YouTube helped them to form the positive learning habits such as learning at home, taking notes of difficult phrases for later use and choosing favourite clips to watch.

The findings suggest several courses of action for the administrations, the teachers and students in general English classes. For the administrators, they should either allow more time for the general English course or reduce the number of students in classes. Besides, they should allow the course to take place in well-equipped classrooms or laboratories. In particular, the administrations or the faculty should organize workshops, training courses, and demonstration classes related to the practice of teaching by YouTube. Furthermore, the school and faculty should call for more research on this field. For the English teachers, they have to make sure that students fully understand the effectiveness of clips on YouTube. What is more, they should promote the interaction among students in the classrooms by creating a more supportive classroom environment. Last but not least, the teachers should design both in-class and out-of-class tasks with more activities for the students. To the students in general English classes, they should be aware of the importance and usefulness of YouTube to improve speaking skills.

References

Arianti, A., et al. (2018). A media for teaching speaking using YouTube video. *Advance in Engineering Research, 175*, 71-73.

Berj, R. A. (2009). Multimedia teaching with video clips: TV, movies, YouTube, and mtvU in the college classroom. *International Journal of Technology in Teaching and Learning, 5*(1), 1–21.

Borko, H., et al. (2008). Video as a tool for fostering productive discussions in mathematics professional development. *Teaching and Teacher Education, 24*(2), 417-436.

Burgess, J., & Green, J. (2009). *YouTube: Online video and participatory culture.* Malden: Polity Press.

Efrizal, D. (2012). Improving Students' speaking through communicative language teaching method. *International Journal of Humanities and Social Science, 2*(20), 127-134.

Gunada, I. W. S. (2017). *Using YouTube video: An IT-based media to improve students' speaking skill* (Undergraduate thesis). Ganesha University of Education, Singaraja.

Hadijah, S. (2016). Teaching by using video: Ways to make it more meaningful in EFL classrooms. *ISELT, 4*, 307-115.

Heriyanto, D. (2015). The effectiveness of using YouTube for vocabulary mastery. *English Teaching Journal, 6*(1), 1-12.

Mazouzi, S. (2013). *Analysis of Some Factors Affecting Learners' Oral Performance. A Case Study: 3rd Year Pupils of Menaa's Middle Schools* (M. A. Dissertation). Department of Foreign Languages, English Division, Faculty of Letters and Languages, Mohamed Khider University of Biskra.

Prakoso, K. (2009). *Lebih Kreatif dengan YouTube.* Yogyakarta: Andi.

Riswandi, D. (2016). Use of YouTube-based videos to improve students' speaking skill. *Proceeding of the 2nd International Conference on Teacher Training and Education, 2*(1), 298-306.

Rivers, W. M. (1968). *Teaching Foreign Language Skills.* Chicago: University of Chicago Press.

Singhkhachorn, S. (2014). *Development of learning and teaching by social network.* Paper presented at the Asian Conference on Society, Education, and Technology, Bangkok.

Stempleski, S., & Tomalin, B. (2001). *Film.* Oxford: Oxford University Press.

Patel, T. (2009, January 3). YouTube for ELT. ELTWeekly [Blog post]. Retrieved July 7, 2021, from http://eltweekly.com/2009/01/eltweekly-issue4-article-youtube-for-elt-by-tarun-patel/

Watkins, J., & Wilkins, M. (2011). Using YouTube in the EFL classroom. *Language Education in Asia, 2*(1), 113-119.

Zaremba, A. J. (2006). *Speaking professionally.* Canada: Thompson South-Western.

Lessons from a Pandemic for the Future of Education
European Distance and E-Learning Network (EDEN) Proceedings
2021 Annual Conference | Madrid, 21-24 June, 2021
ISSN 2707-2819
doi: 10.38069/edenconf-2021-ac0005

EXPLORING ENGAGEMENT IN ONLINE VIDEOS FOR LANGUAGE LEARNING THROUGH YOUTUBE'S LEARNING ANALYTICS

Maria Dolores Castrillo, Universidad Nacional de Educación a Distancia (UNED), Jorge Mañana-Rodriguez, Universidad Carlos III de Madrid, Spain

Abstract

Until a few years ago, video analytics were not accessible to learning stakeholders, mainly because online video platforms did not share the users' interactions on the system with stakeholders. However, this scenario has changed, and currently YouTube, the world's largest media sharing site, offers these data. YouTube is also the main tool for transmitting audio-visual content in Language MOOCs (massive open online courses), and its video engagement data can be monitored through the YouTube Studio channel, which provides free and open access to video analytics. In this paper we present our research based on the analysis of viewers' engagement with 35 videos of the Language MOOC entitled *Alemán para hispanohablantes: basic principles* (German for Spanish-speakers). The data provided by the YouTube Studio Learning Analytics platform has enabled new insights related to participants' watching of these videos in Language MOOCs (LMOOCs). The results of our study provide pedagogical implications for Foreign Language instructors concerning the use of videos in language learning.

Introduction

The first Language Massive Online Open Courses (LMOOCs) started to appear in October 2012. The Spanish University for Distance Education (UNED), the world pioneer in offering LMOOCs, started to offer on that date, among other courses, the LMOOC *German for Spanish-speakers*, coordinated and taught by one of the authors of the present study. The main contents of this LMOOC (which continues to be taught and updated without interruption to date) are transmitted mainly through video-pills, which according to recent investigations have turned out to be "the most powerful learning objects in this type of online courses" (Martín-Monje et al., 2018; p.4). It is specifically an xMOOC, characterized by the use of video lectures as the main tool for delivering content. In the first edition of the LMOOC, the videos were broadcast through two open channels: UNED's own channel (CanalUNED) and YouTube. Almost a decade after these 35 videos were recorded and broadcast, at the time of this study, the videos had received more than 2,000,000 views on the YouTube channel. As research confirms, student retention is an outstanding issue in LMOOCs, and we believe that analysis of students' engagement with the videos contained in the LMOOC can help us understand why they drop out of these courses. Engagement is usually measured by video watching time, so our research begins with the assumption that there are meaningful differences in the retention of different groups of viewers, and that the retention also varies depending on the intrinsic difficulty of the videos. It is noteworthy that this study could not have been carried out only a few years ago, since video analytics were not accessible to learning stakeholders, mainly because online video platforms did not share the users' interactions on the system with stakeholders. However, this scenario has changed: YouTube, the world's largest media sharing site, now offers these data. So, the data provided by the YouTube Studio Learning Analytics platform has enabled us to gain new insights into participants' watching of these videos in our LMOOC. As stated by Ruipérez (2020; p.86) the impact on practice of the field of the Learning Analytics area, notwithstanding the popularity take-off, has been quite limited; with this study we are aiming for practical outcomes and improvements in use of video recordings for language learning. The objective of our research is, therefore, to explore if there are variables that allow to predict a certain level of retention and to define the factors that contribute to it, as a result of the Learning Analytics (LA) process. Video analytics should provide us with insights into student learning activity and their engagement. The results of our study should provide pedagogical implications for FL instructors concerning use of videos for language learning.

Online videos and language learning

Noetel et al. (2021) in their systematic review of the effects of video on learning in higher education conclude that under certain conditions videos can provide "better student learning than many other teaching methods, even when compared with face-to-face teaching" (p.227). While it is true that videos have been used in education for almost half a century (Wright, 1976), the educational use of online videos has experienced exponential growth due to the progressive incorporation of online learning by universities. Furthermore, in response to the COVID-19 pandemic in early 2020, there was a further disruptive increase of online learning and consequently also of online educational videos. Online videos have become an important content-delivery tool for Language Learning in flipped, blended, and online courses in recent years (Castrillo & Martín-Monje, 2016). They are integrated as part of face-to-face courses, serve as a base of many blended courses, and are usually the main content delivery tool in online courses (Brame, 2016). The effectiveness of using video to enhance language learning is clear and had already been established prior to the proliferation of MOOCs (Chun & Plass, 2000). As video lectures are clearly the main tool for delivering content in LMOOCs (Castrillo & Mañana-Rodríguez,

2018), video analytics should provide insights into student learning activity and their engagement. Student retention is an outstanding issue in MOOCs, and we believe that the analysis of their engagement with the videos contained in the LMOOC can help us understand why they drop out of these courses. Engagement is usually measured by the watching time of videos, thus our research begins with the assumption that there are meaningful differences in retention by different groups of viewers, and that the retention also varies depending on the intrinsic difficulty of the videos.

YouTube's Learning Analytics tool

In 2019 YouTube launched its app YouTube Studio, a new version of the old Creator Studio. It is a tool specifically designed so that content creators can access the metrics of the videos and carry out meticulous management of their channel. Among other options, it includes a video analytics page. Each video has its own analytics page, split into four tabs: Overview, Reach, Engagement, and Audience:

- The Overview tab shows the key metrics for the channel. The main graph shows watch time, views, and subscribers. There is also a graph for real-time activity, so one can see how people are interacting with the video at that very moment, and tables for likes versus dislikes, and for audience retention which is how well a video keeps people watching, i.e. do they watch it all the way to the end or leave to view something else after a few seconds.
- The Reach tab shows a similar graph to the Overview but focuses on impressions instead of views. An impression is how many times a thumbnail for a video is shown on YouTube, with a view being recorded if someone clicks on a thumbnail to visit the video page. The Reach tab also provides information about traffic sources.
- The Engagement tab has a graph that focuses on watch time in hours but also average view duration. The same tabs for audience retention and likes vs. dislikes are also provided on this tab.
- The Audience tab gives more insight into who is watching the video, including their age and gender, countries, and languages. The main graph shows returning and new viewers, unique viewers, and channel subscribers.

Methodology

The methodological approach used in this research begins with the assumption that there are meaningful differences in the retention of different groups of viewers, and that the retention also varies depending on the intrinsic difficulty of the videos. Retention can be defined as the average length of the video that the viewers watched on average. Nevertheless, it should be noted that because of the exploratory nature of this research, the identification of statistically significant differences or relationships between variables does not have the aim of testing a specific hypothesis (which in a confirmation study would be the appropriate interpretation of the results). Its interpretation should not be understood as equivalent to that of regular statistical tests in terms of reliability or inference capacity. The growing incidence of data dredging practices makes the previous statement necessary.

Course description

The course, entitled *Alemán para hispanohablantes: nociones fundamentales* (German for Spanish-speakers) consists of a total of 35 videos which have the ultimate goal of providing the students with a basic knowledge of the German tongue, designed for the specific needs of Spanish-speakers. The channel has been available since 2012. The videos in the channel have been seen (or, at least, accessed) over 2 million times since their initial publication. It should be noted that the videos can also be viewed through the UNED's own channel with a significant number of visits not contemplated for this study. It is worth noting that this course received the first award for the best MOOC on the Telefonica MiriadaX platform in 2013 by the Spanish Education Ministry.

It is important to highlight that the videos were developed following guidelines that subsequently proved to be the most successful for retention (Guo et al., 2014), highlighting the following two characteristics: shorter videos are much more engaging (each video's duration is between 4 and 15 minutes) and informal talking-head videos are more engaging (our videos were recorded using this format). Prensky (2011) stated that Khan's videos are, above all, explanation. Our videos also basically consist of explanations of German structures in an analytical, practical and functional way, always following a principle of economy of learning: only rules that work and are proven to work are described and explained. We are convinced that the real issue for German students is that they miss important basic concepts of the German language and it is difficult for them to cover them again and progress in their learning. Our goal was not just to allow students to access the contents on demand with the video lessons but, most importantly, to give them the opportunity to replay at their own pace those contents which they may find especially complex, hence making learning much more flexible and achievable.

Data origin, description and transformations

Through YouTube Studio, a range of the most important variables in the platform was selected. These include: retention, total visualizations, total visualization time (hours), average visualization time (hours), total subscribers, total impressions, percentage of clicks of the impressions, visualizations (women), average duration of visualizations (women), percentage seen (women), visualization time (women), visualizations (men), average duration of visualizations (men), percentage seen (men), visualization time (men), and finally, the average duration of the visualizations, average percentage seen and visualization time for the set of subjects with ages between 25 and 34 years. Although there are data available on the last three variables for other age ranges, these include large amounts of missing cases (from 37% to 100%), which has led to the exclusion of this information in the data set. It is worth noting that, although the updated YouTube Studio tool has been available since 2019, the data for the videos is available from their beginning.

Also, in order to characterize the sets of videos according to their retention, two new variables were created: "Over or equal to the median of retention" (a video with a retention value equal or over the median would have a 1 value and 0 otherwise) and "First quartile of retention", another dichotomous variable that presents the value *one* only if the retention value is over the 25th centile of the list of videos, ordered decreasingly by retention.

All the aforementioned variables have been included in the analyses carried out in this study. The initial hypothesis states that retention is not independent of the variables considered in this study.

Data analyses and tests

A battery of standard statistical techniques has been applied to the data set in order to identify the existence or otherwise of relationships between variables alongside the initial assumptions with an exploratory aim. First, the descriptive statistics were calculated for each variable (except for the two created variables, which are dichotomous). Then, an outlier analysis was performed over all continuous variables using the 1.5 inter-quartile range criterion, evidencing the lack of outliers in the variables. This was followed by the calculation of a correlation matrix of all the continuous variables using Spearman's correlation. A Kolmogorov-Smirnov test was then applied in order to test the hypothesis of normal distribution, which led to the conclusion that that a number of variables did not follow such distribution. The next step was the application of Mann-Whitney in order to identify differences between men and women regarding the continuous variables. This was followed by the application of a CHAID decision tree (minimum cases in the parent node = 2, minimum cases in child node = 1), having as dependent variable the belonging of each video to the group of videos over or equal to the median of retention, with no variable showing statistically significant differences that would lead to a segmentation of the videos. The same test was then applied having as dependent variable the belonging of the videos to the first quartile of retention distribution or otherwise.

The retention of the videos, ordered as they appear in the course, was plotted, which showed a declining tendency as the course progressed. This observation led to the application of a K-means cluster (three clusters were requested, all videos were classified) to the full set of variables, keeping the cluster of belonging of each video as a new variable, together with the distance to each cluster's centroid for each video. Finally, in order to identify statistically significant differences between the videos belonging to each cluster in retention, a one-way ANOVA was applied to the full set of videos divided into clusters of belonging.

Results

The first results of the methodology applied are a set of correlations derived from the general correlation matrix between all the variables. Of particular interest are the correlations between the retention percentage and the rest of the variables. The most relevant correlations can be observed between the average duration of visualizations for men (Rho = .755), average percentage seen for men (Rho = .702), percentage seen for women (Rho = .660) and average duration of visualizations for women (Rho = 0.579). These correlations are, nevertheless, as expected since the retention is necessarily related to the average duration of the session and, particularly, to the percentage seen. Nevertheless, it is worth knowing if these apparent differences in visualization time are in line with the results of a Mann-Whitney U test for men and women in visualizations and visualization time.

There are statistically significant differences between men and women in the two variables. Men present a significantly greater number of visualizations (mean rank = 48.64) than women (mean rank = 24.36); $U(36) = 211.000$, $z = -4.934$, $p < .00.$). The same applies to the visualization time (mean rank for men = 47.88; mean rank or women = 25.13); $U(36) = 238.500$, $z = -4{,}634$, $p < .001$. It is important to mention here that these are the two variables in which statistically significant differences have been identified: the same tests were carried out for the rest of the continuous variables without significant results. In order to apply the CHAID segmentation tree, the dependent variable requires its transformation into a dichotomous variable. For this purpose, and given the limited range in the values displayed by "retention" (between 49.3 and 79.5), the videos with the first 25% accumulated retention were encoded as *1* (including 9 videos) and the rest of the videos as *0* (27 videos). The segmentation tree was then applied to the full set of variables, excluding those with an obvious relationship to retention (total visualization and percentage seen), since these would yield a segmentation tree including only those two variables.

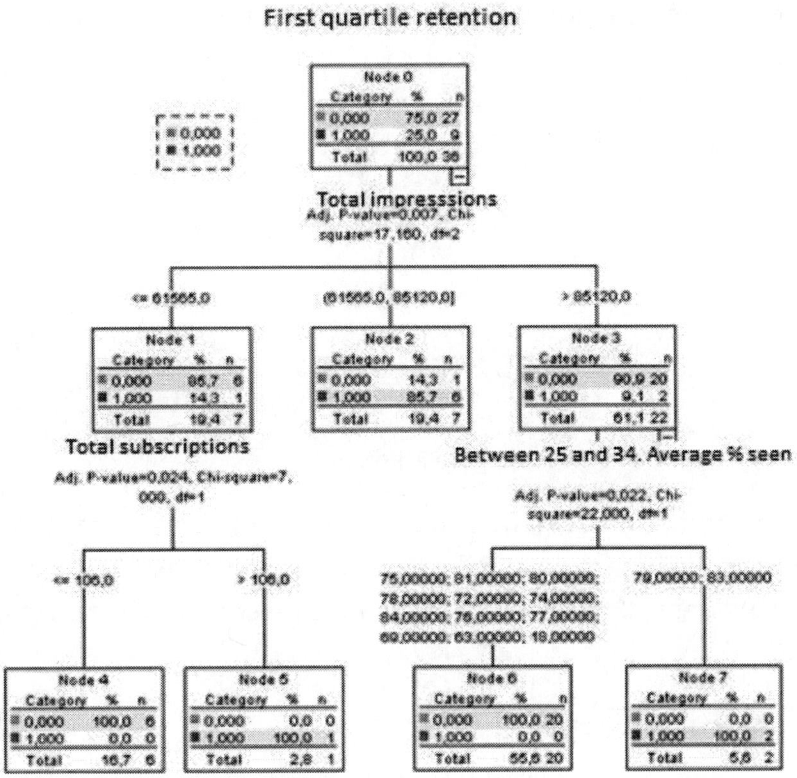

Figure 1. First quartile retention

The first split variable is the number of impressions, that is to say, the number of clicks on advertisements. The videos with an intermediate value of impressions show the greatest fraction of videos in the first quartile of retention (6). For the group with the smaller number of impressions, the most important split variable is the total number of subscribers, although the number of subjects in each node is discrete. For the group with the largest number of impressions, the videos with a percentage seen between 79 and 83%, for the segment of viewers between 25 and 34 years, are in the first quartile of retention. The overall correct classification rate of the model is 97% (96.3% for videos not in the first quartile of retention and 100% for videos in the first quartile of retention). The risk estimations provide positive results, both with the re-substitution method (Estimate = .028, Standard Error = .027) and the Cross-Validation approach (Estimate = .25, Standard Error = .072).

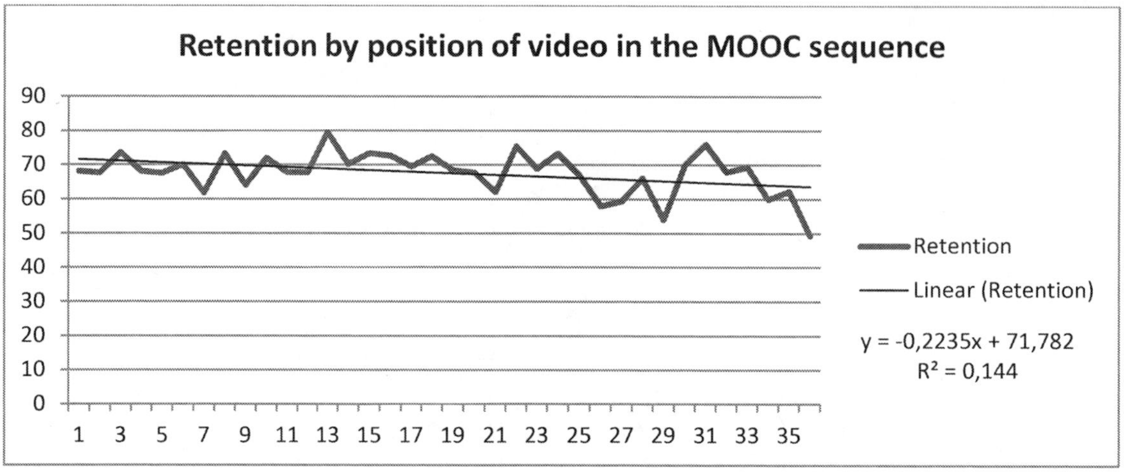

Figure 2. Retention

The retention shows strong variations across the course (in terms of the order of the videos within the course), although the variability seems to be much greater in the second half of the series. Also, the general tendency interpolating the series by a linear equation shows a negative slope.

Discussion and conclusions

In the present study we have explored if there are variables that allow to predict a certain level of retention and what factors contribute to it, as a result of a video Learning Analytics (LA) process. Student retention is an outstanding issue in LMOOCs, and we believe that the analysis of their engagement with the videos contained in the LMOOC can help us understand why participants drop out of these courses. The results of our data analysis show that there are statistically significant differences between men and women in the total number of views and total viewing time, with men viewing significantly more than women. This result is very striking, since an intensive study of the socio-demographic analysis of the participants of this LMOOC showed that in all editions there are more women than men (Castrillo & Mañana-Rodriguez, 2017). This is corroborated by recent subsequent studies of socio-demographic profiles in LMOOCs such as that of Díez-Arcón (in press): it seems to be proven that the predominant gender of LMOOC participants is female. However, analysis of the video analytics of this study indicates that the videos are mostly followed by men. The reason for this imbalance requires further research, but, in the first instance, it could be related to the different types of intelligence and differences in cognitive processes between men and women pointed out by neuroscientists and psychologists (Halpern & LaMay, 2000; Halpern, 1997; Lim, 1994) and reinforce the theories that point to the need to create learning objects in different digital formats to adapt to the profiles of the participants.

Another result is that retention decreases, albeit with a lot of variability between videos, as the course progresses. The courses can be grouped into three sets: one, with 17 videos, which seem to be more interesting for men and for subjects aged 25 to 34, a second set (9 videos) characterized by higher user interaction (subscriptions and impressions) and higher overall interest for women, and finally, a set of 22 videos that show high levels of retention. There are differences in retention between the videos in the first set and the third, but not between the first and the second or the second and the third. The decrease in retention along as the course advances might be due to a multiplicity of factors, some of the most plausible being the increasing difficulty of the contents of each video.

The results can be incorporated into the design of future LMOOCS by splitting the course into sections with similar difficulty, potentially increasing the retention time for each section by addressing audiences with different initial levels and expectations and other variables associated with retention rate.

References

Brame, C. J. (2016). Effective educational videos: Principles and guidelines for maximizing student learning from video content. *CBE—Life Sciences Education, 15*(4), es6.

Castrillo de Larreta-Azelain, M. D., & Martín-Monje, E. (2016). Students' engagement in online language learning through short video lessons. *Porta Linguarum: revista internacional de didáctica de las lenguas extranjeras, 26*, 177-186.

Castrillo, M. D., & Mañana-Rodríguez, J. (2017). Evolución del Perfil Sociodemográfico del Participante en MOOC (2013-2016): Estudio de un Caso en Lenguas Extranjeras. In EMOOCs-ES (pp. 15-24).

Chun, D., & Plass, J. L. (2000). Networked multimedia environments. In M. Warschauer, & R. Kern, R. (Eds.), *Networked-based Language Teaching. Concepts and Practice* (pp. 151-170). Cambridge: Cambridge University Press.

Díez-Arcón, P. (in press). *Perfiles del participante en cursos masivos en línea de lenguas extranjeras (LMOOC): análisis bibliográfico y estudio de caso.*

Guo, P. J., Kim, J., & Rubin, R. (2014). How video production affects student engagement: An empirical study of MOOC videos. *Proceedings of the first ACM conference on Learning@ scale conference*, 41-50. ACM.

Halpern, D. F. (1997). Sex differences in intelligence: Implications for education. *American Psychologist, 52*(10), 1091-1102. https://doi.org/10.1037/0003-066X.52.10.1091

Halpern, D. F., & LaMay, M. L. (2000). The Smarter Sex: A Critical Review of Sex Differences in Intelligence. *Educational Psychology Review, 12*, 229-246 https://doi.org/10.1023/A:1009027516424

Khan, S. (2012). *The one world schoolhouse: Education reimagined.* London: Hodder & Stoughton.

Lim, T. K. (1994). Gender-related differences in intelligence: Application of confirmatory factor analysis. *Intelligence, 19*(2), 179-192.

Martín-Monje, E., Castrillo, M. D., & Mañana-Rodríguez, J. (2018). Understanding online interaction in language MOOCs through learning analytics. *Computer Assisted Language Learning, 31*(3), 251-272

Noetel, M., Griffith, S., Delaney, O., Sanders, T., Parker, P., del Pozo Cruz, B., & Lonsdale, C. (2021). Video Improves Learning in Higher Education: A Systematic Review. *Review of Educational Research, 91*(2), 204-236. https://doi.org/10.3102/0034654321990713

Omnicore (2021). YouTube by the Numbers: Stats, Demographics & Fun Facts. Retrieved from https://www.omnicoreagency.com/youtube-statistics/

Prensky, M. (2011). Khan academy. *Educational Technology, 51*(5), 64.

Ruipérez-Valiente, J. A. (2020). El Proceso de Implementación de Analíticas de Aprendizaje. RIED. *Revista Iberoamericana de Educación a Distancia, 23*(2), pp. 85-101. http://dx.doi.org/10.5944/ried.23.2.26283

Wright, A. (1976). *Visual Materials for the Language Teacher.* Essex: Longman.

Acknowledgements

The research presented has been undertaken with the support of Universidad Nacional de Educación a Distancia (UNED) in the context of the Teaching Innovation Group GLOBE (Innovative Didactic Group for Languages in Open and Blended Environments (GID2016-10) and the ATLAS (Applying Technology to Languages) Research Group.

Lessons from a Pandemic for the Future of Education
European Distance and E-Learning Network (EDEN) Proceedings
2021 Annual Conference | Madrid, 21-24 June, 2021
ISSN 2707-2819
doi: 10.38069/edenconf-2021-ac0006

LEARNING ANALYTICS IN A TIME OF PANDEMICS: MAPPING THE FIELD

Paul Prinsloo, University of South Africa, South Africa, Mohammad Khalil, University of Bergen, Norway, Sharon Slade, Earth Trust, United Kingdom

Abstract

The coronavirus pandemic has impacted global society in many ways, not least education, with schools and universities moving many teaching and learning practices online. This paper examines the response of educational institutions in employing learning analytics, an approach which includes the collection and analysis of student data to understand and optimise teaching and learning. A systematic review of publications is undertaken and key themes identified in an attempt to answer the question: How did learning analytics allow educators to respond to learners' risks and challenges during the pandemic? This study illustrates issues around the rapid adoption of technological solutions outside of the institution; inequality of internet access; considerations of data privacy and longer term consequences; and the need for an agile, but considered policy response.

Introduction

It is estimated that 1.5 billion students have been affected by a rapid move to online learning which has provided the potential to "reshape schools, the idea of education, and what learning looks like in the 21st century" (Anderson, 2020; par.4). Despite its significant impact, it may be argued that the pandemic has also created space to reconsider how to create evidence-informed learning with technology in higher education.

Williamson et al. (2020) suggest that "Education has become an emergency matter, and along with it, educational technologies have been positioned as a frontline emergency service" (p.107). As institutions pivoted to and Emergency Remote Online Teaching (EROT), some technology providers have identified an opportunity "with potentially long-term consequences for how public education is perceived and practised long after the coronavirus has been brought under control" (Williamson et al., 2020; p.108). EdTech companies have had space to claim that education is broken and that technology can fix it (Teräs et al., 2020). We might conclude that "At the present time, public education has been *forcibly decentralised* into students' own homes, *largely disaggregated from the institutions* and practices of education and instead repositioned as a form of home-schooling mediated by technology tools, edu-businesses and other institutions" (Williamson et al., 2020; pp.108-109; emphasis added).

While it is possible to overestimate the permanent impact of the pandemic on education, there is little doubt that it has changed the relationship between education and educational technology providers (Teräs et al., 2020). There are indications that the massive adoption of technology to ameliorate the impact of the disruption has shifted the use of technology "from just content dissemination to augmenting relationships with teachers, personalization, and independence" (Anderson, 2020; par.8). Much of this change emerges from and depends on data, and more specifically, on student data. Fonseca et al. (2020) state that "Educational data usability and accessibility is even more relevant in the context of the global pandemic" (p.1). The bibliometric mapping and analysis by Rodrigues et al. (2020) identifies learning analytics as one of the topics most studied in 2020.

As higher education has moved online, institutions have had significantly greater access to student data (Khalil & Belokrys, 2020). Where Learning Management Systems (LMSs) had functioned primarily as digital repositories for materials and resources for many, they now became indispensable aspects of teaching and learning during Covid. Taking on "an enhanced infrastructural role, moving from a background position to being a dominant medium through which institutions, staff and students interact" (Williamson & Hogan, 2021; p.28). In the process, LMS providers "built interoperable integrations with third-party platform plug-ins to enable data mining at scale from the increasing participation of students in digitally-mediated education" (Williamson & Hogan, 2021; p.28).

At the same time, teaching and learning also moved to digital spaces *outside* of the LMS, such as Zoom, to social media and to Instant Messaging Services such as Facebook's Messenger and WhatsApp. Previously, teaching and learning were largely centralised in the LMS, but became effectively unbundled, not only with regard to the use of other digital spaces, but also the number of providers having access to students' data. The adoption of, for example, digital proctoring "solutions" to ensure examination integrity and uses of "tracing" apps to ensure Covid-safe campuses, "introduce bio-surveillance and epidemiological monitoring on to campuses, thereby raising critical issues related to data security, privacy and ethics, as well as the risk that health data might be repurposed or monetised in the 'after-life' of the pandemic" (Williamson & Hogan, 2021; p.50).

The variety, volume and granularity of student data and its use to provide educators with glimpses of the complexities of learning have always been central to learning analytics. Empirical findings demonstrate how learning analytics has positively impacted on student success and retention (Ifenthaler & Yau, 2020); informed instructional design (Macfadyen et al., 2020); work and cognitive load (Curum & Khedo, 2021); and, through learner-facing dashboards, provided students and instructional teams with insight into student progress and the potential of failure (Verbert et al., 2020). So given its potential to offer insight, how did learning analytics facilitate the response of institutions and educators to support learning during the pandemic?

Research Design and Methodology

A well-defined research question that is "unanswered but answerable" (Alexander, 2020; p.7) forms the foundation for systematic reviews. Such reviews are explicit and systematic about the methodology to identify, select and evaluate relevant research, resulting in an analysis of included studies (Moher et al., 2009; Okoli, 2015). The central research question for this systematic review was: How did learning analytics allow educators to respond to learners' risks and challenges during the pandemic? In conducting this systematic review, we used the guidelines and checklist of PRISMA (Preferred Reporting Items for Systematic Reviews and Meta-analyses) (http://www.prisma-statement.org) to ensure transparency not only in the research process, but also in the analysis (Moher et al., 2009).

Search parameters

After establishing the question guiding the systematic review, we must define the boundaries or parameters that delimit the search. This review used the research database Scopus, the largest interdisciplinary database of scholarly articles (Schotten et al. 2017). Scopus yielded a total number of 162 downloadable articles for the search terms "learning analytics" AND "Covid" (51% of found articles), as well as "learning analytics" AND "pandemic" (31%), and "learning analytics" AND "corona" (11%), and after duplicates were removed, resulted in 80 articles. As comparison, a search on Web of Science (WoS) with these search terms only produced in 8 articles.

Specifying the Corpus of Search Terms

As highlighted above, the three searches shared "learning analytics" as a key term and alternated with "Covid", "pandemic" or "corona" across all fields. The corpus of search terms is directly related to get the widest possible sense of any published research referring to a combination of relevant terms. While it is generally accepted that the Covid pandemic emerged in late 2019, we did not impose a limiting timeframe for the Scopus search.

Delimiting the Search

Delimiting the search may have excluded other scholarly considerations for how educators collected, analysed and used student data without specifically mentioning "learning analytics". As this systematic review aimed to address "learning analytics" as research focus and practice, we considered the delimitation justified.

Overview of the iterative process of inclusions and exclusions

Figure 1 gives an overview of the cycles of search results per research term corpus as discussed above.

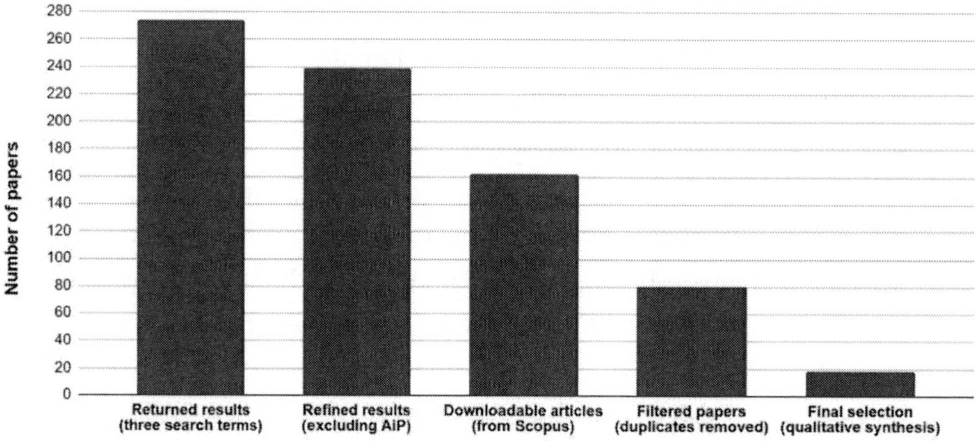

Figure 2. An overview of the outcome of the iterative process of inclusions and exclusions

There were 274 initially identified articles within Scopus - after excluding articles-in-press (AiP), there were 239 articles, of which 162 were downloadable. Removing duplicates brought about by the three search terms resulted in 80 articles. After qualitative synthesis, 18 papers were flagged for further scrutiny and analysis.

Trustworthiness

To reduce the risk of bias among the selected papers for inclusion or exclusion, Fleiss kappa was used to evaluate the inter-rater agreement among those carrying out the systematic review. Fleiss et al. (1981) explain that Fleiss kappa values over .75 indicate excellent value for agreement, .40 ~ .75 suggests fair to good, and below .40 indicates a poor level of agreement. In our case, two authors scanned all filtered papers and identified papers for inclusions and exclusions. The IRR value at this stage was ($\kappa = 0.368$, $p < 0.005$). To resolve differences, all authors undertook further discussion and resolved contradictions. The final IRR kappa value indicated an excellent reliability level of agreement ($\kappa = 0.774$, $p < 0.005$).

Ethical considerations

Though ethical considerations in "conducting systematic reviews in educational research are not typically discussed explicitly" (Suri, 2020; p.41), we acknowledge that every step has ethical implications, whether searching and selecting literature, evaluating, interpreting and distilling evidence, making connections, and choosing an "audience-appropriate transparency" (Suri, 2020; p.41). In addition to following the guidelines offered by PRISMA, it is also important to acknowledge interpretivism as our own epistemological orientation.

Limitations

In line with prescriptions for quality in systematic reviews (Alexander, 2020; Moher et al., 2009) we have acknowledged the criteria for inclusions and exclusions, and also the complexities and the implications of these. Limitations to this systematic review are recognised as using only the Scopus database and not excluding "learning analytics" from the corpus of search terms.

Analysis and findings

The final list of 18 articles was then deductively analysed to identify the relationship between "learning analytics" and the three different variations of terms for the pandemic. The analysis was concerned with what the literature reveals about learning analytics during the pandemic (so far). Table 1 presents an overview of research foci into learning analytics. The focus was not to document the findings of these different studies, but rather to map the use of types of learning analytics or claims regarding opportunities offered by learning analytics to understand and improve student learning and support, and teaching during the pandemic.

Table 1: An overview of the selected articles' reference to learning analytics

Reference	Learning analytics in a time of pandemic
Cornide-Reyes et al. (2020)	The potential of multimodal LA (1)
Rosenberg & Willet (2020)	Preserving students' privacy while enhancing learning using LA (2)
Villegas-Ch et al. (2020a)	Adaptive learning and LA (3)
Dias et al. (2020)	Predictive analytics (4)
Choi and McClenen (2020)	Adaptive learning and LA (3)
Huang et al. (2020)	Predictive analytics (4)
Abou-Khalil et al. (2021)	Student behaviour and engagement (5)
Villegas-Ch et al. (2020b)	Big Data and Artificial Intelligence (6)
Gonzalez et al. (2020)	Student behaviour and engagement (5)
Choi and Cho (2020)	Student behaviour and engagement (5)
Carter Jr et al. (2020)	Artificial Intelligence (Support of SRL) (6)
García-Peñalvo et al. (2020)	Artificial Intelligence (6)
Raffaghelli et al. (2020)	Data literacy (7); ethics and privacy (2); datafication (6)
del Carmen Olmos-Gómez et al. (2020)	Teacher development and improving the quality of learning (8)
Yilmaz et al. (2020)	Teacher development (8)
Jost et al. (2021)	Student behaviour (Support of SRL) (5)
Rasmitadila et al. (2020)	Teacher development (8)
Beerwinkle (2020)	Ethics and privacy (2)

Discussion: Thematic analysis

A total of eight themes were identified and are discussed below, in no particular order:

1. Multimodal – While research and practices involving multimodal learning analytics are on the increase (Blikstein & Worsley, 2016), only one paper covered multimodality and learning analytics in the context of the pandemic. Cornide-Reyes et al. (2020) reviewed the usefulness of a multimodal approach called NAIRA to provide real time feedback to the students to foster collaboration.
2. Student perceptions and student privacy – Under this category, two papers referred to ethics, privacy and student perceptions of their data collection. Rosenberg and Willet (2020) and Beerwinkle (2020) suggested that there should be more focus on the ethical considerations and the data collected during the pandemic in the light of the haste institutions, educators and students responded in the move to EROT.
3. Adaptive learning – Two papers focused on adaptive learning. Choi and McClenen (2020) claimed that adaptive learning is important to provide correct information and personalized data to students in the time of COVID-19, and Villegas-Ch et al. (2020a) refer to Learning Analytics as a driver to analyse large volumes of data to offer adaptive educational models.
4. (and 6.) AI, machine learning and predictive analytics – Five papers were found to specifically address the potential, challenges and implications of AI, machine learning and predictive analytics. An editorial by García-Peñalvo et al. (2020) points to the potential of AI to support learning during the pandemic (also Carter Jr, Rice et al., 2020). Villegas-Ch et al. (2020b) propose improvement to an online model that prioritises an individual student's learning (based on progress and other known information), provides prompts to the student, and notifications to a teacher. The paper proposes student-centred educational models by using AI and big data to improve engagement and reduce drop out with a mention of COVID as a life changer for education. The Dias et al. (2020) paper looks at analysing student interaction with online platforms and generating predictive analytics. The last article by Huang et al. (2020) reviewed the response of the Chinese government to put in place online and distance learning during the pandemic, highlighting the promise of Learning Analytics to identify students at risk in the Chinese context.
5. Student behaviour and engagement – Four papers were identified. Abou-Khalil et al. (2021) explored student perceptions of engagement strategies during emergency online learning and concluded that students prefer engagement with content over engagement with teachers or other students. Social network analysis was used to build a Learning Analytics framework for systems of assessments as a means of understanding learners' paths during the pandemic (Choi & Cho, 2020). Gonzalez

et al. (2020) drew on the potential of Learning Analytics for improving and evaluating the assessment in higher education during pandemics. In a different context, Jost et al., (2021) used Learning Analytics methods to highlight the importance of Self-Regulated Learning during pandemics.

7. Data literacy – The editorial by Raffaghelli et al. (2020) for a special issue on data literacy, highlights the importance of data literacy in the context of the increased collection, analysis and use of learning analytics during the pandemic. The authors point to the emergence of "pandemic pedagogies" and foreground concerns around ways that educators make sense of student data and the broader datafication of education and the emergent practices and concerns. Raffaghelli et al. (2020) express concerns that educators' data literacies have not received the necessary attention.
8. Teacher development – There are three articles that themed "Teacher development". Learning analytics was suggested as a means of comparing teacher performance for development purposes (Yilmaz et al., 2020), to support teacher development through smart learning environments (del Carmen Olmos-Gómez et al., 2020), and to foster teacher use of ICT (Rasmitadila et al., 2020).

Reflections on learning analytics in a time of a pandemic and beyond

Student data is always an invitation to a conversation (Prinsloo, 2019), and considering the huge impact of the pandemic on our students' lives – personal, professional and in their learning – their data could potentially tell many stories and invite many conversations.

Looking at findings from this systematic review, both in terms of quantity and depth of consideration in the nexus between learning analytics and the pandemic, one should be careful not to conclude that learning analytics may have missed an opportunity to appropriately and ethically engage with student data during the pandemic. We may yet see more findings and more detailed analyses of how learning analytics responded during the pandemic going forward. Having said that, based on this review, the following might be considered with regard to learning analytics post-pandemic.

Firstly, as students and educators found ways to communicate and engage in different ways, using multiple devices and platforms, synchronously and asynchronously outside of the institutional LMS, questions can be raised as to the capacity of data limited to the LMS to provide institutions with a detailed view of how students are progressing and learning. Secondly, the pandemic illustrated how unequal access to the internet is, and this inequality of access is gendered, raced and geo-political. While reference to the digital divide prior to the pandemic often called forth images of internet connectivity in the Global South, the pandemic starkly illuminated disparities in access and use of the internet also in the Global North. With learning analytics dependent on internet access, this raises concerns of the generalisability and representativeness of our data sets, as well and introduces a question as to the contribution of learning analytics in "data-poor" contexts, where not all students have access to and/or use the LMS regularly or where the majority of students' engagement happens outside of the LMS.

A third point worthy of consideration is whether the haste in responding to the emergency resulted in institutions, educators and students choosing technologies and applications without due consideration of privacy and ethical issues and concerns. While this lapse of institutional oversight could be rationalised on utilitarian grounds given the urgency to reach out to students, it may be hard to disentangle these practices and arrangements from teaching and learning practices once the pandemic has eased.

The fourth and final point for reflection is how nimble and responsive both the policy environment (both on national, regional and institutional) and digital infrastructure were in terms of responding to the increasing digitalisation and datafication of education.

Conclusion

The pandemic, and institutional responses to it, provide huge scope for reflection. In many ways the pandemic revealed and destabilised many assumptions and beliefs that have become naturalised and gone unquestioned, such as student and staff access to the internet, the affordability and sustainability of access, and so forth. The pandemic may also have led us to realise that we may not yet fully understand student learning and therefore that our support initiatives may be inappropriate or ineffective.

Learning analytics has promised, since its emergence in 2011, to help us understand student learning better, in order to teach and support students more effectively, and to help students to make more informed decisions. If there ever was a time when we needed to better understand what students were experiencing and how they were coping, the pandemic and the move to EROT have provided us with such an opportunity.

As such we were curious to look at research published during the pandemic (to date) and to get a sense of how learning analytics had responded. This systematic review provides us with an initial glimpse of how scholars and researchers have researched and reflected on the potential of learning analytics during the pandemic.

References

Abou-Khalil, V., Helou, S., Khalifé, E., Chen, M. A., Majumdar, R., & Ogata, H. (2021). Emergency Online Learning in Low-Resource Settings: Effective Student Engagement Strategies. *Education Sciences, 11*(1), 24.

Alexander, P. A. (2020). Methodological Guidance Paper: The Art and Science of Quality Systematic Reviews. *Review of Educational Research, 90*(1), 6-23.

Anderson, J. (2020, March 30). The coronavirus pandemic is reshaping education. Quartz [Blog post]. Retrieved from https://qz.com/1826369/how-coronavirus-is-changing-education/

Beerwinkle, L. (2020). The use of learning analytics and the potential risk of harm for K-12 students participating in digital learning environments. *Education Tech. Research Dev., 69*, 327-330.

Blikstein, P., & Worsley, M. (2016). Multimodal learning analytics and education data mining: Using computational technologies to measure complex learning tasks. *Journal of Learning Analytics, 3*(2), 220-238.

del Carmen Olmos-Gómez, M., Luque-Suárez, M., Mohamed-Mohamed, S., & Manuel Cuevas-Rincón, J. (2020). Validation of the Smart City as a Sustainable Development Knowledge Tool: The Challenge of Using Technologies in Education during COVID-19. *Sustainability, 12*(20).

Carter Jr, R. A., Rice, M., Yang, S., & Jackson, H. A. (2020). Self-regulated learning in online learning environments: strategies for remote learning. *Information and Learning Sciences, 121*(5/6), 321-329.

Choi, Y., & Cho, Y. (2020). Learning Analytics Using Social Network Analysis and Bayesian Network Analysis in Sustainable Computer-Based Formative Assessment System. *Sustainability, 12*(19).

Choi, Y., & McClenen, C. (2020). Development of Adaptive Formative Assessment System Using Computerized Adaptive Testing and Dynamic Bayesian Networks. *Applied Sciences, 10*(22), 8196.

Cornide-Reyes, H., Riquelme, F., Monsalves, D., Noel, R., Cechinel, C., Villarroel, R., Ponce, F., & Munoz, R. (2020). A Multimodal Real-Time Feedback Platform Based on Spoken Interactions for Remote Active Learning Support. *Sensors, 20*, 6337.

Curum, B., & Khedo, K.K. (2021). Cognitive load management in mobile learning systems: principles and theories. *Journal of Computers in Education, 8*(1), 109-136.

Dias, S. B., Hadjileontiadou, S. J., Diniz, J., & Hadjileontiadis, L. J. (2020). DeepLMS: a deep learning predictive model for supporting online learning in the Covid-19 era. *Sci Rep, 10*, 19888.

Fonseca, D., García-Peñalvo, F. J., & Camba, J. D. (2020). *New methods and technologies for enhancing usability and accessibility of educational data.* Universal Access in the Information Society.

García-Peñalvo, F. G., Casado-Lumbreras, C., Colomo-Palacios, R., & Yadav, A. (2020). Smart Learning. *Applied Sciences, 10*(9), 6964.

Gonzalez, T., de la Rubia, M. A., Hincz, K. P., Comas-Lopez, M., Subirats, L., Fort, S., & Sacha, G. M. (2020). Influence of COVID-19 confinement on students' performance in higher education. *PLoS ONE, 15*(10), e0239490.

Huang, R., Tlili, A., Chang, T. W., Zhang, X., Nascimbeni, F., & Burgos, D. (2020). Disrupted classes, undisrupted learning during COVID-19 outbreak in China. *Smart Learning Environment, 7*(19).

Ifenthaler, D., & Yau, J. Y. K. (2020). Utilising learning analytics to support study success in higher education: a systematic review. *Educational Technology Research and Development, 68*(4), 1961-1990.

Jost, N. S., Jossen, S. L., Rothen, N., & Martarelli, C. S. (2021). The advantage of distributed practice in a blended learning setting. *Education and Information Technologies, 26*(2).

Khalil, M., & Belokrys, G. (2020). OXALIC: an Open edX Advanced Learning Analytics Tool. *Proceedings of the 2020 IEEE Learning with MOOCS (LWMOOCS) Conference*, 185-190. IEEE.

Macfadyen, L. P., Lockyer, L., & Rienties, B. (2020). Learning design and learning analytics: Snapshot 2020. *Journal of Learning Analytics, 7*(3), 6-12.

Moher, D., Liberati, A., Tetzlaff, J., & Altman, D. G. (2009). Preferred reporting items for systematic reviews and meta-analyses: The PRISMA Statement. *Annals of Internal Medicine, 51*, 264-269.

Okoli, C. (2015). A guide to conducting a standalone systematic literature review. *Communications of the Association for Information Systems, 37*(43), 879-910.

Prinsloo, P. (2019, Sept). Tracking (un)belonging: At the intersections of human-algorithmic student support. *Proceedings of the 9th PCF Conference, Edinburgh.* Retrieved from http://hdl.handle.net/11599/3373

Raffaghelli, J. E., Manca, S., Stewart, B., Prinsloo, P., & Sangrà, A. (2020). Supporting the development of critical data literacies in higher education: building blocks for fair data cultures in society. *Int. J. Educ. Technol. High. Educ., 17*(58).

Rasmitadila, Aliyah, R. R., Rachmadtullah, R., Samsudin, A., Syaodih, E., Nurtanto, M., & Tambunan, A. R. S. (2020). The Perceptions of Primary School Teachers of Online Learning during the COVID-19 Pandemic Period: A Case Study in Indonesia. *Journal of Ethnic and Cultural Studies, 7*(2), 90-109.

Rodrigues, M., Franco, M., & Silva, R. (2020). COVID-19 and Disruption in Management and Education Academics: Bibliometric Mapping and Analysis. *Sustainability, 12*(18), 7362.

Rosenberg, J. M., & Staudt Willet, K. B. (2020). Balancing' privacy and open science in the context of COVID-19: a response to Ifenthaler & Schumacher (2016). *Education Tech Research Dev., 69*, 347-351.

Schotten, M., el Aisati, M., Meester, W., Steiginga, S. & Ross, C. (2017). A Brief History of Scopus: The World's Largest Abstract and Citation Database of Scientific Literature. In F.J. Cantu-Ortiz (Ed.), *Research Analytics* (pp. 31-58). New York: Taylor and Francis.

Teräs, M., Suoranta, J., Teräs, H., & Curcher, M. (2020). Post-Covid-19 education and education technology 'solutionism': A seller's market. *Postdigital Science and Education, 2*(3), 863-878.

Verbert, K., Ochoa, X., De Croon, R., Dourado, R. A., & De Laet, T. (2020, March). Learning analytics dashboards: the past, the present and the future. *Proceedings of the Tenth International Conference on Learning Analytics & Knowledge, Frankfurt*, 35-40. https://doi.org/10.1145/3375462.3375504

Villegas-Ch, W., Roman-Cañizares, M., Jaramillo-Alcázar, A., & Palacios-Pacheco, X. (2020a). Data Analysis as a Tool for the Application of Adaptive Learning in a University Environment. *Applied Sciences, 10*(20), 7016.

Villegas-Ch, W., Román-Cañizares, M., & Palacios-Pacheco, X. (2020b). Improvement of an Online Education Model with the Integration of Machine Learning and Data Analysis in an LMS. *Applied Sciences, 10*(15), 5371.

Williamson, B., Eynon, R., & Potter, J. (2020). Pandemic politics, pedagogies and practices: digital technologies and distance education during the coronavirus emergency. *Learning, Media and Technology, 45*(2), 107-114.

Williamson, B., & Hogan, A. (2021). *Pandemic Privatisation in Higher Education: Edtech & University Reform.* Education International Research. Retrieved from https://issuu.com/educationinternational/docs/2021_eiresearch_gr_covid19_commercialisation_digit?fr=sNTdjNzI5MTkzMTM

Yilmaz, Y., Lal, S., Tong, X., Howard, M., Bal, S., Bayer, I., Monteiro, S., & Chan, T. (2020). Technology-Enhanced Faculty Development: Future Trends and Possibilities for Health Sciences Education. *Med.Sci.Educ., 30*, 1787-1796.

Lessons from a Pandemic for the Future of Education
European Distance and E-Learning Network (EDEN) Proceedings
2021 Annual Conference | Madrid, 21-24 June, 2021
ISSN 2707-2819
doi: 10.38069/edenconf-2021-ac0007

METHOD OR MEDIA: 10 DO'S AND SOME DON'TS FOR USING MEDIA IN ONLINE POST-SECONDARY EDUCATION

Albert Schram, University of Maryland Global Campus (UMGC) – Europe, Italy

Abstract

For effective online teaching and learning there is no short-cut for good instructional design, as well as following well-established pedagogical practices. For universities in the post-pandemic era, the main challenges for delivering quality online programs are, first, to provide good access through high quality digital infrastructure, and, secondly, to assure that all lecturers are trained in modern pedagogical approaches, basic instructional design principles for online teaching, and media usage.

In my own experience, following the eight QM "Quality Matters" standards, will go a long way in improving online instruction and student engagement. These standards provide a simple, proven and robust framework, even for the inexperienced to design and deliver an effective and engaging course. Universities that have consistently applied QM standards, for example, dominate the rankings for best online programs in the USA (QM 2020). Uniquely, QM offers a low-cost training program on online teaching that can be rolled out at scale for lecturers at member universities and schools, that includes all elements for developing and delivering effective online courses, including the use of media.

The use of media in any course is always optional. Recent research, however, shows that the use of media, in particular asynchronous video in combination with other learning materials, can lead to substantial improvements in learning. This research found that the combination of solid instructional design and the appropriate use of asynchronous media in online or hybrid courses can be more effective than traditional face-to-face teaching, due to more focused content, and students being able to rewind thus avoiding feeling overwhelmed (Noetel et al., 2021). Finally, I offer 10 helpful pointers for developing and delivering online courses using media, for those of us who are not experienced online instructors, or instructional designers.

Introduction

In this paper, I will discuss some of the implications of using media in teaching adults, following a recently published, and rather definitive meta-study on the topic (Noetel et al., 2021). First, I will give a general introduction to what constitute good pedagogical practices and solid instructional design during an ongoing technological revolution in both face-to-face as well as online teaching and learning. Secondly, I will summarize research showing that the use of asynchronous videos in courses can substantially improve learning. Thirdly, I will list the practical implications for development of online courses, and the practices and tools for delivering them effectively. Some media turn out to be more apt for specific learning objectives than others, and this must be taken into account when designing a course, or when selecting specific type of media.

Background

The history of technology of the past centuries suggests that broad impact of a technological innovation often occurs four decades or more after initial implementation, when the technological revolution really takes place (David, 1990). Since the mobile internet is now barely twenty years old, what we are seeing today therefore may just be the start of a technological revolution. The use of media in teaching adults has become more common, since now every cell phone has good a camera and microphone with the capability to produce high-quality videos or audio.

Recently, we have seen false optimism about how technology can improve learning. The emergence of Massive Open Online Course (MOOCs) with recorded lectures in the early 2010s, for example, turned out not to be such a technological revolution after all, with only a small percentage of participants actually finishing the courses (Parr, 20139.

In post-secondary education, the process of digitalization and use of artificial intelligence, has meant services once delivered by a single institution can now be offered separately, or in different combinations. This unbundling of educational services driven by digitalization was recently accelerated by the need to develop online teaching due to the COVID19 pandemic. As Lawrence Summers, President Emeritus of Harvard University wrote: "Certainly there are challenges ahead, but surely also opportunities for those bold enough to seize them. The potential unbundling is a certainly a threat, but those who re-bundle well will find they have reinvented higher education for the 21st century." (Barber et al., 2013; p.v).

The discussion on what works and what does not in education can be confusing and spans the whole range from overly simplistic and optimistic techno-visions about dynamic classrooms (Craig, 2017), to utter pessimism about the possibility to measure educational outcomes in adults. The truth is somewhere in the middle. It seems unlikely that there are simple technological fixes for good teaching, such as superior recording equipment or systems that mimic the physical classroom. Conversely, it is too pessimistic to say that no agreement will ever be achieved about what the desired learning outcomes for post-secondary programs will be, as the ill-fated AHELO surveys by the OECD showed (OECD, 2013).

Method: what works and what doesn't in face-to-face and online teaching and learning?

For face-to-face teaching, educational research gives a good indication of what works, and what does not. Some of us, intersperse our lectures with probing questions which we sometimes call "the Socratic method". Nobel Prize winner Carl Wieman at Stanford was mystified by their PhD students still being unable to do physics. He developed what he called experimental teaching, which "puts the problem first". Through rigorous experimental research he was able to show that with improved teaching learning gains increased an order of magnitude (Adams & Wieman, 2011; Deslauriers, Schelew, & Wieman, 2011; Wieman, 2014).

When sticking to the traditional lecture format, however, it is hard to consistently "put the problem first" in all your classes. Since the 1960s problem-based learning (PBL) has addressed this challenge. It has taught the lecturers to withdraw and leave more control to the students. PBL is widely used in medical education, but also in engineering, though only a dozen or so universities in the world use it consistently across all disciplines. Maastricht University, for example, has developed a structured 7-step PBL approach, which is quite robust and at the same time flexible. There is extensive literature on the benefits of PBL, including higher retention rates (Moust, 2007). PBL is more effective because it starts with a problem, and it challenges the learners to take responsibility for their own learning and progress by formulating learning objectives and producing content themselves. Though it is essential a small group teaching method with lots of interaction among students, it can be adapted to larger groups (Roberts et al., 2005).

In addition to face-to-face pedagogy, what are the particular challenges in online teaching and learning? About 15 years ago several universities in the USA decided to set up QM "Quality Matters", a non-profit that has now over 1,700 members in 27 countries. QM is based on the premise that there is no short-cut for good instructional design and alignment. It starts with research and then incorporates best-practices identified by a community of practitioners. According to QM, there are essentially six variable that determine the success of online teaching and learning: starting with course design, course delivery and course content, which the lecturer can control. Institutional infrastructure, the learning management system, faculty members and students' readiness also play an important role.

Moreover, QM has formulated an eight standards presented in a rubric form on which online teaching and learning should be based. These standards are support by leading educational research, but also on extensive experience of lecturers at member university who form a community of practices and discuss regularly what works and what does not in online education.

The eight general standards of the QM rubric cover the following themes:

1. Course Overview and Introduction;
2. Learning Objectives (Competencies);
3. Assessment and Measurement;
4. Instructional Materials;
5. Learning Activities and Learner Interaction;
6. Course Technology;
7. Learner Support;
8. Accessibility and Usability.

The key challenge for course development is to achieve alignment between Learning Objectives (Competencies) (2.1, 2.2), Assessment and Measurement (3.1), Instructional Materials (4.1), Learning Activities and Learner Interaction (5.1), and Course Technology (6.1). When these elements work together, students achieve desired learning outcomes. As to standard 3 regarding assessment and academic integrity, we assume here that issues of academic corruption and plagiarism are successfully being addressed by the institutions general policies and quality standards. QM has separate and somewhat different standards for higher education, K-12, and Continuing Professional Education, but the 8 general standards remain the same (QM 2021). Similarly, general pedagogical principles discussed above still hold, and can easily be combined with the 8 standards.

Media: what role for asynchronous video?

While it may seem like it is important to know whether instructional design or media use makes the largest difference in learning gain, in reality that both are important. Good course design can work without videos, while videos cannot work without good course design. According to cognitive theories of multimedia learning, both face-to-face classes and video conferences, as well as asynchronous videos can all maximize the use of our cognitive infrastructure, since operate both visually as well as through sound (Mayer, 2008). A picture says more than a thousand words, and a video with text can be even more eloquent.

The meta-analytic study by Noetel et al. (2021) analysed 105 past randomized trial studies including 7,776 students, and examined at the effects of videos on learning as compared to the use of other teaching mediums, such as in-person lectures and assigned readings. Overall, when students got videos instead of usual form of teaching their average grades increased from B to B+, but when videos were given in addition to their existing class, the effect was stronger, moving students from a B to an A. The study found that videos were more effective for teaching skills than for transferring knowledge. The two main explanations for these results are that first, videos give students the ability to better control their own pace of learning, thus reducing the likelihood of them feeling overwhelmed, and secondly that pre-recorded videos allowed lecturers to fine-tune how they present information, and thus avoid some of the noise and confusing information that can creep into in person lectures.

From this study, it seems clear therefore, that as a complement to traditional text-based teaching materials, asynchronous videos can be a very power tool to enhance student engagement and learning.

Teaching Strategy and Your Toolbox

The key question concerning teaching strategy is: what do you want the students to do before class, and what do you want to do during and after the class? It is hear that media can play an important role. Before class, we need to have assurance that students understand basic concepts and have mastered essential information. Given the diverse educational backgrounds of especially non-traditional students, those with families and older than 24 years, this has become essential to conducting any meaningful class discussion.

The instructor is left to figure out how better curriculum design and course delivery can enhance active learning and student-centred teaching. The bewildering diversity of types of media can make this task challenging. Video, and audio can be used for course introduction, course promotion, personal introductions, module introduction, instead of traditional lectures or for lecture capture, student feedback, course announcements, interview, event or debate recording, role play, case study or scenario, students' presentations in project, problem or case-based learning, etc. Media is more than just video, and you can use audio recording, voice over slide presentation or screen-casting to demonstrate a website or software.

So what can I recommend based on my recent experience teaching online? I found it most efficient to prepare the whole structure of the course with its learning objectives offline in a spreadsheet, with matching self-assessment, quiz and examination questions. This assures maximum coherence and minimizes waiting times of working online directly in the Learning Management System. Next classify selected video into three categories: short introductory 2-3 minutes, and somewhat longer content rich, teaching videos 5-10 minutes for students to do before each class, and finally mini-lectures or traditional lectures cut up in pieces of 10-15 minutes to stimulate class debate and reflection.

For activating existing knowledge or going over the basics, identify short video's with transcripts and provide it to the students, either auto-generated on YouTube. Provide transcripts for the mini-lecture videos, and complementary readings, providing self-assessment questions for each step. You can produce an introductory video, but the students really don't need to see your face online each session. Classify video's to stimulate interest and engagement vs. video's to stimulate thinking and discussion. Include an online discussion board when appropriate, and provide a message reinforcing what has been learned at the end. Finally, for a hyflex design, those students who cannot attend your (online) class can be asked to answers self-assessment questions and contribute online to the class debate, using Google Docs, or a discussion tool like Kialo or Perusall. To stimulate reflection after class, you can post a recording of presential class debates, or record a short video summary yourself.

10 Do's

In order to break online course development down even further, keeping in mind what I said above about method and media, here are 10 Do's and a 5 don't, reflecting what I learned from over a decade of online teaching. I hope it will be useful for you, although you will have to adapt according to your own objectives and teaching style.

1. IT: set up your PC properly, including automatic backups. If you don't have a new computer with the latest proprietary operating system, you should consider installing open-source Linux distribution.
2. Course structure. Curriculum development need not be done online, rather you can prepare the whole structure of the course with its learning objectives in your spreadsheet, with matching self-assessment, quiz and exam questions.
3. Video selection. Select short videos three kinds: short introductory 2-3 minutes, and somewhat longer content rich, teaching videos 5-10 minutes for students to do before each class. In class, you can use recorded lectures, your own or other people's, but you need to chunk it up in section of no more than 10 or 15 minutes. Provide transcripts of the videos, and optionally complementary readings, providing self-assessment questions for each step. You can produce an introductory video, but the students really don't need to constantly see your face online each session.

4. Classify video's to stimulate interest and engagement vs. video's to stimulate thinking and discussion. Include activities, either self-assessments for all activities and polls to stimulate discussion.
5. Transcripts and YouTube lists. For activating existing knowledge or going over the basics, identify short video's with transcripts and provide it to the students, either auto-generated on YouTube. Remember some students are good at listening, others need to read the text.
6. Learning Management System. Use any Learning Management System, but remember no LMS offers all functionality you may want. Use the import function on your LMS to assure consistency in the self-assessment, quiz and exam questions.
7. Formative assessment. Include mandatory self-assessment, and feed these into slightly more complicated quiz questions. These can all be automatically graded multiple choice, true/false of fill-in-the-blanks questions. Rather than an examination, it is advisable to include some assignments with open questions or problems to solve.
8. Required vs recommended materials. Provide additional information in text or video, so as to show multiple perspectives or extensions. Give links to YouTube list, but do not rely on it as the only source.
9. Online discussion boards. Include an online discussion, and provide a message reinforcing what has been learned at the end. Summarize the online discussion by conducting and summarizing online polls.
10. Chunking. Finally, in the classroom provide extra material by presenting a video lecture in bite sized bits of no more than 10 minutes with self-assessments.

Elsewhere, I have described which software tools I personally use to make it easy to include media into your courses, including Google slides, Polleverywhere, Edpuzzle, Nearpod, and others.

Some Don'ts

Here are some things that I suggest should be avoided:

1. Do not try to replicate a face to face lecture online. Effective teaching is like parenthood, it is all about letting go. Do not try to control all content, all dynamic, and make yourself the centre of to the students' learning experience.
2. Do not fixate on giving your own lectures, and acting as if only synchronous activities can produce learning. On Open Course repositories or YouTube you will find instructional videos, or recordings of public lectures and debates of people much more knowledgeable than yourself on specific topics.

3. Do not believe technology will fix your teaching issues, you will need to become familiar with basic pedagogy, instructional design concepts.
4. Do not have your groups of students sit for hours and hours behind their screens looking at you lecture, without engaging with each other, with learning materials or doing any other meaningful learning activity.
5. Do not talk about online learning and teaching as inherently inferior to face to face teaching, and something to be avoided as soon as the pandemic is under control.

Final Remarks

Using asynchronous videos in your courses can be a powerful tool (Noetel et al., 2021), but you have to be clear for what purpose you want to use media by consistently applying widely accepted instructional design standards such as QM. In addition, it helps to have a theory-based, student-centred pedagogical approach such as Problem Based Learning.

With the right tools, course preparation does not have to take much longer than for any other regular class. Finding alignment between materials, activities and assessments through proper preparation, certainly beats the centuries' old tradition of producing the teaching materials on the white board in class for one time use only.

The avalanche of digital and information technology, online delivery of courses, and unbundling of services is coming towards us. How fast it travels and whether it will affect all players in equal measure is still unclear. The COVID pandemic has certainly accelerated these processes, and lecturers and students alike have found positive things about online teaching, which will be here to stay.

References

Adams, W. K., & Wieman, C. E. (2011). Development and Validation of Instruments to Measure Learning of Expert-Like Thinking. *International Journal of Science Education, 33*(9), 1289-1312. https://doi.org/10/cfzxhr

Craig, R. (2017, January 20). The Top 10 Higher Education Issues We All Agree On. Forbes [Blog post]. Retrieved from https://www.forbes.com/sites/ryancraig/2017/01/20/the-top-10-higher-education-issues-we-all-agree-on/#1c7f3a61fa87

David, P. A. (1990). The Dynamo and the Computer: An Historical Perspective on the Modern Productivity Paradox. *The American Economic Review, 80*(2), 355-361. Retrieved from http://www.jstor.org/stable/2006600

Deslauriers, L., Schelew, E., & Wieman, C. (2011). Improved Learning in a Large-Enrollment Physics Class. *Science, 332*(6031), 862-864. https://doi.org/10/c3jj3m

Moust, J. (2007). *Introduction to problem-based learning: a guide for students* (2nd rev. ed.). Wolters-Noordhoff.

Noetel, M., Griffith, S., Delaney, O., Sanders, T., Parker, P., del Pozo Cruz, B., & Lonsdale, C. (2021). Video Improves Learning in Higher Education: A Systematic Review. *Review of Educational Research, 91*(2), 204-236. https://doi.org/10/gjmdv6

Organisation for Economic Co-operation and Development – OECD (2013). Measuring Learning Outcomes in Higher Education: Lessons Learnt from the AHELO Feasibility Study and Next Steps. Retrieved from https://www.oecd.org/site/ahelo/

Parr, C. (2013, May 10). Not Staying the Course. New study of low MOOC completion rates. Inside Higher Ed [Blog post]. Retrieved from https://www.insidehighered.com/news/2013/05/10/new-study-low-mooc-completion-rates

Roberts, C., Lawson, M., Newble, D., Self, A., & Chan, P. (2005). The introduction of large class problem-based learning into an undergraduate medical curriculum: an evaluation. *Medical Teacher, 27*(6), 527-533. https://doi.org/10.1080/01421590500136352

Wieman, C. E. (2014). Large-scale comparison of science teaching methods sends clear message. *Proceedings of the National Academy of Sciences, 111*(23), 8319-8320. https://doi.org/10/gd6fw3

Lessons from a Pandemic for the Future of Education
European Distance and E-Learning Network (EDEN) Proceedings
2021 Annual Conference | Madrid, 21-24 June, 2021
ISSN 2707-2819
doi: 10.38069/edenconf-2021-ac0008

CREATING MATURE BLENDED COURSES: THE EUROPEAN MATURITY MODEL GUIDELINES

Katie Goeman, Faculty of Economics and Business, KU Leuven, Belgium, Wiebe Dijkstra, Teaching & Learning Services, TU Delft, The Netherlands

Abstract

The pandemic has urged European universities and other institutions of higher education to switch in a very limited time from on-campus to remote teaching or to teaching modes that combine online and face-to-face activities. Instructors, as well as other course designers and support service staff are in search of evidence-based frameworks that show how to incorporate proven blended scenarios, adapted to their context. Between 2017 and 2020 seven European project partners collaborated in order to establish a conceptual and operational framework for blended education and teaching, labelled as the *European Maturity Model for Blended Education*. Its aim is to map blended learning practices, conditions, strategies and policies in a systematic manner and to empower higher education institutions to achieve up-scaled blended courses. In this contribution, we focus on what has been developed with regard to the course level. First, we describe the dimensions and indicators of the model, next we indicate blended courses might be altered in terms of their level of maturity using a series of guidelines and open-source tools and materials. We conclude by proposing how to employ the guidelines in a workshop setting.

Introduction

The Covid-19 crisis, as well as other societal demands change the formats and contexts for teaching and learning in higher education institutions (HEIs). In Europe, there is a prominent call for adopting "purposeful digital and innovative education practices" (European Commission, 2018) and to develop a "high-performing digital education ecosystem" (European Commission, 2020). In this regard, *blended* or *hybrid* educational approaches have been repeatedly pinpointed as drivers of personalized, flexible, inclusive, self-directed and effective student learning (e.g., Peterson, 2016; Thai, de Wever, & Valcke, 2017). While there is still ambiguity about the scope and core conceptions (Smith & Hill, 2019), in this study, *blended learning* is defined as "learning as a result of a deliberate, integrated combination of online and face-to-face learning activities". *Blended teaching* is described as "designing and facilitating blended learning activities". While *deliberate* refers to the explicit role of a design which specifies the proportion and sequencing of in a blended course, *integrated combination* designates the logic for using a particular blend of virtual and physical learning spaces.

In response to the Corona pandemic, across HEIs, course designers as well as support service staff are in search of evidence-based frameworks that show how to incorporate proven blended scenarios, adapted to their context. More than ever, it has been experienced how important it is to combat the "transactional distance" (Moore, 2019) and social isolation of students that may arise from online distance education (Rasheed, Kamsin, & Abdullah, 2020), next to supporting more vulnerable students such as freshmen or those enrolled in specific learning programs. Such student groups are found to being "less ready" in terms of self-regulation and technology savviness (Appana, 2008), or they follow courses in which the tactile or applied aspect of learning is prominent (e.g., physiotherapists, veterinarians, engineers, hospitality collaborators). Blended learning environments may tackle these issues and address students' learning needs either easier or better. In these, an instructor wishes to achieve an equilibrium of internet- and human-mediated learning activities that extend the opportunities for learner interaction, strengthen the scaffolds of learner autonomy, improve a course's structure and the learner interface (Bostock, 2018).

Between 2017 and 2020 seven European project partners collaborated in order to establish a conceptual and operational framework for blended education and teaching (Goeman & Ubachs, 2018; Goeman, Poelmans, van Rompaey, Dijkstra, & van Valkenburg, 2019). In May 2020, the European Maturity Model for Blended Education (EMBED) was published (see https://embed.eadtu.eu). Its aim is to map blended learning practices, conditions, strategies and policies in a systematic manner and, ultimately, to identify tracks for optimization or change. It includes 15 dimensions and three levels of maturity which can be used to assess systematically blended courses, programs and institution-wide provisions.

The last project phase was dedicated to the development of implementation guidelines, that is background information, examples, models, tips and tricks, as well as recent predominantly open access references to resources, in line with the foundations of the maturity model (in the following paragraphs abbreviated as EMM). They are specified for each dimension of the model, and target different (groups of) stakeholders, among others, instructional designers and educational managers in institutions for higher education (HE). The guidelines may be applied for assessment and change purposes, yet, also inspire and guide anyone who wants to implement blended practices in his/her institution in a sustainable manner. A number of the guidelines were integrated in the Massive Open Online Course (MOOC) *Making Blended Education Work* which is based on the EMM and the project output (see https://www.futurelearn.com/courses/making-blended-education-work).

The EMM distinguishes maturity at three levels, namely the course, program and institution level. For each level multiple dimensions and indicators are established. These are based on a literature synthesis, a review of proven practices and a three-round Delphi study. In this contribution, we focus on the maturity of blended courses.

Foundations of the European Maturity Model at the course level

The course level refers to the core of the educational system, where both learning processes and instructional processes are situated. It refers to the primary educational process, in other words the development, execution and evaluation of courses. The stakeholders of this level are mainly educators and students, but also instructional designers, learning developers, content developers and sometimes management.

In general terms, the concept of *maturity* relates to the degree of formality and evidence-based character of the design, decision making and continuous quality improvement (CQI) of blended practices, next to institutional conditions and strategies. The EMM explicitly adheres to a design-focused approach of courses and programs. Consequently, growth in maturity is considered as a result of the ability of (teams of) instructors, instructional designers and others involved, to make informed decisions. This includes using design principles and/or instructional theories, from blended course design right up to whole program design, that is the organization, planning and documentation of a structured series of courses or units. As maturity does not equal quality, high- or low-quality approaches can be in place within each of the maturity levels.

Maturity at the course level is assessed at the background of four dimensions: (a) the course design process, (b) the course flexibility, (c) the course interaction, and (d) the course experience. Figure 1 depicts these dimensions along with their sub-dimensions, while Table 1 (Annex) presents the European Maturity Model at the course level in a comprehensive manner.

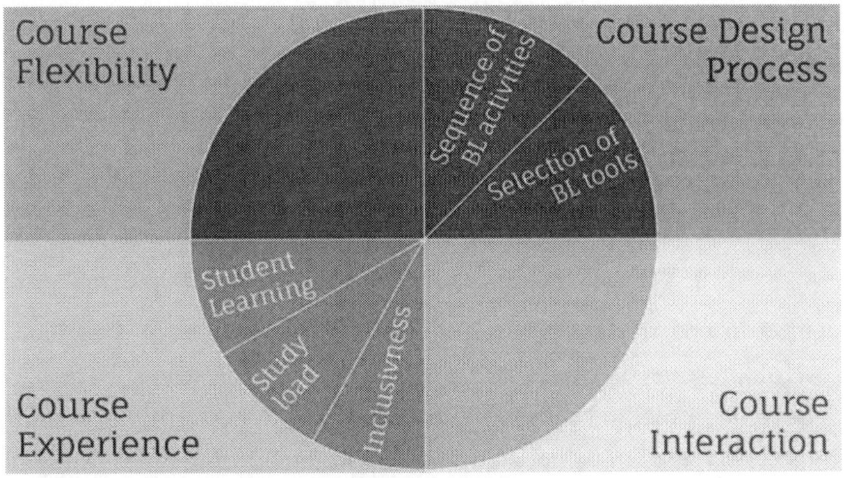

Figure 3. Maturity of blended courses: dimensions and sub-dimensions

Using the EMM guidelines for changing blended courses in terms of their maturity level

Course design process: selection of blended learning activities and their sequencing

Different methods and resources are developed during the last decade in order to guide the decision-making process during the design of blended courses. In their 2013 contribution, eleven authors illustrate there is no "one size fits all" learning design approach, in some cases approaches can be combined (Persico, Pozzi, Anastopoulou, Conole, Craft, Dimitriadis, ..., & Walmsley, 2013). Captured in a design, approaches can be made explicit by means of a type of representation, labelled as follows by Conole (2013): (a) practice-focused (e.g. case studies, lesson plans and patterns), (b) conceptual (e.g. mind maps and metaphorical representations), (c) abstract (e.g. models and vocabulary) or (d) technically-oriented (e.g. diagrams). A series of visual representations, for example, as explained by Conole and Wills (2013) aid practitioners to design, share and discuss practices. These are not considered mutually exclusive; multiple learning designs can be combined, in line with the purpose(s) of the blended teaching practice.

In order to mature in this dimension, one applies a design model or a set of design principles for the selection, integration and sequencing of face-to-face and online learning activities. These refer to particular logics and/or methods to design blended learning. Some examples from the field include the Integrated Course Design (Dee Fink, 2003), the ABC Learning Design method (Young & Perović, 2020) and the Carpe Diem design method (Salmon, 2020b).

To attain the highest level of maturity (Course cycle), adequate quality assurance (QA) principles must be in place in order to continuously improve a course design. Multiple data sources from the ongoing or past runs of a course can be used, i.e. course grades, students experience questionnaires or (group) interviews, interviews with lecturers, learning analytics, etc. These data inform action plans that stipulate how to improve or redesign a course. Frameworks such as the *Quality Assurance Rubric for Blended Learning* (Perris & Mohee, 2020) may provide the actual QA standards hereto.

Course design process: selection of blended learning tools

As to reach maturity level 2 (Design-based) in this dimension, the selection of learning tools during the course design process is based on evidence or previous experience. Authors like Holden and Westfall (2010) or Glover, Hepplestone, Parkin, Rodger, and Irwin (2016) developed media selection guides for blended learning environments. Some HE institutions (HEIs) also developed supporting materials and guidelines, among others the Tool Wheel based on the conversational framework of Laurillard (Last, Jongen, & Hardy, 2020), the Wheel of Pedagogy (Radboud Teaching and Learning Centre, 2020) or the Tool Guide (Educate-it, 2020).

The third maturity level of this dimension is labelled as *Course cycle* because the outcomes of the selection of tools are systematically monitored, evaluated and changed, based on quantitative and qualitative data. These data consist of learning analytics ("How (often) are tools used?"), surveys and interviews with students and instructors ("What are their user experiences?") and/or feedback from tool administrators ("Is the selected range of tools proven to be useful, easy-to-use and efficient?").

Course flexibility

If a course's flexibility is deliberately designed, based on theory or experience it has attained maturity level 2 of the course flexibility dimension. If in search of more background or examples, Andrade and Alden-Rivers (2019), developed a framework for sustainable growth of flexible learning opportunities. Additionally, the report regarding *Flexible pedagogies* (Gordon, 2014) and the report *Flexible Learning* (Universities UK, 2018) show some useful examples to design flexibility.

To obtain maturity level 3 (Adaptive), CQI procedures are embedded to assess and enhance course flexibility on a regular basis. Therefore, quantitative or qualitative user experience accounts from students can be collected to understand how students perceive the course flexibility. These include survey and interviews data, which may be complemented with behaviour data from the learning management system (LMS). Applying techniques such as educational data and process mining leads to further insight into the data (Pechenizkiy, 2012).

Course interaction

Level 2 of the dimension course interaction (Interactive), implies that interaction in a course is deliberately designed, informed by evidence or experience. Such endeavour might be supported by the interaction theory of Anderson (2003) or Stanley's model (2013) which extends Anderson's reasoning and presents *The 5 Interactions of a Robust Blended Learning Model.*

The highest maturity level (Responsive), is characterized by embedded monitoring, evaluation and adjustment of course interaction. In this regard, both the quantity and quality of the interactions are scrutinized in a planned manner, based on user data. Regarding student-content interaction this involves questions such as "How often and how long do students study the materials?", "How do they interact in the online environment?" and "How do they score on tests?". Student-student and student-teacher interactions in the digital and physical learning spaces are observed against the background of models of change and improvement (Sharma & Giannakos, 2020). Recent developments in the field of adaptive learning analytics, eye tracking and multimodal data capturing with or without wearables for analysing complex interactive student or instruction behaviour and their relationship with a plethora of learning outcomes (e.g., Ciordas-Hertel, 2020; Rodríguez-Triana, Martínez-Monés, Asensio-Pérez, & Dimitriadis, 2018; van Goidsenhoven, Bogdanova, Deeva, vanden Broucke, de Weerdt, & Snoeck, M., 2020).

Course experience: student learning

In order to reach maturity level 2 of this dimension (Advanced) it is imperative that features of the blended course facilitate self-regulated learning (SRL). This is possible in various ways, for example by integrating the seven recommendations of Quigley, Muijs, and Stinger (2018) or by integrating technology-supported tools such as pedagogical agents, learning analytics and data visualization (Triquet, Peeters, & Lombaerts, 2017).

The third level (Comprehensive) refers to embedded CQI procedures concerning self-regulated student learning. In general terms, SRL student data are collected and, subsequently, targeted interventions in a blended course are planned in order to improve the facilitation of SRL. This involves adapting or changing specific course features. Triquet and his colleagues (2017) describe 7 methods to measure students' SRL and present two research instruments for practice. Broadbent, Panadero, Lodge, and de Barba (2020) elaborate on technological solutions to enhance SRL, while Paraskeva and colleagues link problem-based learning with SRL in a blended learning environment (Paraskeva, Alexiou, Mysirlaki, Souki, Panoutsos, Gkemisi, & Boutsia, 2017).

Course experience: study load

This dimension refers to the (mis)match between the intended and achieved study load of a blended course. Particular to blended learning environments is that study load is related to both face-to-face and online learning activities. At the second maturity level (Advanced), study load is an estimation based on experience. The Erasmus University (2009) and Radboud University (2018) in the Netherlands, for example, have common guidelines about how to calculate study load. Students are informed on how much time they should spend on a specific topic or an assignment, which aids them to plan and manage their study time. This can be done in a paper-based manner as part of the course syllabus or by incorporating a specific instrument in the LMS.

On level 3 of this dimension (Comprehensive), the calculation of study load is based on evidence as well as experience. Various data sources, both quantitative and qualitative, are employed to monitor, evaluate, and adjust the study load of a course. Examples include statistics from log files that originate from the LMS or other learning tools, next to course evaluations. Qualitative data can be gathered by means of focus groups and interviews with students to gain additional insights related to the study load.

Course experience: inclusiveness

Inclusiveness is an important, yet complex dimension of a blended course. A series of blended course features have to be taken into consideration in order to design or assess its inclusiveness. First of all, it is related to the fact that students feel valued, safe, and have a sense of belonging. Salmon (2020a) has developed a five-stage framework to support incorporation of these aspects into the course design. It covers both the technical and social aspects of learning. Although it aims online learning with so-called *e-tivities* and *e-moderation*, all features may be implemented for blended teaching and learning purposes. Another facet of inclusiveness is that all materials are accessible to diverse learners, also those suffering from physical or cognitive disabilities. For these special need students, it may be required to change the speed of delivery of the contents, to incorporate alternative font styles, to closed captions, transcripts or sign language to video, and include explanatory texts when using images. The University of Edinburgh (2020) offers a useful checklist for assuring the accessibility of both materials and collaborative learning activities. Informed by the experiences of instructors, inclusiveness may be(come) part of the course enhancement processes. At Leiden University Romein (2017), for example, collected 11 teacher stories of inclusive teaching. This booklet can stimulate and inspire others to improve the inclusiveness of their course.

Level 3 of inclusiveness (Comprehensive) requires that the needs of all students must be addressed in and that CQI procedures are embedded with targeted actions to enhance the inclusiveness of a blended course. This means that all the efforts of level 2 should be implemented at the maximum, and complemented with inclusiveness data obtained by means of surveys, focus groups and interviews. Based on the insights, adaptations are suggested and implemented. In Gronseth (2018) one finds the account of an appropriate inclusive blended course design, "connecting" the Web Content Accessibility Guidelines and the Universal Design for Learning.

The EMM guidelines in light of the Covid-19 experience

The pandemic has highlighted the key importance of HEIs being able to transform in the blink of an eye. For achieving substantial changes in teaching and learning, an effective, well-oiled organizational context needs to be in place. *Nil novi sub sole.* Already in 2006, the results of large-scale e-learning research pointed towards four P's in this regard: problem, planning, policy and participation. Any e-learning initiative should solve an educational need (problem). Planning and policy refer to the cyclical process where an organization determines how and when e-learning implementation is to be carried out, communicated, supported and monitored. Participation or the degree to which an organization is able to form effective and efficient collaboration between all stakeholders to decide upon e-learning. Ideally, this involves a transparent communication flow between instructors, students, administrators and policymaking bodies (Goeman & de Vos, 2006). Based on observations during the COVID19 crisis, Elen (2021) emphasised the all-important value of "agency", that is the use of an environment by students (by extension also instructors in the case of free choice). Next to these organizational and individual-level factors, the need for quality teaching and learning services came in evidence during the Covid-19 crisis. Acting as informed matchmakers they glued the needs of all with solutions at hand.

We believe that the stances of the EMM and its guidelines are relevant and useful, both during and after the Covid-19 crisis (see also Dijkstra, 2021). Also, although the EMM initially focused on blended formats of teaching, the central ideas behind the blending are relevant to a wide spectrum of face-to-face and online learning.

First of all, the design-based stance of the EMM puts to the fore the purposefully usage of principles and/or instructional theories to decide upon learning activities and concurrent digital solutions in courses and programs. In light of the COVID experience, this regarded predominantly the (sequencing of) asynchronous and synchronous online events and the onset of particular tools for teaching, learning and assessment. In some instances and for particular groups, blended learning environments were set up. These addressed some issues of remote online learning. At the universities of both authors, for example, several problems were reported with regard to the wellbeing of students and staff, high cognitive load, low motivation, lack of SRL, few interactivity, next to delays in student learning. On the other hand, it was reported that remote online learning worked better for particular types of students. These include, among others, those that are more introvert or those with difficulties to travel to campus. Additionally, both staff and students discovered the benefits of remote and hybrid instances of interaction and feedback, assessment and lecturing, as well as the strengths of video. One could argue that particular barriers were reduced and that courses became more flexible and inclusive. However, sizable time investments were necessary to prepare and build in structure and digital course components. It will be interesting to see how HEIs will embed proven practices and reinvent online and blended learning environments in the post-Covid-19 era.

Working in a design-based manner forces instructional designers and instructors to search for approaches that act upon these issues, and to step away from "belly-based" approaches. The EMM, accompanied by its guidelines for practice, targets both those that have to design from scratch as those that wish to make a transition to blended teaching. In line with the EMM, the institutional conditions and strategies are a leverage for these actions. These may focus on the coherence in course designs, the interoperability and security of tools, the front- and back-end support, the staff's and students' online readiness, as well as their privacy. More than ever, the Covid-19 pandemic has shown the importance of adequate short-to-midterm strategies to cope with challenges and changes. In this regard, it is very interesting to read how South African colleagues acknowledge the crucial role of "eLearning champions", lecturers with a "design thinking mindset". Earlier on, the authors argued that promoting such a mindset in academic staff development interventions would advance the innovative use of technology in teaching and learning (Gachago, Morkel, Hitge, van Zyl, & Ivala, 2017; Patnaik & Gachago, 2021). In the margin, we wonder whether organizational context will gain in prominence in research literature after the pandemic.

Secondly, the stance of the EMM as a linear logic model regarding maturity serves both practical and more theory-oriented purposes. As previously explained, the maturity of blended practices refers to the degree of formality and the evidence-based character of its design, decision making and CQI. The model may be used as a framework for measuring maturity and its growth in descriptive studies, along predefined categories of descriptors. Likewise, it can provide researchers with a detailed snapshot of pre- and post-conditions in intervention studies. For practice, the EMM may be used as a handle to conceive blended practices, to guide discussions and initiate (un)planned changes. By means of the implementation guidelines, (a group of) instructors may guide their progress between different levels of maturity. Important to note is that the model imposes an iterative approach which makes it far from a static framework that could impede a HEI's transformative agenda. The disruptive potential of new digital technologies for teaching and learning is not ignored, on the contrary. It is encapsulated in a CQI loop which aims to derive at the reimaging of teaching and learning experiences in a sustainable manner. In the light of the Covid-19 situation, we observed for example that online learning environments empowered significantly rapid, data-driven informed decision making for course design. It is expected from a HEI to act upon this experience, and further advance their digitally enhanced education ecosystem.

Using the EMM guidelines in a workshop

The model can guide discussions on blended teaching and education in a HE institution, a department, a team of educational managers or instructors. In this regard, one's engagement in such conversations are *in se* more important and deemed valuable than the "scoring" of maturity. It is essential to involve the right stakeholders. These differ according to the subject of the discussions, that is the agreed number of dimensions that will be debated.

Optimally, the model is employed in a team-based, interactive manner, with the aim of reaching consensus. To this end, it seems that a workshop is the most appropriate manner to use the model. In one or more sessions, the participants determine individually and cooperatively the maturity level of the different model dimensions. We recommend to follow the next steps:

1. A facilitator with knowledge of the EMBED framework guides the sessions. This person introduces the EMM, elaborates on the action level (e.g., course, program or institution) and explains the setup of the workshop. It should be clear for all participants which level and what subject matter they will discuss in detail (e.g., which course or which program). Each participant individually assesses the maturity level of each dimension. To this end, both the EMM framework as well as the digital materials (a self-assessment tool and worksheets) support this process (see https://embed.eadtu.eu/working-with-embed_3). In particular, the participants create a radar diagram based on the scores of their present maturity assessment. Such visualization gives a clear overview of the current state of affairs.
2. The facilitator discusses with all participants the results of the self-assessments. The goal of this third phase is to reach consensus on the scoring of the present maturity level of a specific dimension. These are retained and used to justify why a specific level of maturity has (not) been designated to a particular practice). These are used in the following step.
3. The participants create an action plan, which includes what one wishes to change, the reason(s) behind, a specification of who needs to be involved, and when the change should be implemented. A template for such action plan is also

downloadable from the EMBED website (see https://embed.eadtu.eu/working-with-embed). It is recommended that when changes are extensive, it is more useful to initiate a (small) project and involve a project team to design, plan and implement the changes.

4. After the changes are implemented, the results of the action plan or project are evaluated using the same framework and materials.
5. It is further recommended that participants make monitor on regular occasions whether the maturity levels maintain the same level, increase or decrease.

Not only participants of the above described workshop may use the EMM; any individual instructor, instructional designer or team interested in how to mature in blended teaching or education, will find the EMM framework and materials easy-to-use and useful resources or sources of inspiration for introducing (new) blended practices.

Conclusion and future work

The COVID-19 crisis has more than ever shown how important it is to address adequately students' needs in educational contexts characterized by a partial separation of instructors and students in terms of geographic distance or by time. Those in search of a framework for creating blended courses may apply the principles, open-source materials and guidelines as proposed by the project partners of the EMBED project. It allows to assess and alter blended practices in terms of maturity. Initially developed on the basis of thorough literature synthesis, followed by a mixed-method study among educators and experts, the EMM will be further disseminated in real-life HE contexts and refined in order to match to a maximum with the needs of its users.

References

Anderson, T. (2003). Getting the Mix Right Again: An Updated and Theoretical Rationale for Interaction. *The International Review of Research in Open and Distributed Learning, 4*(2), 1-14.

Andrade, M., & Alden-Rivers, B. (2019). Developing a framework for sustainable growth of flexible learning opportunities. *Higher Education Pedagogies, 4*(1), 1-16.

Appana, S. (2008). A review of benefits and limitations of online learning in the context of the student, the instructor, and the tenured faculty. *International Journal on E-Learning, 7*(1), 5-22.

Bostock, J. (2018). A Model of Flexible Learning: Exploring Interdependent Relationships between Students, Lecturers, Resources and Contexts in Virtual Spaces. *Journal of Perspectives in Applied Academic Practice, 6*(1), 12-18.

Broadbent, J., Panadero, E., Lodge, J., & de Barba, P. (2020). Technologies to Enhance Self-Regulated Learning in Online and Computer-Mediated Learning Environments. In M. J. Bishop, E. Boling, J. Elen, & V. Svihla (Eds.), *Handbook of Research in Educational Communications and Technology* (pp. 37-52). Cham: Springer.

Ciordas-Hertel, G. (2020). How to Complement Learning Analytics with Smartwatches? Fusing Physical Activities, Environmental Context, and Learning Activities. *Proceedings of the 2020 International Conference on Multimodal Interaction*, 708-712. New York: ACM.

Conole, G. (2013). *Designing for learning in an open world.* New York: Springer.

Conole, G., & Wills, S. (2013). Representing learning designs – making design explicit and shareable. *Educational Media International, 50*(1), 24-38.

Dee Fink, L. (2003). *A Self-Directed Guide to Designing Courses for Significant Learning.* Retrieved from https://www.deefinkandassociates.com/GuidetoCourseDesignAug05.pdf

Dijkstra, W. (2021). EMBED maturity model. Presentation during the Empower Covid-19 webinar week. Retrieved from https://www.slideshare.net/EADTU/empower-covid19-webinar-week-embed-maturity-model-by-wiebe-dijkstra-6-april-2021

Educate-it (2020). Tool guide. Retrieved from https://educate-it.uu.nl/en/tool-guide/

Elen, J. (2021). Context and agency: Complementarity and interactivity. *Educational Technology Research and Development, 69*(1), 195-197.

Erasmus University (2009). *Calculating study load.* Retrieved from https://www.eur.nl/sites/corporate/files/15_Studielastberekening_juli_2007_ENd.pdf

European Commission (2018). *Communication from the Commission to the European Parliament, the Council, the European Economic and Social Committee and the Committee of the Regions on the Digital Education Action Plan.* Retrieved from https://eur-lex.europa.eu/legal-content/EN/TXT/PDF/?uri=CELEX:52018DC0022&from=EN

European Commission (2020). Communication from the Commission to the European Parliament, the Council, the European Economic and Social Committee and the Committee of the Regions. Digital Education Action Plan 2021-2027. Resetting Education and Training for the Digital Age. Retrieved from https://eur-lex.europa.eu/legal-content/EN/TXT/?qid=1602778451601&uri=CELEX%3A52020DC0624

Gachago, D., Morkel, J., Hitge, L., van Zyl, I., & Ivala, E. (2017). Developing eLearning champions: a design thinking approach. *International Journal of Educational Technology in Higher Education, 14*(1), 1-14.

Glover, I., Hepplestone, S., Parkin, H., Rodger, H., & Irwin, B. (2016). Pedagogy first: Realising technology enhanced learning by focusing on teaching practice. *British Journal of Educational Technology, 47*(5), 993-1002.

Goeman, K., Poelmans, S., van Rompaey, V., Dijkstra, W., & van Valkenburg, W. (2019). Embedding Blended Learning Environments in Higher Education: Towards a European Maturity Model. *Proceedings of the European Distance and E-Learning Network 2019 Annual Conference*, 67-71. Budapest: EDEN. Retrieved from https://proceedings.eden-online.org/wp-content/uploads/2019/06/Annual_2019_Bruges_Proceedings_ISSN.pdf

Goeman, K., & Ubachs, G. (2018). Towards a European Maturity Model for Blended Education (EMBED). *Proceedings of the European Distance and E-Learning Network 2018 Annual Conference*, 305-308. Budapest: EDEN. Retrieved from https://proceedings.eden-online.org/wp-content/uploads/2018/06/Annual_2018_Genova _Proceedings_ISSN.pdf

Goeman, K., & de Vos, E. (2006). Overcoming Barriers to Successfully Implementing e-Learning: The Four P's Framework. *Proceedings of the 5th WSEAS International Conference on E-ACTIVITIES*, 459-466.

van Goidsenhoven, S., Bogdanova, D., Deeva, G., vanden Broucke, S. ., de Weerdt, J., & Snoeck, M. (2020). Predicting student success in a blended learning environment. *Proceedings of the 10th International Conference on Learning Analytics & Knowledge*, 17-25. New York: ACM.

Gordon, N. (2014). *Flexible pedagogies: technology-enhanced learning.* The Higher Education Academy. Retrieved from https://www.advance-he.ac.uk/knowledge-hub/flexible-pedagogies-technology-enhanced-learning

Gronseth, S. (2018). Inclusive Design for Online and Blended Courses: Connecting Web Content Accessibility Guidelines and Universal Design for Learning. *Educational Renaissance, 7*, 14-22.

Holden, J., & Westfall, P. (2010). *An instructional media selection guide for distance learning–Implications for blended learning.* US: USDLA. Retrieved from https://lincs.ed.gov/professional-development/resource-collections/profile-810

Last, B., Jongen, S., & Hardy, P. (2020). Tool wheel. Retrieved from https://tutorials.library.maastrichtuniversity.nl/Tool_Wheel/

Moore, M. (2019). The Theory of Transactional Distance. In M. Moore, & W. Diehl (Eds.), *Handbook of Distance Education* (pp. 32-46). Milton Park: Routledge.

Paraskeva, F., Alexiou, A., Mysirlaki, S., Souki, A., Panoutsos, S., Gkemisi, S., & Boutsia, C. (2017). Applying PBL and SRL to Enhance Learning Strategies and Collaboration in a Blended Learning Environment. *Proceedings of the International Workshop on Learning Technology for Education in Cloud*, 85-96. Cham: Springer.

Patnaik, S., & Gachago, D. (2020). Supporting departmental innovation in eLearning during COVID-19 through eLearning champions. *Proceedings of the 2020 IFEES World Engineering Education Forum*, 1-4. doi: 10.1109/WEEF-GEDC49885.2020.9293653

Pechenizkiy, M. (2012). Educational Data and Process Mining. TU/e Data Mining Expertise Group Research. Retrieved from https://www.win.tue.nl/%7Empechen/projects/edm/

Perris, K., & Mohee, R. (2020). *Quality Assurance Rubric for Blended Learning.* Commonwealth of Learning. Retrieved from http://dspace.col.org/handle/11599/3615

Persico, D., Pozzi, F., Anastopoulou, S., Conole, G., Craft, B., Dimitriadis, Y., ..., & Walmsley, H. (2013). Learning design Rashomon I–supporting the design of one lesson through different approaches. *Research in Learning Technology, 21*, 1-19.

Peterson, D. (2016). The Flipped Classroom Improves Student Achievement and Course Satisfaction in a Statistics Course: A Quasi-Experimental Study. *Teaching of Psychology, 43*(1), 10-15. https://doi.org/10.1177/0098628315620063

Quigley, A., Muijs, D., & Stringer, E. (2018). *Metacognition and self-regulated learning.* Retrieved from https://educationendowmentfoundation.org.uk/tools/guidance-reports/metacognition-and-self-regulated-learning/

Radboud Teaching and Learning Centre (2018). The Educational ICT Toolbox. Retrieved from https://www.ru.nl/lecturers/education-ict/lecture-halls-pc-rooms/pc-rooms-study-halls/what-types-educational-tools-available/

Radboud University (2018). Credits and study load. Course Guides FFTR 2018. Retrieved from https://www.ru.nl/prospectus/2018/fftr/rules-regulations/courses-exams/credits-study-load/

Rasheed, R., Kamsin, A., & Abdullah, N. (2020). Challenges in the online component of blended learning: A systematic review. *Computers & Education, 144*, 103701.

Rodríguez-Triana, M. J., Prieto, L. P., Martínez-Monés, A., Asensio-Pérez, J. I., & Dimitriadis, Y. (2018). The teacher in the loop: Customizing multimodal learning analytics for blended learning. *Proceedings of the 8th International Conference on Learning Analytics and Knowledge*, 417-426. New York: ACM.

Romein, D. (2017). *Teacher's tales: On the road to inclusive teaching.* Leiden University. Retrieved from https://www.universiteitleiden.nl/binaries/content/assets/algemeen/diversiteit/boekje-teachers-tales-webversie.pdf

Salmon, G. (2020a). Five Stage Model. Retrieved from https://www.gillysalmon.com/five-stage-model.html

Salmon, G. (2020b). Carpe Diem – A team based approach to learning design. Retrieved from https://www.gillysalmon.com/carpe-diem.html

Sharma, K., & Giannakos, M. (2020). Multimodal data capabilities for learning: What can multimodal data tell us about learning? *British Journal of Educational Technology, 51*(5), 1450-1484.

Smith, K., & Hill, J. (2019). Defining the nature of blended learning through its depiction in current research. *Higher Education Research & Development, 38*(2), 383-397.

Stanley, T. (2013). The 5 Interactions of a Robust Blended Learning Model. Retrieved from https://www.teachthought.com/learning/the-5-interactions-of-a-robust-blended-learning-model/

Thai, N., de Wever, B., & Valcke, M. (2017). The impact of a flipped classroom design on learning performance in higher education: Looking for the best "blend" of lectures and guiding questions with feedback. *Computers & Education, 107*, 113-126.

Triquet, K., Peeters, J., & Lombaerts, K. (2017). *Self-Regulated Learning Online: Benefits, Empirical Foundations, Multi-level, and Multi-modal Promotion & Evaluation thereof for Teacher Professional Development.* A policy experimentation co-funded by Erasmus+. Deliverable D1.1: Gaps in ITE and CPD provision report. Retrieved from http://teachup.eun.org/documents/556205/1092039/TeachUP_D1.1b_Self-Regulated-Learning-Online.pdf/3d155d94-8a05-4cde-b18c-d6a33f4fc2b9

University of Edinburgh, The (2020). Accessibility Checklist. Retrieved from https://www.ed.ac.uk/information-services/learning-technology/accessibility/checklist

Universities UK (2018). *Flexible learning: The current state of play in UK higher education.* Retrieved from https://www.universitiesuk.ac.uk/policy-and-analysis/reports/Documents/2018/flexible-learning-the-current-state-of-play-in-higher-education.pdf

Young, C., & Perović, N. (2020). ABC Learning Design @ UCL. Retrieved from https://blogs.ucl.ac.uk/abc-ld/

Acknowledgements

We explicitly thank the EDEN conference reviewers for their comments on the first version of this paper. A complete chapter was added as a response to their critical reflections.

Annex

Table 5: Dimensions, subdimension and indicators at the course level, according to the European Maturity Model*

Dimension Subdimension	Description	Maturity level Level 1	 Level 2	 Level 3
Course design process	The process of planning, designing, developing and evaluating a blended learning course.			
Selection of blended learning activities and their sequencing	The rationale for the deliberate selection and integration of face-to-face and online learning activities.	Explorative No considered selection and integration of face-to-face and online learning activities.	Design-based Learning activities (both face-to-face and online) are deliberately selected, integrated, and sequenced based on a design method or design principles.	Course cycle Blended learning activities are deliberately selected, integrated, and sequenced; based on a design method or design principles. QA procedures are embedded in order to continuously improve a course in an iterative manner.
Selection of blended learning tools	The rationale for selecting tools for the delivery and organization of blended learning activities	Tool-based The selection of particular tools is based on their availability at the HE institution.	Design-based The selection of particular tools is based on learning activities, informed by evidence or experience.	Course cycle The selection of particular tools is based on blended learning activities, informed by evidence or experience. This process is monitored, evaluated and changed based on quantitative and qualitative data.
Course flexibility	Opportunities for learners to adjust particular features of the blended learning course, based on their needs and preferences. This includes features such as the selection of learning activities, the selection of resources, the mode of delivery (online/face-to-face activities), pace (educator-paced/self-paced).	No flexibility No deliberate course flexibility.	Flexible The course's flexibility is deliberately designed. Its design is based on evidence or experience.	Adaptive flexible The course's flexibility is deliberately designed, based on evidence or experience. CQI procedures are embedded in order to enhance course flexibility.
Course interaction	Extent to which the blended course facilitates learners' interaction (learner-content, learner-learner, learner-educator).	Non-responsive No deliberate course interaction.	Interactive Interaction in the course is deliberately designed, informed by evidence or experience.	Responsive Interaction in the course is deliberately designed, informed by evidence or experience. Interactions are monitored, evaluated and changed based on data and feedback.

Course experience	The extent to which a course enhances students' learning and eliminates any obstacles that stand in the way of learning.			
		Standard	Advanced	Comprehensive
Student learning	The use of blended course features which facilitate students' self-regulated learning (orienting and planning, monitoring, adjusting and evaluating).	No deliberate consideration of student learning.	Particular blended course features are incorporated in order to facilitate student learning, informed by evidence or experience.	Particular blended course features are incorporated in order to facilitate student learning, informed by evidence or experience. CQI procedures are embedded in order to enhance student learning.
Study load	The match between the intended and achieved study load of a course (distribution and correctness).	The calculation of course study load is an educated guess.	Course study load is calculated based on experience. Different course elements are taken into consideration for the calculation of the study load.	Course study load is calculated based on data and experience. All course elements are taken into consideration for the calculation of the study load. The study load is monitored, evaluated and changed based on quantitative and qualitative data.
		Standard	Advanced	Comprehensive
Inclusiveness	The consideration for the diverse needs (including accessibility aspects) and backgrounds of all students to create an online and face-to-face course experience where all students feel valued, safe, have a sense of belonging, and where all students have equal access to learn	No deliberate consideration for inclusiveness.	Initial attempts to address the diverse needs and backgrounds of all learners. Special attention is paid to social belonging and identity in the online course environment. This process is informed by evidence or experience.	The diverse needs and backgrounds of all learners are addressed. Students feel valued, safe, and have a sense of belonging. The attainment of inclusiveness is based on evidence or experience. CQI procedures are embedded in order to improve inclusiveness in the course.

Note. QA=quality assurance, CQI=continuous quality improvement

* As compared to the published version on the EADTU website, minor differences in terms of wording of the model components are present. This is done for reasons of enhanced comprehension.

Lessons from a Pandemic for the Future of Education
European Distance and E-Learning Network (EDEN) Proceedings
2021 Annual Conference | Madrid, 21-24 June, 2021
ISSN 2707-2819
doi: 10.38069/edenconf-2021-ac0009

HYBRIDISM – THEORETICAL LEARNING RESPONSE TO THE GROWING DIVERSITY IN HIGHER EDUCATION

Christian-Andreas Schumann, Anna-Maria Nitsche, West Saxon University of Zwickau, Kevin Reuther, University of Leipzig, Claudia Tittmann, West Saxon University of Zwickau, Germany

Abstract

The transition from a knowledge society to a network society leads to growing globalisation, networking and a sudden increase in networked knowledge. Higher education and further education, like vocational training, must react with hybrid forms of generalisation and specialisation, in which way complexity and diversity are rapidly increasing in the education systems. In addition, digitalisation and the consequences of the pandemic are pushing this development. Hybridisation can make a theoretical and practical contribution to finding an answer to the complexity of mastering these processes. The consistent further development of learning theory approaches in the context of modelling and applying hybrid systems and automata leads to hybridism and thus to the expansion of the spectrum of learning theories.

Introduction

Human existence relates to perceiving and recognizing the environment. The question of how to recognize objective reality is of existential importance (Audi, 2010). Signals are based on stimuli. They describe changes of state that serve a communication or information purpose and can trigger behavioural consequences or reactions (Hoffmeister & Ziegler, 2021). The process of acquiring and changing behaviours and cognitive structures, consciously or unconsciously, is called learning. In this process, knowledge, skills, and abilities are acquired, and feelings, behaviours and ways of thinking are formed in combination of psychological, emotional, social, and physical aspects (Sandweg, 2017).

Building blocks of cognition consist of elements which are subject to certain laws of construction. Structures are self-regulating wholes and consist of a system of elements and relations that can be subjected to transformations. Building blocks of cognition are characterized by groups of schemata that determine how humans typically deal with classes of environmental conditions. Schemata serve to structure knowledge during storage, recall, embedding, formation, and representation of knowledge (Rumelhart, 1978). Due to the active confrontation with the environment, which every organism permanently engages in by scanning stimuli and comparing information, it is therefore given per se that humans go through a continuous, lifelong process of learning, independent of the form of learning, the learning method, the learning motivation, the learning technology, etc. The learning theories do not describe whether learning can be shaped or promoted, but rather how it can be inhibited.

Learning is defined as a process that integrates individual and environmental experiences and influences to acquire, enrich, or change knowledge, skills, values, attitudes, behaviours, and worldviews. Learning theories develop hypotheses that describe how this process occurs. Major learning theories include behaviourism, cognitivism, and constructivism, which are complemented and extended by learning concepts such as social constructivism, experiential learning, multiple intelligences, situational learning, and community of practice (UNESCO, 2021).

The current accentuation of relevant learning theories, as described in the UNESCO contribution, testifies to two fundamental tendencies, on the one hand the constant further development and diversification of the body of theories and on the other hand the generation of new theories which, like connectivism, take account of new and contemporary forms of teaching and learning in reality. High interconnectedness and networking through globalization and digitalization were the impetus for a new theoretical consideration of learning, but also growing complexity and diversity of influences on learning in the form of multiple hybrid dimensions will be reflected in theory and practice.

Issue of growing complexity and diversity

The development of science is closely connected with the concept of holism, documented, for example, by Aristotle's statement that the whole is more than the sum of its parts. Moreover, in this context, he discussed aspects of diversity and hybridity in his work "The Metaphysics", which are obviously related to holistic approaches (McMahon, 2008).

The holistic approach is becoming more and more established in the systematic analysis and systematic design of various fields of knowledge, including education. If large educational systems are considered with their interactions with other social systems, the multitude of objects and relations involved leads to so-called large systems with an extremely high complexity. To better manage this complexity, decompositions are used to break down the whole into smaller units. The sectional view through decomposition generates simplifications and thus better controllability, but also limitations regarding the model quality.

Despite this pragmatic approach, the fact remains that complexity exists in reality. Oversimplifications lead to inaccurate statements, which is why the realisation that a holistic approach is necessary to guarantee the reflection of real conditions in a corresponding quality is becoming more and more accepted. The increasing emphasis on interdisciplinary and transdisciplinary approach and the demand for the growing number of professional competences further increase the complexity (Schumann et al., 2019). The change of educational systems in the sense of holistic and systemic approaches reflects the changes of real systems in society in general and in education in particular (Heidling et al., 2019).

The volume of information and knowledge is growing exponentially, from the industrial society to the knowledge society to the network society. They are transferred and made available in ever greater quantity and density, but the half-life of their topicality is continuously decreasing. The learning process is becoming a lifelong process with many different types of learning objects, knowledge transfer methods, means and methods in combination with multimedia and computer-based information systems as a highly complex network for mastering knowledge transfer and adequate learning processes (Schumann, Tittmann, & Tittmann, 2008).

Since education always reflects real systems in essential elements, the transfer of these insights leads to analogous challenges in the content-related, organisational, and structural design of new globalised and diversified offerings in higher education. Diversity characterises the variety, manifoldness, and multiplicity of objects and relationships, processes, and functions as well as actors and roles in learning in social groups. Diversity is thus an organisational principle. It is part of any organisational development, especially its strategic orientation. Four strategies are essential to the overarching vision, mission, and strategy of the organisation, which determine the aspirations of diversity management: Managing Representation, Managing Demographic Relationships, Managing Diverse Talents and Managing All Strategic Diversity Mixes (Roosevelt, 2010).

Digitalisation and globalisation reinforce the trend towards diversification. Digital technologies and digital products enable more virtual mobility and access to appropriate digital offerings. This process is accelerated by learners' interactions in social networks. This creates increasing pressure for diversification on the supply side to help satisfy growing individualisation on the demand side. The multiple choices, in turn, increase the individual pressure for learners to make decisions. They are in constant exchange with other actors to choose the best offer without necessarily entering a rigid commitment to one or more educational organisations (Schumann et al., 2019).

Focus on hybridisation in higher education

Hybridisation has always been part of the development of learning forms and methods. This is due to the generality of the term hybridity. It was originally used in biology and botany, but later transferred to cultural phenomena also in the context of innovation and creativity (Canan, 2015).

Since, in turn, cultural aspects are related to all other areas of society, including education, and thus learning, it is used in different contexts nowadays. The concept of hybrid states was adapted within the framework of systems theory and is thus not only relevant in biological, social, and cultural terms, but is used in all areas that can be considered by means of systems theory approaches. Either two originally separate manifestations of different systems or two manifestations of a system are combined in such a way that different hybrid forms are created.

Hybrid forms of teaching, learning and assessment in the interplay of face-to-face and distance learning have been in vogue since the appearance of distance learning several decades ago. This trend has been further strengthened by the possibilities of online learning. However, this is already an overlap of two hybrid forms, which in turn can also be combined with each other: Face-to-face teaching and distance learning as well as offline and online learning. A hybrid form of face-to-face and distance learning is possible, whereby the respective proportion can usually be adjusted as desired and can in turn be combined with a hybrid form of offline and online learning, whose proportions can also vary between two poles. These models have been developed and discussed in the professional world for many years (Doering, 2006; Horn, Crouser, & Bers, 2012).

Its importance has increased enormously with the worldwide, extensive transition from face-to-face to internet-based distance education in the context of the measures to cope with the Corona pandemic. Integration and complementarity of face-to-face and distance education in this context are discussed and analysed worldwide and lead to new approaches of educational strategic concepts and up to educational policy. However, it is not a pure opposition of face-to-face and distance education. The hybrid system is not reduced to one or two hybrid forms of learning, but rather already discussed in the context of other aspects that may well be hybrid in nature, such as educational platforms, individual and group work, special teaching and learning methods, competences to be developed, teaching materials, human resources, etc. (Opertti, 2021 February).

It follows inevitably from these considerations that a stronger emphasis on the holistic nature of educational strategy concepts is called for. It is emphasised that any kind of one-dimensional or disciplinary approach misses the reality of what learners will demand and need from new forms of teaching and learning in the future. The digital transformations that are increasingly triggering these changes are multi-layered in nature and not only technology driven. There are already many forms in the areas of teaching material, learning planning, type of learning, etc. that can take on different hybrid states for the benefit of the learners or can be adjusted accordingly (Opertti, 2021 March).

Complex investigations lead to hybrid systems in education, for example, hybrid learning configurations, hybridity in learning spaces, hybrid learning courses, hybridity in recognition management, hybrid study programmes, hybrid home study, etc. What they all have in common are holistic investigations that establish the connection between complexity, diversity, and hybridity (Cremers & et al., 2017; Cook, Mor, & Santos, 2020; Olapiriyaku & Scher, 2006; Kislova, 2019; Schumann & et al., 2016; van der Merwe & Schoonwinkel, 2019; Schumann & et al., 2019).

Hybridism as complementary learning theory

In principle, a learning theory must meet the requirements that are placed on theories in general. The special feature is the description of how knowledge can be transferred from one person to another or how knowledge can be gained from the confrontation with the environment. This requires a set of models and concepts that serve as a theoretical whole to systematically observe, analyse, describe, explain, and interpret learning and its peripheral processes. The construction of a learning theory is an attempt to classify knowledge about learning. Learning theories support a conceptual framework vocabulary for arriving at interpretations and understanding through observations. The dominant, classical learning theories are behaviourism, cognitivism, and constructivism. In the age of digitalisation, connectivism has been developed as another learning theory that puts the mentioned classical learning theories into a new context based on the digital networking of learners and knowledge (Duke, Harper, & Johnston, 2013).

From an eclectic view, there is a re-evaluation of classical learning theories and the formulation of a new theory that places learning in the context of digitalised knowledge networks and educational systems. Connectivism was developed among several other learning theories, but now occupies a prominent position alongside classical learning theories. It includes elements of chaos theory, self-organisation, and network theory. Individual and organisational learning in knowledge networks with corresponding nodes and connections is placed at the centre of theoretical considerations. Free, network-based access to knowledge resources for the purpose of learning is propagated and theoretically founded (Siemens, 2005).

Through the development of connectivism theory, limits of traditional learning theories are shown, but at the same time new limits are set in a networked world through the uncontrolled access to information and knowledge in learning. The debate about whether connectivism is a pedagogical approach rather than a learning theory is explained by the fact that learning is placed in a new network-based context. But connectivism addresses learning processes per se, which makes it at least a learning theory derived from what exists (Kop & Hill, 2008).

The challenge of the growing complexity of the body of knowledge and the increasing number of access points for learners must be met, whereby the use of taxonomy for class formation in education opens the way to better systematisation (Anderson et al., 2001).

This approach can be further developed in terms of systems theory with the integration of object orientation, whereby states of systems, subsystems, objects, attributes, or attribute values are taken as a basis. These states are mapped independently of the object class via dimensions that can be used to describe hybrid states during learning (Rühling et al., 2010).

The learning process is considered primary, as in all learning theories. The process elements, objects or properties of the objects are understood as dimensions and can assume either continuously or discretely defined states within defined boundaries. Each dimension associated with the learning process can thus assume a hybrid state. Any number of hybrid dimensions can be combined. The resulting hybridity of the entire knowledge transfer system and the associated learning processes allows the derivation of a learning theory, hybridism. The approach can now be pursued to map the interaction of the dimensions by means of hybrid systems and automata (Ábrahám, 2012).

However, automata are also the prerequisite for the controllability and regularability of processes. In the special case of learning processes, a hybrid system would therefore help to model learning in highly complex knowledge networks, as they are increasingly characteristic of the network society, in such a way that the learning processes can be controlled or regulated.

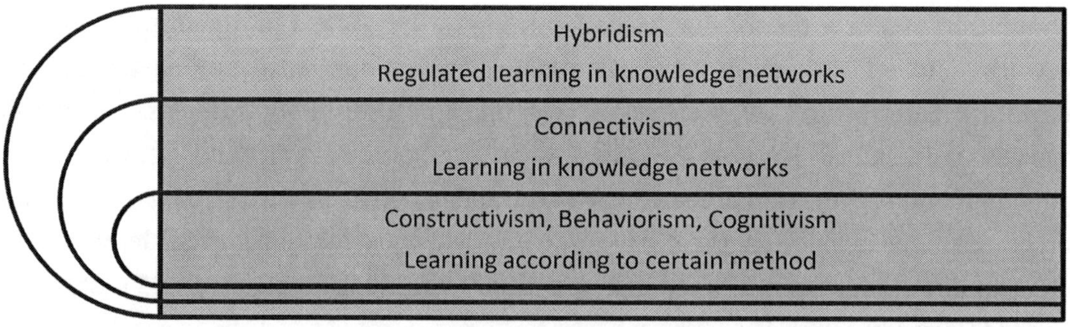

Figure 4. Learning theories and their causal classification in an overall context

The contribution that can be made by expanding the set of learning theory approaches using hybridism is the multidimensional description of hybrid states in modelling learning processes within the framework of single knowledge bases or knowledge networks.

Individuals learn in a system of one to several, hybrid dimensions to expand their knowledge and experience as well as to be able to conclude how to change their behaviour. In addition, there is the option not only to organise their learning process themselves in a multi-talented and networked world of knowledge, but also to actively influence the absorption of information and knowledge as well as the resulting possible change in behaviour by actively influencing hybrid learning space dimensions by changing their states individually or for social groups. Teachers also have the possibility to optimise learning processes of third parties by providing prefabricated, optimised sets of the setting of hybrid states of the dimensions or by learning process-accompanying changes of the hybrid states of the dimensions for individuals or groups of individuals.

Conclusions and outlook

Hybridism integrates self-determination, networking, and multi-dimensionality of changeable variables in stationary or networked learning spaces for learning processes and thus determines how learners acquire knowledge and experience or modify their behaviour in a self-directed, externally directed or uncontrolled way, also in combination. The type and quantity of the dimensions involved as well as their possible hybrid states are defined and optimised in relation to the goals of learning, thus enabling learner-centredness, objectification and self-control in highly complex and networked systems of knowledge transfer. Through the permanent possibility of changing the setting of the hybrid states of the dimensions as well as the combination of the dimensions, learning processes can be made dynamic and adaptively controllable. Theoretical preliminary work on hybrid systems and automata can be used for modelling hybrid learning processes.

In the future, natural and artificial intelligence will not only complement each other, but rather work together collaboratively. In smart systems, influencing variables are combined multi-dimensionally. They can be hybridised in their states and modified to influence the behaviour of the system. It will be interesting to see what potentials can be tapped through convergence and adaptation of the learning processes between natural and artificial objects and systems through hybridisation.

References

Ábrahám, E. (2012). *Modeling and Analysis of Hybrid Systems. Lecture Notes. Theory of Hybrid Systems.* Faculty of Mathematics, Computer Science, and Natural Sciences. Aachen: RWTH Aachen University.

Anderson, L. W., Krathwohl, D. R., Airasian, P. W., et al. (2001). *A Taxonomy for Learning, Teaching, and Assessing: A Revision of Bloom's Taxonomy of Educational Objectives.* Abridged Edition. New York: Longman.

Audi, R. (2010). *Epistemology: A Contemporary Introduction to the Theory of Knowledge* (3rd ed.). New York and London: Routledge.

Canan C. (2015). Was ist Hybridität? In *Identitätsstatus von Einheimischen mit Migrationshintergrund, 51*. Wiesbaden: Springer.

Cook, J., Mor, Y., & Santos, P. (2020) Three cases of hybridity in learning spaces: Towards a design for a Zone of Possibility. *British Journal of Educational Technology, 51*(4), 1155-1167.

Cremers, P. H. M., Wals, A. E. J., Wesselink, R., & Mulder, M. (2017). Utilization of design principles for hybrid learning configurations by interprofessional design teams. *Instructional Science, 45*(2), 289-309.

Doering, A. (2006) Adventure Learning: Transformative hybrid online education. *Distance Education, 27*(2), 197-215. New York and London: Routledge.

Duke, B., Harper, G., & Johnston, M. (2013). Connectivism as a digital age learning theory. *The International HETL Review, Special Issue 2013*, 4-13.

Heidling, E., Meil, P., Neumer, J., et al. (2019). *Ingenieure und Ingenieurinnen für Industrie 4.0.* Studie des Institutes für sozialwissenschaftliche Forschung. 15-70. München: Institutes for social science research.

Hoffmeister, H., & Ziegler, C. (2021). Freies Lehrbuch der Biologie. Chapter 05. GNU Free Documentation License Version 1.3. Retrieved March 26, 2021, from https://hoffmeister.it/index.php/biologiebuch

Horn, M. S., Crouser, R. J., & Bers, M. U. (2012). M.U. Tangible interaction and learning: the case for a hybrid approach. *Personal and Ubiquitous Computing, 16*, 379-389. Springer Nature. https://doi.org/10.1007/s00779-011-0404-2

Kislova, A. (2019). Hybrid Homework – Blending Blended Learning and Face to Face in four Undergraduated Programmes. In M. Brown, M. Nic Giolla Mhichil, E. Beirne, & E. Costello (Eds.), *Proceedings of the 2019 ICDE World Conference on Online Learning* (Vol. 1, pp. 511-520). Dublin: Dublin City University.

Kop, R., & Hill, A. (2008). Connectivism: Learning theory of the future or vestige of the past? *International Review of Research in Open and Distance Learning, 9*(3).

McMahon, J. H. (2008). *The Metaphysics. Aristotle translated by McMahon.* New York: Cosimo Classics.

van der Merwe, A., & Schoonwinkel, A. (2019). Student Access and Success through Hybrid Learning: A South African University's Business and Delivery Model. In M Brown, M. Nic Giolla Mhichil, E. Beirne, & E. Costello (Eds.), *Proceedings of the 2019 ICDE World Conference on Online Learning* (Vol. 1, pp. 981-989). Dublin: Dublin City University.

Olapiriyaku, K., & Scher, J. M. (2006). A guide to establishing hybrid learning courses: Employing information technology to create a new learning experience, and a case study. *The Internet and Higher Education, 9*(4), 287-301.

Opertti, R. (2021, February). *Ten clues for rethinking curriculum.* In-Progress Reflection No. 42. IBE/2021/WP/CD/42. 17-18. Geneva: UNESCO International Bureau of Education.

Opertti, R. (2021, March). *Education in a post-COVID world: Additional considerations.* No. 43. IBE/2021/WP/CD/43. 13-14. Geneva: UNESCO International Bureau of Education.

Roosevelt, Th. (2010). *World Class Diversity Management.* San Francisco: Berrett-Koehler Publishers.

Rühling, S., Schumann, C.-A., et al. (2010). Typology and Illustration of Generic Competencies in a Hybrid Learning Environment. In A. Szücs, & A.W. Tait (Eds.), *Media Inspirations for Learning. e-Proceedings: EDEN 2010 Annual Conference,* Valencia. Budapest: European Distance and E-Learning Network.

Rumelhart, D. E. (1978). *Schemata: The Building Blocks of Cognition.* Volume 79 of Technical report. University of California, San Diego. Center for Human Information Processing.

Sandweg, K. (2017, July 14). Lerntheorien: Wie lernen wir eigentlich? CogniFit [Blog post]. Retrieved March 20, 2021, from https://blog.cognifit.com/de/lerntheorien/

Schumann, Chr.-A., Marr, R., Mißbach, P., & Weber, J. (2016). Recognition Management for promoting and accelerating the academic careers of professional learners. *GUIDE Journal "Digital Universities: International Best Practices and Applications" ISSUE, 2016*(1), 3-16.Roma: GUIDE Association.

Schumann, C.-A. et al. (2019). Key role of modularization for new global pathways expanding access to multiple study programs. In M. Brown, M. Nic Giolla Mhichil, E. Beirne, & E. Costello (Eds.), *Proceedings of the 2019 ICDE World Conference on Online Learning* (Vol. 1, pp. 833-845). Dublin: Dublin City University.

Schumann, C.-A., Tittmann, C., & Tittmann, S. N., (2008). Merger of Knowledge Network and Users Support for Lifelong Learning Services. In *Learning to Live in the Knowledge Society* (pp. 149-152). Springer: Boston.

Siemens, G. (2005). Connectivism: A learning theory for the digital age. *International Journal of Instructional Technology and Distance Learning, 2*(1), 3-10.

UNESCO. (2021). *Most influential theories of learning. General Education System Quality Analysis/Diagnosis Framework (GEQAF).* Retrieved March 23, 2021, from http://www.ibe.unesco.org/en/geqaf/annexes/technical-notes/most-influential-theories-learning

Lessons from a Pandemic for the Future of Education
European Distance and E-Learning Network (EDEN) Proceedings
2021 Annual Conference | Madrid, 21-24 June, 2021
ISSN 2707-2819
doi: 10.38069/edenconf-2021-ac0010

REDESIGNING POST-GRADUATE COURSES FOR FUTURE MUSEUM EDUCATORS IN TIME OF A PANDEMIC: AN EXPERIENCE FROM UNIVERSITY ROMA TRE

Antonella Poce, University of Modena and Reggio Emilia, Maria Rosaria Re, Mara Valente, University Roma Tre, Italy, Francesca Amenduni, Eidgenössisches Hochschulinstitut für Berufsbildung, Swiss

Abstract

The present paper aims to illustrate the reorganization of the second year course "Standards for museum education" of the two-year post-graduate course "Advanced Studies in Museum Education" promoted by the CDM (Museum Education Centre) – Dept. of Education at University Roma Tre, that was carried out during the Covid-19 pandemic, and to analyse the educational strategies adopted in terms of museum educators' professional development to face the 2020 Covid-19 lockdown of Italian museums and universities. The results, taking into consideration the activities and digital tools proposed, show in university students the efficacy of the course reorganization, in terms of transverse and professional skills development, critical thinking and collaboration in particular. Moreover, the data analysis offers useful indications in terms of university online lectures, e-learning laboratory activities and practices, evaluation tools and methodologies aimed at promoting professional development of in-training museum educators in a university learning context.

Introduction

The Creative Industries Education context, such as museums, galleries, and libraries, presents a low emphasis on the use of new digital technologies, entrepreneurship promotion, digital abilities and transverse skills development (Poce, 2019; European Commission, 2017). Both newly graduates and existing employees, especially adult professionals, in fact, lack fundamental skills (OECD, 2018) for their future careers, consequently having less opportunities to improve their development and to add new forms of digital expression to their work (European Commission, 2018). However, the use of web, mobile, social, and analytical tools is becoming more and more popular in the field of Cultural and Creative Industries. These communication channels proved to be essential for cultural institutions in general, and museums in particular, to face the challenges posed by the current world-wide health emergency. In a report published on the EUR LEX website, the need for stronger partnerships between the cultural and creative sectors, social partners and education and training providers, both through initial training and continuous professional development was highlighted. Such closer connections should provide these sectors with the combination of skills needed for creative entrepreneurship in a rapidly changing environment.

The research context

Considering the above conditions, the CDM (Centre for Museum Studies) – based at Dept. of Education of University Roma Tre – has designed and provided a revised version of the second-year course "Standards for museum education" of the two-year post-graduate course aimed at the professional development of future Museum Educators, offered in a blended teaching mode (face-to-face – f2f – and online) on a dedicated platform.

The biennial course "Advanced Studies in Museum Education" is addressed to those interested in deepening the museum education theoretical references and those who wish to employ educational research methods in such a context: to analyse various categories of visitors' needs and to train on standards in museum education, that are set according to the results of the latest international research in the field. The course provides an international dimension to all its initiatives. Experts from the museum education field teach f2f classes (UCL, Loughborough Univ., Tate Modern, National Gallery – UK; Sorbonne – Fr; ICOM; Universidade Aberta – P; UNED, Murcia Univ. – SP; Smithsonian – USA). An academic year involved about 294 hours of f2f lessons, 217 hours of e-learning via the orbisdictus.it platform, 206 hours of internships and project works, 33 hours of guided visits and 750 hours of self-study. In terms of distance learning, online activities were divided into theoretical and multimedia teaching units, with assessments and educational support from teachers. Internship activities took place at partner companies (e.g. MOMa S.p.a. and CoopCulture) or at public or private museums in Italy and abroad (Poce & Iovine, 2015).

Methodology

From the beginning of March 2020, the spread of COVID-19 imposed an immediate reorganization of the post-graduate course. Even before the emergency, it was designed to promote students' digital, transverse and entrepreneurial skills. The mobilization of the world of culture – in particular of the one of cultural heritage – further encouraged the post-graduate course managing staff to create specific online teaching units aimed at understanding the current state of cultural heritage institutions and at figuring out which educational activities could have been effective for heritage institutions going massively online. The implementation and adaptation of the course contents were carried out together with the readjustment of the e-learning platform normally used for distance learning.

The VLE was re-designed to host a new section entirely dedicated to "extra" activities planned to deal with the emergency (see Table 1).

Table 6: Online activities to face the COVID-19 emergency within the post-graduate course

Enhanced online activities after the COVID-19	Institutions involved	Methodologies and tools
Videos with constant updatings on the course schedule	University Roma Tre	e-learning video-recordings
Video-interviews with entrepreneurial stakeholders (Museum, galleries and other CIs)	Italian Creative Industries stakeholders (Teleskill, Links, BSDesign, L'Erma, Eulotech, ETT)	e-learning video-recordings
Virtual Hands-on learning activities	UCL ARENA (UK)	e-learning, cooperative learning, group discussions and presentations.
New online module: - Cultural heritage education in the digital era; - How can museums become more entrepreneurial during the times of COVID-19; - How Italian museums provide virtual support to schools; - Building relationships through heritage - Educational research methodology - Museums and social networks	University of Graz; University of Prague, John Hopkins University; National Lottery Heritage Fund(UK); University Roma Tre	e-learning, cooperative learning, group discussions and presentations, OERs, project-based learning, problem based-learning, Social Networks.
Online internship and training activities: Design thinking and service design	University Roma Tre	e-learning, OERs, project-based learning, problem based-learning
External MOOC	OpenVM Erasmus+ project, DigiCulture Erasmus+ project; National Gallery Washington	e-learning, forums, OERs, textual resources, webinars.

The materials shared in the Orbis Dictus VLE are OERs which are considered powerful educational tools for various reasons: in our case, students and teachers can use these online resources without any cost or limit (Poce, Agrusti, & Re, 2015). OERs include periodically updated PDF files, streaming videos, apps, podcasts, assessment tests, quizzes, etc. available to students on the e-learning platform. A section of the VLE has been reserved for video-updates where students are periodically informed about the activities progress and how to proceed in the course completion. Another large section has been devoted to video-interviews with stakeholders working in the field of new technologies for the fruition of cultural heritage, museum services, and specialized publishing. The video contributions of experts have represented a resource of primary importance, as they created new chances of interaction and cooperation between students and Creative Industries, partner institutions of the course. As far as f2f teaching and learning is concerned, national and international experts and teachers involved in the post-graduate course training activities agreed in redesigning conventional lectures and adapting them to the new digital educational context, meeting the challenge and collaborating to outline redesigned online programs (see Table 2). The students interested in attending one of the modules proposed by the experts were involved according to the following model: introduction of the activity, presentation of the issue, task description and live sessions to discuss and elaborate on the topic. Students were in fact invited to join a virtual classroom on Microsoft Teams© and to participate in live sessions where group discussions, tasks performances, group activities and presentations were held.

Table 2: New modules and activities introduced in the e-learning mode

Title	Acronym	Introduction
Virtual Hands-on learning activities	OBL	Theoretical and practical lessons on object-based learning methodology
Cultural heritage education in the digital era	CHDE	Studying interactions between museums and social media users to understand the relationship between museums and digital audience and improve online communication
How can museums become more entrepreneurial during the times of COVID-19	MME	Strategies to make museums more entrepreneurial at the time of a pandemic
How Italian museums provide virtual support to schools	MVSS	In-depth studies and case studies on what kind of support museums can offer to Italian schools in the educational field and in the use of new digital technologies
Building relationships through heritage	BRH	The role of museums and heritage in supporting communities by building social capital and cohesion within the Covid19 pandemic context
Educational research methodology	ERM	The main methodological research guidelines in the educational field. Providing knowledge about the creation and use of the main tools for data collection in the museum didactics field as well
Museums and Social Networks	M&SN	Deeply investigating the activities of three selected museums on social networks during the Covid-19 pandemic to plan an educational-didactic activity to accompany the museum chosen out of the three in being spread through social networks.

Above all, a new perspective of the post-graduate course aimed at enhancing awareness and reflection on cultural heritage fruition and communication, as imposed by the ongoing pandemic, was promoted.

The renewed e-learning teaching modules offered a stronger possibility for the students to continue the undertaken path without interruptions or program changes. All the activities planned during the health emergency, as well as the live lessons, have been made optional, so that students were free to choose the courses that sparked more their interest and to carry out the activities that caught their attention the most.

The didactic modules carried out in e-learning, as mentioned above, consisted for a part of the study of materials provided by the teachers, proposals of practical activities usually organized in small groups through the use of online sharing and discussion platforms, and a live lesson by the teacher in which the theoretical subjects were further elaborated and the activities carried out by each group were discussed. The teachers gave their feedback on the work of the groups at the end of the live session, highlighting the positive aspects and pointing out what needed to be reviewed or modified; a Q&A session was planned for the last part of every lesson, in which, through questions asked to the professors, any doubt was clarified, and any in-depth analysis of the most interesting aspects was explored.

Data collection and data analysis

The main aim of the learning experience here presents is finding out how the kind of activities mentioned above could encourage 4C skills development, promoting teamwork and Cooperation, Creativity, Critical Thinking, and Communication among students. The post-graduate course managing staff and lecturers involved in the learning activities have designed the evaluation plan of the objectives achieved by the participating students as follows.

- Formative assessment activities: during the course, different assessment tools are used to monitor the level of knowledge acquisition and the transverse skills development. Two evaluation tools are used for formative assessment: a self-assessment survey of the skills developed (consisting of both open-ended and closed questions), filled in by the students at the end of each teaching module, and a closed-ended evaluation test to assess the level of knowledge acquired. The results of the self-assessment survey will be analysed through automatic qualitative and quantitative analysis programs, while the results of the closed-ended evaluation test will be analysed through statistical analysis tools.
- Summative assessment activities: students are asked to produce an empirical research project in the field of museum mediation and cultural heritage fruition. The research product was assessed by a group of lecturers and tutors of the course through a Critical Thinking Evaluation Rubric, already used and validated in previous research (Poce, 2017). The rubric is applied to see whether Critical Thinking skills improve. Moreover, a final evaluation survey of the course will be filled in by the students to evaluate the general course progress, the specific educational activities, and the tools and teaching methodologies used.

Results

- The group of students who took part in the learning experience attend the second year "Standards for museum education" of the two-year post-graduate course "Advanced Studies in Museum Education" at the University Roma Tre, Department of Education. In total, there are 17 students attending the second year of the post-graduate course. Of these, only 1 is a male student, while the rest is all female. The average age of the students is 30 years old and almost all of them have a master's degree in Art, while just a few of them are graduates in Archaeology or Pedagogical sciences.

The first module *Virtual Hands-on learning activities* (OBL) was attended by a total of 13 students, like the second one, *Cultural heritage education in the digital era* (CHDE); the third module, *How can museums become more entrepreneurial during the times of COVID-19* (MME), and the fourth one, *How Italian museums provide virtual support to schools* (MVSS), were attended by 9 students; the fifth module, *Building relationships through heritage* (BRH), was attended by 8 students; the sixth module *Educational research methodology* (ERM) was attended only by 1 student and the seventh module *Museum and Social Networks* (M&SN) was attended by 2 students. In addition to the feedback received from the teachers during the live session, students expressed their opinion about the activities and lessons through a self-assessment survey. From the results visible in the Figure 1, all the activities were judged in a generally positive way by the students.

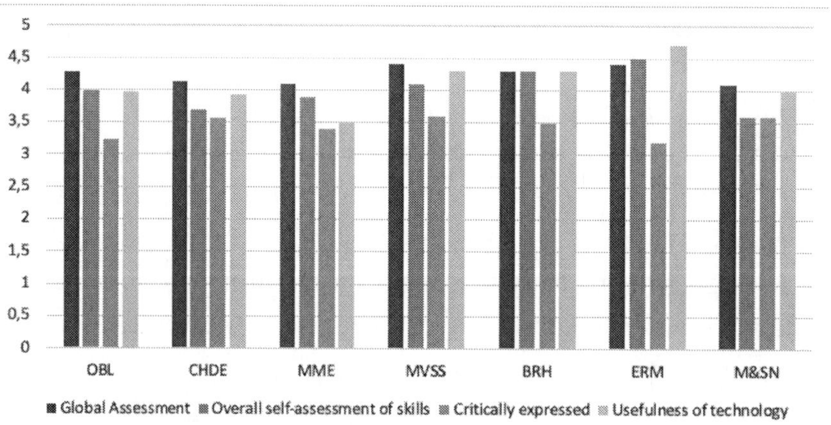

Figure 5. Evaluation results of course modules

With regards to the proposed activities' contents quality evaluation, it has registered most of the times, on a scale from 1 to 5 (1 = *lowest quality*; 5 = *highest quality*), a score equal to or higher than 4, highlighting therefore that the proposed modules have transmitted easily comprehensible contents, with a high relevance to the themes and objectives of the post-graduate course, a clear structure, contents and language used by the teachers, with an average level of difficulty attributed to the assignments and activities the students have carried out in groups; the clearness, exhaustiveness and effectiveness that distinguished the contents and documents used during the lessons were also judged highly.

Regarding the self-assessment of the acquired knowledge, the students stated with a medium-high score that they learned what they expected from the lessons. Their expectations were met through mostly gradual learning: they easily understood the activities assigned to them and the tasks that had to be carried out. As to the information shared by the teachers, it was perceived as adequately delivered and mostly not taken for granted, with the amount of content always proportioned to the lesson. The students also considered the lessons, and in particular the topics dealt with, so interesting as to encourage them to carry out further in-depth studies on the subject.

Analysing the increase of transverse skills, considered one of the main aims of the course, the most solicited skills have been: Creativity, Innovation, Communication, Critical Thinking, Attitude to Research and Collaboration. The students had a medium-high increase in the Problem-solving skill, Memory and Entrepreneurship. On a scale from 1 to 5, the average scores assigned to the activities have almost always exceeded the value of 4, thus attributing a much more than favourable judgement to them.

Concerning the self-assessment survey data, the use of technology, according to the students' opinion, has significantly increased motivation and personal involvement, greatly facilitating the collaborative and participatory aspects of teaching, considerably increasing the confidence with technological tools, thus improving the quality of online teaching thanks to the daily use of new tools and VLE, that support and facilitate the sharing of materials with other colleagues.

Discussion and conclusive remarks

The use of web, mobile, social and media tools proved to be essential for cultural institutions in general and museums in particular to face the challenges posed by the current world-wide health emergency. Thus, future museum educators need to develop a critical approach towards the use of digital mediation and communication tools in order to creatively adopt them in the museum learning path, including university museum exhibitions.

The present research has shown how, thanks to the critical use of technological and digital supports, it has been possible to entirely reorganize the activities of the second year of a biennial post-graduate course that normally includes face-to-face lectures, laboratory activities and practices at the museum. Everything has been made possible smoothly from home thanks to the infinite possibilities offered by the internet and in particular by the digital resources made available by museums. It is no coincidence that, just to mention an example, in the Virtual Hands-on learning activities module, the Object based virtual learning activities were made possible thanks to the use of the digital objects collection made available by the Patrie Museum of the University College of London.

Given the overall very encouraging results, especially if we take into consideration the evaluations given by the students themselves, it is possible to rethink a reorganization of the course that involves both in presence and at distance activities, that we plan to concretely experiment next autumn. It is surely necessary to promptly review the possibility of increasing the number of laboratory activities in e-learning, which have proved to be the most requested by the students. The same goes for encouraging critical reflection activities, maybe through collaborative project proposals linked to concrete and current scenarios, to be submitted periodically to the students, thus stimulating Collaboration, Entrepreneurship and Problem-solving skills that, according to the students themselves, should be strengthened.

Authors' statement

The authors of the present paper contributed to the writing of this article as follows: A. Poce (Introduction, The research context, Discussion and conclusive remarks), M. R. Re (Methodology), M. Valente (Results), F. Amenduni (Data collection and data analysis).

References

European Commission (2017). Europe's Digital Progress Report EDPR 2017. Retrieved from https://ec.europa.eu/digital-single-market/en/news/europes-digital-progress-report-2017

European Commission (2018). Digital Education Action Plan. Retrieved from https://eur-lex.europa.eu/legal-content/EN/TXT/?uri=COM:2018:22:FIN

Facione, P. (1990). *Critical thinking: A statement of expert consensus for purposes of educational assessment and instruction* (The Delphi Report). Millbrae, CA: California Academic Press.

Falk, J. H., Heimlich, J., & Bronnenkant, K. (2008). Using identity-related visit motivations as a tool for understanding adult zoo and aquarium visitors' meaning-making. *Curator: The Museum Journal, 51*(1), 55–79. doi:10.1111/j.2151-6952.2008.tb00294.x

Not, E., & Petrelli, D. (2018). Blending customisation, context-awareness and adaptivity for personalised tangible interaction in cultural heritage. *International Journal of Human-Computer Studies, 114*, 3-19. doi:10.1016/j.ijhcs.2018.01.001

OECD (2018). *Education at a Glance: OECD Indicators.* Paris: OECD Publishing.

Poce, A., Agrusti, F., & Re, M. R. (2015). Sviluppo di uno strumento di valutazione delle risorse aperte (Oers). *Cadmo, 2*, 81-98. doi:10.3280/CAD2015-002008

Poce, A., & Iovine, A. (2015). From cultural to socio-economic capital: lessons from a postgraduate course in 'standards for museum education'. In H. Chatterjee, & L. Hannan (Eds), *Engaging the Senses: Object-Based Learning in Higher Education* (pp. 177-191). London: Routledge.

Poce, A. (2017). *Verba Sequentur. Pensiero e scrittura per uno sviluppo critico delle competenze nella scuola secondaria.* Milano: Franco Angeli.

Poce, A. (2019). Information and data literacy skills development in Creative Industries Adult Education: the Digiculture project. *PEDAGOGIA OGGI, 17*(2), 184-201. doi: 10.7346/PO-022019-12

Lessons from a Pandemic for the Future of Education
European Distance and E-Learning Network (EDEN) Proceedings
2021 Annual Conference | Madrid, 21-24 June, 2021
ISSN 2707-2819
doi: 10.38069/edenconf-2021-ac0011

UNIVERSITY TEACHERS' DIGITAL EMPOWERMENT FOR BLENDED TEACHING: AN ONLINE TRAINING DESIGN

Pablo Baztan, Teresa Romeu, Montse Guitert, Marc Romero, Universitat Oberta de Catalunya, Spain

Abstract

Because of the impact of the pandemic in the different sectors of society, blended training solutions have acquired, in the field of education, an important relevance, speeding up a change that would normally require years to be developed.

Teachers from all levels of education had to adapt and develop their practices using digital technologies without enough knowledge to do it properly. Considering this context, this paper will present the design of an online training that seeks to empower university teachers to take advantage of the potential of digital technologies to design and implement educational practices in blended settings while they acquire Digital Competences. This training will be applied with a challenge-based learning methodology and from a collaborative perspective. In addition, participants will develop the role of students and teachers at the same time in order to design blended educational practices that respond to the needs of their own students.

The proposed training, that will be designed by teachers from the Open University of Catalonia with wide experience on training in Digital Competences and online teaching, will be implemented in 6 countries around Europe (Italy, Spain, Ireland, Greece, Cyprus and Finland), will be developed in the framework of the European project Empower Competences for Onlife Learning in HE (ECOLHE).

Introduction

The rapid and constant changes technology is experiencing and the changes it causes to different sectors of society require an updating of the understanding and knowledge about digital technology continuously. It is not enough anymore to have basic skills of using computers. In fact, the DigComp framework defined by the European Commission (Carretero Gomez et al., 2017) considers more complex dimensions such as information literacy, communication and collaboration or safety. Actual citizens must acquire these skills to properly develop their lives in the digital society, so education has an important role to provide it. This condition causes the need of teachers to develop these new skills, as the European Framework for Digital Competence of Educators, DigCompEdu highlights. This framework (Redecker & Punie, 2017) responds to the awareness of member states that educators need a set of specific digital skills for their work as teachers, in order to take advantage of the potential of digital technologies for improvement and innovation in education. The view from the teaching practice and intervention in the classroom becomes the key and responsible for the integral development of its students, both personally and professionally, in a cultural scenario dominated by digital technologies.

These skills take more relevance in the actual situation of a pandemic, which forced teachers to adapt to online and blended settings without having the necessary technical and methodological skills to do it.

Considering this context, the European project Empower Competences for Onlife Learning in HE (ECOLHE) (co-funded by the Erasmus+ Programme of the European Union) aims to examine the way in which the idea of an E-learning European HE Area has been translated into practice at national level by Academic Bodies. This project, which gathers a consortium from 6 EU partner countries (Italy, Spain, Ireland, Greece, Cyprus and Finland), is an action research project that aims to create the best conditions for an exchange of best practices, at European level, in:

- Teaching digital skills in HE;
- Training course for teachers and tutors for improving online teaching in HE in the logic of LLL, inclusion and innovation recalled by High-Level Group on the Modernization HE;
- Recognition and validation of teaching competences in HE for teachers' professional development and
- Recommendation for Academic Bodies.

This paper is focused on the second point, the background and design of the Training for teachers and tutors, seated on a "Training Pilot for online teaching in HE" to implement online training to empower educators to perform online/blended learning, more responsive to the qualitative dimensions of human interaction. This training will be designed by the Open University of Catalonia (UOC) partners, taking profit of the experience developed on training in Digital Competences and Online teaching for almost 25 years.

Training Pilot for online teaching in HE: background and objectives

Blended Learning (BL) is more than a combination of face-to-face and online elements. Following Armellini and Padilla (2021), "BL is an approach that incorporates a range of dimensions that interact with and shape one another in an educational intervention". They represent these dimensions in a cross chart, where any BL proposal can move integrating them in between each axis extremes. Some other dimensions that can be taken into account are, as example: Synchronous – Asynchronous, Individual work – Collaborative work, Peer assessed – Tutor assessed, etc.

The flexibility of this vision of BL allows and requires us to design a training in which participants can move along each axis. Therefore, different methodologies, sources and tools will be shared, opening the possibility to follow different paths to be engaged in BL, depending on the needs of each participant, with some of these possible routes illustrated with an active practice involving participants.

The training will have to empower teachers to be competent for the design, implementation and assessment of online/blended teaching activities through the improvement of their digital competences and promoting their professional development. This research adopts the definition of digital competence seated by Ferrari (2012) because of its openness and in context application:

> *"Digital Competence is the set of knowledge, skills, attitudes (thus including abilities, strategies, values and awareness) that are required when using ICT and digital media to perform tasks; solve problems; communicate; manage information; collaborate; create and share content; and build knowledge effectively, efficiently, appropriately, critically, creatively, autonomously, flexibly, ethically, reflectively for work, leisure, participation, learning, socialising, consuming, and empowerment".*

The training will be online, and it will be led by Universitat Oberta de Catalunya (UOC) that will prepare and manage directly the training modules considered essential for emerging teaching skills in the digital era. The rest of universities involved in the project participate firstly giving feedback about the global design and content, and secondly piloting the training within their universities: around 150 people totally 25 for each of the 6 study cases among teachers, researchers, PhD students, tutors and academic staff who are already involved in teaching innovation processes and who are therefore interested in updating their methodological digital and soft skills.

To achieve these objectives, the Training Pilot will regard the following activities:

- the training in digital competences for online teachers,
- the training for online teaching emerging methodologies,
- the training in soft skills and communicative skills for digital environments,
- the creation and dynamization of an international community of practice among teachers,
- provide tutorial for trainers, training materials (contents, resources, OER etc.) and
- generate a final evaluation and report to assess the overall piloting result.

During the four months dedicated to piloting, partner countries involved will have the opportunity to discuss the progress of the investigation. ECOLHE Moodle Platform will be the main tool through which partner countries will collaborate to the resolution of any question and to facilitate collaborative work.

After de Pilot implementation and its evaluation, the experience and outcome learnings will provide an innovative training model that can be replicable to other HE institutions to promote online teaching and key teaching competences in the digital era.

Training Pilot for online teaching in HE: design

One of the most frequently used Instructional Design strategies is the ADDIE framework. ADDIE consists of the following five phases: Analysing a learning situation, Designing objectives and principles to address the learning situation, Developing of resources, Implementing the learning resources in the learning situation, and Evaluating how these resources addressed instructional needs.

To develop the training proposal, the ADDIE framework is adopted twice, as a fractal in two different scales: as a guide to develop the training itself, and as a guide to develop each training activity. Figure 1 shows how ADDIE is applied to design the whole training:

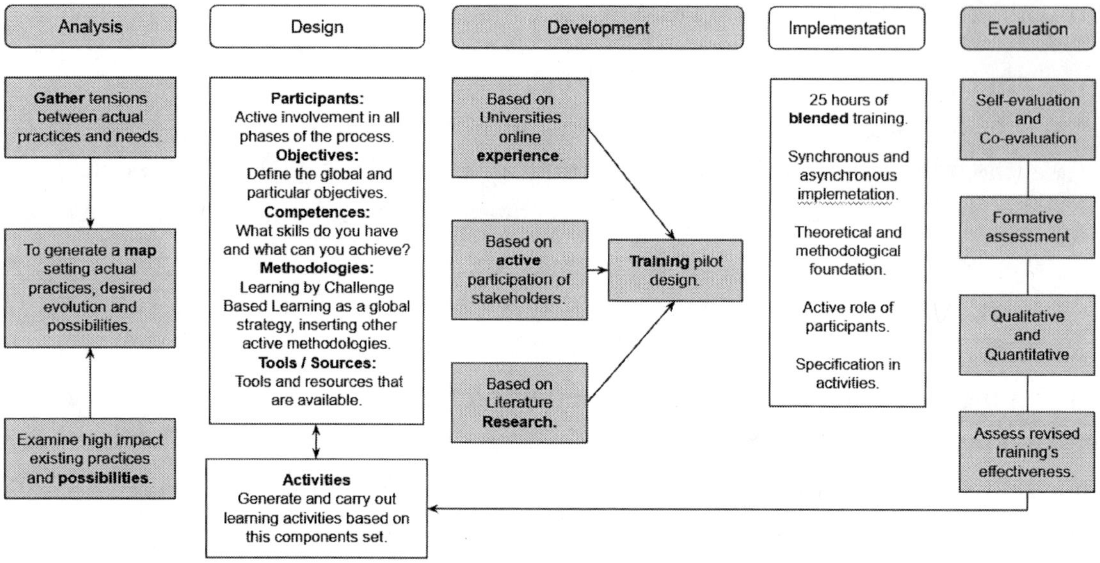

Figure 1. ADDIE model applied to the global training design. Own elaboration based on Nichols and Greer (2016)

Following the ADDIE model, and with the focus in design the training pilot description is specified below:

The main objective of the training is to update emerging digital competences for online and blended teaching in HE, for increasing teachers' ability in the use of digital technologies through online collaboration environments in HE.

Regarding the competences that participants will acquire, it is necessary to choose the ones they will develop when designing any training or activity. In this case, the proposal includes the Digital Competence as cross competence, and some specific competences related to blended teaching design and teaching strategies implementation.

We take DigComp.Edu as a competence framework for Digital Competence, and we choose some of the competences that this framework defines.

To provide space for reflection and practical application, Competences Areas and Competences from the DigCompEdu framework will be collaboratively selected for this training and associated with each activity. The areas of DigCompEdu that will be considered are the following:

- Professional engagement,
- Digital Resources,
- Teaching and Learning,
- Assessment,
- Empowering Learners,

- Facilitating Learners' Digital Competence.

The training will be developed through Challenge Based Learning (CBL). This methodology involves the definition of a solution to a real and very relevant situation linked to participants' environment, in this case involves the collaborative design, implementation and evaluation of a learning situation directly applicable to participants' teaching practice.

When developing their own activities, participants will choose specific methodology (such as Project Based Learning, Case Study or Problem Based Learning) from a wide range that will be described in the training guides.

Bearing in mind that the training will be conducted fully online, training activities will be developed in a Moodle environment and all contents will be presented with a set of digital and open educational resources (OER) organized by the competences of the training. Guides, tutorials, rubrics and other evaluation instruments will be also created.

The training presented will be designed and implemented following both macro and micro perspectives, as previously stated, there will be implemented as a training pilot in order to validate a training model that could be exported to other university contexts.

Training Pilot for online teaching in HE: development, implementation and evaluation

During the pilot, participants will be involved not only receiving theoretical training on online teaching, but also designing, implementing and evaluating their own online activities. A space for reflection and work based on the teaching practice will be created to acquire the teachers' digital competence. The training participants have an active role and will work collaboratively in teams, playing teachers' and students' roles in different phases of the training.

Regarding its planning, the training pilot is structured in different activities, two synchronous and four asynchronous, with a total workload of 25 hours.

Activities description

The activities of the training will be organised as follows:

Introduction – Synchronous

This activity, developed in a webinar format, will consist in a synchronous activity sharing the Training with the involved partners, including an introduction, training development, methodology, materials, etc.

Activity 1: Analysis of a learning activity – Asynchronous

During this activity, participants will analyse an online training proposal developed by UOC for students. In this activity, participants will work in collaborative groups, guided by a template and share their analysis with the rest of participants. This activity is focused on knowledge of a set of digital resources (OER) organized by the seminar competences.

Activity 2: Activity design – Asynchronous

In this activity, participants will apply what they will be learning during the training and will collaboratively design a blended learning activity addressed to their students.

Activity 3: Activity implementation – Asynchronous

Each university manages two of the designed learning activities playing two roles. As teachers implementing one of these activities, and as students performing the other activity designed by another group.

Activity 4: Activity evaluation – Asynchronous

Each group evaluates the implemented activities following an evaluation guide provided by UOC.

Conclusion and training evaluation – Synchronous

Involving all the participants, a final synchronous activity to evaluate the training pilot will be conducted.

The assessment of the pilot is based on continuous assessment and takes into account the different agents involved in the learning process. The teacher will provide feedback to participants during the seminar in order to guide their training process. Participants are also an active part of the assessment process performing self- and co-assessment activities. In addition, participants will assess the training itself.

References

Alammary, A., Sheard, J., & Carbone, A. (2014). Blended learning in higher education: Three different design approaches. *Australasian Journal of Educational Technology, 30*, 440-454.

Armellini, A., & Padilla Rodriguez, B. C. (2021). Active Blended Learning: Definition, Literature Review, and a Framework for Implementation. In Rodriguez, B. C., & Armellini, A. (Eds.), *Cases on Active Blended Learning in Higher Education* (pp. 1-22). IGI Global. http://doi:10.4018/978-1-7998-7856-8.ch001

Carretero Gomez, S., Vuorikari, R., & Punie, Y. (2017). *DigComp 2.1: The Digital Competence Framework for Citizens with eight proficiency levels and examples of use.* Luxembourg: Publications Office of the European Union.

Ferrari, A. (2012). *Digital competence in practice: An analysis of frameworks.* Seville: Joint Research Centre, Institute for Prospective Technological Studies. doi:10.2791/82116.

Nichols Hess, A., & Greer, K. (2016). Designing for Engagement: Using the ADDIE Model to Integrate High-Impact Practices into an Online Information Literacy Course. *Communications in Information Literacy, 10*(2), 264-282. https://doi.org/10.15760/comminfolit.2016.10.2.27

Redecker, C., & Punie, Y. (2017). *Digital Competence of Educators DigCompEdu.* Luxembourg: Publications Office of the European Union.

Lessons from a Pandemic for the Future of Education
European Distance and E-Learning Network (EDEN) Proceedings
2021 Annual Conference | Madrid, 21-24 June, 2021
ISSN 2707-2819
doi: 10.38069/edenconf-2021-ac0012

DIGITAL LEARNING ENVIRONMENT EMBEDDED IN A LARGER NATIONWIDE ONE: A CASE STUDY OF A HIGH SCHOOL

Cecilia Fissore, Department of Foreign Languages and Literatures and Modern Cultures, Francesco Floris, Marina Marchisio, Italy2Department of Molecular Biotechnology and Health Sciences, Sergio Rabellino, Computer Science Department, University of Torino, Italy

Abstract

The outbreak of COVID-19 and national measures undertaken to tackle the spread of the virus may cause significant disruption to the provision of education opportunities for learners and teachers. In Italy, most schools did not practice online teaching before the emergency, and in a short time head teachers, teachers, students had to face new technological tools and deal with a new type of teaching. The PP&S – "Problem Posing and Solving" – project offered to all Italian teachers and schools, for free, a way of carrying out Online Education through a nationwide integrated Digital Learning Environment (DLE). In this paper we present a case study of a high school that used one DLE for online teaching of the entire school, embedded in a larger DLE at national level. The goal of this research is to present the integrated DLE of the project and the reasons why this case study can represent an effective model for online teaching of a school under different dimensions (technological, human and pedagogical). The results show that the teachers and the school head agree with our point of view. Most teachers are very supportive of using one DLE and think that this facilitates students and collaboration among teachers. Being included in a larger project allows teachers to compare, collaborate and share experiences and materials with teachers from all over Italy, and to have continuous technical and training support.

Introduction

In the spring of 2020, 74% of the world's students, about 1.2 billion children from 186 countries, switched to Distance Learning, without most of the education systems being structured and prepared to support digital education. A survey conducted with 4,859 respondents in 40 countries shows that the majority of teachers (67%) did online teaching for the first time in their careers in the last year (School Education Gateway, 2020). The outbreak of COVID-19 and the necessary national measures undertaken to tackle the spread of the virus may cause significant disruption to the provision of education, training and mobility opportunities for learners and teachers. A year after the outbreak of the pandemic, there are many studies, research and reports that have been done at European level to try to learn from this crisis, during which technology is used on an unprecedented scale in education and training. The best known example is the Digital Education Action Plan to help ensure continuity in education and training activities and to adapt the related systems to the digital age (European Commission, 2020).

In Italy, the new school year 2020/21 began in September, after the highly emergency educational activities of the months from March to May 2020. Most schools did not practice online teaching before the emergency, and in a short time head teachers, teachers, students (and often their parents) had to learn how to use new technological tools and deal with a new type of teaching (in Italy often called "DaD – Didattica a Distanza" which means Distance Learning). In the design and implementation of Online Education, a decisive factor is the choice of the Digital Learning Environment (DLE) to be used. At the beginning of the pandemic emergency, this aspect was particularly delicate in Italy. Many schools were not digitally equipped and school staff were not sufficiently trained in this field, so each teacher independently chose the tool to be used for online teaching. This choice had the risk of confusing students with multiple different platforms and above all of encountering data privacy issues. In the following months, many platforms and digital tools were proposed by the Ministry of Education to support teachers in Online Education. In June 2020, the Ministry of Education published a decree that provided a reference framework for planning the start of school activities in September, asking schools to equip themselves with a school plan for integrated digital teaching. The Guidelines have provided indications to be adopted in case of need to contain the contagion or if it is necessary to suspend the teaching activities in presence again. One of the indications was precisely "the identification, by each school, of a platform that [...] ensures an easy performance of the synchronous activity and which is usable with any type of device or operating system" (MIUR, 2020). In this new school year, secondary schools are implementing almost exclusively online teaching.

The PP&S project (available at www.progettopps.it), headed by the Italian Ministry of Education, promotes since 2012 the training of teachers of secondary schools on innovative teaching methods through the use of digital technologies (Brancaccio et al., 2014). The PP&S project, intended for teachers of the STEM disciplines but opened in the emergency to teachers of all disciplines, offered for free to all Italian teachers of secondary schools and to all Italian schools the possibility of carrying out Online Education through an integrated DLE (Fissore, Floris, et al., 2020). For all teachers it also offered great support in the transition from face-to-face to online teaching, as well as a wide range of online training activities (Barana et al., 2020; Fissore, Marchisio, et al., 2020b). In March 2020, a high school in the city of Turin in northern Italy decided to use the PP&S platform for online teaching of the entire school, for all teachers and for all students. After a first positive experience, the choice of the platform was also confirmed for the school year 2020/21. The goal of this research is to present this case study and to answer the following research questions: What are the benefits of using one DLE at school level, embedded in a larger DLE at national level?

Online Education and the situation in Italy

In Italy, not many national reports have been made on the development of Online Education during the Covid-19 pandemic. Most of the investigations focused on the technological availability (PCs, mobile devices and internet connection) of teachers and students in order to investigate the worrying school dropout. In December 2020, the National Institute for Documentation, Innovation, Educational Research published a report on the teaching practices of teachers during the months of emergency teaching (INDIRE, 2020). Some of the topics covered in the survey were: Didactic strategies, Quality of the DaD and Training. According to this report, the teaching strategies most practiced by Italian teachers can be considered the transposition of traditional frontal teaching into distance teaching. Most of the teachers carried out "videoconferencing lessons" and "making resources available for study and exercises" to be carried out independently. A minority of teachers have experimented with laboratory practices. The teachers more inclined to a laboratory type teaching found higher levels of satisfaction than the other teachers. Teachers who had online training experiences during the lockdown underlined the need for training on digital skills and their willingness to bridge the technological gap to support learning processes.

In our opinion, distance learning and online teaching are not the same thing. Online teaching should not be a mere transfer of face-to-face lessons in synchronous online mode via web conference, and it cannot consist of a simple transmission of materials and tasks and exercises (Hodges et al., 2020). Online teaching is a form of teaching that consists of resources but also and above all asynchronous activities that are always available, which students can carry out when they can and when they prefer. In fact, online learning allows students to study from home respecting their own times and independently organizing the time schedule of the study. Resources and activities can be the result of the integration of different media to facilitate students' understanding and personalization based on each person's characteristics. The peculiarities of online teaching are: multimedia (use and integration of different techniques and tools); multimodality (presentation of a concept or carrying out an activity in different ways); granularity (design and development of content for micro topics); non-linearity (alternation of different tools and contents in a non-linear way); and interactivity. These characteristics require a rethinking in the choice of contents and materials to be used, which cannot always be replicated in the same way of face-to-face teaching.

An embedded DLE for online teaching

A fundamental ingredient for Online Teaching is the DLE, a virtual space useful for teaching, learning, developing digital skills, online activities in classroom-based, remote or blended settings. It comprises a human component, a technological component, and the interrelations between the two. The human component consists of one or more learning communities, whose members can be: teachers or tutors, students or learners together with their peers, the administrators of the online environment. The technological component includes a Learning Management System integrated with different tools. Within it, students can be provided with multiple resources and numerous synchronous and asynchronous online activities. The activities carried out by students can be evaluated, alone or in a group, and it is possible to monitor the students' actions on the platform and the learning objectives achieved. The DLE of the PP&S is based on a Virtual Learning Environment, VLE, a Moodle-learning platform, integrated with an Advanced Computing Environment, an Automatic Assessment System and a web conference system (Fissore, Marchisio, et al., 2020a). In the case study we study, the school had the opportunity to have a dedicated DLE for the whole school embedded in the larger nationwide one. In it, the following courses were created: courses for each teacher (of any discipline) for each class of students in which they teach; a course with all students for school communications and activities; and the courses of the departments for each discipline. This design was intended to recreate the school environment as much as possible, to facilitate the organization of activities and communications between teachers, students and between teachers and students, and to encourage collaborative teaching and learning. At the same time, the school's DLE joined the much larger DLE of the PP&S Project, shared by secondary school teachers from all over Italy. This allows the school to maintain its own entity but at the same time to be in contact with teachers from other schools, who have experience within the Project. Within the Teacher Community, where synchronous online training activities also take place, there are many materials for self-training, forums and database of materials for sharing between teachers. For this reason, in answering the research question we will alternate two dimensions: the school level (level 1) and the national level of the PP&S project (level 2). We believe that the use of one DLE for the school embedded in a larger nationwide DLE represents an effective model for online teaching of a school because it presents many benefits under different dimensions.

Technological dimension

In this case, level 1 and level 2 coincide because the school's DLE is embedded in the larger one of the PP&S and acquires all its characteristics. In particular, the following aspects are guaranteed.

- *System reliability*: Guarantee of the functioning of the platform even with large numbers of teachers and students connected at the same time. In addition, the head teacher and individual teachers do not have to worry about technical aspects related to setting up and maintaining the platform because they are guaranteed by the PP&S' technical staff.
- *Interoperability among various systems*: Use of the various integrations of the platform for educational activities.
- *Efficiency with respect to the resources invested*: The possibility of having a dedicated DLE available free of charge and the continuous advice of technical support, thanks to the fact that the project is promoted by the Ministry of Education.
- *Activated services*: E-mail assistance for the school (design of the DLE and for the resolution of problems in which the school acts as an intermediary between students/parents and technical support); assistance for teachers through the helpdesk and forum of the Teachers' Community (resolution of technical problems and support on the use of proposed technologies); assistance for the student (support in access problems and in using the platform).

Human dimension

- *Community of Teachers*: At level 2, teachers can: participate in multiple activities of continuous professional development (synchronous and asynchronous); improve digital skills; confront and collaborate with teachers from all over Italy and with trainers; and have a repository of materials and activities ready to use in their teaching. At level 1, teachers can easily interact and compare remotely with their colleagues, collaborate in the creation of activities and resources and exchange experiences and advice. In general, being part of a community helps teachers not to feel alone in the difficult task of learning new teaching tools and methodologies and the constant support of colleagues and trainers supports lifelong learning.
- *Community of students*: At level 1, the identity of students as belonging to the school does not fail. Students, being all placed in a unique virtual environment, feel part of a community, share the same experiences of using the platform and can discuss didactic activities and easily interact with each other and with the teacher. They can also develop digital skills and collaborate with their peers on the platform. In general, interactions and communications are safeguarded at the level of the individual student, at the class level and at the school level. For the moment, level 2

is not contemplated for this sub-dimension, but in the future interactions between students from different schools throughout Italy could be planned.

Pedagogical dimension

- *Environment born for collaborative teaching* (level 1 and 2 coincide): The design and development of Moodle are guided by the socio-constructivist teaching philosophy based on the concepts of constructivism, constructionism and social constructionism. Dual aspect of the role of the teacher: At level 2, the teacher within a community learns and collaborates with other teachers, experimenting with the use of the platform from a student's point of view. At level 1, teachers manage the DLE and make their students collaborate and learn by creating a learning community.
- *Interdisciplinarity* (level 1): the use of one DLE for all teaching subjects favours the conduct of interdisciplinary activities and the connection among different disciplines.
- *Automatic formative assessment in the various disciplines* (level 1 and 2 coincide): the didactic methodology of automatic formative assessment supports the learning process and the involvement of students, through immediate and interactive feedback (Barana et al., 2019).
- *Inclusion* (level 1 and 2 coincide): Thanks to the integration of the DLE with the highly accessible EasyReading font and the customization of activities and resources, the platform is accessible for all users (even those with specific learning disabilities).
- *Vertical curriculum* (level 2): The project includes first and second grade secondary school teachers who can exchange views with each other in order to encourage the development of a vertical curriculum.

Data and methodology

To answer the research question, the following data were used: data from the platform (number of teachers and students involved, number of courses created for the school); questionnaire to all teachers of the school; and interview with the school head teacher. The questionnaire submitted to the teachers was divided into three parts: general data of the teacher and involvement within the project; reflections on online teaching (characteristics of online teaching, types of teaching activities and tools used); use of DLE PP&S for the whole school (possibilities offered by the platform to students, teachers and the school; technical support and open questions on significant teaching experiences and comments). The interview with the school head instead analysed the motivations and strengths in the choice of adopting one DLE for the whole school (in particular that of the PP&S) and particularly significant aspects (satisfactions, difficulties encountered, appreciation, etc.)

reported by teachers and students. After extracting the data from the platform, the questionnaires were analysed according to the model proposed in the previous paragraph and extracts from the interview were reported to the school header.

Results

The numbers of the high school within the PP&S Project are: 117 teachers of different subjects (some of them enrolled in the project since before the pandemic); 1604 students (from grade 9 to grade 13); 590 courses (1 course for the student community, 8 courses for departments and 581 courses for teaching activities). The departments of the school are natural sciences, physical education, religion, foreign languages, literature, mathematics and physics, philosophy and history, drawing and art history. 55 teachers from different subjects answered the questionnaire: natural sciences (11%), religion (5%), foreign languages (11%), literature (25%), mathematics and physics (32%), philosophy and history (11%), drawing and art history (5%). 79% of the teachers who answered were female. The average age of the teachers is 54 and on average they have been teaching for 25 years. 25% of the school teachers were enrolled in the PP&S project even before the pandemic emergency, all of them from scientific disciplines. Of these, the majority (71%) have been enrolled in the project for more than three years. As also emerged from the INDIRE report, the teachers who answered the questionnaire organized the teaching activities in a mainly synchronous mode (18% in completely synchronous mode and 62% mainly in synchronous). 14% of teachers in equal mode between synchronous and asynchronous and 4% in completely asynchronous mode. This result may be due to the fact that most of the teachers used the DLE for online teaching for the first time. The teachers evaluated the support received to facilitate online teaching (on a scale from 1 = *not at all* to 5 = *very much*) with the following average scores: from the technical staff via email (3.3), from the technical staff via HelpDesk (3.0), from tutors through forums (3.2), from tutors through online synchronous training meetings (3.2), from other teachers through forums (2.9) and from other teachers through the sharing of material (2.8). They positively assessed the aspects concerning the technological dimension, slightly less those relating to the human component. This may be due to the fact that becoming part of a community of teachers in a period of strong emergency has not been easy for some teachers, especially those of non-scientific disciplines that are less represented within the community. Using the same scale, the teachers evaluated the support received to facilitate online teaching in terms of: search for innovative solutions to better achieve the educational objectives (2.8), customization of the virtual learning environment (2.7), creation of resources and activities (3.0), resolution of problems related to use and access to the platform (3.0). The teachers reflected on the human dimension of the community of teachers and students, and they assessed with the same scale as before how much the DLE allows for different aspects for both communities (Table 1).

Table 1: Reflections of teachers on the human dimension a level 1 of the community of teachers and students

DLE allows students to:	Mean	Dev.St.	DLE allows teachers to:	Mean	Dev.St.
Easily have all teaching materials available	3.9	1.0	Participate together with colleagues in training activities	2.6	1.0
Be part of a learning community	3.0	1.1	Develop digital skills	3.2	0.9
Carry out different types of synchronous and asynchronous activities	3.5	1.0	Collaborate in the creation of activities and resources	3.1	1.0
Having a learning environment that recreates the school environment	2.6	1.0	Discuss the activities carried out with students	2.9	1.1
Interact with your peers	2.4	0.9	Share activities and resources	3.2	1.0
Interact with the teacher	2.7	0.9	Sharing reflections and ideas	2.8	1.1

As for the students, teachers agree that the platform contributes to the creation of a learning community and that it is easy for students to find teaching materials and carry out different types of activities. Surely the DLE will never be able to recreate the school environment and the interactions that teachers and students are used to in face-to-face teaching. This may explain the slightly lower scores in the latter aspects. As for the Community of Teachers, the teachers agree that the DLE allows to: collaborate in the creation of activities and resources; sharing activities and resources and considerations, experiences, ideas on teaching activities; discuss the activities conducted with students and develop digital skills together. 82% of teachers answered yes to the question: "Is the use of a unique platform for the whole school a strength?". Some of the most significant reasons were: "Because the use of multiple platforms is very dispersive", "Yes, because it is easier for students to use the same mode with different subjects", "It gives students and teachers an idea of school as a community and allows support between colleagues", "Facilitates interactivity between teachers and students". Some of the motivations of the teachers who answered no were: "It is necessary to be able to use different platforms, in order to choose the ones that have the greatest potential", "Different teaching subjects need different tools". The most significant impressions and opinions of students on the use of the platform for online teaching reported by the teachers were: "Some students use the platform without problems. Other students ask to return to "traditional" lessons", "Learners find the platform very useful for practicing tests with formative assessment or for repeating the tests even an unlimited number of times", "In the beginning there was concern about the possibility of overloading tasks, now they consider it a valid subsidy". Finally, some of the difficulties in using the platform reported by the teachers were: "Initially, it is necessary to be available for training and experimentation, also through trial, error and other attempts.", "At the beginning, due to my lack of knowledge of the platform". 25% of the teachers said there were no difficulties. According to the school head, the choice of one digital environment allows the development of knowledge and use of multimedia technologies and facilitates the transition from a more transmissive traditional teaching to experimentation with different and innovative teaching methods. It also allows the school to invest in teacher training in a homogeneous way and aimed at the shared use of the digital tool and to provide a "common ground" for comparison, support and exchange of experiences and materials. A number of teachers highlighted various initial difficulties with regard to the new technologies proposed. In this sense, online training and tutoring were highly appreciated and favoured the use of the platform. The school head would advise all colleagues to use one platform, presenting it to the school as a precious opportunity and not as an obligation. It involves investing in technical and professional resources and in the training of teachers to support the development of innovation in teaching methodologies through the use of new technologies that are best suited to support teaching paths that offer the best learning opportunities of disciplinary, transversal, digital and inclusive skills for all students.

Conclusions

A case study of the use of one DLE by the whole school embedded in the PP&S nationwide DLE was presented. We discussed the integrated DLE of the project and the reasons why this case study can represent an effective model for online teaching of a school under different dimensions (technological, human and pedagogical). The results show that the teachers and the school head agree with our point of view, especially for the first two dimensions. Most teachers are very supportive of using one DLE and think that this facilitates students and collaboration among teachers. Being included in a larger project allows teachers to exchange views, collaborate and share experiences and materials with teachers from all over Italy, without feeling alone in the learning process. In this context, the teachers greatly appreciated the technical support guaranteed by the project and the various training opportunities offered. Most of the teachers joined the project after the start of the pandemic, in an emergency period. Probably for this reason they have not fully understood the potential of DLE. The analysis presented will be deepened by dividing the teachers between humanities and scientific subjects to study teaching strategies and compare them. Doing online teaching now definitely allows teachers to acquire new skills and to prepare teaching materials that can be used in future teaching. Online teaching should be understood as an additive and not a substitute paradigm for classroom teaching.

References

Barana, A., Fissore, C., & Marchisio, M. (2020). From Standardized Assessment to Automatic Formative Assessment for Adaptive Teaching. *Proceedings of the 12th International Conference on Computer Supported Education*, 285-296. https://doi.org/10.5220/0009577302850296

Barana, A., Marchisio, M., & Rabellino, S. (2019). Empowering Engagement through Automatic Formative Assessment. *Proceedings of the 2019 IEEE 43rd Annual Computer Software and Applications Conference (COMPSAC)*, 216-225. https://doi.org/10.1109/COMPSAC.2019.00040

Brancaccio, A., Demartini, C. G., Marchisio, M., Pardini, C., & Patrucco, A. (2014). The PP&S computer science project in school. *Mondo Digitale, 13*(51), 565-574.

European Commission. (2020). *Communication from the Commission to the European Parliament, the council, the European economic and social committee and the committee of the regions.* Digital Education Action Plan 2021-2027: Resetting education and training for the digital age (COM/2020/624 final).

Fissore, C., Floris, F., Marchisio, M., Rabellino, S., & Sacchet, M. (2020). Digital competences for educators in the Italian secondary school: A comparison between DigCompEdu reference framework and the PP&S project experience. *Proceedings of the International Conference E-Learning 2020*, 47-54.

Fissore, C., Marchisio, M., & Rabellino, S. (2020a). Online tutoring through an integrated platform to support learning Mathematics at lower secondary school. *Proceedings of International Conference E-Learning 2020*, 71-78.

Fissore, C., Marchisio, M., & Rabellino, S. (2020b). Secondary school teacher support and training for online teaching during the covid-19 pandemic. *European Distance and E-Learning Network (EDEN) Proceedings*, 311-320.

Hodges, C., Moore, S., Lockee, B., & Trust, T. (2020). The Difference between Emergency Remote Teaching and Online Learning. *Educause review, 27*, 1-12.

INDIRE. (2020). *Indagine tra i docenti italiani: Pratiche didattiche durante il lockdown—Report integrativo dicembre 2020.*

MIUR. (2020). *Adozione del Documento per la pianificazione delle attività scolastiche, educative e formative in tutte le Istituzioni del Sistema nazionale di Istruzione per l'anno scolastico 2020/2021.*

School Education Gateway. (2020). *Sondaggio sull'apprendimento online e a distanza: Risultati.* Retrieved from https://www.schooleducationgateway.eu/it/pub/viewpoints/surveys/survey-on-online-teaching.htm

Lessons from a Pandemic for the Future of Education
European Distance and E-Learning Network (EDEN) Proceedings
2021 Annual Conference | Madrid, 21-24 June, 2021
ISSN 2707-2819
doi: 10.38069/edenconf-2021-ac0013

DIGITAL STORYTELLING IN MUSEUM EDUCATION CONTEXT: HOW TO PROMOTE CRITICAL THINKING SKILLS THROUGH DIGITAL TOOLS WITHIN SECONDARY SCHOOL PUPILS

Maria Rosaria Re, Department of Education, University Roma Tre, Italy

Abstract

The present paper aims to analyse the use of Digital Storytelling (DST) methodology in museum education context for the development of Critical Thinking (CT) skills within secondary school pupils. Starting from a brief literature review about CT promotion and cultural heritage education, an overview of active learning methodologies used in museum education for CT development is introduced. Moreover, the paper presents the first data obtained from a quasi-experiment carried out at the Galleria Lapidaria in the Capitolini Museums in Rome, which is focused on the use of DST for the promotion of CT skills for secondary school pupils within an integrated formal and informal education path.

Critical thinking and Heritage Education

Given the inclusion of Critical Thinking (CT) as a fundamental transverse competence for the cognitive and personal growth of the learner and the contemporary citizen (Dewey, 1910; OECD, 2005; P21, 2007; Trilling & Fadel, 2009, Griffin et al., 2012; Poce, 2018), formal and informal education has become interested in the definition of strategy, methodologies, experiences and tools useful for the above-mentioned competence, developing, also, diversified and interdisciplinary forms and learning experiences within different education contexts. For some years, heritage education, in particular museum education, has implemented a series of empirical experiences in which the work of art has been placed at the centre of sensory and intellectual experiences aimed at soliciting analysis, reflection, interpretation, both individual and group, skills as well as personal and creative reinterpretation.

The relationship between humanist and artistic culture and the promotion CT skills in formal education is well discussed by Martha Nussbaum in her work *Not for profit: Why Democracy Needs the Humanities* (2010). The interference of the economic profit in the field of education has led, according to the author, to a scientific shift in the educational paths of the globalized world, which identify in the development of technical-scientific knowledge and skills the most important tool to technological, economic, and social development. On the contrary, the strong limitation in the educational field of humanist culture hinders social development, especially in a democratic sense: "intellectual capacities for reflection and critical thinking are fundamental to keep democracies alive and well" and to allow them to "face, in a responsible way, the problems that await citizens as parts of an interdependent world" (Nussbaum, 2010; pp.42-43). The emphasis in Nussbaum's study on the connection between the education of the critical citizen and the enjoyment of the arts, literature, and music, defined as essential in any educational system, consolidates the relationship between individual's well-being and humanist education and determines its urgency from a pedagogical point of view.

The literature on the promotion of CT skills in museum education contexts confirms how museums are to be considered as places of learning suitable for the acquisition of knowledge in a critical way, "because they seem to be places that naturally encourage people to do the kind of things that characterize constructivist learning theory: explore and discover their own interests, interact with numerous stimuli and use their background and previous knowledge as explicit reference frameworks for building knowledge" (Tishman et al., 2007; p.3). The museum and the works of art have an impact on the pupils' cognitive capacities for reflection, as well as on their affective abilities (Terrassa et al., 2016; p.13): the aesthetic experience allows for continuous and reasoned reflection, comparative analysis of information, construction of solutions to complex problems. The relationship with a new museum object activates knowledge already acquired in order to interact with it and build reasoned and as correct inferences as possible (Ritchhart, 2007).

In the field of museum education, the promotion of CT is often link to the promotion of creative thinking (Foley, 2014), although the differences between the two constructs are still substantial: the imaginative and the unexpected are the prerogative of creative thinking, logic, rationality and analysis are typical characteristics of CT (Forrester, 2008). Encouraging the development of CT can prevent the user from being manipulated, thus allowing his/her intellectual independence and the development of creativity and innovation (Browne & Keely, 1993; Mayfield, 1997; Paul, 1995).

Although the definitions of CT used in museum education contexts are different, artistic education and cultural heritage education agree on the need to promote these skills both through activities aimed at a specific audience and by generally stressing their function within the educational role of museums (Smith, 2007).

Effective learning methodologies for CT promotion through museum objects

In the museum context, the learning methodologies defined more congruent with the new idea of transverse skills promotion, especially CT, are those concerning interactivity, both in terms of relationship with the object (hands-on methodology) and with other users (cooperative learning) (Macdonald, 2006; p.322). Marstine (2006) states how the changes in the design of educational paths in museums have led to the new definition of the visitors' experience, now describable in social, immersive and participatory terms: "In educational terms, all this indicates the objective of creating a space for participatory experience, which can lead to moments of self-realization by the visitor" (Marstine, 2006; p.135).

Since Willingham's definition (2008), for which CT implies "thinking in a detached way, demanding that statements be supported by evidence" and also "seeing all parts of a problem and being open to new evidence that does not confirm one's ideas" (p.21), museum and heritage education experiences highlight the need to use discussion groups to improve important cognitive skills, such as interpretation, comparison between different points of view and information, reflections review (Terrassa et al., 2016; p.23). The detailed planning of the educational experience, especially if aimed at promoting reflection and analysis skills, is essential in an educational environment that, not being the traditional classroom environment, could lead to a series of problems, especially logistical ones (Behrendt & Franklin, 2014).

Hands-on and Object Based Learning (OBL) are particularly effective for the promotion of CT skills, especially in artistic and cultural heritage contexts (Hubard, 2011). In the last two decades, OBL has been widely used as a learning strategy from secondary school to adult education contexts (Wiley, 2000; Paris, 2002; Lane & Wallace 2007). However, as Poce (2018) points out, even in primary education, hands-on object manipulation is quite widespread, despite numerous studies demonstrating its efficacy, especially in terms of deeper knowledge acquisition (Triona et al., 2005, Krontiris-Litowitz, 2008).

A further learning strategy defined effective by the literature in the field is Visual thinking (VT), linked to group discussion activities and Inquiry-based learning approach (Hubard, 2011). Although generally associated with STEM education (Audet & Jordan, 2005), Inquiry-based learning allows pupils to get involved in the discovery and construction of new knowledge, promoting a range of cognitive skills and mental dispositions that support this acquisition. Teachers and museum educators promote a critical observation of the museum object, asking pupils to dwell on certain details, to make inferences and to arrive at interpretations, thus promoting VT. Housen showed that the use of VT for CT promotion is associated with creative and aesthetic thinking development (Housen, 2001).

Storytelling can also be an excellent strategy for promoting CT in cultural heritage education context: works of art, such as paintings and sculptures, can be defined as tools through which the artist has deployed his need to recount events and emotions. Storytelling pedagogy places communication at the centre of the educational process: the understanding of messages of different genres and complexity takes place using various languages (verbal, symbolic) and through different media (paper, computer and multimedia). From these assumptions, the classic action of storytelling has further developed into an innovative learning strategy, Digital Storytelling (Meadows, 2003), which involves the creation of a story through technological tools. The methodology of Storytelling foresees a close relationship with the museum object that supports the motivation of pupils participating in learning (Grever et al., 2012). The involvement of the museum users is long-term, whether the museum is narrated directly (Storytelling about the museum), indirectly (Storytelling about a museum object or collection) or participatory (Storytelling created by a group of visitors and entered into the museum display).

Starting from these assumptions, the following paragraph will present the research questions, methodologies and results of a part of the research project *Nomina sunt consequentia rerum* which has seen the realization of Digital Storytelling activities to encourage the stimulation of CT and creativity within the context of Galleria Lapidaria of Capitolini Museums in Rome.

The quasi-experiment "Nomina sunt consequentia rerum" and the realization of Digital Storytelling products

Research questions and methodology

The project *Nomina sunt consequentia rerum* was designed and realized for secondary schools pupils who are not studying the Latin language as part of their educational path. It has been defined by starting from the particular characterization of the Latin inscriptions: the combination of artistic, historical and textual values contained in the epigraph makes this object potentially effective for the promotion of CT. The quasi-experiment was conceived starting from the following research questions:

- Can CT be developed in an epigraphic museum context?
- Does contact with the Latin inscription facilitate the promotion of language skills, analysis and reflection?
- Can active learning methodologies support the acquisition of Latin inscription knowledge and the promotion of CT skills?

Two upper secondary schools in the province of Rome participated in the experimentation, including a total of 144 pupils. This group was then split with 86 pupils participating in the empirical activities and 58 pupils taking part in the control group. Part of the experiment was carried out at the Lapidary Gallery in the Capitolini Museums in Rome, where the experimental classes participated in educational activities on site aimed at the interpretation of selected Latin inscriptions.

The educational path for the promotion of CT skills has been constructed on three main activities:

- a first meeting, realized at school, using the methodology of VT and deploying inductive and cooperative learning strategies, placed the pupils in relation to Latin inscriptions;
- a second meeting, at the Lapidary Gallery of the Capitolini Museums, was carried on through OBL methodology, thus developing activities of reading, analysis and interpretation of selected Latin inscriptions;
- a third meeting, which took place at school, was defined as a mini-workshop of DST and was addressed to collaboratively realize a digital storytelling video.

More specifically, during the third meeting, the pupils, divided into groups, selected one of the Latin inscriptions analysed during the museum-based activities. The inscriptions were made available to the pupils through a shared Google Drive folder: the pictures of the inscriptions were accompanied by the transcription of the Latin text and its translation into Italian. The pupils were also provided with a *Storyboard template* in which they wrote the collaborative creative narrative. Depending on the digital tools provided by the schools, the pupils' groups wrote on digital support (tablets) or paper. The choice to create a mini workshop on DST is aimed at promoting pupils' CT skills, as well as solicitating other transverse skills associated with the activity, such as communication, through different types of support (digital and paper), creativity, through the creative narrative writing activity, and collaboration, given the group activity (see Liguori & Bakewell, 2019).

In total, 13 short stories and 13 DST videos were realized within the project. Participating pupils showed great interest in the activity, finishing the task in time and producing a video linked to the indications set out at the beginning of the task.

DST evaluation tool

The DST videos were evaluated through an evaluation grid designed ad hoc for the learning activity. The evaluation tool, adapted from the one presented in Poce (2015), is composed by eight different indicators for a maximum of 20 points in total, as follows.

Table 7: The DST evaluation grid

Indicators	Descriptors	Scores
Relevance of the topic	Deep and reworked content development Relevant and substantially content development Lack of relevance and/or content	High – 3 Average – 2 Low – 1
Narrator and focus	The choice of the narrator is consistent with the structure of the story and focus The use of focus and the choice of the narrator are not always consistent The use of focus and the choice of the narrator are not consistent, the relationship between them is too confusing or wrong.	High – 2 Average – 1 Low – 0
Structure	The structure of the story is clear, and the stages of narration have a purpose within the story. The structure of the story is a bit chaotic but still defined in different stages. The structure lacks definition, the phases are confused, and the purpose is unclear.	High – 2 Average – 1 Low – 0
Setting	There is a description of the place, adequate and related to the content of the story. The description of the place is not very definite and is poorly linked to the content of the story. Within the story there is almost no description of the place in which the narrative takes place.	High – 2 Average – 1 Low – 0
Characters	The characters are accurately described and their role in the story is well defined. The characters are described fairly flat and evenly, without the right weight being given to their role. The characters are almost totally lacking in description.	High – 2 Average – 1 Low – 0
Form and expression	Always correct form and smooth propensity. Rich and functional language Form and expression with some errors. Generic but rather functional language. Numerous errors in morphology, syntax, punctuation, spelling; expression not fluent. Neglected and improper language.	High – 3 Average – 2 Low – 1
Originality and creativity	Processes the topic with confidence, accuracy, high creativity and provides valid personal interpretations The elaboration is essential and summary. It presents discrete elements of originality and creativity Lacks originality, creativity and reworkability.	High – 3 Average – 2 Low – 1
Quality of digital production	The sounds, images and video effects are of good quality, appropriate to the content of the elaborated story and consistent. The sounds, images and video effects are sometimes randomly inconsistent with the text or not very functional for use. Sounds, images, and video effects do not support the enjoyment of digital production and/or are inconsistent	High – 3 Average – 2 Low – 1

All the videos (No. 13) made by the groups of pupils participating in the empirical activities of the project were evaluated using the above grid by one external evaluator.

Analysis and results

From a first data analysis, all the evaluation indicators reach or exceed the sufficiency score for each digital product realized. The central trend measurements of the 8 indicators show a position of the mode, mean and median scores at the top of the distribution and a presence of the standard deviation contained or absent.

Table 2: Central trend measures of evaluation indicators

	Relevance	Narrator and focus	Structure	Setting	Characters	Form and expression	Originality and creativity	Quality of digital production
Mode	2.62	2.00	1.69	2.00	1.62	2.46	2.92	2.69
Mean	3	2	2	2	2	2	3	3
Median	3	2	2	2	2	2	3	3
Dev.St.	0.51	0.00	0.48	0.00	0.51	0.52	0.28	0.48

The frequencies of high scores tend to be higher than those of medium scores. No low scores at all: this data confirms a satisfactory achievement of the objectives by the pupils in terms of consistency, digital processing, use of the language and personal interpretation of DST video. The content macro-indicator sees high scores assigned to all the papers evaluated in relation to *Setting* and *Narrator and Focus* indicators. The groups of pupils participating in the experiment have realized storyboards that are exhaustive from a narrative and content point of view, with particular attention to the key elements of the narrative.

Conclusion

The definition, realization, evaluation and implementation of museum education paths aimed at stimulating transverse competences are currently some of the most urgent priorities in terms of Lifelong learning promotion through heritage. The realization of the quasi-experiment *Nomina sunt consequentia rerum* is aimed at identifying learning strategies, tools and methodologies effective in terms of Latin inscriptions understanding for CT development within secondary school pupils. The mediation of museum objects that are complex from the point of view of content and interpretation is also a contemporary challenge, because of the solicitation of skills and dispositions that are pivotal in the complex globalized world in which secondary school pupils operate.

The first results from the DST workshop carried out within the research demonstrated the activity was generally successful: pupils were able to combine elements of creative storytelling, linguistic expression and digital tools and realize DST videos. Participating pupils showed that they were able to interpret the information linked to Latin inscriptions in an critical and original way, elaborating accurate and coherent narrative texts. The achievement of these results in a collaborative way underlines the effectiveness of DST methodology for the group re-elaboration of artistic and cultural heritage, supporting the realization of a common and shared construction of new interpretations of museum objects. Data analyses highlight that pupils' CT skills was solicited through DST activity also within the Lapidary Gallery in the Capitolini Museums in Rome: the mediation of Latin inscriptions contents through specific active learning methodologies facilitated analysis, reflection and language skills within not-specialized users, together with collaboration and creativity.

Although, given the project characteristics and evaluation methods, generalizations are not possible: the research results suggest the need for more experimentation in the field of CT development within heritage education context, in order to promote and stimulate transverse competences, knowledge and skills, which could be used in different educational contexts and for different category of users.

References

Audet, R. H., & Jordan, L. K. (Eds.) (2005). *Integrating Inquiry across the Curriculum.* Thousand Oaks, CA: Corwin.

Behrendt, M., & Franklin, T. (2014). A Review of Research on School Field Trips and Their Value in Education. *International Journal of Environmental and Science Education, 9*(3), 235-245.

Browne, N., & Keely, S. (1993). *Asking the Right Questions: A guide to critical thinking.* Englewood Cliffs, New Jersey: Prentice-Hall.

Dewey, J. (1910). *How we think.* Boston: DC Heath and Company.

Foley, C. M. (2014). Why creativity? Articulating and championing a museum's social mission. *Journal of Museum Education, 39*(2), 139-151.

Forrester, J. (2008). Thinking creatively; Thinking critically. *Asian Social Science, 4*(5), 100-105.

Grever, M., de Bruijn, P., & van Boxtel, C. (2012). Negotiating historical distance: Or, how to deal with the past as a foreign country in heritage education. *Paedagogica Historica, 48*, 873-887.

Griffin, P., McGraw, B., & Care, E. (2012). *Assessment and Teaching of 21st Century Skills.* Dordrecht: Springer Netherlands.

Housen, A. C. (2001-2002). Æsthetic thought, critical thinking and transfer. *Arts and Learning Research, 18*(1), 99-132.

Hubard, O. (2011). Rethinking Critical Thinking and Its Role in Art Museum Education. *The Journal of Aesthetic Education, 45*(3), 15-21.

Krontiris-Litowitz, J. (2008). Using manipulatives to improve learning in the undergraduate neurophysiology curriculum. *Advances in Physiology Education, 32*(1), 81-5.

Lane J., & Wallace A. (2007). *Hands On: Learning from Objects and Paintings. A Teacher's Guide.* Glasgow: Scottish Museums Council.

Liguori, A., & Bakewell, L. (2019). Digital Storytelling in Culture and Heritage Education: a Pi-lot Study as Part of the DICHE Project. In Poce, A. (ed.) *Studi Avanzati di Educazione Muselae.* Napoli: ESI.

Macdonald, S. (Ed.) (2006). *A companion to museum studies.* Malden: Blackwell.

Marstine, J. (Ed.) (2006). *New Museum Theory and Practice. An Introduction.* Malden: Blackwell Publishing.

Mayfield, M. (1997). *Thinking for Yourself: Developing critical thinking skills through reading and writing.* Belmont, CA: Wadsworth Publishing Co.

Meadows, D. (2003). Digital storytelling: Research-based practice in new media. *Visual Communication, 2*,189-193.

Nussbaum, M. (2010). *Not for profit. Why Democracy Needs the Humanities.* Princeton: Princeton University Press.

OECD (2005). *The definition and selection of key competencies.* Executive Summary. Retrieved from http://www.oecd.org/pisa/35070367.pdf

P21 (2007). *Framework for 21st Century Learning.* Retrieved from http://www.p21.org/our-work/p21-framework

Paris, S. G. (2002). *Perspectives on Object –Centred Learning in Museums.* Mahwah, NJ: Routledge.

Paul, R. (1995). Critical Thinking: *What every person needs to survive in a rapidly changing World.* Rohnert Park, CA: Center for Critical Thinking and Moral Critique, Sonoma State University.

Poce, A. (Ed.) (2015). *Tecnologia critica, Creatività e Didattica della Scienza.* Milano: Franco Angeli.

Poce, A. (2018). *Il patrimonio culturale per lo sviluppo delle competenze nella scuola primaria. Cultural Heritage and the Development of XXI Century Skills in Primary Education.* Milano: FrancoAngeli.

Ritchhart, R. (2007). Cultivating a culture of thinking in museums. *The Journal of Museum Education, 32*(2), 137-154.

Smith, M. M. (2007). From the Editor. *Journal of Museum Education, 32*(2), 189-190.

Terrassa, J., Hubard, O., Holtrop, E., & Higgins-Linder, M., (2016). *Impact of art museum programs on students: Literature review.* Alexandria, VA: National Art Education Association.

Tishman, S., McKinney, A., & Straughn, C. (2007). *Study center learning: An investigation of the educational power and potential of the Harvard University Art Museums Study Centers.* Cambridge, MA: Harvard University Art Museums and Harvard Project Zero.

Trilling, B., & Fadel, C. (2009). *21st Century Skills: Learning For Life in Our Times.* San Francisco: Jossey-Bass.

Triona, L. M., Klahr, D., & Williams, C. (2005). *Point and click or build by hand. Comparing the effects of physical vs. Virtual materials on middle school student's ability to optimize an engineering design.* Paper presented at Proceedings of the 27th Annual Conference of the Cognitive Science Society, 21-23 July 2005.

Wiley, D. A. (Ed.) (2000). *The instructional use of learning objects.* Bloomington: Indiana Association for Instructional Technology and Association for Educational Communications and Technology.

Willingham, D. T. (2008). Critical Thinking: Why Is It So Hard to Teach? *Arts Education Policy Review, 109*(4), 21-32.

Lessons from a Pandemic for the Future of Education
European Distance and E-Learning Network (EDEN) Proceedings
2021 Annual Conference | Madrid, 21-24 June, 2021
ISSN 2707-2819
doi: 10.38069/edenconf-2021-ac0014

RECONSTRUCTING SUBJECTIVE STUDY EXPERIENCES DURING SHUTDOWN IN PANDEMIC TIMES

Laura Eigbrecht, Ulf-Daniel Ehlers, Baden-Wurttemberg Cooperative State University Karlsruhe, Germany

Abstract

The article reports on a qualitative study based on interviews with students systematically conducted online since March 2020. A total of 13 individual and eleven group interviews on the personal study situation during the Corona shutdown have been conducted, analysed and evaluated. The students' perspectives provide insights into how they subjectively reconstruct and classify the experiences they have made, what conclusions can be drawn from this for future higher education and how higher education institutions must evolve in order to support students in the best possible way. In addition to numerous challenges, the pandemic has brought forth the potential of students to shape and reflect on their learning processes in a self-determined and self-organised way and to contribute as experts to shaping the future of higher education.

Introduction

The Corona Shutdown has challenged students in higher education institutions to adapt to a local shift of study from the campus to their own homes and an almost complete digitisation of teaching in the form of distance learning modes. In the process, the Corona pandemic has placed higher education institutions in one of the largest field trials to date in the area of new teaching-learning methods (Nascimbeni & Ehlers, 2020; p.II). While the situation of teachers was addressed immediately after the shutdown occurred in the form of support measures, this happened little with the situation of students in the public discourse at first. Larger empirical studies that focus on the students' perspective have been released towards the end of 2020 and feature primarily quantitative, standardised approaches (e.g. Marczuk et al., 2021; Traus et al., 2020; Gestung et al., 2021). In order to classify the new study situation beyond quantitative parameters, this article analyses the results of interviews with students that have been conducted systematically since the beginning of the pandemic, constituting a qualitative-explorative approach to the students' situation.

The aim was to find out how students experience their studies during the shutdown in terms of their abilities and the prevailing framework conditions, how they organise their studies and learning themselves, and what potentials and challenges they see for (future) higher education. For this purpose, students have been interviewed since March 2020 and asked about their study experiences during the Corona shutdown. Parts of the interviews were also published as podcasts and represent the most comprehensive podcast series to date on the situation of students during the Corona period throughout Europe (next-normal.eu and studium-im-shutdown.de). The data provides insights into how students subjectively reconstruct the experiences they had. The qualitative approach is particularly suitable for describing and analysing subjective study experiences. In the second chapter, the research methodology and the research questions are described, and in the third chapter the results are presented and analysed and then summarised.

Research Methodology

The study follows a qualitative design based on online interviews with students. Our qualitative approach focuses particularly on strategies with which students react to the new situation of studying in the shutdown.

Research question

The study is about investigating subjective learning and study preferences that students perceive and describe with regard to their study situation during the shutdown. The main open question is: how do students experience their studies during the shutdown in terms of their abilities and in terms of the prevailing framework conditions in order to organise their studies and learning themselves, and which study and learning strategies do they have or develop? The aim is to investigate whether and how students deal with the new study situation not only in the sense of reactive "coping" (see, for example, Grabowski et al., 2007; pp.674 ff.), but in the sense of a subjectively productive approach (as suggested, for example, by subjective learning and socialisation theories, see Ehlers (2004) for a summary), and how the subjective reconstructions provide indications of study opportunities and support needs that can be of importance for the organisation of studies during the shutdown. The main question is concretised in three sub-questions:

1. From the students' perspective, what are the preferences and quality requirements for higher education teaching in the shutdown?
2. How do students describe their participation opportunities and requirements in higher education teaching in the shutdown?
3. How do students in the Corona Shutdown describe and reconstruct their own study strategies, especially with regard to self-organisation and self-regulation?

Research Design

The qualitative interviews have been conducted and recorded as a Zoom conference since March 2020 with German students as well as with students from various European countries. For this purpose, students were interviewed in semi-structured, guideline-based individual and group interviews lasting up to 80 minutes about their study situation during the Corona Shutdown. The digital recordings were coded using the data analysis software MAXQDA according to the method of qualitative content analysis (Mayring, 2015). Beforehand, a code tree was generated in a theory-based procedure in order to be able to work out the subject-related subjective assessment of the students.

Sample selection, interview situation and limitations

The interviews were conducted from two weeks after higher education institutions had to switch to an online teaching mode. Some of them were made available to the public as podcasts, which had two objectives: to gain insights into the situation of students with regard to the above-mentioned questions and to give students a voice in the public discussion, to describe their current situation. To date, 13 individual interviews and eleven group discussions have been conducted. In accordance with the principle of maximum contrast (Dimbath et al., 2018), students were selected who covered a diverse range of subjects in terms of the degree programmes they studied and who differed in terms of the type of higher education institution they attended in order to be able to capture the breadth of the student experience. The interview partners were selected on the one hand through personal contacts and on the other hand through external requests to the interview team. For publication as podcasts, the interviews, which were available as raw material, were edited and supplemented with moderation parts. They were then published on format-specific websites and well-known podcast platforms and promoted via social media.

Aspects such as data selection and sampling as well as the quality of the data limit the validity of empirical studies (Baur & Blasius, 2014; Häder, 2019). Due to self-selection effects, it is assumed that students who are more reticent regarding public statements might not even agree to participate in the interviews and that those who feel comfortable speaking in public are more likely to have their say. This is likely to be equally true for those students who are overwhelmed by their current study situation. With these limitations, it can be assumed that all study situations and challenges are represented to a very limited extent, which limits the validity of the qualitative material.

Analysis and processing of the results

Subjective preferences and quality requirements for higher education teaching in the shutdown

Using the qualitative interview material, we first reconstruct what, from the learners' point of view, are preferences and quality requirements under conditions of digital higher education teaching. The coded segments of the qualitative interviews were assigned to subcodes (evaluative statements on forms of digital teaching; on framework conditions; statements on the topic of digital social presence; wishes and demands for current and future higher education teaching) and are analysed in this chapter with regard to information about their own learning preferences and the subjective reconstruction of their study situation. The investigation of subjective quality preferences was first conducted for learning in online settings by Ehlers (2004).

In our study, clear quality preferences of students could be evaluated in a differentiated way and quality potentials for digital teaching could be derived from this. Overall, it can be observed that the ongoing situation brings more framework conditions into view that influence the perceived quality of online teaching – therefore, subjective quality requirements increase with the duration of the pandemic situation. The qualitative statements show a picture of students who reconstruct the current study experience primarily in terms of the dimensions of flexibility, individualisation, personalisation and digital social presence. There are students who experience greater challenges with regard to the dimensions mentioned and others who currently find favourable study conditions for themselves with regard to these dimensions. The development of capacities, concepts and experiences in the area of digital social presence can be seen as a particularly important point. The following table relates subjectively perceived barriers, conducive conditions and potentials for quality in digital teaching and learning.

Table 1: Subjective reconstructions of quality requirements

Subjectively perceived barriers to quality	Subjectively perceived conducive conditions	Subjectively identified potentials
Discrepancy between differentiated quality requirements of students and actual teaching	Face-to-face lectures meet the need for structure; asynchronous formats meet the need for flexibility	Richer learning environments and holistic digitisation of courses that meet quality requirements
Stressful experience due to increased workload; general conditions negatively influence the need for equal participation in studies	Need for support is met through organisational flexibility and support services	Good accessibility of contact persons as well as individual support and solutions
The need for social contacts and exchange is not sufficiently met	The need for social contacts is fulfilled in individual cases, for example in group work; exchanges at eye level with lecturers are perceived as positive and fulfil the need for respect and solidarity.	Creating new solutions and space for digital social presence
Concern that teaching has not developed further compared to before the pandemic	The need for quality and further development of teaching is met by involving students and reflecting on experiences made	Maintain flexibility and openness and further develop teaching with students

Participation opportunities and requirements in higher education teaching during the shutdown

In her "Participative Media Didactics", Mayrberger describes that "the digitalisation of teaching and learning can only succeed if sufficient experiential spaces are provided for the relevant actors so that they can experience and authentically experience self-directed learning and participation – and critically relate to it" (Mayrberger, 2019; p.44). The depth of participation or involvement of actors is often classified using stage models (Arnstein, 1969; Wright, 2016). Füchtenhans et al. and other researchers describe that student participation and co-design in teaching and research are not yet established and taken for granted, even if this results in a better consideration of their interests and strengthens the personal responsibility and maturity of students for their learning process (Füchtenhans et al., 2018; Hofhues, 2013; Barrineau et al., 2019) in order to be able to address current and future challenges of higher education teaching (Mayrberger, 2020). This also corresponds to a subjective quality perspective described earlier, in which learners themselves are empowered in their responsibility for their learning process.

The forms of participation can be divided into more active and passive forms of participation. Furthermore, they can be divided into participation at the micro (learning, seminar), meso (institution) and macro level (educational initiatives, political level), examples of which can be found in the students' statements. The qualitative data shows that there is a strongly elaborated corpus of requirements for participation that concerns all organisational levels and is much differentiated in terms of participation levels and contexts. They are linked to values, attitudes and corresponding needs that students can articulate and demand more or less consciously through participation opportunities – be it in the joint design of (digital) teaching, in the involvement and co-determination in institutional strategic decisions or in supra-regional and political engagement. An awareness of the quality of higher education teaching seems to go hand in hand with a stronger active demand for it and participation in the design of teaching. The statements on participation opportunities and requirements are summarized in the following table.

Table 2: Statements on participation opportunities and requirements during the shutdown

Micro level	Meso level	Macro level
Actively shaping: Now		
Encouraging teachers to actively formulate feedback; co-designing teaching & learning	Survey by student representatives with recommendations to institutional management; greater openness when students want to place and advance issues; digital engagement; visibility of organised student participation has increased	Petition for non-valuation of the semester
Actively shaping: Future		
Openness to be maintained Maintain; strengthen digital engagement supra-regionally; stronger organised student engagement		
Passive: Now		
Lecturers solicit feedback on how students feel and evaluate course design; participation in teaching not possible due to technical and social conditions	Professors approach student council to work out solutions together	
Passive: Future		
Lecturers should seek specific feedback from students	Include disadvantaged student groups in the design of future teaching; transparent communication	Higher education teaching should become more inclusive, fair, student-centred and equal

Description and reconstruction of own study strategies in the 'shutdown'

The qualitative interview material can also be used to reconstruct statements about students' study and learning strategies with which students structure and organise their everyday study and learning process. The data show that studying in times of pandemic challenges students more on an individual level through spatial and social isolation, increases degrees of freedom and choices – and thus the potential for developing self-organisation and self-regulation (Probst, 1987), with which they influence or control actions and internal processes (Baumeister & Vohs, 2004).

In the qualitative interviews, students make statements about subjective strategies with which they cope with the demands of their studies – it can be concluded that the awareness of corresponding competences increases due to the current situation. Students make statements about self-organisation strategies in relation to the organisation of their own everyday learning and studying, in relation to media use, which are gaining in importance through the digitalisation of teaching, as well as in relation to local conditions. The material shows that students know, reflect on and apply numerous self-organisation strategies and consider them significant. The challenges of digital study take increasingly place at the individual level, require more self-regulation and self-organisation and can thus also become a burden. Therefore, conditions that limit the effectiveness of these strategies are also mentioned. It can be deduced from this that studying has become an even more individual challenge and increasingly demands and expands self-organisation competences. The following table summarises the statements made by students on hindering and supporting factors with regard to self-organisation strategies:

Table 3: Hindering and facilitating factors for self-organisation

Hindering factors for self-organisation	Facilitating factors for self-organisation	Solutions
Delayed or un-regular provision of learning materials	Conscious routines and learning plans	Importance of self-organisation strategies increases
Media distractions	Increase in media literacy; digital tools considered helpful	Necessity of a strategic learning approach in relation to media use
Distraction due to disturbances and work in the household; problematic spatial restriction	Focusing and immersion easier at home	Deliberate spatial separation of living and working space; Redesigning spaces and using them creatively
Increased workload; mental stress; challenges at individual level	Experience in self-organisation and self-learning	Support services

Summary and conclusion

Due to the special study situation, students in the shutdown have become familiar with different ways in which studying is possible. By reflecting on what constitutes good teaching for them, students become aware of individual quality dimensions and requirements – and perceive strengths and weaknesses of different teaching settings. Furthermore, they articulate the extent to which they use conscious self-organisation strategies to organise their daily study routine, which can be individually professionalised through support services. Through close exchange with lecturers, students could often communicate or demand their own preferences and wishes. Higher education institutions can use these new participatory competences and benefit from student perspectives in order to jointly design future teaching and learning processes in participatory settings. In addition to numerous challenges, the pandemic has thus also brought forth the potential of students to shape their learning processes in a self-determined and self-organised way, to reflect on them and to contribute to shaping future higher education teaching and learning as experts. This is a strong signal for including students' voices in the debate on higher education in times of Covid-19 and in the future to provide quality education accessible to all.

References

Arnstein, S. R. (1969). A Ladder of Citizen Participation. *Journal of the American Institute of Planners, 35*(4), 216-224. https://doi.org/10.1080/01944366908977225

Barnat, M., Hofhues, S., Kenneweg, A. C., Merkt, M., Salden, P., & Urban, D. (Eds.) (2013). *ZHW-Almanach: Vol. 1. Junge Hochschul- und Mediendidaktik. Forschung und Praxis im Dialog*. Hamburg.

Barrineau, S., Engström, A., & Schnaas, U. (2019). *An active student participation companion.* https://doi.org/10.23865/hu.v9.1734

Baumeister, R. F., & Vohs, K. D. (Eds.) (2004). *Handbook of self-regulation: Research, theory, and applications.* New York, NY: Guilford Press. Retrieved from http://www.loc.gov/catdir/description/guilford051/2003020013.html

Baur, N., & Blasius, J. (2014). *Handbuch Methoden der empirischen Sozialforschung.* Wiesbaden: Springer Fachmedien Wiesbaden. https://doi.org/10.1007/978-3-531-18939-0

Dimbath, O., Ernst-Heidenreich, M., & Roche, M. (2018). *Praxis und Theorie des Theoretical Sampling.* Methodologische Überlegungen zum Verfahren einer verlaufsorientierten Fallauswahl. Advance online publication. https://doi.org/10.17169/FQS-19.3.2810

Ehlers, U.-D. (2004). *Qualität im E-Learning aus Lernersicht.* Wiesbaden: VS Verlag für Sozialwissenschaften. https://doi.org/10.1007/978-3-663-11211-2

Füchtenhans, S., Koch-Thiele, A., Witt, T., & Zilles, K. (2018). Förderung studentischer Partizipation am Beispiel einer hochschuldidaktischen Tagung. *Die Hochschullehre, 4*, 345–360.

Gestung, V., Hettler, I. S., Badermann, M., Deuer, E., & Meyer, T. (2021). Online-Lehre während der COVID-19-Pandemie: Die studentische Perspektive. *Forschungsbericht 7/2021.* Retrieved from https://www.dhbw.de/fileadmin/user_upload/Dokumente/Schrifterzeugnisse/Forschungsbericht_7_2021_Online-Lehre_waehrend_der_COVID-19-Pandemie.pdf

Grabowski, J., Smith, E. E., & Nolen-Hoeksema, S. (Eds.) (2007). *Atkinsons und Hilgards Einführung in die Psychologie* ([2. Aufl., Übers. und Adaption der amerikan.] 14. Aufl.). Heidelberg: Spektrum Akad. Verl. Retrieved from http://deposit.d-nb.de/cgi-bin/dokserv?id=2966314&prov=M&dok_var=1&dok_ext=htm

Häder, M. (2019). *Empirische Sozialforschung.* Wiesbaden: Springer Fachmedien Wiesbaden. https://doi.org/10.1007/978-3-658-26986-9

Hofhues, S. (2013). Offenheit als Stolperstein: Partizipation mit und an Hochschullehre. In M. Barnat, S. Hofhues, A. C. Kenneweg, M. Merkt, P. Salden, & D. Urban (Eds.), *ZHW-Almanach: Vol. 1. Junge Hochschul- und Mediendidaktik. Forschung und Praxis im Dialog* (pp. 161–166). Hamburg. https://doi.org/10.3278/HSL1314W

Marczuk, A., Multrus, F., & Lörz, M. (2021). *Die Studiensituation in der Corona-Pandemie.* Auswirkungen der Digitalisierung auf die Lern- und Kontaktsituation von Studierenden. https://doi.org/10.34878/2021.01.DZHW_BRIEF

Mayrberger, K. (2019). *Partizipative Mediendidaktik: Gestaltung der (Hochschul-) Bildung unter den Bedingungen der Digitalisierung.*

Mayrberger, K. (2020). Jahrbuch Medienpädagogik 17: Lernen mit und über Medien in einer digitalen Welt. *MedienPädagogik: Zeitschrift Für Theorie Und Praxis Der Medienbildung, 17*(Jahrbuch Medienpädagogik), 59-92. https://doi.org/10.21240/mpaed/jb17/2020.04.26.X

Mayring, P. (2015). *Qualitative Inhaltsanalyse: Grundlagen und Techniken* (12., überarb. Aufl.). Beltz Pädagogik. Weinheim: Beltz. Retrieved from http://content-select.com/index.php?id=bib_view&ean=9783407293930

Nascimbeni, F., & Ehlers, U. D. (2020). Open teaching: Research and practice on open, innovative and engaging pedagogies: Editorial. *Journal of E-Learning and Knowledge Society, 16*(4), I–IV. https://doi.org/10.20368/1971-8829/1135423

Probst, G. J. B. (1987). *Selbst-Organisation: Ordnungsprozesse in sozialen Systemen aus ganzheitlicher Sicht.* Biologie und Evolution interdisziplinär. Berlin: Parey.

Traus, A., Höffken, K., Thomas, S., Mangold, K., & Schröer, W. (2020). *Stu.diCo. – Studieren digital in Zeiten von Corona.* https://doi.org/10.18442/150

Wright, M. T. (2016). *Partizipation: Mitentscheidung der Bürgerinnen und Bürger.* https://doi.org/10.17623/BZGA:224-I084-1.0

Lessons from a Pandemic for the Future of Education
European Distance and E-Learning Network (EDEN) Proceedings
2021 Annual Conference | Madrid, 21-24 June, 2021
ISSN 2707-2819
doi: 10.38069/edenconf-2021-ac0015

HOW PORTUGUESE SCHOOLS NAVIGATED THROUGH THE PANDEMIC FIRST WAVE: VIEWS FROM HEADTEACHERS

Ana Cristina Torres, Angélica Monteiro, Center for Research and Intervention in Education, Faculty of Psychology and Education Sciences of the University of Porto, Ana Mouraz, Department of Education and Distance Education, Open University, Lisbon, Portugal

Abstract

The transition from emergency remote teaching schemes to effective online learning ones has posed just as much similar as specific challenges to different countries and regions during school closures of the COVID-19 pandemic first wave. In Portugal, the specific challenge of a notably aged teaching workforce that admits being underprepared for pedagogically meaningful use of digital technologies in education has become more evident. Focusing on the views of seven interviewed schools' headteachers, this paper presents and discusses the reported facilitators and barriers/constraints of their schools' transition from emergency remote teaching to online learning, during the first pandemic wave and relates those factors with the particular issues of veteran teachers' engagement with online learning. The paper introduces the rekindle+50 project under which the data collection and analysis took place and underlines the extreme importance of continued investment in teacher professional development and collaboration to enhance more effective use of online learning tools and platforms in times of uncertainty.

Introduction

The COVID-19 pandemic and corresponding sanitary crisis that resulted in school closures caused an unprecedented disruption in education systems. The abrupt changes that were demanded of schools, teachers, students and families with the adjustment to distance teaching schemes accentuated existing vulnerabilities and educational inequalities worldwide (UN, 2020). Educational sectors and schooling levels were faced with just as many similar challenges, such as issues of hardware and connectivity, as specific circumstances, such as the ones related to conditions to practical or lab work and support for special needs children and young people. How effectively educational systems responded to such challenges depended as much on how well those systems were prepared for them as on the types of responses and resources that were put forward to tackle them.

In Portugal, schools' closure during the first pandemic wave was nationwide from the 16th of March until the end of the school year. It implied a loss of in-presence instructional time during 14 weeks with an Easter break in the middle. Most schools and teachers took the first weeks to organize the remote teaching routines in this emergency scenery with occasional contacts with students and families asking or recommending learning activities, clearing doubts, reviewing assignments, many times without fixed schedules (DGEEC, 2020). During this time, measures at a national level were mostly about setting up centralized platforms and resources to help teachers, students and families, including partnerships with important entities in the field of online learning (e.g., Open University), as well as making guidelines available for schools to design and implement their Distance Education Plans. At regional and local levels, schools, local authorities, social institutions and enterprises partnered in designing solutions to reach all students and providing them with resources and conditions to remain engaged in learning activities. After the Easter break, in early April, and as new communication and teaching routines were better established for most schools and schooling levels, concerns became more focused on issues such as the inclusion of vulnerable and special needs students, and the monitoring, assessing and certifying of student learning (DGEEC, 2020). Moreover, the government investment was then concentrated on training school leaders nationwide to support other teachers in the progressive transition from an instrumental use of technologies in emergency remote teaching, to a quality digital education, in collaborative and constructive environments (Moreira, Henriques, & Barros, 2020) and on launching educational programming for basic education students on-air in a TV open channel, in an additional attempt to reach students who still lacked the needed equipment or Internet connectivity (Menezes Junior, 2020).

The measures put in place to continue students' learning during school closure, especially through online platforms, were increasingly dependent on families and students' availability of resources, connectivity, competence and autonomy to use specific hardware and software. But they were also strongly dependent on teachers' preparedness to support digital learning, both in terms of hardware and software availability, and technical and pedagogical skills to use it. In this respect, the personal and professional features of the Portuguese teaching workforce became salient as well as the pre-pandemic existing teacher support initiatives and incentives.

When the pandemic spread and forced schools to close, a team of Portuguese researchers was investigating the teacher ageing phenomena and its relationships with the use of digital technologies in education. We were organizing a set of teacher professional development sessions and together investigating its potential to promote the renewal of veteran teachers' commitment to teaching and curricular innovation mediated by digital technologies.

In this context, the paper draws on qualitative data collected within this project to present and discuss the challenges schools and their veteran teachers faced during these exceptional times. Focusing on the views of headteachers, its objectives are i) to identify the main facilitators and barriers/constraints factors of these schools transition from emergency remote teaching to online learning, during the first pandemic wave; ii) to relate the identified factors with the particular issues of veteran teachers engagement with online learning. The paper introduces the rekindle+50 project under which the data collection and analysis took place, as well as some of its main findings to contextualize the situation of veteran teachers in Portugal and the challenges they pose to schools. Afterwards, it presents and discusses the views of some headteachers of the schools where the participant veteran teachers worked.

The rekindle+50 project: study context

The project "Digital migrations and curricular innovation: giving new meaning to experience and rekindle teaching profession after 50" (rekindle+50) focused on teachers over 50 years old and on renewing their commitment to teaching and curricular innovation, mediated through the use of digital technologies. Its purpose was to foster the relationship between the essential aspects of curricular agency assumed by teachers and the practices of educational action mediated by digital technologies (Mouraz, Lopes, Morgado, & Torres, 2020). Methodologically, this project associated research, intervention and the professional development of primary and secondary school teachers. It convened two academic educational research centres and two in-service teachers' education centres from the North and Centre of Portugal. These later hosted two editions each – 2019 and 2020, of a course for pre-school, basic and secondary school teachers with 50 years old or more about Innovative Educational Environments and specific new methodologies in teaching with the use of digital technologies to address student demotivation and school achievement (Morgado, Lencastre, Freires, & Bento, 2021). The research component of the project included diversified data collection moments and methods spanning from an initial online questionnaire, to observing the training sessions, analysing teachers' digital learning diaries held on the Padlet platform by the participants and analysing reflections produced by the teachers throughout and by the end of the courses. Moreover, we organized focus group discussions with some of the veteran teachers participating in the courses, approximately six months after the courses' end, and interviewed their schools' headteachers in looking for more institutional perspectives of the introduced changes in teaching practices related to the training. The second edition of the teacher education courses had started in January 2020, when like so many other teaching and training initiatives, it had to reshape its program to adjust to online learning and, most importantly, to the participant veteran teachers' needs arising from the abrupt changes of school closures due to the sanitary crisis.

Portuguese veteran teachers and the challenges of digital education: establishing a background

In 2018, the average age of the teaching workforce in Portugal was 44 years old (OECD, 2019a), with more than 40% of teachers having more than 50 years old. This ageing trend has been related to the increase in life expectancy and correspondent delay of the retirement age, as well as with the decrease in the school population and correspondent decrease in new teachers' recruitment. Older teachers usually accumulate a professional experience of twenty or more years being frequently identified in the literature as "veteran teachers" (Carrilo, & Flores, 2018; Monteiro, Mouraz, & Dotta, 2021; Orlando, 2014). Though rich in professional experience, Portuguese veteran teachers have suffered from a lack of career progression and erosion of working conditions and well-being (EC/EACEA/Eurydice, 2021) as well as of the perceived social value of the teaching profession (Alves & Lopes, 2016). Internationally, Portuguese teachers experience one of the largest numbers of instructional hours and with the least sense of self-efficacy on the use of class time (OECD, 2019a; OECD, 2019b). When combined with growing pressures to change and innovation challenging their pedagogical knowledge and the experience accumulated in years of practice (Orlando, 2014) and with generational students accentuated by the rapid evolution and incorporation of ICT in youth cultures, many suffer from professional exhaustion, stress and discouragement (Alves & Lopes, 2016; EC/EACEA/Eurydice, 2021). Though the crucial role of the use of digital technologies in improving the quality of education has been well established, many teachers still feel underprepared for the use of technologies in teaching (OECD, 2019b), especially in ways that improve its pedagogical potential in education.

Besides the above-mentioned challenges, the abrupt digitalization of education due to the pandemic lockdown increased the pressure to curricular and pedagogical innovation and the need for immediate responses from educational institutions, with the aggravating factor that there was not enough time to properly prepare teachers for careful planning of meaningful online learning practices. Such constraint led to emergency remote teaching responses, which the main objective is to "provide temporary access to instruction and instructional supports in a manner that is quick to set up and is reliably available during an emergency or crisis" (Hodges et al., 2020; Emergence remote teaching section, para.1).

Though much expectation has been placed on the possibility of the transition to online learning enabling the sustainability of innovative pedagogical practices once schools come back to in-presence teaching, most findings from the rekindle+50 project have shown otherwise that this shift of instructional delivery may not represent, at first, a sustainable pedagogical change. For instance, according to Morgado, Mouraz, and Freires (2019), only the promotion of a culture of technology in teaching-learning contexts can enhance a movement of pedagogical innovation, which has to settle on curricular agency and educational practices mediated by digital technologies. Such innovations require sound strategies to mobilize a sustainable digital culture in the daily life of schools, which constantly tackle constraints that interfere with the construction and implementation of new practices. For the case of veteran teachers, such constraints include professional and personal aspects (Morgado, Lencastre, Freires, & Bento, 2021; Dotta, Monteiro, & Mouraz, 2019). The professional aspects are related to pedagogical relationship (Postic, 1984), encompassing conditions for effective online communication, feedback for formative assessment and opportunities for peer interaction. It also includes the management of time and student online behaviour, which in some cases may contain episodes of distraction, agitation, indiscipline and disrespect. The personal aspects are related, in part, to insecurity, lack of digital competencies, sense of loneliness, fatigue, lack of motivation, fear of change, loss of status and authority (Dotta, Monteiro, & Mouraz, 2019). Usually, veteran teachers can handle technology for personal purposes but need to realize how technology and pedagogy can be combined in meaningful ways, being important to prompt new experiences and to create comfortable and safe places for experimentation (Morgado, Lencastre, Freires, & Bento, 2021). As such, the authors also highlight the importance of school leaders' support, as well as pedagogical and technical support delivery by Training Centres, to the introduction of innovations in professional practices of veteran teachers. In this sense, Mouraz, Lopes, Morgado, and Torres (2020) sum up that school leadership, collaborative work among peers, professional development that aims to place teachers and their curricular decisions at the heart of training actions and digital technologies are essential elements in changing and innovating practices. Teachers' participation in exchange projects also provides them with more resilience to face problems, such as the ones related to the intergenerational gap.

Methodology

The study follows a qualitative approach based on interviews with headteachers of schools with a huge ratio of veteran teachers. It intends to highlight and map the facilitators and constraints lived in schools in the transition to online from the school leaders' perspectives. In this section, we start to introduce the participants of the study moving on, afterwards, to describing the study's data collection and analysis procedures.

Participants: the interviewed headteachers and their schools

This study participants were headteachers from seven school clusters of the North and Centre regions of Portugal (N = 7) who kindly agreed to be interviewed. The veteran teachers that participated in the rekindle+50 project training courses worked in these school clusters, and most of the interviewing process had some relation with the effects of the rekindle+50 project training courses on the schools' veteran teachers. Table 1 introduces some basic features of the interviewed headteachers, as well as the proportion of veteran teachers in their schools.

Many headteachers pointed out the increasingly marked ageing amongst pre-school teachers and a few teachers from disciplinary groups of Basic Education, mainly from the 5th and 6th grades, which corresponds to the national trend (OECD, 2019a). We should also highlight that school A is the headquarters of one of the country's in-service teacher training centres more specialized in digital learning, including innovative learning environments. School B embodies a trend of schools in the inner part of Portugal, suffering from the depopulation, decrease in the school population and corresponding lack of renewal of the teaching staff that retired.

Table 8: Interviewed headteachers and proportion of veteran teachers in their schools.

Headteacher	Gender	Age	Time serving as headteacher	Education	The proportion of veteran teachers in his/her school
A	Male	65	33 years	Electronic engineering	50 to 60%
B	Male	61	21 years	Financial audit and Educational administration	58%
C	Female	56	11 years	History	50 to 60%
D	Female	54	8 years	Philosophy and Educational administration	70 to 80%
E	Male	47	7 years	Portuguese language; Special Education; Educational Administration	40 to 50%
F	Female	55	11 years	English and Educational Administration	40 to 50%
G	Female	57	17 years	Maths and Natural Sciences	40 to 50%

Data collection and analysis

The data was collected in interviews conducted online in June 2020 to headteachers from schools of veteran teachers participating in the rekindle+50 project. The interviews protocol pursued three aims as following specified: (a) to identify the composition of the school teaching staff and their renewal trends; (b) to highlight cultural dynamics and concerns of each school related to curriculum and pedagogical development, collaborative work among teachers and teaching in the transition to online and distance learning; iii) to identify the main challenges and opportunities headteachers identified concerning their teaching staff skills to face the post-pandemic times.

The interviews recordings were transcribed and analysed through a content analysis performed by using NVivo® and combining a mix of pre-determined categories and emergent sub-categories. Pre-determined categories encompassed facilitators and barriers/constraints posed to schools in the transition to online learning environments, whereas sub-categories emerged from the headteachers' discourses.

Results: the headteachers' views

Facilitators of the transition to online learning

Amongst the main facilitators of the transition, the interviewed headteachers referred to institutional actions of planning, supporting and monitoring distance education and raising equipment to make it available to students (all headteachers), collaboration processes (C, D, E, F and G), previous experiences and training with digital education (A, C, E, F and G) and motivational factors including pressures to change through technologies (D, E, F and G).

One of the first main *institutional actions* most schools undertook to facilitate the transition to online learning was to raise equipment, support and expand connectivity through internal resources and partnerships with community entities such as local municipalities (referred by A, B, C and G). Headteachers A and G also highlighted extra care with communication through being open to the educational community concerns and sending clear, continued and equal information to all the educational community members, and particularly to students, to contradict the physical distance of school closure. For most schools, the first two weeks were essentially dedicated to establishing infrastructure, including digital platforms and institutional emails for teachers and students (referred by B, C, D and F). It was also a period to identify and assemble key resources and specialized staff due to *previous experiences and training with digital education* in the schools. Headteachers A, C and F highlighted existing expertise in their schools from past experiences with digital platforms (Moodle and Google Apps), whereas headteachers E and G pointed out some teachers expertise due to past engagement in Erasmus+ cooperation and exchange projects. When in March 2020, the Ministry of Education recommended schools to assemble internal technical support teams, the headteachers recruited teachers from such experiences, and many highlighted the extreme importance of such teams in supporting not only other teachers but also students and families (A, C, F and G). Internal professional development initiatives were provided to the teaching staff mostly to help the exchange of experiences and expertise (referred by A, C, D, E and F) including workshops and production or recommendation of tutorials. Headteacher C also highlighted the provision of specific schedules for teachers to work collaboratively.

For the interviewed headteachers, such institutional actions opened avenues to enhance and sediment formal and informal *collaboration processes* essential for the teachers' capacity to effectively transition to the new teaching and learning environments. The collaborative support and work between teachers were highlighted by all headteachers except A and B as the most important facilitator of the transition. It was also a facilitator particularly underlined when the teachers' age and experiences were added to the equation, as illustrated by this idea that teachers "worked pretty well and I don't see any problem, any difference between new and old teachers within the same disciplinary groups" (C). Elaborating this idea, another headteacher explained that "in this difficult process, the older teachers tried hard not to be left behind, seeking help in some of the younger teachers" (G).

Concerning the specific engagement of veteran teachers, some *motivational factors* were also mentioned, that included the urge to keep up with the pace of educational changes and the efforts to adapt to new learning tools and environments responding to pressures from students and peers (E, F, G).

Barriers/constraints to the transition to online learning

In which concerns barriers/constraints to an effective transition to online learning, the headteachers pointed out motivational factors (A, B, C, E, F, G), relational and pedagogical constraints (B, D, D, E, F and G), the extensive inequalities in terms of access to equipment, connectivity and engaging special needs students (B, C, D, F, G) and related lack of digital competence from some teachers, students and families (C, D, E, F). Two headteachers also pointed out the lack of preparation to distance education given the novelty of the situation (school B) and the difficulty to navigate the excess of available digital platforms and tools, as well as of top-down daily issued legislation and recommendations (school C). Once again, apart from some motivational factors, most were posed to the whole teaching staff regardless of their age. After dealing with the establishment of infrastructure and lack of equipment and connectivity, most schools faced the challenges of poverty and disengagement of some students and families, and, most importantly, the lack of competence and autonomy of students to independently use the digital tools that were adopted or simply to complete the assigned tasks even if in more traditional supports (worksheets, textbooks). This often related to the more *relational and pedagogical constraints* that were mentioned. An initial problem was the excess of tasks that teachers assigned to students and the difficulty of students in managing tasks and schedules. The close presence of the teacher to deal with the students' struggles and the lack of student autonomy was referred with the idea that "students usually studied just for tests and did not have the kind of work they now have to do independently to learn. In the end, they have to learn alone, they have to look for stuff alone" (D). The change in the pedagogical relation implied struggles in feedback and learning assessment. Some headteachers pointed out how teachers felt insecure about the validity of the assessment they made of student learning as well as of the feedback they provided to students and families. One headteacher explained that teachers "were not adapted to trust the kind of learning assessment that is being made, because we are insecure of what is on the other side (...) and if students are learning as well as of the feedback we produce" (B). Finally, the impossibility or refusal of some students and families to have their cameras on and some fears for data protection issues were also initial, though rarer, constraint in terms of pedagogical relation between students and teachers.

The more referred *motivational constraint* was the lack of commitment of some older teachers to the needed changes due to proximity to retirement, which led them to reproduce online the traditional methods they used in the classroom. The huge time and learning investment teachers had to made to produce learning resources with digital tools discouraged some of engaging with the online learning demands, as thus explained: "it is assumed that building resources in such tools take too long, and the investment people make is huge, which increases the teachers' tend to fall into traditional methods" (F). The already installed fatigue, discouragement and self-perception of insufficient preparation posed an extra challenge to those veteran teachers when facing the forced entrance in the emergency remote teaching scenery during the school closures of the COVID-19 pandemic first wave.

Final remarks

This paper draws attention to the need to reshape communication channels with students as one of the main barriers/constraints of schools' transition from emergency remote teaching to effective online learning during the first pandemic wave. The interviewed headteachers underlined the need to surpass the lack of equipment and connectivity, but also the challenges of poverty and disengagement of some students, and most importantly, the lack of students' autonomy to independently use the digital tools and engage in learning tasks. The headteachers also pointed out the inefficacy of some teachers' option to directly transpose pedagogical methods and learning activities to online environments. This was especially the case for those older teachers close to retirement. Such inefficacy was evident when teachers reproduced online the more traditional methods they used in the classroom and especially problematic when involving assessment features as also found in other studies (Doucet et al., 2020).

On the other hand, the main facilitators of the transition highlighted by the headteachers constituted the collaborative efforts from teachers and institutions to rapidly overcome problems related to "first aid" support: connectivity, equipment availability and usability. The collaborative support and work between teachers were also emphasized as a key factor of effective transition to a new pedagogical challenge.

As in all the participant schools, veteran teachers accounted for the majority of the teaching staff, the headteachers could not refer to a specific factor in this group. On the contrary, when having participated in innovation and exchange projects, some of those veteran teachers were agents of change and sustainers of innovation in their schools.

One can conclude that the "online challenge" could be seen as a renewal of teachers' commitment to teaching and curricular innovation mediated by digital technologies. This assumption is also valid for veteran teachers. However, to reach this aim, it seems that continuing to invest in professional development and collaboration to enhance more effective use of online learning tools and platforms with schools reopening is still urgently needed.

References

Alves, K., & Lopes, A. (2016). Professores e o envelhecimento: realidades e especificidades no contexto português [Teachers and aging: realities and specificities in a portuguese contexto]. *Trabalho & Educação, 25*(2), 61-77. Retrieved from https://periodicos.ufmg.br/index.php/trabedu/article/view/9511

Carrilo, C., & Flores, M. A. (2018). Veteran teachers' identity: what does the research literature tell us? *Cambridge Journal of Education, 48*(5), 639-656. doi:10.1080/0305764X.2017.1394982

DGEEC. (2020). *Estamos On com as Escolas: conhecer para apoiar. Medidas educativas e resultados do questionário às escolas* [Were On with schools: to know to support. Educational measures and results from a survey to schools]. Lisboa, Portugal: Ministry of Education, Directorate-General of Education and Science Statistics, Retrieved from https://www.dgeec.mec.pt/np4/474/

Dotta, L., Monteiro, A., & Mouraz, A. (2019). Professores experientes e o uso das tecnologias digitais: Mitos, crenças e práticas [Experienced teachers and the use of digital technologies: myths, beliefs and practices]. *Eduser: revista de educação, 11*(1), 45-60, doi:10.34620/eduser.v11i1.124

Doucet, A., Netolicky, D., Timmers, K., & Tuscano, F. J. (2020). *Thinking about pedagogy in an unfolding pandemic* (An Independent Report on Approaches to Distance Learning during COVID-19 School Closure). Work of Education International and UNESCO. https://issuu.com/educationinternational/docs/2020_research_covid-19_eng

European Commission/EACEA/Eurydice (2021). *Teachers in Europe: Careers, Development and Well-being. Eurydice report.* Luxembourg: Publications Office of the European Union. Retrieved March 24, 2021, from https://eacea.ec.europa.eu/national-policies/eurydice/content/teachers-europe-carreers-development-and-well-being_en

Hodges, C., Moore, S., Lockee, B., Trust, T. & Bond, A. (2020, March 27). The Difference between Emergency Remote Teaching and Online Learning. Educause Review [Blog post]. Retrieved March 30, 2021 from https://er.educause.edu/articles/2020/3/the-difference-between-emergency-remote-teaching-and-online-learning

Menezes Junior, P. (2020). *A Educação nos Tempos da Peste: uma análise sobre a representação da educação nos média na primeira vaga da pandemia* [Education in Times of plague: an analysis of the representation of education in the media during the pandemic first wave]. Porto, Portugal: Faculdade de Psicologia e Ciências da Educação da Universidade do Porto, Unpublished Master thesis.

Monteiro, A., Mouraz, A., & Dotta, L. T. (2021). Veteran teachers and digital technologies: myths, beliefs and professional development. *Teachers and Teaching, 26*(7-8), 577-587. doi:10.1080/13540602.2021.1900809

Moreira, J. A., Henriques, S., & Barros, D. M. V. (2020). Transitando de um ensino remoto emergencial para uma educação digital em rede, em tempos de pandemia [Moving from emergency remote teaching to digital education in times of pandemic]. *Dialogia, 34*, 351-364. Retrieved January 15, 2021, from https://periodicos.uninove.br/dialogia/article/view/17123/8228

Morgado, J. C., Lencastre, J. A., Freires, T., & Bento, M. (2021). Smart Education as Empowerment: Outlining Veteran Teachers' Training to Promote Digital Migration. *Technology, Knowledge and Learning*. doi: 10.1007/s10758-021-09494-6

Mouraz, A., Lopes, A., Morgado, J. C., Torres, A. C. (2020). Veteran teachers and the challenges of curriculum innovation. In R. Dorczak, & A. Portela Pruaño (Eds.), *Generational diversity and intergenerational collaboration among teachers: perspectives and experiences* (pp. 153-165). Cracow: Spraw Publicznych Uniwersytet Jagiellonski.

OECD (2019a). *Country note. Portugal. Education at a Glance 2019.* Paris: OECD Publishing.

OECD (2019b). *TALIS 2018 Results: Teachers and School Leaders as Lifelong Learners.* Paris: OECD Publishing.

Orlando, J. (2014). Veteran teachers and technology: change fatigue and knowledge insecurity influence practice. *Teachers and Teaching, 20*(4), 427-439. doi:10.1080/13540602.2014.881644

Postic, M. (1984). *Relação Pedagógica.* Coimbra: Coimbra Editora.

UN (2020). Policy Brief: Education during COVID-19 and beyond. Retrieved January 19, 2121, from https://unsdg.un.org/resources/policy-brief-education-during-covid-19-and-beyond

Acknowledgements

This work was co-funded by the European Regional Development Fund (ERDF), through the Operational Programme for Competitiveness and Internationalisation (COMPETE 2020 Programme), and by National Funds through the Portuguese funding agency (FCT—Fundação para a Ciência e a Tecnologia, IP) (project no. PTDC/CED-EDG/28017/2017 - POCI-01-0145-FEDER-028017). The research was also supported by the FCT within the multi-year funding awarded to CIIE [grants no. UIDB/00167/2020 and UIDP/00167/2020]. Ana Cristina Torres and Angélica Monteiro also acknowledge the FCT funding for their research contracts at CIIE, established under the transitional rule of Decree-Law 57/2016, amended by Law 57/2017. Angélica Monteiro acknowledges as well FCT for her new post in the framework of the Scientific Employment Stimulus Individual Programme (2020.01982.CEECIND).

Lessons from a Pandemic for the Future of Education
European Distance and E-Learning Network (EDEN) Proceedings
2021 Annual Conference | Madrid, 21-24 June, 2021
ISSN 2707-2819
doi: 10.38069/edenconf-2021-ac0016

#OPENTEACH: OPEN COURSE, OPEN ONLINE TEACHING, OPEN TEXTBOOK

Orna Farrell, James Brunton, Caitriona Ní She, Eamon Costello, Dublin City University, Ireland

Abstract

This paper will explore the experiences of the #Openteach project team in developing a flexible and evidence based approach to support professional learning for those who teach online. The project had a number of phases, which included a needs analysis of online students and educators about effective online teaching, the publication of a review of the literature entitled Teaching Online is Different, and a pilot evaluation report. The #Openteach open course ran in March 2020 and focused on five key aspects of teaching online: social presence; facilitating discussion; collaboration online; live online teaching; and supporting online students. The final phase of the project involves the creation of an open textbook bringing together all of the project outputs, due for publication in summer 2021. Drawing on qualitative and quantitative data collected from online educators pre and post the initiative, this paper reports on two aspects of the #Openteach project in detail: the design, development and delivery of the open online course and the process of creating the #Openteach open textbook.

Introduction

The #Openteach: professional development for open online educators project aimed to develop a flexible and evidence based approach to support professional learning for those who teach online. The #Openteach: Professional Development for Open Online Educators project, was funded by the National Forum for the Enhancement of Teaching and Learning in Higher Education in Ireland from 2019-2020 and was based in Dublin City University (DCU) in Ireland.

Figure 6. #Openteach channels

The #Openteach project aimed to develop a flexible and evidence based approach to support professional learning for those who teach online, see figure 1 above from project channels. The project targeted two groups of educators in particular: part time educators and online educators. The rationale for this was Continuing Professional Development (CPD) is recognised as crucial to the upskilling of educators to enhance the student learning experience. However, an important gap exists in the provision of CPD for part-time and online teachers. As they rarely have the opportunity to avail of campus-based resources they may consequently have limited access to professional development. The #Openteach project sought to address this gap by creating a flexible online open access course about teaching online which was grounded in evidence based practice.

Project phases

The #Openteach project had five phases, see the Figure 2 below:

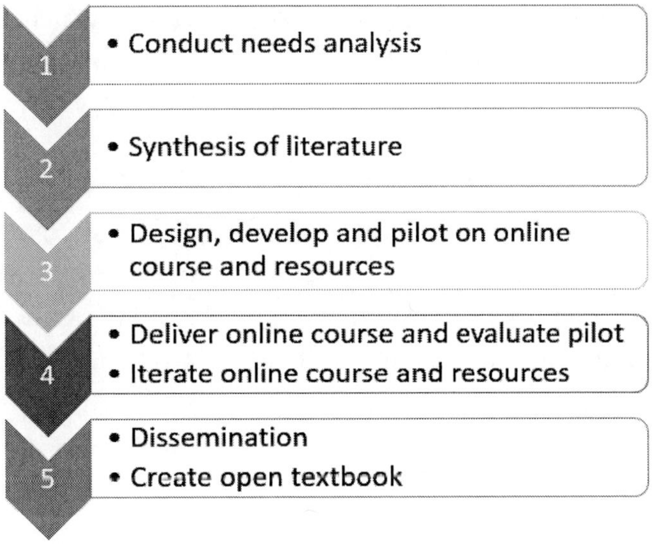

Figure 2. #Openteach project phases

Phase 1

In phase one, we conducted a needs analysis of online educators and online students based in Dublin City University. Data was collected through online focus groups and several questionnaires. We then produced a report detailing our findings called *An investigation of effective online teaching: a needs analysis of online educators and online students* (Farrell, Brunton, Costello, Donlon,Trevaskis, Eccles, & Ní Shé, 2019). Key findings from this report were five key areas that educators identified to enhance through professional development:

1. Technical skills for teaching online;
2. Online learning & teaching pedagogy;
3. Online facilitation skills/approaches;
4. Encouraging online interaction;
5. Community of online educators.

Further, the findings indicated that both online educators and online students found that interpersonal professional skills and clear communication were key features of effective teaching online.

Phase 2

In phase two, we examined the literature around teaching online and conducted a literature synthesis. Following this we published our literature report called *Teaching online is different: critical perspectives from the literature* (Ní Shé, Farrell, Brunton, Costello, Donlon, Trevaskis, & Eccles, 2019). The report examined the literature about online teaching since 2010 and examined the roles and competencies which characterise effective teaching online, as well as approaches to supporting the professional development of online educators.

Phase 3

In phase three, we used the information from the needs analysis report and literature report to begin design and developing the #Openteach open online course. The course was designed following the ABC Learning design approach, which resulted in a ten hour, fully online professional development course (Ní Shé, Farrell, Brunton, Costello, Donlon, Trevaskis, Eccles, 2019). You can read more about the design process in our ABC case study. The course focused on five aspects of teaching online:

1. Presence;
2. Collaboration online;
3. Synchronous teaching;
4. Asynchronous teaching;

5. Supporting online students.

The #Openteach course followed a scenario based approach and participant engagement was largely asynchronous and self-paced as this provided the flexible approach recommended in the literature. The course was designed and delivered on the DCU Moodle site called Loop, and used a variety of tools such as H5P, video, audio, discussion forums, quiz, and workshop in its design, see figure 3 below.

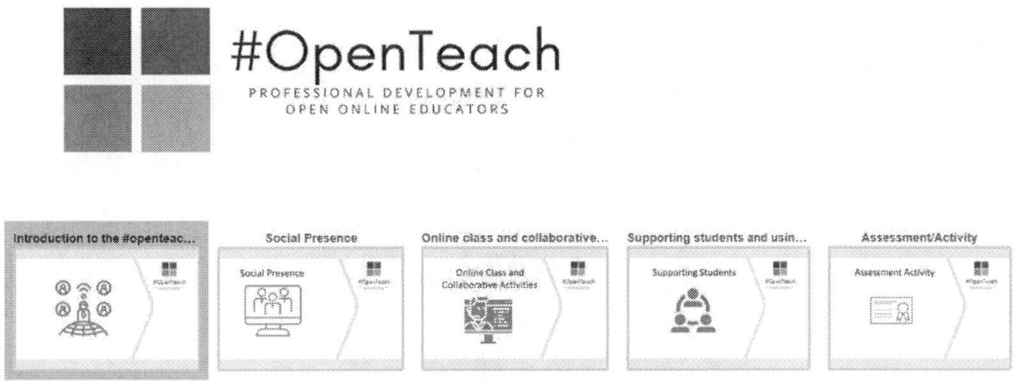

Figure 3. #Openteach Loop course

Phase 4

Phase 4 involved running the course for the first time. The #Openteach online course was free and participation was open to anyone, from anywhere, with the capability to join an online course. The #Openteach open course ran for the first time in March 2020 and the second time in September 2020. The first run coincided with the start of the Covid-19 pandemic, which resulted in a much higher number of participants than we had expected, 450. Following the first course run, we conducted an evaluation study to explore and understand participants learning experiences of the course. An evaluation report was produced called *The Openteach Pilot Evaluation Report* (Farrell, Brunton, Costello, Donlon, Trevaskis, Eccles, Ní Shé, 2020).

The evaluation study yielded a number of interesting findings in relation to the #Openteach course pilot and educators' experiences of professional learning in four thematic areas:

1. Knowledge and understanding of online pedagogy;
2. Community of Educators;
3. #Openteach course design;
4. The Covid-19 Pandemic context.

We present a short extract of our findings from the *The Openteach Pilot Evaluation Report* in the next section (Farrell, Brunton, Costello, Donlon, Trevaskis, Eccles, & Ní Shé, 2020).

Knowledge and understanding of online pedagogy

When asked if participation in the #Openteach course increased their knowledge of online teaching, 98% of 101 respondents answered Yes, 1% responded no and 1% responded maybe.

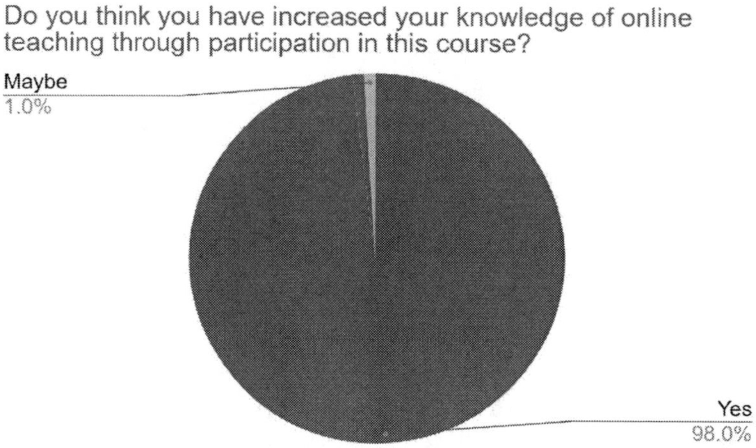

Figure 4. #Openteach impact on knowledge of online teaching

The data shows that the #Openteach course impacted participants' knowledge and understanding of teaching online in a number of ways:

Building confidence about teaching online;

> *"I had no knowledge of online teaching beforehand and I feel I could teach online with my learners now. I have small groups and individuals so I would be comfortable working online with them now."*

Developing new knowledge about online teaching including key theories, technology, and strategies for encouraging student interaction;

> *"I particularly liked the emphasis on pedagogy. The course suited my needs perfectly and allowed me to deepen my knowledge and raise my awareness of the need for carefully designed learning pathways. Online is definitely different to the traditional classroom"*

Gaining insights into online learning by experiencing it from a student perspective;

> *"Experiencing a fully online course and seeing the different tips and strategies for engagement in an online environment"*

Developing ideas and strategies about engaging students in both asynchronous and synchronous environments.

> *"Suggestions on how to better engage students – specifically some of the suggestions on how to use breakout activities, polls etc. Opportunity to read all the very useful suggestions from others on the course, in the various forums"*

Covid-19 Pandemic Context

The release of the #Openteach course coincided with the COVID-19 pandemic in March 2020. Due to the fact that #Openteach was an open and free professional development course about teaching online, the numbers that signed up increased rapidly in a matter of days from 120 to 450. The sudden pivot online by those in the further and higher education sectors thrust many educators into teaching online for the first time.

For those who were teaching online for the first time, the #Openteach course provided them with reassurance, support, and encouragement during a challenging time.

> *"I am a true beginner so my participation has been limited, but I got a good feel for what is involved in this essential area of teaching"*

A number of challenges related to the rapid pivot online were reported in the data by educators. These challenges included problems relating to working from home, poor broadband, underdeveloped digital competencies, time management issues, caring responsibilities, and workload.

> *"Because we were in crisis, I was not able to give the time I would usually give to new learning. I was fitting this in among a hundred other demands, so I was more stretched than I would ideally be when learning."*

> *"I was working from home due to the lockdown and my internet is not consistent, some days I couldn't get online at all"*

Phase 5

The principle of openness was at the heart of the #Openteach project. All of the resources and intellectual outputs were Creative Commons licensed and openly shared through social media and the project website http://www.openteach.ie throughout the project phases. In order to make the impact of the project sustainable in the long term the project team decided to create a free open access online book using the Pressbooks platform. The book is due to be published in June 2021.

The process of remixing and repurposing the #Openteach course into a textbook proved to be an exercise in backwards design. Using the Pressbooks platform, we rewrote, reorganised, rethought activities in order to adapt the course content and activities to suit the book genre. In addition, we added new content activities drawn from project blog and included participant generated content. One affordance of the Pressbook platform was the ability to integrate video and H5P content activities drawn from the course seamlessly into the book.

Project Impact

The #Openteach project has had significant impact on the professional learning of educators at a number of levels: at a local university level, at national and international level, see table 1 below for details of the projects impact.

Table 9: #Openteach project impact by numbers

Website traffic	28 000 unique visitors, 700 000 hits
Twitter	594 followers, 475 tweets, max impressions 10 779
YouTube	5 188 views
Teaching online is different report	36 citations, 5 900 reads
Research publications	3
National conference/workshop	17
International conference/workshop	11
Course participants	1002
Course completers	203

Final thoughts

Over the course of the project, the #Openteach project team learned numerous lessons from the design, development, and delivery of the course about online educators experiences of professional learning, and we share these now as our final thoughts. Professional learning about online pedagogy should be situated online, and the experience of being an online student is invaluable for online educators as it facilitates empathy with students learning in online contexts. Participating in and building a learning community contributes positively to the learning experience for educators. Time management and workload are major challenges for educators, therefore professional learning should allow for flexible engagement. Building confidence and reducing the fear of online teaching is an important aspect of professional learning related to online education. Developing understanding and knowledge of online pedagogy is an important element of professional learning about teaching online. Finally, confidence and competence with the tools and technologies for teaching online are important threshold digital competencies for online educators.

Reference

Farrell, O., Brunton, J., Costello, E., Donlon, E., Trevaskis, S., Eccles, S., & Ní Shé, C. (2019). *An investigation of effective online teaching: a needs analysis of online educators and online students.* Dublin: #Openteach Project. Retrieved from https://openteach.ie/wp-content/uploads/2020/07/Openteach-Needs-Analysis-Report-v2-1.pdf

Farrell, O., Brunton, J., Costello, E., Donlon, E., Trevaskis, S., Eccles, S., & Ní Shé, C. (2020). *Openteach Pilot Evaluation Report.* Dublin: #Openteach Project. (Version 2). Zenodo. http://doi.org/10.5281/zenodo.4599607. Retrieved from https://openteach.ie/wp-content/uploads/2020/07/Openteach-Pilot-Evaluation-Report.pdf

Farrell, O., Brunton, J., Costello, & Ní Shé, C. (2021). *#Openteach: professional development for open online educators.* Dublin: Pressbooks.

Ní Shé, C., Farrell, O., Brunton, J., Costello, E., Donlon, E., Trevaskis, S., &Eccles, S. (2019). *Teaching online is different: critical perspectives from the literature.* Dublin: Dublin City University. doi: 10.5281/zenodo.3479402. Retrieved from https://openteach.ie/wp-content/uploads/2019/11/Teaching-online-is-different.pdf

Ní Shé, C., Farrell, O., Brunton, J., Costello, E., Donlon, E., Trevaskis, S., & Eccles, S. (2020). DCU Case Study: Using ABC to Design an Online Teaching Course for Open Online Educators. ABC Learning Design Website. Retrieved from https://abc-ld.org/casestudy/dcu-case-study2/

Lessons from a Pandemic for the Future of Education
European Distance and E-Learning Network (EDEN) Proceedings
2021 Annual Conference | Madrid, 21-24 June, 2021
ISSN 2707-2819
doi: 10.38069/edenconf-2021-ac0017

INTERPROFESSIONAL LEARNING IN AN ONLINE PROGRAMME: A SWOT ANALYSIS

Josef Trapani, Maria Cassar, Ermira Tartari, Faculty of Health Sciences, Veronica Montebello, Faculty of Dental Surgery, Adrienne Grech, Michelle Camilleri, Faculty of Health Sciences, University of Malta, L-Imsida, Malta

Abstract

The unprecedented COVID-19 pandemic has forced educators individually, and educational institutions collectively, to rethink their teaching and assessment modes. Several universities have seen a sudden shift from traditional face to face teaching and learning to online approaches. The aim of this case study is to share the authors' experience in the design, coordination, delivery and evaluation of a fully online post-registration programme. Now in its twelfth year, this is an interdisciplinary course and caters for qualified health professionals from various sectors and with various levels of experience seeking a baccalaureate qualification. The paper uses the SWOT analysis technique to highlight the programme's strengths and weaknesses, and to reflect on its opportunities for, and threats to, further development. In so doing, it discusses some considerations underpinning the shift from a face to face to an online, mainly asynchronous, mode of delivery for this post-registration academic top-up programme. The paper explains the challenges encountered and the lessons learnt through feedback from the students, stakeholders, and external examiners. The good practices that were developed as a result, including strategies to foster a community of learners, may be of interest to, and applied by, educators in other settings.

Background

In several countries, members of the same healthcare profession have similar qualifications at the point of entry as practising clinicians in healthcare settings. In Malta, however, several healthcare professions include members who would have entered the profession with the same professional qualification but a different academic qualification. This led to the need of academic top up programmes to enable professionals with a traditional/vocational qualification, a diploma or a higher diploma to upgrade their academic qualification to a bachelor's degree. Initially these were delivered face to face, with significant challenges for people with young families and in full time employment and also difficulties in being released from the clinical area to attend lectures. The University of Malta's B.Sc. (Hons) Health Science programme was launched in 2009 to address this need and just under 350 students have completed it thus far.

This is a fully online programme leading to a European Qualifications Framework Level 6 (Bachelor's) academic qualification, delivered mainly asynchronously with some synchronous elements and uses Moodle as a virtual learning environment platform. It aims to help healthcare professionals develop their academic reading and writing skills, clinical reasoning and critical thinking through questioning their practice and ultimately becoming more effective in their work. Concurrently, it enables course participants to upgrade their traditional, diploma or higher diploma qualification to a bachelor's level, thus maximising their career opportunities. Graduates are eligible for second cycle programmes leading to a Master's degree (University of Malta, 2021).

To complete the programme, students need to obtain between 60 and 90 ECTS credits, depending on previous qualifications; these include three core modules (on evidence-based practice, research methods and a dissertation) and a number of elective modules, each of which is worth 10 ECTS credits. Each academic year, a student may complete between one and four modules. The course is, therefore, considerably flexible in terms of intensity and duration. Depending on their other commitments, students may complete the programme over between 1½ and 4 years, and they are allowed to change the intended duration along the course.

This paper uses the SWOT analysis technique (Schooley, 2019) to discuss the strengths and weaknesses of this programme, as well as its opportunities for and threats to its further development. It is based on feedback obtained from stakeholders (including students and external examiners), the literature, and the authors' own reflections, now that the course is in its twelfth year.

Strengths

The programme has a number of strengths. It is one of the first fully online courses at the University of Malta and its flexible distance-learning and mainly asynchronous nature allows full time clinicians with multiple commitments to participate, while maintaining a favourable work-family balance (Grzywacz & Butler, 2007; Andrade & Matias, 2017). Educators and learners on the programme are well supported by the Information Technology (IT) Services team. The programme has a strong interprofessional education (IPE) element as it is delivered by a multidisciplinary team of committed educators coming from a range of academic and/or clinical backgrounds and accepts students from various health professions. There are multiple channels of communication between the students, educators, academic coordinators and administrators.

Organisational and Pedagogical Strengths

A number of standard operational procedures, set up through a team effort by the educators, are rigorously adhered to. These include:

- A minimum standards checklist for each module, catering for both content and delivery but essentially based on ensuring sufficient cognitive, teaching and social presence (Garrison, 2007; Garrison, 2009);
- An administration guide and a *roadmap* for each module, which include clear learning outcomes, study plans, key resources and a schedule of learning activities and assessments, which empower students by covering the fundamental concepts designed to help them actively engage and be successful in their studies;
- Standardised assessment rubrics which enhance harmonisation within and between modules;
- Netiquette guidelines, in both textual and infographic format, displayed prominently on the administration guide and on the VLE area for each module.

Other strengths of the programme include a clear congruence between the intended outcomes, instructional strategies and assessment methods (Asunda & Ware, 2015; Santhanam, 2002); and clarity of expectations and their rationale. Detailed and timely feedback and feedforward constitute a cornerstone of the programme. Feedback is both formative and summative in nature, and thus enables students to improve their work in the same and subsequent modules, and eventually the dissertation, which is congruent with the principles of instructional scaffolding (Al Mamun et al., 2020; Shaw, 2019). It is delivered to students individually but is often accompanied by comments to the entire cohort to enhance group learning. Feedback delivery is occasionally followed up by a synchronous session to clarify concerns and take-home points.

The programme is designed in a way that attracts higher student engagement and interaction, with specific attention given to the affordances available to healthcare professionals working within a clinical environment. Thus the programme offers inherent opportunities for students to apply their learning in an authentic context, which constitutes "real world relevance" (Herrington, Oliver, & Reeves, 2006).

Another strength of the programme is its inclusive teaching and learning style which is upheld throughout the various modules. Delivery of content accommodates different learning styles and different speeds of cognitive learning, and subject material is often presented in a variety of formats. The programme has an element of cultural inclusivity by ensuring that its pedagogy and curriculum are flexible, adaptable and relevant to students from diverse cultural backgrounds. This reflects the multi-ethnic character of the national health service workforce.

Fostering a Community of Learners

There is a strong emphasis on establishing and maintaining a community of practice (Lave & Wagner, 1991), based on the premise that, through regular interaction, groups of people who share a concern or a passion for something do and learn better as a group than individually. This is imparted early on and sustained throughout the programme. The underlying principles are that educators are also learners and students may also be educators; therefore, all members learn at different moments in the programme (Lave & Wegner, 1991; Garrison, 2011). The educators generally adopt a postmodernist approach of teaching, based on more open-ended discussion and which encourages students to work together to co-construct knowledge rather than being too prescriptive. Consequently, the educators' role on the programme is to provide opportunities for learners to take the lead in their own learning, which is fundamental in creating successful online learning communities (Palloff & Pratt, 1999).

Various strategies and activities are utilised towards this end. Students are requested to set up their profile (with a clear photo and a brief bio) at the beginning of each module. Initial exercises are used as icebreakers and also to enable students and educators to share their expectations from the course and the anticipated challenges. Apart from several learning forums, through which moderated online discussions regularly takes place, each module includes a number of general forums, namely:

- A *Q&A Forum* for posting general queries about the module;
- An *Assessment Forum* for queries about the assignments, presentation, collaborative group task or any other form of assessment pertaining to a respective module;
- A *Technical Queries Forum* where students can seek help about the VLE and other IT-related issues;
- A *Virtual Café*, which serves as a means of purely social (non-academic) interaction but also to share insights and resources with fellow members of the virtual community of learners.

Students are encouraged to answer each other's queries rather than waiting for a lecturer to answer. Also, students are invited to post their queries publicly, rather than contacting a lecturer privately. Subsequently, more students may learn from the same query and students are acting as educators and facilitators of other community members' learning.

Weaknesses

On reflection, the programme is impeded by a number of weaknesses. First, it may be argued that the elective modules on offer do not adequately reflect all students' disciplines. However, flexibility has helped to turn this into an interesting, if challenging, opportunity for students to expand their horizon and learn beyond what is traditionally within the remit of their profession. Second, despite the coordinators' efforts to ensure harmonisation, there may be some discrepancies between modules in terms of commitment of the convenor, and possibly quality. Third, the administration and delivery of the programme had to retrospectively fit the university's existent (and often considerably rigid) structures and procedures. These include assessment regulations, methods for formal module evaluation, recognition of academic effort and remuneration of visiting staff, which were mainly developed with face to face courses in mind and may not always reflect the realities of online teaching and learning.

So far, almost all participants have been locally based. This suggests that the online and predominantly asynchronous nature of the programme may be further exploited. Efforts to recruit international participants are presently underway. Limited human resources, but most notably the unavailability of course engineers or instructional designers, mean that each module coordinator must concurrently act as educator, course designer and assessor, and must concurrently troubleshoot most technical queries. Despite being intended as an interdisciplinary programme, the very large majority of the students are nurses, which means that the programme is not yet reaching its potential of a truly interprofessional education programme.

Opportunities

Despite these potential and actual limitations, there are several opportunities for further development, partly based on attempts to address the identified weaknesses. Efforts are made to reach out to potential students, including clinicians in various disciplines and clinical settings, final year students on the Higher Diploma in Health Science programme and online marketing to attract both local and foreign students. Plans are underway to offer certain elective modules as stand-alone continuing professional development courses, thus rendering them more viable in cases where relatively few students on the course choose the module. Being originally designed as an online course, the programme is very amenable to virtual student mobility (Gaebel, 2020) through the networks the educators are already involved in, such as the ERASMUS+ programme (European Commission, 2021) and the European University of the Seas (SEA-EU) (2021) project.

There are constant efforts to maintain and improve the programme's quality and relevance. Part of the brief for external examiners assigned to the programme includes providing constructive feedback and professional development workshops for the educators on this programme; this is done both individually and collectively. Students are provided several opportunities for providing feedback during and after their participation in specific modules and about the programme in general. This is done in an anonymous manner, either via online questionnaires or through meetings with the external examiner with none of the module coordinators present. The external examiner typically synthesises such feedback for the module coordinators' action.

Perhaps the most important, even if intangible, opportunity arising from the interdisciplinary nature of the programme is the fact that it enables clinicians to become more aware of practices and approaches to care in different entities, contexts and countries by members of their own or different professions. Indeed, open discussions and sharing of ideas are often inspirational for students and the educators themselves.

Threats

Since so many aspects of everyday life now occur in an online setting, there is a risk of the programme being impacted by the public's fatigue of anything online (Lee, 2020; Vassou, 2020). Among fellow educators and students, some scepticism about online education and insecurity in using an e-learning platform persist; these are mainly addressed through dedicated professional development courses but, perhaps more effectively, through sharing of experiences and mentoring by more experienced colleagues.

Apart from competition from similar (local and international) online courses that are now available, the programme faces the threat of there being fewer potential students who need to complete an academic upgrade, because several health professions now require at least a bachelor's degree at point of entry and also because it is becoming increasingly possible for applications without a bachelor's degree to be accepted on a master's programme. Dwindling numbers of students may render some elective modules unsustainable, which is one of the reasons why efforts for attracting students from other countries are being reinforced.

The module coordinators on this programme are conscious of an evolving student population. In the early days of the programme, the vast majority of the students were professionally mature clinicians who were finally given the opportunity of reading for a bachelor's degree. The student population has now mainly shifted to newly qualified staff who have just finished their higher diploma programme. This swing has undoubtedly impacted the depth and quality of the online discussions, enthusiasm, commitment to course participation and the joy of learning that characterised earlier student cohorts.

Although the importance of regular and timely participation in asynchronous online discussions is highlighted, there is still evidence of occasional lurking, where some students only contribute towards the end of an online discussion, when this becomes (almost) meaningless (Beaudoin, 2002; Küçük, 2010). Well-designed work-portfolios, which are used in some of the modules on this programme, can help mitigate lurking (Rowley, 2016) by enabling students to write about their own experiences and if they wish to have feedback from their peers, they need to contribute (Liu & Carless, 2006). Group work, which is actively encouraged in various modules due to its well documented contribution to online learning (Mcgribbin, 2013), tends to be unpopular with students, partly because of frustrations arising from perceived and actual variations among group members' involvement, efforts and commitments. This has partly been addressed by reassuring students that, even in group work, students' work is assessed individually on the basis of the quality and quantity of their own contributions.

Finally, in spite of the previously highlighted efforts to maintain open communication channels with and between students and the various forms of support available, some students still do not reach out for help and do not feel a sense of connection with classmates. Thus, despite all efforts, the online course may be perceived as a lonely journey for some students (Burns, 2016; Myles, 2020).

Conclusions and Lessons Learnt

Being involved in the design, coordination, delivery and evaluation of this programme since its inception, and on reflection on its strengths, weaknesses, opportunities and threats, a number of lessons have been learnt. First, designing and delivering an online team-based learning programme should ideally draw together an eclectic team with different forms and levels of knowledge and expertise. Second, an education programme should be planned in view of, and be responsive to, the specific context in which it is to be delivered; for instance, our milieu was originally the Maltese health care workforce around twelve years ago, but now the backdrop is the international healthcare workforce. Thus, programme adjustments and further development may be necessary. The students' context and circumstances should be constantly kept in mind. Finally, to quote Voltaire, "perfect is the enemy of good" (Hegel et al., 1991). Therefore, it is often worth trying a good idea without waiting for the ideal conditions, resources or a perfect team. This programme has run successfully for 12 years and we are grateful for the opportunity to implement it. Nonetheless, we recognize and are cautious of the dangers and risks of inadequate preparedness and the seriousness of compromising quality. Institutional and departmental safeguards in these regards were and always have to be in place. We are all still learning from our own successes and failures, but in our case, vision, determination and some pedagogical and IT skills set us, as a team, en route for running and updating a course for over a decade.

References

Andrade, C., & Matias, M. (2017). Adding school to work–family balance: The role of support for Portuguese working mothers attending a master's degree. *Journal of Adult and Continuing Education, 23*(2), 143-161. https://doi:10.1177/1477971417721717

Asunda, P. A., & Ware, S. (2015). Applying the Congruence Principle of Bloom's Taxonomy to Develop an Integrated STEM Experience through Engineering Design. *JOTS – Journal of Technology Studies, 41*(2). https://doi.org/10.21061/jots.v41i2.a.3

Beaudoin, M. F. (2002). Learning or lurking? Tracking the "invisible" online student. *The Internet and Higher Education, 5*(2), 147-155.

Burns, M. (2016, April 13). The loneliness of the long-distance learner. GPE Transforming Education [Blog post]. Retrieved from https://www.globalpartnership.org/blog/loneliness-long-distance-learner

European Commission (2021). *ERASMUS+ Programme.* Retrieved from https://ec.europa.eu/programmes/erasmus-plus/node_en

European University of the Seas (2021). *Mission Statement and Manifesto.* Retrieved from https://sea-eu.org/mission-statement/

Gaebel, M. (2020, June 30). Erasmus+ should embrace the benefits of virtual mobility. University World News [Blog post]. Retrieved from https://www.universityworldnews.com/post.php?story=20200630082558805

Garrison, D. (2007). Online Community of Inquiry Review: Social, Cognitive, and Teaching Presence Issues. *Journal of Asynchronous Learning Networks, 11*(1), 61-72.

Garrison, D. R. (2009). Communities of inquiry in online learning. In P.L. Rogers, A. Berg, B. E. Boettcher, C. Howard, L. Justice, & K. D. Schenk (Eds.), *Encyclopedia of distance learning* (2nd ed.). IGI Global.

Garrison, D. R. (2011). *E-learning in the 21st century: A framework for research and practice* (2nd ed.). Routledge.

Grzywacz, J. G., & Butler, A. B. (2007).Work–Family Balance. In G. Fink (Ed.) *Encyclopedia of Stress* (2nd ed., pp-868-871). Academic Press. https://doi.org/10.1016/B978-012373947-6.00694-2

Herrington, J., Oliver, R., & Reeves, T.C (2006). Authentic tasks online: A synergy among learner, task and technology. *Distance Education, 27*(2), 233-248

Hegel, G. W. F., Wood, A. W., & Nisbet, H. B. (1991). *Elements of the Philosophy of Right.* Cambridge University Press.

Küçük, M. (2010). Lurking in online asynchronous discussion. *Procedia – Social and Behavioral Sciences, 2*(2), 2260-2263.

Lave, J., & Wegner, E. (1991). *Situated Learning: Legitimate Peripheral Participation.* Cambridge: Cambridge University Press.

Lee, J. (2020, November 17). A neuropsychological exploration of Zoom fatigue. Psychiatric Times [Blog post]. Retrieved from https://www.psychiatrictimes.com/view/psychological-exploration-zoom-fatigue

Liu, N. F., & Carless, D. (2006). Peer feedback: the learning element of peer assessment. *Teaching in Higher education, 11*(3), 279-290.

Mcgribbin (2013, February 19). Advantages of Online Group Work. Center for Online Learning, Research and Service [Blog post]. Retrieved from https://blogs.uis.edu/colrs/2013/02/19/advantages-of-online-group-work/

Al Mamun, M. A., Lawrie, G., & Wright, T. (2020). Instructional design of scaffolded online learning modules for self-directed and inquiry-based learning environments. *Computers & Education, 144,* 103695. https://doi.org/10.1016/j.compedu.2019.103695

Myles, J. M. (2020, February 11). The loneliness of the online learner. University Affairs [Blog post]. Retrieved from https://www.universityaffairs.ca/opinion/in-my-opinion/the-loneliness-of-the-online-learner/

Palloff, R. M., & Pratt, K. (1999). *Building Learning Communities in Cyberspace: Effective Strategies for the Online Classroom.* San Francisco, CA: Jossey-Bass.

Rowley, J. (2016). *E-Portfolios in Australian Universities.* Singapore: Springer Singapore Private. Limited.

Santhanam, E. (2002). Congruence of teaching, learning, assessment and evaluation. *Teaching and Learning Forum 2002: Focussing on the Student.* Retrieved from https://litec.curtin.edu.au/events/conferences/tlf/tlf2002/refereed/santhanam.pdf

Schooley, S. (2019, June 23). SWOT Analysis: What It Is and When to Use It. Business News Daily [Blog post]. Retrieved from https://www.businessnewsdaily.com/4245-swot-analysis.html#:~:text=A%20SWOT%20analysis%20is%20a,in%20making%20a%20business%20decision

Shaw, A. (2019). Scaffolding Learning in the Online Classroom. Center for Teaching and Learning. Retrieved from https://ctl.wiley.com/scaffolding-learning-in-the-online-classroom/

University of Malta (2021). Course information – Bachelor of Science (Hons) Health Science. L-Università ta' Malta. Retrieved from https://www.um.edu.mt/courses/overview/UBSCHHSPDL9-2021-2-O

Vassou, A. (2020, October 16). Yes, online fatigue is real. Ideadeco [Blog post]. Retrieved from https://medium.com/ideadeco/yes-online-fatigue-is-real-92288269117b

Lessons from a Pandemic for the Future of Education
European Distance and E-Learning Network (EDEN) Proceedings
2021 Annual Conference | Madrid, 21-24 June, 2021
ISSN 2707-2819
doi: 10.38069/edenconf-2021-ac0018

EVALUATION OF ONLINE PROGRAMMES: CONSTRUCTING THE SEA-EU TOOLKIT

Josef Trapani, Maria Cassar, Ermira Tartari, Faculty of Health Sciences, Veronica Montebello, Faculty of Dental Surgery, Adrienne Grech, Faculty of Health Sciences, Stefan Attard, Faculty of Theology, Michelle Camilleri, Faculty of Health Sciences, University of Malta, L-Imsida, Malta

Abstract

The COVID-19 pandemic brought online learning to the forefront of education across the globe. Educational institutions were forced to develop and deliver online programmes of study at a manner and pace that left many unprepared. A year and a half into the pandemic, the need for review and evaluation of swiftly developed online programmes is clearly indicated. This paper presents the process of developing a toolkit for evaluating online programmes by academics from the six partners of the European University of the Seas (SEA-EU) project. The toolkit provides a user-friendly guide for educators, managers and stakeholders in the education field, seeking to assess the quality of online programmes. The toolkit development process is extensively described in order to highlight its potential and the usefulness of collaborative work amongst international academic partners.

Introduction

The last two decades have witnessed new approaches to education wherein digitally mediated teaching and learning have slowly increased as a result of higher demand. With the COVID-19 pandemic, the education programmes of more than 1.38 billion learners were abruptly disrupted due to physical campuses being shut down to prevent the spread of infection (McCarthy, 2020). As a result, education providers and students across the globe had to shift to, optimise, or increase online learning endeavours, often without adequate pedagogical and practical preparedness. For educators with digital experience, the new, and now contemporary, reality of online dominance in the field of education triggered by the pandemic, was easily embraced and opportunities for evaluation of online programmes enhanced. Educators with less technological expertise may feel less confident.

In this context, this paper describes the process of developing a toolkit which guides the design, delivery and evaluation of an online programme. The comprehensive and user-friendly nature of the toolkit should empower educators with variable levels of proficiency and confidence in technology and online education. The toolkit was constructed by a team of academics from the six partners of the European University of the Seas (SEA-EU) project, namely the University of Cádiz (Spain), University of Malta (Malta), University of Gdańsk (Poland), University of Split (Croatia), Université de Bretagne Occidentale in Brest (France) and Kiel University (Germany). A description of the process and its evaluation is presented, in view of highlighting the potential of this resource, the usefulness of collaborative work amongst international academic partners as well as lessons learnt from the process.

This toolkit fits the rollout of the European Commission (EC)'s wider action plan regarding digital education, in that it contributes towards the engagement of educators in assessing and evaluating online programmes, despite disparities in their training and experience in online teaching and learning. Indeed, through its Digital Education Action Plan, the EC is committed to support the equal development of online and digital education across all member states, irrespective of the emergence and intensity of the COVID-19 pandemic (EC, 2018).

Toolkit development process

Preparation

The toolkit was developed during an online five-day workshop with representatives from all six SEA-EU members. The process included a variety of strategies and a balance between different guiding principles. In particular, the investigators wanted to achieve a balance between:

- A top-down and a bottom-up approach (Dudinik & Berge, 2006; Martinich, 2016);
- Adopting an emergent design while retaining a loose underpinning structure;
- Using the existent literature and the participants' experience and perspectives as sources for the toolkit;
- Having a pre-established schedule while being sensitive to the need to adapt it according to the developments of, and work completed along, the workshop, in the spirit of collaborative practice;
- Safeguarding all the participants' right to make their input noted while ensuring that the toolkit was devised within the allocated time of one week.

Prior to the workshop, the organisers identified four key themes that were proposed as the starting blocks of the toolkit. The themes were (a) *building a community of learners* (Garrison, 2007), (b) *teaching presence in online learning* (Anderson et al., 2001), (c) *scaffolded learning and teaching strategies* (Jumaat & Tasir, 2014; Shaw, 2019) and (d) *approaches to assessment*. These themes were determined on the basis of a literature search and on the organisers' own experience in designing and delivering online programmes. The organisers of the workshop were all experienced academics who had received training in online learning.

The first day of the workshop was dedicated to presentations by the delegation from each of the six partner universities about the strategies to online learning adopted at their institution and a keynote speech about what needs to be evaluated in online learning. The aim of both activities was to trigger the participants' reflection about their own and other participants' achievements and limitations in online learning and to enhance their sensitivity to the necessary considerations in achieving the main intended outcome of the workshop – that of collaboratively creating a comprehensive toolkit to evaluate online programmes.

Work in thematic groups

On the second day, following a brief presentation about the value of toolkits in education in general and in online learning in particular, the participants were divided into four groups according to the theme they had chosen at registration, on a first-come-first-served basis. Discussion took place in previously created Zoom breakout rooms.

The work within the thematic groups commenced by looking at a working definition of the respective themes. The pedagogical approaches of scaffolding (Jumaat & Tasir, 2014), building a learning community (Garrison, 2007), teaching presence (Garrison & Cleveland-Innes, 2005) and assessment strategies are well supported in both face to face and online learning environments (Lave & Wegner, 1991; Thompson & Macdonald, 2005; Shea et al., 2006). The thematic groups identified different working approaches, with some opting to carry out a literature search for any relevant theoretical background and others drawing upon their experiences in online education to inform the salient aspects of the toolkit.

Building a community of learners

The first thematic group acknowledged that building communities online is an increasingly challenging task, when compared to face-to-face education (Slagter van Tryon & Bishop, 2009). Thus, the group commenced by focusing on barriers that students face when engaging and trying to form part of an online community and shifting the perspective from a course designer to a learner. To minimise these challenges, the concept of universal design and accessible social content were implemented within the framework. The availability of different platforms and methods through which learners can participate in online environments, with a focus on achieving learning outcomes using different active learning strategies, was a predominant theme in these discussions. The initial working document of this thematic group consisted of the distribution of concepts within three phases of online programme evolution: introduction, implementation and evaluation. The introductory phase included assessment of learner needs and expectations, netiquette guidelines, programme policies, creation of profile pages, calendars and icebreakers, as well as the creation of fora for communication. The implementation phase focused on strategies that facilitate discourse and engage learners in knowledge and skill competencies. The concluding phase incorporated the evaluation of strategies used in the overall teaching and learning, in relation to timely feedback and self, peer, external and learner evaluation. Initially all strategies were further divided into strategies for learners and educators. However, the group decided to remove this distinction since, in itself, it created an unnecessary divide within the community of learners that was being promoted, with the educator being a learner as well.

Teaching presence in online learning

This thematic group discussed the need to shift the emphasis from preparing face-to-face sessions to (a) designing course-units which define learning goals; (b) plan effective feedback and assessment; and (c) identify what teaching and learning activities will be used to support students achieve such learning goals. The group proposed an evaluation checklist to guide course development, planning and implementation and to improve course delivery, with the aim of understanding students' expectations and needs. In the second stage, the group discussed instances during the students' learning journey where teaching presence could influence learning and further categorised teaching presence into facilitation of discourse, engaging students, monitoring learning and content delivery. A list of activities and practices which may be used by educators to evaluate the categories of teaching presence was created including: icebreakers, netiquette policies, the importance of encouraging, acknowledging and reinforcing students' contributions, and prompting and guiding discussions to focus on the learning outcomes. Active feedback from students at regular intervals, peer evaluation, self-evaluation and self-reflection with an opportunity for professional growth were identified as effective evaluation methods for teaching presence during course delivery. Participants discussed how teaching presence is also determined through focused direct instruction, which encompasses scholarly leadership and pedagogic competence. Faculty members tasked with online teaching should be provided with online education related to course development and instructions on proper technology use to ensure they are adequately trained to provide high quality online programmes. The working group offered insight into the need to evaluate programme delivery in terms of whether the minimum course expectations were reached by analysing data from results of tests, exams, tasks and using social media and associated diagnostics for evaluation. Evaluating teaching presence after online programme completion was deemed vital. Formal, documented self-evaluation, peer evaluation, evaluation by external examiners/experts, evaluation through computer analytics and data metrics and student evaluation are all methods which may be used for this purpose.

Scaffolded teaching and learning

This thematic group identified the necessary criteria that would assist educators to effectively embed the technique of scaffolding in the very matrix of an online programme. First, the main literature on this technique was consulted, discussed and sifted through, in order to select that which was highly scholarly. Second, a brainstorming session of the most pertinent elements of scaffolding was carried out, making sure to cover as large a span of the online programme as possible, particularly the design and delivery phases. Third, a *Scaffolded Technique Checklist* was developed. This took practically every facet of the learning process into consideration in order to ascertain that a variety of tools are employed to enhance knowledge in the resulting well-structured, smooth running programme. Hence, for instance, the following topics were analysed and incorporated into the Checklist: the learning outcomes; the use of a roadmap and a clear timeline; tools and activities adopted in order to attain the learning outcomes; awareness of knowledge gaps and diverse learning types of students; the use of rubrics; student interaction through peer feedback; and tutor feedback to students given over a particular period of time.

Approaches to assessment

The final thematic group discussed and compiled standards for educators in relation to approaches to assessment for online learning. The focus of the discussion revolved around aspects of measuring and gauging the effectiveness of evaluation strategies in online learning environments. Ongoing self-evaluation by educators and learners during all the phases of the course (before, during and upon course completion) is paramount. Through continuous feedback and regular appraisal mechanisms, the students' satisfaction, participation and progress can be observed and assessed. An evaluation of the possibility to learn from errors and a tolerance for discussion must be fostered in order to accommodate the above. The aim of direct and indirect assessments should be in line with course objectives, irrespective of the process itself. The group engaged in brainstorming, which identified the importance of accounting for learners' different needs and allowing for flexibility. Regular revision of facilitation methods, based on virtual learning environment data analytics and students' feedback on the learning experience, lead to constant improvement and enhancement of a programme. Providing students with individual and timely feedback was identified as a crucial element highlighting the importance of taking action on feedback provided by students and ways and means of relaying the feedback back to the learners and educators. Formative assessments consisting of ongoing evaluation of teaching effectiveness and student learning are important and should be performed multiple times during an online programme. Summative assessments are recommended to evaluate learning at the end of the programme and to identify if the intended learning outcomes have been achieved. The group also identified all the elements of assessment throughout the stages of online learning. A wide range of assessment tools and methods to evaluate the learning progress, knowledge and skill acquisition by adapting to the educational needs of the students were discussed.

The collective outputs of the thematic groups consisted of:

- A working document identifying the salient elements to be considered in view of adopting a scaffolded approach to learning;
- A question based checklist for evaluating strategies in relation to building a community of learners within each phase of an online programme;
- A diagrammatic representation of the central components which are to be considered when evaluating effective teaching presence.
- An algorithm incorporating key elements of assessment at different stages of the online learning process that need to be taken into account when planning, coordinating and delivering online learning.

Collating and refining the toolkit

The following questions were shared to help each group refine and report their work to the rest of the participants:

- Which of the points identified by this group are most important/relevant in evaluating the process of online teaching and learning?
- What points identified by this group work are less important/relevant in such evaluation?
- What modifications do we need to make in our group work to fit the overall toolkit?

The subsequent discussion revealed substantial commonalities and overlap across the outputs of the first two (*Building a community of learners* and *Teaching presence*) and the last two (*Scaffolded learning/teaching strategies* and *Approaches to assessment*) thematic groups. Thus, participants were accordingly regrouped into two larger groups. By the fourth day, the emerging toolkit incorporated two distinct, yet interrelated, elements: textual and diagrammatic. Therefore, participants were reassigned to two groups on the basis of their preference and perceived potential contribution to the artistic or the linguistic element of the emerging toolkit. These realigned groups respectively produced: (a) a set of guiding principles and reflective questions directing the evaluation of online programmes; and (b) a roadmap visually depicting various strategies and methods of evaluation in different phases before, during and after the delivery of an online programme.

On the final day of the workshop, three teams were formed. The first team formulated a preamble and the general guiding principles and intended outcomes of the toolkit. The second team refined the reflective questions for evaluating each phase of an online programme and their location in the emerging roadmap. The third team built a glossary of key terms used in the toolkit and collated a set of external resources that may be helpful to its users. The last part of the workshop was dedicated to discuss plans for dissemination. Final editorial refinements to the entire toolkit were addressed by the organisers. Since this is intended as a 'live' toolkit, a rotation between partners for its maintenance along the duration of the SEA-EU project was agreed by all universities.

The Outcome

Several strategies included in the toolkit draw upon concepts of the Community of Inquiry (COI) framework (Garrison, 2016), through supportive discourse and setting the appropriate climate for the facilitation of social connectedness, promoting a culture of collaboration and encouraging self-reflection. Garrison identified three pillars that relate to online educational experiences: teaching, social and cognitive presence. Teaching presence refers to how well the educator communicates goals and learning objectives, motivates and engages participants and provides timely feedback. Social presence occurs when participants identify with the online community and develop relationships with both peers and faculty. Cognitive presence encourages participants to foster critical thinking and integrate learning principles into real life practical situations. The interaction between all three pillars is fundamental to foster positive learning outcomes (Garrison, 2016).

By the end of this project, it was clear that the COI framework not only positively impacted the design and development of the toolkit, but, in a parallel process, we too, as academics, were also using Garrison's three pillars of teaching, social and cognitive presence, particularly as a result of the diversity amongst all involved. The optimal and maximal contribution of several delegates from all participating partners was challenging in many ways, such as having limited shared knowledge of each individual's expertise, diverse knowledge and experience in teaching online, as well as some participants leaving the workshop periodically due to other commitments. The organisers sought to mitigate challenges in various ways, for example, by creating shared documents that can be worked upon simultaneously over a period of five days, even if participants were not in attendance of a group meeting. This allowed for asynchronous participation and provided a space for reflection and opportunities for reviewing individuals' contributions.

In the spirit of a developing community of inquiry, a toolkit was created. This consists of: (a) a preamble delineating its intended aims and process of updating through the duration of the SEU-EU project; (b) an introductory section explaining the underpinning elements of online teaching; (c) a roadmap and explanatory notes facilitating its use; (d) definitions, objectives and guiding questions for evaluating the introductory, implementation and concluding phases of an online programme; (e) a glossary and bibliography. A segment of the toolkit under construction is presented in Figure 1. The toolkit shall be presented more extensively in a forthcoming collaborative publication by the SEA-EU project.

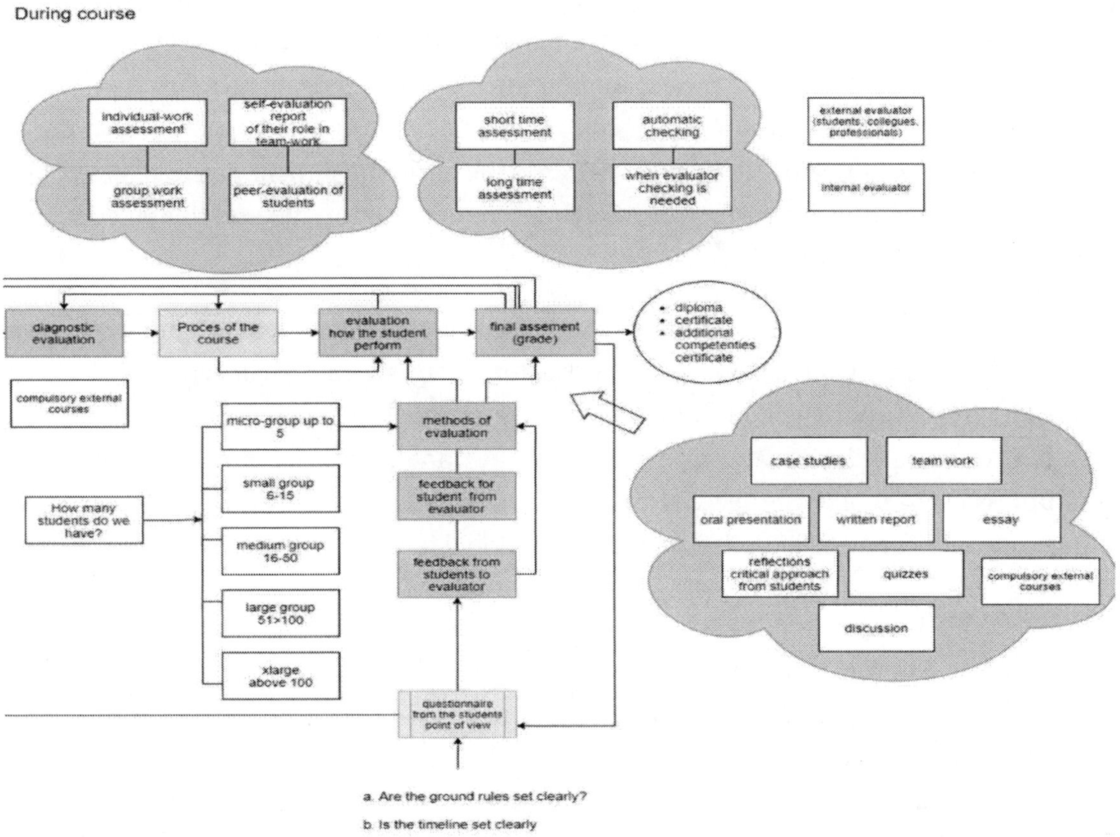

Figure 1. A segment of the SEA-EU toolkit for evaluating online programmes under construction

Process Evaluation

Feedback from the participants was sought at the end of the workshop. The vast majority of the respondents were very satisfied with the process and outcome of the workshop. Most of the participants felt that their intended outcomes were achieved to a substantial (46.7%) or to a large (26.7%) extent, and almost all the participants felt that their perspective about online learning had changed, either slightly (73.3%) or substantially (13.3%). The participants praised the collaborative nature of the workshop across different universities, the sharing of good practices and the moderators' balance between leading and incorporating the participants' input. The use of smaller breakout rooms and the moderators' flexibility and openness to the participants' views, not only about the content of the toolkit being developed but also about the process used in the different stages of the workshop, were received favourably. Less positive feedback included the intensive work involved, the varying commitment of other participants and an occasionally rushed pace with inadequate time for reflection.

Conclusion

The SEA-EU toolkit provides a basic framework and set of instruments for assessing the design, delivery and evaluation of an online programme. Against a backdrop of the sudden rise in the demand and use of online programmes, it is believed that this toolkit is relevant and timely. The basic nature of the toolkit and the methodological process used to develop it, involving an eclectic group of educators, should lend themselves well towards its effective use. This, in turn, augurs well towards the accomplishment of the referred EC's (2018) commitment to supporting the equal development of online and digital education across its member states.

The potential of this toolkit stems from the process of its development, which was described in paper, wherein a group of educators from six European tertiary education institutions drew upon the literature, theory, experience and knowledge in a collaborative manner. The adopted methodology is believed to be underpinned by significant robustness and fitness of the toolkit produced as its output, and should be considered of relevance to educators and managers at national and international levels.

References

Anderson, T., Rourke, L., Garrison, D. R., & Archer, W. (2001). Assessing teaching presence in a computer conferencing context. *Journal of Asynchronous Learning Networks, 5*(2), 1-17. Retrieved from https://olj.onlinelearningconsortium.org/index.php/olj/article/view/1875/706

Dudinik, G., & Berge, Z. L. (2006). Balancing Top-Down, Bottom-Up, and Peer-to-Peer Approaches to Sustaining Distance Training. *Turkish Online Journal of Distance Education, 7*(3), 144-153. Retrieved from https://dergipark.org.tr/en/download/article-file/156430

European Commission (2018). *European Commission Digital Education Action Plan.* Retrieved from https://eur-lex.europa.eu/legal-content/EN/TXT/?uri=COM:2018:22:FIN

Garrison, D. (2007). Online Community of Inquiry Review: Social, Cognitive, and Teaching Presence Issues. *Journal of Asynchronous Learning Networks, 11*(1), 61-72. Retrieved from http://eric.ed.gov/?id=EJ842688

Garrison, D. (2016). *E-Learning in the 21st Century: A Community of Inquiry Framework for Research and Practice* (3rd ed.). London, UK: Routledge.

Garrison, D., & Cleveland-Innes, M. (2005). Facilitating cognitive presence in online learning: Interaction is not enough. *The American Journal of Distance Education, 19*, 133-148. doi:10.1207/s15389286ajde1903_2

Jumaat, N. F., & Tasir, Z. (2014). Instructional scaffolding in an online learning environment: A meta-analysis. *Proceedings of the IEEE*, 74–77. doi:10.1109/LaTiCE.2014.22

Lave, J., & Wenger, E. (1991). *Situated learning: Legitimate peripheral participation.* Cambridge, UK: Cambridge University Press.

Martinich, L. (2016). Excellent execution: Balancing top-down and bottom-up management. *IEEE Engineering Management Review, 44*(2), 20-22. doi:10.1109/EMR.2016.2568720

McCarthy, N. (2020, March 26). COVID-19's Staggering impact on global education. World Economic Forum. World Economic Forum [Blog post]. Retrieved from https://www.weforum.org/agenda/2020/03/infographic-covid19-coronavirus-impact-global-education-health-schools/

Shaw, A. (2019). Scaffolding Learning in the Online Classroom. Center for Teaching and Learning. Retrieved from https://ctl.wiley.com/scaffolding-learning-in-the-online-classroom/

Shea, P., Sau Li, C., & Pickett, A. (2006). A study of teaching presence and student sense of learning community in fully online and web-enhanced college courses. *The Internet and Higher Education, 9*, 175-190. doi:10.1016/j.iheduc.2006.06.005

Slagter van Tryon, P. J., & Bishop, M. J. (2009). Theoretical foundations for enhancing social connectedness in online learning environments. *Distance Education, 30*(3), 291-315. doi:10.1080/01587910903236312

Thompson, T. L., & MacDonald, C. J. (2005). Community building, emergent design and expecting the unexpected: Creating a quality eLearning experience. *The Internet and Higher Education, 8*(3), 233-249.

Acknowledgements

The authors gratefully acknowledge the support and contribution of Ms Giuliana Longworth, Professor Godfrey Baldacchino and Professor Fiona Smart.

Lessons from a Pandemic for the Future of Education
European Distance and E-Learning Network (EDEN) Proceedings
2021 Annual Conference | Madrid, 21-24 June, 2021
ISSN 2707-2819
doi: 10.38069/edenconf-2021-ac0019

REMOTE TEACHING DURING THE LOCKDOWN – EVOLUTIONS AND TRANSFORMATIONS OF PEDAGOGICAL PRACTICES

Pascale Catoire, Manuel Schneewele, Sonia Tesson, Elodie Tricard, Laboratoire Ercaé, Université d'Orléans, France

Abstract

The lockdown, announced on March 16, 2020, led to a massive use of digital tools to offer pedagogical continuity. The objective of this exploratory research is to highlight the digital practices of 1, 994 teachers took part in this research from May to July 2020. A questionnaire measuring their digital practices during the lockdown, as well as the factors of change, was sent to them by email. Although the use of digital tools increased during the lockdown, the underlying pedagogical practices have not changed much. Teachers report that they mainly used digital tools to maintain communication as well as for the deposit, storage and sharing of content, thereby reproducing what is done in class. The results of this study targeting teachers' practices support the idea that the appropriation of digital tools should be considered over a long period of time and through a change in teaching practices.

Introduction

On March 16, 2020, the lockdown was announced in France; all schools and institutions were closed, and all teachers were told they would have to continue teaching their students online. The news came suddenly, many teachers did not feel digitally prepared, they could feel that they lacked equipment, guidance and training to implement this remote teaching.

The aim of this exploratory research was to find out what transformations the necessary and massive use of digital tools had brought in the pedagogical practices of primary school, secondary school, and higher education teachers. What could account for the evolutions observed? Did they depend on the level of the target students?

Digital practices at different levels of education in France

Many studies such as the latest by Tricot and Chesné (2020) state the digital revolution has not taken place in French schools and institutions.

In primary schools, the Talis report (OECD, 2019) showed that France was lagging behind other countries in terms of digital integration, with only 14% of teachers who have their students use digital tools in class. Similarly in secondary schools, the Becchetti-Bizot report (2017) stated that digital tools were little used in class, due to a lack of autonomy left to teachers and schools, and to a lack of support for innovative experiences. In higher education, Duguet and Morlaix (2018) showed that beside some innovative practices, many courses at university were still held in a traditionally and transmissive way.

Processes of appropriation and change in the use of technological tools

From the works of Engeström (1987), Rabardel (1995) and the activity theory (Vygotsky, 1980), we know that appropriation comes from an evolution in the use of these tools, that gradually evolves from a stabilised and well-known practice to another use, as the person tries to overcome the constraints of a given object in order to accomplish a project. In doing so, the person may use the tool differently from what the designer imagined for this very tool. More recently, Derboven et al. (2017) showed that in a virtual learning environment, teachers tended to use generic tools and modify them through a process of appropriation. We could therefore imagine that teachers during the lockdown would use generic tools but would use them differently.

What could encourage teachers to evolve in their pedagogical practices to use the necessary digital tools that would allow remote teaching?

In 1958, Kelman identified three processes of attitude change: compliance, identification, and internalization. We may comply with new tools and attitude because we expect a favourable reaction from another person or group. A symbolical or real reward from the higher educational institutions could have motivated teachers to adopt new tools and attitude (Malhotra & Galleta, 1999). Yet, French teachers are quite independent from these institutions. The identification process could have worked for teachers if they perceived the use of digital tools as a possibility to maintain good social relationship with peers. However, French teachers are used to working on their own. Maintaining relationship with their students and students' families could play a role. Internalization occurs when the new behaviour is intrinsically rewarding because it corresponds to the core values of the person (Malhotra & Galleta, 1999). As teachers place a high value on maintaining contact with their students so that they will not drop out, they might have been convinced by the use of remote teaching.

The theory acceptance model proposed by Davis (1989) and then Venkatesh et al. (2003) showed that determining factors in the acceptance of digital tools were: perceived usefulness and perceived ease of use, which led in turn to the acceptability of these new tools. Digital tools probably appeared as extremely useful to the teachers who were forced to teach online when schools closed. The perceived ease of use could explain the choice of some tools over others.

Nevertheless, we must keep in mind Paquelin's (2009) works around the resistance to change, and particularly the fact that individuals tend to use the tools they know best as much as they can in order to save the energy that is needed when adopting new tools.

Objectives of this research

We conducted this exploratory research with four objectives; we wanted to describe:

- What digital tools teachers used or modified during this time of remote teaching.
- To what extent pedagogical practices were modified.
- What motivated the teachers to change their practices.
- To what extent the adaptations depended on the target students (primary, secondary, or higher education).

Method used for collecting data

We originally collected 3165 answers from teachers all over France to the questionnaire we sent online, collected between May 4 and July 1, 2020; we didn't keep the 865 people who had quit the questionnaire before the end or spent less than 7 minutes on it. We also didn't consider the 313 trainee teachers in this study because their profile was different. Over the 1994 answers that constitute the base for our study, 702 came from teachers in primary school (with students from 3 to 11years old), 1034 came from French teachers in secondary school (with students from 11 to 18 years old), and 258 came from higher education teachers.

Several types of questions were asked: first of all about themselves (age, gender, years in the job, place of work), about material conditions (we will not use these data here), about the tools used (multiple choices fell into 7 categories of pedagogical practices). We also asked if they felt they had used some tools with an intention different from its original design, if they had the impression of having changed their pedagogical practices, why they had started or stopped using certain tools.

We collected and analysed the data thanks to the software Sphinx IQ2. The rise in percentages given below refer to the rise among the total number of teachers surveyed (total sample).

Results

Evolution in the use of different tools before and during remote teaching

The first digital tool mentioned by 70% of the teachers before and during lockdown is *the mail.* Before the lockdown, 63% in primary school said they used the mail, 84% in secondary school, 95% in higher education. With remote teaching, the evolution was +20% in primary school (83% of total sample), +3% in secondary school, -7% in higher education.

Forms and surveys (which enable to question students and parents directly or indirectly) were used by 19% in primary school, 21% in secondary school, 34% in higher education before the lockdown. With remote teaching, the evolution was important: +14% in primary school, +15% in secondary school, +35% (69% of total sample) in higher education.

Online resource data bases (which provide teachers with institutional ready-to-use material) were used by 20% in primary school, 16% in secondary school, 7% in higher education before the lockdown. With remote teaching, there was little evolution: +13% (33% of total sample) in primary school, +5% in secondary school, -1% in higher education.

Online learning management systems (such as Moodle) were used very differently before the lockdown: 4% in primary school, 29% in secondary school, 58% in higher education. With remote teaching, there was an important evolution: + 40% (44% of total sample) in primary school, +38% in secondary school, +5% in higher education.

Tools to share and store files with students were used by 25% of primary school teachers, 51% in secondary school, 65% in higher education before the lockdown. With remote teaching, the evolution was +27% in primary school (52% of total sample), +12% in secondary school, +3% in higher education.

Video conference systems (which enable online classes) were little used in primary and secondary education before the lockdown (less than 3%, contrary to higher education 31%). Those figures jumped with remote teaching: +40% in primary school, +38% in secondary school, +50% (81% of total sample) in higher education.

60% of the interviewees answered they had changed their practice with remote teaching. About a third said they changed it right away (34% in primary school, 33% in secondary school, 38% in higher education), while another third said they adapted gradually (37% in primary school, 35% in secondary school, 22% in higher education). Less than a fifth said they tried to transfer the same pedagogical practices from the class to remote teaching (19% in primary school, 14% in secondary school, 16% in higher education). Some said they continued using the same digital tools as before (10% in primary school, 18% in secondary school, 24% in higher education). A small part of the teachers answered they had used no digital tools (2% in primary school, 21% in secondary school, 4% in higher education) during the lockdown.

About a fifth of the teachers thought they had used digital tools with an intention different from their original design (17% in primary school, 21% in secondary school, 21% in higher education). Those were mainly communication tools such as Zoom, WhatsApp, Discord which were not part of their professional practices before.

Justifications for the use of the digital tools used during remote teaching

Pedagogical usefulness is the first reason why the teachers say they have used new tools (82% in primary and secondary school, 61% in higher education). From more important to less important, here are the different objectives assigned to the digital tools used during remote teaching:

- To give access to learning content (for 90% in secondary school and higher education, 70% in primary school);
- To give access to activities online (for 60% in primary school and higher education, 80% in secondary school);
- To allow human interaction (for 59% in secondary school and higher education, 63% in primary school);
- To assess students (for 17% in primary school, 57% in secondary school and 60% in higher education).

Only 20% of the teachers in primary and secondary school take *institutional requirements* into account when choosing new tools, contrary to 47% in higher education.

The fact that *students (families) may ask for certain tools* does not constitute a reason for adopting new tools for most teachers (8% in primary school, 15% in secondary school, 20% in higher education).

To an open question on the advantages of remote teaching, some primary school teachers stated that it would allow more interaction, contact and involvement of the students' families. Some secondary school teachers said it enabled them to get in touch with shy students and could favour students' autonomy. Some higher education teachers valued the time students saved on transport and the possibility for students to go deeper into the reflexion started in class.

Analysis

As we had imagined, teachers used more digital tools with remote learning even if a few say they have not used any (between 2 and 21% depending on the level they teach). They favoured tools which enabled them to carry on teaching. The use of tools for videoconferencing increased greatly, as well as tools for sharing and storing files in primary school, online learning management systems in primary and secondary school, and the mail for primary school teachers. The increase may be due to the necessity to favour interactions and keep in touch despite the distance. The greater use of online learning management and video conference systems in higher education may account for the decreased use of the mail at that level. We expected the teachers to use more online data and resource data bases, but they only did so in primary schools. French secondary school teachers are used to editing their own teaching resources; they continued to do so during the lockdown.

Even if some tools were used more extensively to adapt to remote teaching, teachers did not seem to change their pedagogical practices fundamentally: they used digital tools mainly for giving access to learning content, for sharing and storing files which shows they still relied on a traditional and transmissive approach. However, a majority of teachers declared they had changed their practices. This apparent contradiction may be explained by the difference which exists between feeling and reality: they may have had the impression of teaching differently because remote teaching was different; yet the tools they chose were those they used before. This is probably due to the principle of economy referred to by Paquelin (2009). They mainly reproduced what they were doing in class, which may account for the large choice of activities online they proposed. French educators know the importance of keeping students active and of constructivist theories for learning. We remember that the appropriation of new tools is a long and complex process. Despite the institutional demands, the new tools that were provided and advertised, the training sessions online which existed, the little time that had been given to teachers was not enough to enable them to innovate and take advantage of the distance to promote other pedagogical uses with the tools they use in daily life (e.g. WhatsApp).

The institutional requirements or the wishes of the students and families did not account for choosing new tools, which was mainly driven by pedagogical usefulness. French teachers are independent and social identification plays a minor role in their choices. As pointed by Davis (1989) perceived usefulness and perceived ease of use are essential as long as they are compatible with the organisation of time and space (Tricot & Chesné, 2020).

We have seen that the choices and uses vary according to the target students. Three reasons may explain the differences in evolutions. Firstly, the increase is more important for the tools that appeared absolutely necessary in the new context. This can account for the high increase of the mail and tools for storing and sharing files in primary school where they were little used before the lockdown. Similarly, the use of online learning management system did not increase much in higher education because they were already quite developed before the lockdown, probably due to the age and autonomy of the students.

This leads us to the second factor explaining the differences among teachers: the high increase of forms and online surveys in higher education may be explained by the age of the students whose opinions can be considered; they also enable to maintain interaction with the high number of students enrolled in a university course. The important use of tools to assess in higher and secondary education, contrary to primary school, may be accounted for by the place final exams have in these institutions. The advantages of digital tools the teachers put forward depend on the needs of different students at different stages. In primary school, it seemed essential during that time of remote teaching to maintain interaction with students and families. In secondary schools, teachers considered digital tools as a way to increase their students' autonomy. In higher education, teachers highlighted that digital tools would enable students to think by themselves and would simplify their daily life by saving on transport time.

The third factor for the differences among the teachers' answers lies in the role the institution plays. Higher education teachers seemed to take institutional demands into account. The link with their institution (the local university) where the decisions are taken is tight enough. On the other hand, as secondary school teachers and primary school teachers are very independent in their schools where the Head does not have any hierarchical pressure, they may have been less inclined to follow the requirements of their institution and may have felt isolated at home. The secondary school teachers who are recruited nationally are probably those who feel the least concerned by institutional demands; this could account for the 21% among secondary school teachers who answered they had not used any digital tools (as opposed to 2% in primary school and 4% in higher education).

Conclusion

Observing remote teaching during the lockdown led us to 4 conclusions which are correlated. Some tools which enabled to maintain interactions and to keep teaching as in class increased, but teaching practices were not modified fundamentally. The tools were firstly used according to the teachers' perception of their pedagogical usefulness and to the perceived needs of their students which differed according to their ages. They enabled primary school teachers to keep in touch with families, secondary school teachers to favour autonomy and activity for their students, higher education teachers to give more time to their students to organize themselves and to assess final exams. The link between these different categories of teachers and their institutions played a role in their adoption of new digital tools and practices. Because of the short time that was given to teachers, there was little appropriation of the new tools which were promoted by the institutions.

The limit of our study is that it relies on an online digital questionnaire, since we could not observe their practices. Teachers were preoccupied and very busy at the time when they answered our questionnaire, which might have had an influence on how they responded. Besides, they may have misunderstood or interpreted our questions differently from what we intended them to be. This probably accounts for the numerous people who quit the questionnaire before the end or the many questions left unanswered, which we had to take out of our study.

The results we obtained could lead us to other studies, a comparison between the answers of trainee and expert teachers, or a study on the material and psychological conditions of teachers during that time. Other statistical studies could be made from these data, to compare the results between the different categories of teachers, depending on the level they teach, on gender. This was not the goal of this exploratory research which aimed at shedding light on the digital practices of different teachers before and during the lockdown.

Beyond the very particular context of the lockdown, our study raises questions as to what encourages or discourages students to adopt new digital tools and pedagogical practices, and how to train teachers for these new uses.

References

Becchetti-Bizot, C. (2017). *Repenser la forme scolaire à l'heure du numérique.* Rapport IGEN. Retrieved from https://www.education.gouv.fr/repenser-la-forme-scolaire-l-heure-du-numerique-vers-de-nouvelles-manieres-d-apprendre-et-d-2678

Davis, F. D. (1989). Perceived usefulness, perceived ease of use, and user acceptance of information technology. *MIS Quarterly, 13*(3), 318-339.

Derboven, J., Geerts, D., & de Grooff, D. (2017). Appropriating virtual learning environments: A study of teacher tactics. *Journal of Visual Languages & Computing, 40*, 20-35.

Duguet, A., & Morlaix, S. (2018). Le numérique à l'université : facteur explicatif des méthodes pédagogiques? *Revue internationale de pédagogie de l'enseignement supérieur, 34*(3), 1-18. Retrieved from https://hal.archives-ouvertes.fr/halshs-01976864

Kelman, H. C. (1958). Compliance, identification, and internalization three processes of attitude change. *Journal of Conflict Resolution, 2*(1), 51-60.

Engeström, Y. (1987). *Learning by expanding: An activity-theoretical approach to developmental research.* Helsinki: Orienta-Konsultit.

Malhotra, Y., & Galletta, D. F. (1999). Extending the technology acceptance model to account for social influence: Theoretical bases and empirical validation. *Proceedings of the 32nd Annual Hawaii International Conference on Systems Sciences* (HICSS-32). January 5-8, 1999, Maui, Hawaii, USA.

Organisation for Economic Co-operation and Development – OECD. (2019). *TALIS 2018 Results (Volume 1): Teachers and School Leaders as Lifelong Learners.* Retrieved from https://www.oecd.org/education/talis/TALIS2018_CN_FRA.pdf

Paquelin, D. (2009). *L'appropriation des dispositifs numérique de formation : du prescrit aux usages.* Paris: l'Harmattan.

Rabardel, P. (1995). *Les hommes et les technologies ; approche cognitive des instruments contemporains.* Paris: A. Colin.

Tricot, A., & Chesné, J.-F. (2020). *Numérique et apprentissages scolaires : rapport de synthèse.* Paris: Cnesco. Retrieved from http://www.cnesco.fr/wp-content/uploads/2020/10/201015_Cnesco_Numerique_Tricot__Chesne_Rapport_synthese.pdf

Venkatesh, V, Morris, M. G., Davis, M. G., & Davis, F. D. (2003). User Acceptance of Information Technology: Toward a Unified View. *MIS Quarterly, 27*(3), 425-478. Retrieved from https://www.jstor.org/stable/30036540?seq=1

Vygotsky, L. S. (1980). *Mind in society: The development of higher psychological processes.* Harvard University Press.

Lessons from a Pandemic for the Future of Education
European Distance and E-Learning Network (EDEN) Proceedings
2021 Annual Conference | Madrid, 21-24 June, 2021
ISSN 2707-2819
doi: 10.38069/edenconf-2021-ac0020

OPEN EDUCATIONAL PRACTICES IN LEARNING AND TEACHING OF COMPUTER SCIENCE

José Luis Delgado, Covadonga Rodrigo, National Distance University of Spain, Spain

Abstract

This paper shows several actions that address the use and development of open educational resources (OERs) and the utilisation of open source machine virtualization tools for Moodle course instantiation in a Computer Science-based Teacher Training course. The training is dedicated to show the basic characteristics and tools present in e-learning environments and to transmit the knowledge to develop educational resources and personalize different learning environments. The learning activities have been designed following the constructive approach, in the form of practical tasks that ensure the training of students in the self-implementation and personalisation of e-learning courses embedded into virtual machines. Students learn how to do the pedagogical design, to set up a delivery, and perform to develop their own resources and re-use from others. Finally, students have to assess the quality of the OERs following the UNE71362 standard. As a transversal pedagogical objective of the Master's course, the learning aims to help the dissemination and awareness of the UNESCO's Sustainable Development Goal 4 (SDG4) which ensures inclusive and equitable quality education and fosters lifelong learning opportunities for all. In this sense, specific OER development for gender inclusion and accessibility for all learners has been promoted.

Introduction

Since the UNESCO Paris Declaration on OER (Open Educational Resources) adopted by the global community in June 2012, there have been a number of new developments, such as new authoring tools or distribution systems. Providing OERs and open software-based tools to the students also offer the flexibility of learning and benefits to all learners. The "open pedagogy" concept is closely associated with the creation, use, and sharing of open educational resources (OER). Weller (2013) states that open pedagogy "makes use of...abundant, open content (such as open educational resources, videos, podcasts), but also places an emphasis on the network and the learner's connections within it" (p.10). Or as Cronin (2017) has defined the related term "open educational practices," as "a broad descriptor of practices that include the creation, use, and reuse of open educational resources (OER) as well as open pedagogies and open sharing of teaching practices" (p.16).

The "open" in open educational resources indicates that these materials are licensed with copyright licenses that provide permission for everyone to participate in the 5R activities – retain, reuse, revise, remix, and redistribute (Wiley & Hilton III, 2018). The Open Educational Quality Initiative (OPAL, 2011) defines open educational practices as "a set of activities around instructional design and implementation of events and processes intended to support learning. They also include the creation, use and repurposing of Open Educational Resources (OER) and their adaptation to the contextual setting. They are documented in a portable format and made openly available" (p.13).

In constructive learning (Connolly & Stansfield, 2007), students use technology tools to connect new information to their prior knowledge rather than to passively receive information. The Constructive characteristic describes learner-centred instruction that allows students to use technology tools to connect new information to their prior knowledge. This characteristic is concerned with the flexible use of technology to build knowledge in the modality that is most effective for each student.

In this work, the authors seek to help their students, (futurable teachers in secondary and high schools, to recognize the added-value derived from using and developing their own OERs and implementing their own course styles and personalization. This involves defining an OER value chain that will help stakeholders identify the various sub-systems in the chain that link the individual teacher's or learner's contribution relating to OER use. For constructive learning, all tasks defined to develop the different sub-systems allow students to use the proposed technology tools to connect the new content information to their prior knowledge and scaffold their new knowledge. Finally, following open pedagogy principles, a network to enhance learner's connections and peer-to-peer interaction has been implemented.

Implementation of AEi instructional design

Within the Spanish Education System, teaching in the field of Vocational Training requires obtaining a relevant qualification, which is embodied in the Master's Degree in Teacher Training for Compulsory Secondary Education and Baccalaureate, Vocational Training and Language Teaching. This degree consists of a set of subjects related to aspects of Education and Innovation, and another set of subjects related to specific topics of the specialty of Computer Science. This second group includes the subject Learning and Teaching of Computer Science (hereinafter, AEi), with a total load of 6 ECTS credits.

It is not only necessary to know and master the discipline of Computer Science, but the teaching staff must be able to assume the management of the teaching-learning process. That is to say, it is necessary to have the necessary knowledge to structure didactically the matter applying appropriate teaching methods. AEi instructional design has been structured mainly around this philosophy. Therefore, students are encouraged to personalize their own virtual-classroom, to develop their own learning resources and share them through an on-line repository, to complete the associated LOM (Learning Object Metadata), to package them under SCORM (Sharable Content Object Reference Model) standard, to re-use learning resources from other peers within a community of practice and to assess the quality level of their developed materials.

Thus, there are three main axes on which it should be possible to focus the effort to update the teaching of AEi:

- Virtualization: in many cases, the development of different Computer Science subjects requires the installation and configuration of different tools that are not always easy to implement and based in many cases on operating systems that are not within the reach of students for different reasons (for not being in the field of habitual use, for requiring certain hardware resources not available or other similar ones). That is why the existence of virtualized environments might be part of the solution to this problem.
- OERs: it is essential to focus the different subjects towards the development of a set of open educational resources that cover the entire discipline to be covered. In this open environment, the reuse of resources is more than desirable, so aspects such as platform interoperability and access to resource repositories are essential.
- Learning platforms or LMS: all of the above requires to be implemented in some LMS system that allows the development of a learning scenario that allows the distance development of the subject or subject in question. Among the different alternatives, Moodle is probably the most widespread platform in this field and allows the established objectives to be met.

Regarding the Constructive Learning descriptors defined in the Technology Integration Matrix (FCIT, 2005) by Harmes, Welsh, and Winkelman (2016) for the instruction of real-world skills, all of the above activities are included into level four: Adaptation Level, which main characteristics help the students to independently use the technology for building knowledge, with student choice and exploration:

- Students begin to use technology tools independently to facilitate construction of meaning. With their growing conceptual understanding of the technology tools, students can explore the use of these tools as they are building knowledge.

- The teachers create instruction in which their students' use of technology tools is integral to building an understanding of a concept. We, the teachers, give our students the access to technology tools (Virtual Machines-VM, and authoring tools) and guide them in exploring and choosing appropriate resources.
- Technology tools that facilitate the construction of meaning are available to students for conventional uses.

At the same time some characteristics of level 5 Transformation level have also been achieved, in particular:

- The setting includes robust access to a wide variety of technology tools, robust access to online resources and a specific community built in the on-line repository, and the ability to publish new content online.

The following sections will show the way in which AEi is articulated according to the three main axes indicated above.

Lab virtualization for Moodle instantiation

The virtues of using virtualization are widely known: simple, fast and efficient implementation of different work environments within the same computer, better use and exploitation of available resources, the possibility of distributing these environments in a simple manner and platform interoperability (Ogunyemi & Johnston, 2010).In this regard, platforms such as Oracle's VirtualBox and EMC Corporation's VMware are probably the two most widely used and widespread virtualization environments in the educational environment. But most of the Spanish autonomies educational authorities have opted for free operating systems based on Unix / Linux and that use VirtualBox as virtualization software already pre-installed in them (for example, MAX of the Community of Madrid or Lliurex of the Community of Valencia), so opting for this virtualization option has been considered the most interesting.

In the field of IT teaching in vocational training centres, one of the main handicaps that appear is the installation and configuration of different services in the classroom (web service, mail service, LMS service, etc.), that can be addressed in two ways:

- Virtualization from scratch: in this case, the development of the virtualized environment starts from scratch. A host operating system is installed and configured from scratch, and then a specific service is installed, along with its corresponding configuration.
- Virtualization by adaptation of a previous system: in this case, the starting point is either a host operating system that has already been installed, or even a system that already contains the desired service perfectly configured.

From the learner's learning point of view, virtualization from scratch gives the possibility to carry out the whole necessary process from the point of formulation of the need until the need (service) is covered and perfectly functional. On the other hand, virtualization by adaptation proposes a quick and transparent implementation of the service for the student. Thus, everyone will have a virtualized environment perfectly configured and in an optimal state of operation, in addition to having an identical configuration that can be easily managed by the teacher. The main disadvantage is that this system gives the student the feeling that he/she has a "black box" whose start-up process is unknown to him/her, and therefore, learning is reduced to its operation and maintenance, and not to the initial installation and configuration process. In AEi we have considered that applying the concept of reuse and refactoring to virtualization is a desirable aspect that should be worked on, so the course proposes the use of an already existing virtualized environment adapted to certain needs.

After these practical experiences, students are able to design other virtual machines to cope with other different areas of vocational training studies. For instance, they could easily develop new VMs for teaching Operating Systems, such as Windows or Linux / Unix, as there already exist pre-configured environments that can be selected to create a full virtual lab, avoiding many typical problems like administrative difficulties of software installation and usage (Stoker et al., 2013). Bitnami is a company dedicated to the packaging of different services using different distribution scopes. As they have many different types of solutions, all ready to use, it is possible that most of the academic services that are needed within the classroom already have an initial implementation in Bitnami that could be adapted and customized.

The practice proposed to AEi students has been the adaptation of a virtual Bitnami machine on VirtualBox that allows the development of a Moodle environment. Moodle LMS delivers a powerful set of learner-centric tools to build a collaborative learning environment that empowers both teaching and learning. This open-source platform is backed by a large community of developers and educators constantly looking for ways to enhance the online learning experience, and there exist a lot of plug-ins and add-ons that extend and customise the functionality of Moodle. The use of this open-source platform contributes to the development of cognitive interest and motivation of the students, developing critical, professional pedagogical thinking and many forms of practical skills of the future teachers (Mykolaiovych et al., 2018). Students can choose on their own, which subject (from vocational training studies) is going to be implemented, but they are requested to develop at least one full lesson, using all kinds of multimedia resources.

Open Educational Resources development, uploading into repository and re-useness

Nowadays learning environments include the use of educational resources present on the Internet, such as digital books, presentations, videos, podcasts, etc., which are already part of the day-to-day life in the virtual classrooms. The study carried out by the Open Research Hub (de Los Arcos et al., 2015) shows the high degree of use of these resources for educational purposes. A broader knowledge of the existence of OER repositories and specific norms to evaluate their quality, together with some basic notions of computing, would allow the educators to create or reuse educational materials with the assurance of intellectual property and adapted to the varied needs of their learners (Rodrigo & Tabuenca, 2020).

Procomún is one of these OER repositories, supported by Spanish Ministry of Education. It stores more than 95,000 OERs along with educators' experiences, constituting an intelligent, social and distributed network. The repository is destined mainly for educational purposes but is open to a wider audience. Everyone can search, consult and download OERs in different formats. A semantic layer has been built on top of the existing platform and the services offered have been expanded by working with structured and Linked Data within the framework of the semantic web standards. The incorporation of a faceted search engine allows the user to find educational objects by restricting the global set of results through multiple criteria or facets based on their reasoning. The other fundamental element of the Procomún space is the Social Network closely linked to educational resources built by educators themselves, enriched with a social labelling system, such as user votes, educational contexts, recommendations for use and links to specific learning communities.

The activities promoted in this work also try to diminish four of the revealed six tensions that drive developing practices around OER in adult learning (Falconer et al., 2013). In particular:

- Open versus free: Low awareness of licensing is pronounced among adult educators and lifelong learners; common practice is to use free (no cost) resources without worrying unduly about IPR. Therefore, IPR issues are explained in detail, and students have to fill in the related metadata in the LOM section.
- Traditional versus new approaches: The majority of OER providers have traditional Higher Education views of teacher-directed pedagogy that are out of line with the direction in which adult learning is heading. The findings raise the possibility that approaches that work well in a university context may be less appropriate elsewhere. Therefore, the activities shown in this paper try to enhance cross-sector

collaboration between universities and high schools that could lead to more effective use of the resources.

- Community versus openness: Community-building is seen by initiatives as essential for successful uptake of OER. Communities can raise awareness, spread practice, and boost confidence. In 2017, authors created a social community linked to the Procomún repository to create a community of practice amongst learners (see Figure 1). The objective of this community is to explore the extent to which educators enrolled in their HE teaching qualification in Computer Science ("Master in Secondary Education, Professional Training and Language teaching") achieve the skills to develop quality OERs.
- Mass participation versus quality: The ability of the masses to participate in production of OER – and a cultural mistrust of getting something for nothing – give rise to user concerns about quality. This is particularly significant given the low ability of lifelong learners to evaluate resources for themselves.

Figure 1. UNED's social community linked to the Procomún repository

Belief in quality is a significant driver for OER initiatives, therefore students are trained to assess their resources with the UNE71362 Quality for Digital Learning Resources standard (UNE, 2020). Learners are trained within the master programme to assess their OERs following this standard that covers indicators of technological, pedagogical and accessibility compliance (Moreno et al., 2019). Students can develop their own diagrams to organize data in a logical way, showing the level of achievement with each of the fifteen criteria:

- pedagogical: didactic description, quality of content, ability to generate learning, adaptability, interactivity and motivation);

- technical: format and design, reusability, portability and robustness;
- usability and accessibility: navigation, operability, accessibility of audio-visual content and accessibility of textual content.

In 2021, the social community comprises more than 126 members and hosts 43 new resources. Created by Computer Science learners using eXeLearning authoring tool connected to the Procomún, thus allowing direct publishing, metadata filling-in and specification of intellectual property. Some of the more recently developed resources are:

- A practical guide for educators that contributes to the dissemination of techniques for the creation and reuse of OERs for learners with hearing impairment.
- A case study for the use of Computer Vision techniques to improve the accessibility of visual OERs for learners with visual impairment.
- Three OERs based on the inquiry-based methodology to empower the presence of women in the field of Computer Science. The resources have been built around the biography of three well-recognised professionals: Hedy Lamarr, Joan Clarke and Evelyn Berezin.
- Two OERs based on project-based learning devoted to raising awareness among learners of the importance of equality in society, particularly in gender.

Discussion and Conclusions

This paper aimed to showcase several innovative experiences that have been tested at a course on Learning and Teaching of Computer Science at the Master's Degree for Teachers Training at Secondary, High School and Vocational Education Programs. It showed that inclusive and sustainable development goals are closer to being achieved through the dissemination of best practices for future teachers, although we have also found some facts to improve in the tools we used:

- There still exists a huge potential in the development of OERs for the Computer Science field in the Procomún repository. The resources mainly available are focused in Compulsory Secondary Education.
- There exists a huge potential in re-useness of the Procomún resources but there is still a lot of work to do on the use of Open Linked Data in OER repositories for improving the searches and recommendations for retrieving the best resources for each teacher and pedagogical context through the faceted search engines.
- Unfortunately, Procomún does not use accessibility metadata standards for labelling their resources, decreasing the potential of the amount of OERs hosted to be reused in educational contexts to address students with accessibility needs or special education needs.

- The use of standards, such as UNE 71362 to evaluate the quality of OERs, is beneficial for all stakeholders of the learning environment and assures a minimum level of quality and accessibility. In addition, this allows the comparison between equivalent OERs in order to get the most suitable one (depending on the subject or the object students) using certain quality parameters provided by UNE 71362.

References

Connolly, T., & Stansfield, M. (2007). Developing constructivist learning environments to enhance elearning. In N. Buzzetto-More (Ed.), *Principles of effective online teaching* (pp. 19-38).

Cronin, C. (2017). Openness and praxis: exploring the use of open educational practices in higher education. *The International Review of Research in Open and Distributed Learning, 18*(5). doi:10.19173/irrodl.v18i5.3096

eXeLearning (2021). Descarga directa de las últimas versions. Retrieved from https://exelearning.net/descargas/

Falconer, I., McGill, L., Littlejohn, A., & Boursinou, E. (2013). *Overview and analysis of practices with Open Educational Resources in adult education in Europe.*

Florida Center for Instructional Technology (2005). The Technology Integration Matrix – Constructive Learning. Retrieved from https://fcit.usf.edu/matrix/project/constructive-learning/

Harmes, J. C., Welsh, J. L., & Winkelman, R. J. (2016). A framework for defining and evaluating technology integration in the instruction of real-world skills. In S. Ferrara, Y. Rosen, & M. Tager (Eds.), *Handbook of research on technology tools for real-world skill development* (pp. 137-162). Hershey, PA: IGI Global.

de Los Arcos, B., Farrow, R., Pitt, R., Perryman, L. A., Weller, M., & McAndrew, P. (2015). *OER Research Hub Data 2013-2015: Educators.* Open Education Research Hub.

Mykolaiovych, K. O., Mykolaivna, S. N., Vasylivna, B. V., & Mykhailivna, P. S. (2018). Improving professional and pedagogical training of future teachers by Moodle platforms (On the example of the course" Pedagogy"). *Научен вектор на Балканите*, (1).

Moreno, L., Fernández-Pampillón, A. M., Sarasa, A., Rodrigo, C., García-Villalobos, J., González, Y., & García-Mata, R. (2019). How to interweave accessibility with didactic and technological quality of digital educational materials. *Journal of Accessibility and Design for All, 9*(2), 141-168.

Ogunyemi, A., & Johnston, K. (2010). *The use of virtual machines to support hands-on learning experiences undergraduate systems oriented courses.* Paper presented at the 4th International Conference of Development Informatics IDIA 2010.

Open Educational Quality Initiative (2011). *Beyond OER: Shifting the focus to open educational practices. The 2011 OPAL Report.* Retrieved from http://duepublico.uni-duisburg-essen.de/servlets/DerivateServlet/Derivate-25907/OPALReport2011_Beyond_OER.pdf

Procomún (2021). Red de Recursos Educativos en Abierto. Retrieved from http://procomun.educalab.es/

Rodrigo, C., & Tabuenca, B. (2020). Learning ecologies in online students with disabilities. *Comunicar. Media Education Research Journal, 28*(62), 53-65.

Stoker, G., Arnold, T., & Maxwell, P. (2013) Using Virtual Machines to Improve Learning and Save Resources in an Introductory IT Course. *SIGITE '13: Proceedings of the 14th Annual ACM SIGITE Conference on Information Technology Education.* October 2013

UNE 71362 (2020). *Calidad de los materiales educativos digitales.* Retrieved from https://www.une.org/encuentra-tu-norma/busca-tu-norma/norma/?Tipo=N&c=N0063263

Weller, M. (2013). The battle for open – A perspective. *Journal of Interactive Media in Education, 2013*(3), Art. 15. doi: 10.5334/2013-15

Wiley, D., & Hilton III, J. L. (2018). Defining OER-enabled pedagogy. *International Review of Research in Open and Distributed Learning, 19*(4).

Lessons from a Pandemic for the Future of Education
European Distance and E-Learning Network (EDEN) Proceedings
2021 Annual Conference | Madrid, 21-24 June, 2021
ISSN 2707-2819
doi: 10.38069/edenconf-2021-ac0021

DIGITAL COMPETENCE IMPROVEMENT BY LITHUANIAN SCHOOL TEACHERS DURING COVID-19

Estela Daukšienė, Elena Trepulė, Airina Volungevičienė, Vytautas Magnus University, Lithuania

Abstract

Distance teaching and learning in Lithuanian schools during COVID-19 pandemic was a booster for teacher digital competence development. The paper analysis the experiences of Lithuanian school teachers to reveal the challenges schools and teachers faced while switching from traditional face to face teaching and learning to distance education. The research revealed existence of different level teacher digital competences at a school and uneven competence development in each school. The analysis of experiences of Lithuanian school teachers through the lens of DigCompEdu framework revealed that professional development competence was the background for other competence areas to develop. The need for digital resources for teaching online contributed to the teacher digital competence development of this area. Digital assessment was indicated as the main challenge that remained unsolved in many cases. Research found that technological peculiarities were easier to learn and showed the need to develop teacher social and didactical competences which are necessary for distance teaching. Lack of activities to empower learners and develop their digital competences was recorded. Teachers themselves acknowledged great improvement of their digital competence.

Introduction

All teachers know the potential of using technologies for teaching and learning, however until the need comes only some of them find time to learn how to use new technologies and use them for teaching and learning. Teacher digital competence development has been the focus for a long time, however the lockdown situation due to the COVID-19 pandemic initiated different needs and approaches. With the need to social distancing and staying at home came the necessity to organize distance teaching and learning for schools, which used to organize learning face-to-face. Were they prepared for that? How this challenged them and contributed to their digital competence?

The digital competence is usually understood as an ability to use technologies for different activities and depending on the selected framework may have different elements or stress the use of technologies for different activities and in different areas. The most popular framework to define digital competences in Europe is the DigComp framework (Digital Competence Framework for Citizens) which was introduced in 2013 (Ferrari, 2013) and updated in 2016 (Vuorikari et al., 2016) and 2017 (Carretero Gomez et al., 2017). Some countries (such as Spain) have adapted and applied this framework for defining and developing teacher digital competence; they link the 5 digital competence areas indicated in the framework, to the courses or in service training programmes that are provided for teachers.

The recent European Framework for the Digital Competence of Educators DigCompEdu (Redecker, 2017) was developed in 2017. It is broadly used and applied in Europe as the core resource, defining teacher digital competences. DigCompEdu framework defines 3 blocks and 6 areas of teacher digital competence: (a) educator's professional competences – professional engagement; (b) educators pedagogical competences – digital resources, teaching and learning, assessment, and empowering learners; and (c) learners competences – facilitating learners' digital competence. In all these competencies a teacher needs to use technologies for different activities to be competent. This paper aims to analyse the experiences of Lithuanian school teachers while teaching online during COVID-19 pandemic first wave (March–October 2020) with the focus to reveal the development of teacher digital competence in all 6 areas of DigCompEdu framework.

Methodology and background

Before March 16th, 2020 when all Lithuanian schools were closed due to the spread of COVID-19 pandemic, only several Lithuanian schools had a possibility to organize distance teaching and learning. There existed regulation for a school to receive the approval from the Lithuanian Ministry of Science and Education to organize distance teaching and learning. The created limitation led to the situation that there were only several schools in the country which had part of their school learners or just some subjects taught online. Thus, a very small number of teachers had experience in teaching online before COVID-19, and the need to organize distance teaching and learning for a traditional school was a real challenge.

In March 2020, when the pandemic stopped the regular processes globally, in Lithuania all schools were closed for two weeks to prepare for teaching online. During those two weeks a school had to agree on how the process would be organized, what tools to be used, what schedule to follow, what devices and internet connection pupils and teachers had and which were possible to be used, and much more to agree upon to start distance teaching at the end of March. It was a tough period for all – school administration, teachers, IT specialists, etc. During those two weeks there were lots of webinars organized nationally for school representatives by universities, politicians and those who could provide some guidance either for teachers or school leaders, however having no experience it was difficult to plan. Thus this leads to many different scenarios and experiences.

To reveal the experiences of the Lithuanian school communities the qualitative research approach was selected. Two research data collection methods were applied: expert interviews with school administration representatives were organized to reveal the experiences of school leaders; and focus groups with teachers, with upper grade pupils and with parents of lower grade pupils were organized to reveal the experiences of different participants of learning process. The targeted convenient selection of participants created a possibility to choose the most proper research sample (Rutkienė & Tandzegolskienė, 2013; Žydžiūnaitė & Sabaliauskas, 2017) for the empirical research. For the selection of schools to participate in the research the following selection criteria were indicated: different technological scenarios and platforms (focusing on selecting schools with different chosen technological scenarios), different school experience in organizing distance teaching and learning; different type of schools (ensuring the variety to be represented – from primary to upper secondary); different Lithuanian region (to include bigger and smaller towns and rural areas).

Eight Lithuanians schools were selected according to the selected and described criteria. There were eight expert interviews with the representatives from administration of the selected Lithuanian schools; the person had to have a leading role in managing distance learning at school. There were five focus groups with teachers (8-9 teachers each) organized. They were participated by 41 teacher of different subjects – Lithuanian language and literature (7), history/geography (5), Math (4), chemistry (3), English language (3), Music (3), and other. The age of teachers ranged from 22 to 69. There were two focus groups with upper grade secondary school pupils (8-9 pupils each) and two focus groups with parents of lower grade pupils (6-7 parents each, half of the parents had more than one child of school age). Most parents were of age 30-49, and all pupils were from 16 to 18 years old (there were 30 parents and pupils in total). The empirical research was conducted in September-October 2020 to reveal the experiences of the first pandemic wave in March-June 2020 and the preparation steps (September-October) for the second wave which started in October-November 2020 (depending on the situation in the regions).

The participants of expert interviews (school administration representatives) were coded as A1, A2, A3, etc., while participants of focus groups were coded with 2 letters and 2 numbers, indicating the research method (F for Focus group), the number of the school, the target group participant (T for teacher, P for parent and S for pupil/student) and number of the participant in the group, such as F1T2 stands for a focus group organized in school No.1, Teacher No. 2, F2S4 stands for the school No.2 student(pupil) No.4, and F4P3 stands for the school No.4 parent No.3.

Qualitative data of the expert interviews and focus groups were analysed through thematic analysis, based on the steps which include several phases indicated by the researchers (Braun & Clark, 2006; Clark & Braun, 2013; Nowell et al., 2017). It was started with familiarization with the collected data; was followed by generation of initial codes, search for, review and naming of the themes; and finalized with the production of the report. To ensure the privacy of data and research participants the following research principles of ethics (Žydžiūnaitė & Sabaliauskas, 2017) were followed in all research stages: respect to persons (research participants were coded) and their privacy (research participants were not fostered to reveal more than they openly shared), confidentiality and anonymity (all details that might reveal participant identity or school were anonymized, the researched schools were known only to the research team), beneficence and non-maleficence (time for interview and focus group were adapted to participant preferences, also following the same principle in agreeing if the meeting was to be held face-to-face or virtual; negative ideas and approaches that were identified during research were impersonalized), and justice (research participants agreed to participate in the research; an obligation to provide correct statements by research participants were followed).

Research results

The thematic map of the themes identified from all research participants are presented in Figure 1. The discussion of research results is followed by the different themes from the thematic map.

The analysis of research data revealed that possession of teacher digital competencies varied not only between schools and different subject teachers, but also there were huge differences on the level of digital teacher competencies in the same school. Some teachers lacked digital competences [A5, F4P6], didn't know how to use videoconferencing tools [F4P6, F3P1] or

> *"were afraid to click anything not to destroy the devices" (A2).*

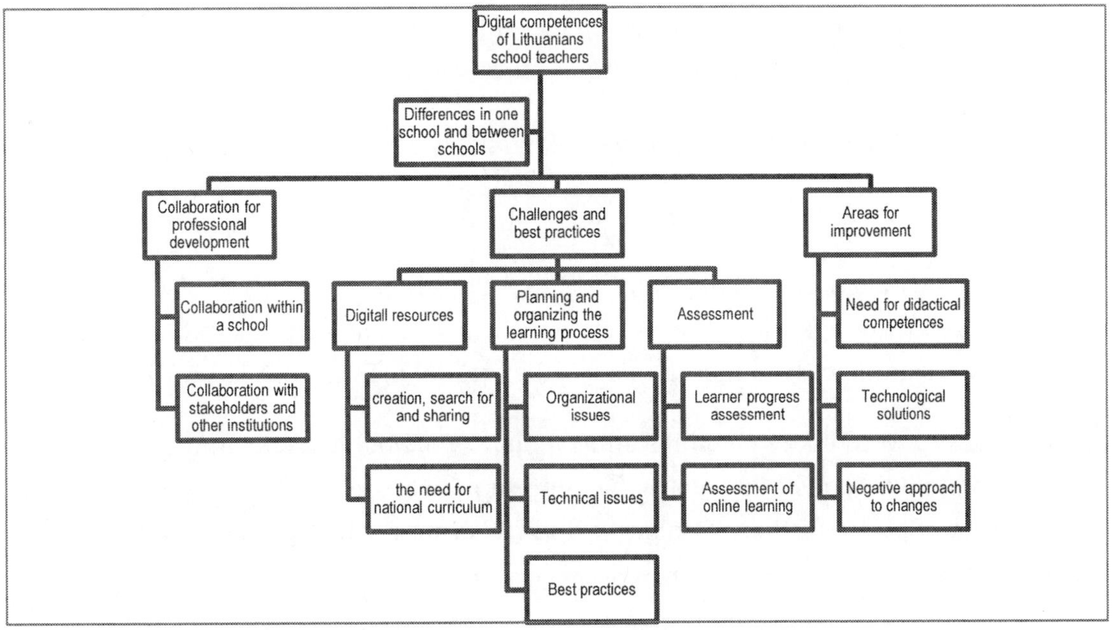

Figure 1. The thematic map of digital competence development of Lithuanian school teachers during the first wave of COVID-19 (March–October, 2020)

There were some schools which were satisfied if the teachers somehow connect to synchronous video lessons [A4, A6] and use videoconferencing tools to provide assignments for pupils [A2, A5] or organize synchronous lessons [A6, A7], while there were some schools where the quality of distance learning was the focus from the very start [A8]. The schools which organized distance learning earlier [A8] or had some teachers with advanced digital competences before pandemic [A1, A2, A5, A7] were able to come up to creative solutions [F2M5, A7] or organize teacher to teacher consultations [A1, A2, A7]. There were teacher methodical groups created for teacher collaborations [A1, A2, A8] in some schools; younger teachers or social staff were assigned to the teachers who lacked experience or knowledge in technology use in other schools [A7].

Collaboration for professional development

The deteriorating epidemiological situation and the overarching challenge of bringing the educational process to the digital space have brought many teachers closer together, enabling intensive professional collaboration between members of the school community [A1, A2, A,3 A7, F2T8]. The latter remains one of the positive effects of quarantine: professional cooperation between teachers in methodological groups has even strengthened and increased [F1T5, F2T3, F2T8].

To maintain a sense of community and encourage teacher collaboration, schools have developed: a virtual "coffee break" [A1, A2], a collaboration activity called "boss hour" [A1], or a "virtual teacher room" [F1T5], where teachers met remotely every morning, and the administration not only used the possibility to discuss current issues, but also supported or encouraged each other psychologically [A7]. School community collaborated and helped each other in this non-traditional situation:

> *"pupils helped teachers, pupils helped pupils" (A5)*

> *"pupils also helped each other" (A3)*

Collaboration with parents usually were organized by class mistresses [F3P2, F4P6, F3P1], who organized meetings with parents remotely. The attendance of parents at the remote meetings was significantly higher than at regular school meetings [A3, A6, F1T5].

Although there were many meetings and events, the school leaders emphasize that they lacked productive cooperation with the representatives of the Ministry of Education, Science and Sport (further Ministry) and a clearer strategy and focus for the implementation of distance learning [A1, A2, A3, A5]:

> *"we were expecting more guidance and clear proposals from the Ministry and the municipality, e.g. when selecting tools. What we have received cannot be called even guidelines, just a patchwork of existing opportunities, which can be found on the Internet" (A1).*

Cooperation between school leaders and the municipality has in many cases taken place using video conferencing tools [A1, A2, A3, A4, A5] or social networking facilities [A4]. Some school leaders were very pleased with the productive collaboration with the municipality (school stakeholders) and the fact that the collaboration continued [A2], but in some schools the collaboration of school leaders and municipalities was idle [A6].

Challenges and best practices: Digital resources

The analysis of the research data revealed that all schools organizing teaching and learning during pandemic used both – digital learning content F3P2] in combination with traditional textbooks [F1M, F4T3, F4T5]:

> *"yes, we used digital resources and teachers shared places where to find this kind of material" (A6)*

> *"we used mixed content" (A3)*

Teachers created digital content themselves [A7, F4T8], shared and used their developed learning content or open educational resources [A1, F5T1, F5T2] and other types of open digital content:

> *"we used online digital lessons that were found on internet and were available" (A2)*

This was the commercial learning content which was temporarily made open in many cases [A3, A8, A6, A7, A2]. Research participants mentioned an unequal amount of prepared and appropriate digital content for different subjects, different subject topics [A3, F5T1], and the absence of digital content for some subjects:

> *"There have certainly been subjects where there was no digital content, or there existed but much less than teachers needed" (A5)*

The lack of nationally developed digital content was stressed [F1P3]. The later might be used by all schools when the need to organized distance learning arises:

> *"Digital content should be freely available to schools, freely, it should not be commercialized" (A2)*

It was emphasized that there is no common strategy [A3, A5] and that schools should have access to digital learning content on a shared platform [A3]. Digital content – theory and complementary exercises or tasks [F5P1, F2P2] are necessary, and they should encourage students' creativity and active learning, and not just answering of multiple choice questions [A3].

Challenges and best practices. Teaching, learning, and assessment

The organization of distance education was chaotic, the question was raised about what can be called a quality lesson in distance learning [A8]. It was acknowledged that not all the possibilities of the chosen platforms were used, because teachers simply did not know them and therefore applied small variety of methods, limiting group learning [A8], or active online learning F2S7]. The tasks mostly were performed on paper and a photo of them was sent via different channels – email [F2T5], messenger [F2T4] or online grading book [F4T2] – which were not always appropriate for big volume files so creating challenges to open some documents [A5]. Incompatibility of equipment has also contributed to the chaos of online learning as pupils used different devices – tabs, phones, or computers.

Some schools used Moodle [F2P6] or MsTeams [A1] for learning management. However, there were some schools which let teachers choose and use what they know [A4]. Thus, teachers used a variety of tools [F2M5, F2M1, F2M4, F2M8, F2P1, F3P2, F4P4, F2P1]. Not only the variety of technologies, but also the variety of teaching strategies used existed in one school leading to challenges for pupils:

> *"five teachers do things differently – the tasks can be found anywhere. Thus, in the beginning the challenge was to understand the teacher strategy, the rules, the tactics, how he teaches" (FIM8)*

Lack of technological knowledge and instructions on how to use technologies lead to the lesson with 200 participants instead of one class pupils joining a lesson [A2]. The need for clear instructions [A1, F3T4] and coherent planning [F5T4] were indicated by different research participants, where the lesson plans that were prepared and shared with learners in advance were mentioned as the main success factors [F2S5, F2T5]. The need for tasks, which help pupils plan their time and learn independently, were also stressed [F1T1, F2T6]

Assessment was indicated as a biggest challenge [A1, A2, A7, F4P6, F2P5] that was not solved by some subject teachers [A1, A2, A7]. Teachers didn't know technological solutions for creating online tests or such tasks that would not lead to cheating. However, they used technologies for self-check activities or applied various methods for collecting feedback from learners regarding distance learning process. The preparation for these activities were very time consuming, leading to many teachers working unlimited number of hours [A6, F4T8].

Areas for improvement. Teacher didactical competences to engage learners and improve their digital competences

The analysis of data revealed the need for digital didactical competences. It was easier to learn some technical or technological peculiarities, to use technologies, but it was more difficult to teach online, to organize the distance learning process. In the beginning most teachers tried the same teaching and learning methods and approaches that they use to implement in face to face classes [A4];

> *teachers "turned on video cameras and worked the same way they used to work at school, just in video lessons ... synchronously ..." (A2)*

However later came the feeling that it was not enough to do the same things that were done in the classes to reach better results [A8]. And even after several months online it was indicated that

> *"not all teachers found the methods that work" (A2)*

The questions regarding the principles of time management during online lesson were raised [F4P6, F3P1], the need for more teacher social skills, for new ways of communication online were stressed [A1, A2, A7]. Not all teachers had a positive approach to changes that were initiated due to pandemic. Thus, there were some teachers who left the school after the first months of teaching online. The reasons for leaving were several – unwillingness to apply technologies for teaching or to improve digital competences and change practices that they used to apply [F4P3, A2], or internal limitations and protest [A5, A7, A8]. Some teachers denied the existence of COVID-19 stressing that online learning will disappear [A7].

Research shows that many teachers had a possibility to start using the tools that earlier they never found time for start using, and this lead to advanced teacher digital competences: [F1P2, F2P1, F1P8, F1P3, F5P5, F2P2, F5P2, F5P1, F2M5, F3T6, A3, A4, A5]:

> *"we've learnt a lot of things, in deed" (F3P3)*

> *"we learnt what we never knew of existing. We see how it is useful" (F3P8)*

However the activities organized by teachers while teaching online have not focused on engaging learners, nor improving their digital competences. But summing up their digital competence improvement teachers acknowledge:

> *"Let's be open and sincerely say: Thank you, Corona, for forcing us to improve, greatly" (A4)*

Conclusions

The research showed that the digital competences of Lithuanian school teachers varied in the same school from those who were basic users to advanced ones. This created a place for teacher collaboration for a learning process to be implemented successfully – methodological groups of teachers collaborated on certain subject teaching peculiarities, younger and more advanced teachers and specialists helped those who lacked digital knowledge and skills; good practice sharing webinars were organized to share what works. Different situations were recorded analysing the use of digital content for teaching and learning online, as different subject teachers faced different challenges in finding or creating the curriculum themselves. Teacher cooperation was recorded in this area as well. Distance teaching revealed the need for teacher social and didactical competence development, as technical peculiarities were easier to learn. Some good practices in applying different learning methods were recorded, however tasks that would improve pupils' digital competences were not recorded. Learner assessment was indicated as the main remaining issue. Pupils called for more interactivity, confirming the need for teacher digital didactical competence development.

"Real change often takes place in deep crises, and this moment holds the possibility that we won't return to the status quo when things return to 'normal'" (Schleicher, 2020; p.26). This idea may also be supported by Lithuanian teachers' thoughts that they were forced to try technologies for learning, but this revealed a number of possibilities to be used in future.

References

Braun, V., & Clarke, V. (2006). Using thematic analysis in psychology. *Qualitative Research in Psychology, 3*, 77-101. https://doi.org/10.1191/1478088706qp063oa

Ferrari, A. (2013). DIGCOMP: A Framework for Developing and Understanding Digital Competence in Europe. In Y. Punie & B. Brecko (Eds.), *EUR 26035.* Luxembourg: Publications Office of the European Union. http://dx.doi.org/10.2788/52966

Carretero Gomez, S., Vuorikari, R., & Punie, Y. (2017). *DigComp 2.1: The Digital Competence Framework for Citizens with eight proficiency levels and examples of use.* EUR 28558 EN. Luxembourg: Publications Office of the European Union. http://dx.doi.org/10.2760/38842

Clarke, V., & Braun, V. (2013). Teaching thematic analysis: Overcoming challenges and developing strategies for effective learning. *The Psychologist, 26*(2), 120-123. http://dx.doi.org/10.1191/1478088706qp063oa

Nowell, L. S., Norris, J. M., White, D. E., & Moules, N. J. (2017). Thematic Analysis. Striving to Meet the Trustworthiness Criteria. *International Journal of Qualitative Methods, 16*, 1-13, http://dx.doi.org/10.1177/1609406917733847

Redecker, C. (2019). European Framework for the Digital Competence of Educators: DigCompEdu. In Y. Punie (Ed.), *EUR 28775 EN.* Luxembourg: Publications Office of the European Union. http://dx.doi.org/10.2760/178382

Rutkienė, A. & Tandzengolskienė, I. (2013). Gebėjimo veikti savarankiškai raiška universitetinių studijų metu (socialinių mokslų srities atvejis). *Acta Paedagogica Vilnensia, 31*, 69-83. https://doi.org/10.15388/ActPaed.2013.31.2514

Schleicher, A. (2020). *The impact of COVID-19 on Education – Insights from Education at a Glance 2020.* Retrieve https://www.oecd.org/education/the-impact-of-covid-19-on-education-insights-education-at-a-glance-2020.pdf

Vuorikari, R., Punie, Y., Carretero Gomez, S., & van den Brande, G. (2016). *DigComp 2.0: The Digital Competence Framework for Citizens. Update Phase 1: the Conceptual Reference Model.* EUR 27948 EN. Luxembourg: Publications Office of the European Union. http://dx.doi.org/10.2791/607218

Žydžiūnaitė, V., & Sabaliauskas, S. (2017). *Kokybiniai tyrimai principai ir metodai.* Vilnius: Vaga.

Lessons from a Pandemic for the Future of Education
European Distance and E-Learning Network (EDEN) Proceedings
2021 Annual Conference | Madrid, 21-24 June, 2021
ISSN 2707-2819
doi: 10.38069/edenconf-2021-ac0022

DISTANCE TEACHER TRAINING DURING THE FIRST COVID PANDEMIC BY THE UNIVERSITY OF CRETE ELEARNINGLAB

Panagiotes Anastasiades, Konstantinos Kotsidis, Christos Synnefakis, Alexia Spanoudaki,
University of Crete eLearning Lab, Greece

Abstract

The closing of schools at the beginning of spring 2020, because of the Corona Virus pandemic, featured the need for School Distance Education (SDE). Nevertheless, teachers did not have previous experience in SDE and as a result, they were in need of support in this urgent situation. The Laboratory for Advanced Teaching Technologies for Lifelong Learning and Distance Education (e-Learning Lab) of the University of Crete, attempted to contribute with its own means to the support of teachers who struggled to respond to the challenges of distance teaching resulting from the suspension of schools. Within the above framework, fast track distance seminars were designed and implemented, aiming at the support of teachers on pedagogical issues of Distance Education. During the period from 19 March to 29 April 2020, 20 distance training seminars were conducted, in which more than 40,000 teachers of primary and secondary education from around Greece participated. The overall presentation and assessment of the training actions showed not only the enormous interest of the teaching community but also the need for such training actions with particular emphasis on the principles and the methodology of SDE, on synchronous and asynchronous learning environment as well as the designing or planning of teaching scenarios based on the pedagogical approaches compatible with Distance Learning.

Introduction

Supporting the teachers with key issues regarding Distance Education became a major priority during the first lockdown, as till then teachers had no previous experience on School Distance Education. The Department of Primary Education of the University of Crete and most specifically e-Learning Lab, responding to the need for teacher support, designed and implemented fast-paced, free distance learning programs for primary and secondary education teachers.

The purpose of this paper is on the one hand to summarize the training activities that took place in the first period of the ban / Lockdown in the direction of introductory training of teachers on issues related to School Distance Education and on the other hand to investigate teachers' attitudes regarding participation in training.

The structure of the paper is as follows: In the first section, a first approach is attempted regarding the issues of the implementation of the School Distance Education in an emergency situation, such as Covid-19. The second section summarizes the contribution of the University of Crete and the e-Learning Lab, in the support / training of teachers in introductory issues related to School Distance Education focusing on the pedagogical dimension of the whole project. In the third section, a first attempt is made to make a comprehensive assessment of the training activities during the first period of the ban / Lockdown (March–April 2020). The paper is completed with the conclusions section.

School Distance Education in Periods of Emergency (Pandemic, Covid-19)

The term "School Distance Education" refers to the provision of education for primary and secondary education, which is provided remotely, is addressed to school-age individuals and is distinguished into autonomous and complementary (Vergou, Koutsoumpa, & Mouzakis, 2016).

During the first period of the Covid-19 pandemic, 80% of the global student population was affected by restrictive measures in 138 countries (Chang & Yano, 2020), the impact of which has not yet been studied (Flores & Gago, 2020). The need to address the negative impact of the suspension of the educational process pushed the shift to distance learning not as an option but as a coercive de facto enforcement (Toquero, 2020).

Therefore, emphasis in this first period of the pandemic was placed on (Anastasiades, 2020):

- ensuring access to Panhellenic School Network services, technological tools and infrastructure;
- reconnection of students in an emergency with classmates and teachers in an educational environment of technological mediation.

The response of the teaching community exceeded all expectations as it managed to significantly restore a first contact with the students, despite the technological problems and mainly the fact that teachers lacked the training. Obviously, the indiscriminate transfer of the philosophy of Face-To-Face Teaching methods and techniques into purely technological / technocentric terms in Distance Education Environments created risks of considering distance education as a problematic choice.

The absence of the minimum pedagogical conditions for the basic implementation of the School Distance Education was more than obvious. It was therefore necessary to try to support teachers on the basis of pedagogical approaches based on the fundamental principles of distance education, such as the interaction between learners, learners with teachers and learners with educational materials (Moore, 1989), practice communities and the three dimensions of the Exploration community model (Social, Teaching and Cognitive Presence) (Garrison, Anderson, & Archer, 2001), for the design and implementation of distance learning school activities with an emphasis on social interaction.

Case Study Description

The e-Learning Lab of the Department of Primary Education of the University of Crete, responding to the need to support Primary and Secondary Education teachers in their efforts to implement introductory activities of distance education with their students, in the period of March – April 2020, designed and implemented fast-paced seminars with the method of distance education.

Objective

The objective of the training actions is divided into 3 Thematic Units:

1. Fundamental principles of Distance Education: Basic Theories, differences between Distance Education and in person teaching, the importance of educational material, Social dimension, etc.
2. The Pedagogical utilization of ICT in a School distance education environment (synchronous, asynchronous environments and blended Learning environments).
3. Design of Educational material: introductory activities for the critical utilization of the existing material with the methodology of Distance Education / Development of scenarios of teaching intervention based on the methodology of Distance Education.

Target group

Primary and secondary school teachers.

Implementation Methodology

Each training seminar lasted 9 hours and was structured on two levels:

A. Synchronous School Distance Education (3 hours): Each training seminar provides one (1) training meeting, in which interested parties could participate:

- via video conference for a limited number of participants (150);
- via real time streaming (Live Streaming) for an unlimited number of participants.

For the most effective coverage of the needs of practice and the thorough support of the trainees, the solution of the two tutors was chosen. The first tutor focused on the synchronous e-learning environment (teleconferencing), presented the activities and interacted with the participants in the teleconference, while the second one focused on social networks and interacted with the users who watched the live broadcast of the seminar. He received their questions and transferred them to the video conference room, giving answers via chat while helping as well to coordinate the training activity.

B. Synchronous Distance Education (3 hours): In each training seminar

The seminars were complemented with interactive educational material, specially designed with the method of distance education, which the trainees had the opportunity to study asynchronously in space and time of their choice, aiming at their own support. Finally, in the context of the training, the trainees were asked to do an optional task related to the creation of a teaching scenario using the methodology of distance education, so as to establish a direct connection between theory and practice in the context of sharing good practices.

Implementation of Training Seminars

In the context of the above actions in the period of March – April 2020 were carried out a total of:

- 20 Teleconferences with the participation of 1560 trainees,
- 6 Live Streaming Sessions with 15,000 participants in the "main hall" and another 25,000 from notifications from a total of 175,000 unique viewers.

Finally, the website with the educational material (www.edivea.org) was visited by over 60,000 unique visitors.

Research methodology

Purpose

The purpose of this research is to explore the views of trainee-teachers regarding their impressions of their participation in this training program.

Research Questions

1. How satisfied are the participants with their participation in the Training Seminar in terms of trainers?
2. How satisfied are the participants with the technological environment of the teleconferencing / Live Streaming (quality of audio, video, chat, etc.)?
3. How satisfied are the participants with the training material?
4. How satisfied are the participants with the possibility of utilizing the new knowledge in their educational work?

Methodological Framework

The survey was conducted in March and April 2020. It is an action survey that was synchronous, field-based and quantitative. A questionnaire was used as a means of data collection, which included closed-ended questions.

Sample

The sample of the research is the 4239 teachers of different specialties.

Presentation of Results

Table 10: Participants via Teleconferencing/ Livestreaming

	Participants via Live Streaming		Participants via Teleconferencing		Total	
	N	percentage %	n	percentage %	n	percentage %
Male	609	21.6	242	17	851	20.1
Female	2209	78.4	1179	83	3388	79.9
Total	2818	100	1421	100	4239	100

Table 2: Degree of Satisfaction from the Training Program of participants through Teleconferencing

How satisfied are you with your participation in the Training Seminar regarding	Participants via Teleconferencing												
	Low level of ICT literacy			Medium Level of ICT literacy			High Level of ICT literacy			Total			
	n	M.O	S.D.	N	M.O	S.D.	N	M.O	S.D.	N	M.O	S.D.	sig
a. the trainers	90	4.4	0.761	808	4.33	0.781	513	4.26	0.85	1412	4.31	0.805	0.151
b. the technological environment of Telecoferencing/Live Streaming	90	4.07	0.872	808	3.96	0.94	513	4.02	0.937	1412	3.98	0.934	0.36
c. the training material	90	3.81	0.959	803	3.82	1.012	512	3.83	1.066	1406	3.82	1.028	0.987
d. the possibility of utilizing new knowledge in your educational work	90	3.88	0.934	803	3.96	0.952	512	3.94	0.987	1406	3.94	0.963	0.757

According to the results of the research, the participants in the Training Seminar via Teleconferencing stated that they were quite satisfied (4.31) with the trainers. In relation to technological environment of Teleconferencing, the participants were moderate to quite satisfied (3.98). Also, the participants were moderate to quite satisfied (3.82) with the training material and the possibility of utilizing knew knowledge in their educational work.

Table 3: Degree of Satisfaction from the Training Program of participants through Livestreaming

How satisfied are you with your participation in the Training Seminar regarding	Participants via Livestreaming												
	Low level of ICT literacy			Medium Level of ICT literacy			High Level of ICT literacy			Total			
	n	M.O	S.D.	N	M.O	S.D.	N	M.O	S.D.	N	M.O	S.D.	sig
a. the trainers	133	4.18	0.869	1556	4.34	0.763	1128	4.46	0.720	2817	4.38	0.755	0.000
b. the technological environment of Telecoferencing/Live Streaming	133	3.63	1.041	1556	3.65	0.975	1128	3.82	0.982	2817	3.71	0.984	0.000
c. the training material	133	3.78	1.054	1556	4.06	0.945	1128	4.19	0.922	2817	4.10	0.946	0.000
d. the possibility of utilizing new knowledge in your educational work	133	3.29	1.077	1556	3.77	1.016	1128	4.07	0.979	2817	3.86	1.023	0.000

According to the results of the research, the participants in the Training Seminar stated that they were quite satisfied (4.38) with the trainers. In particular, there was a slight variation in the already large satisfaction depending on the level of ICT literacy: participants with very low ICT literacy, appeared quite satisfied (4.18), participants with a moderate level of ICT literacy, felt quite satisfied (4.34) and participants with a high level of ICT literacy, felt quite satisfied (4.46). The difference of the GPA is considered statistically significant ($p = 0.000$). In relation to the technological environment of Live Streaming, the participants expressed their satisfaction (3.71). In particular, a slight variation was observed depending on the level of ICT literacy, where moderate to very satisfied (3.63) appeared the trainees with a low level of ICT literacy, as well as the trainees / students with a moderate level of ICT use and trainees with a high level of knowledge of ICT use, felt moderate to very satisfied (3.65 and 3.82 respectively). The difference of the GPA is considered statistically significant ($p = 0.000$). Also, the participants were quite satisfied (4.10) with the training material. In particular, there was a slight variation in the already large satisfaction (3.78), participants with a moderate level of ICT literacy, felt quite satisfied (4.06) and participants with a high level of ICT literacy, felt quite satisfied (4.19). The difference of the GPA is considered statistically significant ($p = 0.000$). Lastly, the trainees felt moderate to quite satisfied (3.86) with the possibility of utilizing new knowledge in their educational work. In particular, a slight variation was observed depending on the level of ICT literacy, where moderate (3.29) appeared the trainees with a low level of ICT literacy, the trainees / students with a moderate level of ICT use were moderate to quite satisfied (3.77) and the trainees with a high level of knowledge of ICT use, felt quite satisfied (4.07). The difference of the GPA is considered statistically significant ($p = 0.000$).

Conclusions

In conclusion, the participants in the Training Seminar via Teleconferencing were quite satisfied with the trainers. In relation to technological environment of Teleconferencing, the participants were moderate to quite satisfied. Also, the participants were moderate to quite satisfied with the training material and the possibility of utilizing knew knowledge in their educational work. On the other hand, the participants in the Training Seminar via Livestreaming were quite satisfied with the trainers. In relation to the technological environment of Live Streaming, the participants expressed their satisfaction. Also, the participants were quite satisfied with the training material.

The hasty introduction of Distance Education in emergency conditions, has highlighted readiness problems not only in central planning but also in the school units. According to recent research, the training of prospective teachers often lags behind the preparation for distance learning (Debruler, Denton, McKay, & Sicilia, 2020).

E-Learning Lab designed and implemented 20 fast-paced seminars from March 19 to April 29, 2020, through the teleconferencing platform of Webex Meetings, while they were also broadcast live (live streaming) on the page of the University of Crete I e-Learning Lab and in social networking media (Facebook). Emphasis was placed on the principles and methodology of Distance Education, the environments of synchronous and asynchronous DE, as well as the design or formulation of teaching scenarios based on pedagogical approaches compatible with DE in order to support teachers.

The satisfaction of 40,000 teachers of all levels for the whole training process highlighted the importance of the pedagogical approach in the design and implementation of the seminars which was based on the practical training of the trainees in both synchronous and asynchronous distance learning environments.

A key role in the design and implementation of these seminars was played by the experience accumulated by:

- the distance training of teachers within the Major Training Program of the Pedagogical Institute (Anastasiades, 2012; Anastasiades et al., 2011) and the training of expatriate teachers within the Expatriate Education Program of the University of Crete (Anastasiades, 2007; 2012; Damanakis & Anastasiades, 2005);
- conducting distance learning programs for teachers;
- distance education through the ODYSSEUS program, which is the first systematic effort to design and implement an integrated complementary school environment with the use of ICT in Greece through the pedagogical utilization of Interactive Teleconferencing in Primary schools of Cyprus during the period 2000–2003

(Anastasiades, 2003) and Greece during the period 2004-2020 (Anastasiades, 2017; Anastasiades, 2003; 2009).

References

Anastasiades, P. (2003). Distance Learning in Elementary Schools in Cyprus: The evaluation Methodology and Results. *Computers & Education, 40*(1), 17-40.

Anastasiades, P. (2007). Blending Interactive Videoconferencing and Asynchronous Learning in Adult Education: Towards a Constructivism Pedagogical Approach. A Case Study at the University of Crete (EDIAMME). In S. Negash, M. Whitman, A. Woszczynski, K. Hoganson & H. Mattord (Eds.), *Handbook of Distance Learning for Real-Time and Asynchronous Information Technology Education* (pp. 24-64). Hershey, PA: Idea Group Inc.

Anastasiades, P. (2009). *Interactive Videoconferencing and Collaborative Distance Learning for K-12 Students and Teachers: Theory and Practice.* New York: Nova Science Publishers Inc.

Anastasiades, P. (2012). Design of a Blended Learning Environment for the Training of Greek Teachers: Results of the Survey on Educational Needs. In P. Anastasiades (Ed.), *Blended Learning Environments for Adults: Evaluations* (pp.230-256). Hershey, PA: Idea Group Inc.

Anastasiades, P. (2017). "ODYSEYS 2000-2015": Complementary school distance education using ICT: evaluation of the research contribution. *Open Education – The Journal for Open and Distance Education and Educational Technology, 13*(1), 88-128.

Anastasiades, P. (2018). Learning & Social Network at the University of Crete [eLearning Lab]. In A. Volungeviciene & A. Szűcs (Eds.), *Exploring the Micro, Meso and Macro Navigating between dimensions in the digital learning landscape: European Distance and E-Learning Network (EDEN) Conference Proceedings, 17-20 June 2018* (pp. 598-605). Genoa: EDEN.

Anastasiades, P. (2020). Distance learning in the era of COVID-19, focusing on the Greek Educational System. *Open Education – The Journal for Open and Distance Education and Educational Technology, 16*(2), 20-48.

Anastasiades, P., Kaga, E., Loukeris, D., Mantas, P., & Trantas, P. (2011). Major Teacher Training Program: A study to investigate the training needs of teachers. *Comparative and International Educational Review, 16-17*, 126-154.

Chang, G. C., & Yano, S. (2020). *How are countries addressing the Covid-19 challenges in education?* A snapshot of policy measures. Retrieved October 01, 2020, from https://www.gecv.ac.in/uploads/ssip/UNESCO%20snap %20shot%20for%20maintaining%20education.pdf

Damanakis, M., & Anastasiades, P. (2005). Life Long & Distance Learning and the Diaspora: Implementing a Virtual Learning Environment at the University of Crete. *Themes in Education, 6*(1), 83-96.

Debruler, K., Denton, C., McKay, A., & Sicilia, E. (2020). Supporting Michigan Educators through the Transition to Online Learning. In R. Ferdig, E. Baumgartner, R. Hartshorne, R. Kaplan-Rakowski, & C. Mouza (Eds.), *Teaching, Technology, and Teacher Education During the COVID-19 Pandemic: Stories from the Field* (pp. 191-196). AACE-Association for the Advancement of Computing in Education.

Flores, M., & Gago, M. (2020). Teacher education in times of COVID-19 pandemic in Portugal: national, institutional and pedagogical responses. *Journal of Education for Teaching, 46*(4), 507-516.

Garrison, D. R., Anderson, T., & Archer, W. (2001). Critical thinking, cognitive presence, and computer conferencing in distance education. *American Journal of Distance Education, 15*(1), 7-23.

Moore, M. G. (1989). Three Types of Interaction. *American Journal of Distance Education, 3*(2), 1-7.

Toquero, C. M. (2020). Emergency remote education experiment amid COVID-19 pandemic. *IJERI: International Journal of Educational Research and Innovation, 15,* 162-176.

Vergou, M., Koutsoumba, M., & Mouzakis, H. (2016). Supplementary Distance Learning for Infants: an Action Research based on Museum Education. *Open Education – The Journal for Open and Distance Education and Educational Technology, 12*(2), 24-39.

Lessons from a Pandemic for the Future of Education
European Distance and E-Learning Network (EDEN) Proceedings
2021 Annual Conference | Madrid, 21-24 June, 2021
ISSN 2707-2819
doi: 10.38069/edenconf-2021-ac0023

LESSONS LEARNT FROM THE CARDIFF CPD DEVELOPMENT PROGRAMME

Francisco Iniesto, Martin Weller, Sarah Roberts, The Open University, United Kingdom

Abstract

The Cardiff Commitment Continuing Professional Development (CPD) programme was a collaboration between Cardiff Council, Cardiff and Vale College and The Open University (OU). Initial contact with Cardiff Council's Cardiff Schools Service (Cardiff Council) began with discussions around supporting teacher CPD needs through a co-designed teacher focussed workshop. The Global Covid19 Pandemic resulted in this collaboration being extensively redesigned to reflect the need for teaching staff to support their learners via a blended online distance learning model. Cardiff and Vale College also agreed to join the initiative. This programme ran between November '20 and March '21 with a total of 12 workshops and a sample of 32 teachers and lecturers from across 23 institutions. Key benefits identified to participating staff included the professional development and upskilling opportunity, input into the co-creation of resources for peers and the wider sector and effecting change within their organisation and wider cluster through peer to peer approach.

Background and aims

There exist many recent international initiatives to support blended learning in primary, secondary, and further education (FE) sectors. For example, the European Maturity model for Blended Education provided criteria and instruments to assess the degree of maturity of blended education and innovation (Valkenburg et al., 2020). The blended learning essentials projects facilitated a free suite of online courses for the FE sector to promote effective practice and pedagogy in blended learning (Deepwell, Palmer, & Greig, 2019). While the Bringing Learning to Life project offered functional skills courses through the OpenLearn online learning platform (Farrow, 2019). These needs have increased with the Covid19 pandemic where various initiatives have promoted the pivoting of blended learning environments (Maguire, Dale & Pauli, 2020; Marinoni, Van't Land, & Jensen, 2020).

When thinking about blended learning initiatives in the Welsh context, where this research is contextualised, the Welsh Government has published several documents and guidance for schools and setting on learning and supporting distance learning (Welsh Government, 2020).The Learning Partnership Wales offers bespoke training for schools, clusters of schools and larger groups too during Covid19. Finally, The Digital 2030 Framework, focused on enhanced learning, was published in the summer of 2019 and updated in 2020 to include agreed Standards for digital skills (based on the FE and Work-based learning professional standards and aligned to Digital 2030) (Wells Government, 2019).

The Cardiff Commitment Continuing Professional Development (CPD) programme was a collaboration between Cardiff Council, Cardiff and Vale College and The Open University (OU). Initial contact with Cardiff Council's Cardiff Schools Service (Cardiff Council) began with discussions around supporting teacher CPD needs through a co-designed teacher focussed workshop. The Global Covid19 Pandemic resulted in this collaboration being extensively redesigned to reflect the need for teaching staff to support their learners via a blended online distance learning model. Cardiff and Vale College also agreed to join the initiative. In collaboration with Cardiff Council and Cardiff and Vale College, the OU in Wales has developed and delivered a model consisting of agreed work streams that support teaching staff within schools and colleges in the online pivot and promote blended learning pathways.

The global Covid19 pandemic coupled with the imminent new curriculum for Wales posed challenges and opportunities to develop skills and approaches to distance teaching and learning pedagogy. Many teaching staff have adapted well in their approach to blended learning during the circumstances imposed in the past year, whilst others are still finding their way. The OU has been an established provider of high-quality higher education through flexible distance learning for over 50 years and is excited to share experiences, whilst learning alongside peers within schools and the FE sector. This collaboration recognised the demand on teaching staff across the education sector has never been more challenging, with many schools adapting to ever-changing circumstances. In collaboration, the OU has delivered a series of interactive online workshops, focused on pedagogy and effective learning design. Workshops were delivered to an invited cohort of teachers and lecturers identified by Cardiff Schools Service and Cardiff and Vale College (Phase 1). A series of workshops were then delivered (and recorded for others) to complement learning (Phase 2). Through the workshops and community created, insights were captured to potentially inform bilingual resources to support participants in peer learning within clusters and faculty. This programme ran between November '20 and March '21. The completion of this project has been successful in upskilling school and college staff in online teaching and blended learning pedagogy; in part to support preparation for the new curriculum in Wales. The programme has demonstrated key components of pedagogy such as reflection and co-creation, as well as to reflect the peer to peer aspect of the new curriculum. It has been an example of sharing practice and expertise across education levels and institutions.

Methodology

A cohort of 32 teachers and lecturers from across 23 institutions identified by Cardiff Schools Service and Cardiff and Vale College were invited to participate in the project (Phase 1 and Phase 2). From those 46.87% belonged to the primary level, 31.25% to secondary, 15.62% to FE level and 6.25% to Music Service and Regional Consortium. In terms of job roles, participants covered a varied spectrum of teachers (different years), lecturers, and leaders from various areas, with a predominance in science, technology, engineering, and mathematics (STEM). For Phase 2 the invitation was extended through the Cardiff Schools Service, Cardiff and Vale College email distribution lists and other contacts in the education sector.

Alongside fellow Cardiff schoolteachers (across primary, secondary, and special schools) and lecturers from Cardiff and Vale College, participants were supported to actively participate in a series of workshops. These took the form of information sharing as well as discursive sessions online using the Microsoft Teams platform. The intention was for learning and skills developed through this collaboration to be shared with teachers and lecturers more widely. For that reason, Phase 2 workshops were recorded to be available in Hwb (Learning and teaching for Wales repository) including handouts (available in English and Welsh) to accompany each workshop recording summarising the key points. This sharing of practice was led by the programme partners in various ways and over time, but there was also a requirement for participating staff to consider peer to peer learning throughout their school, cluster, or faculty. During the process, participants were asked to use reflective practice and input into evaluation, and participation to shape elements together from the initial workshops in a participatory and co-creation approach (Jull & Graham, 2017). For mapping the workshops, the new curriculum for Wales was considered.

Phase 1 was organised by OU's Learning Design team (LDS), as a series of online workshops exploring pedagogy including activity design and assessment with the objectives of building knowledge and community through the series of workshops. While the first two workshops in Phase 1 were already set up, topics for the next workshops could be voted within the participants including the date and time. Organisers proposed 2 weeks in between workshops to give participants more time to put some things into practice, to encourage participants to reflect on the workshop and use a reflection journal to help their capacity-wise but without losing momentum (Bassot, 2016). Phase 2 was designed as stand-alone workshops and were delivered in a shorter space of time (one workshop or even two per week), topics for the workshops were proposed by experts from the Institute of Educational Technology (IET) at the OU. Input into the topics was explored from the several proposed options which were discussed and shaped together during Phase 1. For Phase 2 the participation was open to a wider audience of lecturers and teachers. For that purpose, Eventbrite events were created for each of the 6 workshops included in this phase, events information was provided both in English and Welsh. Table 1 summarises the workshops included in the programme and the attendance, in Phase 2 between parentheses are the participants which were part of the sample for Phase 1. As it can be seen the participation decreased during the programme.

Table 11: Workshops during the programme and attendance

Workshops	Date	Content	Attendance
Phase 1 (November '20 to January '21)			
Workshop 1	Thursday 5 Nov	Introduction	30 (93.75%)
Workshop 2	Thursday 12 Nov	Activity Design	22 (68.75%)
Workshop 3	Thursday 26 Nov	Assessment	18 (56.25%)
Workshop 4	Monday 14 Dec	From assessment to classroom	7 (21.87%)
Workshop 5	Wednesday 20 Jan	Collaborative activities	9 (28.12%)
Workshop 6	Wednesday 3 Feb	Reflection and strategy	9 (28.12%)
Phase 2 (February to March '21)			
Workshop 1	Tuesday 23 Feb	Supporting Inquiry learning design	6 (6) (18.75%)
Workshop 2	Thursday 4 March	Using & Creating OERs	8 (3) (9.37%)
Workshop 3	Tuesday 9 March	Feedback and Online Assessments	11 (2) (6.25%)
Workshop 4	Tuesday 16 March	Harnessing online communities & networks	1 (1) (3.12%)
Workshop 5	Friday 19 March	Designing Exceptional Learning Moments	2 (2) (6.25%)
Workshop 6	Tuesday, 23 March	Representing learners' online study journeys	1 (1) (3.12%)

The methodology design proposed combined the use of mixed methods (Terrell, 2012). A survey was used at the beginning of the programme to have a better understanding of the participants, their roles and teaching contexts, how Covid19 has impacted their teaching and the responses to this, their professional development experiences, and expected gain from the programme. This first survey had a response rate of 84.37%. Two further surveys were then used during, and at the end of the programme to support comparison to assess gaps and gains in confidence in designing and delivering blended learning, digital literacies and skills for online teaching, and confidence in supporting students in blended pathways, during Phase 1 and 2. The final survey of the programme has been designed to cover the experience of the programme as a whole and individual activities, the extent to which the learning outcomes have been achieved, and to identify expected changes to their practice. For Phase 1 the response rate was 21.87%, 15.62% for Phase 2, and 28.12% for the whole programme.

Several approaches to gathering qualitative information have been conducted in the middle and late stages, providing a richer understanding of the needs of the participants and their experiences and benefits drawn from the programme. This included the last workshop of Phase 1 as a reflective experience from the participants and a focus group with 9 (6 OU, 2 Cardiff Council and 1 Cardiff and Vale College) members from the programme partnership, to better understand the strength and difficulties of the project and move the partnership forwards.

Results and discussion

Participants and partners perspectives are disclosed using the different sources of data included in the methodology.

The participants perspectives before the programme started

The experience of participants before Covid19 was predominantly face-to-face (Figure 1), while the experience of adjusting their teaching practice to blended learning was challenging. The pandemic has impacted participants teaching in different ways including students and families' engagement, the use of online platforms and online teaching methods, and the design of educational resources.

The expectations of participants to gain from the programme workshops included a better understanding of blended learning, professional development, gaining skills, sharing ideas and networking. Participants' topics to develop during the programme included learning about online tools, step by step guides to create educational resources, and assessment and feedback methods.

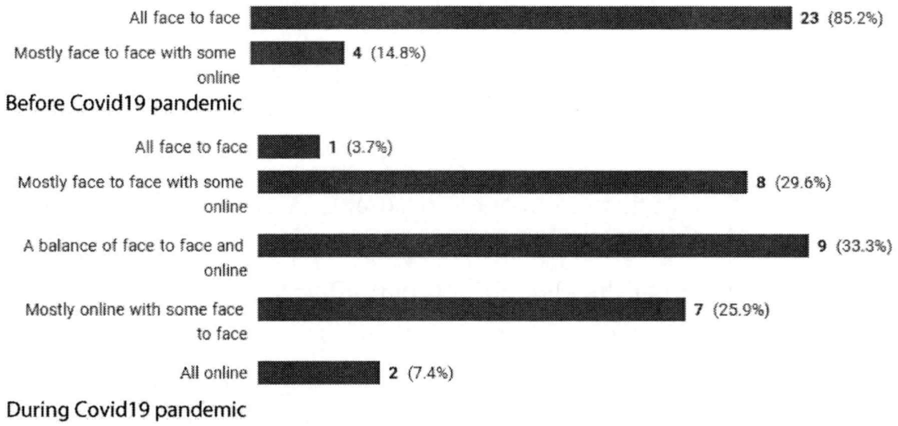

Figure 7. Before and during Covid19 pandemic teaching

The participants perspectives after each Phase and once the programme finished

Participants teaching practice during Phase 1 was used to create online educational resources and teaching in live sessions, increasing confidence. In that sense, participants indicated a better understanding of online activities and assessments, and practice with online tools after Phase 1. Participants engaged in working together, sharing experiences and collaborative ideas. In that sense mentoring has helped to support each other.

> *"We are doing everything pre-recorded at the moment, we are doing live check-ins and pre-recorded lessons, it feels a bit scary to do the live sessions, we have learnt about the flexibility and being open about what works and what doesn't." (Participant from reflective workshop)*

> *"We acknowledged we can't do everything at once, it takes time to introduce things and embed them into the organisation, it was good to see other people who agree you can't do everything in one go. We liked the idea of collaboration, but we questioned how best to do that, because we are involved in so many tools." (Participant from reflective workshop)*

Phase 1 participants suggested future learning needs to be focused on building more flexible collaborative activities and assessments. Participants found valuable the use of Teams break out rooms, Padlet activities and pools to decide the content of the workshops. Participants found the workshops based on online assessment particularly useful, this indicates the interest in online assessment through the programme. Phase 2 participants understood the benefits of using Open Educational Resources (OERs) and open practices, the potential of using feedback in online assessment to increase engagement and updating the learning design to teaching needs. Participants wanted to learn more on how to employ citizen science and supporting student journeys online. Participants showed varied confidence with the tools introduced during the programme (see Table 2).

Participants agreed online learning is an appropriate way to overcome barriers during the pandemic and that they will make greater use of online learning because of taking part of the programme. They also agreed taking part in the CPD programme has improved their views on the quality of online learning (see Table 3). The main areas where this has contributed to their professional development identified by participants were the development of activity design principles, a better understanding of distance learning and practical implementation of ideas in their classroom activities. In their future, participants indicated their desire to trial the content of the programme and share it with other colleagues. Participants acknowledged the CPD programme supports changing the approach to teaching in their department or institution and suggested the need for more support in blended learning training considering the appearance of the new curriculum.

Table 2: Confidence with the use of tools

	No experience	Not confident	Somewhat confident	Confident	Very confident
Phase 1 (n=7)					
Word cloud and interactive whiteboard			28.6%	14.3%	57.1%
Use of VLE discussions			28.6%	28.6%	42.9%
Group research and creation of a WIKI			42.9%	42.9%	14.3%
Infographics (CANVA or Piktochart)		14.3%	28.6%	28.6%	28.6%
Mind mapping (MindMeister)		14.3%	28.6%	42.9%	14.3%
Adobe connect Online Rooms		14.3%	71.4%		14.3%
OpenLearn courses		14.3%	57.1%	14.3%	14.3%
Phase 2 (n=5)					
Citizen science websites and apps (iNaturalist)	40%	40%	20%		
Creating and sharing Open Educational Resources	20%	40%	40%		
Learning design including the use of tricky topics	20%	20%		60%	
Networking tools (Twitter, Facebook, forums)		20%	20%	40%	20%
Tools for supporting student journeys (Our Journey)	40%	20%		20%	20%

Table 3: Attitude and values

Attitude and values (n=9)	Disagree	Neither agree nor disagree	Agree	Strongly agree
Online learning is the best way to overcome barriers during the pandemic		22.2%	22.2%	55.6%
I will make greater use of online learning because of taking the CPD programme		11.1%	33.3%	55.6%
Online learning can be of equal quality to face to face learning	33.3%	11.1%	44.4%	11.1%
Taking part in the CPD programme has improved my views on the quality of online learning		11.1%	55.6%	33.3%
I intend to share what I have learnt on the CPD programme with other colleagues		44.4%	44.4%	11.1%

The partners perspectives

Partners considered organising the programme from the logistical point of view was difficult to address and time-consuming, while the project has been inclusive and the response from participants involved in the workshops has been always positive. Partners believed engagement among participants was better after the first workshops. Partners credited that with the new curriculum there is an opportunity to do things differently and programme materials can impact the way the new curriculum is delivered.

> *"I have to say, it's been an absolute joy working on this project, because people did engage really well. And when we split them up into groups to work together, they always fed back really well and seem to enjoy them talking. I've been really pleased with the engagement. And of course, on top of everything that's happening at the moment, it's not easy to leave what you're doing come to a series of training." (Participant from focus group)*

> *"I know they've got a lot out of it from people I've spoken to the went on it. Just having sometimes having that relationship to chat through problems with other people has a bigger impact when being shown how to use a tool that can help. I think it might not have had an impact in terms of using more technology in the classroom, but it might have an impact on their confidence in using things and sharing with others and communicating about technology for teaching and learning. Because I think a lot of the ones that went from our college, they were quite savvy with tech before." (Participant from focus group)*

Partners considered teachers have limited time for their professional development, the new curriculum, should be more supportive and encourage collaboration across departments. The programme might have an impact on teachers' confidence in using tools and sharing with others and communicating about technology for teaching and learning. In that sense for those participants on the course, it has been invaluable to be able to learn good practice in the use of technology. Through the programme, there has been an improvement in the quality of educational resources produced. Partners were satisfied with the partnership during the project. It has followed a participatory approach to take decisions and for input, there has been a sense of commitment and enthusiasm considering the circumstances. It was positive to have all the sectors that share the same problematics involved in change. Finally, partners were engaged to participate in similar projects in the future.

Conclusions

Participation in the programme has been affected by several factors, teachers returned to the classroom part way through this programme and there was a second lockdown after the Christmas holidays. It was less flexible with accessing online workshops during school hours. Promotional time for Phase 2 varied depending on when organisers received some information and the capacity of partners to pass on the information. The impact of the project at this point is still limited to the reported experiences. It is expected meaningful impact will come from teachers and lecturers' practices in collaboration and sharing of knowledge, behaviours already identified during the programme. The resources produced during the programme such as Phase 2 workshops are expected to be available through the

Hwb repository including handouts in Welsh and English, Microsoft Teams shared space will remain open for mentors to potentiate its use and the Welsh version of the OU course "Teaching Online" in OpenLearn is available.

As participants have reported, the programme has facilitated more confidence in designing and delivering blended learning and in supporting their students studying in that environment, the programme has extended the resources for digital literacies and skills for online teaching. In that sense as identified by the partners, the programme has been a professional development opportunity, including input into the co-creation of resources for peers and the wider sector. With the new curriculum for Wales, projects such as the Cardiff Commitment CPD programme promote effecting change within organisations and wider cluster through peer to peer approach and a chance to share practice, learn from one another and collectively work towards addressing the needs of teaching staff across the school system, FE and higher education.

References

Bassot, B. (2016). *The reflective journal.* Macmillan International Higher Education.

Deepwell, M., Palmer, T., & Greig, S. (2019). *Blended Learning Essentials Project reports. Project Report.* Association for Learning Technology.

Eventbrite (n.d.). Now is your time. Retrieved from https://www.eventbrite.com/

Farrow, R. (2019). Bringing Learning to Life: Evaluation of Everyday Skills in maths and English. Open Education Research Hub. The Open University (UK). CC-BY 4.0 Retrieved from http://oro.open.ac.uk/67478/

HWB (n.d.). Curriculum for Wales. Retrieved from https://hwb.gov.wales/curriculum-for-wales

HWB (n.d.). Resources. Retrieved from https://hwb.gov.wales/repository/

Jull, J., Giles, A., & Graham, I. D. (2017). Community-based participatory research and integrated knowledge translation: advancing the co-creation of knowledge. *Implementation Science, 12*(1), 1-9.

Learning Partnership Wales, The (n.d.). Ongoing Support for Schools. Retrieved from https://tlpwales.co.uk/ongoing-support-for-schools/

Maguire, D., Dale, L., & Pauli, M. (2020). *Learning and teaching reimagined: a new dawn for higher education?* Retrieved from https://repository.jisc.ac.uk/8150/1/learning-and-teaching-reimagined-a-new-dawn-for-higher-education.pdf

Marinoni, G., Van't Land, H., & Jensen, T. (2020). *The impact of Covid-19 on higher education around the world.* IAU Global Survey Report.

Microsoft (n.d.). Microsoft Teams. Retrieved from https://www.microsoft.com/en-ww/microsoft-teams/group-chat-software

Open University, The (n.d.). New course to help teaching and lecturing online. Retrievd from https://www.open.ac.uk/wales/en/news/new-course-help-teaching-and-lecturing-online

Open University, The (n.d.). OpenLearn. Retrieved from https://www.open.edu/openlearn/

Terrell, S. R. (2012). Mixed-methods research methodologies. *Qualitative Report, 17*(1), 254-280.

van Valkenburg, W., Dijkstra, W., de los Arcos, B., & Goeman, K. (2020). European Maturity Model for Blended Education. Retrieved from https://embed.eadtu.eu/

Welsh Government. (2019). A strategic framework for post-16 digital learning in Wales. Retrieved from https://gov.wales/sites/default/files/publications/2019-06/digital-2030-a-strategic-framework-for-post-16-digital-learning-in-wales.pdf

Welsh Government. (2020). Guidance on learning in schools and settings from the autumn term. Retrieved from https://gov.wales/sites/default/files/publications/2020-07/guidance-learning-schools-settings-from-autumn-term.pdf

Acknowledgements

The Cardiff Commitment Continuing Professional Development (CPD) programme has been funded by the Higher Education Funding Council for Wales - Cyngor Cyllido Addysg Uwch Cymru (HEFCW).

Lessons from a Pandemic for the Future of Education
European Distance and E-Learning Network (EDEN) Proceedings
2021 Annual Conference | Madrid, 21-24 June, 2021
ISSN 2707-2819
doi: 10.38069/edenconf-2021-ac0024

ARGUMENTE: AN ONLINE ARGUMENTATION SYSTEM FOR FORMAL AND NON-FORMAL EDUCATION

Larisa Enríquez Vázquez, Myrna Hernández Gutiérrez, Universidad Nacional Autónoma de México, México

Abstract

ArguMente is an online system that offers two types of learning spaces. On the one hand, a close group space that implements a student-centred teaching strategy, the purpose of which is to automate the Dialogue Design System model for written argumentation (DDS). On the other hand, it offers a space for the exercise of an argued debate under a non-formal environment of education that calls for the creation of learning communities. Experiences for teaching argumentative skills and for teaching teachers have taken place through the first space, the closed classroom, while the second space, the open classroom, is being used to promote the autonomous argumentative dialogue.

Introduction

Argumentation is a linguistic process that is used to defend a position that we assume before a certain problem or situation. Whether in writing or orally, it must be understood as an interaction contextualized in other discursive types, which leads to questioning beliefs and testing one's own points of view. (Pérez, 2014). That is why argumentation is considered, not only as a competence in itself, but as a transversal competence that contributes to better learning since, as Hyland points out, disciplinary argumentation is a practice of inquiry, construction and communication of knowledge made by members of certain scientific communities, making use of academic discourse(Hyland, 2016).

Asterhan and Schwarz (2016), referring to several authors, mention that "Providing reasons why a certain explanation idea or opinion is faulty not only allows one to propose convincing arguments to refute that position in a discussion but also is likely to strengthen his or her understanding of the correct concept in the process"; this understanding and the skills involved in the generation of an argumentation occur in educational spaces, both formal and non-formal.

Formal and non-formal education

The Institute for Lifelong Learning of the United Nations Educational, Scientific and Cultural Organization (UNESCO, 2012) considers that learning comprises a wide range of educational opportunities formally offered through schools (from basic education to postgraduate and higher education); but it also extends beyond formal education, encompassing non-formal and informal learning for youth and adult citizens who are out of the school system.

Considering that currently the didactic process is centred on learning, it can be defined as formal learning the learning that takes place in education and training institutions, recognized by the relevant national authorities and leads to the obtaining of diplomas and qualifications; it is structured according to criteria such as curricula, qualifications and teaching-learning requirements. On the other hand, non-formal learning refers to the kind of learning that has been acquired additionally or alternatively to formal learning. In some cases it is also structured according to education and training criteria but, in a more flexible way. It usually occurs in community contexts, in the workplace or through activities of non-governmental organizations. Non-formal learning, through recognition, validation and accreditation processes, can also lead to qualifications and other types of academic certification.

We agree with UNESCO that it is necessary to recognize and develop mechanisms for the recognition, validation and accreditation (RVA) of non-formal and informal learning in contemporary educational and economic policies. For this reason, we consider that education in the current context must integrate different scenarios to learn, that is, to resume training from the classroom to learn in formal and non-formal contexts and in them, develop the necessary skills in learners and citizens of digital contexts. One of the fundamental skills to learn to learn is argumentation since it considers the application of logical thinking for the development of critical thinking. We also agree with Scott, (2015), especially in the context of the pandemic, on the importance of students having the combination of critical thinking, creativity, and collaboration and communication skills, all of them necessary to deal with the new unexpected situations they will face.

ArguMente

ArguMente is a web system that supports different simultaneous processes in relation to argumentation that respond to a vision of contributing to the training of more active, more critical students, with the capacity to dialogue in order to face different day-to-day situations. ArguMente considers two types of spaces to exercise written argumentation: a closed classroom that takes up the idea of the school environment and formal education. In it, the teacher gathers a group of students and proposes theses to argue under a format of a card, called Idea card; these are registered and graded with the specific feedback concerning the written argumentation proposed by the student. The other space, the open classroom, considers a freer environment for argumentation and, as its name implies, it is open. In this non-formal space, each user can create communities that summon people interested in the subject and propose theses to be discussed without a time restrain.

By working with ArguMente, students are immersed in a dynamic that forces them to progressively improve their argumentation and communication skills and competencies, either with the help of other colleagues (from the community or the group) and / or teachers.

Closed classroom

The closed classroom integrates the DDS model, where the teacher presents the unit or concept that will be developed throughout the week and prepares a thesis to reflect and / or discuss in greater depth on the subject. In the automation of this process, to generate a thesis in the system, the professor enters an area of the system in which a file is presented, in this file the teacher writes the statement corresponding to the thesis, the subject with which is related, the subject to which it corresponds, the level of studies in which it should be applied (baccalaureate or degree), the first argument and the first counter-argument derived from the thesis. The mandatory data in this file are the thesis, the argument and the counter argument; in this way, enough information will be stored so that the thesis can be applied by another professor or in other groups or even proposed in the open classroom. ArguMente is a web system that supports different simultaneous processes in relation to argumentation which respond to a vision of having more active university students, facing different situations they encounter every day. When working with ArguMente, students are immersed in a dynamic that progressively requires them to improve their argumentation skills and competencies, with the help of other classmates, staff students and teachers. In previous experiences, working with Idea cards allowed students to rescue main ideas from the academic readings or topics or as conclusions for each didactic unit reviewed. In several cases, these Idea cards supported them to improve their understanding, but also to prepare for exams. This is mainly because it forces them to analyse and synthesize ideas and have strong basis (evidence) that support their arguments. Although the methodology has been used primarily with social science students, this exercise can be applied to any area of knowledge. Figure 1 shows the student's interface in the closed classroom. The menu on the left side shows the options offered to the student in order to review the different theses that he/she has worked on or that he/she still has to work on. The thesis can be consulted in two ways, from the general concentration of all the theses or, through the groups created by the teachers and in which he/she is registered.

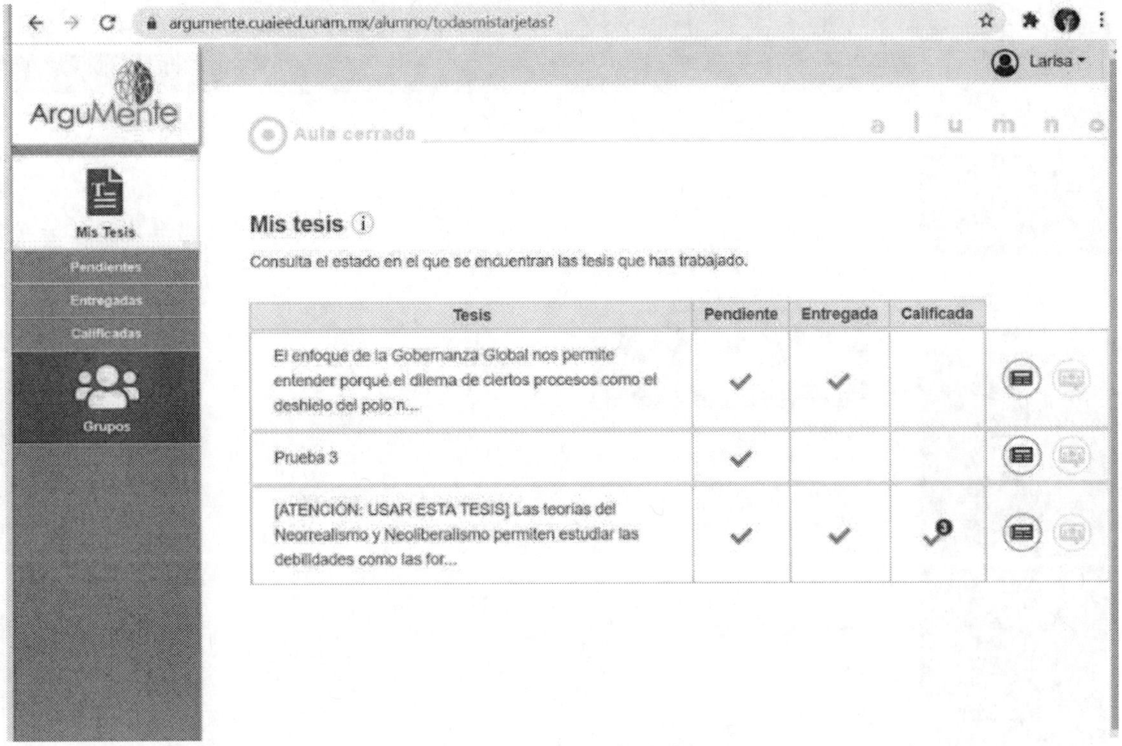

Figure 1. Student's interface

Figure 2 presents the teacher's who, in addition to being able to review and grade the cards that they have given to the students, either from the Thesis or My groups option (as in the case of students), also they have the options to create theses and to consult the catalogue of theses that have been proposed by all other teachers who use ArguMente.

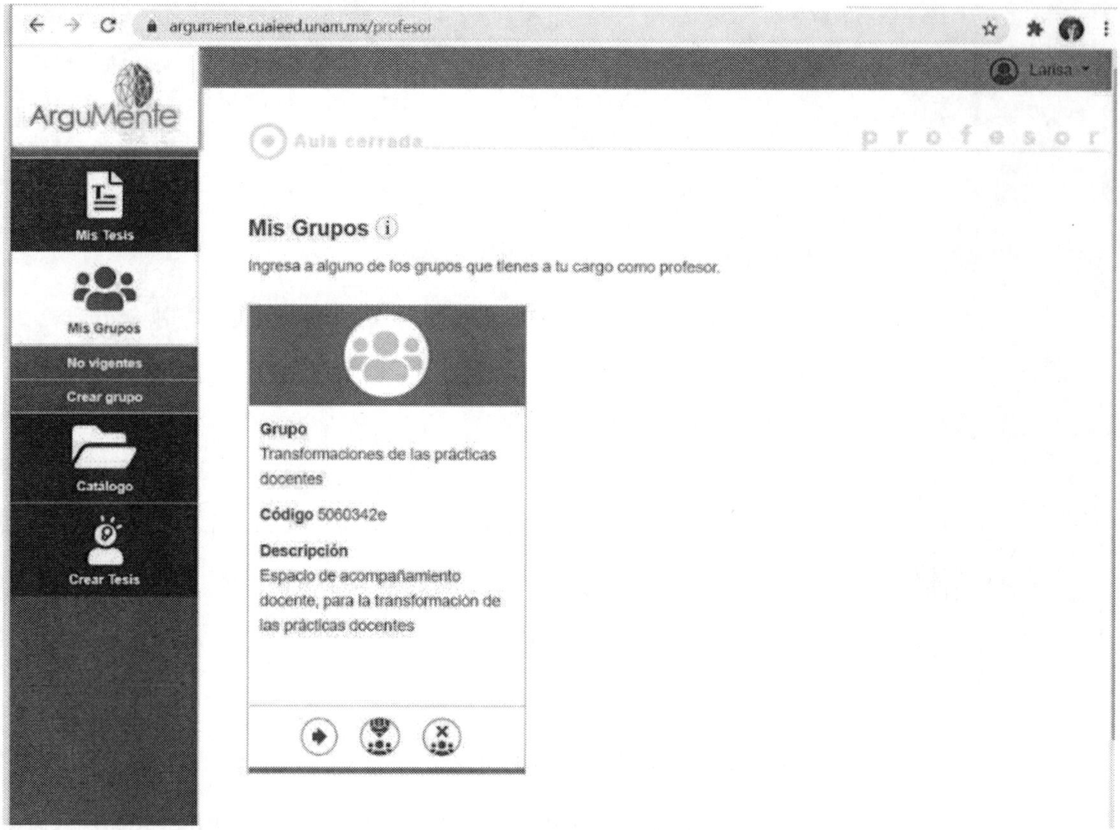

Figure 2. Teacher's interface

Open classroom

The open classroom, unlike the closed classroom, provides a space for argumentative debate where all people who are interested in it can participate. It is a space that raises a horizontal structure where anyone can submit a thesis as well as participate in any debate or dialogue that is taking place within a community and in which they are interested in participating. The open classroom only considers two types of users: the argumentator who actively participates in argued discussion, and the observer, who probably is someone interested in participating.

The way in which argued discussions are organized in this space is through communities, which can be proposed by the argumentator; Each debate begins with a thesis where one argument in favour and one against is shown, this allows the debate to be opened and the other argumentators can take positions and reinforce them with new arguments; with this they are forming discussion threads. Figure 3 presents the argumentator's interface, in the open classroom, for a specific community. It is possible to see the thesis that is being discussed along with an argument and a counterargument to it. The argument is in purple and the counterargument in orange. The argumentator who wants to join this discussion, will be able to select the button for or against, either for the main thesis or for a specific supporting argument and, from there, write his/her own argument and add the supporting evidence.

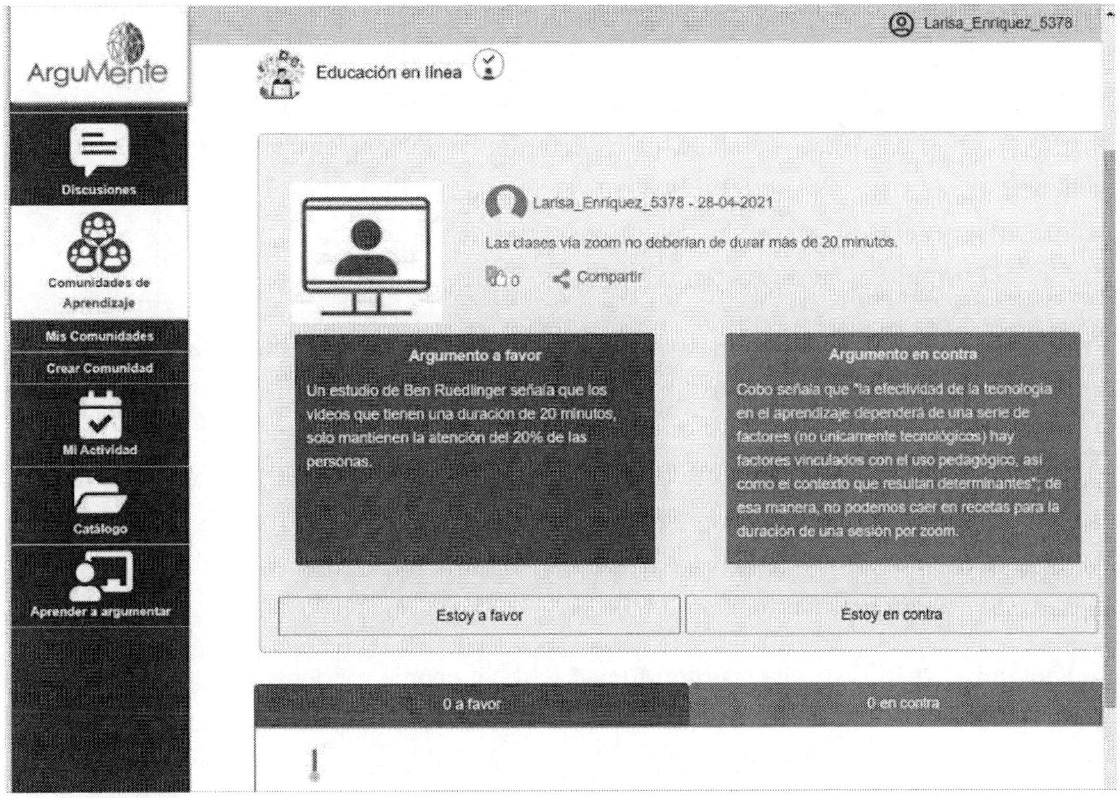

Figure 3. Argumentator's interface at the open classroom

Experiences using ArguMente

The first version of ArguMente's closed classroom was put to the test during 2020, through two different types of interventions; one with students from the Faculty of Political and Social Sciences at UNAM and another, for teacher training within the framework of a seminar on autonomous learning.

For the case of the political and social science students, as part of the doctoral research project of one of the authors, an assessment on the progression of the argumentative skills that the students were exercising, took place. The assessment endured 1 semester, 18 students of the Faculty of Political and Social Sciences voluntarily participated. During the 16 weeks that the semester lasted, the students worked on 4 theses, by solving idea cards. In particular, it was identified that students strengthened skills such as applying:

- strategies that guide a current speech, to identify aspects that are actually happening, and ask key questions about them;
- concept mapping strategies that identify important concepts and summarize knowledge;

- strategies that use connecting words as signals to stimulate thought and support the elaboration of a specific point;
- analytical strategies to identify information necessary to support a point, reflecting an implicit understanding of common argumentation schemes.

In the case of using ArguMente with teachers, a positive change in attitude was identified in them. They got more involved in the seminary; they progressively read more and widened their research sources as well as increased the quantity and quality of the arguments, generating more consistent and solid arguments than when they started the seminar (Enríquez & Hernández, 2020).

Regarding the open classroom, although this space has barely been released, there is important information from evaluations to identify user needs and usability tests. Although from the beginning of ArguMente's proposal it was considered that the open classroom would allow users to build an argued dialogue with other people, it was thought that the space would integrate some functions from the closed classroom, such as the thesis catalogue, the possibility to create thesis and to view idea cards that students from the closed classroom would have shared.

In September 2020, a survey was conducted with 84 people to identify aspects that ranged from their understanding of the debate and argumentation concepts, to the interest in participating in a space that allowed argued debates, in an environment of communities of interest. Based on the results, 8 of the respondents were contacted to interview them and thus obtain more precise information on the operation of the open classroom. As a result of these interviews, the following functionalities were also added:

- to publish and promote the debate of the month;
- to value as "I like" or "I do not like" the arguments presented by argumentators;
- to follow up on discussions and arguments in which a particular user participates;
- to follow up on communities of interest;
- to register in the communities where you want to participate.

Results

Teachers and students who had previously worked with the DDS model, found in ArguMente, great advantages, both for the creation, organization and review of the theses, as well as for the resolution, review and sharing of the Idea cards. Teachers and students who were not familiar with DDS identified a pedagogical advantage, both for teaching and learning.

Table 1 presents the results of the assessment carried out at the end of the semester, with the students who used ArguMente. It can be seen that in general, students liked the system, found it easy to use and considered that the functions were sufficient to develop the argumentation activity. It can also be seen that 50% of the students indicated that they would like to continue using ArguMente.

Table 1: Students' assessment results about ArguMente

	1 Totally disagree	2	3	4	5 Totally agree
The functions that the system contains were enough to make my arguments.	0.0 %	10.0 %	20.0 %	20.0 %	50.0 %
Navigation within ArguMente was easy to do.	10.0 %	10.0 %	10.0 %	10.0 %	60.0 %
Retrieving and viewing the graded idea cards was easy.	0.0 %	10.0 %	10.0 %	20.0 %	60.0 %
The system in general seemed simple to me.	10.0 %	0.0 %	10.0 %	20.0 %	60.0 %
I consider it necessary to have a tutorial or instructions to use the system.	0.0 %	10.0 %	50.0 %	40.0 %	0.0 %
The interface design is intuitive.	10.0 %	0.0 %	10.0 %	30.0 %	50.0 %
The design of the system looks nice to me.	10.0 %	0.0 %	10.0 %	10.0 %	70.0 %
I would like to continue using ArguMente.	10.0 %	0.0 %	20.0 %	20.0 %	50.0 %

Regarding the open classroom, the evaluations carried out so far indicate that those users who had previously worked with the closed classroom found the new proposal very easy to navigate and attractive, while those who did not know ArguMente, indicated some aspects to improve usability.

Conclusions

The online system ArguMente was developed considering the interaction in learning environments for different types of users with specific tasks for each of them. This characteristic allows developing the ability to argue in a teacher-directed manner or freely with other people who are interested in presenting arguments and evidence to support their positions. It seems to us of great relevance to generate options that allow students to develop fundamental skills in the current context, with the integration of formal and non-formal educational environments and scenarios, as it is proposed in lifelong learning, and that the various areas of their reality will also be transformed with this trend of lifelong learning. ArguMente has involved the experience and ideas of teachers, researchers and students. This collaboration and multidisciplinary work, in addition to creating a product that will benefit the university community, has allowed to generate, in the group in general and in the project participants in particular, a deep reflection, which has considered different perspectives, research interests and problems from each of the disciplines that participate, managing to build a comprehensive solution.

References

Asterhan, C., & Schwarz, B. (2016) Argumentation for Learning: Well-Trodden Paths and Unexplored Territories. *Educational Psychologist, 51*(2) 164-187. doi:10.1080/00461520.2016.1155458

Enríquez, L., & Hernández, M. (2020). Teacher training through argumentation to promote autonomous learning in educational environments mediated by technology. In S. Kucina Softic, A. Teixeira, & A. Szucs (Eds.), *Short Paper Book – Enhancing the Human Experience of Learning with Technology: New challenges for research into digital, open, distance & networked education* (pp. 30-37). The EDEN Research Workshop, 21-23 October, Universidade Aberta, LE@D, Portugal.

Hyland, K. (2011). Academic discourse. In K. Hyland & B. Paltridge (Eds.), *Continuum Companion to Discouse Analysis* (pp. 171-184). London: Continuum.

Pérez, H. (2014). *Argumentación y comunicación. Desarrollo De La Competencia Comunicativa.* Neisa.

Scott, C. L. (2015). *El futuro del aprendizaje 2 ¿Qué tipo de aprendizaje se necesita en el siglo XXI?* [Documentos de Trabajo ERF, No. 14].Paris: Investigación y Prospectiva en Educación UNESCO.

UNESCO (2012). *Directrices de la UNESCO para el reconocimiento, validación y acreditación de los resultados del aprendizaje no formal e informal.* UNESCO. Retrieved from http://unesdoc.unesco.org/images/0021/002163/216360s.pdf

Acknowledgements

ArguMente is part of the research project "DDS en línea" which is funded by UNAM-DGAPA-PAPIIT program, with registration number IT400518. We would like to thank DGAPA for the support.

We also thank and recognize the commitment and work of the students Luis Flores, Mayra Aceves and Valeria Gómez as well as Antonieta Rodríguez, Estefania Prieto.

Lessons from a Pandemic for the Future of Education
European Distance and E-Learning Network (EDEN) Proceedings
2021 Annual Conference | Madrid, 21-24 June, 2021
ISSN 2707-2819
doi: 10.38069/edenconf-2021-ac0025

"MISSION POSSIBLE": SUPPORTING AN ADOPTION OF A DISTANCE LEARNING MODEL FOR SCHOOLS DURING THE PANDEMIC

Maria Spilker, Antonieta Rocha, Ana Afonso, Lina Morgado, Laboratory of Distance Education and eLearning (LE@D), Open University, Portugal

Abstract

This investigation relates to the professional development of in-service teachers on online teaching in K-12/P-12 schools during the COVID-19 pandemic. The main questions concerned the autonomy and support from/in schools, alternatives found and implemented. A model was developed and applied in different institutions. This article will focus on analysing the results of one Portuguese school.

The study follows a Design-Based-Research methodology. The results revealed teachers have knowledge gaps regarding intermediate/advanced digital skills. Through the training course, teachers' awareness was raised about the distinction between Remote Education and Distance Learning and some skills inherent to online teaching were developed.

Introduction

After the World Health Organization (WHO) declared the COVID-19 circumstance, on March 11th 2020, as a pandemic Portugal tries to slow down the SARS-Cov 2 virus dissemination by decreeing emergency measures and subsequent confinement. These measures include, among others, teleworking and the closure of institutions and organizations, with the main purpose of promoting social distance and avoiding contagion. All the educational institutions, private and public, were included in these measures.

The suspension of face-to-face school activities as a result of the enacted measures and, the need to ensure the continuity of the school year, leads to the Portuguese Government recommendation of implementing Distance Learning solutions for all educational institutions. The lockdown of educational institutions introduced some puzzlement about the concepts in use, specifically, the meaning of distance and its affordances in education. In this sense, though very briefly, it is important to distinguish Distance Learning (DL) from Emergency Remote Teaching (ERT) (Hodges et al., 2020). The DL is characterized by a physical and temporal distance of the main educational actors, but this distance can be blurred by using the adequate balance between cognitive, social and teaching presence (Garrison & Anderson, 2003). A careful instructional design is key for the success of DL and the role of technology should not be named crucial, neither underestimated. The ERT seeks to provide rapid responses to emergent situations such as the one lived during the pandemic. Conducting a sudden classroom closing off and a forced physical separation between teacher and students, the first impulse was to transpose contents, lecture-based classroom and assessment to the virtual space. The solutions found were based on synchronous sessions (Minghat et al., 2020), still determined by the school hours and, at least, as long as the "normal" classes. The ERT was dictated by curriculum requirements and the intuitive use of web-conferencing as a substitute of the "affordances" (Laurillard, 2002) already existing at the presence teaching environment, rather than scaffolding new paths.

Like other schools worldwide, the Portuguese schools were asked for rapid solutions as an attempt to overcome the suspension of face-to-face teaching, with the enormous need on the part of the schools to self-organize for the benefit of its students (Flores & Gago, 2020). The Portuguese Government defines that teaching must continue at distance, to allow regular contact between students and their teachers and colleagues, and consolidation and development of learning. For this operationalization, the Government suggested that each educational institution should create a Distance-Learning-Plan. This plan should include the constitution of an own support team, if necessary, the taking place of training courses aiming to fill teachers' gaps concerning technological knowledge. Along these lines school support websites was created that provides publications, educational resources, a space for sharing examples of (good) practices, a selection of advisable tools and examples of methodologies to be used. Although these solutions are continuously named as DL, the Portuguese schools offered what Bozkurt and Sharma (2020) call "remote classes".

Aware of the existing inequalities in Portugal, both in terms of the access to own devices and quality broadband, alongside with some digital (il)literacy, the Portuguese government, by March 2020, relaunched and reinforced the maxim of the Program "Portugal INCoDe 2030 National Digital Competencies Initiative" which, on its Axis 2, advocates: (a) Training pre-school, primary and secondary education teachers; (b) Program for training primary and secondary school teachers, with the participation of the Schools Association Training Centres and higher education institutions. Following these measures, the European Digital Transition Action Plan was launched in September 2020, which foresees (a) making individual equipment available for teachers and students; (b) ensuring free mobile connectivity for teachers and students; (c) access to quality digital resources; (d) digital teachers' training plan according to the European Digital Competence for Educators (European Commission/EACEA/Eurydice, 2019). This idea is supported by the recent analysis of OECD on the potential impact from COVID-19 confinement measures which highlights the unpreparedness of teachers to support digital learning: "ICT skills are particularly important given the radical shift towards online teaching during the COVID-19 lockdown in many OECD countries..." (Schleicher, 2020).

It is the general recognition of the unpreparedness of the majority of teachers (and students), of the most varied teaching cycles, to use and implement DL solutions leading to quality learning, that inspires the training proposal for teachers presented on the following pages. Induced by the lockdown, during the confinement, students realized they had to become more autonomous and teachers assumed new roles in the virtual teaching-learning experience. The changes were not a planned or structured, instead, it was perceived as a difficult experience for both students and teachers.

The pandemic can be perceived as the beginning of change for Portuguese schools. Digital transformation carries new possibilities, more interaction, flexibility and autonomy, the possibility for collaborative learning, developing critical thinking, resilience... This whole situation required, on the part of teachers (and alongside technological literacy) a change in their practice and even teaching culture. In support of this idea, Portuguese teachers reacted proactively to the disruptive context emerging from the COVID-19 pandemic and, recognizing their unpreparedness for the transition from face-to-face classes to the required ERT solutions, creating, for instance, groups for sharing of practices and supporting of each other on teaching in this new context, namely through teachers' associations, as well as scientific community experts in the e-Learning field.

Regarding the cases reported for Europe, we may conclude that the options align with the options also implemented by the Portuguese government. However, cases of countries, such as Finland (Rasmitadila et al., 2020), are reported, where VLEs are already established practice and, therefore, the pressure of an unexpected transition was not felt. On the other hand, in the Portuguese context, Flores and Gago (2020) state that, although there were no mandatory recommendations by the Government, it was important to insure the interaction between students and teachers, to teach online, taking into attention the necessary adjustments in pedagogy and assessment.

Methodology

This investigation emerges from several requests for advice from different non-higher and higher education institutions to face, effectively, the challenge of the emerging situation, namely of the transition from classroom teaching to "real" online teaching. Within this article, we will only focus on analysing the results of a Portuguese school in Lisbon. Based on a design-based research methodology (DBR) (McKenney & Reeves, 2012), the development of intensive and rapid training, in emergency distance learning modality, was carried out in different stages. In this article, we will present the three first stages, while the last ones, Maturing Intervention and Theoretical Understanding, are still work in progress.

Analysis Stage (DBR)

Literature Review Stage

Initially, the authors made a review on very recent literature concerning the pandemic and its implications at the education system, at an international and national level, alongside with the reports on distance education and remote (emergency) education. This literature review was continuously updated, along with all phases of the research, and the results already presented at the beginning of this article.

Diagnostic Stage – Focus Group

As a first contact moment with the educational institution and to better design a training course to find an answer for the emerging needs, an interview was made to the institutions' stakeholders. The interview was focussed around the following topics: How are teachers coping with the pandemic situation? How are teachers handling the necessity of "teaching from home"? How are teachers getting support, for instance, from the school, colleagues, Ministry of Education? Which are the main barriers (pedagogical and technological) faced by teachers? Overall, how do teachers evaluate the process so far?

To collect information about the pandemic school scenario and gather some (preconceived) ideas, we used a focus groups methodology (Krueger, 2014) with a multidisciplinary group (including school stakeholders, teachers and elearning experts). For instance, the focus group participants stated:

> *"Technology is an obstacle here. I only use it for everyday life and to organize my teaching work." (Teacher #1)*
>
> *"I believe we need a training on how to adapt these tools to distance learning (...) not on technology. We cannot overload students with zoom lessons." (Teacher #7).*

In summary, the following conclusions and concerns can be pointed out: teachers felt unprepared for online teaching; teachers reflected on their emergency practices and were aware that they were not implementing Distance Education; teachers felt the need for initial training on pedagogical strategies to support DL, as well as the need for adequate mastery of some teaching support tools; teachers were compiled to relate and communicate differently with the students' families. Furthermore, those involved were motivated and receptive and willing to develop high-quality teaching.

Diagnostic Stage – Survey

Alongside, a survey online was applied to the teachers. The survey comprised multiple-choice questions: 4 to characterize the target audience; 10 to know the level of knowledge about digital tools; and 2 about EaD experience. The questions were arranged based on the literature relevant to the purpose of the research. The survey had 42 respondents. Besides the professional and demographic characteristics, it gathered information about the use of technology in the classroom and the perception of their digital competence.

Participants' characterization

Forty-two teachers answered the questionnaire, of which 78.6% were female and 21.4% male. Ages ranged from 20 to 29 age groups (16.7%) and those over 60 years (4.8%), being in the age group of 30-39 years about 35.7% and 28.3% in the age group 40-49 years. Regarding the levels of education at which the respondents were educators and/or teachers: Kindergarten (3 to 5 years) – 8 educators; 1st cycle (6 to 10 years) – 23 teachers; 2nd cycle (10 to 12 years) – 15 teachers; 3rd cycle (12 to 15 years) – 14 teachers. Likewise, we observed that teachers sometimes assume the teaching of more than one discipline (two to four), resulting from their qualifications and the curricular group(s) to which they belong.

Digital Competence previous to the training

Regarding digital tools, we were interested not only in understanding the level of (non) knowledge but also the level of their (non) use. Thus, it was important to assess the level of digital literacy of this group, as well as their level and intensity (occasional or regular) of the use and applicability of these tools in school context pre-pandemic. Given the diversity of the offer as well as the specific features and applications, we have chosen to separate into different categories: (a) LMS platforms; (b) presentation tools; (c) video editors; (d) image creators and editors; (e) image banks; (f) sources; (g) video excerpts; (h) cloud; (i) online questionnaires and forms and, (j) editing and screen capture.

At the educational level, respondents mostly used email as a communication tool. Regarding the Virtual Learning Platforms themselves the respondents know and use the paid and closed-access educational platform online named *Escola Virtual* and also Google Classroom. Regarding other digital tools, although free and available online, the respondents revealed their lack of knowledge in the context of creating and offering content to their students. The results are quite concerning, as they are not aligned with the European Framework for the Digital Competence of Educators: DigCompEdu (European

Commission/EACEA/Eurydice, 2019). These results were an important starting point, both for the definition of the model and for structuring the training course itself, in which we brought together the offer of digital tools and which provided a starting point and awareness of the OER.

Distance teaching experiences previous to the training

When asked about previous online training courses, 81% of respondents said they had never taken an online training course. Of the remaining 19%, only 4.8% claimed to have had contact with this teaching regime during their formal qualification; 6.8% promoted by guardianship; 6.8% in free training courses. Finally, when asked about tools used in an educational context in approximately one month (between the beginning of confinement and the training course), the respondents stated that they had mainly used Virtual School (18.2%), email (11.4%) and Zoom (14.8%).

These results were also evidence of an option for "traditional", lecture-based teaching, without using new technologies or mobile learning. With institutions having computers, this non-use seems to be a "missed opportunity". As such, and in a lockdown context, this fact led to an increased effort to technologically update and upgrade, but also to an opportunity to meet and adopt new practices, ideally collaboratively, and in communities.

Design Stage

From the collected data emerged the need for designing differentiated scenarios of DL, taking into attention various age ranges and different teaching/learning cycles and adapted to each specific case. This was made through a simplified Analysis, Design, Development, Implementation and Evaluation methodology (Durak & Ataizi, 2016). For the development of content for the intensive training online, the authors used the Rapid eLearning Development methodology: after an analysis of the training need, the objectives were defined; it was paid special attention to the previously gathered characteristics of the target audience; a training plan was designed; content was developed and outlined e-activities, to be performed by the educators and teachers; and, finally, the modality for evaluating trainees and the course itself has been defined.

MIREAD

The MIREAD (*Modelo de Intervenção Rápida em Ensino a Distância* – Rapid Intervention in Distance Learning Model) was developed based on the characteristics of DL, such as described by Anderson and Dron (2011), centred on asynchronous communication and punctual synchronous one. In the following sections, the different MIREAD's aspects are shortly explained. MIREAD was developed based on literature review and the analysis of information and data gathered and in the experience of the team. From this, 4 guiding vectors for the model were reified.

1. Actors' previous ideas: It is necessary to deconstruct teachers' previously conceived ideas (Moscovici & Doise, 1991) about DL (e.g. Distance Education is synonymous with video conferencing) and, also, to reflect upon the role of communication in online contexts (Quintas-Mendes et al., 2008).
2. Access and familiarity with online technology and culture: It is important to develop digital literacy and soft skills for teaching online, which go beyond the simple mastery of web tools, thus really embracing cyberculture (Santos, 2014).
3. Asynchronous versus synchronous communication: The first impulse of many schools was to use video conferencing systems to replicate the traditional (mostly theoretical) classes. The setback was, like Wiederhold (2020) states, "... people are now beginning to recognize a new phenomenon: tiredness, anxiety, or worry resulting from overusing virtual video conferencing platforms—something researchers and journalists have begun calling 'Zoom fatigue'." Within the framework of MIREAD, we propose the use of synchronous communication, with specific pedagogical goals, in a balanced way, thus maintaining temporal flexibility (Shambaugh, 2016).
4. Moving from a physical to a virtual space: The transition from the face-to-face classroom to online learning requires resources, materials, technology and human resources, as well as a pedagogical design and strategy, and a constant reassessment of the whole process and relationships between the different actors (Pimentel & Gomes, 2019).

MIREAD's main components

In line with the 4 vectors, the two main MIREAD's components are the Weekly Digital Learning Tool (WDLT) and the selected Virtual Learning Environment (VLE).

The WDLT

The WDLT is a planning and communication tool, for teachers and students, which is on the foundations of the pedagogical assumptions of the MIREAD. It provides the students with an overview of the weekly learning tasks to be accomplished, indicating all the tools, resources, schedules and outcomes required. It also must take into account that we are dealing with lower age groups and, therefore, it also plays an important role in helping the caring adult become a mentor of the student in the concretization of the WDLT. It should also not be ignored that the WDLT must take into account particular constraints (Rasmitadila et al., 2020). The WDLT is a structuring component of the MIREAD, as it operates as a connection element that mediates the pedagogical experience between teachers-students-content and families. It helps the teacher to plan the activities for a class and how to mediate the teaching-learning process. It is the teacher that chooses the resources in line with the activities and their duration (taking into account the workload of each class). It also presents how and when the student is going to be evaluated (for instance through the artefacts uploaded to the VLE) and receives feedback.

The VLE

The second component of MIREAD is the VLE, herein understood as the technological platform that hosts the pedagogical experience. We would like to note that, according to the results of the analysis stage previously conducted, we realized that until the moment of the training implementation, the educational institution was using the email as a communication tool with the students. It was also verified that the teachers had no previous knowledge about VLEs and its use. Taking into account the specific context of the educational institution, it was necessary to find a suitable VLE: rapid implementation; with no additional costs; with a flat learning curve; user-friendly and appropriate children under 12. The VLE should support asynchronous communication, in one place, and integrates a synchronous communication tool, avoiding cyberbullying or zoom-bombing, to make possible all the pedagogical strategies that the teacher wants to apply. It was important to deconstruct the idea that the class should be taken as face-to-face and with the same time slot. During the training, the teachers were sensitized (and felt that themselves) that an online session can be tiring. So the sessions should be delimited in time and with specific aims, also covering social-emotional aspects of the students.

Course Design

In Portuguese schools, the face-to-face classroom essentially prevails. The need to teach online has put many teachers facing enormous challenges. The offer of short-term and intensive training, personalized and to fill gaps, was the solution found to meet the pressing and emerging needs. Thus, MIREAD includes a training course that includes aspects such as DL awareness (main characteristics of DL; Emergency DL model), Online Teaching (Synchronous Communication vs. Asynchronous Communication) and Online Educational Resources and Tools. In this article, we focus only on two aspects that we find to be of greater importance: the Weekly Digital Learning Tool and the VLE selection and use.

Evaluation Stage

Artefacts and study units conceived by the trainees

Based on our observations and feedback given by the trainers to all educators/teachers concerning the implementation of the MIREAD model some results can be presented. The final activity of the training course to be carried out by the trainees consisted of designing and implementing an asynchronous environment for a discipline and outlining a Weekly Digital Learning Tool – WDLT for a specific class. The vast majority performed the activity and in the last training session, some of the final products were presented to the group. Briefly, we observed that the Weekly Digital Learning Tool was decisive short-term planning for the discipline.

Trainees were careful to create interdisciplinary activities, aligning in the timeline the sequence of activities developed in the different units. For example, in the 2nd Cycle of Basic Education, an activity was developed in the Portuguese study unit about a given author, followed by creative work in the Visual and Technological Education unit, as well as a poem in the Musical Education unit. Subjects such as Physical Education, whose teachers initially expressed concern about the operationalization of physical activities at a distance, developed alternatives such as working on theoretical aspects of the subject (e.g. rules of Collective Sports Games), making available videos on collective and individual sports games, and performing physical activities at synchronous weekly meeting times. Foreign Language subjects have chosen to resort to videos on YouTube; to the creation of videos by the teachers themselves, to video recording, via smartphones, by students; focusing on orality training in synchronous sessions.

Trainees' achievements

Overall, the trainees were collaborative, enthusiastic, proactive, open to suggestions and change and, most of all, willing to implement and promote changes (technological and pedagogical) on behalf of students' success. For instance, teachers stated:

> *"The training reassured me because I got an idea of how I can work with my students at a distance without having to resort to a wide range of platforms. Realizing that with only 2 tools (Classroom and Zoom) I will be able to do asynchronous and synchronous work with the students was very reassuring and allowed me to start outlining action plans." (Teacher #1)*

> *"I believe that this training is truly important to overcome all the challenges that lie ahead during the 3rd period in DL and, above all, to bring us closer to our students and to provide them with all the necessary motivation and support." (Teacher #8)*

When looking back at the training conducted, an overview of the trainees' achievements highlights several strengths and weaknesses that may be transversal to teachers from other educational institutions, and that should be taken under consideration in the next iteration of this research.

As for the strengths, we may point out that the trainees showed the capacity to explore and openness for the later adoption of previously unknown digital tools. They were pro-active and searched for solutions through autonomous research. It was rewarding to see real teamwork and a climate of mutual help (especially among colleagues of the same education cycle), sharing practices. The feedback provided by the colleagues and by the training team was always well-received and transposed to (new) practice). The course was perceived as a trigger for teachers to reflect on their classroom practices (physical and virtual) and to strive for better performance by applying the recommendations made throughout the training modules.

As for the weaknesses, we may highlight that there were some operational difficulties associated, namely, with multidisciplinarity in primary school and, more specifically, concerning the design of the unit subject, which encompassed several areas of knowledge (adoption of strategies to avoid the scroll of death). Also, it was not lineal that there is a need to provide detailed guidance to students and to pay special attention to the temporal and/or modular segmentation of activities.

The course was only able to raise awareness on topics related to open educational resources (OER) versus property-based educational resources (such from Virtual School); copyright issues (Creative Commons) and open educational practices (OEP). Furthermore, teachers were generally aware of problems related to issues such as children's data protection. Teachers awarded the training course great importance in that it proved to be a transformative experience of the teaching practices (in an online or face-to-face context) far beyond the objectives initially outlined and specifically associated with distance education.

Further research is being planned, to collect and analyse follow-up information, such as, for instance, how DL was implemented and, effectively, took place, and how the change was evaluated by the stakeholders involved. This will include analysing post-training questionnaire analysis and conducting interviews, to evaluate and improve the model developed, entering a new DBR cycle and aiming for new insights on this field. When professionals "(...) speak about their own crisis of confidence, they tend to focus on the mismatch of traditional patterns of practice and knowledge to features of the practice situation – complexity, uncertainty, instability, uniqueness, and value conflict – of whose importance they are becoming increasingly aware" (Schön, 2006; p.18). However, after the pandemic challenge, the education professionals "are able to 'practice' their practice" (Schön, 2006; p.60).

Final considerations

The world-scale lockdown imposed by the COVID-19 pandemic had a profound impact in all areas of society and education was not excluded. This emergency situation brought with it a challenge for families, students, teachers and researchers from education-related areas but it's also true "that opening up to uncertainty offers opportunity, diversity and a politics of hope" (Scoones & Stirling, 2020). As Carretero et al. (2021; p.7) in their report highlight "Several lessons for the future can be drawn from schooling practices during the spring 2020 lockdown". Moving from traditional face-to-face educational systems to DL systems is a rather complex process that requires, not only technological infrastructures and human resources, but also the adoption of specific pedagogical principles, features, and practices, supported by scientific research in DL.

Recognizing that occasional ERT solutions, like those generally implemented during the pandemic, require competence and characteristics quite different from those needed at DL, this article focuses on lessons learned from the authors work in responding to training requests from schools during the lockdown scenario. This work led to the development of a Rapid Intervention in Distance Learning Model (MIREAD), mainly based on asynchronous interaction, with some moments of synchronous interaction, to support a community of teachers and schools, in the implementation of an effective and true DL solution. Supported by the assumptions that distance teaching and learning should neither replicate nor simulate face-to-face models; that it should preserve temporal and local flexibility, based on asynchronous communication and that it is based on teacher-student-content interaction, MIREAD was developed as a DL model which encompasses the conceptualization, implementation and monitoring of DL solutions.

MIREAD foresees that the work with the students is based on weekly planned activities proposed by the teacher, with the support of the offered materials (educational resources in digital format). The interaction must be mainly asynchronous with punctual synchronous sessions limited to the essential: one per discipline, per week, lasting 20 to 40 minutes. The importance of the solution proposed in this article lies in the response to pressing problems. Notwithstanding, this solution is also intended to be perceived as a first step towards DL in a broader sense. Distance teaching/learning scenarios have specific characteristics and, request, both from teachers and pupils, singular competence and skills, for instance, concerning the communication online and the workload estimation. This means that, for instance, while designing the WDLT, teachers should be aware of the time needed by students to conclude a proposed activity. The teacher should also take into consideration that this learning modality requires more autonomy, greater time management skills, and higher levels of motivation from the students and these should be well-supported by a detailed WDLT.

In this context, which might be the teachers' task? After they designed and delivered the WDLT to the students, they have to moderate the different kinds of messages that are posted into the asynchronous environment. The students' messages can include help requests on the content, presentation of the produced artefacts, or social messages. The teacher, online, should pay attention to his workload. It is not expected that the teacher should be 7days/24hours online. On the other hand, the level of students' anxiety tends to grow, so answering relevant questions should be well-timed. In other words, the teachers must be aware and have skills on how to use properly and efficiently the asynchronous communication channels, such as forums, demonstrating how it is expected from the students themselves. The pandemic raised awareness to the urgency of a digital transformation, having implications in the educational area, but also of a cultural transformation, requiring, for instance, open-minded and curious teachers, willing to explore new technologies in the classroom. The next steps of this research aim to assess the teachers' development of competence through rapid and personalised training units and the adequacy of the model to answer the challenges set by the situation of emergency, being sure that it is through education that cultural revolutions take place.

References

Anderson, T., & Dron, J. (2011). Three generations of distance education pedagogy. *The International Review of Research in Open and Distributed Learning, 12*(3), 80. https://doi.org/10.19173/irrodl.v12i3.890

Bozkurt, A., & Sharma, R. (2020). Emergency remote teaching in a time of global crisis due to CoronaVirus pandemic. *Asian Journal of Distance Education, 15*(1), 1-6.

Carretero, S., Napierała, J., Bessios, A., Pugacewicz, A., Ranieri, M., Triquet, K., Robledo-bottcher, N., & Montanari, M. (2021). *What did we learn from schooling practices during the COVID-19 lockdown?* Insights from five EU countries. https://doi.org/10.2760/135208

Durak, G., & Ataizi, M. (2016). The ABC's of Online Course Design According to Addie Model. *Universal Journal of Educational Research, 4*(9), 2084-2091. https://doi.org/10.13189/ujer.2016.040920

European Commission/EACEA/Eurydice. (2019). *Digital Education at School in Europe. Eurydice Report.* Publications Office of the European Union. https://doi.org/10.2797/376130

Flores, M. A., & Gago, M. (2020). Teacher education in times of COVID-19 pandemic in Portugal: national, institutional and pedagogical responses. *Journal of Education for Teaching, 46*(4), 507-516. https://doi.org/10.1080/02607476.2020.1799709

Garrison, D. R., & Anderson, T. (2003). *E-Learning in the 21st Century: A Framework for Research and Practice.* RoutledgeFalmer.

Hodges, C., Moore, S., Lockee, B., Trust, T., & Bond, A. (2020). The Difference between Emergency Remote Teaching and Online Learning. Educause Review.

Krueger, R. A. (2014). *Focus groups: A practical guide for applied research.* Sage publications.

Laurillard, D. (2002). Rethinking Teaching for the Knowledge Society. *Educause Review, 37*(1), 16-25. https://doi.org/10.1080/0305792022000007463

McKenney, S., & Reeves, T. (2012). *Conducting Educational Design Research.* Routledge.

Minghat, A. D., Ana, A., Purnawarman, P., Saripudin, S., Muktiarni, M., Dwiyanti, V., & Mustakim, S. S. (2020). Students' Perceptions of the Twists and Turns of E-learning in the Midst of the Covid 19 Outbreak. *Revista Romaneasca Pentru Educatie Multidimensionala, 12*(1Sup2), 15-26. https://doi.org/10.18662/rrem/12.1sup2/242

Moscovici, S., & Doise, W. (1991). *Dissensões e Consenso.* Livros Horizonte.

Pimentel, E. P., & Gomes, A. S. (2019). Ambientes Virtuais de Aprendizagem para uma Educação mediada por tecnologias digitais. In E. O. Santos, M. Pimentel, & F. Sampaio (Eds.), *Informática na Educação: autoria, mídia, letramento, inclusão digital.* Sociedade Brasileira de Computação.

Quintas-Mendes, A., Morgado, L., & Amante, L. (2008). Online Communication and E-Learning. In T. T. Kidd & H. Song (Eds.), *Handbook of Research on Instructional Systems and Technology: Vol. II. Information Science Reference.*

Rasmitadila, R., Aliyyah, R. R., Rachmadtullah, R., Samsudin, A., Syaodih, E., Nurtanto, M., & Tambunan, A. R. S. (2020). The Perceptions of Primary School Teachers of Online Learning during the COVID-19 Pandemic Period: A Case Study in Indonesia. *Journal of Ethnic and Cultural Studies, 7*(2), 90. https://doi.org/10.29333/ejecs/388

Santos, E. (2014). *Pesquisa-Formação na Cibercultura* (1st ed.). Whitebooks.

Schleicher, A. (2020). *The impact of covid-19 on education insights from education at a glance.* OECD Publishing.

Schön, D. A. (2006). *The reflective practitioner.* Ashgate Publishing Limited.

Scoones, I., & Stirling, A. (2020). *The politics of uncertainty: Challenges of transformation.* Taylor & Francis.

Shambaugh, N. (2016). Interactivity and Immediacy in Online Academic Programs. In S. D'Agustino (Ed.), *Creating Teacher Immediacy in Online Learning Environments* (pp. 76-90). IGI Global. https://doi.org/10.4018/978-1-4666-9995-3.ch005

Wiederhold, B. K. (2020). Connecting through Technology during the Coronavirus Disease 2019 Pandemic: Avoiding "zoom Fatigue". *Cyberpsychology, Behavior, and Social Networking, 23*(7), 437-438. https://doi.org/10.1089/cyber.2020.29188.bkw

Lessons from a Pandemic for the Future of Education
European Distance and E-Learning Network (EDEN) Proceedings
2021 Annual Conference | Madrid, 21-24 June, 2021
ISSN 2707-2819
doi: 10.38069/edenconf-2021-ac0026

PERCEIVED EFFICACY OF E-PROCTORING SOFTWARE FOR EMERGENCY REMOTE ONLINE BASED ASSESSMENT: PERCEPTIONS OF PROCTORED EXAMINATIONS

Chinaza Ironsi, Near East University, Cyprus

Abstract

The switch from traditional teaching methods to emergency remote online learning as a result of the outbreak of COVID-19 necessitated a change in approaches to measurement and evaluation in our educational system. A lot of methods were adopted yet the need for credible, properly monitored, valid and reliable assessment continues to be an issue of debate. E-proctoring as a popular strategy for monitoring and administering online-based examinations has witnessed tremendous success over the years yet ethical issues and many more are yet to be extensively examined. While a teacher may embrace the use of this software for monitoring examination, the perception of preservice teachers has not been explored adequately, much more the opinions of the instructors and preservice teachers on the level of efficacy with regards to the use of e-proctoring strategy for monitoring online-based examinations in a hybrid/emergency remote online educational model has not been investigated. It is in this light that this study intends to examine the perceptions of instructors and preservice teachers on the use of e-proctoring devices during online-based assessments, two research questions were investigated through a quantitative research design. A structured questionnaire was used to elicit information from 40 participants comprising of 36 students and 4 teachers on their perceptions of the effectiveness and efficacy of the e-proctored software while administering and monitoring examinations. Findings from the study will be beneficial in drawing valid conclusions on the use of e-proctored devices in monitoring emergency remote online-based assessment. The conclusions will prepare school administrators and equip them with the possible approaches to adopt in ensuring that a credible valid and reliable evaluation process is conducted during the post-COVID 19 semesters.

Introduction

Online learning is an integral part of contemporary education globally, a study which was carried out by ambient insight research does suggest that more than 1.2 million learners carried out learning through an online learning platform, yet a recent study confirms that more than 80% of learners have been engaged in online learning (Kesharvas & Hulus, 2019). The switch to emergency remote online learning as a result of the COVID-19 pandemic outbreak suggests a redesign and implementation of most instruction delivery to an online format and recently to a hybrid. While instruction delivery continues in a hybrid format, and the world looks forward to a second wave of the pandemic/ possible lockdown (which is already on-going in some parts of the world), there is a need for educational researchers to reconsider key aspects and areas of educational instructional delivery, one of such areas includes; curriculum design, educational evaluation, and assessment. Particularly, in the area of educational evaluation and assessment, there is a recent call for rethinking and redesigning the way we administer examinations to ensure that the mode of administering assessments are credible, produces positive learning outcomes, promotes positive academic integrity, transparency, malpractice, and anxiety-free (Hopfenbeck, 2020; Wald & Harland, 2020; Isinkaye, Soyemi, & Arowosegbe, 2020; Mathwasa & Sibanda, 2020; Ossai, Ethe, & Edougha, 2020). For decades, one of the most popular ideas in the pedagogy of education especially with regards to assessment in literature is the idea of online-based assessment (Bhagat, Wu, & Chang, 2016). There are growing appeals for a review of online assessments to ensure that educational assessments are valid, reliable, and properly monitored. Research on online assessment has a long tradition though issues of validity, reliability of test items, and the nature of examination monitoring have continued to pose a serious challenge (Bates, 2018). A recent strategy used for monitoring online examinations is through e-proctoring software (Cramp, Medlin, Lake, & Sharp, 2019; Kayser, 2016; Lilley, Meere, & Barker, 2016) which are yet to be adopted by educational institutions especially during the Covid-19 era. These approaches to online exam supervision have been influential in the field of education because of their success in ensuring that examinations are carried out in a conducive remote environment devoid of malpractices (Lilley, Meere, & Barker, 2016). This field has gradually broadened as many are focusing on the use of proctoring software for future online examinations, especially for post-COVID-19 semesters.

Recently, the development and use of e-proctor software for administering examinations are gaining momentum as a recent poll indicates that more than 50% of educational institutions use these proctoring devices in their universities (ProctorU, 2020; Grajek, 2020), yet there is a need to review the results achieved thereafter especially on areas of cheat detection, cheat misrepresentation and other ethical issues. It is well documented in the literature that the utilization of online platforms especially e-proctored examinations enhances assessment delivery by ensuring that examinations are administered and monitored in a credible and convenient means (Butler-Henderson & Crawford, 2020; Clark, Callam, Paul, Stoltzfus, & Turner, 2020; Bates, 2018). Though the level of convenience, reliability, transparency, moral/ethical adherence, and credibility of these monitored examinations are yet to be ascertained or examined by researchers. These aforementioned are serious concerns for numerous authors who posit that while e-proctored examinations may have yielded results, issues of student dishonesty during examinations, malpractice, transparency, and software malfunctioning related issues continues to linger (Udechukwu, 2020; Lee, 2020; Coghlan, Miller, & Paterson, 2020, Binstein, 2015). These lead to myriads of problems as online-based examinations may not be seen as promoting academic integrity, or fostering credible, effective, efficient means of administering malpractice free and anxiety free examinations in a hybrid/ EROT model. Studies on proctored examinations have been too general in discussing these issues especially as e-proctored examinations may have not been utilized during hybrid/EROT model scenarios until recently. One way to solve this problem is to carry out a study that will elicit information from instructors and preservice teachers on their perceived efficacy of the use of e-proctoring software for administering and monitoring online-based examinations in a hybrid educational model. This will assist to re-evaluate the entire online examination process, eliciting information on the overall performance of the e-proctored software in administering credible malpractice free examination devoid of anxiety and stress.

Literature review

The use of technology makes learning more effective and efficient (Davis, Rand, & Seay, 2016; Karim, Kaminsky, & Behrend, 2014), especially in the array of benefits that it brings to education (Cramp, Medlin, Lake, & Sharp, 2019), this is evident in the advancement of the use of proctoring software for examination invigilation and supervisions to avoid the issue of examination malpractices and cheating (Kayser, 2016; Toquero, 2020). This is because technological advancements are essential in improving the student learning experience, enhancing the quality of instruction delivery, and ensuring positive learning outcomes as well (Adkins, 2011; Atoum, Chen, Liu, Hsu, & Liu, 2017; Ironsi, 2020a). Studies agree that the use of such devices like proctors will be beneficial to education by ensuring that credible examinations that are devoid of cheating, stress, and anxiety are conducted while using online-based instruction delivery (Atoum et al., 2017; Daffin Jr & Jones, 2018). True as it may seem that developments in the use of technology have benefited the educational sectors, there are also growing challenges in this sector especially during these unprecedented times of the Covid-19 pandemic outbreak. There is a need for schools to re-evaluate the use of technology in administering and monitoring examinations to ensure that credible examinations are administered during these times of pandemic and emergency, as this will uphold academic integrity. While some may argue the need to keep the affective filter of the learner at the barest minimum during test situations (Ironsi, 2017), others believed that the pandemic outbreak was a time to offer student assistance, administering of examination following strict regulations may not be the best.

For example, previous research showed that universities in Spain have embarked on online examinations during this pandemic outbreak utilizing e-proctoring tools (González-González, Infante-Moro, & Infante-Moro, 2020). A series of recent studies have identified e-proctoring tool as the use of artificial intelligence integrated electronic tools for monitoring of remote online-based examinations (Sutton, 2019; Alessio, Malay, Maurer, Bailer, & Rubin, 2018; Davis, Rand, & Seay, 2016). Several studies suggest that though electronic proctoring tools have been used in previous times, most universities are resolving to the use of this tool for online examinations during this pandemic era (García-Peñalvo, Abella-García, Corell, & Grande, 2020; González-González et al., 2020). Previous studies have shown that there is a demand for the use of tools and devices which will ensure that the quality of most evaluation process in online-based assessment is improved (Woldeab, Lindsay, & Brothen, 2017; Bandyopadhyay, Barnes, & Bandyopadhyay, 2015), yet some believed that this increase in demand led to the rampant emergence of e-proctoring software (Daffin Jr & Jones, 2018; Karim et al., 2014). Prior research suggests that e-proctoring is majorly used in MOOCs whose major problems lie within conducting and monitoring credible and reliable examinations within the online space (Woldeab, Lindsay, & Brothen, 2017; Kayser, 2016; González-González et al., 2020). This has also been explored in prior studies that try to showcase the level of credibility that exist in using e-proctoring for online-based evaluation process (Lilley, Meere, & Barker, 2016; Sutton, 2019). Previous studies on the use of e-proctoring have emphasized that this tool allows for visual and auditory surveillance during examinations (Li, Chang, Yuan, & Hauptmann, 2015; Atoum et al., 2017), the majority of prior research has showcased the functionality of visual and auditory surveillance where the audio and cameras of the learner who is taking the examination are being monitored (Cramp, Medlin, Lake, & Sharp, 2019; Davis, Rand, & Seay, 2016).

Furthermore, most early studies, as well as current work, further shows that there are tools that could be integrated which allows the teacher to see the computer screen of the test taker while administering a test (Davis et al., 2016; Kayser, 2016). For instance, the following studies were conducted on the use of an e-proctoring tool for conducting an online based examination and it was uncovered that special browsers were incorporated in the e-proctoring device which assists in preventing the test takers from leaving the examination while the examination is ongoing (Li et al., 2015; Lilley et al., 2016), yet studies on proctoring are well documented as it is also well acknowledged that the use of special browser assists in preventing test takers from accessing the web browser or search engines for searching for answers (Cramp, Medlin, Lake, & Sharp, 2019; González-González, Infante-Moro, & Infante-Moro, 2020). Several authors have recognized that most proctors ensure that additional tools are added that disables the test takers' web browser, which makes it impossible for the students to cheat during examinations (Atoum et al., 2017; Kayser, 2016). Yet some authors have also suggested that the integration of additional tools that will enhance its functionality will foresee that most universities begin to switch to the use of online-based assessment soon (Li et al., 2015; Rios & Liu, 2017). Again, a study suggests that more than 500 universities in Arizona State University and California State University make use of proctoring for their examinations (González-González, Infante-Moro, & Infante-Moro, 2020).

Practically, e-proctors have contributed a lot to monitoring online-based examinations though many may argue that the use of e-proctoring has not completely erased the issue of cheating or malpractice in online examination (Udechukwu, 2020). This has been discussed by a great number of authors in literature as they emphasized that a lot of deception and dishonesty are seen in online-based examinations that are proctored (Hylton, Levy, & Dringus, 2016; David et al., 2016). For example, research has provided evidence for deceptions in the online-based examination as a result of the unmonitored nature of these examinations where test-takers involve in malpractices during such examinations (David et al., 2016), these questions the integrity, credibility, validity, and reliability of such examinations as well as academic integrity. As has been previously reported in the literature, there is usually misconduct in some online-based examinations (Bhagat et al., 2016) as a large number of existing studies in the broader literature have examined online-based assessments and they pinpoint that nearly 80% of the surveyed examinations showed misconduct and malpractice during the examinations (Witherspoon, Maldonado & Lacey, 2012; Hylton, Levy, & Dringus, 2016; Mellar, Peytcheva-Forsyth, Kocdar, Karadeniz, & Yovkova, 2018; Bilen & Matros, 2020; Bhagat, Wu, & Chang, 2016; Witherspoon, Maldonado, & Lacey, 2012; Karim, Kaminsky, & Behrend, 2014; Udechukwu, 2020).

There are also works of literature that ponders on certain concerns for e-proctoring as they posit that the cost-effectiveness of e-proctoring devices makes it difficult for most educational institutions to acquire, others complain that the use of e-proctoring may induce stress and text anxiety (Song & Luximon, 2020), some literature suggests that examinations should be carried out in conducive environments where the affective filter is reduced to a minimum (Ironsi, 2017) and this aligns with other literature that indicates that the use of proctors for examination may induce stress and anxiety which would affect the academic performance of the test takers (Regehr & Goel, 2020; Song & Luximon, 2020). Proctoring devices have become essential in these challenging periods where most institutions have switched to remote online learning, and there is a need to assure test takers and the entire academic community that online-based assessment would be of high quality devoid of malpractice and cheating. For instance, recent research suggests that the higher education Opportunity act of 2008 in the United States of America mandates all universities to ensure and verify the identities of test-takers to ensure that those who register for online courses are the same individuals participating throughout the course duration (Kraglund-Gauthier & Young, 2012), this is a measure to help reduce impersonation and cheating in online-based instructions and assessments. Again, it is important to state that some private companies are already utilizing proctor's software for profit maximization without adequately considering ethical related issues – this creates more issues for debate. Many may argue that the use of e-proctoring has not erased the issue of cheating or malpractice in online examination (Karim, Kaminsky, & Behrend, 2014; Udechukwu, 2020; Lee, 2020). While educational institutions may claim to have achieved success in supervising and administering credible, transparent examination through the use of e-proctoring software, a lot of controversies and criticisms have emerged recently (White, 2020). The focal point of this disagreement hinges on issues of ethical credibility of e-proctored software and technologies, its appropriateness for use in administering online-based examinations, especially in hybrid/ EROT model scenarios. There is numerous evidence in literatures that points to issues of cheating in online-based examinations (Hylton, Levy, & Dringus, 2016; Bilen & Matros, 2020; Bhagat, Wu, & Chang, 2016), which in turns affects academic integrity. The use of e-proctored devices requires technological devices and internet connections which its availability may vary with test-takers. Poor internet connection which disconnects may void online-based examinations (Swauger, 2020).

However, while a recent study claims that e-proctored examinations are better than traditionally invigilated examinations which many presume is filled with cheating and malpractice (Dimeo, 2017), there are possible uncertainties with regards to how artificial intelligence may detect and identify a "cheating behaviour". Numerous e-proctoring websites have explained how they compute "red flags" to detect cheating yet it is difficult to ascertain how reliable a man-made technological configured device may attain 90% efficiency in detecting cheating behaviours or misjudging behaviours as cheating (Swauger, 2020; Peters, 2020; Buolamwini & Gebru, 2018). Another issue is privacy, privacy seems a broad philosophical issue and the use of e-proctoring software for online-based examinations raises more ethical and moral concerns on privacy-related laws and policies which may not be addressed by institutions. Much more, certain legal authorities may possess privacy laws that have not been adequately formulated to cover areas of data collection, data storage, image capturing, and biometric identities of test-takers. These ethical, moral, privacy-related issues and many more are serious issues of debate that needs to be addressed to maintain transparency, credibility while administering and monitoring online-based examinations using e-proctoring software. The main problem is that the lockdown as imposed by the government would not allow for face-to-face invigilation of examinations as has been the case before the outbreak of the Covi-19. There is a further problem with using only assignments, presentations, or end-of-term projects as means of measuring students, there is also a need to test, measure, and grade their performances afterward (Cheng et al., 2020). This seems to be a common problem as online examination needs to be credible, properly monitored, valid, and reliable enough to measure learning outcomes, and where this is impossible, problem arises with regards to the quality of educational instruction (Sutton, 2019). This study anticipates that there is a need for schools to be prepared for the post-COVID-19 semester to be able to deliver quality educational instruction and also to administer credible valid and reliable examinations that are properly monitored to promote academic integrity.

The present study

However, while a lot has been written on proctored examinations, very limited studies cover these arrays of issues with regards to conducting and monitoring credible, transparent, and reliable online-based examinations. Also, studies have not discussed the use of proctored applications like *safe exam browser* for administering examinations during a hybrid/emergency remote online teaching scenario. The practical contributions of e-proctored examination through utilizing Safe Examination Browser (SEB) in ensuring credible and reliable examination in a hybrid/EROT educational model is yet to be properly investigated. There is no previous research that has investigated the use of an e-proctoring approach to online-based examinations, especially while using a hybrid/emergency remote online based instruction and this remains an area to be investigated. As far as we know, little or no previous research has examined the successes and possible challenges of utilizing e-proctoring software for monitoring examinations, especially during hybrid/ emergency online learning.

Furthermore, other studies have examined the use of proctoring software for online-based examination but have failed to discuss its use for emergencies, ethical related issues, and the results achieved so far have not been thoroughly examined. One way to overcome these gaps in literature is to examine critically the use of e-proctoring software for monitoring examinations in a hybrid/emergency remote online-based instruction, to unveil the successes achieve and challenges as well. This study anticipates that there is a need to investigate the utilization of e-proctored software like SEB while administering and monitoring examinations during the post-pandemic semester. This will give much insight into the future of organizing more credible, properly-monitored, transparent, and reliable examinations for post-pandemic education through the use of proctored software. Importantly, this study would document several key contributions that would be made to the fields of education with a special focus on areas of measurement and evaluation. This study will make several significant contributions to the field in showcasing instructors' and students' opinions on the utilization of proctors for administering and monitoring online based examinations, especially in a hybrid educational model. To achieve these the use of the following research questions was investigated:

- What is the perception of preservice teachers on the efficacy of e-proctoring software for monitoring examinations?
- What are the opinions of instructors on the effectiveness of e-proctoring software for examinations?

Method

Research Design

The study adopted a quantitative research design that makes use of questionnaires in eliciting information from participants with regards to their views and opinions on an issue (Black, 1999). This research design was deemed suitable for this study as it will make use of questionnaires in eliciting information from teachers and students on the use of e-proctoring for emergency remote online-based instruction. The study employs the use of *Safe Exam Browser* which is an e-proctoring software using for monitoring online-based examinations. This software was utilized for monitoring examinations during the Fall semester. This software was used during the remote online-based instruction for midterm examinations and summative assessments. The period of instruction delivery lasts for 15 weeks, midterm examinations were conducted after 7 weeks for 1 week afterward the summative assessment lasted for 2 weeks. All the assessments were administered utilizing the safe exam browser as a proctor for monitoring the examinations.

Participants

The participants comprise 36 preservice teachers and 4 language instructors. They were chosen through a purposive sampling technique majorly for this study as the objective of the study was to elicit information from preservice teachers and instructors on their perception of the use of e-proctoring for emergency remote online-based assessment. These participants were chosen from a private university in North Cyprus after agreeing to participate in the study, they also gave oral consent to participate throughout the study.

Data Collection

A structured 15 itemized questionnaire was the main instrument for data collection. This instrument was structured on a 5 point Likert type scale of *Strongly Agree* (5) *Agree* (4) *Neutral* (3) *Disagree* (2) and *Strongly Disagree* (1). The instrument was face validated by two experts in the field of education who examined the questionnaire items to carry out a superficial assessment of question items before administering the same to participants. The face validation leads to the rewording of some items and a final version of 15 items was obtained. The items were piloted with 10 students who were randomly chosen to determine the reliability of the instrument and a Cronbach alpha index of .86 was obtained affirming that the items were consistent in measuring the opinions of the participants on the use of e-proctoring for emergency remote online-based instruction. Afterward, this instrument was administered to all the participants and collected for analysis.

Data Analysis

After administering the questionnaire, the researcher collected the instrument and analysed the same using SPSS analytical tool to carry out descriptive analysis to ascertain the mean responses of the participants on the various items of the questionnaire. The results obtained were organized in tables and presented below;

Result and Discussion

This section summarizes the findings and contributions obtained after the analysis of the data collected, they are presented according to the research questions and in tables.

Table 1: The perception of preservice teachers on the efficacy of e-proctoring for monitoring examinations

Scale	N	M	SD
Examinations are usually credible using e-proctor software	36	2.02	1.48
Using e-proctors erases cheating and malpractice	36	2.55	1.44
Test takers are relaxed while sitting for examinations	36	2.72	1.38
Overall evaluation progress becomes transparent	36	4.15	0.52
E-proctored examination are seen as valid methods of evaluation	36	3.02	0.56
An E-proctored examination is highly reliable	36	2.45	1.62
Administering reliable examinations during emergencies are possible	36	4.45	0.68
E-proctored examination improves the integrity of instruction	36	4.60	0.42
Anxiety levels are minimal while conducting e-proctored exams	36	2.17	1.55
A conducive environment for evaluation is fostered in e-proctored exams	36	4.55	0.45
E-proctoring software enhances auditory and visual surveillance	36	4.68	0.52
E-proctored software is affordable	36	1.88	1.78
Issues of impersonation are tackled through e-proctored evaluations	36	4.95	0.72
Students are bothered about the safety of their privacy &personal details	36	4.92	0.69
Test takers are bothered about invasion into their computers	36	4.78	0.66

The table presents the mean values on preservice teachers' perception of the use of e-proctoring for monitoring examinations. The result showed that the preservice teachers did not perceive examinations to be credible using e-proctor software neither did they affirm that using e-proctors for examination erases cheating and malpractice, rather they thought that test takers were not relaxed while sitting for examinations as a mean value of 2.02 (SD 1.48), 2.55 (SD1.44) and 2.72 (SD1.38) was obtained for these items. However, they thought that using e-proctoring enhances transparency in the evaluation process, a mean value of 4.15 (SD 0.52) was obtained for this item yet they were neutral when asked if e-proctored exams are seen as valid methods of evaluation, a mean value of 3.02 (SD 0.56) was obtained. They were affirmative that the e-proctored examination was not reliable, a value of 2.45 (SD 1.62) was obtained for this item.

Moreover, they perceived that using e-proctors makes it possible to administer examinations during situations of emergency and improves the integrity of the entire instruction, a mean value of 4.45 (SD 0.68), and 4.60 (SD 0.42) was obtained for these items. Again, the results indicate that the teacher believed that anxiety levels were not minimal during e-proctored examinations even as they affirmed that using e-proctored software for examinations creates a conducive environment that fosters the use of auditory and visual surveillance while administering a test, with mean values of 2.17 (SD1.55), 4.55 (SD 0.45) and 4.68 (SD0.52) was obtained for these items. When the teachers were asked to indicate if e-proctor software is affordable, a negative response was obtained with a mean value of 1.88 (SD 1.78). With regards to impersonation, the participants thought that impersonation related issues were tackled while administering an e-proctored examination, a mean value of 4.99 (SD 0.72).

Table 2: The opinions of instructors on the use of e-proctoring for examinations

Scale	N	M	SD
Examinations are credible using e-proctor software	4	2.32	1.18
Using e-proctor erases cheating and malpractice	4	4.26*	0.50
Test takers are relaxed while taking examinations	4	1.41	1.93
Overall evaluation progress becomes transparent	4	1.11	1.85
E-proctored examination are seen as valid methods of evaluation	4	1.62	1.70
An E-proctored examination is highly reliable	4	2.42	1.42
Administering reliable examinations during emergencies are possible	4	4.05*	0.78
E-proctored examination improves the integrity of instruction	4	3.10	0.73
Anxiety levels are minimal while conducting e-proctored exams	4	2.07	1.45
A conducive environment for evaluation is fostered in e-proctored exams	4	2.34	1.62
E-proctoring software enhances auditory and visual surveillance	4	4.66*	0.47
E-proctored software is affordable	4	3.03	0.68
Issues of impersonation are tackled through e-proctored evaluations	4	4.15*	0.82
Students are bothered about the safety of their privacy & personal details	4	4.65*	0.74
Test takers are bothered about invasion into their computers	4	4.72*	0.81

Table 2 above presents the opinions of instructors on the use of e-proctoring for examinations. The findings indicate that a mean value of 2.32 (SD 1.18) was obtained when the participants were to indicate if examinations conducted using e-proctoring were credible, this response indicates a negative notion on the credibility of e-proctored examinations. However, they affirmed through their responses that the use of e-proctoring during examination erases issues of cheating and malpractice as a mean value of 4.26 (SD 0.50) was obtained for this item. Clearly, the results show that the participants thought that test-takers were not relaxed during examinations, the evaluation process was not transparent, not valid, not reliable as a mean value of 1.41 (SD1.93), 1.11 (SD1.85),1.62 (SD1.70), and 2.42 (SD1.42) were obtained for these items. However, the results indicate that the instructors were positive that administering reliable examinations in emergencies was possible through the use of an e-proctored examination, a mean value of 4.05 (SD0.78) was obtained for this item. They were neutral on the integrity of instruction using e-proctored examination, a value of 3.10 (SD 0.73) was obtained for this item. Similar to the response of the students, the result shows that the instructors believed that anxiety levels were not minimal during exams conducted using e-proctors nor did the e-proctored exam ensure a conducive environment for evaluation, a mean value of 2.07 (SD 1.45) and 2.34 (SD 1.62) was obtained. They were neutral with regards to the affordability of e-proctor software as a mean value of 3.03 (SD 0.68) was obtained for this item. They were affirmative that the use of e-proctoring enhances auditory and visual surveillance as issues of impersonation are tackled as well, a mean value of 4.66 (SD0.47) and 4.15 (SD 0.82) was obtained for these items.

Discussion

From the short review above, key findings emerge: The notion that e-proctored examination is usually credible were debunked as the participants thought otherwise, Contrary to the findings of some studies (García-Peñalvo, Abella-García, Corell, & Grande, 2020; Woldeab, Lindsay, & Brothen, 2017; Cramp, Medlin, Lake, & Sharp, 2019), we did not find any corroboration that suggests so. Our findings at least hint that there could be a possibility that the use of an e-proctor for monitoring examination could eliminate the issue of malpractice, impersonation though the issues of transparency or integrity of instruction could not be ascertained. A further novel finding is that issues of anxiety, ethical issues, privacy-related issues, validity, reliability, and affordability of e-proctor software continue to be an issue to ponder. The findings of this study were contrary to the suggestions of similar studies which opine that e-proctored examination are credible, valid, reliable, and affordable means of conducting a quality examination that is devoid of anxieties or stress (Davis, Rand, & Seay, 2016; Kayser, 2016; Karim et al., 2014; Li, Chang,

Yuan, & Hauptmann, 2015; Udechukwu, 2020). While the teachers were affirmative that the use of e-proctoring erases cheating the students thought otherwise. This finding contradicts the assertion of some studies which posit that the utilization of proctor erases cheating and malpractice during online-based examinations (Woldeab, Lindsay, & Brothen, 2017; Kayser, 2016; González-González et al., 2020) while buttressing the points of some authors who have argued that the use of proctors has not eliminated cheating and malpractices during online examinations (Witherspoon, Maldonado, & Lacey, 2012; Hylton, Levy, & Dringus, 2016; Mellar, Peytcheva-Forsyth, Kocdar, Karadeniz, & Yovkova, 2018; Bilen & Matros, 2020; Bhagat, Wu, & Chang, 2016; Udechukwu, 2020). Also, the present study to an extent confirmed the findings of other studies which suggest that e-proctored examinations are usually suitable for emergencies, as the environment for conducting such examination are conducive as plugins for auditory and visual surveillance were used (Daffin Jr & Jones, 2018; Bandyopadhyay, Barnes, & Bandyopadhyay, 2015; Lilley, Meere, & Barker, 2016; Song & Luximon, 2020). True as it may seem, care must be taken to ponder on the reason why an examination conducted in a conducive environment breeds anxiety and stress on the examinees, this is another area that needs further investigation. The results demonstrate two things; first, though e-proctoring was useful in administering examination during an emergency, the level of its credibility, validity, and reliability is to a large extent yet to be addressed, though this could be contextual as well. Second, the result affirms that there is a need for re-evaluation of e-proctoring software as ethical and privacy-related issues are yet to be critically addressed.

Conclusion and recommendation

The objective of the study was to elicit information from teachers and students on the use of e-proctoring software in administering assessments, in conclusion, it would appear that e-proctor software plays a paramount role in ensuring that test takers do not engage in examination malpractice during online examination yet more efforts need to be made towards improving this software ensure more reliability and validity of evaluations conducted using these platforms. The paper concludes by arguing that though a lot of literature exists on the positive roles of e-proctoring in online examinations, the authors concluded that its usefulness needs to be re-evaluated to ensure wider coverage especially with regards to its use for valid credible, and reliable examinations. This allows the conclusion that e-proctoring plays a paramount role in conducting an online examination, especially in emergencies though careful efforts must be made to ensure that this software is overhauled and used in a way that does not induce fear, trepidation, or anxiety on test-takers. This may be considered a further validation for the re-evaluation of the software which will lead to redeveloping other areas that require enhancement. Broadly translated our findings indicate that while teachers may consider some positive sides of using e-proctoring for monitoring examinations, the students did not perceive the software as a useful tool for examination supervision or monitoring. The students were more concerned with the biometrics features of e-proctoring software, questions of where their details are stored, and privacy right related issues that were yet to be resolved. It is difficult to arrive at any conclusions concerning variations in opinions and perception of the participants in this regard yet despite the limitations these are valuable in light of the positive role of e-proctoring software as viable tools for conducting online examination especially in emergencies which was the case during the COVID-19 pandemic outbreak.

Limitations

The major limitation of this study was the sample size of the participants which was relatively small. The outbreak of the pandemic made a lesser number of students enrol for studies for the fall semester. We affirm that a larger sample size could produce different findings on the same topic. Another limitation was the inability of the study to investigate the perception of instructors and students from other universities instead of choosing only one particular university. We believe that different results may be obtained if the study investigated the opinions and perceptions of other instructors and teachers at other universities. This study was a perception-based study and like every other perception-based study, perceptions of participants can be influenced by other groups and this may affect the results obtained.

References

Adkins, S. S. (2011). *The US market for self-paced eLearning products and services: 2010-2015 forecast and analysis.* Ambient Insight.

Alessio, H. M., Malay, N., Maurer, K., Bailer, A. J., & Rubin, B. (2018). Interaction of proctoring and student major on online test performance. *International Review of Research in Open and Distributed Learning, 19*(5), 166–185. https://doi.org/10.19173/irrodl.v19i5.3698

Atoum, Y., Chen, L., Liu, A. X., Hsu, S. D., & Liu, X. (2017). Automated online exam proctoring. IEEE Trans. *Multimed. 2017*(19), 1609-1624. doi:10.1109/TMM.2017.2656064

Bandyopadhyay, K., Barnes, C., & Bandyopadhyay, S. (2015). An investigation of the factors that influence the use of proctoring in online courses. *Proceedings of the Association of Collegiate Marketing Educators; ACME: USA*, 49-50.

Bates, T. (2018). The 2017 national survey of online learning in Canadian post-secondary education: Methodology and results. *International Journal of Educational Technology in Higher Education, 15*(1), 29.

Bilen, E., & Matros, A. (2020). *Online cheating amid COVID-19.* Available at SSRN 3691363.

Binstein, J. (2015, January) How to Cheat with Proctortrack, Examity, and the Rest. Jake Binstein [Blog post]. Retrieved from https://jakebinstein.com/blog/on-knuckle-scanners-and-cheating-how-to-bypass-proctor

Bhagat, K. K., Wu, L. Y., & Chang, C. Y. (2016). Development and Validation of the Perception of Students towards Online Learning (POSTOL). *Educational Technology & Society, 19*(1), 350-359.

Black, T. R. (1999). *Doing quantitative research in the social sciences: An integrated approach to research design, measurement, and statistics.* Sage.

Buolamwini, J., &Gebru, T. (2018). Gender Shades: Intersectional Accuracy Disparities in Commercial Gender Classification. *Proceedings of Machine Learning Research, 81*, 15.

Bulent, B., Murat, Y., & Selahattin, G. (2016). Attitude Scale towards Web-Based Examination System (MOODLE) – Validity and Reliability Study. *Educational Research and Reviews, 11*(17), 1641-1649.

Butler-Henderson, K., & Crawford, J. (2020). A systematic review of online examinations: A pedagogical innovation for scalable authentication and integrity. *Computers & Education*, 104024.

Cheng, L., DeLuca, C., Braund, H., Yan, W., & Rasooli, A. (2020). Teachers' grading decisions and practices across cultures: Exploring the value, consistency, and construction of grades across Canadian and Chinese secondary schools. *Studies in Educational Evaluation, 67*, 100928.

Clark, T. M., Callam, C. S., Paul, N. M., Stoltzfus, M. W., & Turner, D. (2020). Testing in the time of COVID-19: A sudden transition to unproctored online exams. *Journal of Chemical Education, 97*(9), 3413-3417.

Coghlan, S., Miller, T., & Paterson, J. (2020). Good proctor or" Big Brother"? AI Ethics and Online Exam Supervision Technologies. arXiv preprint arXiv:2011.07647.

Cramp, J., Medlin, J. F., Lake, P., & Sharp, C. (2019). Lessons learned from implementing remotely invigilated online exams. *Journal of University Teaching & Learning Practice, 16*(1), 1-18.

Daffin Jr, L. W., & Jones, A. A. (2018). Comparing Student Performance on Proctored and Non-Proctored Exams in Online Psychology Courses. *Online Learning, 22*(1), 131-145.

Davis, A. B., Rand, R., & Seay, R. (2016). Virtual proctoring: The effect of proctoring on grades. In D. Feldman, & T. J. Rupert (Eds.), *Advances in accounting education: Teaching and curriculum innovations* (pp. 23–50). Melbourne, Australia: Emerald Publishing. https://doi.org/10.1108/s1085-462220160000018002

Dimeo, J. (2017, May 10). Online exam proctoring catches cheaters, raises concerns. Inside Higher Ed [Blog post]. Retrieved from https://www.insidehighered.com/digital-learning/article/2017/05/10/online-exam-proctoring-catches-cheaters-raises-concerns

García-Peñalvo, F. J., Abella-García, V., Corell, A., & Grande, M. (2020). *La evaluación online en la educación superior en tiempos de la COVID-19.*

González-González, C. S., Infante-Moro, A., & Infante-Moro, J. C. (2020). Implementation of E-proctoring in Online Teaching: A Study about Motivational Factors. *Sustainability, 12*(8), 3488.

Grajek, S. (2020, April 10) COVID-19 QuickPoll Results: Grading and Proctoring. EDUCAUSE Review [Blog post]. Retrieved from https://er.educause.edu/blogs/2020/4/educause-covid-19-quickpoll-results-grading-and-proctoring

Hopfenbeck, T. N (2020). Rethinking validity in educational assessment. *Assessment in Education: Principles, Policy & Practice, 27*(6), 585-587. doi:10.1080/0969594X.2020.1866866

Hylton, K., Levy, Y., & Dringus, L. P. (2016). Utilizing webcam-based proctoring to deter misconduct in online exams. *Computers & Education, 92–93*, 53-63. https://doi.org/10.1016/j.compedu.2015.10.002

Isinkaye, F. O., Soyemi, J., & Arowosegbe, O. I. (2020). An Android-based Face Recognition System for Class Attendance and Malpractice Control. *International Journal of Computer Science and Information Security (IJCSIS), 180*(1), 78-83.

Ironsi, C. S. (2017). *Effect of test anxiety on academic performance of EFL Learners.* Lambert Academic Publishing, ISBN:978-620-2-070620-3

Ironsi, C. S. (2020a). Learners' perception on the use of e-learning platforms during the Covid 19 pandemic outbreak. Paper presented at the EDUCCON 2020 Empower Teaching Studies, December 12, 2020, Turkey.

Ironsi, C. S. (2020b). Strategies for student engagement in remote online learning. A case study of Northern Cyprus. *RUNAS Journal of Education and Culture, 1*(2), 18-31. https://doi.org/10.46652/runas.v1i2.19

Ironsi, C. S. (2021). From flipped learning to emergency remote online learning: A post-Covid-19 concise narrative. *Narrative on Online Education, 1*(1), 45-58.

Karim, M. N., Kaminsky, S. E., & Behrend, T. S. (2014). Cheating, reactions, and performance in remotely proctored testing: An exploratory experimental study. *Journal of Business and Psychology, 29*(4), 555-572.

Kayser, M.N. (2016). *Online Proctoring Success Factors & Best Practices.* Paper presented at the Minnesota eLearning Summit, Saint Paul, MN, USA.

Kennedy, A. B., Riyad, C. N. Y., Gunn, L. H., Brown, A. G., Dunlap, K. B., Knutsen, M. E., & Dahl, A. A. (2020). More Than Their Test Scores: Redefining Success with Multiple Mini-Interviews. *Medical Science Educator, 30*(3), 1049-1060.

Keshavarz, M. H., & Hulus, A. (2019). The Effect of Students' Personality and Learning Styles on Their Motivation for Using Blended Learning. *Advances in Language and Literary Studies, 10*(6), 78-88.

Kraglund-Gauthier, W. L., & Young, D. C. (2012). *Will the Real "John Doe" Stand up? Verifying the Identity of Online Students.* Emerald Group Publishing Limited.

Lee, J. W. (2020). Impact of Proctoring Environments on Student Performance: Online vs Offline Proctored Exams. *The Journal of Asian Finance, Economics, and Business (JAFEB), 7*(8), 653-660.

Lilley, M., Meere, J., & Barker, T. (2016). Remote live invigilation: A pilot study. *Journal of Interactive Media in Education, 2016*(1), 1-5. https://doi.org/10.5334/jime.408

Li, X., Chang, K.-M., Yuan, Y., & Hauptmann, A. (2015). Massive open online proctor: Protecting the credibility of MOOCs certificates. *Proceedings of the 18th ACM conference on computer supported cooperative work & social computing*, 1129-1137. New York, USA. https://doi.org/10.1145/2675133.2675245

Mathwasa, J., & Sibanda, L. (2020). The Effect of Examination-Related Anxiety on Career Pathway for High School Graduates. In S. G. Taukeni (Ed.), *Addressing Multicultural Needs in School Guidance and Counseling* (pp. 216-237). IGI Global.

Mellar, H., Peytcheva-Forsyth, R., Kocdar, S., Karadeniz, A., & Yovkova, B. (2018). Addressing cheating in e-assessment using student authentication and authorship checking systems: teachers' perspectives. *International Journal for Educational Integrity, 14*(1), 2.

Ossai, M. C., Ethe, N., & Edougha, D. E. (2020). Development, Validation and Standardization of Tertiary Examination Behaviour Inventory: Diagnostic Instrument for Measuring Cheating Tendency in Educational Assessments. *Education Quarterly Reviews, 3*(3).

Peters, J. (2020, June 8) IBM will no longer offer, develop, or research facial recognition technology. The Verge [Blog post]. Retrieved from https://www.theverge.com/2020/6/8/21284683/ibm-no-longer-general-purpose-facial-recognition-analysis

ProctorU (2020). Harnessing the Power of Artificial Intelligence to Improve Online Proctoring, 2020. Retrieved from https://www.proctoru.com/harnessing-the-power-of-artificial-intelligence

Regehr, C., & Goel, V. (2020). Managing COVID-19 in a Large Urban Research-Intensive University. *Journal of Loss and Trauma*, 1-17.

Rios, J. A., & Liu, O. L. (2017). Online proctored versus unproctored low-stakes internet test administration: is there differential test-taking behavior and performance? *American Journal of Distance Education, 31*, 226–241. https://doi.org/10.1080/08923647.2017.1258628

Song, Y., & Luximon, Y. (2020). Trust in AI Agent: A Systematic Review of Facial Anthropomorphic Trustworthiness for Social Robot Design. *Sensors, 20*(18), 5087.

Sutton, H. (2019). Minimize online cheating through proctoring, consequences. Recruit. *Retaining Adult Learn, 21*, 1-5, doi:10.1002/nsr.30434

Swauger, S (2020, April 2). Our Bodies Encoded: Algorithmic Test Proctoring in Higher Education. Hybrid Pedagogy [Blog post]. Retrieved from https://hybridpedagogy.org/our-bodies-encoded-algorithmic-test-proctoring-in-higher-education/

Toquero, C. M. (2020). Challenges and Opportunities for Higher Education amid the COVID-19 Pandemic: The Philippine Context. *Pedagogical Research, 5*(4).

Udechukwu, J. (2020). Digital Proctoring: Challenges and Prospects in Computer-Based Assessment in Nigeria. *European Academic Research Journal, 7*(12).

Wald, N., & Harland, T. (2020). Rethinking the teaching roles and assessment responsibilities of student teaching assistants. *Journal of Further and Higher Education, 44*(1), 43-53.

Witherspoon, M., Maldonado, N., & Lacey, C. H. (2012). Undergraduates and academic dishonesty. *International Journal of Business and Social Science, 3*(1).

White, N. (2020, April 22). 'Creepy' software to stop university students cheating in online exams. Daily Mail Australia [Blog post]. Retrieved from https://www.dailymail.co.uk/news/article-8243637/Creepy-software-used-stop-university-students-c

Woldeab, D., Lindsay, T., & Brothen, T. (2017). *Under the watchful eye of online proctoring. Innovative learning and teaching: Experiments across the disciplines.* Minneapolis, MN: University of Minnesota Libraries Publishing.

Lessons from a Pandemic for the Future of Education
European Distance and E-Learning Network (EDEN) Proceedings
2021 Annual Conference | Madrid, 21-24 June, 2021
ISSN 2707-2819
doi: 10.38069/edenconf-2021-ac0027

LESSON LEARNED: REFLECTIONS OF UNIVERSITAS TERBUKA'S NON-TRADITIONAL ASSESSMENT SOLUTIONS

Ojat Darojat, Rahmat Budiman, Universitas Terbuka, Indonesia

Abstract

Modern technology advancements have been reshaping and reforming education throughout the world. Furthermore, the Covid-19 outbreak is a powerful urge to establish more adaptive policies. Universitas Terbuka (UT) or the Indonesia Open University realizes that students are expecting to have a more individual and flexible learning during the Covid-19 outbreak, including the examination. UT makes uses of new technology and innovations to establish the online proctoring examination that enables students to take the examination at their own places without the present of the human proctors. Requirements to ensure the online proctoring examination meets the quality criteria were established. Previous studies show that students showed positive attitude towards the online proctoring examination. In the context of UT, due to students living in remote islands and the issue of the limited internet access might potentially challenge UT to implement the online proctoring examination. To provide solutions to the challenges, UT is demanded to develop alternative innovative solutions. Therefore, partnership with the government, private sectors, and other organizations is a necessary.

Introduction

Universitas Terbuka (UT) or the Indonesia Open University was established in 1984 to provide high school graduates and working people a greater access to tertiary education. In addition, it aimed to increase in-service teachers' competencies. As the only distance higher education institution in Indonesia, UT has been experimenting significant transformations. The development of modern technology in the last ten years is a key driver in that such transformations. In short, UT has been transforming from a traditional distance learning university to a cyber university. In practice, however, as modern technology and infrastructure, in particular the internet coverage, have not been equally distributed throughout the country, conventional services are still maintained, such as on-site tutorials (face-to-face tutorials) and on-site examinations. Although the number of internet users in Indonesia is increasing, most of the users reside in Java (Asosiasi

Penyelenggara Jasa Internet Indonesia, n.d.). This situation is viewed as challenges and opportunities, at the same time, that enables UT to explore innovations in all aspects of learning services and operational management.

Recently, a Covid-19 outbreak has doubled the challenges to face and the opportunities at the same time, which in turns boost new innovations and development. Due to Covid-19, large scale social restriction policy which is implemented across the nation prevents UT to hold face-to-face tutorials and on-site examinations. On-site online examinations which are held in regional offices and some appointed learning centres are also suspended. To ensure students accomplish the learning competency, UT adopts fixed-scheduled take home exam (FSTHE). As the FSTHE is unsupervised, the questions are developed to measure the high-level thinking skills for all subjects. The FSTHE materials, including the question items, scoring instructions and examination procedures are developed by lecturers and professors from face-to-face universities. In order to improve the quality of the examinations and to ensure all students develop the skills and competencies, UT highlights the importance of further innovations, including the development of online proctoring exam that enables students to take the exam at their own place with close supervision of students during the examinations. This paper is expected to address some insights into the development and practice of online proctoring as study of online proctoring is particularly limited (Woldeab & Brothen, 2019).

Online Proctoring Examination

The idea to develop the online proctoring application emerged three years ago. UT understood and realized that students are expected to have a more individual and flexible learning. In addition, the information technology infrastructures of Indonesia have been developed. In addition, student information technology literacy has also improved. Therefore, UT believed that the idea should be successfully executed. Initially, two teams were formed; one team is to set up the system and application and the other is to prepare the academic policy, including preparing the examination rules and regulations.

System and Application

The application can be installed in student personal laptop. However, to ensure that the examination runs smoothly, several minimal requirements are requested, including:

- Windows 8 operating system;
- Dual Core 2 GHz Processor;
- RAM 4 GB;
- Hard Disk 100 MB;
- Bandwidth 1 Mbps.

Once a student has installed the application, he is able to log in with his student number. The system automatically verifies his identity (face detection in real time), the hardware (microphone and camera), the room or place (student must rotate the camera 360° to ensure he is the only person in the room and there is no other facilities to help him do the examination, such as books, other laptops or personal computers, and other electronic devices), and the internet connection. After all requirements are completed, the students can start the examination. Figure 1 below illustrates the students' verification result.

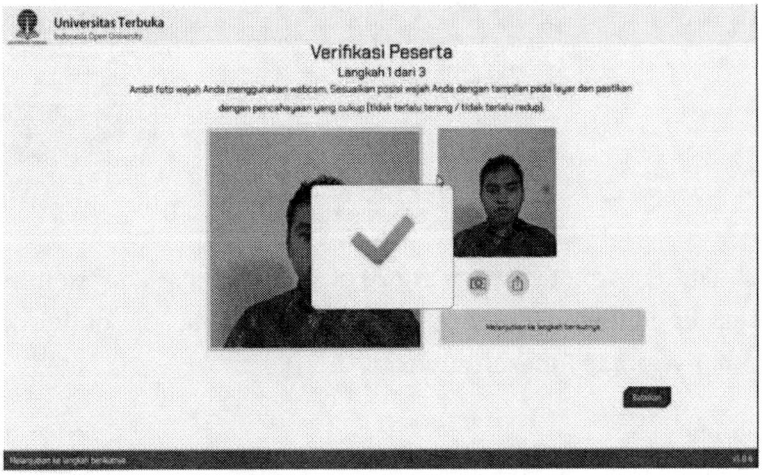

Figure 1. Student Verification

Proctoring process

During the examination, the camera on the laptop or personal computer is recording the student's head and eye movements. The application will recognize any suspicious movement and automatically there is a warning on the monitor to let the student know that he has violated the rules and regulations. This practice is also known as automated proctoring (Hussein, Yusuf, Deb, Fong, & Naidu, 2020). If the violations remain, the application will automatically close. This means that the student fails in the examination. However, if the student follows the rules and regulations, the application remains open as scheduled. After all questions are completed, the student clicks the submit button and the result will appear in several seconds.

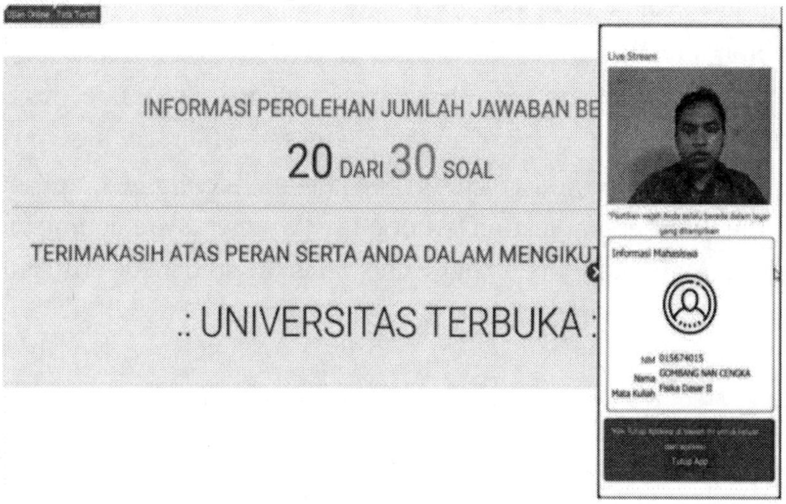

Figure 2. Examination result

Figure 2 shows that the correct answers are 20 of 30 questions. The Examination Center at the UT Headquarter combines the score with, for example, the online tutorial score to generate a cumulative grade for each subject.

Quality assurance

UT has developed internal quality assurance framework that also covers both paper-based examination and online examination. As the online proctoring examination is particularly new, UT is currently developing a quality criteria for the online proctoring examination. The quality criteria are developed based on the standard for the paper-based and online examinations.

To minimize the problem during the online proctoring examination, UT provides an instruction manual to familiarize the students with the application. In addition, to meet with the requirements, UT keeps the recordings at the Universitas Terbuka Data Center for two years in case students complain about the examination results.

Future Trends

Student motivation and interest in taking the online proctoring examination at Universitas Terbuka is projected to increase, as it provides several advantages, including flexibility to take the exams anywhere, cost effectiveness, and instant results. Although majority the internet connectivity enjoyed by people living in urban areas, internet has been more accessible and affordable across the country. The idea to implement the online proctoring examination is supported by a study by Weiner and Hurtz (2017) who suggested that students have positive attitudes of online proctoring.

Students living on remote islands and the issue of the limited internet access might potentially challenge UT to implement the online proctoring examination. Therefore, UT is expected to develop a strategic partnership with the government, private sectors, and other organizations.

References

Asosiasi Penyelenggara Jasa Internet Indonesia. (n.d.). Laporan Survei Internet APJII 2019 – 2020. Retrieved March 22, 2021, from https://apjii.or.id/survei.

Hussein, M. J., Yusuf, J., Deb, A. S., Fong, L., & Naidu, S. (2020). An Evaluation of Online Proctoring Tools. *Open Praxis, 12*(4), 509-525.

Weiner, J. A., & Hurtz, G. M. (2017). A comparative study of online remote proctored versus onsite proctored high-stakes exams. *Journal of Applied Testing Technology, 18*(1), 13-20.

Woldeab, D., & Brothen, T. (2019). 21st Century assessment: Online proctoring, test anxiety, and student performance. *International Journal of E-Learning & Distance Education, 34*(1), 1-10.

Lessons from a Pandemic for the Future of Education
European Distance and E-Learning Network (EDEN) Proceedings
2021 Annual Conference | Madrid, 21-24 June, 2021
ISSN 2707-2819
doi: 10.38069/edenconf-2021-ac0028

ONLINE COMMUNICATION AND ASSESSMENT PRACTICES DURING THE COVID PANDEMIC: A STUDY OF THE PORTUGUESE HIGHER EDUCATION STUDENTS' PERCEPTIONS

Lina Morgado, João Paz, Hugo Pereira, Ana Loureiro, Inês Messias, Paula Cardoso, Ana Paiva, Ana Runa, Carlos Seco, Elisabete Mendes, Márcia Vieira, Nuno Oliveira, Laboratory of Distance Education and eLearning, Universidade Aberta, Portugal

Abstract

This proposal is part of an ongoing research and presents the results on the perceptions and pedagogical practices experienced by students from various higher education degrees in Portuguese higher education institutions, during the period of social confinement determined by the Portuguese Government, due to the COVID-19 pandemic. The main objective of the general research was to understand how Higher Education faculty and students experienced the digital transition to emergency education and the pedagogical practices adopted during the period. The research was based on a mixed methods approach and, in order to address the research objectives and describe the pedagogical practices implemented, specific instruments were developed for data collection. A questionnaire was developed, aimed at students, and interviews aimed at both students and faculty, focusing on technological and pedagogical dimensions, as well as the assessment of the experience. Data collection was carried out after the first lockdown, at the end of the first semester of 2020, and took place in eight higher education institutions. In this paper we will present a preliminary analysis of Questionnaire results related to two dimensions: online communication and assessment.

Introduction

Higher education institutions (HEI) have experienced, in the period of lockdown, new situations that involved the closure of physical campus spaces and a gigantic disruption, in the transition to online, on an unprecedented scale. In general, institutional responses were given with a rapid shift to emergency digital learning, in what Zimmerman (2020) classified as the "Great Online-Learning Experiment" and Wu (2020) defined as a test of organisational agility, which evidenced the resilience of the actors and educational organisations involved. In Portugal, although many HEI already have some experience and dedicated support structures (e-learning offices, distance learning units or support departments for educational technologies), the stages of implementation of strategies in this area are different. This has been shown in the latest annual initiative of institutions and elearning units – eLIES. Another relevant factor is the fact that Portugal lived without specific distance learning legislation until 2019, when was first published the regulation in this field – DL 133/2019. In the context of CoViD-19, all HEI made a move to online by adopting emergency solutions to keep courses running. Thousands of students went to classes online; thousands of teachers gave their lessons online (worldwide, 1.5 billion students were affected (UNESCO, 2020; UNICEF, 2020). In this context, initiatives of experts, and of HEIs have also sprouted, creating online communities of practice and diverse support networks. Open educational resources (OER), open educational practices (OEP) and courses on-the-fly for formal and informal training have been developed and shared. Networks have been created to support teachers and the academic community in a way that no programme or policy initiative for digital inclusion or transition or funding for digital empowerment of teachers, to date, has been able to deliver (INCoDe.2030, or the Horizon Report forecasts, 2019). Crawford, Rudolph, Makawi, Glowatz, Burton, Magni, and Lam (2020) document, through a meta-analysis across 20 countries, the type and speed of responses given in higher education, namely at the time of first lockdown, where they focused mainly on moving content to the online environment without the provision of an appropriate pedagogy adapted for online. In this framework, it is therefore important to stress that we are dealing with what some, like Murphy (2020) call "emergency eLearning" or other, such as Hodges, Moore, Lockee, Trust, and Bond (2020), Emergency Remote Teaching (ERT): "a temporary shift of instructional delivery to an alternate delivery mode due to crisis circumstances. It involves the use of fully remote teaching solutions for instruction or education that would otherwise be delivered face-to-face or as blended or hybrid courses and that will return to that format once the crisis or emergency has abated. The primary objective in these circumstances is not to re-create a robust educational ecosystem but rather to provide temporary access to instruction and instructional supports in a manner that is quick to set up and is reliably available during an emergency or crisis". All this situation has brought distance education to the forefront, introducing inevitable comparisons. From the perspective of Bozkurt and Sharma (2020) the distinction made between ERT and distance education determines "the degree to which educators believe in distance education these days will play a significant role in the prosperity of distance education in a post-COVID world" (p.2). Beyond this aspect, it is important to know the pedagogical strategies implemented and the practices experienced, identifying for example the focus adopted in online communication – synchronous versus asynchronous –, what Lovink (2020) called "living in video space" with levels of digital fatigue (Wiederhold, 2020) or zoom fatigue (Sacasas, 2020), and high cognitive and work overload (Morris, 2020). Replicating the face-to-face pedagogy of the classroom, but with a "zoom pedagogy or zoom university" for teachers and students, plus also ongoing self-presentation efforts in the mediated communication (hyper-communication) (Whalter, 1996; Anderson, 2003; Whats, 2019). In this line, if some pedagogical practices developed tend to be teacher-centred, and not student-centred, as is usual in distance education (Bates, 2019), it was noted the need to look for practices that would contribute to focus the student's attention in the teaching-learning processes, approaching this centrality of the educational process. Thus, with this study, we tried to get to know aspects of the students' experiences which, being sometimes less valued in the normal scenario of face-to-face classes, are inseparable from the design of engaging, meaningful, participatory pedagogical scenarios. At the same time, we considered it important to study the often-widespread idea that the richness of communication is poorer in online environments than in face-to-face environments (Quintas-Mendes et al., 2009) including the assumption that the richness of emotional communication online is linked to the appropriateness of the strategies used (Derks, Fischer, & Bos, 2008; Paiva, Giger, Faísca, & Batista, 2011).

This paper is part of an ongoing general exploratory study (Paiva et al., 2020) that aims to understand students' perceptions of their academic experiences during ERT and to analyse teachers' and higher education students' experiences during this digital transition, as well as to identify facilitating and blocking pedagogical strategies/practices through teachers' and students' narratives. Accordingly, this article presents part of the results obtained in the questionnaires regarding the perceptions of communication and evaluation practices.

Methodological Approach

The present study is of exploratory nature, justified by the current and pertinent topic, having as focus the experience of the rapid digital transition for an "emergency teaching", which is a distinct scenario from distance education. A mixed nature methodology was used (Hesse-Biber, 2010), quantitative and qualitative, while the data collection was made by applying an online survey by questionnaire and a total of 40 interviews through video conference (Salmons, 2012; Archibald et al., 2019), to 20 teachers and 20 students. This study's participants are students and teachers from 8 institutions of the Portuguese Higher Education Network, four are University Education Institutions (3 public and 1 private) and four are Polytechnic Institutes (3 public and 1 private) encompassing the Lisbon and Tagus Valley, Alentejo and Algarve regions (the centre and south of Portugal).

Instrument: questionnaire

For the present research a questionnaire was made, specific for higher education students that have experienced a transition for remote teaching. The specific goals of the questionnaire were the following: (a) characterize the student's profile (demographic, digital, about ODL and online participation of academic activities); (b) identify the perceptions and practices about the synchronous and asynchronous communication situations experienced in the online activities; (c) identify feedback and assessment practices developed; (d) gather the interactive situations proposed on the curricular units, with contents, faculty and students; (e) analyse the cognitive, social and emotional adaptation processes to the online academic activities; (f) identify the communication strategies used in the online academic activities; (g) characterise emotional states associated with experiencing online activities; (h) assess the global evaluation of the academic experience lived during this period. The questionnaire consisted of 53 items, divided into 5 parts. In the first part, an informed consent form was included. The second part consisted of 10 closed and open questions (Q), aimed to ascertain data about the student's profile: sociodemographic and use of technology, previous experience in Distance Education and online participation practices in this period. On the third part, 6 closed questions were presented, asking the students to situate themselves in terms of attendance, using a Likert scale with 4 points to each item (from *Never* to *Very Frequently*). The aim was to know their perception about the experienced synchronous and asynchronous communication situations, as well as the assessment practices developed in the online learning activities. The fourth part incorporated 3 dimensions: interaction-contents. interaction-student-teacher, interaction-peers, divided into 13 statements, with the goal to gather data on their perceptions about the situations created in the curricular units, asking them to position themselves in a 5 points scale (from *Never* to *Very Frequently*). In the fifth part, the goal was to gather data on their perceptions about the used strategies for cognitive adaptation, social and emotional processes to the online academic activities. A scale comprising 20 items was used, where the participants reported their opinion on each item, in terms of agreement, i.e. from 1 (*Totally Disagree*) to 5 (*Completely Agree*). This scale was divided into 3 main dimensions: autoregulation and socio-cognitive strategies, emotional and relational communication strategies and emotions expression strategies.

Data Collection and Analysis

The instruments were approved by the Research Unit Ethics' Committee, and submitted to a previous validation, allowing the adjustment of its adequacy in relation to several characteristics. Data collection took place online, at the end of the second semester, between the end of May and July. Faculty and/or course coordinators were contacted and presented with information about the objectives, procedures, guaranteed data confidentiality and asked for their informed consent. As regards the statistical treatment and analysis, SPSS software was used.

Results

Online Communication Practices and Evaluation

Some of the data characterising the profile of the students who answered the questionnaire are briefly presented. In total, 482 students answered the questionnaire, 78.4% were female and 21.6% male, with the following age distribution: 34.8% between 17-20 years old; 48% between 21-30 years old, 7.8% between 31-40 years old and 7.2% between 41-50 years old. Other data characterising the profile of the students surveyed are: Previous experience of online distance learning (ODL): 52.7% of students stated that they had never had this experience. Of those 43.4% say they have had some contact with ODL, 13.6% have had it infrequently and 14% have had it rarely; Year of the course attended: the distribution of respondents is mostly (67%) in the first two years of the course and 18.7% in the third year.

Regarding Time spent online and types of activities, the answers to Q10 ("Per day, on average, how many hours were you doing online activities (synchronous and asynchronous)") show that a large part of the respondents (43.1%) were more than 6 hours on average per day doing online activities, while 34.9% were between 3 and 5 hours.

Table 1: Select the type of online activities you took part in during the curricular units

Types of online activities	Freq.	Perc.
Submission of assignments in platforms (Moodle, Teams, Google Meet, etc.)	435	90.2
Group work	427	88.6
Oral presentations	410	85.1
Individual work	356	73.9
Formative tests	280	58.1
Participation in Forum Discussions	198	41.1
Video recorded presentations	174	36.1
Online final exam	130	27
Projects	112	23.2
Self-assessments	94	19.5
Simulations	70	14.5
Games	32	6.6
Role Playing	23	4.8

The answers to Q11 ("Select the type of online activities you took part in during the curricular units") show that the most referred activities were the Submission of assignments in platforms (90.2%), Group work (88.6%) and Oral Presentations (85.1%).

Regarding students' perceptions of synchronous online activities, Q12 assessed to what extent they were considered diverse, tiring, monotonous or stimulating (Table 2). Regarding the diversification of synchronous online activities, the highest scores were distributed between *Not Very Frequent* (39.6%) and *Frequent* (46.3%), with a marginally higher value in the latter case. As for the feeling of tiredness caused by synchronous online activities, the highest value was *Frequently* (38.4%), followed by *Very Frequently* (26.8%). With regard to the feeling of monotony caused by synchronous online activities, the highest values were distributed between *Less Frequently* (34.2%) and *Frequently* (30.9%). As regards how stimulating synchronous online activities were, 38% of the respondents considered it to be *Less Frequently* and 32.6% considered it to be *Frequently*. It should be highlighted that 20.3% considered that they were *Never stimulating*.

Table 2: Q12. During Emergency Teaching classes, online activities based on synchronous platforms were:

	1 – Never	2 – Less Frequently	3 – Frequently	4 – Very Frequently
Diversified, because new strategies were developed online	4.4	39.6	46.3	9.8
Tiring, because they were mainly content transmission by the teacher	11.0	23.9	23.9	26.8
Monotonous, because they replicated face to face classes	17.2	34.2	30.9	17.6
Stimulating, because they made communication with the other students easier	20.3	38.0	32.6	9.1

Regarding the asynchronous activities (using the forums), Q13 assessed the extent to which participation in the discussion forums was used to create topics, answer the teacher, engage in discussions or report information about their assignments (Table 3). The respondents' answers show that they considered the use of the discussion forums to create topics *Less Frequently* (40.2%) and *Never* (33.2%), to answer the teacher *Frequently* (43.2%) and *Very Frequently* (23.9%), to engage in discussions *Less Frequently* (37.6%) and *Never* (28.4%) and to report information about their assignments *Frequent* (37.6%) and *Less Frequently* (26.8%).

Table 3: I used the Forums mainly to:

	1 – Never	2 – Less Frequently	3 – Frequently	4 – Very Frequently
Create topics and post my messages	33.2	40.2	22.0	4.6
Answer teacher requests	11.6	21.4	43.2	23.9
Engage in discussions	28.4	37.6	27.2	6.8
Report information about my assignments	17.8	26.8	37.6	17.8

In Q14 we wanted to assess the extent to which online forum-based activities were considered easy, difficult, richer and flexible by students (Table 4). The respondents' answers show that they considered the activities based on the use of discussion forums, easy as *Less Frequently* (33.6%) and *Frequently* (33.4%), difficult *Less Frequently* (42.7%) and *Never* (25.9%), richer *Frequently* (38.8%) and *Less Frequently* (34.2%) and flexible *Frequently* (37.1%) and *Less Frequently* (25.3%).

Table 4: Q14. During Emergency Teaching classes, online activities based on forums were:

	1 – Never	2 – Less Frequently	3 – Frequently	4 – Very Frequently
Easy, because we already used the forums before	25.1	33.6	33.4	7.9
Difficult, because there was too much reading and writing due to other participants' contributions	25.9	42.7	23.9	7.5
Richer, because they enabled multimedia communication	14.9	34.2	38.8	12.0
Flexible, because each student manages his time	18	25.3	37.1	19.5

When questioned about the evaluation practices developed in the online activities by the teacher during this period (Q15, Q16, Q17), the respondents positioned themselves as follows (Table 5): 49.2% perceived continuous feedback *Frequently* and 17.2% *Very frequently*, which translates to a monitoring practice of *proximity*. Despite this, 4% of respondents considered it to be *Less Frequently*, and even 4.8% considered that it *Never* occurred. In the case of the productivity of the feedback given by the teacher, about half (48.5%) of the respondents consider it to have been *Frequently*, plus 13.3% who consider it to have been *Very Frequently* productive feedback. When asked about the customisation of the feedback given by the teacher, the answers were divided: 40.5% considered that it was *Frequently*, 35.7% considered it *Less Frequently* and 10% considered that there was *Never* any effort at customisation.

Table 5: Q15. During Emergency Teaching classes, I felt that teacher feedback to online activities was:

	1 – Never	2 – Less Frequently	3 – Frequently	4 – Very Frequently
Continuous	4.8	28.8	49.2	17.2
Productive	6.0	32.2	48.5	13.3
Customized	10.0	35.7	40.5	13.9
Creative	12.0	43.4	35.7	8.9

When asked about the feedback given by the teacher to the final assignments, i.e. at the end of the semester, the following results were registered (Table 6): the majority 47.9% considered it to be *Frequently*, as being continuous and productive, while 44.6% evaluated it as having been customised, although 40.7% of the respondents rated it Less Frequently as creative. However, this characteristic was perceived by 36.3 % as being a practice of teachers. If we consider the values of the item *Very Frequently* of any of these dimensions, we can conclude that the type of feedback given was in the positive range of the scale (*Frequently* and *Very Frequently*).

Table 6: Q16. During Emergency Teaching classes, I felt that teacher feedback to final assignments was:

	1 – Never	2 – Less Frequently	3 – Frequently	4 – Very Frequently
Continuous	7.7	33.0	47.9	11.4
Productive	8.1	32.0	47.9	12.0
Customized	9.8	34.9	44.6	10.8
Creative	14.3	40.7	36.3	8.7

The question about assessment strategies developed (Q17) was answered as follows (Table 7). Most students consider that teachers have incorporated new assessment techniques, with 40.9% *Frequently* and 11.8% *Very Frequently*. Despite this positive trend, 31.3% perceived this practice by teachers as *Less Frequently*. The same trend is registered when 41.5% of the respondents' state that Enhanced strategies were *Frequently* applied through the use of technologies and media and 10.6% *Very Frequently*, although 36.5% respond that this practice was *Less Frequently* and 11.4% are peremptory opting for *Never*. On the other hand, 41.7% consider that these strategies have not changed since the beginning of the lessons, although 35.5% consider that they have changed *Less Frequently*. When asked to position themselves on whether assessment strategies have been adapted for online remote learning, the trends are more assertive in this respect: 45.4% *Frequently* and 24.9% *Very Frequently* clearly pointing to adaptation to the new scenario (70.3%).

Table 7: Q17. During Emergency Teaching classes, the assessment strategies:

	1 – Never	2 – Less Frequently	3 – Frequently	4 – Very Frequently
Incorporated new evaluation techniques	16.0	31.3	40.9	11.8
Were enhanced by other technologies and media	11.4	36.5	41.5	10.6
Did not change since the beginning of classes	10.8	35.5	41.7	12.0
Were adapted to online remote teaching	7.7	22.0	45.4	24.9

Preliminary Discussion of Results

Types of online activities

The most commonly performed online activities seem to fit into the traditional pedagogical practices of face-to-face teaching, transposed to online. However, it should be noted that some of the activities that can benefit from the potential of online digital technologies and/or LMSs, or are exclusive to them, have high values, as is the case of *Formative tests* (58.1%) and *Participation in Forum Discussions* (41.1%). The value of 36.1%, regarding *Video Recorded Presentations*, shows that more than a third used this procedure, which increases flexibility, allowing students who could not be present in synchronous classes to view them afterwards. However, others such as *Self-Assessments* (19.5%) as well as activities of less typical pedagogies but which could have a good online support, such as *Simulations* (14.5%) or *Games* (6.6%), were less used. It is worth mentioning the value of the *online Final Exam*, which corresponded to 27%, evidencing that it was possible to transfer this assessment online, but only in a quarter of the cases.

Time spent online

The results show that almost 50% of the students spent more than 6 hours a day in online activities. Although it is not possible to disaggregate the results into synchronous and asynchronous hours, the analysis of the open answers and the interviews show that most of them are synchronous hours, corresponding to the direct transposition of face-to-face classes into a synchronous regime and that their perception is of a high workload (one of the points mentioned as less positive in the emergency remote learning experience in the answers was "Many hours at the computer"). Further analysis of the open answers and interviews will allow us to assess whether procedures to minimize phenomena such as zoom fatigue (Bates, 2020) were considered, although the results of the analysis of the answers to Q12 already point to a negative answer.

Synchronous online activities

Synchronous online activities seem to have had some degree of diversification, with the introduction of new online work strategies, given that the results that fall within the positive range of the scale (*Frequently* and *Very Frequently* 56.1%) are marginally higher than the negative range. Regarding fatigue due to the teacher's transmission of content, it seems evident that this was a common activity that will have typical zoom fatigue effects. The results that fall in the positive scale interval (*Frequently* and *Very Frequently* 65.2%) point to a higher frequency of the feeling of fatigue, i.e. about ⅔ consider that the online activities caused fatigue due to being mainly transmission of content by the teacher. Regarding the feeling of monotony due to replication of face-to-face classes, the results do not show a clear trend. The results that fall within the positive range of the scale (*Frequently* and *Very Frequently* 48.5%) are only marginally lower than those that point to a lower frequency, regarding the feeling of monotony due to the activities being a replication of the face-to-face classes. Regarding stimulating effects, the results in the negative range of the scale (*Never* and *Less Frequently*, 58.3%) show that the potential of synchronous communication was not sufficiently valued, exploited or promoted in online activities. In short, synchronous online activities are perceived as tiring due to the transmission of contents by the teacher and, to a lesser extent, not very stimulating by allowing improved communication with other students. However, the feeling of monotony for replicating face-to-face classes, which would be expected to accompany the tiredness values, is less high than this one, which seems to indicate that replicating face-to-face classes was not necessarily monotonous, possibly due to the introduction of some diversification with new online work strategies.

Asynchronous online activities (Discussion Forums)

The answers regarding asynchronous online activities in discussion forums seem to indicate teacher-centred pedagogical practices, with the results on the use of the forum to answer the teacher's questions that fall within the positive range of the scale (*Frequently* and *Very Frequently* 67.1%) being higher. The results on the use of the forum to participate in discussions, which fall in the negative range (*Never* and *Less Frequently* 66.0%), point to an underutilization of online discussion forums, as a means of written and asynchronous communication, and of their specific affordances, for debate activities that allow developing critical and higher-order thinking (Garrison, 2017). As for the students' perceptions of this form of asynchronous communication, the results show that most of them had not found the forums easy because they had used them before (the answers falling in the negative range of the scale, Never and *Less Frequently*, make up 59%), in line with the fact that 52% had no previous experience with distance education. A clear trend shows that they did not find it difficult to use because there would not be much to read and write (the answers falling in the negative range of the scale, *Never* and *Less Frequently*, make up 68.6%). This figure seems to confirm the indications about the type of use of the forums which were noted earlier. On the other hand, There was some recognition of the advantages in terms of flexibility for the management of their learning time, since the answers in the positive range of the scale, *Frequently* and *Very Frequently*, make up 56.6%. Indirectly, it can be perceived that asynchronous activities did not have the same weight as synchronous activities. In other words, it seems that both institutionally and for teachers and students, classes are the synchronous sessions (online equivalents of face-to-face sessions), and asynchronous activities are the equivalent of homework or extra-class activities (data from student interviews clearly point in this direction). The triangulation of these data with the faculty interviews' data will enable us to ascertain how and with what objectives synchronous and asynchronous activities were carried out and if they followed specialized literature recommendations for their use (Watts, 2016), causing the effective students' perceptions.

Feedback and assessment practices

The results point towards the conclusion that online assessment in general activities was perceived by a 60% majority as having occurred continuously and productively, which indicates a very positive teaching practice. On the other hand, this aspect may also have been facilitated by the implementation of synchronous and asynchronous activities allowing for a feedback from the teacher expanded in time. The perception of the feedback received (Savividou, 2017) according to pedagogical, contextual and even relational aspects should be explored in greater depth, crossing with the data from the interviews of teachers and students. However, one of the aspects that stands out in these results is that the feedback occurred continuously and was productive (effective), thus pointing to a good pedagogical practice (Hattie & Timperley, 2007) and the teachers' choice of communication strategies focused on a general feedback and not so much on individualized feedback. These results can also be supported based on the types of assignments carried out and the majority choice of teachers to submit them on platforms (Moodle, Teams, Google Meet), focused on individual (73.9%) and group (88.6%) assignments and on the fact that automatic feedback strategies supported by digital platforms and tools were not used (only in Online Exams – 27%). On the other hand, the strategy of personalised feedback, although mentioned as having been a relevant practice, implies higher teacher workload but ensures the "perception of monitoring" and "being-there". This data can be deepened with the teachers' and students' narratives.

Conclusions

The main conclusions of the study may be summarized as follows:

- Students perceived to be too much time online;
- Data about synchronous activities shows evidence of zoom fatigue effects due to being mainly transmission of content by the teacher and that the potential of synchronous communication was not sufficiently valued, exploited, or promoted by teachers (although there was some diversification of activities);
- Data about asynchronous activities (forums) shows some recognition of the advantages in terms of flexibility for the management of their learning time and no difficulty in having too much to read and write but also an underutilization of online discussion forums as a means of written and asynchronous communication, and of their specific affordances;
- Data about teacher feedback shows fair levels and quality of teacher feedback;
- Assessment strategies were also fairly adapted to online remote teaching.

Recommendations

We propose the following recommendations for similar future practices:

- Rethink synchronous sessions taking in account differences from face-to-face settings;
- Diversify activities exploring affordances of the new medium;
- Implement more asynchronous activities properly designed and not so teacher centred
- Improve teacher feedback (use more creativity);
- Enhance assessment strategies using other technologies and media.

The results presented here are only partial. We intend, with the case studies, through the narratives based on students' and teachers' perceptions, to contribute to discuss good practices, understanding what can be improved and avoided, in the construction of blended or distance learning scenarios, by reflecting on good pedagogical practices rebuilt in the post-pandemic transformation accelerated by the digital experience. There are some clear common trends, but others are less clear, pointing to possible differentiated practices, which only a more in-depth study, namely through the analysis of correlations with other variables, will clarify.

References

Anderson, T. (2003). Getting the Mix Right Again: An Updated and Theoretical Rationale for Interaction. *The International Review of Research in Open and Distributed Learning, 4*(2).

Archibald, M. M., Ambagtsheer, R. C., Casey, M. G., & Lawless, M. (2019). Using Zoom Video Conferencing for Qualitative Data Collection: Perceptions and Experiences of Researchers and Participants. *International Journal of Qualitative Methods, 18*, 1-8.

Bates, T. (2019). *Teaching in the Digital Age.* Tony Bates Associates Ltd.

Bates, T. (2020, March 9). Advice to those about to teach online because of the corona-virus. Online Learning and Distance Education Resources [Blog post]. Retrieved from https://www.tonybates.ca/2020/03/09/advice-to-those-about-to-teach-online-because-of-the-corona-virus/

Bozkurt, A., & Sharma, R. (2020). Emergency remote teaching in a time of global crisis due to Coronavirus pandemic. *Asian Journal of Distance Education, 15*(1), 1-6.

Crawford, J., Butler-Henderson, K., Rudolph, J., Malkawi, B., Glowatz, B., Burton, R. Magni, P., & Lam, S. (2020). COVID-19: 20 countries' higher education intra-period digital pedagogy responses. *Journal of Applied Learning & Teaching, 3*(1), 9-28.

Decreto-Lei nº 133/2019, Regime Jurídico Ensino a Distância, 49-57. Retrieved from https://data.dre.pt/eli/dec-lei/133/2019/09/03/p/dre

Derks, D., Fischer, A. H., & Bos, A. E. R. (2008). The role of emotion in computer-mediated communication: A review. *Computers in Human Behavior, 24*, 766-785.

Garrison, R. (2017). *E-learning in the 21st century: a community of inquiry framework for research and practice.* Routledge.

Hattie, J., & Timperley, H. (2007). The power of feedback. *Review of Educational Research, 77*(1), 81-112. https://doi.org/10.3102/003465430298487

Hesse-Biber, S. N. (2010). *Mixed Methods Research. Merging theory with practice.* The Guilford Press.

Hodges, C., Moore, S., Lockee, B., Trust, T., & Bond, A. (2020, March 27). The Difference between Emergency Remote Teaching and Online Learning. Educause Review [Blog post]. Retrieved from https://er.educause.edu/articles/2020/3/the-difference-between-emergency-remote-teaching-and-online-learning

Lovink, G. (2020, November 2). The anatomy of Zoom fatigue. Eurozine [Blog post]. Retrieved from https://www.eurozine.com/the-anatomy-of-zoom-fatigue/

Morris, B. (2020, May 27). Why does Zoom exhaust you? Science has an answer. The Walt Street Journal [Blog post]. Retrieved from https://www.wsj.com/articles/why-does-zoom-exhaust-you-science-has-an-answer-11590600269

Murphy, M. (2020). COVID-19 and emergency eLearning: Consequences of the securitization of higher education for post-pandemic pedagogy. *Contemporary Security Policy, 41*(3), 492-505.

Paiva, A., Giger, J.-C., Faísca, L., & Batista, L. (2011). 'Mais quente melhor': O impacto do papel informativo das emoções na CMC. *Revista Galego-Portuguesa de Psicoloxía e Educación*, 371-382.

Quintas-Mendes, A., Morgado, L., & Amante, L. (2008). Online Communication and E-Learning. In T. T. Kidd & H. Song (Eds.), *Handbook of Research on Instructional Systems and Technology: Vol. II. Information Science Reference.* doi:10.4018/978-1-59904-865-9.ch065

Salmons, J. (2012). *Cases in Online Interview Research.* London: SAGE Publications

Sacasas, L. M. (2020, April 21). A Theory of Zoom fatigue. The Convivial Society [Blog post]. Retrieved from https://theconvivialsociety.substack.com/p/a-theory-of-zoom-fatigue

Savvidou, C. (2017). Feedback given, feedback received: lessons from a distance learning course. *EDULEARN Proceedings*, 8756-8764. IATED Publications.

Watts, L. (2016). Synchronous and Asynchronous communication in distance learning: a review of literature. *The Quarterly Review of Distance Education, 17*(1), 23-32.

Wiederhold, B. K. (2020). Connecting through Technology during the Coronavirus Disease 2019 Pandemic: Avoiding "Zoom Fatigue". *Cyberpsychology Behavior, and Social Networking, 23*(7), 437-438.

Wu, Z. (2020, March 16). How a top Chinese university is responding to coronavirus. World Economic Forum [Blog post]. Retrieved from https://www.weforum.org/agenda/2020/03/coronavirus-china-the-challenges-of-online-learning-for-universities

UNICEF (2020). *UNICEF and Microsoft launch a global learning platform to help address COVID-19 education crisis.* Retrieved from https://www.unicef.org/press-releases/unicef-and-microsoft-launch-global-learning-platform-help-address-covid-19-education

UNESCO (2020). *COVID-19 education response.* Retrieved from https://en.unesco.org/covid19/educationresponse/globalcoalition

Zimmerman, J. (2020, Mach 10). Coronavirus and the Great Online-Learning Experiment. Chronicle of Higher Education [Blog post]. Retrieved from https://www.chronicle.com/article/coronavirus-and-the-great-online-learning-experiment/

Acknowledgment

This research was supported by the Foundation of Science and Technology – financed national funds through FCT – Fundação para a Ciência e a Tecnologia, I.P., in the project UIDB/04372/2020 with Project number PTIN/UID4372-LE@D/032020

Lessons from a Pandemic for the Future of Education
European Distance and E-Learning Network (EDEN) Proceedings
2021 Annual Conference | Madrid, 21-24 June, 2021
ISSN 2707-2819
doi: 10.38069/edenconf-2021-ac0029

"I FEEL LIKE A GUINEA PIG": EMOTIONAL RESPONSES TO THE ONLINE PIVOT

Elaine Beirne, Mairéad Nic Giolla Mhichíl, Mark Brown, Dublin City University, Ireland

Abstract

This paper reports on the emotional experiences of first year students as they prepared to start their higher education online because of Covid-19 public health precautions. Emotion research holds important insights for the development of pedagogical and institutional strategies to support students adapt to the increased focus on online learning both now and into the future. Students' responses to a survey embedded at the beginning of an online learning preparatory MOOC were analysed to identify (a) the anticipatory emotions they were experiencing towards online learning, and (b) what they perceived to be the sources of those emotions. Findings revealed that anxiety was the prevailing emotion, although positive emotions, such as excitement and hope, were also reported. A thematic analysis identified seven over-arching sources of those emotions as described by the students. This paper concludes by briefly discussing the implications for educators.

Introduction

The Covid-19 pandemic has propelled emotion research to the fore. The challenges faced by teachers and students in the pivot to online learning, has highlighted the need for a "pedagogy of care" in the online domain (Burke & Larmar, 2020). To inform practice in this area, the current study investigates the emotional responses of first year students towards starting their higher education online.

The literature recognises emotion as a crucial factor that can constrain or facilitate the learning experience. Emotions are known to influence attention, self-regulation, motivation, and ultimately, learning success across different learning environments (Linnenbrink-Garcia & Pekrun, 2011; Pekrun, Goetz, Frenzel, Barchfeld, & Perry, 2011; Artino, 2009). According to Schutz et al. (2006), emotional experiences in education emerge from person-environment transactions. It can thus be deduced that a change in the mode of learning has the potential to elicit emotional responses among students that may influence their participation and performance. Understanding learners' emotions under the unique and challenging conditions of transitioning to Higher Education and an online mode of delivery, is, therefore, an important step in supporting students during and after this process.

A limited number of studies in the online domain have explored how students describe the sources of their emotional experiences. Järvenoja and Järvelä (2005) identified five main sources of emotion from students' qualitative accounts of their emotional experiences when learning using computers: (a) self, (2b) context, (c) task, (d) performance and (e) social. O'Regan (2003) found that students expressed their emotions in relation to the various aspects of an online course, such as design and organizational issues, cognitive issues, social issues, time management, and technology. Focusing on adult learners, Zembylas (2008) found that the flexibility of online learning, achievement, and the unexpected emotional nature of online communication were sources of positive emotion. Negative emotions, on the other hand, were evoked by the unknown, technology, time management issues, communication difficulties, and the struggle to obtain a work-life balance. As approaches and technologies evolve, however, more up-to-date research is needed.

In the context of the current pandemic, Espino et al. (2021) collected the emotional responses of middle and high school students towards the pivot to online learning and explored how those emotions related to the specific aspects of the online learning environment outlined in the Community of Inquiry (CoI) framework. They found that students exhibited more negative than positive emotions overall. The negative emotions were exhibited in relation to the instructional format, ability to focus, workload, and interactions with teachers, while the positive emotions were exhibited in relation to the instructional format and the flexibility of the schedule. The current study will extend this line of enquiry to first year higher education students.

Methodology

The current study was guided by the following two research questions:

- What emotions did students experience before starting college/university online?
- What were students' perceived reasons for feeling this way?

Data was collected using a cross-sectional online survey. A link to the survey was embedded in a step at the beginning of the MOOC, *A Digital Edge: Essentials for the Online Learner*. All responses were anonymous, and participation was optional. Ethical approval for the study was obtained from DCU's Research Ethics Committee (DCUREC/2020/150).

"A Digital Edge: Essentials for the Online Learner" was developed by Dublin City University (DCU) in collaboration with the Irish Universities Association (IUA) and

DCU's Students Union. The aim of the MOOC was to support college and university students to adapt to the increased focus on online learning because of Covid-19. Data for the current study was collected during the first iteration of the MOOC which launched in September 2020, prior to the beginning of the first online semester for many students. In this regard, it was a prime opportunity to investigate students' prospective emotions towards learning online at college or university.

Instrument

A list of six discrete emotion states was used to collect data pertaining to participants' emotions. The list was derived from previous studies on learning-centric emotions (Beirne, 2020; Pekrun, Goetz, Frenzel, Barchfeld, & Perry, 2011; D'Mello, 2013). Participants were directed to identify the most prominent emotion they were experiencing in response to the increased focus on online learning because of Covid-19. A further open-ended question prompted respondents to report in their own words the source of that emotion. Data pertaining to the participant's gender and whether this was their first year at university was also collected. The instrument also contained further items unrelated to the current paper.

Participants

Of the 982 MOOC participants who responded to the questionnaire, 663 of them were entering their first year of college or university. These 663 students formed the sample for this study.

Quantitative Results

Figure 1 presents the proportion of respondents who reported each emotion. Anxiety was the most frequently reported emotion, selected by nearly two thirds of the respondents (64%). This was followed by the positive emotions of excitement (14%) and hope (12%). Anger and Hopelessness were rarely reported.

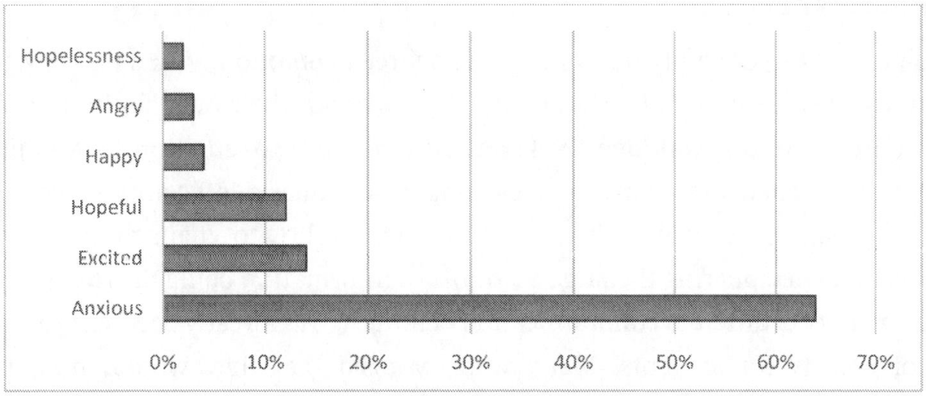

Figure 1. Emotion frequencies

Qualitative Results

Data from the open-ended question, was analysed using thematic analysis. Braun and Clarke's (2006) six step guide was followed (see Table 1). Seven overarching themes or factors influencing learners' emotions were identified: (a) Perceptions of Ability, (b) Technology, (c) Confidence in Provider, (d) The Unknown, (e) Advantages and Disadvantages, (f) Communicating Online, and (g) The Bigger Picture (see Figure 2 for overview). Each of these themes are described below.

Table 1: Thematic Analysis Procedure

Phase	Description
1	Familiarise yourself with data
2	Generate initial codes
3	Search for themes
4	Review themes
5	Define and name themes
6	Produce report

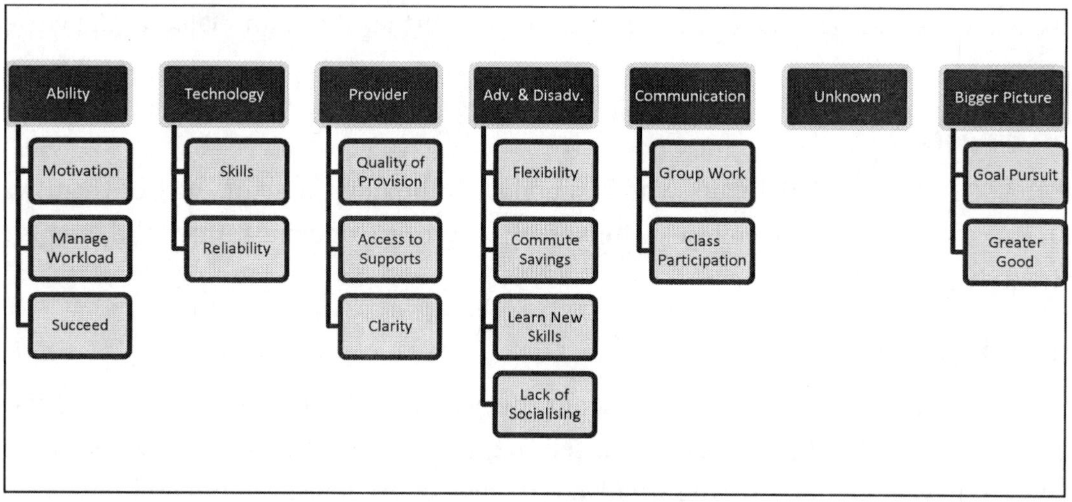

Figure 2. Themes and Subthemes

Perceptions of Ability

Varying perceptions of ability was a pervasive source of emotion. When reflecting on their emotion towards learning online, students' doubts about their own ability to learn in an online environment that was identified as a source of negative emotion. The ability to stay motivated and avoid distractions when learning from home or "off campus" was a concern voiced by students. Students also doubted their ability to manage their workload. Monitoring and deciphering the large amounts of information being provided, sometimes through a variety of different communication channels, was already becoming a prominent source of anxiety for students. Many were worried that they would miss important deadlines as a result. Anxiety, hopelessness, and anger were also brought about by students' doubts about their ability to achieve their learning goals while learning online.

Some people reflected on a negative previous experience, while others who were new to online learning questioned their ability to adapt or held the preconception that it would be harder to learn online.

> *"I feel that I cannot take in information as well as being on campus in a lecture as there are too many distractions at home." (R206)*

> *"I'm anxious to miss a class or an assignment because of the amount of mails I receive every day." (R890)*

> *"I feel overwhelmed by the countless formats through which the same information is dispersed." (R100)*

> *"It's nearly impossible to learn effectively online, so my mind always races on and on about how this will affect my overall experience with university." (R360)*

At the same time, when students were more confident in their ability, positive emotions ensued. Some of the reasons for this confidence were positive previous online learning experiences or the expectation that the online mode of delivery would suit their learning style.

> *"I find it easy and comfortable to learn and study by myself." (R142)*

Technology

The technology used to support online learning evoked emotions among students. Having insufficient digital skills was a source of anxiety for students who were concerned that this deficiency would impede their learning experience. Unreliable internet connections and system stability was also a source of anxiety for students. On the other hand, being comfortable around technology was a source of hope and excitement for students as they embarked on this new experience.

> *"I'm not great with technology and I'm nervous about falling behind, missing important deadlines etc." (R477)*

> *"I have very poor Wi-Fi connection and online learning is very stressful." (R319)*

> *"I've done the ECDL, have good internet and desktop/ laptop so I am well-equipped to move online." (R020)*

Confidence in Provider

The confidence that students had in their college or university being able to provide the teaching and support needed in the online domain was identified as another source of emotion. Anxiety was experienced by those who questioned their access to supports or whether the quality of the teaching would be the same online. Others, who were encouraged by the universities' efforts so far reported feeling hopeful about online learning.

> *"Uncertainty surrounding the quality and level of learning and productivity compared to previous and future years." (R595)*
>
> *"I'm worried we won't be able to get help if we need it." (R287)*
>
> *"I have seen the efforts made by my university to provide a safe and enjoyable year online." (R843)*

The Unknown

Learning online was a first for many of the students. This new experience was a source of both positive and negative emotion. For some, the unknown methodology of online learning was a source of apprehension and anxiety. For others, the unknown was perceived as a new challenge or adventure, which evoked excitement. It was also specified by students that these feelings, both positive and negative, were amplified by the fact not only were they starting online learning for the first time, but they were also starting university for the first time.

> *"University is daunting enough as it is, I feel like a guinea pig with this online learning." (R090)*
>
> *"Anxious towards the idea of an unfamiliar learning style." (R082)*
>
> *"This is a brand-new experience for me. I have never studied at third level and have never studied online. I cannot wait to get started." (R150)*

Advantages and Disadvantages

Perceived advantages and disadvantages of starting university online evoked both positive and negative emotion, respectively. The sources of positive emotion encompassed by this theme include (a) the flexible nature of online learning and being able to learn at your own pace, (b) the opportunity to learn new skills, and (c) the monetary and time savings associated with not having to commute to campus. One or two students even mentioned that starting college in an online capacity made the transition easier.

> *"I feel like I can take control of my own learning. There are less physical stresses such as travelling to campus, being in the right place at the right time. I'm also excited by the challenge of immersing myself with online learning to prepare for my future as with every year that goes by IT skills in every workplace become more and more important." (R328)*

A prevalent source of negative emotion and a perceived disadvantage of online learning was the reduced opportunity to socialise with others. Making new friends was something that many students were looking forward to at university, but they felt that this would be harder online, leading to feelings of anxiety and even anger. Students also mentioned that they felt like they were missing out on a "real" university experience, which was also a source of anxiety and anger. One person in particular reported feeling angry because they felt like the entire year would be a write-off:

> *"I have had my time as a first year stolen from me." (R615)*

> *"I am concerned that online learning will limit and hinder the social aspect of college life that I was looking forward to." (R032)*

Communicating and Interacting Online

The perceived difficulties associated with communicating and interacting with peers and lecturers online was a source of negative emotion for students. They worried about the practicalities of group work, as well as how effectively they would be able share their opinions or ask questions without the face-to-face connection.

> *"It is quite hard to truly express your ideas through a computer screen and it can be off putting not knowing your classmates in person." (R247)*

> *"I am especially concerned about how group assignments would look like." (R714)*

The Bigger Picture

When reflecting on the upcoming semester, some students' emotions went beyond the specifics of the learning context. Goal pursuit was a source of excitement for students, who mentioned that starting university in any format was better than nothing.

> *"I am mainly eager to start university and I am willing to learn in any manner." (R471)*

The other source of emotion encompassed by this theme was the greater good. Students felt hopeful as they agreed with the precautions being taken and felt like they were playing their part to protect others against Covid-19.

> *"I am hopeful that by learning online I can help keep those around me safe." (R278)*

Conclusions

This study examined the emotional experiences of first year higher education students as they prepared to start learning online. The findings contribute to an increased understanding of emotions associated with online and distance learning. As can be expected from the unprecedented nature of the experience, anxiety was by far the most common emotion experienced by the students. However, the reasons behind students' emotions were more wide-ranging. Many of the sources of emotion identified are consistent with previous literature. These include technology, the unknown, workload and time-management, communication difficulties, the ability to focus, and the flexibility of online learning (Espino et al. 2021; Hilliard, Kear, Donelan, & Heaney, 2020; Järvenoja & Järvelä, 2005; O'Regan, 2003; Zembylas, 2008). Other sources identified, such as the socialising concerns and confidence in the provider, were more context-specific but could be relevant to those undertaking full-time online degrees irrespective of the pandemic.

The findings of this research hold important insights for institutional leadership and educators who endeavour to support students in the transition to online learning, both in crisis situations, such as the on-going Covid-19 pandemic, and beyond. Some of the takeaways might include:

- The importance of considering the wide spectrum of digital and other online learning-related competences in the student body. Additional supports may be needed for those who do not have the necessary skills.
- The value of social interactions to students. Social time could be incorporated into live lectures or facilitated outside teaching hours.
- The value of fully leveraging the flexibility afforded by online and distance provision. Flexibility can be incorporated into both instruction and assessment.
- The need to develop and share a clear and consistent communication strategy with students.

In conclusion, the current study captures the emotions expressed by students towards online learning in advance of that experience. A follow-up study after a sustained period of online learning would provide comparative insights to identify how students' emotions change over time as well as the factors contributing to such changes.

References

Artino, A. R. (2009). Think, feel, act: Motivational and emotional influences on military students' online academic success. *Journal of Computing in Higher Education, 21*(2), 146-166.

Beirne, E. (2020). *What a feeling! A multistage, multimethod Investigation of emotions and their antecedents in an Irish language MOOC* (PhD thesis). Dublin City University.

Burke, K., & Larmar, S. (2020). Acknowledging another face in the virtual crowd: Reimagining the online experience in higher education through an online pedagogy of care. *Journal of Further and Higher Education*, 1-15.

D'Mello, S. (2013). A selective meta-analysis on the relative incidence of discrete affective states during learning with technology. *Journal of Educational Psychology, 105*(4), 1082-1099.

Espino, D. P., Wright, T., Brown, V. M., Mbasu, Z., Sweeney, M., & Lee, S. B. (2021). Student Emotions in the Shift to Online Learning during the COVID-19 Pandemic. *Proceedings of the International Conference on Quantitative Ethnography*, 334-347. Springer, Cham.

Hilliard, J., Kear, K., Donelan, H., & Heaney, C. (2020). Students' experiences of anxiety in an assessed, online, collaborative project. *Computers & Education, 143*, 103675.

Järvenoja, H., & Järvelä, S. (2005). How Students Describe the Sources of Their Emotional and Motivational Experiences during the Learning Process: A Qualitative Approach. *Learning and Instruction, 15*(5), 465-480.

O'Regan, K. (2003). Emotion and e-learning. *Journal of Asynchronous Learning Networks, 7*(3), 78-92

Pekrun, R., Goetz, T., Frenzel, A. C., Barchfeld, P., & Perry, R. P. (2011). Measuring emotions in students' learning and performance: The Achievement Emotions Questionnaire (AEQ). *Contemporary Educational Psychology, 36*(1), 36-48.

Schutz, P. A., Hong, J. Y., Cross, D. I., & Osbon, J. N. (2006). Reflections on investigating emotion in educational activity settings. *Educational Psychology Review, 18*(4), 343-360. doi:10.1007/ s10648-006-9030-3

Zembylas, M. (2008). Adult learners' emotions in online learning. *Distance Education, 29*(1), 71-87.

Lessons from a Pandemic for the Future of Education
European Distance and E-Learning Network (EDEN) Proceedings
2021 Annual Conference | Madrid, 21-24 June, 2021
ISSN 2707-2819
doi: 10.38069/edenconf-2021-ac0030

DIFFERENCES IN ACADEMIC RESILIENCY WHEN THE PANDEMIC FORCED COURSES ONLINE: WAS PRIOR ONLINE COURSETAKING PROTECTIVE?

Claire Wladis, City University of New York, Alyse C. Hachey, University of Texas at El Paso, Katherine M. Conway, City University of New York, United States of America

Abstract

We report results from a dataset consisting of all courses taken by students at the City University of New York [CUNY] in fall 2019 and spring 2020. This time frame covers the semester prior to the wide-spread onset of the COVID-19 pandemic in New York City (i.e., pre-pandemic), and the semester when the coronavirus precipitated a rapid and unprecedented forced shift of all courses within the university system to a fully-online mode of instruction early in the term (i.e., pandemic term). Findings indicate that students at two-year colleges, men, and certain racial/ethnic groups had less resilient course outcomes when comparing their rates of pre-pandemic vs. pandemic course outcomes. However, these differences were observed primarily among those students who had not originally chosen to enrol in any fully online courses that year. In contrast, students who had originally chosen to enrol in fully online courses that year were much more resilient, with differences by institution type, gender, and race/ethnicity by and large not exacerbated by the pandemic.

Motivation for the Study

The question has arisen as to whether the forced shift to online learning due to the pandemic impacted course outcomes differentially for different groups. For example, institution type (two-year vs. four-year) was already a significant predictor of college outcomes pre-pandemic (e.g., NCES, 2020a). Gender and race/ethnicity have also been predictive of outcomes in online courses, as well as college courses more generally (e.g., Johnson & Mejia, 2014; Xu & Xu, 2019). It is unclear the extent to which the pandemic has magnified these inequities. It is difficult to tease apart the direct effects of the pandemic from effects of the abrupt mandatory shift to fully online learning, and this is not a causal study; however, we are able to tease apart some of these patterns by considering students separately based on whether they originally chose to enrol in fully online courses prior to the onset of the pandemic. Analysing data collected from the City University of New York

[CUNY] provided a unique opportunity to find answers to these questions for three-fold reasons: New York City had the earliest large-scale severe impact from the COVID-19 pandemic in the U.S.; the CUNY student population is large and widely diverse, allowing for in-depth exploration for different student sub-groups; and CUNY provides the same overall context while including both two-year and four-year colleges. Therefore, in this study, we analysed the course outcome data at CUNY for various groups in fall 2019 (pre-pandemic) vs. spring 2020 (when the COVID-19 pandemic forced all students fully online a third of the way into the semester). Research has investigated whether students are at higher risk of failing online courses in comparison to face-to-face courses with mixed results (e.g. Jaggars & Xu, 2010; Johnson & Mejia, 2014; Shea, & Bidjerano, 2014), but it is not even clear the extent to which these findings are relevant to the forced-online experiences of many students during the pandemic, since students who chose to take online courses in the past typically had different characteristics than those who did not, and many of these characteristics correlate with other factors that are also related to course outcomes (e.g., Giancola et al., 2009; Johnson & Mejia, 2014; Xu & Xu, 2019; Wladis et al., 2018; Wladis, et al., n.d.). Because those who self-select into online courses and those who do not have been found to differ, questions have arisen as to how the forced shift to fully online learning during the pandemic relates to the course outcomes of *all* types students. This study attempts to address this question.

Theoretical Framework

This study draws on the concept of *resilience,* defined as "a phenomenon or process reflecting relatively positive adaptation despite experiences of significant adversity or trauma" (Luthar, 2006; p.6). Resilience has an important role in coping during and after natural disasters and large-scale crises (Bono et al., 2020). In the context of this study, we conceptualize academic resilience as relative—the extent to which a student's course outcomes improved, stayed the same, or worsened during the pandemic term. Evidence relates resilience with socio-demographic factors, employment and academic level, and further, suggests that resilience is malleable to development and improvement through intervention (see review in San Român-Mata et al, 2020).

In addition to the shift to fully online learning, students' resiliency during the pandemic may have been impacted by other factors. Pre-pandemic findings suggest time poverty has a significant relationship with academic momentum, with women, student parents, and minority students generally more time poor (e.g. Wladis et al., 2018). Additionally, pandemic-related stress may have had an impact on students' resiliency (Pariat et al., 2014). Non-traditional students (who, pre-pandemic, enrolled both online and at two-year colleges at higher rates), often face higher levels of external sources of stress (Giancola et al., 2009). For two-year college students at CUNY, findings from Manly et al. (2020) indicate the pandemic amplified existing stressors and created new ones and reduced the time available for college. Research with four-year college students suggests that the impact of the pandemic also had mixed effects on time (St. Amour, 2020). Because we are not able to isolate these variables directly, we considered instead comparisons within groups based on prior voluntary online enrolment: differences that persist across both groups of students (those who did and did not originally choose to enrol online) may be more likely to be related to direct impacts of the pandemic; whereas differences that vanish when we look only at students who previously took online courses may be due to the experiences that students had when they were forced into the fully online course mode involuntarily as a result of the pandemic. This allows us to put forth hypotheses about which students were likely most negatively affected by being forced online—while the results are not causal, they may be helpful in generating hypotheses for future causal testing, and they may serve as preliminary guidelines for institutions who are wondering whether future mandatory fully online courses may be detrimental to some student groups or not.

Method

This study utilizes a dataset consisting of all courses taken by students enrolled in fall 2019 or spring 2020 in the City University New York [CUNY] system, which includes two and four-year colleges (1,564,548 course records taken by 260,784 unique students). We conducted all analyses in Stata, using *mixed* for multi-level linear probability models and *melogit* for multi-level logistic regression models. Logistic regression and linear probability multi-level models were run and both approaches rendered similar results. Our multi-level models were comprised of three levels, including individual course record, the particular student and the college the student attended. With *i* for course records and *j* for students and *k* for colleges, our multi-level model is:

Level 1:

$$Y_{ijk} = \beta_{0jk} + \beta_{1jk}T_{1ijk} + \cdots + \beta_{njk}T_{1ijk} + \varepsilon_{ijk}$$

Level 2. For each $\boldsymbol{l} = \mathbf{0}, \ldots, \boldsymbol{n}$:

$$\beta_{ljk} = \tau_{l0k} + \tau_{l1k}C_{l1k} + \cdots + \tau_{lmk}C_{lmk} + u_{ljk}$$

Level 3. For each $\boldsymbol{l} = \mathbf{0}, \ldots, \boldsymbol{n}$ and $\boldsymbol{p} = \mathbf{0}, \ldots, \boldsymbol{m}$:

$$\gamma_{lpk} = \mu_{lp0} + \mu_{lp1}L_{lp1} + \cdots + \mu_{lpq}L_{lpq} + r_{lpk}$$

Where β_{0jk} are the level-one intercepts, $\beta_{1jk}, \ldots, \beta_{njk}$ are the level-one slopes, and ε_{ijk} represents the random effect for course record i, student j, and college k; τ_{l0k}; for $l = 0, \ldots, n$, τ_{l0k} are the level-two intercepts, $\tau_{l1k}, \ldots, \tau_{lmk}$ are the level-two slopes, and u_{ljk} are the random effects for student j at college k; and for $l = 0, \ldots, n$ and $p = 0, \ldots, m$, μ_{lp0} are the level-three intercepts, $\mu_{lp1}, \ldots, \mu_{lpq}$ are the level-three slopes, and r_{lpk} are the random effects for college k.

Results

Students at two-year colleges had significantly lower rates of successful course completion (final grade of C- or better) in comparison to four-year colleges ($p<0.001$), which is in line with previous research (e.g., Goodman et al., 2014). They also did significantly worse in the forced-online pandemic term than the pre-pandemic term ($p<0.001$). The slope differed significantly for two-vs.-four-year colleges ($p<0.001$), with four-year students having more successful course completion during the spring vs. fall term. (see Figure 1.). Thus, four-year students had significantly more resilient outcomes during the pandemic than two-year students. Control variables (gender, race/ethnicity, age, G.P.A., first-semester freshman status, median household income of zip code) added to the model reduced the size of the difference but did not eliminate any of the observed patterns or significances.

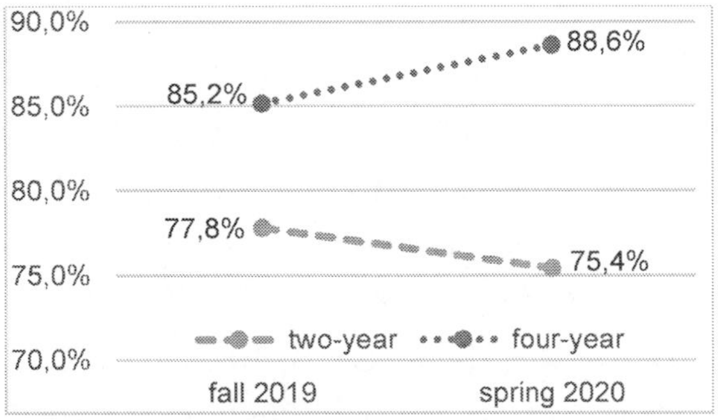

Figure 1. Mean successful course completion rates, by student, two-vs-four year colleges, only those students enrolled both terms

Prior to the pandemic, students were free to opt in or out of online courses and research showed differential rates of online course enrolment by both gender and race/ethnicity, with both women and White students overrepresented online (e.g., Shea & Bidjerano, 2014; Xu & Xu, 2019). Our next analyses assessed how the forced shift to online learning related to these factors. For students at two-year colleges, women had approximately similar rates of successful course completion both terms, whereas men's course outcomes were significantly worse in spring when all courses were forced online ($p < 0.001$). For students at four-year colleges, both genders were more successful in the pandemic spring term than in fall, but there was still a significant interaction, with women's successful course outcomes increasing more during the pandemic spring term than men's ($p < 0.001$). Thus, at both two-and four-year colleges, women's course outcomes were more resilient during the pandemic than men's course outcomes.

Overall differences in course outcomes by race/ethnicity ($p < 0.001$) were also found at both two-and four-year colleges. For students attending two-year colleges, Asian/Pacific Islander students had similar course outcomes in fall and spring, while all other student groups (White, Black, Hispanic and American Indian/Native Alaskan) did worse in the spring pandemic term than the pre-pandemic fall [slope differences were statistically significant ($p < 0.005$)]. In contrast, for students at four-year colleges, all racial/ethnic groups had better outcomes during the spring than in the pre-pandemic fall; however, relative slope patterns were somewhat similar. In one exception, gaps in outcomes between Black or Hispanic vs. White students narrowed slightly during the pandemic spring term.

We explored whether the patterns for gender and race/ethnicity are connected to students' prior online course enrolment, as some research suggests this is a factor (Hachey et al., 2014). Students were classified as "dual-mode" if they had enrolled in at least one online and one face-to-face course in both fall and spring. Students were classified as "traditional-mode" if they enrolled in only face-to-face courses both terms. During the spring pandemic term, even face-to-face courses were forced fully online; we classified students based on their *original* preferred mode(s), to tease out the relationship between their preferences and outcomes. While there were significant increases in the course outcomes gap between men and women during the pandemic term at both types of colleges for traditional-mode students ($p < 0.001$), results indicate no significant interaction between semester and gender for dual-mode students (see Figure 2). Being a dual-mode student seemed to be protective for men during the spring pandemic term, with traditional-mode men at two-year colleges having less resilient outcomes in the pandemic term. There were also significant differences in success rates for traditional-mode students at both two-year and four-year by race/ethnicity by term; these differences tended to be less significant among dual-mode students. The patterns found indicate that conditions during the pandemic term (i.e. forced switch to fully online) correlated with increased success and narrowing of outcome gaps for dual-mode students by race/ethnicity, but a negative impact and widening of the success rate for traditional-mode students by race/ethnicity (see Figure 2).

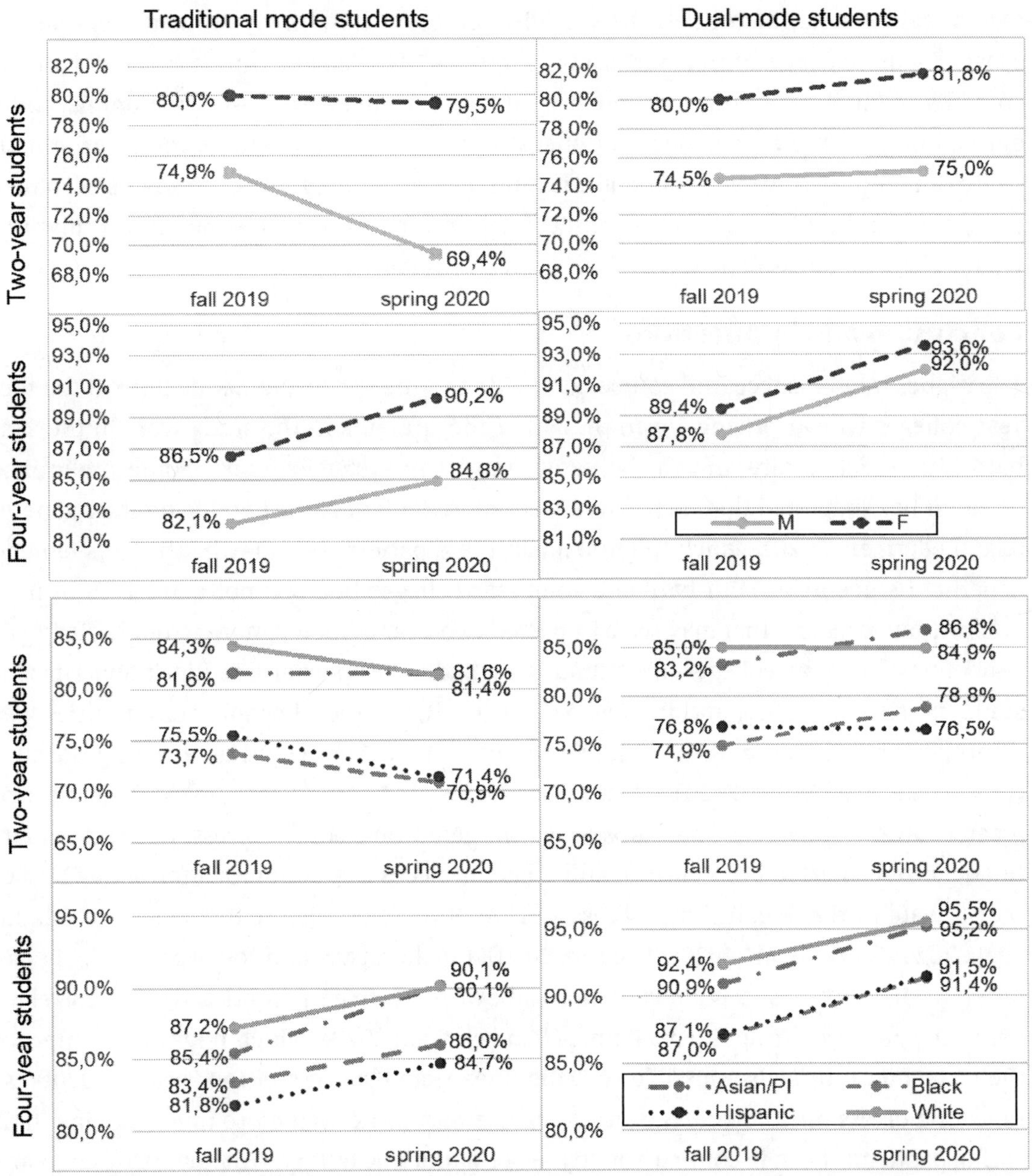

Figure 2. Mean successful course completion, by student, by term, gender or race/ethnicity, and by dual- vs. traditional-mode, at two- vs. four-yr. colleges

Limitations

CUNY students are highly diverse and thus the results of this study are likely generalizable to a wider population; however, caution should be used before extending findings to other groups (e.g., rural campuses). Gender and race/ethnicity were also recorded in a limited way by the CUNY system. During the study time frame, CUNY had only a binary category for gender (male or female). Thus, the gender categories may not fully represent the ways in which students might identify. CUNY also collects race/ethnicity using limited U.S.

federal categories, which likely do not fully represent how many students self-identify, especially those from multiple racial/ethnic groups. We also note that our classification of students as dual vs. traditional mode is an imperfect measure of prior online course enrolment, as this does include traditional students who took an online course prior to the study time frame. However, this classification does accurately reflect student's enrolment preference and online experience immediately prior to the pandemic, and if anything, would likely underestimate rather than overestimate any effects.

Conclusion and Implications

The higher rates of successful course completion in the spring pandemic term at the four-year colleges was surprising, given that all of the students in the study were in the same hard-hit pandemic city and in the same university system context. Some preliminary research has suggested that instructors were more lenient in spring during the pandemic (e.g., Lederman, 2020), which might explain these patterns—it may be that this leniency benefitted students at both two- and four-year colleges but was not enough to override other negative factors that may have impacted two-year students more strongly during the pandemic. Two-year colleges are attended by higher proportions of Black and Hispanic students (NCES, 2020b), and in New York City, Black and Hispanic communities were disproportionately more likely to get sick with and die from COVID-19 during the study (Boston Medical Center, 2020). Recent research also indicates that two-year students faced greater time poverty, an upsurge in environmental stressors (particularly financial/housing/food insecurity), and a lack of necessary conditions for online success (i.e., private workspace, Internet access, devices, etc.) in relation to the pandemic (Manley et al., 2020; Garcia et al., 2020; Osborne, 2020). Further, two- and four-year students have different distributions of characteristics to begin with (e.g., parenthood) that correlated with time poverty during the pandemic (Manley et al., 2020), which might have impacted their outcomes. It is also possible that the unexpected success of four-year students is a reflection of less time poverty (i.e., no commute/less work) and more time studying in the spring pandemic term in comparison to the pre-pandemic fall (St. Amour, 2020), compared to two-year students. Although this research is not causal and there are likely many factors influencing the results, our findings do suggest that the pandemic and the related forced shift to online learning may have worsened educational inequities by institution type already present before the pandemic (Fain, 2020).

The patterns found for gender are unexpected, as research (Heggeness & Fields, 2020) suggests that during the pandemic, women carried the heavier burden of child rearing/home schooling (i.e., higher time poverty); yet it was men (particularly at two-year colleges) who had the worst course outcomes during the spring pandemic term when instruction shifted fully online. This actually reinforces other pre-pandemic research, which shows that women tend to do better than men in college in spite of having more time poverty (Wladis et al., n.d.), and that women are also more likely to enrol in online courses voluntarily, and therefore had on average more experience with them prior to the pandemic (e.g. Johnson & Mejia, 2014), which may have been a factor. This hypothesis is reinforced by patterns observed after disaggregating dual-mode and traditional-mode students, where the interaction between gender and pre-vs-pandemic term was only significant for traditional mode students, and not for dual mode students. Some gaps by racial/ethnic group expanded on average during the pandemic (e.g., Asian/PI vs. Black, White, or Hispanic students); however, this also seemed to be significantly related to whether students were dual-or traditional-mode. Racial/ethnic gaps remained relatively stable and even shrunk in some cases (e.g., Black vs. White at two-year) among dual-mode students, while they tended to increase among traditional mode students. This suggests that students who previously chose to enrol in online courses were more resilient during the pandemic, across racial groups. This introduces questions about exactly which traits, circumstances, or skills distinguished dual- from traditional-mode students, and how this might inform attempts to improve equity in college outcomes among students by institution type, gender, and race/ethnicity, especially as institutions move to offer more fully online courses. It may be important to investigate possible malleable factors of those who self-select into fully online courses, so institutions could work to better support all students succeed online. Further, since many students who self-select into online courses do so out of a need for flexibility in terms of time and space (Jaggars et al., 2013), it may also be that some students who had already opted to enrol online at the start of the semester were better served when all their courses moved fully online during the spring pandemic term—if this were the case, it would suggest that providing these students with more flexibility to take courses fully online in the future, even after the pandemic is over, might be beneficial. Further causal research is necessary to explore this possibility.

References

Bono, G., Reil, K., & Hescox, J. (2020). Stress and wellbeing in college students during the COVID-19 pandemic: Can grit and gratitude help? *International Journal of Wellbeing, 10*(3), 39-57. doi:10.5502/ijw.v10i3.1331

Boston Medical Center (2020, October 27). Black Hispanic individuals hardest hit by COVID-19: Higher death, hospitalization rates compared to non-white Hispanic individuals, variable by race. ScienceDaily [Blog post]. Retrieved from https://www.sciencedaily.com/releases/2020/10/201027111229.htm

Fain, P. (2020, June 17). Higher education and work amid crisis. Inside Higher Ed [Blog post]. Retrieved from https://www. insidehighered.com/news/2020/06/17/pandemic-has-worsened-equity-gaps-higher-education-and-work

Garcia, L. L., Bohling, M., & Adkins, C. (2020, July 10). The early impacts of COVID-19 on the Community College student experience. Diverse Issues in Higher Education [Blog post]. Retrieved from https://diverseeducation.com/article/183750/

Giancola, J., Grawitch, M., & Borchert, D. (2009). Dealing with the stress of college a model for adult students. *Adult Education Quarterly: A Journal of Research and Theory, 59*, 246-263. doi: 10.1177/0741713609331479

Hachey, A. C., Wladis, C. W., & Conway, K. M. (2014). Prior online course experience and G.P.A. as predictors of subsequent online STEM course outcomes. *The Internet and Higher Education, 25*, 11-17. doi:10.1016/j.iheduc.2014.10.003

Heggeness, M. L., & Fields, J. M. (2020, August 18). Working moms bear brunt of home schooling while working during COVID-19. US Census Bureau [Blog post]. https://www.census.gov/library/stories/2020/08/parents-juggle-work-and-child-care-during-pandemic.html

Jaggars, S. S., Edgecombe, N., & West Stacey, G. (2013). *What we know about online course outcomes. Research Review.* Community College Research Center, Columbia University. Retrieved from https://ccrc.tc.columbia.edu/media/k2/attachments/what-we-know-about-online-course-outcomes.pdf

Johnson, H., & Mejia, M. C. (2014). *Online learning and student outcomes in California's community colleges.* Public Policy Institute of California. Retrieved from http://www.ppic.org/content/pubs/report/R_514HJR.pdf

Lederman, D. (2020, April 22). How teaching changed in the (forced) shift to remote learning. Inside Higher Ed [Blog post]. Retrieved from https://www.insidehighered.com/digital-learning/article/2020/04/22/how-professors-changed-their-teaching-springs-shift-remote

Luthar, S. S. (2006). Resilience in Development: A synthesis of research across decades. In D. Cicchetti & D. J. Cohen (Eds.), *Developmental Psychopathology: Risk, disorder and adaptation* (3rd ed.). Wiley.

Manley, C. A., Wladis, C., Hachey, A. C., & Karim, S. (2020). *Deeper Listening: The unexpected relevance of external stressors and time poverty for online students.* Paper presented at the OLC Accelerate Conference, November, Orlando, FL/Virtual.

NCES. (2019). Indicator 23: Postsecondary graduation rates. Retrieved from https://nces.ed.gov/programs/raceindicators/indicator_red.asp

NCES (2020a). Undergraduate retention and graduate rates. Retrieved from https://nces.ed.gov/programs/coe/indicator_ctr.asp

NCES. (2020b). Characteristics of Postsecondary Students. The Condition of Education. Retrieved from https://nces.ed.gov/programs/coe/indicator_csb.asp

Osborne, M. (2020, June 1). 8000+ community college students share their COVID-19 stories. EdNC [Blog post]. Retrieved from https://www.ednc.org/nc-community-college-students-share-covid-19-impact/

Pariat, L., Rynjah, A., Joplin, M., & Kharjana, G. (2014). Stress Levels of College Students: Interrelationship between Stressors and Coping Strategies. *Journal of Humanities and Social Science, 19*(8), 40-46. doi:10.9790/0837-19834046

Shea, P., & Bidjerano, T. (2014). Does online learning impede degree completion? A national study of community college students. *Computers & Education, 75*, 103-111. http://dx.doi.org/10.1016/j.compedu.2014.02.009

San Román-Mata, S., Zurita-Ortega, F., Puertas-Molero, P., Baducu, G., & González-Valero, G. (2020). A predictive study of resilience and its relationship with academic and work dimensions during the COVID-19 Pandemic. *Journal of Clinical Medicine, 9*(10), 3258. doi:10.3390/jcm9103258

St. Amour, M. (2020, June 23). Report: COVID-19 has hurt college students. Inside Higher Ed (Blog post]. Retrieved from https://www.insidehighered.com/quicktakes/2020/06/23/report-covid-19-has-hurt-college-students

Wladis, C., Hachey, A. C., & Conway, K. M. (n.d.). *It's about time: The inequitable distribution of time as a resource for college, by gender and race/ethnicity.*

Wladis, C., Hachey, A. C., & Conway, K. M. (2018). No time for college? An investigation of time poverty and parenthood. *Journal of Higher Education, 89*(6), 807-831. doi:10.1080/00221546.2018.1442983

Xu, D. & Xu, Y. (2019). *The promise and limits of online higher education: Understanding how distance education affects access, cost and quality. American Enterprise Institute.* Retrieved from https://tacc.org/sites/default/files/documents/2019-03/the-promises-and-limits-of-online-higher-education.pdf

Lessons from a Pandemic for the Future of Education
European Distance and E-Learning Network (EDEN) Proceedings
2021 Annual Conference | Madrid, 21-24 June, 2021
ISSN 2707-2819
doi: 10.38069/edenconf-2021-ac0031

OPEN ONLINE COURSES AND THE DEMOCRATIZATION OF KNOWLEDGE FOR VULNERABLE GROUPS

Elena Barcena, Timothy Read, Monica Vilhelm, Universidad Nacional de Educación a Distancia (UNED), Spain

Abstract

This article builds on a body of literature (e.g., Daniel, 2012; Portmess, 2013; O'Mahony & Salmon, 2014) where the potential of MOOCs for the democratization of knowledge has been claimed. The authors highlight four key characteristics that have been seen to be essential in the design, development and deployment of open online courses for vulnerable groups, in order to maximise student participation, interaction, and learning in such educational scenarios. These characteristics are instructional design for social inclusion, three degrees of accessibility, inclusive language, and Activeness. They will be analysed from a practical and experiential perspective in the context of a Language MOOC (massive open online course) developed by the authors' research group, although they are relevant for any other type of open online course. They will be argued to facilitate any future access to information in general, once the course has finished, and as such, represent a catalyst for the democratization of knowledge.

Introduction

The promise of online courses as a way to offer education to people left behind from formal institutional studies has been highlighted in the literature for almost as long as such courses have existed (Fisher, 2018). With the increase of forced migration and displacement, social exclusion, and now the pandemic, more and more people can be seen to belong to so called *vulnerable groups*, requiring such education. Daniel (2012) established a logical link between open education and the idea of the "democratization of knowledge", that is, the possibility to widen and diversify access to higher education that can lead to useful certification and facilitate personal choice and planning. Similar arguments have been presented by other authors such as Portmess (2013) and O'Mahony and Salmon (2014).

While many initiatives have been undertaken to promote open online courses for vulnerable groups, these efforts have not led to a wider uptake of these courses by the student population who could most benefit from them (Read, Sedano, & Barcena, 2018). Given their diversity, evident from their personal circumstances and individual learning needs, care is required when referring to them collectively as members of any single vulnerable group. While this is inevitably true, experience shows that specifically scaffolded open educational solutions can be targeted at such groups, since even if not all of the members benefit from all aspects of the scaffolding, most will benefit from some of them.

In this article the authors highlight four key characteristics that have been seen to be essential in the design, development and deployment of open online courses for vulnerable groups, in order to maximise student participation, interaction, and learning in such educational scenarios. These characteristics are instructional design for social inclusion, three degrees of accessibility, inclusive language, and Activeness. They will be analysed from a practical and experiential perspective in the context of a Language MOOC (massive open online course; henceforth, LMOOC) developed by the authors' research group, although they are relevant for any other type of open online course. They will be argued to facilitate any future access to information in general, once the course has finished, and as such, represent a catalyst for the democratization of knowledge.

Instructional design for social inclusion

When considering the pedagogic structure of online language learning scenarios prepared for vulnerable groups, what needs to be understood, is that regardless of personal differences and difficulties, the amount of exposure to the object of study and the availability of authentic materials, in a conveniently integrated study environment, will always potentiate learning. More importantly, like any other form of learning, language learning should take place under conditions that are as close as possible to real life usage. The reality is that a considerable part of daily communication these days takes place through a technological device (be it a desktop computer or a smartphone). Using this device for learning, therefore, represents a continuation of behaviour and reflects the way that newly learned language competences would be used ordinarily.

Where the instructional design process differs from that of generic LMOOCs, is that the language needs of vulnerable groups cannot generally be met by standard educational resources. Such students are not typically interested in learning, for example, how to describe people in detail in the new language (different types of hair, complexions, etc.) or undertaking small talk. They have well defined purposes for wanting to learn the language: e.g., survival in a new community (often culturally distant, sometimes reluctant to welcome them), social integration, access to the labour market or to formal education, defending their rights. Furthermore, experience has shown that students from such groups have restrictions and reservations about how and where they are prepared to study, that must be taken into account when designing any course for them.

The work undertaken by the authors' research group builds on previous explorations of the adequacy of general MOOCs for inclusion (e.g., de Waard et al., 2014; Read, Sedano, & Barcena, 2018). Instructional design features have been proposed for inclusive LMOOCs and the inherent learner-centred learning approach at the core of the field of Languages for Specific Purposes has been closely followed. The LMOOC being used here as the object of study was designed and developed for displaced people (as an example of members of a vulnerable group) and came to be called Open Doors (part 1 and 2). It is still available at UNED's MOOC platform.

The instructional design process started with a needs analysis. The data was collected from questionnaires, interviews and face-to-face work sessions with teachers, refugees and migrants from NGOs and support associations. Although one of the first things identified was that displaced people were not homogeneous as a group, this needs analysis proved to be useful in finding out which languages they had in common, what digital skills and experience they had (the technological devices they used, what they used them for, and whether they had an Internet connection), and what level of support they would require in an online course.

The analysis of the data collected confirmed in the first place that, despite their heterogeneous profile, the main need of displaced people is to learn the language of their host country for social inclusion and employment. The languages this student population had in common were English, French and Arabic. They mostly had mobile phones as their only technological device, did not always have stable access to Internet, and had a low level of digital literacy. They used the phones for social contact and had no experience of computer assisted learning. As for the level of support needed, they belonged to old educational traditions and showed signs of emotional trauma. Therefore, several workshops were run to explain what LMOOCs were and to jointly identify what their most urgent learning need was: Spanish for beginners (from A1 to A2).

The design, structure and main contents of the course were developed in a workshop based on Design Thinking, a modality first proposed in the literature by Dorst (2011). This is an iterative hands-on method in which the participants attempt to solve a given problem collaboratively whose solution might not be immediately obvious upon first inspection. During this brainstorming session, the question: "What do you need Spanish for?" was raised. A group of refugees took turns to fill up a board with post-its which contained ideas expressed telegraphically. They could be general or specific. The monitor of the session then coordinated the gathering of the post-its in conceptual clouds and this is how everyone present came up with a structure made up of eight situational modules for two MOOCs and some of the main contents therein.

Each LMOOC consisted of four independent situation-specific modules and was designed to be undertaken over a period of six weeks. In each course, the first week was designed for students to introduce themselves and become familiar with the MOOC platform. Four weeks were then dedicated to the learning content, and the last week, to complete any unfinished activities. Each LMOOC required an average of 25 study hours (and was accredited with 1 ECTS upon successful completion).

The materials subsequently developed were presented to a group of refugee students who collaborated with the project and we worked on a number of versions as usual. That is how dialogues were created, which served as the basis for the course activities. Once finished, the teachers and the refugees recorded all the dialogues in UNED's TV studio. In retrospect, this was one the strongest points of the project since the texts that had been produced aligned with the real communicative needs and concerns of the future course participants.

Any democratization of knowledge requires the target community to possess the relevant language skills. Therefore, any open online course that has been developed using a relevant instructional design, in this case for those students who are typically left behind standard education, can be seen as an important step toward this goal.

The three degrees of accessibility

Accessibility is typically used in the academic literature, with regard to online information, to refer to the presentation of information so that everyone, including people with disabilities, can access it. In this work the concept is extended and sub-divided into three types, namely *technological accessibility* (that follows the standard use), *pedagogic accessibility* and *linguistic accessibility*.

Firstly, technological accessibility was achieved by the preparation of the course content and activities for mobile deployment, as a lower common denominator, since the needs analysis had identified that fact that most of the potential students owned a device of this type and intended to use it to follow the course. Furthermore, most materials (including vocabulary, grammar tables, and activities) were also downloadable for those who did not have a permanent Internet connection, so that they could work offline.

Secondly, pedagogic accessibility, is used here to refer to the socio-cultural specifics present in pedagogic approaches that might prove to be a barrier for students from other cultures.

In Western countries as well as belonging to a social culture we also belong to a technological culture and, of course, a learning culture. People share much more in terms on how we process and deliver information than they are probably aware of. This implicit relation must be considered when offering a course to non-Europeans (the principal part of the Open Doors student population). This is why ten very brief guides with supporting videos were written to scaffold the courses (about how to enrol in the course, how to undertake a test, how to watch a video, etc.).

Thirdly and finally, linguistic accessibility, refers to difficulties present in the target language that need to be scaffolded for learners to help them acquire sufficient skills and knowledge to be able to progress in an unhindered manner. Considerable effort was put into preparing bimodal information and materials. Most contents were both textual and audio-visual. Videos had subtitles in Spanish, and transcripts in English, French, and Arabic. Texts in Spanish had translations to support beginners and false beginners. It should be noted that subtitles and translations were undertaken by volunteer students and then revised by the teachers.

Apart from course design and implementation, delivery is key in the success of any course. In order to reinforce the inclusion aspect of the course, facilitation was undertaken by teachers from the support groups plus a few advanced students. Specific instructions on forum management before the courses started were provided. Furthermore, facilitators were requested to go through the whole course as students to become familiar with it.

Given that facilitators were mostly Spanish nationals, the contact that the refugees and migrants participating in the courses had with them in the forums represents a form of implicit social inclusion, since they were actually mixing with people from the country in which they wanted to integrate, which enabled them, to some degree, to experience how the nationals behave in interpersonal communication.

Returning to the democratization of knowledge, the authors argue that scaffolding learning in terms of the three types of accessibility highlighted here, lays the foundation for a skill set that vulnerable students can use to progress in the future, processing facts and information as needed.

Inclusive language

A crucial role that language plays in any human interaction, particularly in online environments where there are no visual clues, is that of integration. Language is key to the creation of emotional tone and in defining a social atmosphere. As Foolen (2015) argued, there is a clear and direct relation between emotion and language. Its effect in learning has been studied since Brown (1991) noted how a combination of empathy, extroversion and assertion may facilitate the merging of cognition and affect, and hence enhance the success of the learning process.

As argued by Barcena, Read, and Sedano (2020), Appraisal Theory offers an appropriate framework that can be extended for modelling inclusive language for use in online courses. These authors identified a set of thirty-three linguistic resources for use in forums and course materials with a potential impact both on group inclusion and positive individual discrimination, based on this Theory. The resources have been grouped around a complex axis: elements for favouring social inclusion or avoiding exclusion, elements for positive or negative individual discrimination, and elements related to Attitude (positive and negative assessments, defined in terms of affect, judgement and appreciation), Engagement (the linguistic phenomena by which authors construe their point of view and the resources used to adopt stances towards other authors' perspectives) and Graduation (force and semantic focus, by which speakers raise or lower the interpersonal impact, intensity or volume of the evaluation), as identified in Appraisal Theory.

There were two type of linguistic elements promoted during the courses, those aimed at promoting a feeling of inclusion / avoiding exclusion, and those aimed at avoiding prejudices, stereotypes and discrimination. Each was structured at different linguistic levels. The former contemplated the phonological level (e.g., marking the use of prosodic patterns, avoiding dialectic varieties), the semantic-discourse level (e.g., use of empathic language, appropriateness in the level of formality), grammatical level (e.g., avoid the use of gender-marked words, use of non-assertive language), and the pragmatic level (e.g., empowering language to the interlocutors and their performance, awareness of culture-driven language). The latter contemplated the semantic level (e.g., no stereotypes were used of origin or gender in professions, no distinctions were made of beliefs, political opinion, social and economic background, race and ethnicity, age, disability, gender, sexual preferences), grammatical level (e.g., by compensation), discourse level (e.g., avoiding the use of patronising and sexist language, no excessive use of emotional language).

The inclusive language not only played a pedagogic role but also supported the students emotionally. This was shown when they talked negatively about aspects of their home countries and other potentially delicate subjects (such as war and terrorism), which received no follow on either from their peers, facilitators or themselves in subsequent messages. Although difficult to prove categorically, there was considerable evidence that facilitators' inclusive language use had an impact on the participants' discourse because more features like these were observed as the course went by.

Once again, when considering the democratization of knowledge, the authors argue that most information is online, so having experienced inclusive language in online courses potentiates students' elicitation strategies when interacting with others in the future. As such they are better able to access knowledge and be able to use it in a more focussed and productive manner.

Activeness

Regardless of how an online course is structured, made accessible (in the three ways highlighted previously), and supported by inclusive language, there is still a missing element for student engagement, namely their adoption of "Activeness" (Read & Barcena, 2021). The authors there define it as "a dynamic psychological and cognitive state where vulnerable students start to exercise control of their learning and progress based on their needs and desired outcomes".

Activeness is a driving force or state for engaged (language) learning and empowerment in the virtual community. It is defined by Read and Barcena (2021) in terms of investment (as a step beyond motivation in capturing the complex relationship of learners to their desire to use what is being learnt), integration (the reciprocal relation with the learning community. This is a form of *integration*, not so much with the educational goals or contexts, but with the people who are actually participating in the learning process,) and performance (something that converts intention into effective action). In this state, vulnerable learners start to exercise control of existence and progress based on their needs and desired outcomes. They draw upon metacognitive processes such as self-regulation and self-efficacy to overtake the inertia of inactivity (often an enforced norm for refugees) and engage with their language learning activities.

The results of potentiating Activeness in the LMOOC were evident. Even though no quantitative analysis was undertaken of the correlation between the percentages of the activities undertaken, forum participation and correct performance in evaluation, and the evidential features of Activeness. However, the facilitators reported that the most salient students (that is, those not necessarily with a high starting level of Spanish), showed evidence of activeness, in terms of the way they followed the proposed schedule, participated in the forums, finished the majority of the course activities at the end of the first five weeks (without needing the final catch-up week), passed the final test and were able to receive the final certification.

Furthermore, other quantitative factors also suggested a positive effect of Activeness on student performance. Firstly, the high degree of interaction in the forum and the number of messages that went beyond single question-answer interactions. Secondly, the number of students who finished the course. MOOCs are known for having high levels of abandonment; typically, figures are around 90% of enrolled students. In this course, more than 700 students finished the first LMOOC, representing a completion rate of over 30%, well above average. Thirdly, the number of messages in the forums, which dropped slightly but did not fall off massively, as is usually the case in MOOCs. While there may be other reasons for these numbers, the students consistently demonstrated throughout the course, and subsequently in the post-questionnaire, their high level of satisfaction overall. As well as the quality of the content and structure of the course, this was arguably thanks to the inclusive language used for communication. Finally, even though it is difficult to prove without a proper evaluation process, there were signs that there was significant progress on the part of those students that accomplished the courses and contributed most actively to the course activities and the forums.

Activeness is quite possibly one of the most important characteristics of student behaviour in the democratization of knowledge. It underpins the psychological tools that they must adopt and apply to overcome the inertia of inactivity and the proactivity required to overcome barriers to accessing and processing information in an effective way.

Discussion and conclusion

This article started by introducing four characteristics (instructional design for social inclusion, degrees of accessibility, inclusive language, and Activeness) the authors believe are key to potentiating open online courses and making them more effective for vulnerable groups as a catalyst for democratizing knowledge.

Participating in a strategically designed and scaffolded LMOOC that promotes both inclusion and activeness serves the triple purpose of enabling more effective target language learning and empowering vulnerable learners to reach their developmental potential to become engaged members of the language learning community, arguably as an important step towards doing the same in the real world. While the example presented in this article is that of a language learning course the characteristics can be included in any open online course, whether intended to be massively followed by students, or not.

Democratizing knowledge via online learning was in the mind of many early MOOC (and before that, other types of open online courses) developers. However, up until now, this has not been the case. Socially inclusive instructional design, degrees of accessibility, inclusive language, and Activeness are argued here to effectively open up LMOOCs for wider, disadvantaged and vulnerable social groups, like refugees and migrants. They also lay the foundation for online learning and the development of a set of skills, which not only enhances target language knowledge and communication, but also increases social inclusion and provide opportunities for a richer and better society.

References

Barcena, E., Read, T., & Sedano, B. (2020). An Approximation to Inclusive Language in LMOOCs Based on Appraisal Theory. *Open Linguistics, 6*(1), 38-67.

Brown, H. D. (1991). Affective variables in second language learning. *Language Learning 23*(2), 231-244.

Daniel, J. (2012). Making sense of MOOCs: Musings in a Maze of Myth, Paradox and Possibility. *Journal of Interactive Media in Education, 3*, 1-20. Retrieved from https://jime.open.ac.uk/articles/10.5334/2012-18/

Dorst, K. (2011). The core of 'design thinking' and its application. *Design Studies, 32*(6), 521-532.

Fischer, G. (2018). Massive open online courses (MOOCs) and rich landscapes of learning: A learning sciences perspective. In F. Fischer, C. E. Hmelo-Silver, S. R. Goldman, & P. Reimann (Eds.), *International Handbook of the Learning Sciences* (pp. 368-379). Routledge/Taylor Francis.

Foolen, A. (2015). Word valence and its effects. In U. M. Lüdtke (Ed.), *Emotion in language: Theory – research – application* (pp. 241-255). John Benjamins Publishing Company. https://doi.org/10.1075/ceb.10.12foo

O'Mahony, B., & Salmon, G. (2014). The role of Massive Open Online Courses (MOOCs) in the democratization of tourism and hospitality in education. In D. Dredge, D. Airey & M. J. Gross (Eds.), The Routledge Handbook of Tourism and Hospitality in Education (pp. 130-142). London: Routledge.

Portmess, L. (2013). Mobile Knowledge, Karma Points and Digital Peers: The Tacit Epistemology and Linguistic Representation of MOOCs / Savoir mobile, points de karma et pairs numériques : l'épistémologie tacite et la représentation linguistique des MOOC. *Canadian Journal of Learning and Technology / La revue canadienne de l'apprentissage et de la technologie, 39*(2). Canadian Network for Innovation in Education. Retrieved from https://www.learntechlib.org/p/178065/.

Read, T., & Barcena, E. (2021). The role of activeness for potentiating learning in LMOOCs for vulnerable groups. *Journal of Interactive Media in Education, In press.*

Read, T., Sedano, B., & Barcena, E. (2018). Tailoring Language MOOC design for migrants and refugees. *Technological Innovation for Specialized Linguistic Domains: Languages for Digital Lives and Cultures Proceedings of TISLID, 18*, 383-396.

de Waard, I., Gallagher, M. S., Zelezny-Green, R., Czerniewicz, L., Downes, S., Kukulska-Hulme, A., & Willems, J. (2014). Challenges for conceptualising EU MOOC for vulnerable learner groups. *Proceedings of the European MOOC Stakeholder Summit 2014*, 33-42.

Lessons from a Pandemic for the Future of Education
European Distance and E-Learning Network (EDEN) Proceedings
2021 Annual Conference | Madrid, 21-24 June, 2021
ISSN 2707-2819
doi: 10.38069/edenconf-2021-ac0032

SERVICE LEARNING FOR ENHANCING STUDENT CIVIC ENGAGEMENT

Ana Skledar Matijević, Teresa Tomašević, Institute for the Development of Education, Croatia, Lasse Lindhagen, Malmö University, Sweden

Abstract

The NEXUS project focuses on cultural diversity and migration within higher education institutions (HEIs), and enhancing student civic engagement by integrating Service Learning elements into second language courses, i.e. teaching the language of the receiving country.

Service Learning as an educational method and as an integral activity of community engagement is crucial for the NEXUS project because it explicitly promotes cooperation between the academic community and the civil sector, putting the students and community engagement at the core of the learning experience. It also contributes to the achievement of the third mission of the university, which directly facilitates the development of the social responsibility of students and other members of the academic community in solving specific societal problems.

A Service Learning idea developed through NEXUS is based on second language courses which contain elements of culture and society of the receiving country and therefore lend themselves to including civic education and civic engagement elements for empowering students in the syllabus.

Introduction

The NEXUS project is an ERASMUS+ project, running from 2019 to 2022, focused on empowering students (especially migrants) to exercise their rights, uphold human values, and contribute constructively to the society around them and the global community in general (promoting the nexus of migrants through active citizenship; nº ref.: 2019-1-ES01-KA203-065861; https://nexus4civics.eu).

In representative and participatory democracies, it is crucial that citizens are engaged in order to be an active part of society (Motti-Stefanidi et al., 2018). However, the 2013 Eurobarometer statistics show that young people in the EU are losing trust in EU-institutions, are becoming less interested in voting because of the feeling that their votes will make no difference and that they are unaware of the democratic processes within the EU (EACEA, 2013). Other studies show that young people are somewhat more engaged in non-governmental organizations than in traditional political parties and that they are using more digital tools, such as social media, when they interact and engage (Motti-Stefanidi et al., 2018). Even if there are significant differences among countries, the trend is still clear that young people are becoming increasingly detached and that there is a need for enhanced engagement among young people in the EU. Newly arrived migrants are especially vulnerable to feeling detachment since they generally risk lacking social identity, sense of belonging and social engagement (Mansouri & Kirpitchenko, 2016)

Therefore, NEXUS aims at innovating the civic educational process resulting in increased participation of students in their communities.

This paper describes the service learning landscape in the context of enhancing civic engagement and the development of a service learning course scenario which will help convert students with migrant backgrounds from objects into the subjects of service learning.

The Contemporary Concept of Service Learning – The Civic Aspect

There are many definitions of service learning since the concept has evolved over time and since there are numerous ways in which it can be implemented in different contexts. A contemporary concept of service learning is reflected by the European Association for Service Learning in Higher Education (EASLHE), which defines service-learning as "an educational approach that enhances students' civic engagement, brings them closer to different social realities while allowing them to work in a real environment. It involves structured and graded student placements in organisations in response to the needs of the community and is different from volunteering because it is part of mandatory coursework" (EASLHE, 2021). This definition of service learning includes all the key elements of contemporary service learning.

The civic aspect of service learning has been explored from the 2000s on. According to Saltmarsh (2005), higher education should include "civic learning" and students should be equipped with "the knowledge, skills, and values necessary to participate as engaged, democratic citizens" (Saltmarsh, 2005) in order to successfully participate in the democratic processes.

According to Bringle et al. (2012) civic engagement refers to "teaching, research, and/or service that is both in and with the community [...] and includes service learning and participatory action research". Instead of student placements common in service learning, partnerships with actors from the community are encouraged which include a "mutually-beneficial collaboration, in which all persons contribute knowledge, skills, and experience in determining the issues to be addressed, the questions to be asked, the problems to be resolved, the strategies to be used, the outcomes that are considered desirable, and the indicators of success" (Bringle et al., 2012). Such an approach ensures further development of higher education institution's civic engagement and public service.

Zlotowski stresses the importance of a "coordinated partnership between the campus and the community, with the instructor tailoring the service experience to the educational agenda and community representatives ensuring that the students' community service is consistent with their goals" (Zlotkowski, 1995). Zlotowski also believes that the following three points are crucial for successful implementation of service learning: "1. integrating service-learning programs into the central mission and goals of the schools and agencies where they are based; 2. establishing a balance of power between educational and community partners; 3. wedding reflection to experience." (Zlotowski, 1995).

This is in line with the goals of service learning defined by Bringle et al. (2004), which include "(a) benefit to community stakeholders (e.g., agency, clients, neighbourhood 4 residents) and (b) academic learning outcomes" (Bringle et al., 2004). They emphasise the importance of combining theory and practice in order to achieve the goals of socially responsive knowledge according to Altman: "(1) to educate students in the problems of society; (2) to let them experience and understand first-hand social issues in their community; and, most important, (3) give students the experiences and skills to act on social problems. (Altman, 1996, pp. 375-376)." (Bringle et al., 2004).

Service Learning Diagram

According to the Fresno State University, service learning can be presented by the diagram below, which shows the position of service learning at the overlap of academic learning, practical experience and civic engagement, student practice, student volunteering and civic education.

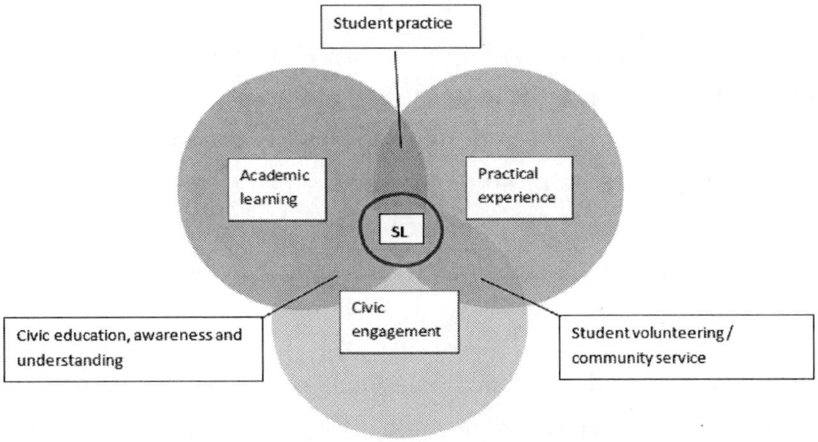

Figure 1. Service Learning Diagram
(source: http://www.fresnostate.edu/csm/arc/service-learning.html)

Principles of service learning

According to Bringle and Hatcher, (1999) "well-designed reflection activities should (a) intentionally link the service experience to course-based learning objectives, (b) be structured, (c) occur regularly, (d) allow feedback and assessment, and (e) include the clarification of values", whereas Begić et al. (2019) emphasise that for a service learning programme to be successful, three principles should observed:

- Reality: student engagement should be based on real, identified and previously researched problems, challenges and needs of a community.
- Reciprocity: all the parties involved should benefit from the exchange of knowledge – the students, the teachers/higher education institution and the community.
- Reflection: a revision of the connection between engagement and educational content must be ensured

Students become equal stakeholders in the learning and teaching process and are focused on proactive and critical thinking. Simultaneously, they become involved in social, community and business processes because they are collaborating with organizations outside the education system which can ultimately provide them with various contacts or their first employment. This is in line with the principles of the Bologna process because it responds to the problem of acquiring theoretical knowledge without practical experience that corresponds to specific social problems (EACEA, 2020) and correspond to the first two stages of Kolb's four stage learning cycle, i.e. concrete experience and reflective observation (Kolb, 2014) .

Service Learning Stakeholders

There are three key stakeholders in a service learning programme: the students, the higher education institution (represented by the teacher) and the external partner. Their roles need to be carefully assigned and managed. The higher education institution should define the learning outcomes, prepare the syllabus, monitor the quality of the process, implement assessment procedures and encourage critical thinking. The external partners should participate in the planning process and monitor, mentor and evaluate the students' progress, and give feedback. The students should actively participate in the defined activities, communicate regularly with other team members, the teacher and the external partner and participate in the reflection activities after their placement has completed.

According to Begić et al. (2019), the benefits are clear for all the stakeholders. The students gain a better understanding of theoretical knowledge in a realistic context by dealing with authentic societal problems. They also develop critical thinking and creativity. The higher education institution develops innovative teaching methods, raises awareness of the impact and the application of academic knowledge in the community and creates a positive image, while the external partners gain a possibility to solve problems in the community through the exchange of (academic) knowledge and a possibility to receive and give new knowledge, information and perspectives.

Using Service Learning to Enhance Civic Engagement

Service learning fits well into the third mission of higher education institutions. The third mission can be described as the development of activities that will link a higher education institution to its surrounding environment. According to Farnell (2020), there is a long tradition of universities' interaction with their communities, and "the benefits of higher education are not limited to students and graduates but extend across society" (Farnell, 2020). By becoming increasingly involved and connecting their activities to both the problems and needs of their communities, higher education institutions can become significant stakeholders in contributing to economic, cultural and societal growth. While the umbrella term *community engagement* is used to "refer to engagement with a broad range of external stakeholders on a broad range of issues" (Farnell, 2020), 'civic engagement' implies "a focus on promoting active citizenship and democratic values" (Farnell, 2020), and this is the aspect that the NEXUS project is focused on.

Students on their part require quality and purposeful study programmes in line with both the labour market trends and current social trends. At the same time, the teaching process requires the introduction of new, innovative and inclusive methods of working, teaching and learning, those that involve the integration of local, regional and global problems in the curriculum. In a broader perspective, it is necessary to ensure a strong connection, i.e. cooperation, collaboration and knowledge exchange between higher education institutions and local communities, as well as a joint response to challenges.

However, even if community engagement is becoming more visible in various forms of visionary strategic documents it is still at an early, peripheral phase in many European higher education institutions, and the central challenge is in placing it at the heart of higher education institutions' DNA. Service Learning, which essentially is community-based learning, can be a possible way for higher education institutions to work better with the local communities to meet their societal needs and harness the power of higher education institutions' diverse knowledge bases to drive a sustainable and inclusive Europe. Higher education institutions' capacity for community engagement can be reinforced by embedding Service Learning into the curriculum and syllabus design so it can be assessed within the course structure. In doing so, students will both gain awareness of different types of societal needs and get first-hand experience of engaging in the community and addressing these needs. This will also help higher education institutions to reach their full potential as valuable actors in their local communities, not only for students and staff but also for those needing change to those not directly involved in teaching or research.

Defining and Reaching the Target Group

The purpose of NEXUS is to primarily reach newly arrived migrant students and promote their civic engagement. However, since migrant students are not a homogeneous group within higher education institutions, but rather they are dispersed through various study programmes at different levels and follow different study paths it was concluded that the receiving country's language courses which higher education institutions offer for newly arrived foreign students are courses with a high probability of migrant students' participation. In order to reach this group within higher education institutions, Service Learning modules connected to second language learning courses offered at higher education institutions are recommended because by addressing these types of courses it is possible to specifically reach students who are new to the receiving country and who will benefit from taking part in a Service Learning module. Regardless of how long these students are planning to remain in the receiving country, the Service Learning experience will build a sense of how the receiving community is organised and how civic engagement contributes to solving societal challenges.

A Service Learning Course Idea

Even though there are numerous examples of good practice regarding Service Learning projects which involve migrants and/or persons with a migration-related background, most of them involve them as objects, i.e. as the end users - the ones who are receiving the students' help and/or benefiting from the students' service learning activities. The NEXUS project aims to make the students with a migration-related background/newly arrived students the subjects in Service Learning projects, i.e. aims to include them in Service

Learning projects as active participants – the ones who implement community service activities in order to achieve the learning outcomes of the courses and at the same time become actively involved in the community and hence increase their level of civic engagement.

A Service Learning idea developed through NEXUS is based on second language courses, as they usually contain elements of culture and society of the country/countries where the languages are spoken so such courses will lend themselves to Service Learning initiatives. Higher education institutions throughout the EU offer second language courses from beginners' level to a high level of proficiency in the target language, levels A1–C2 in the Common European Framework of Reference for Languages (CEFR). The NEXUS project gathered 62 examples of similar courses from Spain, Sweden, Slovenia, Belgium, Italy and Croatia through desk research. Roughly 40% of these course contain explicit contents of culture and/or society.

Target groups for the courses vary, but to a high extent, the courses are aimed at foreign students already enrolled at the higher education institution in question, such as exchange students and international students, so called free movers. Apart from a language proficiency of different levels and language skills, many of the courses have an explicit learning outcome of knowledge of the national culture and/or society. The purpose of including this element in the course may be a method and means to get a wider understanding of the target language, or an outspoken aim to enhance the students' awareness of cultural and societal mechanisms in their new society. An example of the latter is Malmö University's course package aimed at international students, Swedish Language, Culture and Society I–IV (Centre for Teaching and Learning: Education). These courses teach and assess culture and society in English to ensure content on an academic level. This would not be possible in the target language. When connecting these learning outcomes to service learning pedagogy students will gain first-hand experience of working with societal challenges and higher education institutions will increase their presence as stakeholders in the community. We find that it is vital to connect Service Learning to the learning outcomes surrounding culture and society because this will guarantee that the service learning experience remains focused on and directed towards experiencing and working for the development of community engagement.

Choosing the appropriate external partners, i.e. organisations from the community which will provide the students with the opportunity to interact with the community through community service activities is crucial. The external partners are responsible for the first step of implementing a service learning course – defining the problems and social needs in the community. The second step, structuring and organising the community service activities the students will participate in, is done jointly by the higher education institution (the teacher in charge of the course) and the external partners. After the students complete their placement, the external partner organisations give their feedback, which is necessary for the third step of the service learning course—reflection.

For the purpose of this project idea – creating an SL course with the aim to enhance newly arrived students' civic engagement in the local society – the project has chosen to work with courses designed with the explicit learning outcome of an understanding/knowledge/proficiency of the local culture and society, like the one described above. It is also suggested that the choice of external partners includes local organisations engaged in promoting human and civil rights and dealing with other current societal issues of the receiving country, since such an environment will enable students to gain a better understanding of the society and culture and the pressing issues.

Challenges Arising from COVID-19

COVID-19 has imposed a new delivery mode on education in general, by suddenly moving all teaching and learning online. While the preparation part of a Service Learning project in which the students receive instructions from the teacher and the final reflection part in which the student reflect on their community service activities, and even assessment and grading can easily be transferred to an online learning environment, the community service part – the essential part of a Service Learning project – can be adapted, however there are challenges, both technological and conceptual, since community service activities are mostly tasks that are completed on site and depend on interaction with the community. Such in-person interaction, however, has been made difficult by the social distancing rules. This can affect the social component of Service Learning by reducing the opportunities for developing social skills in a traditional way. Online interactions can only partly substitute the in-person interaction and some service learning projects had to be discontinued (comp. EOSLHE). However, there are also examples of successful transition to online activities.

Conclusion

Using Service-Learning as a pedagogical tool in language learning courses in higher education is not a new concept. However, such courses come with the aim to develop the students' language proficiency. The novelty of this suggested course outline is that the academic content for the students to develop in practice – as well as the takeaway for the receiving organization –would be within the field of culture and society. This means that the language course has more the role of a vessel for the Service-Learning outcome in a way that the project has not been able to find elsewhere.

References

Begić, J., Berbić, K., Brajković, L., Matanović, D., Mileusnić, M., Paraga, S., . . . & Zec, K. (2019). *From idea to change: A guide for starting a service-learning program.* Zagreb: Institute for the development of education.

Bringle, R. G., & Hatcher, J. A. (1999). Reflection in Service Learning: Making Meaning or Experience. *Evaluation/Reflection, 23*, 179-185. Retrieved from https://digitalcommons.unomaha.edu/slceeval/23

Bringle, R., Clayton, P., & Price, M. (2012). Partnerships in service learning and civic engagement. *A Journal of Service-Learning and Civic Engagement, 1*(1), 1-20.

Bringle, R., Phillips, M., & Hudson, M. (2004). *The measure of service learning.* Washingtpn, D.C.: American Psychological Association.

Malmö University (n.d.). Centre for Teaching and Learning. Retrieved May 13, 2021, from https://mau.se/en/about-us/faculties-and-departments/faculty-of-education-and-society/the-centre-for-teaching-and-learning/

EACEA. (2013). *Youth Participation in Democratic Life.* Retrieved from https://ec.europa.eu/assets/eac/youth/policy/youth_strategy/documents/youth-participation-study_en.pdf

EASLHE. (n.d.). European Association of Service Learning in Higher Education. Retrieved from https://www.eoslhe.eu/easlhe/

EOSLHE. (n.d.). European Observatory of Service-Learning in Higher Education. Retrieved from https://www.eoslhe.eu/

Farnell, T. (2020). *Community engagement in higher education: trends, practices and policies.* Luxembourg: European Union. Retrieved from https://nesetweb.eu/wp-content/uploads/2020/07/NESET_AR1-2020_analytical-report.pdf

Kolb, D. A. (2014). *Experiential learning: Experience as the source of learning and development.* FT Press.

Mansouri, F., & Kirpitchenko, L. (2016). Practices of active citizenship among migrant youth: beyond conventionalities. *Social Identities, 22*(3), 307-323.

Motti-Stefanidi, F., Pavlopoulos, V., & Asendorpf, J. (2018). Immigrant youth acculturation and perceived discrimination: Longitudinal mediation by immigrant peers" acceptance/rejection. *Journal of Applied Developmental Psychology, 59*, 36-45. Retrieved from https://www.sciencedirect.com/science/article/pii/S019339731730271X

Saltmarsh, J. (2005). The civic promise of service learning. Liberal education. *Liberal Education, 91*(2), 50-55.

Zlotkowski, E. (1995). Does service-learning have a future? *Michigan Journal of Community Service Learning, 2*(1), 123-133

Lessons from a Pandemic for the Future of Education
European Distance and E-Learning Network (EDEN) Proceedings
2021 Annual Conference | Madrid, 21-24 June, 2021
ISSN 2707-2819
doi: 10.38069/edenconf-2021-ac0033

LISTENING TO THE STUDENT VOICE – STUDENT ENGAGEMENT IN PROFESSIONAL HIGHER EDUCATION

Marina Brunner, Ulf-Daniel Ehlers, Baden-Württemberg Cooperative State University Karlsruhe, Germany

Abstract

The practical orientated education and training of professional higher education institutions attract a very diverse student body and more and more non-traditional students are finding their way to higher education institutions in Europe. In order to sufficiently address the different needs of this group, non-traditional students must be given opportunities for student engagement in student organisations and extracurricular activities outside of lectures. Furthermore, the diversity characteristics of non-traditional students within professional higher education institutions need to be analysed, as well as the barriers and challenges to student engagement. With the help of qualitative expert interviews and focus groups, five problem areas were defined and an outlook on possible improvements was given in order to sharpen the view of an inclusive university environment outside of the lecture hall.

Introduction

For years, more and more students have been entering universities and colleges, and the diversity of the student body has increased along with the number of students (Ehlers 2020). Since the academic landscape is very broad, this paper will take a closer look on the so-called Professional Higher Education Institutions (PHEIs). PHEIs focus more on practical experience and can be defined as a "form of higher education that offers a particularly intense integration with the world of work in all its aspects, including teaching, learning, research and governance" (Camilleri et al., 2014; p.24). The PHEI attract a very heterogeneous and non-traditional group of students which are both academically versed and practically interested. For example, adult students, lifelong learners, parent students, students from a migrant background, students with a disability, etc. are enrolled in these institutions (Kramer et al., 2011). In order to respond proactively to this increasing diversity, student engagement is an important tool for PHEIs to create an inclusive higher education institution for non-traditional students and engage them in all aspects of their studies. Student engagement is a multi-layered concept, which in the current debates on inclusion is mainly discussed in the teaching context. When talking about inclusion in the field of student engagement, student engagement in extracurricular student organisations is often overlooked. Yet, student organisations, such as student representation, are increasingly involved in structural decision-making processes within the PHEI and enable a shared creation process of the institution between PHEI leaders and students. If non-traditional students are not sufficiently represented in these student organisations, it is likely that also their opinions will not be represented and their needs will not be reflected in the structures of the PHEIs.

Therefore, non-traditional students must be able to participate in student organisations in order to include them holistically in their university education and ensure that their voices are heard. To achieve this goal, the barriers and challenges regarding student engagement of non-traditional students need to be identified. In this context, this paper addresses two questions:

- What are characteristics of non-traditional students in PHE?
- What barriers and challenges do non-traditional students face particularly in the area of engagement within student organisations?

Non-traditional students and diversity management

Universities are increasingly confronted with growing societal challenges; for example, the demographic change is reflected in a more diverse composition of the student body. In addition, higher education institutions, as socio-political actors, cannot escape current trends and must therefore also react to numerous demands, whether it be the increasing demand for performance, growing international mobility or the desire to be able to reconcile family and education (Nibuhr et al., 2012). With the Bologna Process, the general wish of the EU countries was expressed that "(t)he student body entering and graduating from higher education institutions should reflect the diversity of Europe's populations" (Bologna Process 2018). This new group of diverse students, who are increasingly entering higher education institutions, are also called non-traditional students.

The term non-traditional student can be used to describe all students who, for social, economic, physical or cultural reasons, did not have or have only very limited access to higher education in comparison to other students, the so-called traditional students. Basically, the term non-traditional student refers to groups of students who form a minority in the student body. And as the student body changes, so does the interpretation of the definition of non-traditional students. The definition of a non-traditional student is therefore also context-dependent and can have different connotations depending on the country, institute or field of study. In addition, the boundaries between traditional and non-traditional students are blurred, so a student can be traditional in some aspects and non-traditional in others at the same time (Schuetze et al., 2002).

In order for higher education institutions to embrace this change and meet the complex needs of the growing and increasingly diverse student body, both structural and cultural adjustments need to be made. The keyword for facing these changes is diversity management. In this understanding, diversity management is a well-founded socio-political demand for social participation of all individuals and an economic necessity to utilize the diverse potentials available in society. When managing diversity, the different diversity characteristics must be considered, for example person-related aspects such as age, gender, ethnicity, etc., behaviour-related aspects such as attitudes to thinking, communication and working styles or learning behaviour and strategies. Behavioural aspects differ between individuals and do not automatically derive from certain personal characteristics (Nibuhr et al., 2012).

The Diversity Wheel (see Figure 1) by Lee Gardenswartz and Anita Rowe, based on the work of Marilyn Loden and Judy Rosener provides a good overview of different diversity characteristics. The characteristics are divided into four dimensions. Firstly, personality, which describes the general behaviour of a person and their way of interaction with others. Secondly, the internal dimension with characteristics such as age, gender or mental and physical abilities or social background. The individual cannot self-select or control these characteristics. Thirdly the external dimension includes characteristics such as place of residence, marital status or education; these characteristics are therefore not innate, but rather the results of life events and decisions made. And lastly, the organizational dimension, it includes elements that are dependent on positioning in the world of work (Loden et al., 1991; Gardenswartz et al., 2003). This paper focuses on the internal and external dimensions of diversity.

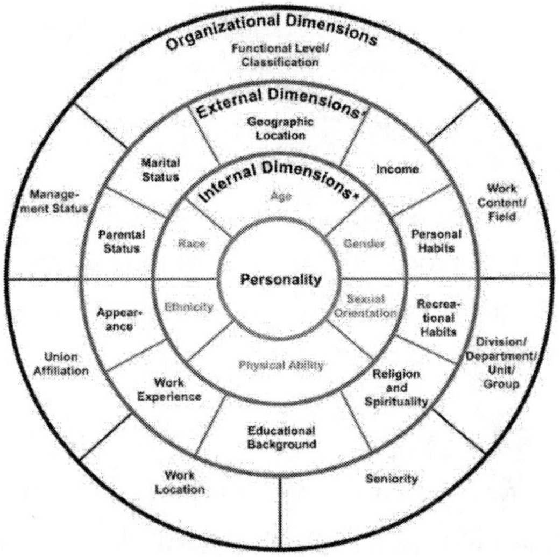

Figure 1. Diversity Wheel (Loden et al., 1991; Gardenswartz et al., 2003)

Student engagement

A diverse student body holds the challenge for PHEIs to create opportunities to include all students in the structural and cultural development and design of the institution and to represent their opinions and needs. This involvement can be strengthened by supporting inclusive access to engagement opportunities to ensure a perspective-rich development and design processes between higher education institutions and students. (National Student Engagement Programme, 2020)

So far, the topic of student engagement has mainly gained attention in teaching, but this official form of student engagement is only one part of the student experience. Ashwin et al. defines student engagement in terms of what is "formed" by students, distinguishing between "formation of understanding" which refers to the individual engagement of students in lectures to produce learning outcomes, "formation of curricula" which focuses more on changing course content, and "formation of communities" which concentrates on the opportunities for students to build networks e.g. in form of student organisations, to change the institution and its structures in a sustainable way (Ashwin et al., 2015). This paper refers to the last form of student engagement.

Student organisations are thematic or political associations of students who come together in groups outside their lectures. Student engagement is hereby linked to participation and means the involvement of students in activities that shape processes within their environment. Participation within organisations such as the PHEI means that students can express their opinions and get involved for example in university committees (Ditzel et al., 2013). Especially through the Bologna Process, these organisations have gained importance and contribute to quality assurance within the institutions. (Higher Education Authority, 2016; p.VIII) Student organisations not only give participants a sense of thematic belonging, but can also provide a social support network for students and thus strengthen the bond with the institution. Furthermore, as Rosch et al. explain, student organisations give students the opportunity to increase self-awareness and develop leadership qualities, as these organisations often represent different roles and structures that can also be found in the professional working world (Rosch et al., 2017). Hence, student organisations also offer good preparation for the professional world it is even more important for non-traditional students to have the opportunity to participate in these extracurricular activities.

Research Methodology

In order to identify the different characteristics of non-traditional students and to expose barriers in relation to the student engagement opportunity, a qualitative expert survey was conducted. In a further step the results were complemented by the results of four focus groups.

Six institutes from Germany, Croatia, Belgium, Spain and Malta participated in the research process. Four of the six institutes are PHEIs and the other 2 are research institutes with a research focus on higher education. All these countries are members of the EU and can therefore be regarded as a relatively homogeneous group, although country-specific differences are to be expected. Nevertheless, the results should not be regarded as a global standard. The qualitative expert survey contained questions on the following topics:

- Dimensions and characteristics of non-traditional students at PHEI.
- Student engagement opportunities at the individual institutes.
- Participation barriers for non-traditional students with a focus on extracurricular activities and student associations.
- Good practices at own institute or from broader society.

The following results are based on a qualitative expert survey conducted in written form between 24.02.21 and 29.03.21. The experts drew their answers from internal studies, their own assessments and conversations with student support staff.

In addition to the information derived from the qualitative expert surveys, four focus groups were conducted by the PHEIs in Malta, Spain, Belgium and Germany. As part of the research project, the opinions of 28 experts, student representatives and non-traditional students were collected and analysed through semi-structured focus groups. Similar to the expert surveys, the online focus groups had the four topic areas: Dimensions and characteristics of non-traditional students, student engagement opportunities, participation barriers and good practices. In order to be able to compare the results more effectively, a semi-structured focus group guideline was provided, which contained a variety of questions on the individual topic areas. To participate in the focus group, the individuals had to either belong to the group of non-traditional students, be a representative of a student organisation or have a professional background as a student-support staff or PHE institutional leader. Table 1 provides an overview of the interview partners (IP), their position and area of experience and their countries.

Table 1: Overview of focus group participants

IP	Position / Area of experience	Country
	1. Focus group	
1	Non-traditional student	Malta
2	Non-traditional student	Malta
3	Non-traditional student	Malta
4	Non-traditional student	Malta
5	Student Support Coordinator	Malta
6	Social Worker and Chaplain	Malta
7	Student Mentor and Part-time Lecturer	Malta
8	Director Outreach Services and Students' Affairs	Malta
	2. Focus group	
9	Student representative	Spain
10	Non-traditional student	Spain
11	Academic Coordinator	Spain
12	Coordinator of University-Business Relations	Spain
13	Member of the Student Council	Spain
14	Dean of the School of Engineering	Spain
15	Non-traditional student	Spain
	3. Focus group	
16	Head of Education and Students Affairs	Belgium
17	Student Support Staff	Belgium
18	Student representative	Belgium
19	Non-traditional students	Belgium
20	Non-traditional students	Belgium
21	Non-traditional students	Belgium
	4. Focus group	
22	Head of Student Counselling and University Communication	Germany
23	Head of the Psychotherapeutic Student Counselling Centre	Germany
24	Representative for students with disabilities and chronic illnesses	Germany
25	Management of the research project on the course of studies	Germany
26	Researcher in the research project on the course of studies	Germany
27	Chairman of the General Students' Committee	Germany
28	Student representative	Germany

Finally, the written expert surveys and focus group reports were analysed and different characteristics for non-traditional students were collected, clustered and then assigned to the different diversity dimensions. Furthermore, the various barriers for non-traditional students with a focus on student engagement were identified and grouped into overarching problem areas.

Diversity characteristics and barriers of non-traditional students

Broken down by internal and external diversity characteristics (see Figure 2), the following student groups were primarily mentioned with characteristics of internal diversity dimension: Students with physical, mental impairments or learning difficulties, gender identity and sexuality, adult students, students with a migrant/multicultural background, women in STEM degree programmes.

External diversity characteristics of non-traditional students could be found in the following groups: first-generation students and the socio-economic background of the parental home, working students, non-traditional previous education, re-entry students, students with caring responsibilities or family burden and international students.

A student may possess several of these characteristics and some additional challenges also arise from the mix of several diversity characteristics.

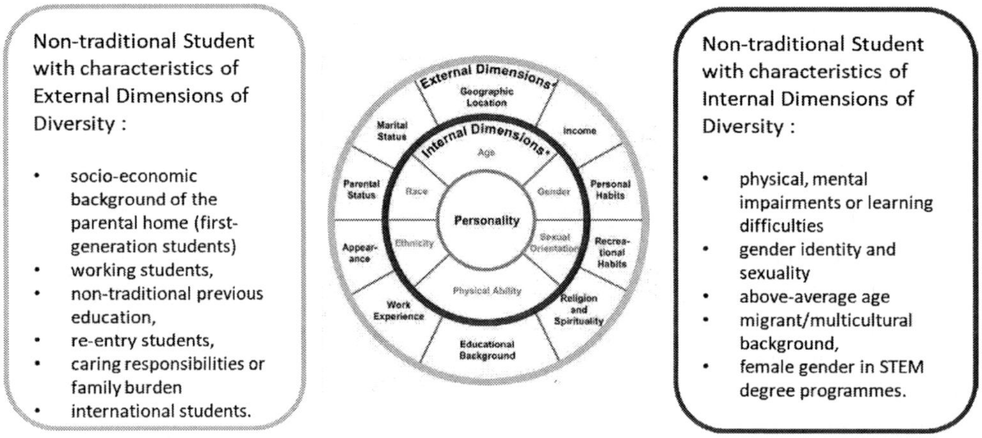

Figure 2. Characteristics of external and internal diversity dimensions of non-traditional students

During the course of the analysis, it became apparent that many of the non-traditional students are confronted with similar problems when it comes to student engagement within student organisations. Five overarching problem areas could be identified: Time problem, visibility problem, identification problem, image problem, accessibility problem.

The *time problem* is common to all groups of students, but is greatest for students who have less time due to the characteristics of the external dimension, such as other part-time jobs or caretaking responsibilities. Especially students who finance their studies themselves already have to balance time and financial resources. As involvement in study organisations often implies a certain time commitment, they are often unable to dedicate additional time resources beyond their study and work commitments. Another concern of students is that the time spend for the engagement student organisations is not compatible with the workload of their studies and thus leads to poorer academic performance. Such a development is particularly harmful for students who finance their studies with a scholarship or foreign students whose visa validity is linked to the completion of their studies. Typical PHEI characteristics, such as the many practical phases and the shorter and limited time on campus, are also cited by some students as reasons discouraging involvement in student organisations.

The *visibility problem* describes the lack of information about student organisations. This mainly revolves around uncertainty regarding the roles and processes within student organisations. Some students do not know what tasks are expected of them and whether they are up to the challenge. Another problem is that some students do not know what the various student organisations at their institution are actually doing, because the results, especially of political initiatives, are often not directly visible.

This also leads to the next problem area, the *identification problem*. Some students, especially those who are not sufficiently represented in student organisations, cannot easily identify with the mission of these groups. Some miss the connection to their own lives and challenges. Furthermore, stereotypes of traditional students are often still used in advertising materials and convey a false message of what kind of members are welcome.

The *image problem* describes a cultural problem that student organisations face. They are partly perceived by other students as popularity contests and as exclusive clubs with special election and selection processes. Furthermore, student organisations are still associated with a strong drinking culture. If the assumption is that the cohesion in these groups can only be strengthened through drinking and partying, for some students this cannot be reconciled with their responsibilities or their cultural background.

The last problem especially concerns students with characteristics from the internal dimension. This pertains to the *accessibility problem*, which mainly affects students with language barriers or mobility difficulties due to disabilities. They have problems physically participating in the activities of student organisations.

Outlook and Conclusion

In addition to the barriers and challenges, the experts also provided existing solutions from their institutes or countries, as well as other potential ideas. The different best practice approaches can be categorised according to the previously identified problem areas. Although target group-specific measures are necessary in some cases, they also bear the danger of assigning students to rigid categories and drawing conclusions about supposed deficits that have no evidence in detail (Nibuhr et al., 2012). The following potential solutions have been briefly listed, but will not be elaborated on as they are not the focus of this research.

Time problem: To solve the time commitment problem, there are possibilities to offer short-term engagement, which refers to short-term thematic projects that students can participate in, but which do not involve a regular time commitment. Furthermore, some universities offer the possibility to include student engagement as an elective module in the course of studies, so that students receive ECTs for their work in student organisations and do not have to decide between study effort and engagement. Another form of compensation would be through financial support for students, which also blurs the line between members in student organisations and student assistants in the university. For students with children, the model of university-owned day-care centres or childcare can also be a great time-saver and thus an opportunity to participate in student organisations.

Visibility problem: Another problem mentioned was the lack of visibility of results and information about tasks, roles and processes within student organisations. PHEI have introduced various measures to give more visibility and recognition to student organisations through student engagement awards or by publishing more success stories of student organisations within the institution but also externally, such as through press releases. In addition, it is important for student organisations to directly contact and target non-traditional students.

Identification problem: In order to counteract the identification problem of non-traditional students, attempts are being made to systematically create more space and visibility for diversity topics within universities. This is done, for example, through awareness-raising campaigns with regard to domestic violence, usage of gender-neutral language, questioning norms of who is represented on PR material and quotas in committees (e.g. for women) to enable a more diverse representation of the student body. Buddy programmes within student organisations can also provide non-traditional students with a sense of belonging.

Image problem: Another problem affecting the student organisations themselves is that student organisations are still perceived as exclusive clubs or associated with a strong drinking or hazing culture. On the one hand, some PHEI have already established initiatives within student organisations to address these issues, such as anti-discrimination and equality chapters in student organisations in order to monitor and consult. On the other hand, external committees of non-traditional students have been formed to write inclusion guidelines for student organisations.

Accessibility problem: Some institutes see emerging opportunities in digital access for students, which has also seen an upsurge due to the Corona pandemic. Digital participation opportunities can give students with limited mobility a more flexible option to participate in student organisations.

A central aspect with regard to the limitations of this research work is the size of the present sample. In order to make a representative analysis of the characteristics and barriers for non-traditional students in PHEI, multiple institutions from several countries need to participate in the expert survey and in the focus groups. Another point to consider in this context is that the knowledge gained about barriers to student engagement is also influenced by the current Corona pandemic. In the present research findings, barriers to student engagement activities that normally take place in presence were investigated. Student engagement opportunities have had to be severely curtailed in the last 18 months and therefore play a minor role in the everyday life of the students. First-year students in particular are less aware of the various extracurricular activities available than they would have been in non-Corona times. As a result, the perception of participation options and barriers e.g. the visibility and accessibility can be biased.

In summary, it can be said that the higher education landscape in Europe is becoming more diverse, but the institutions themselves have not yet sufficiently addressed the needs of non-traditional students. Student organisations provide a good social network for non-traditional students but are still often left out of conversations about inclusion. Studying needs to be seen as a holistic experience in students' lives rather than just a preparation for the world of work. To accommodate its more diverse student body, institutes and student organisations need to make structural and cultural changes to truly represent the needs of all students. This is not about fitting non-traditional students into an existing system, but creating a new system together with all students.

References

Bologna Process (2012). *Bucharest Communiqué.* Available at http://ehea.info/Upload/document/ministerial_declarations/Bucharest_Communique_2012_610673.pdf

Camilleri, A. F., Delplace, S., Frankowicz, M., Hudak, R., & Tannhäuser, A. (2014). *Professional higher education in Europe. Characteristics, practice examples and national differences.* European Association of Institutions in Higher Education. Retrieved from https://www.pedocs.de/volltexte/2015/10873/pdf/Camillieri_etal_2014_Professional_Higher_Education_in_Europe.pdf

Ditzel, B., & Bergt, T. (2013). Studentische Partizipation als organisationale Herausforderung – Ergebnisse einer explorativen Studie. S. M. Weber, M. Göhlich, A. Schröer, C. Fahrenwald & H. Macha (Eds.), *Organisation und Partizipation* (pp. 177–186). Wiesbaden: Springer Fachmedien Wiesbaden.

Ehlers, U. (2020). *Future Skills: Lernen der Zukunft – Hochschule der Zukunft.* Wiesbaden: Springer Fachmedien Wiesbaden GmbH.

Gardenswartz, L., & Rowe, A. (2003). *Diverse Teams at Work: Capitalizing on the Power of Diversity. Capitalizing on the Power of Diversity.* Alexadria, VA: Society for Human Resource Management. Retrieved from https://researchguides.austincc.edu/c.php?g=994136&p=7261002

Higher Education Authority (2016). *Enhancing Student Engagement in Decision-Making. Report of the Working Group on Student Engagement in Irish Higher Education.* Retrieved from http://www.thea.ie/contentfiles/HEA-IRC-Student-Engagement-Report-Apr2016-min.pdf

Kramer, J., Nagy, G., Trautwein, U., Lüdtke, O., Jonkmann, K., Maaz, K., & Treptow, R. (2011). Die Klasse an die Universität, die Masse an die anderen Hochschulen? *Zeitschrift für Erziehungswissenschaft, 14*(3), 465-487. doi: 10.1007/s11618-011-0213-4.

Loden, M., & Rosener, J. B. (1991). *Workforce America: Managing Employee Diversity as a Vital Resource.* Homewood.

National Student Engagement Programme (2020). *The Path to a New National Approach to Student Engagement in Decision-Making.* Discussion Paper for Students and Staff across Irish Higher Education. Retrieved from https://studentengagement.ie/wp-content/uploads/2021/03/NStEP-Framework-Discussion-FINAL-WEB-1.pdf

Nibuhr, C., & Diehn T. (2012). *Vielfalt gestalten. Kernelemente eines Diversity-Audits für Hochschulen.* Essen: Ed. Stifterverband (Positionen).

Rosch, D. M., & Collins, J. D. (2017). The Significance of Student Organizations to Leadership Development. *New Directions for Student Leadership,* 9-19.

Schuetze, H. G., & Slowey, M. (2002). Participation and exclusion: A comparative analysis of non-traditional students and lifelong learners in higher education. *Higher Education, 44*(3/4), 309-327.

Acknowledgement

The research was conducted in the context of the Erasmus Plus project InclusiPHE – Inclusive Engagement of Non-Traditional Students in Professional Higher Education. InclusiPHE is a project funded by the European Union; project partners and contributors: Mondragon University, European Association if Institutions in Higher Education, Baden-Wuerttemberg Cooperative State University, Knowledge Innovation Center, UC Leuven, Institute for the Development of Education, The Malta College of Arts, Science & Technology, European Students' Union.

Lessons from a Pandemic for the Future of Education
European Distance and E-Learning Network (EDEN) Proceedings
2021 Annual Conference | Madrid, 21-24 June, 2021
ISSN 2707-2819
doi: 10.38069/edenconf-2021-ac0034

DIGITAL EDUCATION TO FOSTER THE SUCCESS OF STUDENTS IN DIFFICULTY IN LINE WITH THE DIGITAL EDUCATION ACTION PLAN

Marina Marchisio, Alice Barana, Cecilia Fissore, Marta Pulvirenti, University of Turin, Italy

Abstract

Because of the Covid-19 pandemic, the need to promote digital education has been felt even more, bringing the DELTA Research Group to reflect on how digital education could optimally facilitate the creation of an educating community able to promote and support educational success exclusively through distance learning. In order to answer, in this paper the experience of the 2019/2020 edition of “Scuola dei Compiti” (a recovery project for secondary schools of the poorest suburbs of Turin) is analysed in the perspective of the priority strategies illustrated in the Digital Education Action Plan for the period 2021-2027. Results will show that this was a forerunner experience perfectly in line with the principles and directions outlined in the document. Moreover, thanks to digital education, even a peculiar edition of the project such as this one has been a success: in fact, it has allowed students to improve from a cognitive and metacognitive point of view, even during a time that was very difficult for some families.

Introduction

In Italy, the digital competence level is very low (only 44% of people between 16 and 74 years old have basic digital skills, while the European average is 57%) and the digital divide disfavours social inclusion and the exercise of full democratic citizenship (Selva, 2020). In order to meet this need, since many years the main goal of the DELTA (i.e. Digital Education for Learning and Teaching Advances) research group of the University of Turin is to improve Digital Education. The DELTA Research Group implements its research through trials and projects involving many secondary school students and that aim not only to improve their cognitive and meta-cognitive processes but also to enhance their digital competence (Barana & Marchisio, 2016; Barana et al., 2020b). The DELTA Research Group studies and develops innovative and effective methodologies to promote school success, also with the use of new technologies. In 2020, the global Covid-19 pandemic gave a further boost to the group's research, forcing some of the projects that were meant to be in-person to shift to distance learning only. An example of this implementation is the project against school failure "Scuola dei Compiti" (i.e. "School of Homework") of the University and the City of Turin (Barana et al., 2017). It started in 2013 to support those students from Turin poorest suburb upper and lower secondary schools who needed to reduce failures in STEM subjects (where STEM stands for Science, Technology, Engineering, and Mathematics), foreign and Italian languages. In its first six editions (up to the 2018/2019 one) the project has involved 9564 students from grade 8 to 10. Since its first edition, the project has provided supporting courses with the face-to-face modality (called "traditional" courses) and others called "digital" courses that were making the most of a specific DLE (i.e. Digital Learning Environment) with the blended learning modality that alternated classroom-based and online moments. All courses have always been aimed at disadvantaged students, whose families were in unfavourable economic situations and/or not able to support them in their education. The practical need to redesign "Scuola dei Compiti" in an entirely online mode for the 2019/2020 edition has brought to the following research question: "how can the previously acquired competences of the research group, and in general the digital education, optimally facilitate the creation of an educating community able to promote and support educational success exclusively through distance learning?" The results of this edition of "Scuola dei Compiti" are in line with the promotion of a high-performing digital educational ecosystem and the improvement of digital skills and competences for the digital transformation i.e. the two strategic priorities outlined in the 2020 Digital Education Action Plan (European Commission, 2020). The DEAP is the plan of the European Commission, which outlines the measures for the digital inclusive and high-quality instruction and training that should be adopted by every European country. It covers the programming period 2021-2027 and it defines priorities and corresponding actions on which the EU can provide an added value. Although the DEAP was published in September 2020, the research of the DELTA research group has somehow anticipated most of the fundamental aspects indicated in this document, as will be illustrated in the results section.

The "digital" experience to promote school success

Because of the Covid-19 pandemic, the need to promote the development and adoption of digital learning environments has been felt even more, even in the context of remedial education (Bolondi et al., 2021; Darling-Hammond et al., 2020). "Scuola dei Compiti" was therefore entirely redesigned for its 2019/2020 edition in order to be completely digital and thus be able to reduce educational poverty and promote school success. It became a vast experimentation of a totally online recovery project after only one experience in the past, with smaller numbers, that was carried out in the framework of the project "Ragazzi

Connessi" (i.e. "Connected Youth") (Fissore et al., 2020). Thanks to previous editions and competences developed by the research group over the years, many methodologies have been implemented to favour students in difficulty in order to immediately take the side of the neediest students, who risked being the most fragile in this historical period, which certainly was not the easiest. The project was made possible thanks to the collaboration among the schools, the city of Turin, and the DELTA research group, which cooperates with several departments of the University of Turin. The actors involved have been many: staff of the Municipality of Turin; teachers, trainers, scholarship recipients and tutors of the departments of Molecular Biotechnology and Health Sciences, Mathematics, Foreign Languages, Humanities, Physics, Philosophy, and Educational Sciences; students and their families; teachers, school staff, headmasters of the schools involved. There were multiple goals: not only to reduce early school leaving but also to recover school failures and overcome learning difficulties, increase passion and motivation in studying, reach self-confidence and facilitate the transition from lower to upper secondary school. In a time of global pandemic, it became even more necessary to reach these goals (Giovannella et al., 2020). As in previous editions, the 2019/2020 one also provided tutoring hours held by university students selected on the basis of their study program and their profit and appropriately trained for their role in the school context. The subjects involved were: Chemistry, English, Italian, French, digital Latin, Mathematics, digital Mathematics, Physics, and German (where all courses without the adjective "digital" were "traditional"). Although with the redesign of "Scuola dei Compiti" every course was online, the difference between "traditional" and "digital" courses was still significant, as it will be shown in the results. In fact, at the beginning of February, all tutors had attended a two-meetings initial training: an introduction to the project and a specific pedagogical training. Besides, tutors of "digital" courses attended further training on the most innovative teaching methods for school recovery in a blended perspective, that is, integrating face-to-face moments with online ones; "traditional" tutors did not attend them because their courses were supposed to be held face-to-face. When the project was modified because of the new social distancing rules, this second part of the training was synthetically re-proposed to every tutor in online mode. 87 courses have been activated, each of them for a small group of students (5-10 students) which followed up to two hours of weekly tutoring. The number of weeks was different for each school (from 7 to 15 weeks), to satisfy their different needs; the project ended for all with the closure of schools at the beginning of June. The reprogramming of the project in a totally online way has led to strategic considerations by the people in charge of the project (from the Municipality and the University of Turin but also teachers and headmasters of schools) on how to make the most of digital technologies for a recovery online path. This led to the decision to fully use the integrated DLE (Digital Learning Environment) that was already set for "digital" courses. The DLE would have been the space, shared by tutors and students, where all tutoring activities could take place (Barana & Marchisio, 2021). In fact, thanks to the collaboration with the ICT services of the Department of Computer Science of the University of Turin (Barana & Marchisio, 2020a), the project provides a Moodle platform integrated with the web conference system Adobe Connect, the Advanced Computing Environment Maple through the MapleNet plugin and the Automatic Assessment System (AAS) Möbius (https://www.digitaled.com/products/assessment/). This DLE (available on https://scuoladeicompiti.i-learn.unito.it/) with the described supplements facilitates the implementation of collaborative and cooperative learning, adaptive teaching, and problem-solving, thanks to the possibility of using forums and creating supplementary and interactive activities (Barana et al., 2019a; Barana et al., 2019b; Paiva et al., 2015). The font used by the platform is "EasyReading" (http://www.easyreading.it/it/) which is Dyslexia friendly and accessible.

Methodology

To evaluate the effectiveness of digital education in facilitating the creation of an educating community able to promote and support educational success exclusively through the distance-learning modality, various initiatives have been undertaken, at the beginning of the project, in itinere, and at the end. These included: numerous meetings among the people in charge of the project to reprogram the guidelines according to the new rules of social distancing; various gatherings with teachers to support them and to receive feedback weekly reports sent by tutors. At the end of the project, all the actors involved were asked to fill in online questionnaires. This was critical to obtain evidence and data to monitor progress and improve the understanding of challenges and opportunities of this digital transformation, as indicated in the DEAP as well. All students filled in one Likert-scale questionnaire while their teachers and their tutors filled one for each of their students in order to compare the results for each student from three different points of view. Questionnaires investigated students' improvement at a cognitive and metacognitive level as well as the impact of this vast experimentation of an entirely online recovery project. In the teachers' questionnaire, it was also required to indicate the average mark of a student in a specific subject before starting the course (which will be called "initial mark") and a feedback by teachers on the increase (or decrease) of students' performance in that subject at the end of the school year. This numerical value (which will simply be called "increase" and will be preceded by a minus sign in case of a "decrease") had to be given based on the latest activities of the student carried out together with the teacher during the last months of distance learning and, regardless of the mark, they would have put in the school report. The sum of the "initial mark" and the "increase" will be called "final mark" for brevity.

Results

The following analysis discusses the data collected through these questionnaires and meetings at the beginning, in itinere, and at the end, in the perspective of strategic priorities of the DEAP (European Commission, 2020). These priorities indicates that to promote digital educational ecosystems of high performance it is necessary to: have infrastructures, connectivity, and digital equipment; plan and develop effective digital skills (including effective and up-to-date organizational skills) and digitally competent and confident education and training staff; high-quality content, easy-to-use tools, and secure platforms, respecting privacy and ethical standards.

Infrastructure, connectivity, and digital equipment

Initially, 41 schools were supposed to participate in the 2019/2020 edition of "Scuola dei Compiti" (for a total of 189 courses to activate) but, due to the sudden pandemic, only 21 have decided to continue. This was caused by reasons mainly related to the poor digital infrastructures possessed by their students (connection and devices), which were necessary in order to take part in the project in a fully online mode. Many schools had already provided devices and mobile SIM for connection to the neediest students who, however, were not always the same students enrolled in the project. This highlighted an important factor indicated in the DEAP, namely the need for greater investments in connectivity, and equipment in order to guarantee access to digital education to anyone in the future. The students who actually participated in this edition of the project and who could therefore access the platform amounted to 635; however, fewer questionnaires were received because it was not easy to remotely control their completion. The answers analysed, therefore, refer to 338 questionnaires filled in by students, 453 by tutors, and 415 by teachers. Participation in the project was good, thus underlining the fundamental role of this digital edition in increasing equality and inclusion, allowing the most disadvantaged students, the real target of the project, to continue learning even during the school closing period.

Digital skills and digitally competent and confident education and training staff

Courses were highly attended also thanks to the initial training provided to tutors. Tutors, all aged 22 to 25, were able to quickly acquire the digital skills necessary to use technology effectively and creatively to engage, motivate, and also support their students in the acquisition of digital skills, as indicated in the DEAP. "Digital Latin" and "digital Math" courses were the most popular, after the "German" course that was however only one and attended only by 2 students. The 62 students enrolled in "digital Latin" courses attended on average 17 hours of tutoring while the 51 students enrolled in "digital Math" courses attended on average 14 hours; all the other courses (traditional Math, Chemistry, French,

English, Italian, Physics) had an average attendance of 10 hours each. This highlights that the initial training provided to "digital" tutors, deeper and more detailed, has led to the success of their courses; the subsequent analysis of "initial and final marks" also proves this success. As also highlighted by DEAP it is therefore observed that the greater the skills of educators (in this case of tutors) the greater the probability of success of online courses. The project proved to be a success also from a cognitive point of view: in fact, looking at answers given by teachers to the question "In your opinion, compared to before the 'Scuola dei Compiti' course, has your student improved in the discipline?", 75% of them answered "yes, they have". Furthermore, according to teachers, students who have improved the most are those who have taken courses in "traditional Math", "traditional English", "digital Latin" and "digital Math". In general, before attending the course, students' average marks in the subject were on average 5.16 (out of 10); the average mark of students after attending the course was 5.85: there was, therefore, an average increase of +0.69 points and the difference is statistically significant to a pairwise Student's t-test ($t = 20.66$, $p < 0.001$). The project was in fact aimed at students with minor insufficiency and the data show that it is particularly effective for them as it allows to recover those few points that can lead very close to sufficiency if not full sufficiency. The average increase in "digital" courses is 0.89 out of 10, significantly higher than the increase in "traditional" courses (0.63 out of 10); the difference is significant on an ANOVA test ($p = 0.01$). This shows once again how the different methodologies adopted by "digital" tutors led to a greater success of their students. These data are also confirmed by analysis of the questionnaires completed by students. They state that, at the end of the course, their knowledge of the subject has increased by more than half a point out of 5: from an average value of 2.6 (expressed in Likert scale 1 to 5) before attending the course to 3.2 after attending the course. Confidence also increased from 2.8 to 3.4. Interest in the subject, self-paced study, and participation in lessons with the teacher also increased on average after the course. Despite the course being entirely remote, students declare that they have improved in all these metacognitive aspects. Furthermore, most of the students report that they attended online meetings mainly because they found them interesting and useful (with mode 4 on a Likert scale of 1 to 5), the tutor was young and nice (mode 3), and because they themselves were motivated to improve their skills (mode 4). The role of the tutor has therefore proved to be fundamental in this extraordinary edition of the project; in fact, it was them who guided their students thanks to their digital skills. In so doing, tutors were of great support to teachers, who already had a lot on their plate, dealing with daily teaching with the whole class. As also indicated by the DEAP, a good understanding of the digital world should be part of the formal and non-formal education provided to make basic digital skills part of the key transferable skills, and "Scuola dei Compiti" was a good way to help this process for students and tutors. In fact, a good relationship developed between tutors and students, which was fundamental for the success of the project. 54.8% of students stated that they felt "very" or "very much" comfortable with the tutor (4 or 5 expressed in a Likert scale by 1 to 5); only 0.4% of them responded negatively (the average is 4.1). Students' answers tend to be confirmed by those of the tutors, whose answer to the question "has the student established a good relationship with the tutor?" reached an average of 3.2. To conclude, we report that students greatly appreciated the course they received despite all the difficulties of this historical period: 81% of them declared that, in case of need, they would like to attend a similar course again. Furthermore, students found that the tutors' explanations were interesting (with an average of 3.72 on a Likert scale of 1 to 5), that the number of meetings was sufficient (average of 3.59) and they declare that in such a period of health emergency being able to participate to the project was supportive (average of 3.47).

High-quality content, easy-to-use tools, and secure platforms, respecting privacy and ethical standards

One of the key elements to deliver the project was the Digital Learning Environment made available for the project. As shown in Table 1, students showed that they generally appreciated the opportunities offered by the online platform, in which they found interactive materials, the support of the tutor from home in asynchronous activities, and collaborative activities to be carried out with their peers. These materials and activities were created specifically by tutors from scratch or taken from a database of ready-made materials made available by the research group. This allowed to design high-quality educational content, and digital technology has been crucial, as indicated in the DEAP. Only "digital" tutors have created interactive materials and tests for automatic formative assessment because they have been trained on how to do it: in table 1, the "mean" column only considers answers of those who actually used them; the "N.A." column shows the number of students who replied that they did not use them. We also underline the fact that these data were collected at the end of the project, in June 2020, when we were just emerging from the pandemic situation and all the frustrations it caused.

Table 1: Answers from students about digital content involved in the project

Answers from students	Responses	Mean	St. Dev.	Mode	N.A.
Was the platform easily accessible?	338	3.06	1.213	3	0
Did you appreciate communicating with the platform?	338	3.17	0.985	3	0
Would you like to have a platform also for school lessons?	338	3.11	1.326	3	0
How much did you appreciate having interactive materials?	276	3.57	1.075	4	62
How much did you appreciate tests?	163	3.12	1.027	3	175
Did tests help you to learn from your mistakes?	163	3.49	1.008	3	175

These results are particularly positive if we take into consideration that, for most students, the totally online mode was a novelty that they had never experienced before. In fact, the majority of teachers stated that their students "never" took part in online lessons nor used online material before the health emergency (the mode of answers given is 1 on the Likert scale as shown in Table 2). The project was for many students a first step into their digital literacy and encouraged healthy, safe, and meaningful uses of digital technology, as indicated in the DEAP.

Table 2: Answers from students about their previous digital experience

Before the pandemic has the student ...	Responses	Mean	Mode	St. Dev.
... already taken part in online lessons carried out by the teacher?	415	1.6	1	1.072
... already used online material made available by the teacher?	415	2.02	1	1.064

Furthermore, by asking to specify which type of online resource they had already used before the pandemic, it appears that 51.8% of students had already used handouts in pdf or word format but 31.3% of them had never used any type of interactive material at all given by their teacher. This is an influential factor because it shows even more how difficult it was for students and teachers to adapt to the conditions dictated by the social isolation imposed: in addition to having to attend lessons online without physical contact, students also had to get used to using certain types of resources never used before. Therefore, given that this modality of course delivery was new for most of the students involved, some answers collected in table 3 given by teachers, students, and tutors are very relevant. We asked them which modality they would feel most appropriate in the future for the fruition of the project for the student they were filling out the questionnaire about. For all three actors involved in the project, the best way was the "mixed" one, in which face-to-face tutoring alternates with online tutoring with the support of an online platform. This was also the same modality already offered in the past for courses called "digital" (or "experimental" in the first editions). The second modality chosen is the one with only face-to-face tutorings but always supported by an online platform to have materials available for recovery. It is also meaningful that the majority of actors involved agree that in a future edition they would like to have a platform available to support tutorings (only 14% of the total of the answers collected say they prefer face-to-face tutoring without any platform support).

Table 3: Answers from teachers, students and tutors about the most appropriate modality of fruition of the project

After this experience, what could be the best modality for the next edition?	Teachers	Students	Tutors
Only face-to-face tutorings, without platform	9.6%	14.9%	18.5%
Only face-to-face tutorings, with platform	24.2%	18.9%	33%
Only online tutorings, with platform support to access interactive materials	0%	10.8%	3.5%
In blended modality, both face-to-face and online tutorings and with platform	50.7%	24.2%	37.3%
Missing data	15.5%	31.2%	7.7%
Total	100%	100%	100%

Conclusions

Thanks to the experience of the research group in digital education, it was possible to successfully deliver the project by fully exploiting the most innovative teaching technologies and methodologies that have made students involved improve from a cognitive and metacognitive point of view. It was an action aimed at the most vulnerable, the invisible ones, in a period that was very difficult for some families, and digital education has played a fundamental role in increasing equality and inclusion, allowing even the most disadvantaged students to be able to be involved and not be left behind. It was also an opportunity to make all the actors involved think about how digital technologies can be integrated into education and training and it served for many as a first hint of digital literacy to develop an understanding of risks and opportunities linked to digital technology and to encourage a healthy, safe and meaningful fruition. Furthermore, students and tutors involved have acquired valuable digital skills and competences that should, from this historical period onwards, become part of the formal and non-formal education provided in every education and training institution in order to make the competences become basic digital skills part of the key transferable skills. Rereading the experience of "Scuola dei Compiti" in the light of DEAP (European Commission, 2020) we can see that this was a forerunner experience perfectly in line with the principles and directions outlined in the document. Past experiences of the research group have provided tutors (and therefore students) with high-quality educational content to increase the relevance, quality, and inclusiveness of the recovery intervention; the project has therefore served to facilitate flexible and accessible learning opportunities for the learners involved. This extraordinary edition of the project has served to promote a high-performance digital educational ecosystem, as once again stated in the DEAP. In fact, it has made all the students, tutors and teachers involved understand its potential: 86% of them at the end of the project agree on the fact that "in a future edition of the project they would like to have an online platform available to support tutors". Answering the research question, it can therefore be said that digital education has succeeded in its intent of facilitating the creation of an educating community exclusively through the distance-learning modality able to promote and support the educational success of students in difficulty and to help them in their academic success limiting their school dropout. Obviously, a lot of work still needs to be done in order to be able to reach a complete transformation of education for the digital age, but the information and knowledge gained from this first trial will be useful to improve the understanding of challenges and opportunities of the digital transformation in future education projects. Although this was an entirely online experimentation caused by unavoidable external factors, it is clear that, in the future, the digital component will no longer be missing even in recovery projects; this experience was fundamental to lay the foundations for future projects which, regardless of the pandemic, could adapt more and more to these new modalities. Starting from this very experience, the DELTA Research Group is now implementing, among other things, a new recovery project during the school year 2020/2021: this was designed to be held online from the very beginning, given the excellent results observed during the last edition of "Scuola dei Compiti".

References

Barana, A., & Marchisio, M. (2016). From digital mate training experience to alternating school work activities. *Mondo Digitale, 15*(64), 63-82.

Barana, A., Fioravera, M., Marchisio, M., & Rabellino, S. (2017). Adaptive Teaching Supported by ICTs to Reduce the School Failure in the Project 'Scuola Dei Compiti'. *Proceedings – International Computer Software and Applications Conference*, 432-437.

Barana, A., Conte, A., Fissore, C., Marchisio, M., & Rabellino, S. (2019a). Learning Analytics to improve Formative Assessment strategies. *Journal of E-Learning and Knowledge Society, 15*(3), 75-88. https://doi.org/10.20368/1971-8829/1135057.

Barana, A., Marchisio, M., & Miori, R. (2019b). MATE-BOOSTER: Design of an e-Learning Course to Boost Mathematical Competence. *Proceedings of the 11th International Conference on Computer Supported Education (CSEDU 2019), 1*, 280-291.

Barana, A., & Marchisio, M. (2020a). An interactive learning environment to empower engagement in Mathematics. *Interaction Design and Architecture(s) Journal – IxD&A, 45*, 302-321.

Barana, A., Pulvirenti, M., Fissore, C., & Marchisio, M. (2020b). An Online Math Path to Foster the Transition of Students between Lower and Upper Secondary School. ELearning Sustainment for Never-Ending Learning. *Proceedings of the 16th International Scientific Conference ELearning and Software for Education, 1*, 568-575.

Barana, A., & Marchisio, M. (2021). Analyzing interactions in Automatic Formative Assessment activities for Mathematics in Digital Learning Environments. *CSEDU 2021, Proceedings of the 13th International Conference on Computer Supported Education* (Vol. 1, pp. 497–504). SCITEPRESS. doi: 10.5220/0010474004970504.

Bolondi, G., Del Zozzo, A., Ferretti, F., Garzetti, M., & Santi, G. (2021). Can Formative Assessment Practices Appear Spontaneously during Long Distance Learning? *CSEDU 2021, proceedings of the 13th International Conference on Computer Supported Education* (Vol. 1, pp. 625–632). SCITEPRESS.

Darling-Hammond, L., Schachner, A., & Edgerton, A. K. (with Badrinarayan, A., Cardichon, J., Cookson, P. W., Jr., Griffith, M., Klevan, S., Maier, A., Martinez, M., Melnick, H., Truong, N., Wojcikiewicz, S.). (2020). *Restarting and reinventing school: Learning in the time of COVID and beyond.* Palo Alto, CA: Learning Policy Institute.

European Commission (2020). *Communication from the Commission to the European Parliament, the council, the European economic and social committee and the committee of the regions.* Digital Education Action Plan 2021-2027: Resetting education and training for the digital age (COM/2020/624 final).

Fissore, C., Marchisio, M., & Rabellino, S. (2020). Online tutoring through an integrated platform to support learning Mathematics at lower secondary school. *Proceedings of International Conference E-Learning 2020*, 71-78.

Giovannella, C., Passarelli, M., & Persico, D. (2020). The Effects of the Covid-19 Pandemic on Italian Learning Ecosystems: The School Teachers' Perspective at the steady state. *Interaction Design and Architecture(s) Journal, 45*, 264-286.

Paiva, R., Ferreira, M., Mendes, A., & Eusébio, A. (2015). Interactive and Multimedia Contents Associated with a System for Computer-Aided Assessment. *Journal of Educational Computing Research, 52*(2), 224-256.

Selva, D. (2020). Divari digitali e disuguaglianze in Italia prima e durante il Covid-19. *Culture e Studi del Sociale, 5*(2), 463-483.

Lessons from a Pandemic for the Future of Education
European Distance and E-Learning Network (EDEN) Proceedings
2021 Annual Conference | Madrid, 21-24 June, 2021
ISSN 2707-2819
doi: 10.38069/edenconf-2021-ac0035

DEVELOPING SOFT SKILLS THROUGH ACTIVE LEARNING: STORYTELLING CONCRETE EXPERIENCES THROUGH A MOOC

Alessandra Tomasini, Valeria Baudo, Politecnico di Milano – METID, Italy, Deborah Arnold, AUNEGe – Digital University for Economics and Management, France

Abstract

The eLene4Life project aims to support curriculum innovation in higher education (HE) through the development of active learning approaches for transversal skills, with the ultimate aim of improving students' employability. The MOOC "Active Learning for Soft Skills Development", one of the project outputs, has been put in place as a space for learning through experience sharing and discussion. The MOOC aims at fostering the exchange of results achieved by instructors after the concrete experimentation of active learning methods and at increasing their sensibility and knowledge of the most effective modalities through which to implement those methods. This paper outlines the genesis of the MOOC. Its three main objectives are: (a) collecting and valorising different voices of the teachers who directly experimented one or more methodologies of active learning in their classroom (most of them during the pandemic); (b) embracing and sustaining experiences, as well as addressing doubts coming from a wider audience interested in putting into practice such methods oriented to soft and digital skills' development; (c) offering a non-formal learning opportunity in line with European indications about micro-credentialing through developing synergies with the ECCOE project (European Credit Clearinghouse for Opening up Education).

Introduction

This paper wants to capitalize on the experience gained in the design and realization of an online learning path, a MOOC, in an international context where the storytelling of real experiences "embedded" in the curriculum plays the leading role. There are studies (Succi & Canovi, 2020; Cinque, 2016; Wilhelm et al., 2002) and reports (Manpower Group, 2018, Deloitte, 2017; European Commission, 2013; ISFOL, 2012) that highlight the importance of supporting and strengthening students' development of soft skills to meet the needs of the labour market and fill the existing gaps. Schultz (2008; p.152) says "students participating in a lecture with the aim of learning a hard skill will inevitably and unconsciously practice a range of soft skills. This comes very close to an ideal way of lecturing ... no changes to a programme's curriculum are necessary; instead, the change will be reflected in the lecturers' teaching methodology." A re-design of the course, or part of it (a lesson or a module), putting students at the centre of the learning experience making them active and responsible for their learning, can respond to this need. Active learning methodologies are recommended to educators as a means to promote a wider and general knowledge base and interpersonal skills such as communication, problem solving and teamwork (Prince, 2004; Walker, 2003; Bean, 1996; Sutherland & Bonwell; 1996, Silberman, 1996).

Many universities have already moved in this direction, supporting teaching staff to gain awareness of these approaches and integrating them in their didactics, to improve students' engagement, knowledge retention and results. A survey conducted by the European University Association in 2017 indicates that higher education institutions worked on "the implementation of reforms in quality assurance, credit systems, as well as degrees and qualifications frameworks, emphasized the use of learning outcomes and student-centred learning approaches" (Gaebel et al., 2018; p.77). In such a scenario, the eLene4Life project highlights the importance on how to support and guide lecturers in implementing active learning methodologies to foster soft skills while teaching subject-matter courses.

The eLene4Life project

eLene4life is the sixth project born in the frame of almost two decades of collaboration among institutions participating in the eLene Network. The current project aims at supporting curriculum innovation in higher education through the development of active learning approaches for soft skills' development, with the ultimate aim of improving students' employability. A framework for soft and digital skills has been developed in the previous project "eLene4Work" and it constituted the base from which the eLene4Life activities have been designed.

The MOOC is one of the project outputs, and comes at the end of two main phases. The first one is the analysis of innovative methodologies and activities which foster the acquisition of transversal skills, during which a benchmarking activity and interviews in the Higher Education & Corporate sectors were conducted in parallel. The second phase focused on the production of three closely related outputs:

- the Dynamic Toolkit – a selection of active learning methodologies collected during benchmarking phase;

- the Pilot Projects – 12 Higher Education teachers chose one of the methodologies listed in the Dynamic Toolkit (Figure 1) and designed how to integrate it along their course during academic year 2019/2020 (see more in the Pilot Projects Report);
- the MOOC – aimed at collecting and valorising the Dynamic Toolkit methodologies and the pilot teacher experiences.

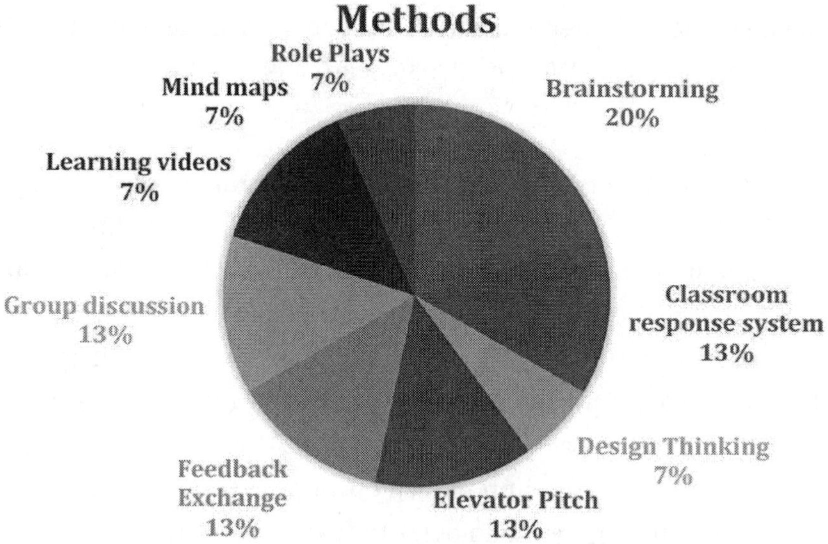

Figure 1. Methods tested during the pilots

The MOOC "Active Learning for Soft Skills Development": a discussion-based MOOC

The MOOC is available on Polimi Open Knowledge (www.pok.polimi.it), the MOOC platform of Politecnico di Milano. Launched in 2014 for MOOC delivery, it currently counts more than 113 000 users from all over the world with 71 MOOCs produced. This MOOC is part of the series of MOOCs 4 teachers, devoted to faculty development. The course has been explicitly designed as a "discussion-based MOOC", a format already tested with success during a past European Project (D-Transform).

The main purpose of the MOOC is the creation of an online environment fostering the exchange of innovative teaching and learning experiences for soft and transversal skills enhancement. Soft skills are crucial more than ever in a volatile, uncertain, complex and ambiguous (VUCA) context.

The MOOC has been designed carefully to be based on the sharing of experience, not only the ones coming directly from the teachers involved in the pilots, but also those coming from MOOC participants. This MOOC is not about teaching the best experience ever in active learning for soft skills' development but is about sharing experiences both those that worked well and those that did not work so well, putting them on the table and discussing with peers to gain insights and tips from their experience. In fact, sharing doubts, ideas, practical experiences is the significant added value of the MOOC.

Although the eLene4Life MOOC is mainly addressed to higher education teachers, it is beneficial also to teachers at other levels and also for the corporate sector, since not only is soft skills' development is crucial for them, but the methods tested and described can also be reused and adapted. Furthermore, the international dimension of exchange among participants highlighted that "teaching" soft skills is not something written in stone, and that different countries used different approaches. In this format of a discussion-based MOOC, the sharing of personal experiences, the possibility to see different implementations of different methods in different countries are the ways in which knowledge passes to participants, since knowledge is not something to be transmitted but something that we build collectively in the learning process itself. The role of the instructional designer in this format is fundamental since he/she is in charge of creating an environment that can be a safe and comfy place for people where everyone is welcomed, and his/her contribution is appreciated.

The course is organised in 7 weeks. The first one is devoted to the exploration of the relationship between active learning and soft skills. The next three are focused on the three elements of the Constructive alignment (Biggs, 2003): Intended Learning Outcomes, Assessment Strategies and Teaching and Learning Activities. The fifth week concentrates on the monitoring and evaluation of the learning and teaching experience. The 6th week is different, and it is devoted to peer assessment, an activity designed to capitalize what the learners discovered during the MOOC, asking them to submit the design project of the activity they'd like to implement in their class to foster soft skills. Finally, the 7th week brings all together the full teachers' interviews involved in the pilot experience.

The main elements taken into consideration in the instructional design process are:

- the *fil rouge* must be the instructors experience during pilots: they should guide the whole learning path.
- to guide novices, who recognise the importance of potentiating students' soft skills, in understanding and designing all steps of integrating an active learning experience in their course.
- to favour an exchange of experiences, doubts and concrete applications coming from the learners (discussion based).
- to offer an online learning experience able to support digital soft skills' development in learners (McAuley, 2010).
- To increase the value and attractiveness of the MOOC, by issuing proof of the achievement of the learning outcomes (micro-credential) (Engels-Perenyi &

Nomden, 2021) through the solutions developed by the sister project ECCOE (European Credit Clearinghouse for Opening up Education).

The design process

The international dimension of collaboration has been a key factor in the MOOC design and development, considering the direct involvement of different stakeholders in the realization of contents. A first proposal for a course index was shared among partners, to give an idea of the pedagogical framework adopted and facilitate the discussion and collection of suggestions with partners. The main MOOC idea was to guide the learner in a first overview on the main aspects to be considered when renovating their own course (or just a small part of it) to better support students' soft skills' development, taking advantage of Biggs' Constructive alignment.

The first content of each week is a video presenting the experiences conducted by the teachers during the pilots that focus on one of those elements. Two critical aspects were considered in the MOOC design phase: teachers' contributions must not be too long, and learners should easily understand what is described in the video. So, when the video content production phase was launched, we opted for the interview format, as this can facilitate a deeper reflection on what they did and on the process they implemented. Their thoughts were presented coherently with the constructive alignment theory and accompanied by an infographic (Playcard) that synthesizes the methodologies implemented. Introducing a graphic element, such as an infographic, had the aim of helping users understand more clearly the specific design elements that instructors decided to implement in their pilot considering their context, constraints, attitudes. Since many videos were recorded at home due to the covid-19 crisis, precise instructions were made considering both technical and methodological aspects useful for self-recording.

The pilot teachers' video storytelling is followed by two different contributions from the partnership: the "Voices from eLene", aimed at highlighting stimuli from pilots enriching them with partners' experience, personal reflection and knowledge, concrete suggestions for learners to be applied; and the "Voice from the expert", aimed at deepening the theory behind the active learning methodologies implemented.

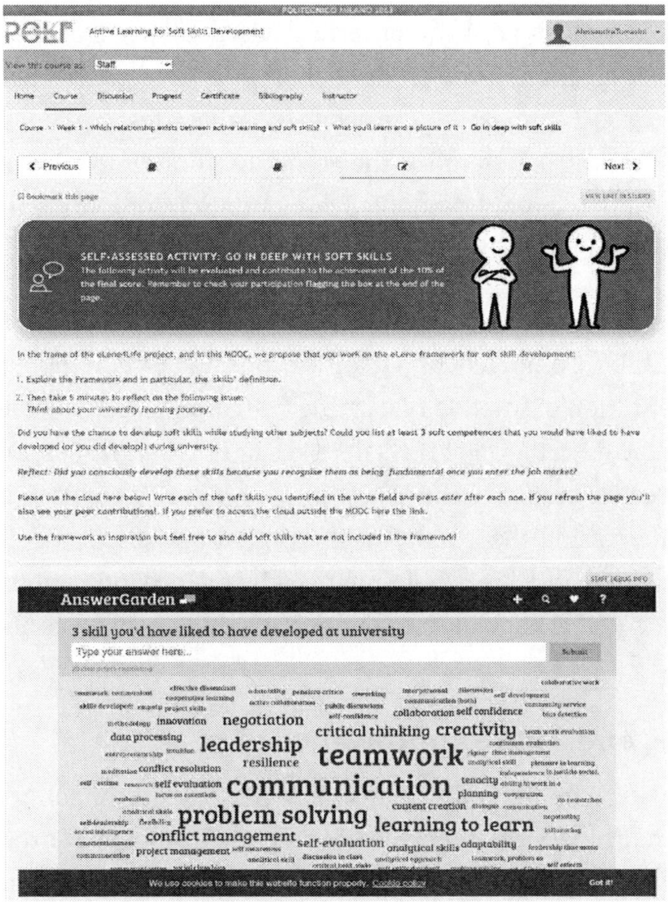

Figure 2. An example of a MOOC activity

A series of collaborative activities were designed to support the "discussion-based" characteristic of the MOOC and to foster experiences able to sustain digital soft skills development of participants:

- Polls and brainstorming tools (e.g. Answer garden and Padlet): these have been used as easy-to-do tasks to stimulate even unforthcoming learners to collaborate. Taking part in these activities requires a small amount of time, allowing users to see immediately their contributions together with the others.
- Peer-assessment activity: at the end of the path, learners have to develop a project about active learning methodologies. Here the activity plays different roles: firstly it is an assessed task, secondly it is an activity based on active learning methodologies itself, so it can be directly experimented by learners, thirdly it is a way to discover concrete implemented projects that can be taken as an inspiration.
- Discussion Forum: this is the virtual space to exchange ideas starting from specific content presented by pilot teachers or from external resources (aimed to deepen certain aspects). This design element is very much appreciated by learners because it adds further points of view to the whole discussion inside the MOOC community.

The eLene MOOC complies with the criteria devised by the ECCOE project to support transparency and recognition of the credential earned through this learning opportunity. The Erasmus+ ECCOE project – European Credit Clearinghouse for Opening up Education – is developing a system for the recognition of digital credentials. The project aims to increase trust in technology-enabled credentials among students, higher education institutions (HEIs) and employers.

To this end, the eLene MOOC complies with the European standards such as EQF and ESCO (European Skills, Competences, Qualifications and Occupations) in terms of course description and definition of Intended Learning Outcomes (ILOs) and assessment. Indeed, ECCOE identified the description of ILOs in terms of ESCO attitudes, knowledge and skills combined with direct reference to the ESCO unique identifier of each individual skill as a key criterion for increasing the quality of the digital credential associated with a given learning opportunity. Quality is further enhanced by precise indications about the kinds of activity that learners will engage in to develop these skills, as well as about the assessment methods mobilised.

Main takeaways and future improvements

At the time of writing, the first edition of the MOOC is still ongoing and the results we present are only preliminary findings. Concerning the number of enrolled users so far, we have reached 450 participants, and the number of people who already finished all the activities and received their certificate of accomplishment is still low. Up to now we can say that one indicator of success is the fact that the forum is active, and the stimuli proposed to the discussion and for self-reflection are effective.

Furthermore, we conducted interviews with selected participants who reported a general positive impression, highlighting the usefulness of contents and theory presented also for those who are already familiar with active learning practice. The integration, in the course, of external resources as elements to enrich the discussion among peers, is particularly appreciated as it brings learners to really engage with them as part of the learning path and not only as an additional resource. Planning some synchronous interactions would be helpful to reinforce the exchange and, as one interviewee indicated, can make the difference on learning impact in terms of "what to take home". As mentioned, the experience of the first edition is still ongoing and further hints and feedback from participants that will be collected at the end of the edition will give more visibility on the strengths and weaknesses of the learning experience. These will be integrated in the presentation for the 2021 EDEN Annual Conference.

This international experience, in terms of instructional design activity and project management, has been very challenging and satisfactory. The strict coordination among all the actors involved has been the key element to structure the whole MOOC since its contents are highly interdependent; a delay on one element creation could have halted the implementation of the entire course. We will continue to work on the enrichment of the MOOC contents and the eLene4Life Dynamic Toolkit with further active methodologies contributed by MOOC participants and the competences acquired will be validated through the delivery of a micro-credential.

References

Bean, J. C. (1996). *The professor's guide to integrating writing, critical thinking, and active learning in the classroom.* San Francisco, CA: Jossey-Bass Publishers.

Biggs, J. B. (2003). *Teaching for Quality Learning at University.* Buckingham: Society for Research into Higher Education and Open University Press.

Cinque, M. (2016). "Lost in translation". Soft skills development in European countries. *Tuning Journal for Higher Education, 3*(2), 389-427.

Deloitte Access Economics (2017). *Soft Skills for Business Success.* Retrieved from https://www2.deloitte.com/content/dam/Deloitte/au/Documents/Economics/deloitte-au-economics-deakin-soft-skills-business-success-170517.pdf

D-Transform (2015). Transforming Universities for the Digital Age. Retrieved from https://www.dtransform.eu/

European Commission (2013). *Improving the quality of teaching and learning in Europe's higher education institutions.* Retrieved from https://op.europa.eu/it/publication-detail/-/publication/fbd4c2aa-aeb7-41ac-ab4c-a94feea9eb1f

ECCOE (2019). European Credit Clearinghouse for Opening up Education. Retrieved from https://eccoe.eu/

eLene4Life (2018). eLene4Life – Learning and Interacting to Foster Employability. Retrieved from http://www.elene4life.eu

eLene Network (2012). eLene public Facebook Group. Retrieved from https://www.facebook.com/groups/eLenenetwork

eLene4Life (2019). Welcome to the eLene4Life Dynamic Toolkit. Retrieved from http://elene4life.eu/dynamic-toolkit/

eLene4Life (2020). Pilot Project Report – Active Learning in Practice. Findings from eLene4Life Pilot Projects. Retrieved from http://elene4life.eu/project-outputs/pilot-projects/

eLene4Work (2017). Soft Skills Framework. Retrieved from https://drive.google.com/file/d/0ByZukJfrU4qGMGhpLVJYcTZ0clE/view?usp=sharing

Engels-Perenyi, K., & Nomden, K. (2021). A European Approach to Micro-credentials - MICROBOL Working Group on Qualifications Frameworks and ECTS. European Commission. Retrieved from https://microcredentials.eu/wp-content/uploads/sites/20/2021/01/European-Commission-expert-report-on-microcredentials_Microbol_27.01.pdf

Gaebel, M., Zhang, T., Bunescu, L., & Stoeber, H. (2018). *Learning and teaching in the European Higher Education Area.* European University Association. Retrieved from https://eua.eu/downloads/publications/trends-2018-learning-and-teaching-in-the-european-higher-education-area.pdf

Istituto per la formazione e il lavoro – ISFOL (2012). LE COMPETENZE PER L'OCCUPAZIONE E LA CRESCITA. Retrieved from http://isfoloa.isfol.it/bitstream/handle/123456789/290/Sintesi_Rapporto_2012.pdf;jsessionid=BFDDAB511439E0C7FD3F81EC18E05341?sequence=4

Manpower Group (2018). *Skills Revolution 2.0 Skills Revolution 2.0 Robots Need Not Apply: Human Solutions for the Skills Revolution.* Retrieved from https://www.manpowergroup.com/wcm/connect/59db87a7-16c6-490d-ae70-1bd7a322c240/Robots_Need_Not_Apply.pdf?MOD=AJPERES&CVID=m6L8fhv

McAuley, A. (2010). *The MOOC model for digital practice.* SSHRC Knowledge Synthesis Grant on the Digital Economy.

Prince, M. (2004). Does Active Learning Work? A Review of the Research. *Journal of Engineering Education, 93*, 223-231. https://doi.org/10.1002/j.2168-9830.2004.tb00809.x

Schulz, B. (2008). The Importance of Soft Skills: Education beyond academic knowledge. *NAWA Journal of Language and Communication, 2*(1), 146-154. Retrieved from https://ir.nust.na/bitstream/10628/39/1/The%20Importance%20of%20Soft%20%20Skills-Education%20beyond%20academic%20knowledge.pdf

Silberman, M. (1996). *Active Learning: 101 Strategies to Teach any Subject.* Needham Heights, MA: Allyn and Bacon.

Succi, C., & Canovi, M. (2020). Soft skills to enhance graduate employability: comparing students and employers' perceptions. *Studies in Higher Education, 45*(9), 1834-1847. https://doi.org/10.1080/03075079.2019.1585420

Sutherland, T., & Bonwell, C. (1996). *Using Active Learning in College Classes A Range of Options for Faculty*. Jossey-Bass Publisher.

Walker, S. E. (2003). Active learning strategies to promote critical thinking. *Journal of Athletic Training, 38*(3), 263-267.

Wilhelm, W. J., Logan, J., Smith, S. M., & Szul, L. F. (2002). *Meeting the demand: teaching "soft" skills*. Retrieved from https://files.eric.ed.gov/fulltext/ED477252.pdf

Lessons from a Pandemic for the Future of Education
European Distance and E-Learning Network (EDEN) Proceedings
2021 Annual Conference | Madrid, 21-24 June, 2021
ISSN 2707-2819
doi: 10.38069/edenconf-2021-ac0036

THE CHALLENGES OF OPEN DATA MOVEMENT FOR EDUCATION: WHAT IS THE SAY OF YOUNG EMPLOYEES AND STUDENTS IN CROATIA?

Branka Mraović, Faculty of Geodesy, University of Zagreb, Croatia

Abstract

This paper aims to shed light on how students and young employees in Croatia assess their education for open data and what is their opinion on the compliance of the central Open Data Portal with the needs of young people as well as how they evaluate open data policy related to the young people in Croatia. This research highlights the lack of technical knowledge as a serious obstacle to the productive use of open data. As many as 56% of respondents from companies that have undergone digital transformation believe that they do not have enough knowledge to participate in open data projects, and the same scepticism is expressed by 59.6% of non-technical respondents and 45.7% of students. The data presented in this paper is part of a broader empirical research on the impact of digitalization on the transformation of the Croatian economy, carried out by the author in late 2018 on a sample of 51 young employees from 10 companies in the city of Zagreb and 70 students from 16 technical and non-technical Faculties of Zagreb University.

Introduction

In this paper, on the example of the reception of the Open Data movement among the young population in Croatia, I want to draw attention to the importance of the proactive role of the education system and its obligation to provide students with action knowledge that will enable them to successfully cope with the challenges of rapid development of high-tech environment. I want to emphasize that education is primarily a cultural phenomenon that should: (a) serve the welfare of society and man; (b) promote the values of cooperation and altruism, and (c) be organized so as to strive for the common good. Under the influence of digitalization, the role of users is changing. In earlier stages of internet development, they were consumers of e-content, and technological development enabled them to convert to e-content creators. The development of advanced technologies, especially 2.0 (social media), Web 3.0 (semantic web), and web 4.0 (Internet of Things – IoT) opens up huge opportunities for governments, companies, institutions and citizens, but also sets new educational demands before them. New technologically mediated forms of learning are at work that require new knowledge and skills. This primarily refers to knowledge of search techniques, knowledge of digital media and data literacy. However, in order to turn the potentials provided by the non-human entities into real benefits for the humans, new mental models of people are needed, with education systems and academic community expected to play a key role in these radical transformations of our lives, work and ways of thinking. The focus of this analysis is how students and young employees perceive open data policy in Croatia, and how they assess their educational readiness for open data.

E-Government and Open Data

In a complex, dynamic and interdependent global community, no one can function as a lonely island, not even the governments. As Schellong (2010) points out, the development of Web 2.0 has changed the understanding of the role of Government and the way it works. "The term Government 2.0 refers to the use of social software and underlying philosophy of Web 2.0, information sharing, transparency or peer production in government" (Schellong, 2010; p.374). Electronic Government (e-Government) or "Open Government" (Obama Administration, Office of Management Budget, 2008; the Malmoe Declaration, European Commission, 2009) or "Government 2.0" is networking Government. The dominant trend of a data-driven society is the constant democratization of data use and protection, in which the European Union regulatory framework takes the lead. Consequently, citizens are perceived as co-creators in policy-making, public management and public service delivery (Schellong, 2010). In the new millennium, the governments around the world are making efforts to develop the open data ecosystems with the goal of using open data to create new value in the business sector. The term "open data of public administration" refers to an information policy that provides a set of management principles aimed at promoting the sharing and reuse data sets that does not restrict privacy and confidentiality, which are produced with public money and are available without restrictions on their use and distribution (Styrin, Luna-Reyes, & Harrison, 2017; pp.132-3). The goal of the open data policy promoted by large international and supranational organizations such as the UN, World Bank, OECD, EU and others is to create a business climate with the aim of improving services and motivating users to be creative and develop new innovative companies. Open data is considered to be one of the key factors that will enable the transformation of public administration and the development of the digital economy. Empirical research by Zhao, Wallis, and Singh (2015) indicated a strong positive reciprocal link between the development of e-government and the digital economy. It also confirmed that the co-evolution between technology and organization continues in the context of the 4th Industrial Revolution and pointed to the importance of national cultural features for the digital transformation of the economy, state and society.

Croatia became a full member of the EU in July 2013 and has since started the process of translating open data policy into the Croatian context. At its 107th session on 19 July 2018, the Government of the Republic of Croatia adopted the Open Data Policy, which represents a strategic direction for further development of the policy of openness and transparency of public administration, whose implementation aims to create and develop an enabling environment for the opening up and re-use of public authority data to create a new social and economic value. According to EU estimates, the open data market in 2020 would amount to at least 75.7 billion euros and open the possibility of new employment for 25,000 people. For the Republic of Croatia, the EU estimated the creation of up to 1,000 new jobs in 2020, and the market value was estimated at EUR 186 million (Government, HR, 2018).

Promoting Open Data, Enabling Proactive Learners

From the conceptual project of digitalization emerges the concept of a Big Society which is realized through a human-machine symbiosis in a wide range of collaborative projects between the corporate and public sector and the academic community. Ekbia et al. (2015) use a term "heteromation" as the term to indicate the new creative role of people in creating the knowledge infrastructure in a high-tech environment and emphasize the "distinction between data generated by people versus data generated about people". This opens up the possibility for individuals and small players to "own" their data and that through shared participation in data collection they are no longer just measured, but also the "measuring subjects". To reduce costs, an increasing number of companies (Amazon, Tesla) and institutions (NASA) use volunteer computing to test software and solve specific algorithmic problems. Through the spread and popularity of open linked data, an increasing number of authors are contributing to the extraction of web data into a semantic web format (Fang, Sheng, Wang, Ngu, & Zhang, 2017; p.121). The idea that is particularly promoted by academic knowledge bases such as Freebase, DBpedia and DeepDive is to enable as many people and machines as possible to share jointly generated knowledge.

The penetration of advanced technologies into all spheres of people's lives, work and thinking, and their universal, pervasive and radical character, poses numerous questions, dilemmas and challenges to engineering professions, scientists, education systems, citizens and politicians. But at the same time, technology affirms the values of civil society and supports the rights of citizens, and expands the influence of local communities. However, as Haraway (2007) categorically argues, every vision implies in itself the power to see and the point of view of interest, and consequently, requires responsibility.

> *"Technologies are skilled practices. How to see? Where to see from? What limits to vision? What to see for? Whom to see with? Who gets to have more than one point of view? Who gets blinkened? Who wears blinkers? Who interprets the visual field? What other sensory powers do we wish to cultivate besides vision?" (Haraway, 2007; p.120).*

Situated knowledge develops from communities, not from isolated individuals, through "decoding" and transcoding plus translation and criticism (Haraway, 2007; p.122), leading to affirmation of partiality, and not universality, which allows the "knowledge of subjugated" to be involved in the paradigmatic model of science. This knowledge can be an important and useful guideline for strategic thinking that facilitates both moving in the desired direction and avoiding undesirable outcomes. Her plea for situated and embodied knowledge aims at "transformation of systems of knowledge and ways of seeing", as being convinced that transformative potentials of knowledge can lead to the organization of the world that will be less dependent on the will to dominate.

National digital strategies around the world recognize open data as a *conditio sine qua non* and as one of the key tools that enable productive, participatory and innovative interactions between citizens and public servants, by expanding the space of experimentation to find new solutions to new problems opened by the development of disruptive technologies in various spheres of the business sector, education, health, culture and politics. The OECD study (2016) as the two main challenges for the open data policy emphasizes the "resistance to publish open data and the lack of human resources with technical training to effectively participate in the process of opening data" (Styrin, Luna-Reyes, & Harrison, 2017; p.146).

Research by Styrin, Luna-Reyes, and Harrison (2017) highlights that the national open data projects depend on political leadership and the involvement of multiple stakeholders such as civil servants, IT developers, entrepreneurs, data activists from NGOs, IT industry, citizens and financial institutions. They identified political leadership as the most vulnerable aspect because it can change periodically with elections. This indicates to the need to cultivate an organizational culture and a positive climate towards open data, for which the USA is a successful example. Cordella and Hesse (2014) point to stakeholder theory as a useful tool for analysing the impact of open data ecosystems on the scope and pace of digital transformation of the state. The authors give an example of the use of ANT as a useful analytical lens to measure the dynamics of e-government projects because they imply the connection and interaction of different actors in complex negotiation processes. Research by Pinochet et al. (2019) sheds light on open data as a new form of activism leading to a collective intelligence that will enable greater transparency of public activities.

They point to young people as an important social group that will play a crucial role in promoting digital education.

Results of the empirical research and data analysis

Research goals

This article presents the data on how students and young employees in Croatia assess their education for open data projects, and what is their opinion on the compliance of the central Open Data Portal with the needs of the Young as well as how they evaluate open data policy related to the young people in Croatia.

Sample of respondents

The author conducted this study late in 2018 on a sample of 51 young employees aged to 35 from 10 companies in the area of the city of Zagreb that use new technologies and work with large datasets and 70 students aged to 25 from 16 technical and non-technical Faculties of Zagreb University. In the group of employees, the sample included respondents from: pure digital companies, companies that have undergone digital transformation and geospatial institutions; small, large and medium-sized companies; public and private; from 10 industry branches (e-commerce, Internet advertisement, University Computing Center, distribution and logistics, energetics, telecommunications, National roads, gas industry, Cadastre Zagreb and Land Registry Law Office).

Hypotheses

In accordance with the formulated goals, the following hypotheses were formulated:

- I expect that there is the probability of relationships between occupation, type of education and level of digitalization of the company and respondents' opinion of their educational readiness for open data projects, and I expect that the observed groups of respondents will differ in measured characteristics.
- I expect that the observed groups of respondents will differ in their views on the compliance of the central Open Data Portal with the needs of the Young, and the way in which they perceive open data policy for the Young

Variables

The pivotal independent variables (predictors) in this article are occupation (students and young employees), a type of education (technical and non-technical), and the level of digitalization of the company (pure digital, companies that have undergone digital transformation, and geospatial institutions). Measured dependent variables are: self-evaluations of the respondent's educational readiness for open data, attitudes towards the work of the central Open Data Portal, attitudes towards open data policy, and perceptions of the most deserving actors for data opening in Croatia.

Methods of data processing

Inferential analysis was done in R statistical package (R Core Team, 2020), while dataset preparation and figures were done in Stata statistical software, version 14.2 (StataCorp, 2015). The data were processed using a hi-square test.

Data analysis

I. Self-evaluation of students and young employees of their educational readiness for open data

The finding obtained showed that students and young employees similarly perceive the level of their education in the field of technical sciences for open data, namely 49% of employees and 32.9% of students believe that they are educated enough to be able to set specific data requirements that will be useful to them ($X^2 = 4.5$, df = 2, $p < 0.106$).

The data show that technical and non-technical respondents differ statistically significantly in their opinion on the sufficiency of their education for open data requirements ($X^2 = 12.4$, df = 2, $p < 0.002$). Also, respondents from pure digital companies, transformed companies and geospatial companies differ statistically significantly regarding this measured variable ($X^2 = 16.2$, df = 4, $p < 0.003$). It is worth noting that as many as 90% of respondents from geospatial companies compared to 62.5% from pure digital and 24% from transformed companies perceive their technical education sufficient for open data (Figure 1).

The high evaluation that respondents from geospatial institutions attribute to their education can be explained by the fact that the sector has been involved for many years in coordinated activities at the global (UN), regional (EU) and national state level aimed at building the Global Spatial Data Infrastructure, and this is also linked to continuing education programs for the Staff (after the EU INSPIRE Directive entered into force on 15 May 2007). This finding confirms some other analyses according to which spatial data are one of the best developed areas in the field of open data in Croatia. On the other hand, the critical attitude of respondents from pure digital companies could be due to the high complexity of the work environment and the rapid changes in the ways of performing work operations imposed by the ICTs development. It is certainly alarming to find that among those respondents who feel that their technical education is not sufficient for active involvement in data-opening processes and their effective use, there are:

- 41.2% of employees and 45.7% of students;
- 59.6% of non-technical and 29.7% of technical respondents;

- 56% of respondents from transformed, 37.5% from pure digital companies and 10% from geospatial institutions.

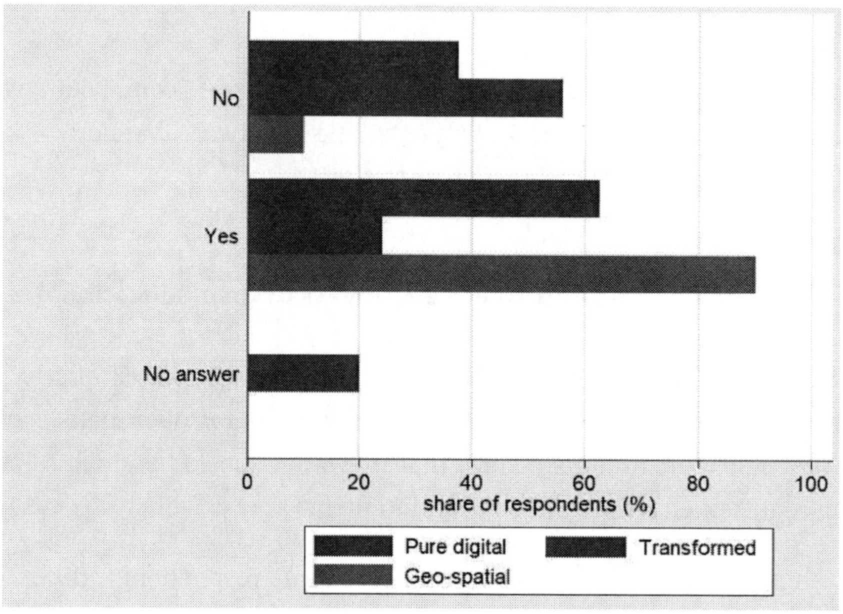

Figure 1. Perceptions of sufficiency of education for setting open data demands

II. Attitudes of students and young employees about open data policy in Croatia

One of the goals of this research is to shed light on how young respondents peive open data policy in Croatia. I operationalized this research question through three close-ended questions: (a) Is the central Open Data Portal (data.gov.hr) sufficiently adapted to young people?; (b) How would you assess the results of the open data policy in Croatia related to the Young so far?; (c) How would you assess the contributions of key stakeholders engaged in data opening in Croatia in terms of promoting user participation: Government; Non-governmental organizations; IT industry; Innovators; Entrepreneurs; Financial institutions; Politicians; Someone else, who. The finding obtained confirmed the initial hypothesis as it shows that the occupation, type of education and level of digitalization of the company have a significant impact on the way respondents assess open data policy in Croatia.

The data show that students and young employees differ statistically significantly in terms of their perception of the adaptation of the central Open Data Portal to young people ($X^2 = 22.5$, $df = 3$, $p < 0.001$). Statistically significant differences regarding the perception of the adaptation of the central Open Data Portal to young people also exist between respondents with technical and non-technical type of education ($X^2 = 9.5$, $df = 3$, $p < 0.023$), and between respondents from pure digital and transformed companies and geospatial institutions ($X^2 = 23.6$, $df = 4$, $p < 0.001$).

The central Open Data Portal is sufficiently adapted to young people according the opinion of:

- 29.4% of employees and 7.1% of students;
- 20.3% technical and 12.3% non-echnical respondents;
- 90% respondents from geospatial institutions, 25% from pure digital companies and only 8% from transformed companies.

The open data policy for young people in Croatia is considered satisfactory by:

- 19.6% of employees and 5.7% of students;
- 12.5% of technical and 10.5% of non-technical respondents;
- 60% of respondents from geospatial institutions, 12.5% from pure digital companies and only 8% from transformed companies.

According to frequencies' orderings, as stakeholders who have given the greatest contributions to the opening of data in Croatia in terms of promoting the participation of users, students identify: (a) IT industry (81.7%), (b) innovators (73.3%), and entrepreneurs (65%), while young employees first place entrepreneurs (82.6%), then the IT industry (80.4%), and financial institutions (69.6%).

III. How familiar are young employees and students with the open data policy in Croatia?

What concerns in particular is the poor awareness of the young population on open data policy in Croatia. Among those respondents who are not familiar with the activities of the central Open Data Portal (data.gov.hr) are:

- 54.3% of students and 39.2% of employees;
- 56.1% of non-technical and 40.6% of technical respondents;
- 52% respondents from transformed companies, 43.8% from pure digital companies and 0.0% from geospatial institutions.

Among those respondents who are not familiar with the Open Data policy for the Young in Croatia are:

- 55.7% of students and 51% of employees;
- 54.4% of non-technical and 53.1% of technical respondents;
- 72% of respondents from transformed companies, 50% from pure digital companies and 0.0% from geospatial institutions.

Conclusions

Respondents from geospatial institutions have the most positive perception of open data policy in Croatia, while respondents from transformed companies are the most critical of it. Respondents from geospatial institutions believe that they are sufficiently educated for open data (90%), believe that the Central Open Data Portal is sufficiently adapted to the young people (90%) and that Croatia has a good open data policy for the young people (60%). This research highlights the lack of technical knowledge as a serious obstacle to the productive use of open data. As many as 56% of respondents from transformed companies believe that they do not have enough knowledge to participate in open data projects, and the same scepticism is expressed by 59.6% of non-technical respondents and 45.7% of students. As stakeholders who have made the greatest contributions to the opening of data in Croatia in terms of promoting user participation, students identify: (a) IT industry (81.7%), (b) innovators (73.3%) and entrepreneurs (65%), while young employees put entrepreneurs first (82.6%), followed by the IT industry (80.4%) and financial institutions (69.6%). What concerns in particular is the poor awareness of the young population on open data policy in Croatia. As many as 55.7% of students, 72% of respondents from transformed companies and 50% from pure digital companies are not familiar with the open data policy, while the level of information of respondents from geospatial institutions is 100%. To embrace artificial intelligence, users need to be helped to understand and love it, and in these intentions, the online learning movement is and can be a motivating leader. Although this is a small sample, the results of this research can undoubtedly be a useful message to the education system and curriculum creators, but also to the media content editors.

References

Cordella, A., & Hesse, J. (2015). E-government in the making: an actor network perspective. *Transforming Government: People, Process and Policy, 9*(1), 104-125. doi:10.1108/TG-02-2014-0006

Ekbia, H., Mattioli, M., Kouper, I., G. Arave, G., Ghazinejad, A., Bowman,T., Ratandeep Suri, V., Tsou, A., Scott Weingart, S., & Sugimoto, C.R. (2015). Big data, bigger dilemmas: A critical review. *Journal of the Association for Information Science & Technology, 66*(8), 1523-1545.

Fang, X. S., Sheng, Q. Z., Wang, X., Ngu, A. H. H., & Zhang, Y. (2017). GrandBase: generating actionable knowledge from big data. *PSU Research Review, 1*(2), 105-126. https://doi.org/10.1108/PRR-01-2017-0005

Haraway, D. (2007). Situated knowledge. In K. Asdal, B. Brenna , & I. Moser (Eds.), Technoscience, The Politics of Interventions (pp. 109-134). Oslo: Academic Press.

Mulholland, J. (2016, September 27). What Obama Did for Tech: Transparency and Open Data. Government Technology [Blog post]. Retrieved from https://www.govtech.com/data/What-Obama-Did-for-Tech-Transparency-and-Open-Data.html

R Core Team (2020). R: A language and environment for statistical computing. R Foundation for Statistical Computing, Vienna, Austria. Retrieved from https://www.R-project.org

Schellong, A. R. M. (2010). Bencmarking EU e-government at the crossroads. A framework for e-government benchmark design and improvement. *Transforming Government: People, Process and Policy, 4*(4), 365-385. doi 10.1108/17506161011081336

StataCorp (2015). Stata Statistical Software: Release 14. College Station, TX (USA): StataCorp LP.

Styrin, E., Luna-Reyes, L. F., & M. Harrison, M. T. (2017). Open data ecosystems: an international comparison. *Transforming Government: People, Process and Policy, 11*(1), 132-156. https://doi.org/10.1108/TG-01-2017-0006

Vlada Republike Hrvatske (2018). Politika otvorenih podataka, srpanj 2018. Retrieved from https://rdd.gov.hr/UserDocsImages/SDURDD-dokumenti/POLITIKA%20OTVORENIH%20PODATAKA.pdf

Zhao, F., Wallis, J., & Singh, M. (2015). E-government development and the digital economy: a reciprocal relationship. *Internet Research, 25*(5), 734-766. doi:10.1108/IntR-02-2014-0055

Acknowledgements

I thank my colleague Marko Lucić for processing this data, commitment and enthusiasm.

Lessons from a Pandemic for the Future of Education
European Distance and E-Learning Network (EDEN) Proceedings
2021 Annual Conference | Madrid, 21-24 June, 2021
ISSN 2707-2819
doi: 10.38069/edenconf-2021-ac0037

SAFE FROM HARM: DEVELOPMENT OF ONLINE CHILD PROTECTION TRAINING FOR SCOUTS NEW ZEALAND

Elizabeth Asbury, Emma Addington, George Orsborn, Whitireia New Zealand, John Williams, SCOUTS New Zealand, New Zealand

Abstract

Introduction: SCOUTS New Zealand place paramount importance on keeping young people safe from harm. New Zealand (NZ) has one of the highest rates of child abuse and child death by maltreatment in the developed world. SCOUTS NZ engage with 14,500 children and young people, supported by 4,500 adult volunteers in 340 locations across New Zealand. SCOUTS wanted to inform and educate all their members about the importance of child protection (CP), while managing the challenges of a geographically disparate population through online learning.

Method: "Introduction to Child and Youth Protection" module was created collaboratively with SCOUTS NZ and online educators at Whitireia NZ. The aim was to provide an accessible, evidence based, self-paced online module illustrating the realities of child abuse and neglect in NZ, while enabling the participants to understand the role of SCOUTS NZ in child and youth protection. The module was developed using "Articulate Storyline", peer reviewed by Subject Matter Experts (SMEs) working in Youth Development and Social Work, and evaluated using the Kirkpatrick framework.

Results: 1102 SCOUTS leaders and volunteers have completed the CP module and evaluation to date. Significant improvements in the learning outcomes "Understanding the realities of child abuse and neglect in NZ" (5.32 ± 1.35 vs. 6.26 ± 0.79, $p < 0.001$), "Understanding the importance of child and youth protection in NZ" (5.99 ± 1.13 vs. 6.51 ± 0.71, $p < 0.001$) and "Understanding the role of SCOUTS in child protection" (5.74 ± 1.22 vs. 6.46 ± 0.79, $p < 0.001$) were found on completion of the module. Participants found the module engaging (95%), useful (97%), applicable (99%) and relevant to their role (99%).

Conclusion: By using tailored, appropriate content, emotive topics can be addressed through online learning, as this successful collaboration has demonstrated.

Introduction

Aotearoa New Zealand has one of the highest rates of child abuse and one of the worst rates of child death as a result of maltreatment in the developed world (Adamson, 2013). On average a child dies every five weeks as a result of violence in New Zealand, the majority of whom are under 12 years of age (New Zealand Police, 2016). Between 2007 and 2016, children under five years of age represented 12% of all homicide victims, while in 2015, 63 children aged 16 years or under were hospitalised as a result of an assault perpetrated by a family member (New Zealand Police, 2016).

Sobering research by Rhouland and Vaithianathan (2018), found that nearly 10% of all children fall victim to substantiated abuse or neglect in New Zealand, and that on average one child dies every five weeks as a result of violence in New Zealand (Doolan, 2004). While physical abuse and violence are often the most recognisable forms of abuse, children can experience emotional abuse, which may involve feeling unsafe at home, feeling degraded, receiving constant criticism or being left alone, while sexual abuse includes inappropriate touching and involvement in any sexual act with an adult. Oranga Tamariki Act (Oranga Tamariki, 1989) defines child abuse as "the harming (whether physically, emotionally, or sexually), ill-treatment, abuse, neglect or deprivation of any child or young person". Sadly, studies have found that one in four New Zealand girls is sexually abused before the age of 15 (Fanslow, Robinson, Crengle, & Perese, 2007) and that Māori girls are at greatest risk. It is also reported that NZ Police respond to one "family violence" call every five minutes (New Zealand Police, 2016), indicating that hundreds of New Zealand children are exposed to abuse and violence every day.

Most child abuse occurs within the family environment but it can happen anywhere: at school, in the larger community, or online (Child Matters, n.d.). The sad reality is that most child abuse occurs in what would otherwise be seen as a 'safe' environment, often undertaken by a trusted family member, friend, church leader, sports coach, teacher or mentor. Unfortunately SCOUTS New Zealand has not been immune from acts of abuse, which has led to a significant overhaul of how SCOUTS keeps children and young people safe from harm.

Every child has the right to a childhood free from harm. With 5,000 volunteers trusted with the care and protection of over 14,500 child and youth members within SCOUTS New Zealand (Scouts New Zealand, 2018), SCOUTS feel they have a critical role to play in ensuring children and young people remain safe. One strategy to keep children in their care safe from harm, is to support their volunteers to understand what child abuse is, how to recognise abuse and what to do should they suspect abuse.

SCOUTS place paramount importance on keeping young people safe from harm, but were struggling to provide comprehensive face-to-face child protection training to all members and volunteers of the 340 SCOUTS groups across New Zealand. SCOUTS identified that online learning could deliver standardised organization-wide child protection training and education, in spite of the geographically disparate nature of participants.

Methods

Educators at Whitireia New Zealand worked with SCOUTS NZ to create an accessible, engaging, and non-threatening eLearning module that allowed the participants to encounter the often alarming and disturbing content associated with child protection privately, independently and at their own pace. This paper presents the evaluative study of the newly created "Introduction to Child and Youth Protection" online learning module, and explores the reality of creating an online environment where participants can explore a challenging content in a positive learning atmosphere.

The development team, consisting of a health and occupational psychologist, educationalist, a nurse education eLearning developer and representatives from SCOUTS NZ, created a researched and referenced module entitled "Introduction to Child and Youth Protection" as the first of three modules addressing child protection for SCOUTS NZ. The objective was to create a suit of objective, interactive modules that explained realities of child abuse and neglect in New Zealand, explored the impact of child abuse in SCOUTS NZ and provided opportunities for participants to reflect on their behaviour in relation to keeping children safe from harm. Subsequent modules examine how to recognise types of abuse, including the behaviour of perpetrators, how to manage a disclosure, and what to do should they suspect abuse. The learning outcomes were designed to mirror those of the traditional, classroom-based pedagogy:

- Understanding the realities of child abuse and neglect in NZ;
- Understanding the importance of child and youth protection in NZ;
- Understanding the role of SCOUTS in child protection.

The eLearning developers worked with SCOUTS NZ and child and youth development subject matter experts to identify suitable content, source material, linked references and real-world scenarios. A storyboard and prototype were then developed, and scenarios were filmed using local Scout groups. The module was designed to take approximately 30 minutes to complete and was comprised of 22 pages of content. The content defined child abuse and neglect, discussed demographic data relating to child abuse, neglect and family violence, and demonstrated real-world scenarios to illustrate best practice. The module was created using Articulate 360 (Articulate, 2017) and was accessed via the CPD@Whitireia Moodle Learning Management System (LMS). Module development tools such as Articulate 360 allow non-programmers such as tertiary educators to create dynamic flexible learning material (O'Donnell, Lawless, Sharp, & Wade, 2015), that can be viewed anytime, at any place and on any device. The ability to access the child protection modules in a safe, non-threatening and comfortable environment selected by the participant was deemed critical in the creation of the module. Once developed, the child protection module was reviewed and tested internally and then by a group of SCOUTS volunteers to check any technical issues, content and suitability.

The evaluation is based on Kirkpatrick's Four Levels of Evaluation model (Kirkpatrick & Kirkpatrick, 2006), which proposes a four level training evaluation approach. The first two levels, Reaction and Learning can be assessed on completion of the course, and include both the participants perceptions of the training and their perceived increase in knowledge. Levels Three and Four explore the extent to which the new learning has been applied and the organizational impact of the training, and fell outside the remit of the current project. The evaluation questionnaire contained three sections. The first section asked participants to rate their reaction to the content and applicability of the module, while the second section explored the response to the various interactive tools in the module. Both sections used a four-point Likert scale response format. The final section explored changes in understanding based on the learning outcomes and were charted on a seven-point sliding Likert scale, from low to high level understanding. Participants were first asked to retrospectively rate their previous understanding of each of the three learning outcomes before having completed the module, and then reflect on their current understanding following module completion.

Results

The "Introduction to Child and Youth Protection" online learning module launched in April 2019. To date 2401 (47%) of the estimated 5021 SCOUTS NZ volunteers (Scouts New Zealand, 2018) have gained access to the modules, while 1102 participants have undertaken the evaluation to date, representing 45% of participants. The average time to complete the module was reported as being between 20 and 40 minutes. Many participants had a long association with SCOUTS, with an average of 9.5 (SD = 10.52) years active (range 1 – 65 years).

Participants were asked to rate their reaction to the modules using a four-point Likert scale response format, from one (*Strongly disagree*) to four (*Strongly agree*). The participant's reactions to the module content is shown in Table One.

Table 1: The percentage of participant's reaction to the "Understanding Child and Youth Protection" module content

	Strongly disagree	Disagree	Agree	Strongly agree
I found the module content engaging	1%	3%	67%	29%
I found the content of the module useful	<1%	2%	61%	36%
The module content is relevant for SCOUTS leaders and volunteers	<1%	<1%	42%	57%
I was comfortable with the content of the module	<1%	1%	49%	49%
I am more confident in my understanding of child protection issues	<1%	5%	59%	35%
I am confident that I can and will apply this understanding to my role in SCOUTS.	<1%	<1%	44%	55%

While 81% of participants were comfortable learning about child and youth protection in an online environment, 80% expressed a preference for online child and youth protection education, rather than a traditional classroom / workshop-based approach. Reactions to the various interactive devices were broadly positive, as shown in Table Two.

Table 2: The percentage of participant's reaction to the "Understanding Child and Youth Protection" interactive devices

	Not at all engaging	Not very engaging	Quite engaging	Very engaging
Sliders	1%	10%	67%	22%
Click and reveal	2%	11%	65%	22%
Filmed scenarios	<1%	5%	48%	46%
Reflective questions	1%	9%	64%	26%

Significant improvements in the learning outcomes "Understanding of the realities of child abuse and neglect in NZ" (5.32 ± 1.35 vs. 6.26 ± 0.79, $p < 0.001$), "Understanding of the importance of child and youth protection in NZ" (5.99 ± 1.13 vs. 6.51 ± 0.71, $p < 0.001$) and "Understanding of the role of SCOUTS in child and youth protection" (5.74 ± 1.22 vs. 6.46 ± 0.79, $p < 0.001$) were found on completion of the module.

Discussion

Child abuse and neglect is an emotive topic, and the statistics relating to child abuse and neglect in Aotearoa New Zealand are particularly shocking. SCOUTS New Zealand is a diverse and inclusive youth organisation, and has embraced the obligation to do everything possible to keep its young people safe from harm. As such, the "Introduction to child and youth protection" module was the first of three online modules focussed on child protection, and sits alongside a raft of new child protection initiatives. These include the new 0508 SCOUTHELP helpline, "Feeling unsafe?" promotion and advertising, along the

"Purple Card" scheme, which places child protection information in the hands of all SCOUTS members, leaders, children and volunteers.

The results show that the module was very well received by participants. User experience ratings were positive for over 95% of participants, and almost all found the module relevant, useful and immediately applicable to their role in SCOUTS. User engagement and subsequent learning can be enhanced if learning is timely and relevant (Brooks et al., 2016), and critically, although the participants had a high level of understanding relating to child protection before undertaking the module, there were significant improvements in knowledge relating to all three learning outcomes on completion.

While all the interactions were predominately reported as engaging, the most engaging were the video scenarios. The scenarios demonstrated SCOUT leaders responding to events in a familiar environment, enabling the participants to reflect on their own practice and how they would respond in a similar situation. Creating a simulated learning environment as an education method in a relevant context, actively engages learners in the learning process (Lamont & Brunero, 2013). The realness of simulation can promote deep experiential learning and awareness due to its perceived relevance to the learner (Peddle, 2011). This educational approach provides real-life, engaging, authentic problem-based learning that requires the learner to reflect on their own SCOUTS practice.

One of the major drivers of this project, was to ensure that education around child and youth protection was accessible to all SCOUTS members, leaders and volunteers. eLearning is a highly effective approach that enables flexible and cost effective competence development, as it is not restricted to physical location or time of use (Jeong & Yeo, 2014). eLearning, such as the Child and Youth Protection eLearning series, enables more people to be educated, at a lower cost and with similar or even better learning outcomes compared with classroom-based learning (Salmon, 2013). The creation of the eLearning child protection modules have increased accessibility to appropriate education on a number of levels. Firstly, the module could be undertaken anytime, anywhere and from any device ensuring that those who are unable attend face-to-face training or are geographically isolated from training in the main centres, were able to participate. Secondly, the modules were accessible, created using audio on each slide, closed captions and plain language to cater for the wide range of learnings styles and reading abilities. Finally, studies have shown that carefully created online education can successfully address sensitive topics and issues of culture safety (Asbury & Orsborn, 2020), illustrating that eLearning can provide a safe environment to engage with challenging content. By creating accessible, authentic eLearning SCOUTS NZ can become a more informed, responsive and proactive organisation in the field of child and youth protection.

References

Adamson, P. (2013). *Child Well-Being in Rich Countries: A Comparative Overview.* Innocenti Report Card 11. UNICEF.

Articulate. (2017). Introducing Articulate 360. Retrieved from https://articulate.com/360

Asbury, E. A., & Orsborn, G. (2020) Teaching Sensitive Topics in an Online Environment: An Evaluation of Cultural Safety E-Learning. *Whitireia Journal of Health, Nursing and Social Services, 27*, 23-31.

Brooks, H. L., Pontefract, S. K., Vallance, H. K., Hirsch, C. A., Hughes, E., Ferner, R. E., ... Coleman, J. J. (2016). Perceptions and impact of mandatory eLearning for foundation trainee doctors: a qualitative evaluation. *PloS One, 11*(12), e0168558.

Child Matters. (n.d.). What is child abuse? Retrieved from http://www.childmatters.org.nz/

Doolan, M. P. (2004). *A Life Too Short: Child death by homicide in New Zealand: An examination of incidence and statutory child protection actions.*

Fanslow, J. L., Robinson, E. M., Crengle, S., & Perese, L. (2007). Prevalence of child sexual abuse reported by a cross-sectional sample of New Zealand women. *Child Abuse & Neglect, 31*(9), 935-945.

Jeong, H.-Y., & Yeo, S.-S. (2014). The quality model for e-learning system with multimedia contents: a pairwise comparison approach. *Multimedia Tools and Applications, 73*(2), 887-900.

Kirkpatrick, D., & Kirkpatrick, J. (2006). *Evaluating Training Programs: The Four Levels.* Berrett-Koehler Publishers.

Lamont, S., & Brunero, S. (2013). 'eSimulation' Part 1: Development of an interactive multimedia mental health education program for generalist nurses. *Collegian, 20*(4), 239-247.

New Zealand Police. (2016). Police Statistics on Homicide Victims in New Zealand 2007 – 2016. *A Summary of Statistics about Victims of Murder, Manslaughter, and Infanticide, 6642*(July 2018), 1-17.

O'Donnell, E., Lawless, S., Sharp, M., & Wade, V. (2015). *A review of personalised e-learning: Towards supporting learner diversity.*

Oranga Tamariki. (1989). *Oranga Tamariki Act 1989 Children's and Young People's Well-being Act 1989.*

Peddle, M. (2011). Simulation gaming in nurse education; entertainment or learning? *Nurse Education Today, 31*(7), 647-649.

Rouland, B., & Vaithianathan, R. (2018). Cumulative prevalence of maltreatment among New Zealand children, 1998–2015. *American Journal of Public Health, 108*(4), 511-513.

Salmon, G. (2013). *E-tivities: The key to active online learning.* Routledge.

Scouts New Zealand. (2018). *Annual Report 2018.*

Lessons from a Pandemic for the Future of Education
European Distance and E-Learning Network (EDEN) Proceedings
2021 Annual Conference | Madrid, 21-24 June, 2021
ISSN 2707-2819
doi: 10.38069/edenconf-2021-ac0038

PANDEMIC AS CATALYST FOR NATIONAL DIGITAL TRANSFORMATION OF HIGHER EDUCATION – A SWEDISH CASE STUDY

Lena Dafgård, Dalarna University, Alastair Creelman, Linnaeus University, Sweden

Abstract

The covid-19 emergency presented daunting challenges for all in higher education, in particular teachers and students who were forced to quickly pivot from the familiar setting of the campus to purely online education in a matter of days. Despite the enormity of this challenge the transition was negotiated successfully in terms of online teaching though issues such as social interaction, student isolation and digital divides remained largely unaddressed. In Sweden, the pandemic response has been a wake-up call to address the lack of national coordination of online and blended education as well as the need for more coordinated approaches to professional pedagogical development. This paper outlines the response of several national networks and stakeholder organisations, notably the Network for IT in Higher Education (ITHU), though the forming of a mutual support group on Facebook to coordinating workshops and sharing resources. A survey of ITHU members revealed a number of key focus areas for national coordination as well as the development of a culture of sharing between teaching staff and educational technicians that did not exist before the pandemic.

Introduction

Pre-Covid Swedish higher education had a relatively uncoordinated approach to online learning and there was a great variation in strategies between different higher education institutions (HEIs). Responsibility for the development of online and distance education was delegated to institutional level where it was largely driven by specialists and enthusiasts in projects and networks. There were of course many examples of good practice and many innovative institutional initiatives but there was no arena to share these and very little collaboration between institutions in terms of pedagogical development. Furthermore, there was no significant culture of sharing and most educational resources were locked behind institutional passwords. The production and use of open educational resources (OER) have been centred around smaller projects and are still far from mainstream acceptance.

Sweden was an early leader in distance education in the 1990s and government coordination and funding led to a sharp growth in distance courses and even degree programmes until around 2008 when the authority responsible for networking and cooperation in higher education (NSHU – Myndigheten för nätverk och samarbete inom högre utbildning – Swedish Agency for Networks and Cooperation in Higher Education) was closed down and responsibility was then delegated to institutional level. Since then, the uncoordinated development described above has resulted in a reduction in the number of distance courses and a focus on campus courses and programmes. The rapid increase in the number of distance courses resulted in many university teachers teaching online courses without any experience or in-service training. The results of a national questionnaire in 2009, which 740 course coordinators teaching online courses answered, demonstrated that only about half of the respondents had participated in any training at all (Dafgård, 2020). About half of those who received training had only up to one week of training or equivalent (Dafgård, 2020).

The authorities questioned the quality of many distance courses due to low completion rates and this led to a reduction in numbers. Many distance and online courses have indeed suffered from lower completion rates, often largely due to an instrumental approach to online education and a lack of pedagogical course design. The Swedish decision on *the dual mode model*, which means that both distance education and campus courses are offered by the same institution, has made it more difficult to allocate funds to develop distance pedagogy, new technology, and production of media materials in the way *the single mode model* institutions did, which specialised in distance education (Moore & Kearsley, 2005). A key factor in the discussion of distance education quality is that of the “transactional distance”, a feature of most course forms (Moore, 1997). “Transactional distance” originates from Dewey and is further developed into the Theory of Transactional Distance” by Moore (Moore, 1997). There is a risk of a higher degree of “transactional distance” in online courses as it refers to the psychological distance, i.e., changed behaviour of students and teachers and the pedagogical effects, which can cause problems in understanding and communication. “Transactional distance” can be reduced by student-teacher interaction (Payne, 1999).

Since the demise of the responsible government authority, NSHU, a voluntary network was formed, ITHU (Swedish Network for IT in Higher Education – http://ithu.se). ITHU is a professional development network that aims to promote and enhance the pedagogical application of IT in teaching and learning. The network also aims to be a forum for the exchange of experience and knowledge in the field in terms of practice, research and development. ITHU consists mostly of educational developers, educational technologists, teachers and librarians. The network has representatives in almost all Swedish higher education institutions.

ITHU's main objectives are to:

- develop the competence of university teachers and other staff in the use of digital media in teaching and learning;
- initiate and coordinate activities, projects and working groups in the field of educational technology;
- act as a pedagogical support for other networks in higher education;
- monitor developments in the field of educational technology;
- cooperate with authorities and other organisations in the field.

Since its inception the network has been an important meeting place for all involved in educational technology and in particular its pedagogical application in teaching and learning. ITHU has established a good collaboration with the relevant government authorities and associations in Swedish higher education, namely UKÄ (Universitetskanslersämbetet – Swedish Higher Education Authority), UHR (Universitets- och högskolerådet – Swedish Council for Higher Education) and SUHF (Sveriges universitets- & högskoleförbund –The Association of Swedish Higher Education Institutions). In recent years there has been a growing awareness among the authorities that there was a need for action in the field of digital online education and the pandemic has acted as a catalyst for a major reassessment of national policies, strategies and actions. One notable joint activity was a national online conference on pedagogical development in September 2019 that attracted over 500 participants, the first major online conference in Swedish higher education.

Covid

As in most countries, the sudden transition to emergency remote teaching resulted in an over-reliance on synchronous video meetings that tried to recreate traditional classroom practice in a digital space. Institutions produced at short notice guides, videos, resources, workshops and webinars to help teachers adapt to the new situation. The vital role of educational technologists cannot be overstated in this context since they were able to help teachers redesign courses and keep them going despite extreme pressure and lack of time. A clear result of the pandemic period has been a sharp rise in status for educational technologists and a recognition of the vital role they play in the institution's core activities.

In order to provide a digital space for sharing ideas, resources and mutual support, ITHU started a Facebook group, *Digital omställning i högre utbildning* (Digital transformation in higher education – https://www.facebook.com/groups/ITHUsamverkan) on 17 March

2021. The target group was all teaching staff, educational technologists, librarians and administrative staff at all Swedish universities. The group became extremely popular and within one week the number of members passed 2,000 with a very high level of activity that has continued since then. By 1 May 2021 the group had 4,008 members and around half of these had been active during the previous month. Membership has been carefully monitored and applicants must first answer questions to gain access. ITHU steering committee members have shared the responsibility of monitoring access as well as encouraging participation by commenting on posts and writing regular reviews of each week's activities in the group. Posts have been tagged by topic and the most popular topics have been (in order of frequency): Zoom, pedagogical discussion, digital tools, recording, examination, webinars, open educational resources, learning management systems (LMS), health/work environment and collaborative learning. The group has contributed to the growth of a sharing culture that did not exist in Sweden to any extent before the outbreak of the pandemic and continues to be a space for discussion and support. One notable success factor has been the mix of competences and disciplines so that teachers' questions about technology or pedagogy are promptly answered by specialists, though of course some questions lead to lively discussions. Another feature has been the international element with educators from Norway, Finland and Denmark actively participating.

Similarly, the Swedish university computer network, SUNET (https://www.sunet.se), played an important role by setting up a web page where webinars and online workshops from different institutions could be visible to all. This enabled educators to participate in relevant workshops arranged by other institutions and save unnecessary duplication of resources.

During the pandemic period several important national reports were published, all strongly recommending better national coordination of digitalisation in higher education with a focus on professional development for teachers and funding for research and development in the field. A report from the government Expert Group on Public Economics (ESO), (Nyman, 2020), examined the state of online and distance learning in Sweden and gave recommendations for a major investment in pedagogical development, development of validation and lifelong learning opportunities, investment in research into online education and an investigation into legal barriers to the development of open educational resources. A survey of opinions and responses to the digital transformation was carried out in early 2021 of ITHU members from all Swedish HEIs: teachers, educational developers, educational technologists, management. The Swedish Higher Education Authority (UKÄ, 2020) published an investigation into pedagogical development with recommendations for a national strategy for teaching and learning in Swedish higher education, a national strategy for digitalisation in higher education and research and the coordination of such efforts by the Swedish Council for Higher Education (UHR). These initiatives were already under way at the start of the pandemic but their impact has been greater in the light of the sudden pivot to online education.

In addition, the Association of Swedish Higher Education Institutions (SUHF) has formed working groups on digitalisation and accessibility as well as digital examination to further strengthen institutional collaboration in these fields.

Results and discussion

The results of the survey of ITHU members will be presented here. The questionnaire was sent to the 300 members of ITHU and the response rate was about 30%, spread over most of the HEIs in Sweden.

Findings indicate that most of the respondents, 83%, had experience of distance education before Covid-19 and nearly 80% of those with experience assess that they have much experience or very much experience and 80% state that their experience of distance education is rather good or very good. This can be interpreted as the members of ITHU have a particular high competence as the respondents have a wide experience from several perspectives of distance education, e.g., as a teacher, as a student, and many had also theoretical studies in distance pedagogy.

For some questions a comparison regarding the results has been made between two groups of respondents: *teachers* and *staff working mainly with development and support* (henceforth, only staff is used for staff working mainly with development and support). The results demonstrate that teachers' biggest challenges (maximum three alternatives could be marked) when teaching online are *practical elements* (39%), *large groups of students* (34%), *adaptation of forms of examination* (34%), and *changing campus courses to distance courses* (30%). The result is similar for staff with the difference that they consider *big groups of students less challenging* (18%) compared to teachers (34%). Staff also regard *adaptation of forms of examination to distance* (48%) compared to 34% for teachers, and *not being able to have written examinations on campus* (33%) *hybrid teaching* (33%), as bigger challenges than teachers do (18%) (hybrid teaching means that students are at a distance and on campus at the same time). The teachers' most important pedagogical opportunities (maximum three alternatives could be marked) in the transition to distance education are *development of technology usage* (50%), that *more people realise that technologies can support pedagogy* (48%), *the development of teaching* (46%), and *a higher degree of flexibility for students* (41%). In comparison to the teachers, nearly twice as many of the staff think that *more people realise that technology can support pedagogy* (85%). However, compared to teachers (50%), less than half of the staff (20%), think that *the development of technology usage is one of the most important pedagogical challenges* (maximum three alternatives could be marked). Staff see *an increased interest in pedagogical issues* (42%) to a higher degree compared to the teachers (25%).

The biggest technical challenges (maximum three alternatives could be marked) that the transition to distance education has entailed are to a high degree similar for the teachers and staff. Both groups have answered that the biggest challenge is *lack of time to learn about new technology* (about 50%). However, there are some differences regarding two of the alternatives. Teachers consider it as a bigger technical challenge *to find the most suitable technology* (about 50%) compared to staff, only about 30%. The alternative *to understand how technology is used in the best way* has about the same result for both groups (about 30%). More of the staff think that *teachers do not have the necessary knowledge about the technology* (about 32%) while it was only about half of the markings from teachers (14%). Both groups see it as a big technical challenge (about 28%), *that more focus is on technology instead of pedagogy.* About 23% of the teachers consider it as one of the biggest technical challenges that they *cannot use the technology they need* (due to lack of licences or that the servers are outside the EU etc.) and staff see this as an even bigger challenge (28%).

According to both groups of respondents, the two most important technical possibilities with the transition to distance education (maximum three alternatives could be marked) are *possibilities to have course meetings at a distance* (Zoom) (66-73%) and that *teachers have become more skilled at using technology* (about 50%). Another important possibility for teachers is that they *use more media in their teaching* (28%). Staff consider the third and fourth most important possibilities are that *teachers' have an increased interest in technology* (51%) and that *teachers have been "forced" to use technology in their teaching* (49%).

Regarding the "new normal" during the spring 2020, nearly 90% of the respondents claimed that *Zoom and other tools for e-meetings were used more than before.* Many respondents also reported that *teaching developed* and that *it was more adapted to distance education. The number of recordings increased* and *LMS were used more* than before the pandemic. Only about 10% have answered that the teaching continued as before the transition.

What do respondents think will be permanent changes after the pandemic? The most ticked alternatives are (in order of frequency); *more flexible teaching forms will be offered, more employees will work from home, the importance of staff's pedagogical digital competence will be strengthened,* and *attitudes to the use of technology will be more positive.* The alternatives *more distance courses will be offered* and *there will be a changed need for rooms for teaching* are less marked, but still have got about 30% of the markings. What that the respondents think will disappear after the pandemic are *teachers' scepticism of using technology*, (nearly 40%), *hybrid teaching*, (23%), and 21% answered that they *did not know.*

The rapid transition to online education, which made it difficult or even impossible to have written exams on campus, made it obvious that it is important to develop *other and alternative forms of examination* and that questions in examinations can be formulated in new ways. Teachers have become more interested in developing creative methods to assess students' knowledge and problematize how these methods can influence student learning. There has been an increased interest in and focus on *course design* to strategically adapt teaching and learning in campus courses to online courses. Teachers, who have not previously taught online courses, have to a higher degree realised their need for professional development in distance education and pedagogical digital competence. There have been more *incentives* and *funding for development projects* and how to develop the possibilities of teaching and learning *practical elements* in courses, which has turned out to be one of the most difficult issues to solve, particularly in professional education and training.

With the fast transition to online courses teachers' teaching environment changed dramatically and made it necessary to work with new methods which required support of technologies. However, the number of tools and platforms they could use were limited due to uncertainty around the interpretation of European regulations on data security, namely GDPR (General Data Protection Regulation) and the 2020 Schrems II judgement on the use of USA-based cloud services. Therefore, a national coordination is required regarding which platforms and tools may be used by government authorities such as HEIs.

The student perspective was presented by Sweden's United Student Unions (SFS) in an overview of the results from surveys of student experience of the pandemic period with results from 12 surveys from 10 institutions (SFS, 2020). The students were in general positive to how their institutions had handled the transition to online education and recognised the challenges involved. However, there were many signs that students' motivation suffered as the pandemic developed and many reported feelings of isolation and stress-related issues. The difficulties of establishing and maintaining social contacts and getting support from colleagues were reported at several institutions.

Recommendations and conclusions

The government authority, UKÄ, compiled a report (UKÄ, 2021) on the effects of the pandemic on Swedish higher education. This was based on contributions from all the relevant university and student organisations as well as a number of networks like ITHU and Swednet (Swedish Network for Educational Development in Higher Education). The cooperation between all the relevant organisations in the field was a significant coordinated response to the crisis.

The main recommendations from this report were:

- National coordination of digitalisation of higher education, especially in terms of digital infrastructure, tools and platforms, professional development and new forms of examination and assessment.
- Greater collaboration between institutions, sharing of resources and the funding of joint initiatives in line with the goals of EUA's vision document Universities without walls – a vision for 2030 (EUA, 2021).
- Development of digital pedagogical competence and coordinated support for pedagogical development initiatives at all HEIs.
- Strategies and coordinated initiatives for development of cloud-based services and technologies which can be used without violating GDPR and Schrems II.
- Collaboration and dialogue between pedagogical and legal perspectives and development of pedagogical-legal competence.
- Special attention to student accessibility issues.

In summary, the covid-19 pandemic has been an unexpected catalyst for national mobilisation in the digitalisation of higher education in Sweden. There is now a higher level of awareness and greater cooperation between HEIs, authorities and stakeholder organisations and the foundations are being laid for a more coordinated approach to digitalisation in the future.

References

Dafgård, L. (2020). *Digital distance education: a longitudinal exploration of video technology* (Doctoral dissertation). Department of Applied Information Technology, University of Gothenburg, Gothenburg. Retrieved from http://hdl.handle.net/2077/62810

EUA (2021). *Universities without walls – A vision for 2030.* European University Association. Retrieved from https://www.eua.eu/downloads/publications/universities%20without%20walls%20%20a%20vision%20for%202030.pdf

Moore, M. G. (1993). Three types of interaction. In K. Harry, J. Magnus, & D. Keegan (Eds.), *Distance education: New perspectives* (pp. 19-24). London: Routledge.

Moore, M. G. (1997). Theory of transactional distance. In D. Keagan (Ed.), *Theoretical Principles of Distance Education* (pp. 22-38). London: Routledge.

Moore, M. G., & Kearsley, G. (2005). *Distance education: A systems view.* Belmont, Californien: Thomas Wadsworth.

Nyman, K. (2020). 2020:5 Uppkopplad utbildning – en ESO-rapport om högskolans digitalisering. Retrieved from https://eso.expertgrupp.se/rapporter/2020_5_uppkopplad_utbildning/

Payne, H. (1999). *A review of the literature: Interactive Video Teletraining in Distance Learning Courses.* Atlanta, GA: Spacenet, Inc. and the United States Distance Learning Association.

SFS. (2020) Hur påverkar coronapandemin studenterna? Sveriges Förenade Studentkårer. Retrieved from https://sfs.se/coronapandemin-sa-har-studenterna-och-hogre-utbildning-paverkats/

Shearer, R. (Ed.) (2007). *Instructional Design and the Technologies: An Overview* (2nd ed.). Mahawah, N.J.: Erlbaum Associates.

UKÄ. (2020). *Pedagogiskt utvecklingsarbete – rapportering av regeringsuppdrag.* Swedish Higher Education Authority. Retrieved from https://www.uka.se/om-oss/var-verksamhet/regeringsuppdrag/pedagogiskt-utvecklingsarbete/pedagogiskt-utvecklingsarbete---rapportering-av-regeringsuppdrag.html

UKÄ. (2021). *The Swedish Higher Education Authority's Pandemic Assignment – Interim Report 1.* Swedish Higher Education Authority. Retrieved from https://english.uka.se/about-us/publications/reports--guidelines/reports--guidelines/2021-04-13-the-swedish-higher-education-authoritys-pandemic-assignment---interim-report-1.html

Lessons from a Pandemic for the Future of Education
European Distance and E-Learning Network (EDEN) Proceedings
2021 Annual Conference | Madrid, 21-24 June, 2021
ISSN 2707-2819
doi: 10.38069/edenconf-2021-ac0039

INSIGHTS FROM A MOOC PLATFORM DURING COVID-19 PANDEMIC IN ITALY

Valeria Baudo, Davide Mezzera, Politecnico di Milano – METID, Italy

Abstract

The COVID-19 Pandemic heavily redesigned our lives and our way of teaching and learning. We have witnessed an exponential growth of MOOC enrolment numbers during pandemic as a general world trend, and a big rise in learners in the MOOC platform of Politecnico di Milano. In this paper we will share insights collected from Polimi Open Knowledge during 2020. This analysis enlightens the role of MOOCs for students and citizens during the pandemic, in relation with the specific period of lockdown in Italy.

Introduction - Polimi Open Knowledge

Polimi Open Knowledge – POK (http://www.pok.polimi.it) is the open knowledge platform of Politecnico di Milano – Polimi, launched in 2014 for the MOOCs delivery. It is based on OpenEdx, an open source learning management system (LMS) developed by MIT and Harvard University to host Massive Open Online Courses (MOOCs). The number of MOOCs and of participants enrolled in POK have steadily grown since its birth. At the time of writing, more than 120,000 enrolled learners can count on 71 MOOCs, provided in Italian or in English (and in some cases in both languages), with up to 2,000 videos and a wide range of educational contents and learning activities.

The underlying philosophy of the platform is to offer educational contents for different target users, according to Collection of courses specifically designed around them:

- MOOCs for students, to improve their knowledge background and their skill set before and during their Bachelor's and Master's degree courses;
- MOOCs for researchers, to help them develop transversal skills, needed for their work;
- MOOCs for professionals, to develop specific technical, hard skills in innovative professional areas and soft skills required by the job market;
- MOOCs for teachers, to support teaching and learning innovation in both Higher Education Institutions and schools;

- MOOCs for citizens, to explore global challenges and citizenship issues and provide opportunities for lifelong learning not strictly related to career enhancement.

The pandemic has brought back attention to online education in general and especially to MOOCs. The first data (AlQaidoom & Shah, 2020; Felipe Torres, 2021; Lohr, 2021; Reda & Kerr, 2020; Shah, 2020) shows an increasing trend for all major MOOC providers. In March 2020 data shows a big rise in the number of learners visiting POK. During 2020 registered users increased by 28% (+24,890 new learners) compared to a 25% growth (+17,412 new learners) in 2019. The total number of registered users at the end of 2020 was 113,108. POK users can be divided into two main clusters: firstly, Polimi users that include all people registered with an institutional account of Politecnico di Milano (most of them are students, but there are also teaching and administrative staff, researchers, alumni, etc.) and secondly external users, such as students from other institutions, teachers from high schools and, generally speaking, all people willing to learn new things or strengthen their knowledge around specific subjects. POK offers the same services to both groups: users have the same chance to access the courses, and to obtain certificates of participation; thus, the use patterns of the platform are somehow comparable between the two groups.

Looking at the series of data collected along POK history, it is evident an increase in the number of daily active users during specific periods of the year (we define "active user" a person who logs into the platform performing an action in a course, on a specific day). Most user activities generally occur in February and in September, concurrently with the start of the first and the second semester, which is an indicator of the integration of MOOCs into curricular activities. During 2020 the above-mentioned periods in February and in September show the usual increase of the activities on the platform, but there is a third, unexpected peak during April 2020; it is possible to notice how this trend is directly related to the situation of total lockdown in Italy.

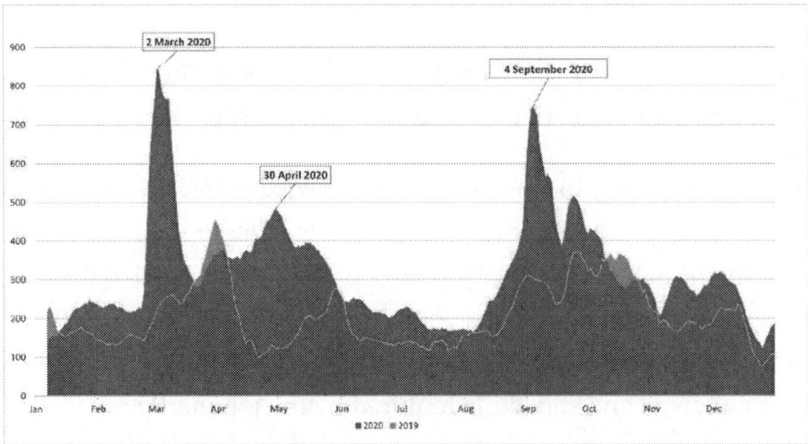

Figure 8. Daily active users on POK: trends of 2019 vs 2020 – 7-day moving average

MOOCs for didactics during lockdown

On the 17th of February 2020 the first Italian cases of COVID-19 were detected in Lombardy, the region where Politecnico di Milano is located. It was something dramatically unexpected, and the university moved its teaching and learning activities totally online in a couple of weeks. The already existing practices of blended learning and flipped classroom, together with the technological solutions provided, made it possible to quickly shift to the fully online mode. In this scenario, MOOCs played a crucial role in supporting and even steering this transformation: Politecnico di Milano was the Italian university that responded sooner and faster to the demanding requirements of social distancing. At the beginning of March all schools – from kindergarten to university – were closed by law, and on the 9th of March the lockdown was officially enacted.

In this emergency scenario, MOOCs arose as a key resource to shift didactic activities online (Kichu & Bhattacharya 2021; Sun, 2020). Integrating and making the most of MOOCs in didactics is one of the several missions of METID, the learning and teaching innovation task force of Politecnico di Milano. METID designs and develops MOOCs and it is in charge of faculty training. Even before the pandemic, MOOCs have been specifically designed to support teaching and learning innovation, blended learning processes and flipped classroom approaches. There are currently more than 150 Polimi courses that officially integrate MOOCs into teaching and learning experiences, and the pandemic disrupted this trend as an easy way to shift to the fully online scenario.

Although we usually experience a peak at the beginning of each semester, during 2020 the numbers were higher than ever. Having a look at the learners' profiles during the first four weeks of the second semester, we notice that more than 60% of active users are from Politecnico di Milano (compared to an average of 37% of institutional users generally in the platform). In addition to that, in the past years some of the MOOCs specifically created for students, were used in teaching, but in 2020 data showed a different model, with MOOCs being used in a shorter period of time, instead of a widespread use during the whole semester, attesting that MOOC were a lever for the fully online scenario.

This is evident in analysed data because there are more than 800 daily active users on average in the first week of March, while in the previous years learners participated in MOOCs in distributed periods of the year. Having a set of MOOCs already available, and in many cases designed in consistency with curricular learning outcomes, these online courses suddenly became a key strategic resource to face the emergency created by the pandemic and allowed the university to promptly respond with a ready-to-use alternative to face-to-face didactics. It is needless to add that they didn't replace classroom experiences completely, but adapting to the emergency was definitely easier, and the level of offering was largely higher than what would have been with no MOOC available.

This trend is evident in the MOOC "Equazioni differenziali lineari del secondo ordine", used in courses such as Mathematical Analysis and Differential Equations. During COVID pandemic teaching staff took advantage of the MOOC as an asset for online didactics, requiring students to use it. In Figure 2 it is possible to notice the difference in the behaviour of active users between 2019 and 2020. In 2020 active users were more numerous, and the actions performed by them are concentrated in time, according to the model of use of MOOC as a key asset in the first phase of the lockdown.

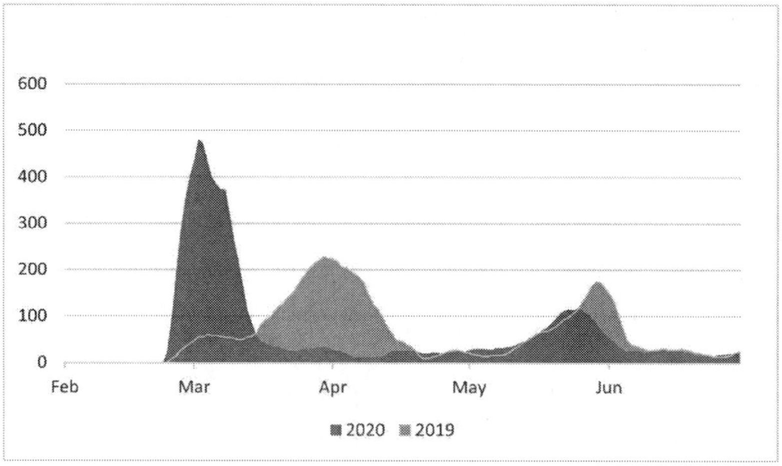

Figure 2. Active users of "Equazioni differenziali lineari del secondo ordine" in 2019 and 2020 – 7-day moving average

MOOCs for citizens during lockdown

Starting from the 22nd of March 2020, the lockdown in Italy imposed a complete restriction of movement and gathering nationwide, and a total closure of economic activities except for essential services. Everyone, except essential workers, had to stay at home.

Looking at the insights from POK, data showed an unexpected side effect of the confinement. People, once locked down, were keen to take advantage of their compulsory "free time" to strengthen their skills and to gain new knowledge through MOOCs. In the graph below the line referring to external users has a peak in the period of April-May. This trend is totally new for the platform and it is related to the specific contingency.

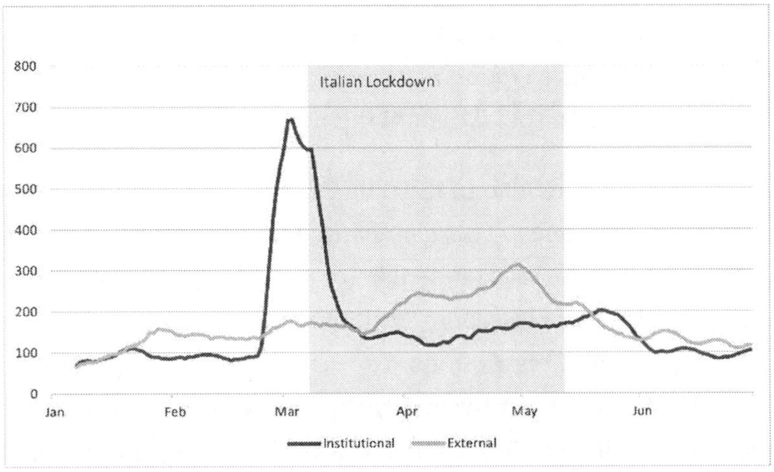

Figure 3. Institutional and external active users during the lockdown – 7-day moving average

The analysis of the most popular courses among external users during April-May 2020 revealed that the most appreciated are basically related to soft skills and personal development (such as "Gestione del Conflitto/Managing Conflicts", "Gestione del cambiamento/Managing Changes") and "Finanza per Tutti", a "MOOC for citizens" on financial education. Looking deeper at the profile of participants, they are basically Italian (it is not surprising since these MOOCs are taught in Italian) and in the age range 35-50 years, the majority of them being in the labour market with no specific distinction related to gender.

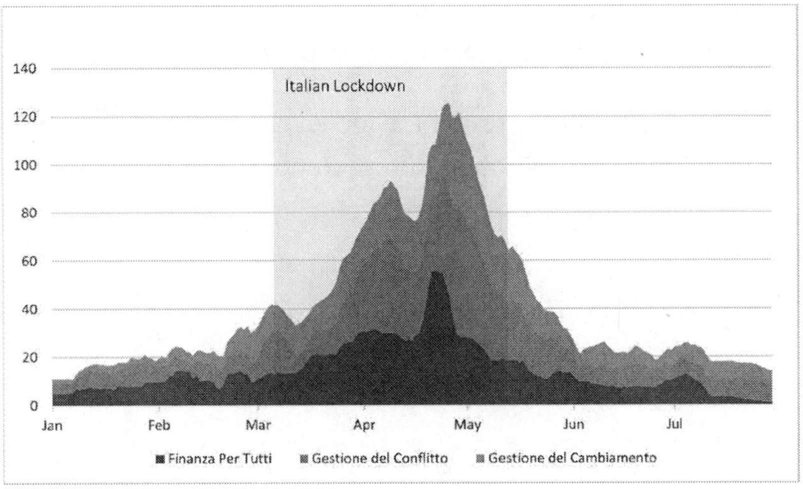

Figure 4. The cumulative increase of no-institutional active users in the most popular MOOC during lockdown

The use of MOOC in HyFlex Classroom setting

In the last period of the year, right after summer, the situation changed again. The second wave of COVID-19 reached Italy in autumn. A new lockdown was decided, with small differences from the previous one of March 2020. More people were allowed to go to work (although remote working was highly encouraged), more commercial activities were open with limitations, some schools reopened, and universities were allowed to teach partially in presence in compliance with social distancing norms.

This situation had consequences also in the data from the platform: in fact, the most active users were the institutional ones. The classes in Higher Education started following a hybrid model, combining face to face presence (for people willing/able to do so) and remote teaching. The so-called HyFlex classroom, in Italian called "classe estesa", is the way that universities are using to face restrictions due to the pandemic. This model combines instructors teaching students in a physical classroom and – at the same time – students participating online via video-conferencing software. In some experimentations, teachers themselves are online and students go physically to class. It is an interesting model that requires an accurate design of the teaching and learning experience (Beatty, 2019; Cohen, Nørgård, & Mor, 2020; Hodges, Moore, Lockee, Trust, & Bond, 2020; Irvine, 2020)

Online resources and MOOCs play a crucial role in this setting. Although we still lack a set of data about it, since it is still an ongoing experience, it is possible to offer insights from a MOOC that has been integrated in didactics following a different approach in teaching in September 2020. The course is "Introduzione alla Matematica per l'università: Pre-calculus" and it is offered to our first-year students to deepen or review some basic mathematical concepts. The MOOC is part of Polimi refresher courses that are generally offered in presence but moved online in 2020: the integration with the MOOC changed, shifting from a flipped classroom approach to a virtual flipped approach.

This course does not specifically represent the model of HyFlex courses, but it can be used as a "litmus test" and can give ideas about future trends.

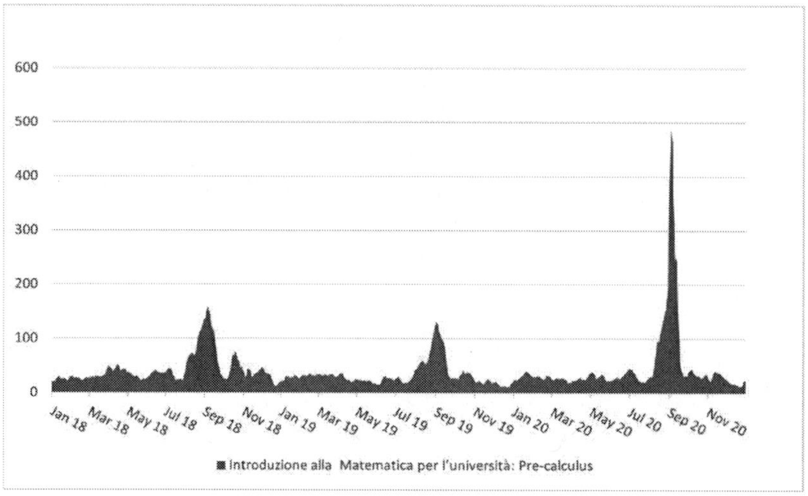

Figure 5. Active users in "Introduzione alla matematica per l'Università" from 2018 to 2020 – 7-day moving average

The number of active users in "Introduzione alla Matematica per l'università: Pre-calculus" MOOC in September 2020 reached impressive numbers, increasing by 400% the active users in specific days. The newly adopted model integrates a strong schedule for MOOC participation, less free than it usually is in the "traditional" flipped classroom approach. Learners are requested to show up online in the MOOC, according to specific timing in specific days; they watch listed videos, then do the quizzes; then they move back to the online virtual classroom in Microsoft Teams and meet the teachers, they can ask them questions to solve their doubts regarding contents and exercises; finally, they come back to the MOOC and post in the forum the results of their exercises. Teachers themselves have been positively impressed by the results of this learning path and noticed a growing sense of comfort and familiarity of first-year students with online teaching and learning and, more in general, with MOOCs. Although it is not possible to empirically provide evidence so far, this might be related with these students' previous experience in online didactics (in Italian "Didattica a Distanza", DAD) at the end of their high school learning path, due to the pandemic.

Conclusion and limits

However, the main caveat of this paper is that pandemic is still ongoing, and it is not possible to infer that the insights shown are a new trend or a unicum due to current contingencies. Although some studies recently published stressed the importance of the MOOC in the so-called "new normal" in higher education, not enough data and literature have been published so far to confirm that.

This study is limited to one University and one MOOC platform, while a combination of studies on different universities and on different platforms can provide a more complete picture. Furthermore, this analysis can be fruitfully integrated with a qualitative approach, in order to give back a more complete overview.

Despite these limits, the data shown in the paper highlighted the important role of MOOCs for higher education institutions and for citizens during the pandemic.

References

AlQaidoom, H., Shah, A., (2020). The Role of MOOC in Higher Education during Coronavirus Pandemic: A Systematic Review. *International Journal of English and Education, 9*(4).

Beatty, B. J. (2019). *Hybrid-flexible course design. Implementing student directed hybrid classes.* Provo, Utah: EdTech Books. https://edtechbooks.org/hyflex

Cohen, A., Nørgård, R. T., & Mor, Y. (2020). Hybrid learning spaces--Design, data, didactics. *British Journal of Educational Technology, 51*(4), 1039-1044. https://doi.org/10.1111/bjet.12964

Eradze, M. et al. (2020). Hybrid Flexible Learning with MOOCs: A Proposal to Reconceptualize the COVID19 Emergency beyond the Crisis. *IEEE Learning with MOOCS*, 174-179.

Farnell, T., Skledar Matijević, A., & Šćukanec Schmidt, N. (2021). The impact of COVID-19 on higher education: a review of emerging evidence. NESET report, Luxembourg: Publications Office of the European Union. doi: 10.2766/069216.

Felipe Torres, G, (2021, March 18). Boosted by the Pandemic, MOOCs Are Here to Stay. How Can We Improve Them? Elearning Insight [Blog post]. Retrieved from https://news.elearninginside.com/boosted-by-the-pandemic-moocs-are-here-to-stay-how-can-we-improve-them/

Hodges, C., Moore, S., Lockee, B., Trust, T., & Bond, A. (2020, March 27). The Difference between Emergency Remote Teaching and Online Learning. EduCause [Blog post]. Retrieved from https://er.educause.edu/articles/2020/3/the-difference-between-emergency-remote-teaching-and-online-learning

Irvine, V. (2020, October 26). The Landscape of Merging Modalities, EDUCAUSE [Blog post]. Retrieved from https://er.educause.edu/articles/2020/10/the-landscape-of-merging-modalities

Kichu, M., & Bhattacharya, M. (2021). COVID-19 Pandemic impels surge in MOOC learning and the New Normal: A Literature Review. *IJIRT.*

Li, C., & Lalani, F. (2020). The COVID-19 pandemic has changed education forever. This is how. World economic forum, 29. Retrieved from https://www.weforum.org/agenda/2020/04/coronavirus-education-global-covid19-online-digital-learning/

Lohr, S. (2021, May 26) Remember the MOOCs? After Near-Death, They're Booming. The New York Times [Blog post]. Retrieved from https://www.nytimes.com/2020/05/26/technology/moocs-online-learning.html

Reda, V., & Kerr, R. (2020, March 31). Moocs have helped Italy keep teaching during the pandemic. The World University Rankings [Blog post]. Retrieved from https://www.timeshighereducation.com/blog/moocs-have-helped-italy-keep-teaching-during-pandemic

Shah, D. (2020, December 23). The Second Year of The MOOC: 2020 Saw a Rush to Large-Scale Online Courses. EdSurge [Blog post]. Retrieved from https://www.edsurge.com/news/2020-12-23-the-second-year-of-the-mooc-2020-saw-a-rush-to-large-scale-online-courses

Sun, Y. (2020). Reflection on MOOCs in the Special Period of Anti-coronavirus. *Theory & Practice in Language Studies*. doi: 10.17507/tpls.1011.23

Lessons from a Pandemic for the Future of Education
European Distance and E-Learning Network (EDEN) Proceedings
2021 Annual Conference | Madrid, 21-24 June, 2021
ISSN 2707-2819
doi: 10.38069/edenconf-2021-ac0040

OPENTEL: LESSONS FROM A PANDEMIC FOR THE FUTURE OF DISTANCE EDUCATION

Francisco Iniesto, Victoria L. Murphy, Eileen Scanlon, Shi Min Chua, The Open University, United Kingdom

Abstract

The move to introduce technology enhanced learning (TEL) is a trend that has been observed for decades. Following the disruption arising from Covid-19 pandemic, there has been a move to remote teaching in universities across the world. This move has put the transformation or digital revolution in the limelight in the media. TEL is of strategic importance to the conduct of teaching, learning and research in education internationally. TEL, when combined with the growing benefits of open approaches to education, leads to a potentially transformational means of learning. In this paper the authors introduce some examples of research projects from the Open University's OpenTEL research grouping. These examples highlight some of the work conducted relating to supporting students, universities, and communities using TEL during the pandemic. OpenTEL research has identified that Covid-19 has exposed the need for better institutional support for students who are facing stress and disruption in their studies; collaboration among higher educational institutions to share knowledge; better engagement in the online pivot ; and understanding of the possibilities (and limitations) for online tools to maintain existing research communities.

Introduction

The Open University (OU) was founded in 1969 and has a mission to be "open to people, places, methods and ideas". In line with this mission, there are no minimum academic qualifications needed to start a degree with the OU. Since its inception, the OU has taken learning to learners, wherever they are, using an evolving range of technologies, supporting learners from across the UK and, more recently, across the globe (Cross et al., 2019). The university has pioneered new approaches to teaching in response to the needs of its diverse set of students who are learning at a distance. The methods used are particularly interesting in relation to the teaching of Science, Technology, Engineering and Maths (STEM) subjects, where innovative methods have been used to ensure that learners can develop practical skills. A range of technologies are used to support learners in all subjects, ranging from broadcasting information via the BBC, to using augmented reality to practice presentations (McFaul & FitzGerald, 2020). Courses at the OU predominantly used a blended approach, combining online study and, where appropriate, posted materials. Prior to Covid-19 it was also the practice of the OU to support students by organising in-person and online tutorials held by hundreds of associate lecturers across the UK. During Covid-19 these tutorials were all moved to an online format.

The OpenTEL research grouping was developed to bring together university-wide interest and expertise in the research on technology enhanced learning (TEL). Coordinated by researchers from the Institute of Educational Technology (IET), we have developed a strong cross-university alliance, open to collaborations across disciplines and units, researching a broad range of topics such as inclusion, accessibility, remote learning and teaching, artificial intelligence in education, and citizen science. The strategic objective of OpenTEL research is to develop and advance understanding of how technology enhanced learning impacts teaching and learning, bringing together international understanding of this field, as well as national and local understanding. We are bringing our OU expertise together to make impacts on both approaches to, and views of, TEL research. Within the OU, OpenTEL has a unique position as a research group dedicated to the use of TEL in a manner befitting the OU's mission, in other words, exploring research-informed ways to "open up" education. Researchers have argued that TEL as a field is inherently applied and multidisciplinary (see e.g. Scanlon & Conole, 2018). This cross-disciplinary approach (both technological and pedagogical) is increasingly needed to address complex contemporary societal challenges. In response to the complexities of effectively using TEL to support students, OpenTEL has developed new approaches, perspectives, and innovative methodologies by establishing an interdisciplinary group of researchers with backgrounds including educational technology, STEM, social science, and organisational studies. The wide diversity of group members' backgrounds allows the exploration of openness and TEL research in ways that can feed into the OU's teaching and we aim to work to ensure that researchers and practitioners can collaborate. OpenTEL provides glimpses of the future with innovative examples of evidence-based TEL.

Since we started our pan-university TEL research community (in 2016), we run regular events, Show and TEL conferences, end of project seminars, Special Interest Group (SIG) meetings, writing retreats and bidding workshops. In 2021 OpenTEL has six main research areas of activity:

1. learning in an open, connected world and at scale,
2. design and analytics in learning,

3. language learning landscapes,
4. citizen science,
5. inclusion, and
6. professional and digital learning.

These areas represent aspects of TEL are central to our research on the future of distance education.

Opening up education

Research projects within these six areas include the following. For example, the European Massive Open Online Course (MOOC) Consortium – Labour Market (*EMC-LM*) which researched higher educational institutes engaging with MOOCs and microcredentials in the labour market aligned with continuing professional development (Farrow, 2020). TEL is also starting to be used to tackle global workplace issues, going beyond the sphere of formal learning, the Learning from Incidents and Implementing Action (*LFIA*) project examined how companies in the energy sector used TEL to learn after incidents and prevent major disasters (Murphy et al., 2018). Another example is the multiple OpenTEL projects that have led to the development of the citizen inquiry platform *nQuire*. nQuire is a platform which was built to support personal inquiry learning among schoolchildren (Scanlon et al., 2020) but has developed into a citizen science platform for all ages.

The *MAZI* project team, on the other hand, combines wireless technology, low-cost hardware and open-source software to open opportunities. They created learning resources which could be accessed by anyone in the surrounding geographical area, without the need for a stable internet connection (Gaved et al., 2019). The different ways that education can be "opened up" are also demonstrated through the work of the Global OER Graduate Network (*GO-GN*). GO-GN is a network of PhD candidates from around the world whose research projects include a focus on open education, open educational resources (OERs) and open educational practices (Weller, Farrow, & Pitt, 2019). Finally, the Assistants to the Disclosure and Management of Information about Needs and Support (*ADMINS*) project created a virtual assistant to help students with accessibility needs navigate complex paperwork that can be a near-impossible task for them without such support (Iniesto, Coughlan, & Lister, 2021).

Response to Covid-19

Contemporary issues, such as learning at scale, open learning, and remote learning, have come to the forefront of discussion during the Covid-19 pandemic.

Understanding the student experience and support needs

OpenTEL responded to the pandemic by supporting individual group members in developing projects. For example, as a data collection tool, nQuire was used by the OU and Young Foundation to collect evidence on the impact of the pandemic on students. Working with the Mental Health Foundation and representatives from across the OU, OpenTEL is developing the concept of a Centre for Democratising Research which builds on our research approach to citizen science inquiry and nQuire. Impact is shown as this citizen science research activity has been recognised with the Guardian Award for Research impact for nQuire in 2020.

Several projects have explored the student experience and understanding the needs of students in extreme circumstances, "the impact of Covid-19 disruption" project (Aristeidou & Cross, 2021) conducted a survey (with 555 responses) during summer 2020 to investigate how OU student learning has been impacted by the Covid-19 disruption. In particular, the responses facilitated further study on undertaking specific learning, assessment, and social activities, and how students' background characteristics relate to any potential impact. The main factors affecting OU students' studies was impact on their mental health and their employment. The project indicated the need of immediate intervention strategies, including institutional and funder support (funded extensions or expedited alternatives), cultivating individual-driven coping behaviours which can be promoted by institution training programs.

With a similar objective, "the student support networks during lockdown" project used techniques from social network analysis to explore who students had been going to for help; support received from social networks are essential for helping students to maintain mental health during times of stress such as Covid-19. Early results from the analysis showed the importance of a university's communication strategy, as getting accurate information on changing policies was highlighted by participants as an important aspect of receiving support during the immediate university response. As the pandemic progressed, the project suggested that the size of students' networks did not change substantially. However, some students did reach out more frequently to their associate lecturer for academic issues, that sometimes included providing emotional support. Nevertheless, it should be emphasised that the experiences of students were very diverse, with some finding that academic studies were a welcome escape instead of an additional stress.

Supporting other universities moving online and creating resources

During the pandemic OU academics have informally shared expertise to other institutions and educators as they engaged in the online pivot for the first time. That involved a series of online informal drop-in sessions for sharing experience and knowledge which, in the end, become popular events (Weller, 2020) for those who needed to make the transition to online teaching quickly.

In line with opening education up beyond traditional higher educational degrees, our response also included support for the development of microcredentials and short courses, re-designing production in terms of agile methods and learning design templates as part of the OU FutureLearn Microcredentials initiative. IET has been involved in developing a FutureLearn microcredential to support anyone to discover how adults learn online – and at a distance – drawing on key theories, evaluating technologies for supporting learning, drawing on a range of experiences and research on how to design engaging and inspiring online courses successfully.

To that end, during the pandemic the OU has developed courses to promote useful support for teachers across Africa. *The Pathways for learning: new approaches in higher education* project, in partnership with the African Council of Distance Education, provided professional development programmes for university lecturers, instructional designers, technical and professional staff, managers, and heads of department who share responsibility for providing quality distance and online learning. It aimed at supporting educators from any discipline or professional role to better understand teaching online. Participants in the project not only gained the knowledge and skills for online teaching, but also experienced online learning themselves first-hand by engaging with well-designed materials, platforms, and experts. This learning experience has built their confidence in online teaching, as some of them reported greater confidence in pushing for change and integrating what they have learnt into their practices as part of the shift to greater online and blended approaches.

Supporting ongoing community

As discussed above, OpenTEL is a cross-university research grouping. To allow knowledge exchange between disciplines, we have hosted monthly SIG events and a two-day annual mini conference called *Show & TEL* for the past five years. To continue the strong sense of community within the group, these events were quickly moved online in response to Covid-19-related restrictions. For some events, this move enabled the group to reach a wider audience and explore different ways of communication. For example, the Open and Inclusive SIG has used technology to great effect, through events such as a practical session on accessibility and TEL for visually impaired students. While these types of events were possible prior to the pandemic, the embrace of TEL as the norm has made potential participants more willing to engage. One highlight was a seminar on student voice attended by over 40 OU staff and students from across the UK. Students were given the opportunity to speak freely and openly about different topics. This stimulated discussion around current and emerging issues regarding accessibility at the OU. Interactive workshops, held on topics as diverse as how Covid-19 has impacted learning experiences and ethical considerations in TEL, have also been a common occurrence. The overall feedback from attendees of these events has been positive, with participants expressing their appreciation for an open and safe forum for their opinions. An advantage of these workshops has also been the opportunity to collect visual summaries of discussions as a feature of workshops, rather than needing to create and distribute summaries. Figure 1 shows a dialogue map that was used to guide and capture conversations on ethics in TEL.

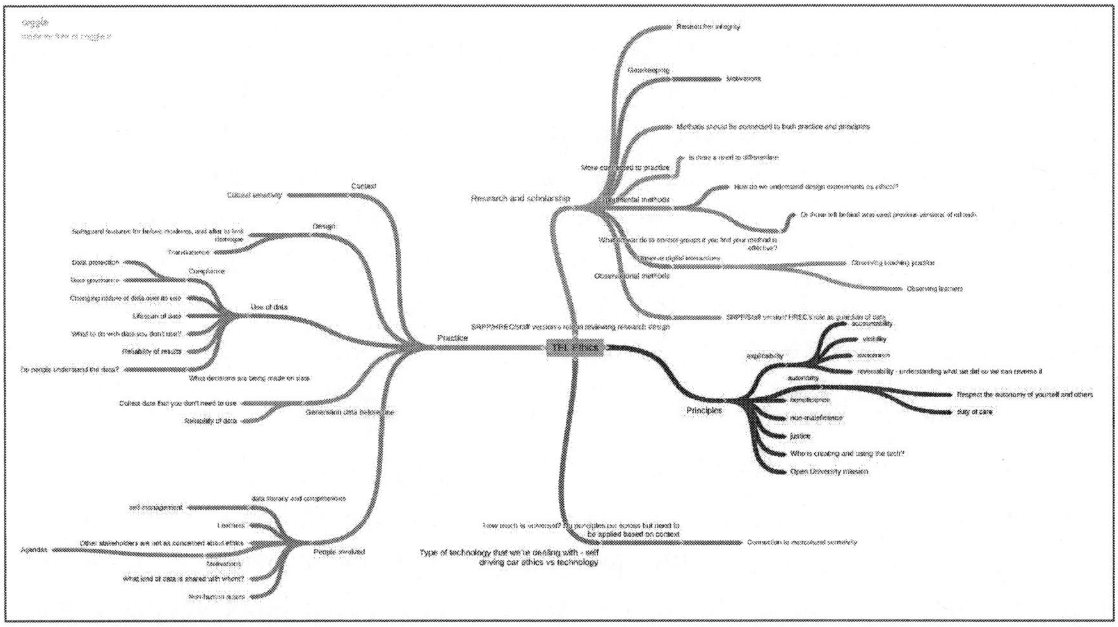

Figure 1. A dialogue map used to guide and capture conversation during an interactive workshop.

In addition to hosting our own events, OpenTEL has supported projects that have promoted the creation of TEL related communities. For example, the Computers and Learning Research Group (CALRG) moved their annual conference to an online format for the first time in 2020. The conference organisation team was funded by OpenTEL to conduct a scholarship project on the experiences of participants and organisers. Twenty-two survey responses and seven interviews allowed the project team to create a guide for others organising similar online events, which is available in full on the OpenTEL blog. A key finding was the ability of interactive asynchronous events to allow participants to take a break from listening but still have a sense of "eventedness". At the CALRG conference, for example, time for a scavenger hunt activity was scheduled during the first day, where participants were set challenges related to the digital platforms used (Microsoft Teams and Adobe Connect). There were also several unique advantages to an online only conference approach. For example, the digital platforms made it easy to naturally collect feedback for presenters; participants had frequently used the chat box for reflections, which could be sent to a presenter. An alternative approach was used during the doctoral consortium (part of the event), when a Google Doc was used to collect a large amount of feedback for students on their presentations. However, there were also difficulties identified with the online format. The volume of emails exchanged before the conference was much larger than it would have been if the organisers had been in the same office. Likewise, there were unexpected practical considerations, such as how to discreetly let the presenter know that the time for their presentation is running out. Perhaps the biggest surprise came when a university wide update of Adobe Connect caused the access link that the organisers had originally advertised to stop working. Planning what to do should the technology completely fail is perhaps a lesson for all. Although there were pros and cons to the digital format, one certainty was that the reduced financial and time costs allowed a greater diversity of participants to both attend and present. The CALRG conference has traditionally been a relatively small-scale event that allowed OU students to present at a friendly event with established academics. In 2020 the conference was attended by over 100 people from seven countries, including several students from other universities. The friendly nature of the conference did not change, meaning students across the world who were starting their academic journey were able to join a likeminded group in a low stakes conference. This is very much in line with opening up education.

Conclusions and lessons learnt

While the press has talked about the acceleration of the digital revolution brought about by Covid-19 (Times Higher Education, 2020), the reality is that higher education has been making increasing use of TEL for decades. Covid-19 has catalysed this, highlighting both opportunities and potential stumbling blocks for the future. The global "experiment" of most universities moving to online teaching over the course of a few months has been a baptism of fire for many in the sector, while many have capitalised on their previous experience. It remains to be seen what this accelerated shift means for the future. We have noted the impact of the increased availability of OERs and the demand for support for the move to online teaching has been filled by rapidly produced online courses. In addition, the search for ways to introduce more interactivity into remote teaching has offered opportunities for platforms such as nQuire. As universities embrace the current possibilities for supporting both formal and informal life-long learning enabled by digital technologies, there must also be caution. As the OU has long been aware, diverse students have diverse needs. TEL can tear down barriers to education, but equally can create others (Lister et al., 2020).

In this paper we have given some examples of the ways in which we have used our developing OpenTEL research capacity to respond to the challenges of the move to digital, three key areas need to further be explored:

- Covid-19 has exposed the need to better provide institutional support for students who are facing stress and disruption in their studies.
- Experiences of collaboration among higher educational institutions to share knowledge and experiences support a better engagement in the online pivot.
- The possibilities (and limitations) for online tools to maintain existing research communities.

Our ambition is to further develop our capacity in evolving the design, content, and delivery of supported open education through research and pedagogical innovation in educational theory, methodology and practice such that we can better respond to emerging issues. We have identified equality and inclusion and learning at scale as areas of priority for us to further develop our work. We also consider that it is important to look at the ways in which we can consider research practices associated with technology enhanced learning which contribute to more sustainable choices.

References

Aristeidou, M., & Cross, S. (2021). *The impact of Covid-19 disruption on the learning activities of OU students.* The Open University.

Conde Gafaro, B. (2021, February 25). OpenTEL – CALRG 2020 Evaluation Report. Retrieved from http://www.open.ac.uk/blogs/opentel/calrg-2020-evaluation-report/

Cross, S., Sharples, M., Healing, G., & Ellis, J. (2019). Distance Learners' Use of Handheld Technologies. *The International Review of Research in Open and Distributed Learning, 20*(2).

eSTEeM – The OU centre for STEM pedagogy (2021). Students' support networks during lockdown. Retrieved from https://www.open.ac.uk/about/teaching-and-learning/esteem/projects/themes/other/students%E2%80%99-support-networks-during-lockdown

European MOOC Consortium – EMC (2020). European MOOC Consortium Labour Market. Retrieved from https://emc.eadtu.eu/emc-lm

Farrow, R. (2020). The role of MOOCs in promoting social inclusion through employability: a rapid assessment of evidence. *Italian Journal of Educational Technology, 28*(3), 189-209.

FutureLearn (2021). Microcredentials. Retrieved from https://www.futurelearn.com/microcredentials/online-teaching

Gaved, M., Calderón Lüning, E., Unteidig, A., Davies, G., & Stevens, J. (2019). *Power, Roles and Adding Value: Reflecting on the Challenges of Bridging Across Research and Action on an International Community Networking Project.* Paper presented at the 17th CIRN Conference 2019. Monash University, Italy, 6-8 November.

Global OER Graduate Network – GO-GN (2021). Retrieved from http://go-gn.net/

Guardian, The (2020, November 25). Research impact: award winner and runners-up. Retrieved from https://www.theguardian.com/education/2020/nov/25/research-impact-award-winner-and-runners-up

Holmes, W., Porayska-Pomsta, K., Holstein, K., Sutherland, E., Baker, T., Shum, S. B., & Koedinger, K. R. (2021). Ethics of AI in Education: Towards a Community-Wide Framework. *International Journal of Artificial Intelligence in Education*, 1-23.

Iniesto, F., Coughlan, T., & Lister, K. (2021). Implementing an accessible Conversational User Interface applying feedback from University students and disability support advisors. *Proceedings of the 18th International Web for All Conference,* 1-11. Taipei, Taiwan, 20-21 April. New York: Association for Computing Machinery.

Lister, K., Coughlan, T., Iniesto, F., Freear, N., & Devine, P. (2020). Accessible Conversational User Interfaces: Considerations for Design. *Proceedings of the 17th International Web for All Conference,* 1-11. Taipei, Taiwan, 20-21 April. New York: Association for Computing Machinery.

MAZI (2020). Developing a DIY networking toolkit for location-based collective awareness. Retrieved from http://www.mazizone.eu

McFaul, H., & FitzGerald, E. (2020). A Realist Evaluation of Student use of a Virtual Reality Smartphone Application in Undergraduate Legal Education. *British Journal of Educational Technology, 51*(2), 572-589.

Mental Health Foundation (2021). Good mental health for all. Retrieved from https://www.mentalhealth.org.uk/

Murphy, V. L., Littlejohn, A., Rienties, B., King, S., & Bryden, R. (2018, April). *How do you know if you're learning from incidents?* Paper presented at SPE International Conference and Exhibition on Health, Safety, Security, Environment, and Social Responsibility. Society of Petroleum Engineers.

nQuire (2021). Home. Retrieved from https://nquire.org.uk/

Open University, The (2020). OU supports online and mobile learning in Africa during COVID-19. Retrieved from https://www.open.ac.uk/research/news/ou-supports-online-and-mobile-learning-africa-during-covid-19

Scanlon, E., & Conole, G. (2018). Interdisciplinarity in Technology Enhanced Learning: An Interview Study. *Journal of Interactive Media in Education, 2018*(1), 1-8.

Scanlon, E., Herodotou, C., Sharples, M., & McLeod, K. (2020). nQuire: Citizens Acting as Scientists in Massive Open Online Learning. *Proceedings of the Seventh ACM Conference on Learning@ Scale*, 257-260. Virtual Event, USA, 12-14 August. New York: Association for Computing Machinery.

Times Higher Education (2020). The Future of Digital Assessment: Covid-19, Short Courses and Beyond. Retrieved from https://www.timeshighereducation.com/hub/inspera/p/future-digital-assessment-covid-19-short-courses-and-beyond

Weller, M. (2020, March 20). Open University help for other institutions – drop in sessions. The Ed Techie [Blog post]. Retrieved from http://blog.edtechie.net/ou/open-university-help-for-other-institutions-drop-in-sessions/

Weller, M., Farrow, R., & Pitt, B. (2019). *GO-GN: Lessons in Building an Open Research Community*. Paper presented at the Pan-Commonwealth Forum 9 (PCF). Edinburgh, 9-11 September. Burnaby: Commonwealth of Learning.

Young Foundation, The (2021). Putting people at the heart of social change. Retrieved from https://www.youngfoundation.org/

Acknowledgements

Our thanks are due to the many members of OpenTEL who have collaborated on this work over the past 5 years.

Lessons from a Pandemic for the Future of Education
European Distance and E-Learning Network (EDEN) Proceedings
2021 Annual Conference | Madrid, 21-24 June, 2021
ISSN 2707-2819
doi: 10.38069/edenconf-2021-ac0041

STILL OPEN DURING THE COVID-19 LOCKDOWN: AN ANALYSIS OF ONLINE STUDENTS' ENGAGEMENT WITH THE VIRTUAL CAMPUS

Julià Minguillón, Julio Meneses, Anna Calvo, Jordi Serres, Xavi Aracil, Universitat Oberta de Catalunya, Spain

Abstract

The global pandemic caused by the Covid-19 outbreak and the subsequent mandatory lockdown made university students spend more time at home, changing their daily habits including studying, as a consequence of the forced self-confinement. In this article we describe the changes observed in the connection patterns to the institutional learning management system of the students enrolled in a Spanish online university during the lockdown. Our results show that the students were more likely to connect to the virtual campus, they did so more evenly over the days of the week, and more concentrated in a few hours in the central part of the days. Interestingly, the changes in students' connection patterns were not associated with their socio-demographic characteristics, although they were affected by their academic trajectory and their academic enrolment.

Introduction

In 2020, a global pandemic caused by the worldwide spread of the Covid-19 coronavirus shattered all aspects of everyday life. Higher education was not an exception, as most institutions were forced to switch from face-to-face to remote instruction in a very short period of time, without any methodological support and, in some cases, with scarce resources (Abou-Khalil et al., 2021). Students were locked in their homes fulfilling the mandatory self-confinement enforced by governments, while higher education institutions had to transition to a fully online scenario and use the available means (mainly the institutional website and some video conferencing tools), and do so without the proper pedagogical knowledge and support (Crawford et al., 2020). On the other hand, online universities were already providing students with online teaching before the pandemic crisis, and their adaptation to the new situation caused by the mandatory lockdown was not so dramatic. Nevertheless, all face-to-face activities such as the final evaluations had to be completed online, and some additional flexibility measures had to be offered to students in order to help them to keep their path throughout the academic semester.

In the case of online universities, there was an important factor that also shaped the impact of Covid-19 on students' study habits and academic engagement. A large majority of the students in these institutions are non-traditional students (Sánchez-Gelabert, Valente, & Duart, 2020), that is to say, compared to traditional ones, they are adults, with professional and family commitments (Samra, Waterhouse, & Lucassen, 2021). During lockdown, some of these commitments were also affected, so the students had more available time to study and participate in the proposed learning activities (Gonzalez et al., 2020). On the other side, the main challenge faced by the institutions in which they were enrolled was to ensure the additional support needed to meet their increased academic demands during self-confinement, and maintain their engagement throughout the semester.

In this article we analyse the change in the connection patterns of the students of an online distance university during the lockdown period by posing the following research questions:

- RQ1: Did students change their attendance due to the Covid-19 lockdown?
- RQ2: Are there differences in their weekly and daily connection patterns during the lockdown period?
- RQ3: Regarding persistence throughout the semester, are there differences between groups?

Methodology

Context

This study was carried out at the Open University of Catalonia (UOC), an open, distance, and fully online university in Spain. Most of the students attending at the UOC are adults with a profile that hardly could fit into the traditional university system. In this sense, they value the UOC as an opportunity to start their academic trajectory or finish their previous studies, in a very innovative environment characterized by a pedagogical model that promotes continuous assessment (Sangrà, 2002). The underlying asynchronous model allows students to enrol part-time in their studies and follow their own pace according to the schedule of planned learning activities, empowering them to accommodate any competing demand or adverse circumstance they may face in their lives (Kember, 1999). Regarding the global pandemic, on 31 January 2020, the Spanish government confirmed the first Covid-19 infection. In the following days, the number of cases exponentially increased due to community transmission, which forced the declaration of the "state of alarm" and a complete lockdown on March the 14th. This enforced lockdown was periodically extended until June the 21st. Therefore, during the Spring 2020 semester all

Spanish students, enrolled in traditional and online institutions, had to remain self-confined at their homes. This situation had an important impact in their daily routines, affecting their lifestyle habits and, from the perspective of our aims in this study, changing the connection patterns to the Virtual Campus.

Data

Students' connections to the virtual campus and their enrolment data were gathered from the institutional Learning Record Store (Minguillón et al., 2018). Three academic semesters were analysed, namely Spring 2020 (affected by the pandemic crisis), Spring 2018 and Spring 2019, which were used as a reference to establish a pre-Covid scenario to compare with. We focused on students taking an official undergraduate program, and excluded students residing outside of Spain given that the lockdown restrictions were different in other countries. Table 1 shows students' demographic characteristics and enrolment data for the selected semesters. All three populations of students show a similar distribution according to their demographic and academic characteristics, being mainly non-traditional, adult part-time learners (Sánchez-Gelabert, Valente, & Duart, 2020).

Table 1: Students' socio-demographic and academic characteristics in the selected academic semesters

		Spring 2018	Spring 2019	Spring 2020
Students	Total	27,009	29,428	31,502
Gender	Male	12,439 (46.06%)	13,473 (45.78%)	14,227 (45.16%)
	Female	14,570 (53.94%)	15,955 (54.22%)	17,275 (54.84%)
Age	18-24 years old	3,970 (14.70%)	4,664 (15.85%)	5,468 (17.36%)
	25+ years old	23,039 (85.30%)	24,764 (84.15%)	26,034 (82.64%)
Academic trajectory	Freshmen	3,389 (12.55%)	3,809 (12.94%)	3,696 (11.73%)
	Rest of the students	23,620 (87.45%)	25,619 (87.06%)	27,806 (88.27%)
Academic enrolment	Part-time (< 30 credits)	24,526 (90.81%)	26,543 (90.20%)	28,183 (89.46%)
	Full-time (≥ 30 credits)	2,483 (9.19%)	2,885 (9.80%)	3,319 (10.54%)

The teaching period of any academic semester at the UOC lasts 103 days, with an initial short week 0 starting on Wednesday, and fourteen complete weeks (Monday to Sunday). Self-confinement started March the 14th, 2020, and corresponds to the day 25 of the Spring 2020 semester. Although the lockdown was officially declared at 00:00, it must be noted that the Spanish population was *de facto* self-confined at their homes the day before (day 24 of the academic semester). Therefore, in order to define two periods and being able to compare students' connection patterns to the institutional LMS, in this research we have considered a pre-lockdown period that comprises from day 1 to day 23, and a following lockdown period from day 24 to day 103.

Measures

In order to analyse the changes in connection patterns, we used three different measures as a proxy to the students' engagement with the virtual campus: Attendance, weekly / daily connections, and persistence. Attendance was measured as the percentage of unique students connected to the virtual campus each day of the academic semester. Connection patterns were measured as the total number of connections to the Virtual Campus per specific time period, namely day of the week (from Monday to Sunday) and hour of the day (from 00 to 23), after normalizing by the total number of enrolled students. Finally, persistence was measured as the averaged percentage of days that students have connected to the virtual campus divided by the total number of days since the beginning of the academic semester, as an indicator of the students' involvement level.

Results and discussion

RQ1: Changes in students' attendance between pre-lockdown and lockdown periods

Figure 1 shows the percentage of different students connected to the virtual campus per day, comparing Spring 2020, Spring 2019, and Spring 2018.

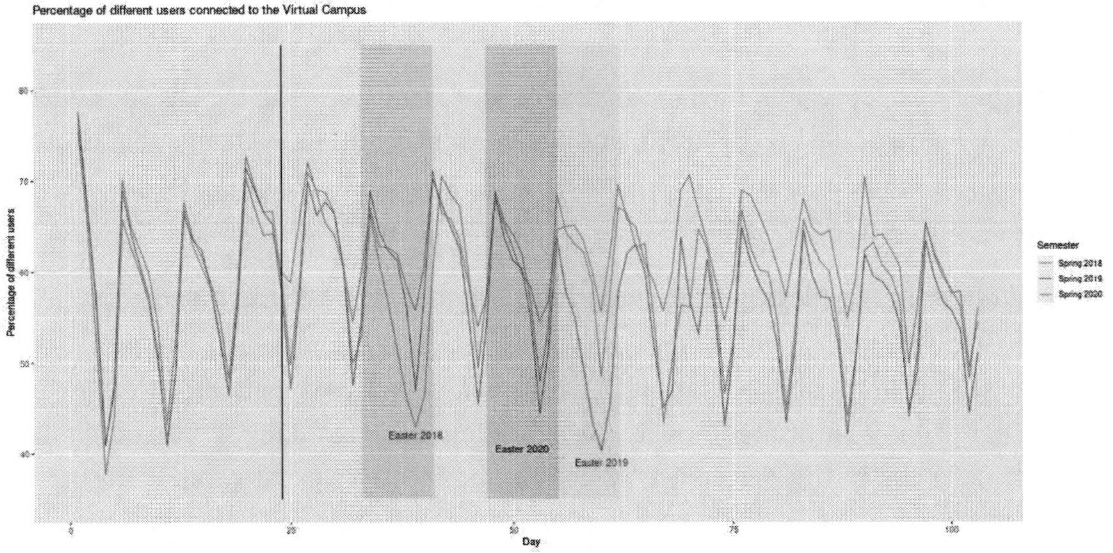

Figure 1. Percentage of different students connected to the virtual campus by day

Figure 1 reveals two interesting facts. First, all semesters showed the same weekly connection patterns during the pre-lockdown period, marked by a black line on day 24. After day 24, during the lockdown period, a clear difference can be seen in the case of Spring 2020, as students kept up or even increased their attendance around 55% and 70% (marked with a blue line). Interestingly, Spring 2019 and Spring 2018 showed a different pattern with a constant decrease in both cases that roughly ranged between 45% and 65%

(red and green lines). Similar results regarding the changes in connection patterns were described in Favale et al. (2020). Second, Spring 2020 (marked with a blue area) exhibited a different pattern during the Easter week, showing no impact on the students' connection to the virtual campus that could be reasonably attributed to the mobility constraints that kept them self-confined at home in comparison to the previous semesters (red and green areas) in which students took a few days off and were less likely to connect. Table 2 shows the average number of total connections to the virtual campus for each academic semester, splitting the users' connections according to the pre-lockdown (P) and lockdown (L) periods. Comparing both time periods, the average number of daily connections per student increased substantially in Spring 2020 during the lockdown (+0.19). On the other hand, for the two previous semesters, the difference was minimal or even reversed (+0.05 and –0.02, respectively).

Table 2: Total and daily average (inside the parentheses) number of student connections to the virtual campus

Semester	Total (daily)	Pre-lockdown period (P)	Lockdown period (L)	Difference (L-P)
Spring 2018	173.27 (1.68)	38.29 (1.66)	136.98 (1.71)	+0.05
Spring 2019	161.63 (1.57)	36.83 (1.60)	126.27 (1.58)	-0.02
Spring 2020	163.95 (1.59)	33.40 (1.45)	131.58 (1.64)	+0.19

To sum up the evidence presented in this section, our results show an increase in students' attendance between the pre-lockdown and the lockdown periods, a change that could be reasonably attributable to the consequences of the self-confinement experienced by the students in the Spring 2020 semester.

RQ2: Changes in students' weekly and daily connection patterns during the lockdown period

We analysed the impact of self-confinement during the lockdown period on the students' connection patterns, measured weekly (days of the week) and daily (hours of the day). Figure 2 (left) shows the percentage of connections to the virtual campus during the lockdown period (days 24-103) according to the day of the week. Although the three semesters included in our analysis followed the same pattern, the difference between the day in which students were more connected (Monday) and the less connected (Saturday) was clearly lower in Spring 2020 than in 2018 and 2019 (3.87% vs. 7.39% and 6.55%, respectively), when the self-confinement probably blurred the difference between weekends and weekdays (Favale et al., 2020). On the contrary, Spring 2019 and Spring 2018 exhibited a different, almost identical pattern. Regarding the hour of the day, Figure 2 (right) shows that there were also differences between Spring 2020 and the previous semesters. In fact, students were more connected between 10:00 and 19:00 and less connected during the rest of the day in Spring 2020, a trend that is consistent with the changes in household energy consumption observed during the lockdown (Santiago et al., 2021).

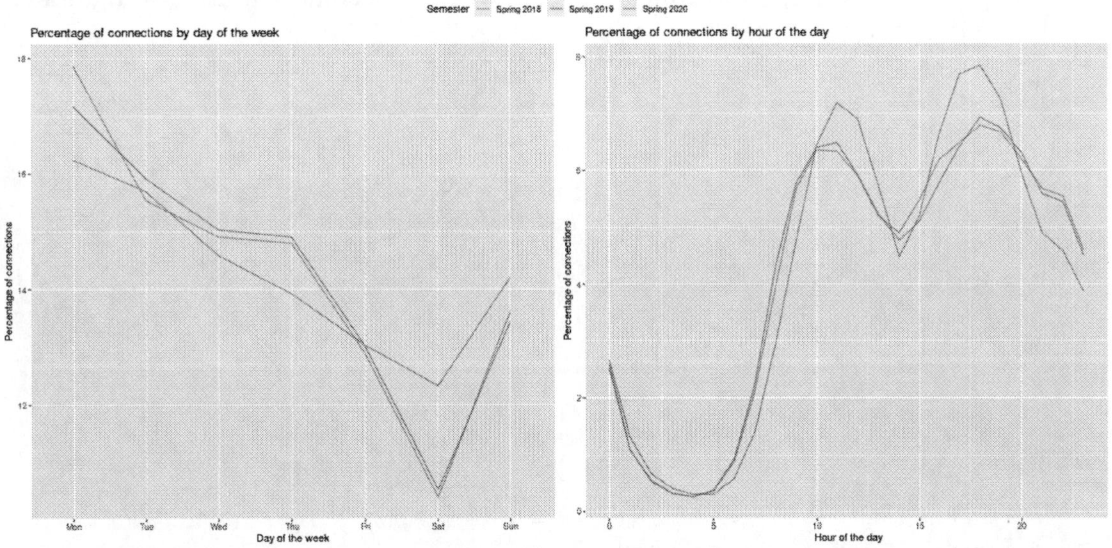

Figure 2. Percentage of student connections to the virtual campus by day of the week (left) and hour of the day (right)

In light of these results, we can conclude that there were differences in students' weekly and daily connection patterns in the Spring 2020 semester, a change in their connection habits that could be reasonably explained because of the increase in available time over the whole week and, particularly, the central part of the days. Additionally, taking into account the blurring of the perceived distinction between weekends and weekdays during the lockdown, the gap between Mondays and Saturdays previously observed was significantly reduced.

RQ3: Differences in students' persistence between pre-lockdown and lockdown periods by group

Finally, we also compared the differences in persistence for the different groups of students shown in Table 1. Due to space limitations we only show the most interesting results. However, it is worthwhile to note that women and men did not show substantial differences in their behaviour, although women slightly increased their connection rate to the virtual campus during the lockdown period. Regarding the students' age, both traditional (i.e. 18-24 years old) and non-traditional (i.e. 25+ years old) students showed a quite similar behaviour, although the younger students showed a more diverse behaviour, and were slightly more connected to the virtual campus than their counterparts during the lockdown period. Taking into account their academic trajectory, Figure 3 shows an interesting difference between freshmen and more advanced students. Actually, freshmen were the only group in which persistence declined during the Spring 2020 semester, but less than in the two previous semesters. Due to its definition, persistence shows greater fluctuations (due to differences in the number of connections per day of the week) at the beginning of the semester, stabilizing at the end, where it becomes almost a straight line.

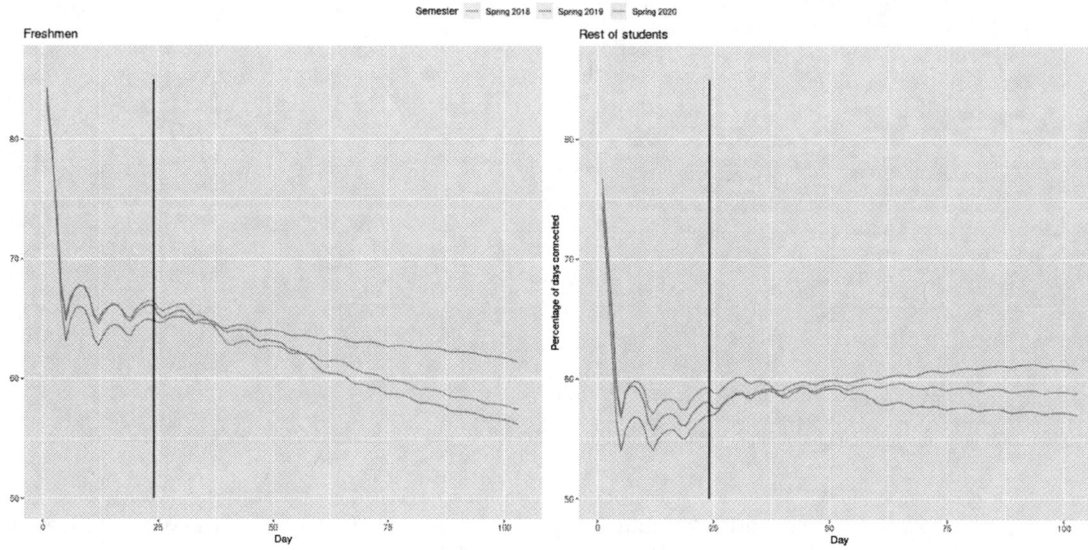

Figure 3. Average percentage of days connected to the virtual campus by academic trajectory

Finally, Figure 4 shows an interesting difference between part-time and full-time students. As expected, full-time students were more connected to the virtual campus over the three semesters than their part-time counterparts. However, although their persistence was almost constant in the second half of the previous academic semesters, full-time students kept increasing their connection patterns roughly up to a 75% in Spring 2020, that is to say, they were connected three out of four days on average. Interestingly, part-time students kept their persistence levels or even slightly improved them in Spring 2020, a distinctive behaviour that contrasts with previous semesters, in which these students showed a slight decrease in their connection to the virtual campus over the same period.

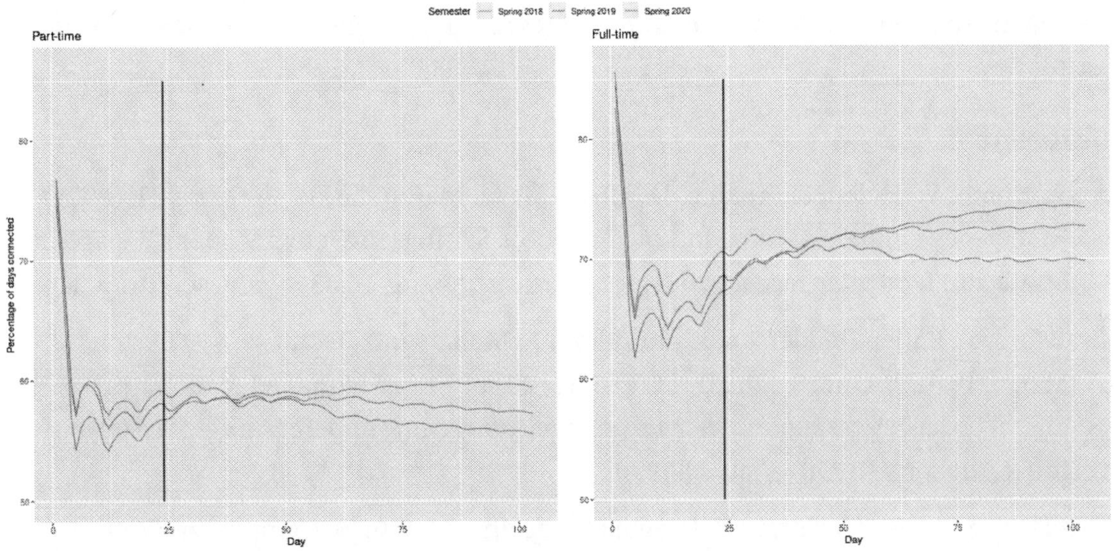

Figure 4. Average percentage of days connected to the virtual campus by academic enrolment

Therefore, we can answer RQ3 as follows: the period of confinement affected all students regardless of the group to which they belonged, but freshmen students were the only ones who did not increase their persistence.

Conclusions

In this paper we have analysed the changes in the connection patterns to the institutional learning management system of the students enrolled in an online distance university during the Covid-19 lockdown. Before summarizing our results, it must be noted that our approach has some limitations. First, students' engagement is a much more complex phenomenon than just getting connected to the virtual campus, which in fact acts as a proxy measure of students' study habits. Second, no data was available on the employment status or the family obligations that our students had during the self-confinement. Despite such limitations, we can draw some interesting conclusions. From an institutional point of view, facing the Covid-19 crisis was not a haunting issue as the University was already operating in a remote teaching scenario compared to other traditional institutions that had to adapt their everyday functioning in a very short period of time and, in some cases, with scarce resources. Nevertheless, an adaptation to the situation was still required as far as the students and the teaching staff were affected by a pandemic crisis that had personal implications for them and their families. In this sense, it must be acknowledged that the students showed a positive reaction and decided to increase their engagement, changing (mainly, by increasing) their connection patterns to the virtual campus. As we have evidenced, Spring 2020 students were more connected than their counterparts from previous semesters, and also did so more continuously by changing their daily and hourly connection pattern. Actually, their persistence increased over the semester, but for freshmen, the group that showed the greatest impact of self-confinement during the lockdown.

References

Abou-Khalil, V., Helou, S., Khalifé, E., Chen, M. A., Majumdar, R., & Ogata, H. (2021). Emergency Online Learning in Low-Resource Settings: Effective Student Engagement Strategies. *Education Sciences, 11*(1), 24. https://doi.org/10.3390/educsci11010024

Crawford, J., Butler-Henderson, K., Rudolph, J., Malkawi, B., Glowatz, M., Burton, R., Magni, P. A., & Lam, S. (2020). COVID-19: 20 countries' higher education intra-period digital pedagogy responses. *Journal of Applied Learning and Teaching, 3*(1), 09-28. https://doi.org/10.37074/jalt.2020.3.1.7

Favale, T., Soro, F., Trevisan, M., Drago, I., & Mellia, M. (2020). Campus traffic and e-Learning during COVID-19 pandemic. *Computer Networks, 176*, 107290. https://doi.org/10.1016/j.comnet.2020.107290

Gonzalez, T., de la Rubia, M. A., Hincz, K. P., Comas-Lopez, M., Subirats, L., Fort, S., & Sacha, G. M. (2020). Influence of COVID-19 confinement on students' performance in higher education. *PLOS ONE, 15*(10), e0239490. https://doi.org/10.1371/journal.pone.0239490

Kember, D. (1999). Integrating part-time study with family, work and social obligations. *Studies in Higher Education, 24*(1), 109-124. https://doi.org/10.1080/03075079912331380178

Miller, M. & Lu, M.-Y. (2003). Serving Non-Traditional Students in E-Learning Environments: Building Successful Communities in the Virtual Campus. *Educational Media International, 40*(1-2), 163-169. https://doi.org/10.1080/0952398032000092206

Minguillón, J., Conesa, J., Rodríguez, M. E., & Santanach, F. (2018). Learning Analytics in Practice: Providing E-Learning Researchers and Practitioners with Activity Data. In J. M. Spector, V. Kumar, A. Essa, Y.-M. Huang, R. Koper, R. A. W. Tortorella, T.-W. Chang, Y. Li, & Z. Zhang (Eds.), *Frontiers of Cyberlearning: Emerging Technologies for Teaching and Learning* (pp. 145–167). Springer. https://doi.org/10.1007/978-981-13-0650-1_8

Samra, R., Waterhouse, P., & Lucassen, M. (2021) Combining and managing work-family-study roles and perceptions of institutional support. *Distance Education, 42*(1), 88-105. https://doi.org/10.1080/01587919.2020.1869530

Sánchez-Gelabert, A., Valente, R., & Duart, J. M. (2020). Profiles of Online Students and the Impact of Their University Experience. *The International Review of Research in Open and Distributed Learning, 21*(3), 230-249. https://doi.org/10.19173/irrodl.v21i3.4784

Sangrà, A. (2002). A New Learning Model for the Information and Knowledge Society: The Case of the Universitat Oberta de Catalunya (UOC), Spain. *The International Review of Research in Open and Distributed Learning, 2*(2). https://doi.org/10.19173/irrodl.v2i2.55

Santiago, I., Moreno-Munoz, A., Quintero-Jiménez, P., Garcia-Torres, F., & Gonzalez-Redondo, M. J. (2021). Electricity demand during pandemic times: The case of the COVID-19 in Spain. *Energy Policy, 148*, 111964. https://doi.org/10.1016/j.enpol.2020.111964

Lessons from a Pandemic for the Future of Education
European Distance and E-Learning Network (EDEN) Proceedings
2021 Annual Conference | Madrid, 21-24 June, 2021
ISSN 2707-2819
doi: 10.38069/edenconf-2021-ac0042

E-LEARNING APPLICATION IN MUSICAL EDUCATION: NEEDS AND POSSIBILITIES

Zrinka Šimunović, University of Slavonski Brod, EDUDpt, Croatia

Introduction

Technological progress, or in other words, the digital revolution, a name that more clearly describes the speed and manner in which this process takes place, is changing our world in multiple areas and across multiple levels. Due to the complexity and the organization of the formal education system, the implementation and the use of technological resources does not take place sufficiently and at the same speed in all schools. The entry of technology into teaching depends on the users' capabilities and technical resources, i.e. on each individual teacher and the technological equipment at his disposal (Nart, 2016). And while the offer of digital tools for creating, performing and sharing music has become widely available and financially acceptable to the general population, which according to Savage (2007) has accelerated the process of technological change in music, the usage of technology in schools with traditional music practice is very rare (Mills & Murray, 2000). The availability of ICT resources in music schools, such as technological equipment and licensed computer programs designed to assist learning and teaching in the users' mother tongue (especially those intended for music education), the lack of teachers' competencies required to use technology in teaching, as well as the absence of methodological frameworks that could support planning and executing of such lessons are the main reasons for this delay of technology implementation in the music education system. According to a 2018 study by the Organization for Economic Co-operation and Development (OECD), more than 60% of teachers said that they did not feel ready to use digital technology in teaching. By contrast, in a public consultation launched by the European Commission in 2021 on the new Digital Education Action Plan (2021-2027), over 60% of teachers stated that they had improved their digital skills and that the crisis caused by COVID-19 forced them to use technology more than usual. In the near future, it is realistic to expect that ICT will be integrated into the usual music teaching curriculum (Crow, 2005). Teachers should advance from being the passive users of digital tools to becoming the digital innovators capable of using technology to improve their teaching skills and consequently achieving greater success with learning outcomes (Koehler & Mishra, 2005).

But how much is technology changing us as music teachers? How much is our teaching changing? And formal music education in general? What is good about this change and what is not good for our students? We are discussing and emphasizing the benefits that technology provides in music teaching, however, certain special demands, that such education requires, technology cannot fulfil yet. For instance, demonstrating proper body posture, along with correct arm and hand position, avoiding injuries while performing music (Waddell & Williamon, 2019) or delivering online teaching at a high artistic level (Adileh, 2012). These are all actions that, in addition to multidimensional activities, presuppose a "live" teacher (Ruismäki & Juvonen, 2009), a "live" model observed and followed by the students with more of their senses than just sight and hearing. Through the method of interviews with music school teachers, we will try to find answers to the questions posed here and some additional ones. The aim of this paper is to encourage the scientists and teachers in music education to think about and find the best solutions for optimal and purposeful use of new technological achievements.

Methodology

The conducted research is qualitative in nature. The obtained data were processed by classical content analysis (Leech & Onwuegbuzie, 2008) including the induction process (Creswell, 1994). In qualitative research, such a process involves multiple reading of the obtained data in order to get sufficient knowledge of the researched material. The data are then coded in the first- and second-level codes, which are again categorized and grouped according to the correlation between the research data and the theories.

Participants

The process of selecting participants for this study comprised of the non-probability sampling method, i.e. convenience sampling. The condition for selecting the teachers who participated in the research was that at the time of the research they were employed in the same institution as the researcher herself. According to Lava and Kvale (1995; p.220) the criteria by which the researcher is part of the group being tested is one of the most important conditions that qualitative research should meet. The music school in which the research was conducted includes primary and secondary music education with an emphasis on one of the areas: instrumental, theoretical, singing and dance. When selecting teachers, one of the criteria was to have representatives in all of the listed areas of work and in both levels of music education. The convenient sample consisted of 8 teachers, four instrument teachers, two music theory teachers, one dance teacher and one voice teacher. Of these, two teachers work in secondary school, three teachers work in both primary and secondary school, and three teachers work only in primary school. The work experience of the participants ranges from 5 to 30 years.

Instruments

Data were collected by a semi-structured interview guided by a flexible interview protocol and supplemented by follow-up questions and comments (adjusted according to Price, 2020, which, according to Ayres (2008), is suitable for research that requires a deeper analysis and personal experience of the participants). Questions covered areas such as participants' experiences while they were still students themselves and their encounters with technology in that process, participants' use of technology in their current role as teachers, their attitudes towards online teaching and the changes that it brings in curriculum planning and teaching performance, e.g.:

> *"During your student experience, what methods (briefly describe) and what technology (including video / audio devices) did your teachers use while teaching?"*
>
> *"When did you start using technology in your teaching?"*
>
> *"What role does technology play in your lesson planning?"*
>
> *"What is the biggest change in your teaching methods over the last few months?"*
>
> *"What are the limitations of online teaching?"*

Process

Selected participants were offered the opportunity to take part in the research. The purpose and the importance of the research were presented. Participants were guaranteed anonymity and ethical data management. After the preliminary interviews, a recorded interview was conducted, after which the data were transcribed in the literal sense. The interview lasted approximately 30 minutes.

Data analysis

The obtained answers were coded and the first- and second-level codes were extrapolated. Figure 1 shows thematic categories that were labelled by summarizing the sentences with related meaning of the studied statements of the participants. The main topic is "E-learning in Music Education" which is divided into two categories named "Transformation of teaching" and "Technology in main role". The aforementioned categories were then divided into subcategories related to specific areas, which were determined using the method of extrapolating the most frequently used words in the participants' answers.

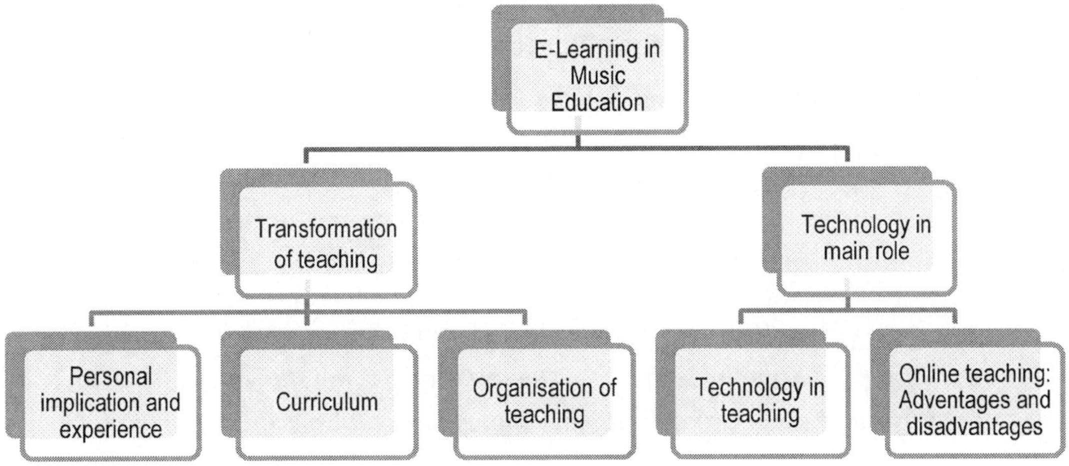

Figure 9. Category Analysis

Results

At this point, we are going to present the results of the study organized in the following six categories:

Personal implication

This category includes questions related to the teachers' previous experiences, while back when they were still students themselves. When asked about the motivation that prompted them to start teaching, some teachers (N = 3) indicated teaching as their second choice that they were in a way constrained to choose because they didn't succeed as concert musicians due to life circumstances. Nevertheless, the other part of the participants (N = 5) is devoted to both the teaching profession and the transfer of knowledge to young artists. One of them says:

> *"I've soon realized that some of the non-standard methods of teaching and explaining that I've been using (while trying to help my colleagues) proved as being highly effective and that most of 'my students' mastered the material very quickly and successfully."*

When asked how much and what type of technology in particular their teachers once used during the teaching process, participants answered according to expectations that technology was used to a much lesser extent in comparison to today. The most common answers regarding the specific devices were TV sets, video and audio devices, cassette tapes and compact discs, which were used to familiarize the students with the performances of famous musicians.

Curriculum

The curriculum by which the participants were taught while they were students did not meet their needs at the time. Therefore, immediately after they started working as teachers themselves, they implemented their own curriculum, combining ideas gathered at permanent teacher's training courses with the use of technology. In addition to the increased use of technology in their teaching, when compared to their teachers in the past, participants also invest time in adapting teaching methods and strategies to the individual needs and abilities of each of their students, such as:

> *"I suggest my students record their playing and try to improve it by noticing the mistakes. To motivate them to rehearse, I advise my students to listen to the performances of certain musical compositions and specific performers. "*

The participants unanimously agree that classroom teaching curriculum and online teaching curriculum differ greatly and that learning expectations and outcomes in online teaching are lower than in classroom teaching.

Organisation of teaching

Lesson planning for the three participants is the same in both classroom and online teaching. Three out of eight participants plan their lessons in the same way in both classroom and online teaching. However, the other five participants have stated some specific characteristics of online lesson planning: it is more extensive and detailed than preparing for classroom teaching, browsing the Internet for ideas is more common than in classroom teaching, giving up on the improvement of student's performance, and also completely omitting certain content that is otherwise easily performed in a regular classroom environment. Online lessons generally last the same as classroom lessons for all participants, except for one participant who organizes her online lessons in such a way that students send recordings of their performances, and then she analyses them and talks to students about them. Changes in the organization of teaching caused by online teaching are visible in the number of hours spent in front of a computer, the use of digital tools, but also some particularities such as:

> *"Insisting less on the perfect student's performance, and putting more emphasis on maintaining student's motivation."*

> *"Enabling students to work independently."*

Technology in teaching

Participants describe their first use of technology in teaching differently. Two participants first started using the technology during the last year (due to the pandemic), while the others have been using it since the very beginning of their teaching career. The participants themselves have most often found the motivation and ideas to start implementing technology in their teaching on the Internet, or through conversations with other colleagues, and somewhat less often from their university professors. In the preparation of teaching, technology plays an important role for most participants because it enables them to find sheet music, ideas, varied selection of compositions, it also helps improve the teaching process and facilitate communication with colleagues and students. One participant distinguishes the amount of technology used in the preparation of live classroom lessons where she practically does not use it at all compared to her online teaching, while another participant does not care much about technology in his lesson preparation. When asked how and whether technology has affected the changes in their teaching, the participants state that students have become more independent and conscientious in their work. The participants also have a better insight, because they are able to devote more time and analyse the technical part of playing skills when studying recordings that their students make and send. They also mention that they themselves, through technology, have advanced in the profession and improved their teaching. The smartphone is used for both private and teaching purposes by all participants. They believe that the exclusion of the smartphone would affect the delivery of online classes, which would not even be possible, the process of teaching and learning the content would slow down, and there would be a lack of creative ideas because there would be no exchange on the Internet. However, one participant claims the exact opposite:

> *"With the help of a smartphone, you acquire other people's ideas and knowledge, but when you are alone, you encourage your own creativity."*

Online teaching: Advantages and disadvantages

How the participants see the benefits of online teaching, which has lately been the most commonly used way. The advantage of online teaching lies in the fact that it is the only possible way of teaching when the classroom teaching is not an option, so consequently it is the best possible choice. Students are more responsible and conscientious in their approach to work than in live classroom teaching, they are more independent. Teachers and students are protected from the virus infection. Everyone is becoming acquainted with the useful side of technology. Online teaching encourages students to self-evaluate more, which positively affects the learning outcomes. Disadvantages of online teaching differ in individual and group teaching. Participants who are instrumentalists most often mention the impossibility to directly influence the position of the hand, arm and body posture while their students are playing and also the impossibility of tuning musical instruments when teaching younger students:

> *"A student who fails to understand the required instructions in interpretation during an online lesson is deprived of the teacher's help in-person and thus fails to correct the wrong posture or find the correct tone."*

For older students, the disadvantages of online teaching are related to the extent and quality of the program:

> *"Older students lack progress in their artistic expression and the completion of the music program, especially high school graduates."*

All participants agree that online teaching has its limitations and that the lack of physical contact is irreplaceable in this type of teaching.

Conclusion

With this research, we tried to get teachers' answers to several key questions regarding the use of technology in music education. We have started from the theoretical frameworks in which the increase in the use of technology in education has been visible in the last few years, and especially in the last year due to the COVID-19 crisis (European Commission, 2021). Our participants, music educators, confirmed this fact by comparing their personal schooling, their prior teaching experience and the current situation. They all agree that today they are forced to use technology much more and in a much more complex way than they had the opportunity to see from their teachers or compared to how they used it themselves a year ago. The biggest change relates to the transition from in-person teaching to online teaching. Accordingly, the participants have noted increased effort necessary to adapt the curriculum as well as the teaching methods and strategies to the individual needs and abilities of each of their students. There are far more advantages of technology-assisted teaching and when used in a purposeful and planned manner, it significantly helps in achieving teaching objectives. Nevertheless, the participants agree, that without the knowledge and practical skills that music educators can provide to their students, music education cannot fulfil its purpose. In this sense, online teaching is a good temporary solution to which they have adapted, mostly on their own, or using the ideas of their colleagues that they found on the Internet. The results obtained by this research are insufficient for a more in-depth analysis of the use of technology in music education and they need to be extended with quantitative data. Digital Education Action Plan 2021-2027 (European Commission, 2021) predicts, among other things, the improvement of education that will be obtained by analysing the data and anticipating possible situations. This research, expanded by the increased number of participants along with the corresponding quantitative analysis, could serve for a clearer concept of music education in the near future.

References

Adileh, M. T. (2012). Teaching music as a University eclective course through e-learning. *Australian Journal of Music Education, 1*, 71-79. Retrieved from https://files.eric.ed.gov/fulltext/EJ1000246.pdf

Ayres, L. (2008). Semi-structured Interview. In L. M. Given (Ed.), *The Sage encyclopedia of qualitative research methods* (pp. 810-811). Los Angeles, London, New Delhi, Singapore: SAGE Publications.

European Commission (2021). *Digital Education Action Plan (2021-2027).* Communication from the Commission to the European Parliament, the Council, the European Economic and Social Committee and the Committee of the Regions. Retrieved from https://ec.europa.eu/education/education-in-the-eu/digital-education-action-plan_en

Creswell, J. W. (1994). *Research design – Qualitative and Quantitative Approaches.* London – New Delhi: Sage Publictions. Thousand Oaks.

Crow, B. (2005). Music-related ICT in education. In C. Philpott (Ed.), *Learning to Teach Music in the Secondary School: A Companion to School Experience* (pp. 115-139). London: Rautledge Farmer.

Koehler, M. J., & Mishra, P. (2005). What happens when teachers design educational technology? The development of technological pedagogical content knowledge. *Journal of Educational Computing Research, 32*(2), 131-152. doi:10.2190/0EW7-01WB-BKHL-QDYV

Lave, J., & Kvale, S. (1995). What is anthropological research? An interview with Jean Lave by Steinar Kvale. *International Journal of Qualitative Studies in Education, 8*(3), 219-228. doi:10.1080/0951839950080301

Leech, N. L., & Onwuegbuzie, A. J. (2008). Qualitative data analysis: A compendium of techniques and a framework for selection for school psychology research and beyond. *Psychological Association, 23*(4), 587-604. doi:10.1037/1045-3830.23.4.587

Mills, J., & Murray, A. (2000). Music technology inspected: good teaching in Key Stage 3, *British Journal of Music Education, 17*(2), 129-56. Retrieved from https://www.cambridge.org/core/journals/british-journal-of-music-education/article/music-technology-inspected-good-teaching-in-key-stage-3/C5A96D8CB330B739DA59907E47544078

Nart, S. (2016). Music software in the technology integrated music education. *Turkish Online Journal of Educational Technology (TOJET), 15*(2), 78-84. Retrieved from https://files.eric.ed.gov/fulltext/EJ1096456.pdf

OECD (2018). *Development Co-operation Report 2018: Joining Forces to Leave No One Behind.* Paris: OECD Publishing. doi:10.1787/dcr-2018-en.

Price Jr, D. F. (2020). *Experience, Technology and Curriculum for Today's Online Instrumental Music Educator* (Doctoral dissertation). Boston University, Boston. Retrieved from https://search.proquest.com/openview/7bb022ae95a07934f159b85547fcb25e/1?pq-origsite=gscholar&cbl=18750&diss=

Ruismäki, H., & Juvonen, A. (2009). The new horizons for music technology in music education. The Changing Face of Music Education. *Music and Environment*, 98-104. Retrieved from https://www.swsu.ru/sbornik-statey/pdf/The_new_horizonts_for_music_technology.pdf

Savage, J. (2007). Reconstructing music education through ICT. *Research in Education, 78*(1), 65-77. Retrieved from https://www.researchgate.net/profile/Jonathan_Savage2/publication/233514091_Reconstructing_Music_Education_through_ICT/links/556f0e9308aeab7772282a04/Reconstructing-Music-Education-through-ICT.pdf

Waddell, G., & Williamon, A. (2019). Technology use and attitudes in music learning. *Frontiers in ICT, 6*, 11. doi:10.3389/fict.2019.00011

Lessons from a Pandemic for the Future of Education
European Distance and E-Learning Network (EDEN) Proceedings
2021 Annual Conference | Madrid, 21-24 June, 2021
ISSN 2707-2819
doi: 10.38069/edenconf-2021-ac0043

E-LEARNING CHALLENGES FROM THE STUDENTS' POINT OF VIEW

Daiva Rimkuvienė, Vytautas Magnus University, Lithuania, Anna Vintere, Latvia University of Life Sciences and Technologies, Latvia, Eve Aruvee, Estonian University of Life Sciences, Estonia

Abstract

E-learning has become mandatory at all levels of educational institutions due to the coronavirus pandemic. This paper analyses the learning difficulties that university students have encountered as a result of this changed situation. Empirical research includes a survey of students at three Baltic universities: Latvia University of Life Sciences and Technologies (LLU), Vytautas Magnus University (VMU) and Estonian University of Life Sciences (EMÜ). The aim of our article is to compare opinions on the challenges faced by students of Baltic States during mandatory remote learning. The results of this study revealed that there were no statistically significant differences between respondents in the countries participating in the survey in terms of the opinions expressed on the availability of appropriate hardware, communication with teacher and interaction with classmates and difficulty focusing on remote studies. Students who prefer face to face learning style mentioned difficulties in paying attention to studies, In addition, the majority of respondents indicated that they often had problems communicating with teachers. It was found that not only achieving learning outcomes, implementing practical works, and the volume of study works caused challenges but also lack of digital skills and interaction with classmates.

Introduction

The COVID-19 pandemic outbreak forced many educational units to suspend typical face-to-face classes to ensure the safety of students, lecturers (Mukhtar et al.; 2020; Baczek et al., 2021; Rahiem, 2021). Universities are struggling to find options to deal with this challenging situation.

Modern ICT provide enormous opportunities for effective communication (Bravo-Agapito et al., 2021). E-learning programmes and courses were already available for people who were mentally and economically ready for such learning (Popovici & Mironov, 2015).

Although many academic units of Universities in Baltic countries have also started blended or online learning, still a lot of them are stuck with old procedures, that is, they follow the traditional set up of face-to-face lectures in classrooms. Baltic universities remote learning in Moodle environment took many years to be implemented. However, the majority of taught courses integrated only the presentation of the educational material. Part of the courses was adapted to be learnt through a blended learning approach when students could take part of the course in classrooms. The assessments of the students were performed only at the University. However, it should be noted that students had an opportunity to choose different study forms. Usually, both teachers and students preferred face-to-face communication as a more effective way to communicate information.

The sudden shift to full online instruction led universities members to adjust their teaching plans, teaching styles and assessment methods (Orlov et al., 2021). In the 2020 Spring semester, both university teachers and students faced many problems. There was an urgent demand for computer equipment, teachers had to learn to deliver lectures, and students had to comprehend online material. Lectures were taught through various video conferencing software, as for example, AdobeConnect, BigBlueButtons (BBB), MsTeams, and Zoom. There were cases when the systems crashed due to the high number of connected users. Teachers of various courses experienced problems with the material presentation. For example, for teaching mathematics, the usual practice is to present solutions to problems on the board. For social sciences, it is necessary to ensure the opportunity for students to communicate and develop discussions. Students also faced the challenge to quickly adapt to the "new normal" in a higher education setting (Lapitan et al., 2021; Toquero, 2021). It is evident that students found a new teaching method unusual and causing many learning difficulties. Looking at the challenges of remote learning, technological knowledge, communication skills and time management skills are the ones that determine the effectiveness of remote learning (Martin et al., 2020).

For the Autumn semester, the university community has prepared better. As distance learning was already expected, universities were provided with the necessary equipment and training in advance. VMU, LLU, EMÜ use Moodle as the main learning environment. MsTeams is recommended as the main platform for video conferencing software at VMU. Studies at LLU were provided remotely using the video conferencing system BigBlueButton (BBB) integrated in the Moodle system. The Zoom platform was often used for individual consultations and additional classes, depending on its accessibility to teachers. The Zoom is most commonly used for lectures and communication at EMÜ. The work in the Autumn semester has started in the classrooms by keeping a safe distance. However, due to the dramatic deterioration of the situation in the country, since the middle of October in Lithuania and the middle of December in Estonia, Baltic countries has returned to remote learning. Remote learning was continued in the 2021 Spring semester.

Literature sources provide a number of analytical articles on learning challenges during learning at home and highlight certain factors such as levels of motivation, teachers' knowledge of e-learning techniques and pedagogy, and the structured learning environment influencing student satisfaction with their remote learning experience during the COVID19 pandemic (Baber, 2020). While understanding that this way of teaching is forced and temporary, it is useful to know what challenges students have faced and what suggestions they make. The aim of our article is to compare opinions on the challenges faced by students of Baltic States during remote learning.

Materials and methods

Empirical research includes a survey of students at three Baltic universities: Latvia University of Life Sciences and Technologies, Vytautas Magnus University and Estonian University of Life Sciences on the challenges and benefits of remote learning during the COVID-19 pandemic. The questionnaires are available at: https://ej.uz/ATT_S (in Latvian), https://ej.uz/estudies_EE (in Estonian) and https://ej.uz/estudies_LT (in Lithuanian). 387 students from various specialities participated in this research.

The questionnaire included questions related to the students' attitudes towards challenges posed by remote learning. Students had four answers to choose from: *never* (1), *rarely* (2), *often* (3), and *always* (4). Students were also asked for suggestions to improve remote learning.

Respondents' answers are analysed from two perspectives: (a) Are there differences between countries? (b) Is there a difference, depending on learning style preferences?

As well, Principal Component Analysis (PCA) was performed in order to observe an underlying structure in a complex system of variables.

To perform data analysis, the Cronbach's alpha test was used for assessing the reliability of the questionnaire, Kruskal-Wallis test and Wilcoxon test – for comparing between groups, as well as Tukey test – for pairwise comparison. A statistically significant value of $P < 0.05$ was considered.

The data were analysed using the statistical package R version 4.0.3 (R Core Team, 2020).

Results

The data analysis showed that 266 fully completed questionnaires were submitted. 91 Estonian, 54 Lithuanian, and 121 Latvian students completed the questionnaire.

Table 1 presents the distribution of respondents' opinions on the learning style preferences. Having analysed the preferences of students' learning style, statistically significant differences by country were identified (chi-square = 24.18, $p < 0.001$). Even 61.5% of Estonian students prefer *face to face with a teacher learning style.* 31.5% of Lithuanian respondents indicated that they prefer e-learning and a similar proportion (29.6%) mentioned that they prefer face to face learning.

Table 1: Learning style preferences

	learning face to face with a teacher	e-learning/ remote learning	learning in a group	learning by myself	other
Estonia	61.5 %	18.7 %	12.1 %	1.1 %	6.6 %
Latvia	43.0 %	24.8 %	19.8 %	9.9 %	2.5 %
Lithuania	29.6 %	31.5 %	16.7 %	14.8 %	7.4 %

In order to find out what problems students encountered when studying remotely, we asked 11 questions (Cronbach's alpha = 0.77). The average response rates are shown in Table 2. Letters *a*, *b* and *c* means that these groups are different, and *ab* indicates that there is no difference in the groups. Regarding the results presented in the table, it can be seen that the answers of Lithuanian students fall into the group *a*. That is, they were more likely to say that they rarely or never encountered the problems mentioned. There were no statistically significant differences between the opinions of students from different countries when answering the questions about *Availability of appropriate hardware / smart devices / software at home, Communication with teachers, Personal motivation/desire to complete assignments* and *Difficulty focusing or paying attention to remote studies.*

The most contrasting opinions were found in the choice of answers to the questions on *Digital skills to use distance learning platforms/tools offered by teachers.* This lack of digital skills was mainly experienced by Latvian students. 62.0% of students noted that they had problems with the platforms offered by the teachers.

Unfortunately, the results of the analysis show that most respondents indicated that they often encountered problems in communicating with teachers. In this case, there were no statistically significant differences in the analyses of all countries. Moreover, the Latvian students have indicated that they more often faced challenges on the *Implementation of practical / laboratory work / practice*, Lithuanian students on the *Difficulty of focusing or paying attention to remote studies*, and Estonian respondents on the *Volume of study works.* Latvian and Estonian students encountered challenges regarding the *Availability of appropriate hardware / smart devices / software* at home the least, while Lithuanian students encountered challenges regarding *Digital skills to use remote learning platforms / tools offered by teachers.*

Table 2: Challenges posed by remote learning. Questionnaire results by countries

	Latvia mean (group)	Lithuania mean (group)	Estonia mean (group)	Kruskal-Wallis	p-value
Q1. Availability of information on e-learning opportunities / remote study process	2.47 (b)	2.04 (a)	2.19 (ab)	11.28	0.003
Q2. Volume of study works	2.32 (a)	2.41 (a)	2.93 (b)	27.29	<0.001
Q3. Implementation of practical / laboratory work / practice	2.80 (b)	2.04 (a)	2.10 (a)	32.49	<0.001
Q4. To achieve the study results provided for in the study courses	2.73 (b)	2.06 (a)	2.07 (a)	28.60	<0.001
Q5. Availability of appropriate hardware / smart devices / software at home	2.12 (a)	2.17 (a)	1.97 (a)	2.91	0.234
Q6. Internet connection instability	2.58 (b)	2.24 (a)	2.57 (b)	0.23	0.013
Q7. Difficulty focusing or paying attention to remote studies	2.72 (a)	2.83 (a)	2.74 (a)	1.05	0.591
Q8. Personal motivation/desire to complete assignments	2.63 (a)	2.57 (a)	2.63 (a)	0.14	0.931
Q9. Digital skills to use distance learning platforms / tools offered by teachers	2.75 (c)	1.98 (a)	2.40 (b)	28.62	<0.001
Q10. Communication with teachers	2.91 (a)	2.83 (a)	2.96 (a)	0.81	0.668
Q11. Interaction with classmates	2.60 (b)	2.25 (a)	2.48 (ab)	6.38	0.042

It was also examined whether the problems encountered by students during remote learning are dependent on learning style preferences. Wilcoxon test ($W = 5863$, $p < 0.001$) has shown there is a statistically significant difference in assessing *Difficulty focusing or paying attention to remote studies* between students, who prefer *face to face* learning style and the ones who prefer *e-learning style.* It is obvious that those who prefer learning *face to face* have faced more difficulties in *Focusing attention on studies.*

The performed Principal Component Analysis (PCA) shows that when all variables are included, three components explain only 54% of the variation and four components explain 63%. When the variables Q1–Q6, Q9 and Q11 are included, three components explain 68% of the variation, four – 78%. Therefore, the more detailed analysis was performed by including only the aforementioned variables. Figure 1 presents the graphic interpretation of *cos2* of variables. A high cos2 indicates a good representation of the variable on the principal component.

The first principal component Dim1 explains 43% of the variation and is moderately correlated with six of the original variables (Figure 1a): Q3 – Implementation of practical / laboratory work / practice (0.42), Q4 – Achieving the study results provided for in the study courses (0.44), Q11 – Interaction with classmates (0.40), Q1 – Availability of information on e-learning opportunities / remote study process (0.38), Q6 – Personal motivation/desire to complete assignments (0.38), Q9 – Digital skills to use distance learning platforms / tools offered by teachers. This component may be described as flexible adaptation.

The second principal component (Dim2) explains 13% of the variation and is highly correlated with Q2 – Volume of study works (0.74)

The third principal component (Dim3) explains 12% of the variation and is highly correlated with Q5 – Availability of appropriate hardware / smart devices / software at home (0.87).

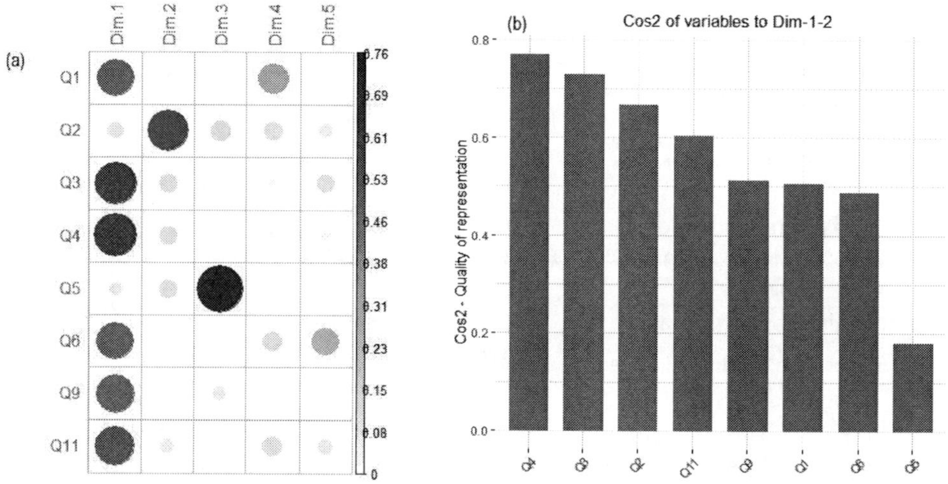

Figure 1. The quality of representation of the variables on factor map: graphic interpretation of cos2 of variables

As can be seen in Figure 1 (b), the most important variables are related to the main learning challenges Q4, Q3, Q2 and Q11, i.e. how to achieve favourable learning outcomes despite changes in the learning environment. The challenge of the same significance is *Interaction with classmates.*

Finally, it was relevant to find out what recommendations have been made by the students for the improvement of remote learning. Only 49.6% of Latvian, 51.9% of Lithuanian, 67.3% of Estonian respondents gave answer to the question: "In your opinion, what is needed (what e-learning improvements, improvements, etc.) to make e-learning more accessible, efficient and ensure higher quality of education?"

20.6% of Latvian, 12.9% of Lithuanian and 5% of Estonian students answered, everything is satisfactory and the study materials are enough. In addition, some even point out that only the willpower is needed to learn and master everything. 7.9% of respondents indicated that they are against distance learning in general and want to resume full-time studies. It should be noted that opinions vary. Some students would prefer pre-recorded classes, thus avoiding possible technical problems. Others prefer live discussions and the opportunity to ask questions.

Respondents note that not all teachers are provided with quality equipment such as good microphones and graphic tablets. They also emphasise the need to improve the assessment of given tasks. They appreciate the changed and thus broader possibilities of teaching methods and suggest more varied ways of presenting material and tasks. In addition, they would like to be provided with more descriptions in their mother tongue after, for example, reviewing online entries, as not all specific subject terms are easy to perceive. pointed to the need to ensure better operation of the BBB server and Internet connection, as there had been various cases (especially at the beginning of remote studies) when video lectures lost their Internet connection, that nothing could be understood from the lectures and they had to be moved. Sometimes the e-learning system got a little stuck, prevented from connecting to the BBB or even thrown out of it. But 6.3% of responses of Latvian students indicated flaws in the Moodle e-learning platform related to file upload, deletion / retention of previous versions and their availability to teachers, etc.- During the tests, which were placed in e-studies and were given a set time, the students had to wait a long time until the next task appeared. They also had to wait a long time for the study materials placed in e-studies to open. Students also recommend improving the interface of the Moodle system, for example, using an online platform with integrated microphone push-to-talk.

Admittedly, some of the answers (11.1% of Latvian, 16.7% of Lithuanian, 10.9% of Estonian respondents) also include teachers' knowledge of e-learning techniques and pedagogy. Students believe that teachers should take advantage of study opportunities and post materials on all topics so that they do not have to use e-mail where something may be lost. They pointed out the need to record lectures with appropriate computer programs so that they can be played, as well as to place lecture presentations in the e-learning system. It would be very helpful for students to have more independent work in all subjects, which would have to be submitted later and evaluated. This would help to focus more on learning. In study subjects where it is necessary to solve tasks, lecturers are advised to show the course of solutions in the course of online lectures, rather than leaving the solution of tasks to students.

Students pointed to the need for more interactive lessons, i.e. to try to involve students more in online lectures, using various tools (quiz, questions, games, etc.). Students would also like more group work. In the tests, ask what was taught, because there are subjects in which teachers ask for what they have no idea or little talk about. It would also be necessary for teachers to record all lectures, because teachers speak too fast and the most important is difficult to make notes.

A few quotes are provided:

> *"More in quantity and more engaging self-study, e. g. more engaging tasks, is needed."*
>
> *"Taking exams is complicated and very stressful as there is very limited time given and no possibilities to go back to questions."*
>
> *"To my mind, the attitude towards remote learning of both students and teachers should change. In my personal opinion, remote learning is easier as I can concentrate more at home than in a classroom."*

Having analysed the answers of the students, it might be stated that the same challenge of achieving the best learning outcomes remained. As well, there are new challenges, such as problems related to software and hardware, and interaction with classmates.

There are some limitations to our study that should be noted. The most important limitation is the sampling technique used. The research sample was selected in a non-random way. It should be noted that no analysis has been carried out with regard to students' subjects, choice of specialisation and year of study. The students were reached remotely and the responses were given on a voluntary basis, thus, the study can only be seen as preliminary and as a possible source for further research.

Conclusions

Based on the pandemic situation, challenges arise in migrating from a physical classroom to a mandatory remote learning environment. Both teachers and students had to change their teaching and learning habits, style and perspective to e-learning. Students' viewpoints towards the problems they face are not homogenous. Part of the students regards the transition to remote learning as acceptable and convenient. Though, a larger group of respondents would prefer learning face to face with a teacher. The comparison of opinions of respondents from Baltic countries shows no statistically significant differences in the evaluation of the availability of appropriate hardware and software at home, a difficulty of concentrating on studies, communication with teachers, interaction with classmates. Opinions contrasted the most on the problems related to digital skills of using remote learning platforms/tools offered by teachers, which was rated by Latvian students as the most frequent difficulty they encountered. The analysis shows that some of the biggest problems are related to regular challenges on how to achieve good learning outcomes and how to perform the given tasks. Problems related to communication with both peers and teachers also emerged. Respondents offered suggestions for improving their studies, which may be useful in the post-epidemic period. These include the need for technical improvement, more interactive classes as well as pre-recorded material, a more structured course in a Moodle environment with several teachers, as well as more engaging tasks. It could be argued that the suggestions made by students are in turn a challenge for teachers, who have a lot of work ahead of them to change their teaching style and adapt to sudden changes in the teaching environment. On the other hand, it will be an incentive to improve the quality of teaching in the future. Remote learning has come to stay.

References

Baber, H. (2020). Determinants of students' perceived learning outcome and satisfaction in online learning during the pandemic of COVID 19. *Journal of Education and e-Learning Research, 7*(3), 285-292.

Baczek, M., Zaganczyk-Baczek, M., Szpringer, M., Jaroszynski, A., & Wozakowska-Kaplon, B. (2021). Students' perception of online learning during the COVID-19 pandemic: A survey study of polish medical students. *Medicine, 100*(7). Retrieved from https://journals.lww.com/md-journal/Fulltext/2021/02190/Students__perception_of_online_learning_during_the.87.aspx

Bravo-Agapito, J., Romero, S. J., & Pamplona, S. (2021). Early prediction of undergraduate student's academic performance in completely online learning: A five-year study. *Computers in Human Behavior, 115*, 106595. https://doi.org/10.1016/j.chb.2020.106595

Lapitan, L. D., Tiangco, C. E., Sumalinog, D. A. G., Sabarillo, N. S., & Diaz, J. M. (2021). An effective blended online teaching and learning strategy during the COVID-19 pandemic. *Education for Chemical Engineers, 35*, 116-131. https://doi-org.ezproxy.vdu.lt:2443/10.1016/j.ece.2021.01.012

Martin, F., Stamper, B., & Flowers, C. (2020). Examining student perception of reading for online learning: Importance and confidence. *Online Learning, 24*(2), 38-58.

Mukhtar, K., Javed, K., Arooj, M., & Sethi, A. (2020). Advantages, Limitations and Recommendations for online learning during COVID-19 pandemic era. *Pakistan Journal of Medical Sciences, 36*(COVID19-S4). https://doi.org/10.12669/pjms.36.COVID19-S4.2785

Orlov, G., McKee, D., Berry, J., Boyle, A., DiCiccio, T., Ransom, T., et al. (2021). Learning during the COVID-19 pandemic: It is not who you teach, but how you teach. *Economics Letters, 202*, 109812. https://doi.org/10.1016/j.econlet.2021.109812

Popovici, A., & Mironov, C. (2015). Students' perception on using eLearning technologies. *Procedia – Social and Behavioral Sciences, 180*, 1514-1519. https://doi.org/10.1016/j.sbspro.2015.02.300

R Core Team (2020). R: A language and environment for statistical computing. R Foundation for Statistical Computing, Vienna, Austria. Retrieved from https://www.R-project.org

Rahiem, M. D. H. (2021). Remaining motivated despite the limitations: University students' learning propensity during the COVID-19 pandemic. *Children and Youth Services Review, 120*, 105802.https://doi.org/10.1016/j.childyouth.2020.105802

Toquero, C. M. (2020). Emergency remote education experiment amid COVID-19 pandemic. *IJERI: International Journal of Educational Research and Innovation, 15*, 162-176. https://doi.org/10.46661/ijeri.5113

Lessons from a Pandemic for the Future of Education
European Distance and E-Learning Network (EDEN) Proceedings
2021 Annual Conference | Madrid, 21-24 June, 2021
ISSN 2707-2819
doi: 10.38069/edenconf-2021-ac0044

WHAT SKILLS ARE INVOLVED IN OPEN VIRTUAL MOBILITY? A STUDENTS' PERSPECTIVE FROM ITALY AND SPAIN

Gemma Tur Ferrer, Universitat de les Illes Balears, Spain, Antonella Poce, Università di Modena e Reggio Emilia, Maria Rosaria Re, Università di Roma Tre, Italy, Sofia Villatoro, Universitat de les Illes Balears, Spain

Abstract

Virtual Mobility can enhance curriculum development in Higher Education by promoting international co-design and collaborative work among students and lecturers through the use of Information and Communication Technologies (ICT). During the spread of COVID-19 pandemic, virtual forms of students' mobility increased considerably, allowing learners to continue or start VM experience even if boarders and campuses around the world were closed. The recent outbreak in interest and activity related to VM requires educational researchers to study this learning practice in depth in order to provide data and effective indications in terms of skills promotion. During the academic year 2020-2021, a team of lecturers of Teacher Education programs from the Roma Tre University (Rome, Italy) and the University of the Balearic Islands (Balearic Islands, Spain) agreed to work in open digital environment, organising specific VM activities for 38 university students. Specifically, students were asked to meet online, design and collaboratively create, in groups from the two countries, Open Digital Resources (OERs) to be used in international online contexts with their future pupils. This paper presents the design of the learning experience together with self-assessment results of the professional and transverse competences promoted. Conclusions also reflect on the new improvements to be done for new editions of the activity.

Introduction

The biggest challenges faced by universities and made more urgent by the spread of the pandemic are clearly globalisation and digital transformation (Buchem et al., 2018; Kaplan, 2020). Virtual Mobility (VM), defined as "a set of ICT supported activities, organized at institutional level, which realize or facilitate international, collaborative experiences in a context of teaching and/or learning" (Op de Beeck, & van Petegem, 2013), should be a valuable support to both challenges, thanks to the possibility, within this kind of activities, of knowledge promotion exchange, intercultural understanding enhancement and digital skills development (Poce et al., 2020a). Moreover, as stated by Ruiz Corbella and Garcia Aretio (2010), VM should be considered a democratic form of learning: thanks to cross-border collaboration with people from different backgrounds and cultures through ICT, university students can have access to a wider institutional market as well as brings greater interactivity and flexibility for the affordances of the technological tools in which it is based. Movement restrictions during the COVID-19 pandemic led many institutions to organise VM experiences instead of physical mobility: according to International Association of Universities data (2020), the virtual mobility provision during the pandemic increased for over 60% of HEIs around the world. In this way, the VM intrinsic characteristics and strengths have been adapted to a more flexible inter-university learning experience, whose design is in line with the learning content of the specific courses in which students are enrolled.

The Virtual Mobility learning design

The learning activity was designed following Rajagopal et al. (2020b) guide for Open Virtual Mobility activities, and in table one there are the main areas and all the elements that were contemplated by the team of teachers.

Table 1: Learning design following the OpenVM guide (Rajagopal et al., 2020b)

	Elements
Virtual mobility Context	Partner teachers. 3 teachers are involved in the design, whereas 6 are involved in the implementation of the VM activity.
	Partner institutions. Two institutions are involved, one from Italy (RomaTre University) and one from Spain (University of the Balearic Islands)
	Level of education and Educational programme. Students from the UIB were doing a subject in year 3, "Technological Means and Resources in the Teaching-Learning Process in Primary Education". In Italy there were students doing the "Educational Research Methodology" (subject in year 1) and "Museum, Experiment and Reading" (subject in year 4). Students from the "Educational Research Methodology" course were at the first year of their Teacher Education program whilst students from the "Museum, Experiment and Reading" course were at their fourth year
	Intended learning outcomes. The activity was mainly designed to promote virtual mobility among student teachers. And as learning aims, the following were the main ones: understanding the concepts of virtual mobility and virtual exchange; creating open educational objects; and, developing virtual mobility skills.

Task and support	Tasks students. Students are introduced for the first time to the field of Virtual Mobility, although the topic for the joint work is known as they are asked to co-design a short proposal for Primary Education. Tasks teacher. The design of the activity is developed by a group of teachers from both contexts and their share interaction with students in the social networked used for the VM activity with students. However, each national team of teachers are responsible for the assessment of their students. Support for students. Students are given an introductory session and written instructions for the activity. Also, they receive support by both teams of teachers in the social network. Being active teachers, with this support, students are expected to self-direct their performance and self-regulate their learning. Support for teachers. Teachers do not have particular support for the VM activity in itself. Support for staff. There is no other staff involved in the VM activity in itself.
Roles and responsibilities	Roles student. Students develop the whole activity in international teams except for the final reflective task. Roles teacher. Teachers follow students weekly as they share the same network groups and can monitor the whole process of exchanges. Teachers agree in one message weekly in order to guide the task during the scheduled period. Responsibilities student. Students take the responsibility to meet and develop the task although they are not free to group themselves. Student characteristics. The group of each University is diverse, with students from local sites but also from abroad, bringing diversity to the final teams made by the two sites. Teacher characteristics. The team of teachers has a rather less diversity. However, students from the UIB are mainly from the educational technology field whereas teachers from RomaTre are from research methods and cultural heritage fields.
Materials and spaces	Materials. All students are given the same instructions, including the description of the activity, and Technical environment. This is the best improvement since first edition and an ethical social network is introduced so students share networks where to meet easily. Also, regarding the videoconferences tools, this year was easy to facilitate institutional platforms. Places. Students interact internationally in social networks and online meetings. Students at local levels share face to face settings, although students in the Balearic Islands also need to do online meetings between them if they are based in different islands. Times. Students are encouraged to meet both synchronously and asynchronously. Institutional embedding. The learning activity is embedded in a subject of their Teacher Students programs of the RomaTre and the UIB universities. Student-created artefacts. Students are asked to submit a joint Open Educational Resources (OER) with the suitable licences.

Students were given a schedule for the VM activity, which was based on the last years' edition. The following table, based on Poce et al. (2020b) presents this current edition calendar and reports the actual events and issues arisen.

Table 2: Schedule of the VM activity

	Recommendation
Week 0 October	Students are introduced to the OpenVM activity in the context of their subjects. They are given the opportunity to choose the activity among many others. Less students than in the course 2019-20, especially from the Spanish University, choose this project.
Week 1 2nd November	Students join the OpenVM activity groups in MEWE, the social and ethical network. When they register, they find a salutation message from teachers. They post their first messages for salutation too. Some students join with some delay. Students of both Universities agree for the meeting date and the VC platform. Some groups use Doodle, and some other agree in the date by exchanging messages in the social network. They prepare the meeting at local level. Groups at the UIB also join students from different islands which adds greater difficulties for communication as this local step also needs videoconference sessions for their meetings and initial agreements.
Week 2 9th November	Students meet using institutional videoconference platforms and take decisions on their topic and learning design. Lecturers at the UIB need to program the online sessions as this is only possible by teachers.
Week 3 16th November	Students work on the joint presentation. Some problems arise in particular due to the low engagement of some students.
Week 4 23rd November	Students add their individual slides to the presentation with reflective texts.
Week 5 30th November	Last editions and submission. Students answer the survey for research aims. Only half of the students answer the survey.

Research

The current study is aimed at exploring the development of the Open Virtual Mobility activity. The following research questions guided our study:

- What is the level of satisfaction among students?
- What skills do students perceive they have developed more?
- What skills do student perceive as more relevant for Primary Education?

To answer these questions, we adopted a descriptive approach, and a mixed methodology was designed, with quantitative and qualitative techniques to explore students' perceptions. So, first of all, data was collected with a Likert-scale survey that was sent to students through the social network used for the learning activity, and each question was written in English and translated into Italian and Spanish in order to ensure correct understanding. The survey was created ad hoc to explore the learning design in general terms and included the following five elements: the learning activity, international context, the social network, the group of peers and the role of teachers. The question on skills development followed the framework by Rajagopal et al. (2020b). The quantitative data is then completed with a text analysis of students' final pieces of reflection and open comments to explore with greater depth their satisfaction and perception on learning skills.

Results

For the first research question, we explored both general satisfaction and also looked for more detailed information on the elements of the learning design. As can be seen in Figure 1, all students with no exceptions were satisfied or very satisfied.

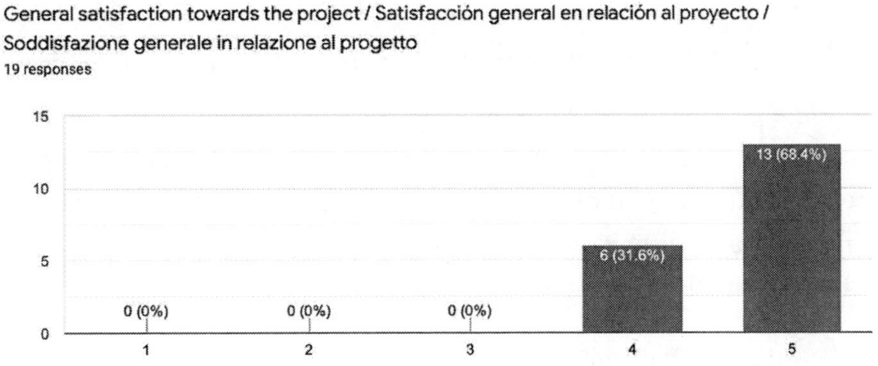

Figure 1. General satisfaction towards the project

Satisfaction was also generalized when asking about five elements of the learning experience (Figure 2), but there are some nuances that allow us to observe limitations to improve for future editions for the activity. In general, it can be seen that again all elements obtain a high level of agreement at higher scores of satisfaction, and among all, it can be highlighted that the social network and the role played by teachers are the elements with better results (11 answers at level 5 and 3 at level 4). However, all questions obtain neutral answers which in general, allow us to think that there is still room to improve the current learning design. There is no element that receives a single answer of total un-satisfaction but nonetheless, the international context of the activity, the social network and the group of peers obtain an answer at level 2, which means a rather unsatisfied student involved in the activity.

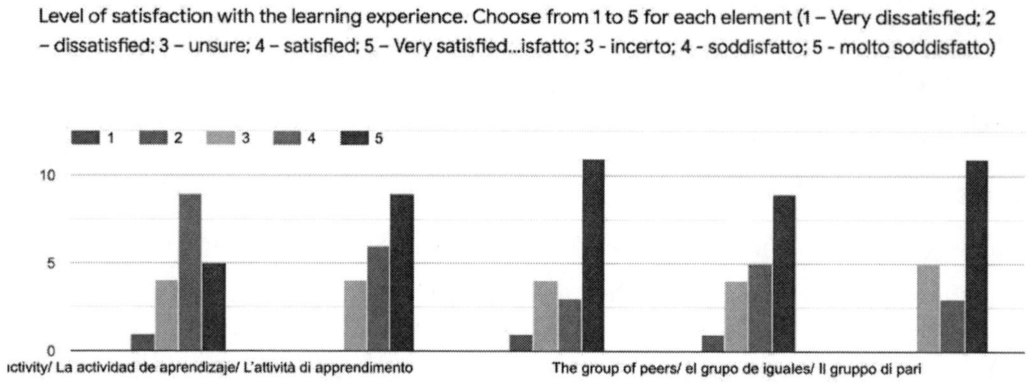

Figure 2. Level of satisfaction towards five elements of the learning design

There are some comments by students that complete the meaning of the quantitative results. In general, although they encountered language and teamwork difficulties, they are satisfied with the experience and the tools that they recommend to repeat it in future courses and they are willing to transfer the experience to their future teaching. The following texts show these ideas (translated from Italian or Spanish):

- Student 2 adds the limitations due to linguistic barriers: "It was an exciting and constructive experience. Even if at times difficult because of the different language but stimulating because of it."
- Student 6 highlights the tools that were new and praises the organization of the activity: "I learnt new tools, both MeWe (an interesting social network with no ads or followers...) Doodle (great for an organisation of this type) and the ones chosen in the group. Undoubtedly a good experience that I would repeat again on another occasion and that in the near future I would like to do with my students. (...)"
- Student 7 recommends new editions of the VM project: "The project seems very interesting and useful to me. I think it should continue so that more courses take a more elaborate form and can collect more content."
- Student 11 enjoyed the activity but points out the difficulties for honest teamwork of all members of the group: "I really enjoyed this experience but not everyone in my group participated :(. Great work from the teachers. Thank you very much."

Figure 3 shows the results for the question about their skill development due to the VM activity, and results are very positive with some nuances to be commented. Again, it is relevant to point out that all questions obtain answers of neutral perceptions, and only three skills seem not to have been developed at all by very few students: the collaborative learning and the active SRL (one student) and, networked learning (two students). All skills obtain more than half of the answers at a highest scores (levels 4 and 5 of agreement).

Open mindedness is the skill with more answers at level 5, and adding together scores 4 and 5, the total of agreement is of 15 students, which is the same results as intercultural skills and attitude, autonomy- driven learning, media and digital literacy, active self-regulated learning, and the knowledge of Virtual Mobility and Open Education.

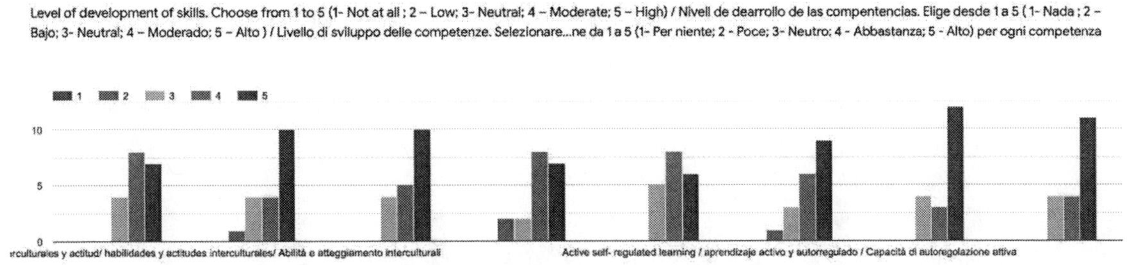

Figure 3. Students' perception for the development of skills

Comments by students highlight the development of some skills (mainly digital, open-mindedness and collaborative, intercultural skills) from the Open Virtual Mobility framework:

- Student 10 focuses on the development of language, digital, open-mindedness and collaborative skills: "This virtual mobility experience was an effective opportunity to practice and enhance our skills in using online learning and research technologies. Collaborating with colleagues in the context of an international learning experience has certainly contributed to improving our language skills but, above all, it has enriched us from a human point of view, prompting us to work on our open-mindedness, on the value of tolerance, thus improving our teamwork skills."
- Student 1 observes the collaborative potential for intercultural learning and the relevance of the activity in the current pandemic times: "In my opinion, this experience was very positive and interesting. The collaboration with the group was active and participative on the part of all those involved. The different realities of which the students are bearers has allowed a greater realisation of the concept of multicultural integration and in a historical moment like the one we are in, having had the opportunity to cooperate and virtually meet new people has certainly produced multiple benefits for the realisation of the project itself, but also for individual development."
- Student 15 highlights the diversity of skills needs for success collaborative projects: "Group work involves multiple skills for success, from digital skills to interpersonal skills. This collaborative work has been very fruitful."

As for their envisioning of the importance of these skills for Primary Education, it is surprising the level of the agreement that there is in most of the skills. Only for the collaborative skills, one student answers with disagreement whereas the vast majority of the group answers with the highest score. The networked learning is the skill with less answers at level 5 although the greatest part of student agree about the need to develop it during Primary Education (14 students' answers levels 4 and 5).

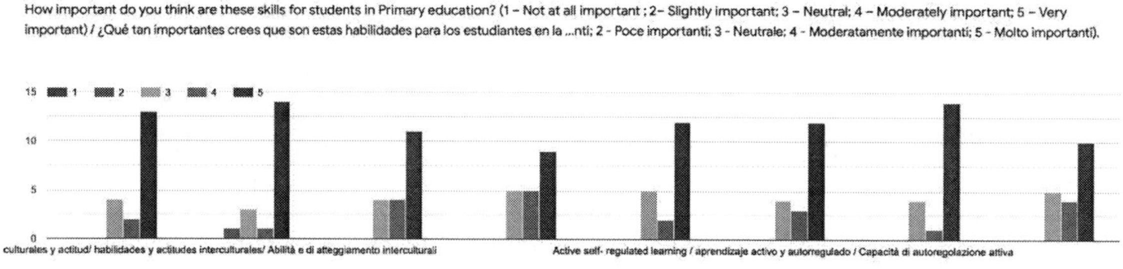

Figure 4.

Discussion and conclusion

This current learning design is a contribution towards the improvement of curriculum based on collaborative and co-designed international projects (Tur & Buchem, 2021). As for the first research question, this second edition has been successful as students' satisfaction may suggest. However, the low number of students that take part from the Spanish university again suggest the need to further improve the VM activity, probably by ensuring understanding and promoting motivation in the subject introduction. The research about the skills seems to confirm the development at different levels of the set of skills defined by Rajagopal et al. (2020a) but extends knowledge on Primary Education. Last year's iteration of the Open VM activity between RomaTre and the UIB allowed us to observe some limitations (Poce et al. 2020b) that have been greatly solved in this current edition, in particular those related to the digital environment: sharing a Virtual Learning Environment, in which students can communicate and share with lecturers at the same time. During preparation, an ethical social network was suggested and it seems that it was a successful decision. However, it stills needs to be improved with the synchronous session of all students for the presentation of all OERs done by students to clarify the objectives and support motivation.

References

Buchem, I., Tur, G., & Urbina, S. (2018). Quality assurance for attainment, assessment and recognition of virtual mobility skills in context of open education. QA Framework in the Open Virtual Mobility project. *EDULEARN18 Proceedings*, 945-952. Edulearn Conference, 2-4 July 2018. Retrieved from https://iated.org/concrete3/view_abstract.php?paper_id=65036

International Association of Universities (2020). *Regional/National Perspectives on the Impact of COVID-19 on Higher Education.* Paris: International Association of Universities (IAU) UNESCO House.

Kaplan, A. (2020). *Covid-19: A (potential) chance for the digitalization of higher education.* ESCP Business School. Retrieved from https://academ.escpeurope.eu/pub/IP%202020-72-EN.pdf

Op de Beeck, I., & Van Petegem, W. (2013). Virtual mobility: an alternative or complement to physical mobility? *ERACON 2011 & 2012 Dual Year Proceedings*, 151-160.

Poce, A., Amenduni, F., Re, M., & De Medio, C. (2020a). Assessing a MOOC users experience in a virtual mobility project: preliminary results for quality enhancement. *Italian Journal of Educational Technology.*

Poce, A., Tur, G., Amenduni, F., & Darder, A. (2020b). *Open Virtual Mobility between student teachers from Italy and Spain: an opportunity for the enhancement of the curriculum.* Poster presented at "Human and Artificial Intelligence for the Society of the Future" EDEN 2020 Annual Conference, 22-24 June 2020.

Rajagopal, K., Firssova, O., Op de Beeck, I., van der Stappen, E., Stoyanov, S., Henderikx, P., & Buchem, I. (2020a). Learner skills in open virtual mobility. *Research in Learning Technology, 28.* https://doi.org/10.25304/rlt.v28.2254

Rajagopal, K., Brouns, F., Firssova, O., & Op de Beeck, I. (2020b). Open VM Design Guide. Retrieved from https://www.openvirtualmobility.eu/topics/outputs/o1-framework-and-guidelines/

Ruiz Corbella, M., & Garcia Aretio, L. (2010). Movilidad virtual en la educación superior: ¿oportunidad o utopía? *Revista Española de Pedagogía, 246*, 243-260. Retrieved from https://reunir.unir.net/bitstream/handle/123456789/3854/MovilidadVirtualEnLaEducacionSuperior.pdf?sequence=1&isAllowed=y

Tur, G., & Buchem, I. (2021). Special issue editorial. Virtual mobility: opening up educational mobilities. *Edutec. Revista Electrónica De Tecnología Educativa, 75*, 1-8. https://doi.org/10.21556/edutec.2021.75.1987

Authors

The present contribution was edited in the following order: Gemma Tur: sections "Results" and "Discussion and conclusion"; Antonella Poce: section "Introduction"; Maria Rosaria Re: sections "The Virtual Mobility learning design" and "Research"; Sofia Villatoro: sections Results" and "Discussion and conclusion".

Lessons from a Pandemic for the Future of Education
European Distance and E-Learning Network (EDEN) Proceedings
2021 Annual Conference | Madrid, 21-24 June, 2021
ISSN 2707-2819
doi: 10.38069/edenconf-2021-ac0045

STUDENTS' ENGAGEMENT WITH PODCAST DURING LOCKDOWN – AN ANALYSIS OF INTERACTION FOOTPRINTS IN A COMPUTER SCIENCE COURSE

Benoit Donnet, Dominique Verpoorten, Université de Liège, Belgium

Abstract

This paper addresses a remote teaching activity that consists, for students, in being exposed to podcasts instead of classic face-to-face theoretical lessons. In particular, the paper discusses potential impact of podcasts on students' engagement in an introductory Computer Science course.

Introduction

During the Higher Education disruption caused by the COVID-19 (Crawford et al., 2020), podcasts were largely used as replacement or complement to the courses that could not take place on campuses anymore. Podcasting is however not new. Since its inception in 2004 (Prince, 2020), this practice has been variously described and delineated. This paper favours the following definition: "Podcasts are regularly produced digital episodes of video or audio content that are available on the Internet and can be downloaded or streamed on demand" (Hatfield, 2018). Yet, it matches the teaching method inspected here: the weekly provision of downloadable video files, released as instalments in a series, and acting as lecture content in a context of temporary online pivot (Nordmann et al., 2020). The purpose of this paper is to analyse how a group of first-year students reacted to the sudden command to study through podcasts. A better knowledge of ins and outs of such a systematic exposure to podcasts is important for the course in question (in a SoTL perspective, Felten, 2013) and, beyond, for more acute approaches of technology-enhanced learning in general (McNamara & Drew, 2019).

Method

The Course

The course "Introduction to Programming" (abbreviated here in "CS1") is provided to first year students (Bachelor level) during the first semester of the academic year (September – December) with exams in January, preceded by a 15-day study period. The CS1 course consists in theoretical lectures (10 sessions), practical sessions (exercises on paper – 10 sessions), laboratory sessions (exercises in front of a computer – five sessions. Lessons and exercises sessions typically last two hours. During the Academic Year 2020-2021, 91 students were enrolled in the course, 74% of them were at their first year at the university, 12% repeated the year, and 14% reoriented from another curriculum. Among the students, 82.4% took the final January exam (organized remotely) for a pass rate of 27%. Those figures are consistent with success rate at the university, for first year students, in our country (Ares, 2013-2014).

Podcasts

Podcasts are provided for each of the 8 chapters (Table 1, column 1) of the CS1 course and uploaded on the institutional intranet. An URL towards each podcast is also posted on the course LMS (Blackboard). The number of podcasts (Table 1, column 3) matches the number of sections in chapters and, according to their respective volume, covers them with varied number of slides (Table 1, column 2) and timespan (Table 1, column 4). Podcasts are released as instalments in a series (Table 1, column 5), largely on time, offering the possibility to students to watch them in advance with respect to the lessons' agenda (Table 1, column 6). Students are supposed to watch podcasts every week and internalize their content like they would do with material covered on regular face-to-face lessons (Table 1, column 6).

Table 12: Description of the course material.

Chapter	# Slides	Podcast		Timeline (mm/dd)	
		# records	total amount of time (min.)	uploaded	lessons
1	73	5	152	09/15 – 09/20	09/23
2	64	3	80	09/22	09/30
3	112	13	226	09/28 – 10/06	10/07 – 10/14
4	67	6	90	10/06 – 10/14	10/21
5	178	18	273	10/14 – 11/02	10/28 – 11/18
6	110	14	205	11/17 – 11/21	11/25
7	51	4	119	11/24	12/02
8	42	7	84	12/01	12/09
Total	697	70	1,229		

The majority of our podcasts lasts between 10 and 20 minutes, which is consistent with Guo et al. (2014). This comes with multiple advantages: (a) it reduces the risk of failure during the recording, (b) the size of the podcast (in mega-bytes) is quite reasonable (52MB/podcast, on average), so that students with poor connections can still view it in (we hope) acceptable conditions, and, (c) it limits the risk students being disconnected of the lesson, due to its duration. A few longer podcasts concern use cases that must be exposed in a single shot, otherwise the whole reasoning would be broken. Most of podcasts are annotated by the teacher during the recording process (Figure 1), somehow as he would do when using a blackboard in a physical classroom. The recording process is as follows:

slides are projected on the laptop, with QuickTime running in background for recording the screen and the audio. At the same time, the slides are also projected on a tablet that is used both for controlling the slides (i.e., remote control) and annotating them using a digital pencil (as a teacher would do on the board during an on-site lesson – an example of annotated slide is illustrated in Figure 1). The recording is then post-processed with QuickTime to reduce its size (i.e., resolution H.264, up to 1280 x 720). Post-processed recordings are then uploaded on the University intranet and an URL is also provided on the course virtual space.

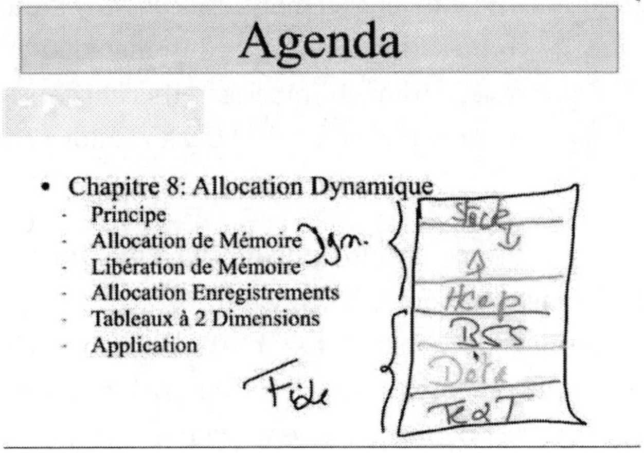

Figure 10. Example of annotated slide (Chapter 8)

Data Sources

Data was collected according to the 3 P's framework (Verpoorten et al., 2017) that recommends to consistently analyse any pedagogical innovation by gathering and meshing three types of data reflecting dimensions of students' learning experience therewith: Participation, Perception, and Performance data.

Participation Data

The University infrastructure on which podcasts are uploaded allows to track the unique number of students accessing a given podcast, as well as the number of cumulative views for each podcast. This data was collected every Friday, 06:00PM, between September 18th and January 11th (the day of the exam). This leads to a sample of 18 weekly series of data. Once uploaded on the University podcast platform, each podcast URL is also posted on the CS1 course blackboard. Our course blackboard comes with basic learning analytics capabilities. In particular, it records when and how often each student visits a given resource, such as a course chapter. As podcasts for a given chapter are grouped in a given repository in the blackboard, learning analytics are gathered on a per chapter basis.

Perception Data

A survey was administered to students just before the final exam. The survey was anonymous, to let the student express themselves freely.

Performance Data

Students were grouped into clusters according to the way they engage with podcasts. This is made possible thanks to Participation data collected from the CS1 course space which provides a view of students' engagement. However, it is worth noting this clustering provides a lower bound on students' engagement. Indeed, any student is always able to access to podcasts directly through the University intranet that provides a direct link towards the CS1 course podcasts. Although imperfect, this clustering provides a valuable insight into students' engagement in podcasts watching and allows the following grouping based on the engagement intensity with podcasts:

- Cluster 1 (the imperceptible) groups students who did not access to podcasts, for a given chapter, through the course blackboard.
- Cluster 2 (the discreet) groups students who did access between one and five times to podcasts, for a given chapter, through the course blackboard.
- Cluster 3 (the subscribers) groups students who did access more than six times to podcasts, for a given chapter, through the course blackboard.

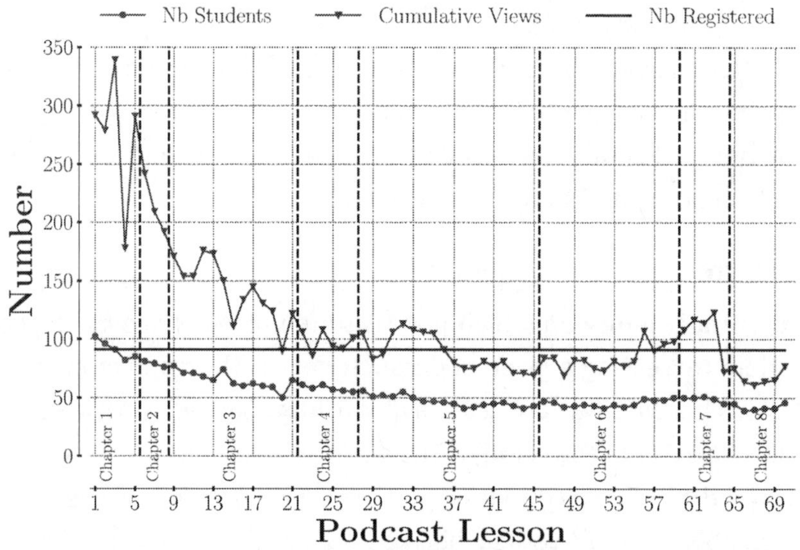

Figure 11. Total podcast viewing at the end of the course (January, 11th)

Results

Participation

Overall, the podcasts were seen 8,147 times (Figure 2, blue line), that is an average view by enrolled students of 89. Most of the podcasts are seen twice (Figure 2, see the gap between the blue curve – cumulative views – and the red curve - unique number of students). Also, the students' engagement tends to decrease over time: unique users fade as well as the number of views. Finally, on Figure 2, the horizontal line provides the number of students registered to the course (91). It may seem odd that, for the first podcasts, the number of unique students is slightly higher than the number of registered students. The reason for this is that a few students have left the curriculum early in the semester because, e.g., they want to reorient themselves. As those students, finally, do not really account during the remainder of the semester, they were removed them from the sample.

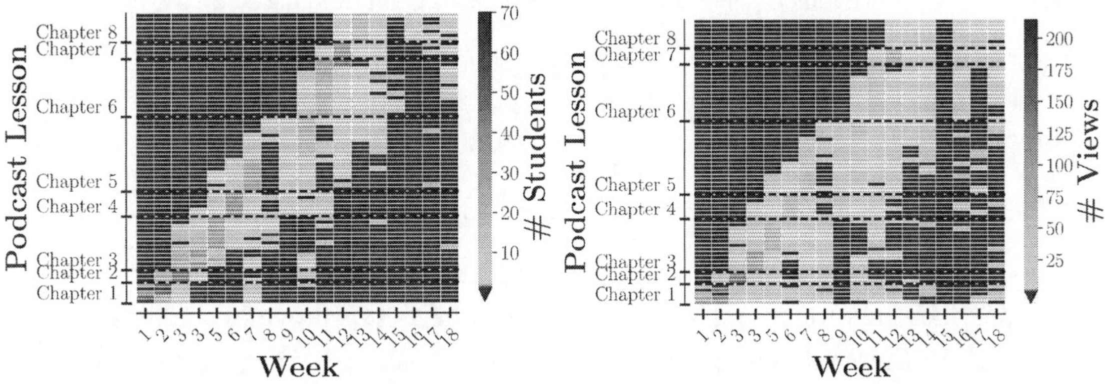

Figure 12. Podcast access over time per student (left) and per viewing (right)

Fig. 3 shows how students interact with the podcasts throughout the semester. The X-Axis gives the time (as week numbers), while the Y-Axis provides the different podcasts, organized by chapter. The colour bar provides either the unique number of students accessing a podcast (Figure 3, left) or the number views of a podcast over the course duration (Figure 3, right). Figure 3 (left) shows that students, typically, follows the podcast publication cycle to access them, except for Week 7 (which corresponds to a Mid-Term exam), where one observes a slight increase. The situation is a little bit different for the number of viewings (Figure 3, right) as chapters seem to be viewed over a (slightly) larger period of time. This is particularly true with Chapter 1 for which podcasts are accessed nearly every week during the semester.

Perception

The questionnaire brought about 79 answers, that is the majority of the students who took the final exam (90%). Main observations are: (a) 77% of respondents estimates having watched more than 75% of the available podcasts (44% having watched all of them – this is consistent with the red curve on Figure 2). (b) 80% of students acknowledges the usefulness of podcast annotations. Finally, the majority of respondents (55%) expresses that the ideal podcast duration is between 10 and 20 minutes.

Performance

The cluster distribution (Figure 3, left) provides a view of students' engagement and tries to trace its effect on performance. Indeed, as shown in Table 2, belonging to Cluster 2 and 3 for a given chapter means that students have covered most of the chapter podcasts.

Table 2: Chapter coverage per cluster. The percentage is computed based on the number of records per chapter (see Table 1).

	Chapter							
	1	2	3	4	5	6	7	8
Cluster 1	0%	0%	0%	0%	0%	0%	0%	0%
Cluster 2	≤ 100%	≤ 100%	≤ 38%	≤ 83%	≤ 27%	≤ 35%	≤ 100%	≤ 71%
Cluster 3	100%	100%	> 38%	> 83%	> 27%	> 35%	100%	> 71%

Figure 4 (right) deepens the analysis by looking at clusters on a per student basis. The X-Axis provides the various course chapters, while the Y-Axis provides students identifier (anonymized). These refined learning analytics show that a portion of students are stable over time, i.e., they never leave their cluster, they stay in Cluster 1 or Cluster 2 throughout the semester. A few students exhibit a "slow start" behaviour, beginning in Cluster 1 and moving to Cluster 2 (sometimes even Cluster 3) as the semester goes by. On the contrary, others suggest a drop-out trajectory, starting the semester in Cluster 2 and slightly plummeting to Cluster 1.

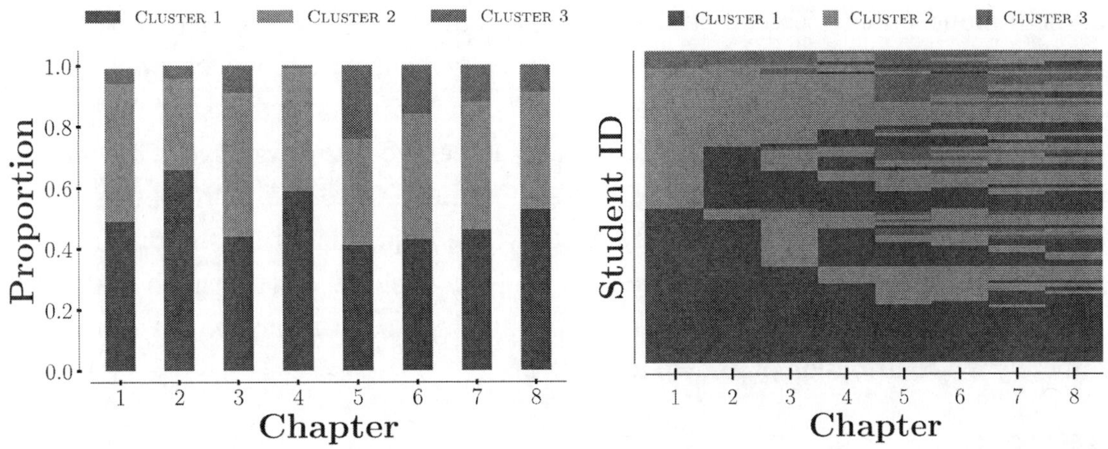

Figure 4. Podcast clustering distribution (overall distribution – left – and per student – right)

Table 3: Probability of succeeding/failing at the exam according to the average cluster membership over the semester (*N = 91*).

	Raw	Percentage
Pr[Pass | Cluster 1]	6	6.6%
Pr[Fail | Cluster 1]	30	33%
Pr[Drop Out | Cluster 1]	4	4.4%
Pr[Pass | Cluster 2]	13	14.3%
Pr[Fail | Cluster 2]	32	35.2%
Pr[Drop Out | Cluster 2]	0	0%
Pr[Pass | Cluster 3]	1	1.1%
Pr[Fail | Cluster 3]	5	5.5%
Pr[Drop Out | Cluster 3]	0	0%

Discussion

The main result of this study is counter-intuitive (but not totally isolated, Williams et al., 2016; Lindsay & Evans, 2021): watching podcasts does not make a difference. Statistical tests confirm what is observable from mere percentages in Table 3: a) not watching podcasts is no absolute reason for failure (Table 3, cluster 1, line 1). As the course evaluation is only practical (i.e., exercises resolution), reading the written material and doing weekly exercises may be enough for some students, b) the percentage of failure is roughly the same among the "imperceptible" and the "discreet" clusters (Table 3, line 2 and line 5), the "subscribers" cluster does not bring home more success (Table 3, line 7 and line 8). This has important consequences for CS1 regulation: is it worth lecturing in podcasts (or even in face-to-face)? Contribution to the field is also noticeable: the lack of relationship between podcast watching and success in the course should exercise caution, when using learning analytics, one is tempted to establish quick connections between interaction footprints somehow reflecting engagement and performance (Wold, 2018). The study also brings about a minor input: while it is often argued by proponents of asynchronous content (screencasts, live lecture captures, Web lectures) that the permanent availability of such resources allows students to study them at their own pace and as much as they need (Nielsen et al., 2018), the results here rather show even use of the podcasts (Figure 3). Students look at them once and do not seem to take advantage of the fact they can watch them again for better fixing the lesson content. Of course, both conclusions can be marred by the major limitation of the study: the impossibility for the researchers to guarantee that, at this early stage of learning analytics exploitation (Hausman et al., 2020), no podcast viewing has escaped their compilation. Although negative, this experienced difficulty is a contribution of its own to the field.

References

Académie de Recherche et d'Enseignement Supérieur (ARES) (2013 - 2014). Indicateurs de l'Enseignement Supérieur. Retrieved from https://www.ares-ac.be/fr/statistiques/indicateurs

Beaubouef, T., & Mason, J. (2005). Why the High Attrition Rate for Computer Science Students: Some Thoughts and Observations. *ACM SIGCSE Bulletin, 37*(2), 103-106. doi:10.37074/jalt.2020.3.1.7

Crawford, J., Butler-Henderson, K., Rudolph, J., Malkawi, B., Glowatz, M. Burton, R., & et al. (2020). COVID-19: 20 Countries' Higher Education Intra-Period Digital Pedagogy Responses. *Journal of Applied Learning & Teaching, 3*(1), 9-28. doi: 10.1145/1083431.1083474

Felten, P. (2013). Principles of Good Practice in SoTL. *Teaching and Learning Inquiry, 1*(1), 121-125. doi:10.2979/teachlearninqu.1.1.121

Guo, P. J., Kim, J., & Rubin, R. (2014). How Video Production Affects Student Engagement: An Empirical Study of MOOC Videos. *Proc. ACM Learning @ Scale Conference (L@S, Melbourne*, 41-50. doi:10.1145/2556325.2566239

Hatfield, E. F. (2018). Narrative Learning Using Podcasts Interpersonal. *Communication Teacher, 32*(4), 236-242. doi: 10.1080/17404622.2017.1372790

Hausman, M., Verpoorten, D., Defaweux, V., & Detroz, P. (2020). Learning Analytics: A Lever for Professional Development of Teachers? In W. Nuninger & J.-M. Châtelet (Eds.), *Handbook of Research on Operational Quality Assurance in Higher Education for Life-Long Learning* (pp. 308-335). IGI Global. doi:10.4018/978-1-7998-1238-8.ch013

Howard, E., Meehan, M., & Parnell, A. (2018). Live Lectures or Online Videos: Students' Resource Choices in a First-year university mathematics module. *International Journal of Mathematical Education in Science and Technology, 49*(4), 530-553. doi:10.1080/0020739X.2017.1387943

Lindsay, E., & Evans, T. (2021). The Use of Lecture Capture in University Mathematics Education: a Systematic Review of the Research Literature. *Mathematics Education Research Journal*, 1-21. doi:10.1007/s13394-021-00369-8

McNamara, S., & Drew, C. (2019). Concept Analysis of the Theories Used to Develop Educational Podcasts. *Educational Media International, 56*(4), 300-312. doi:10.1080/09523987.1681107

Nielsen, S. N., Andersen, R. H., & Dau, S. (2018). Podcast as a Learning Media in Higher Education. *Proc. 17th European Conference on e-Learning (ECEL), Athens*, 424-430.

Nordmann, E., Horlin, C., Hutchison, J., Murray, J.-A., Robson, L., Seery, M. K., & MacKay, J. R. D. (2020). Ten Simple Rules for Supporting a Temporary Online Pivot in Higher Education. *PLOS Computational Biology, 16*(10), e1008242. doi:10.1371/journal.pcbi.1008242

Prince, B. (2020). Podcasts: The Potential and Possibilities. *Teaching Sociology, 48*(4), 269-271. doi:10.1177/0092055X20959837

Verpoorten, D., Parlascino, E., André, M., Schillings, P., Devyver, J., Borsu, O., van de Poel, J.-F., & Jerome, F. (2017). *Blended Learning – Pedagogical Success Factors and Development Methodology.* (Tech. Rep.) Université de Liège, Beligum: IFRES.

Watson, C., & Li, F. W. (2014). Failure Rates in Introductory Programming Revisited. *Proc. Conference on Innovation & Technology in Computer Science Education (ITiCSE), Uppsala*, 39-444. doi:10.1145/2591708.2591749

Williams, A. E., Aguilar-Roca, N. M., & O'Dowd, D. K. (2016). Lecture Capture Podcasts: Differential Student Use and Performance in a Large Introductory Course. *Educational Technology Research and Development, 64*(1), 1-12. doi:10.1007/s11423-015-9406-5

Wold, M. (2018). *Students' Usage Patterns of Video Recorded Lectures in an Undergraduate Mathematics Course.* Paper presented at the INDRUM 2018 Conference, Kristiansand, Norway.

Lessons from a Pandemic for the Future of Education
European Distance and E-Learning Network (EDEN) Proceedings
2021 Annual Conference | Madrid, 21-24 June, 2021
ISSN 2707-2819
doi: 10.38069/edenconf-2021-ac0046

FROM BENCH TO MONITOR – TURNING ADVANCED LIFE SCIENCE COURSES INTO VIRTUAL

Elisabeth M. Zielonka, Yvonne A. Yeboah, Irena Provazníková, Juergen Deka, European Molecular Biology Laboratory, Heidelberg, Germany

Abstract

The European Molecular Biology Laboratory (EMBL) provides advanced training for life science researchers in state-of-the-art technologies and fosters scientific exchange. The heart of the face-to-face advanced course programme is a strong focus on expert led hands-on training combined with theoretical and application lectures, as well as networking opportunities. Due to the pandemic, the face-to-face life science wet-lab and computational courses were converted into virtual formats. The courses are participant centred and focus on real scientific challenges and problems on the given topic. The need for these advanced molecular biology training courses is reflected by the high numbers of applications. Here we describe one solution to the virtual transformation of EMBL's course programme, including the first reactions of our international audience and the effect for the future of cutting-edge advanced training courses for lifelong learning in the life sciences.

Introduction

Methodologies and technologies are rapidly evolving in the life sciences and other STEM (Science, Technology, Engineering and Mathematics) areas. It is key for scientists and academic researchers to stay up to date with the newest developments in their field and also beyond. One solution to overcome this challenge are lifelong learning opportunities. Novel advanced technology training with complex procedures requires particular focus through practical and hands-on sessions.

The European Molecular Biology Laboratory (EMBL) is Europe's leading life sciences organisation. An intergovernmental organisation of 27 Member States, EMBL operates sites in France, Germany, Italy, Spain and the United Kingdom. We conduct world-class life sciences research, provide training for students and scientists, and provide state-of-the-art research infrastructures for a wide range of scientific and experimental services. EMBL pursues five core missions, including advanced training for external scientists through courses and conferences as well as a scientific visitor programme (source: EMBL webpage).

Each year EMBL offers up to 60 face-to-face training courses across its sites, providing life scientists access to the latest methodologies and technologies. The topics are diverse and range from cell biology, genomics, proteomics to structural biology, synthetic biology and bioinformatics. For efficient course delivery, approximately 30 of these courses are take place in the EMBL's Advanced Training Center (Heidelberg, Germany), which harbours training laboratories and computational facilities. Most of the 4- to 11-day courses cover complete experimental workflows, from sample collection, to hands-on wet-lab methodologies, to computational data analysis. The course organizers, trainers and speakers are leading scientists in their research fields, from EMBL and world-wide. All courses receive many applications and positive feedback, as measured by the post-course surveys. The course reputation and quality are supported through the conceptual course design, and the practical and operational support offered by EMBL's external scientific training team.

Due to the Covid19 pandemic the EMBL face-to-face advanced course and conference programme had to be suspended. While the conferences resumed in a virtual format within two weeks, the courses needed more attention to implement their core principles and standards in live virtual designs. The aim was to transform the courses into a format where PhD students, postdocs and staff scientists receive training in cutting-edge hands-on methodologies paired with scientific exchange and networking to create a clear benefit to the scientific community.

Key challenges of the EMBL Heidelberg virtual transformation:

- Time zone management; trainers, speakers and also participants are located worldwide. A tool is needed to manage the various time zones and ensure live participation. In addition, the overall live online time period has to be adjusted to fit all course participants wherever they are.
- Consistency in course delivery; the organizers, trainers and speakers vary from course to course. A course template and various session templates are needed to ensure standards and quality of course content and the delivery.
- Identification of session modes and development of strategies that allow practical scientific methodology training and engaging activities.

Virtualization of EMBL's External Scientific Course Programme

The heart of the EMBL course programme is a learner centred approach paired with engaging activities to foster discussions, scientific exchange and networking. The courses are addressing real scientific challenges and cases, with the aim to enhance the participants' engagement and learning. These elements are also key in the virtualization of the course programme and created the basis for the course designs.

Our technology focused courses address responsible conduct of research by adequate quality controls, standards in the field, advantages and disadvantages of the given methodologies. Generated data, processing and analysis apply the FAIR principles of data management (Wilkinson et al., 2016). Every participant has the opportunity to present and discuss their research project with the fellow participants and key experts in the research field. By integrating active learning principles, the participants also apply the gained knowledge and skills in complementary team activities that address scientific case studies (Laurillard, 2012). As for our face-to-face programme, the quality of the virtual courses is continuously monitored and improved based on organizer/trainer and participant feedback surveys.

Below we illustrate the implementation of our virtual course strategy by crucial sections of the conceptual design.

Learning Management System and software tools

For courses run at EMBL Heidelberg the software EMBL eCampus (EMBL, 2021b) is the centre of the virtual programme. It is a customized Moodle-based learning management system with Zoom integrations serving as a virtual classroom for the live sessions. The platform is hosted on EMBL servers and supported by an IT company called Wunderbyte.

To ensure quality of content and delivery as well as corporate design we invested in consistent course templates (addressed under course design). The participant engagement is supported by the integration of the plug-in tool H5P for creating interactive lectures and quizzes. Participants can interact and network via several options in EMBL eCampus prior to, during, and after the course. We tested integration of the messenger software Slack, which did not bring any advantage as compared to the integral EMBL eCampus tools. Networking and scientific exchange are important elements of EMBLs course programme. To facilitate these sessions, we make use of speed networking, online games like Pictionary or use interactive gathering tools like Gather.town.

Course organizer and trainer support / templates

EMBL's scientific courses differ in their scientific organizers and trainer teams. To ensure the quality of the virtual course delivery, we created template courses and programmes in EMBL eCampus. These programmes structure the course into an engaging learning experience and support the organizing teams in the virtual transformation of their advanced training courses.

Furthermore, EMBL eCampus itself provides an introductory course for trainers and organizers about the utilization of the platform. Organizers, speakers and trainers are supported by the external scientific training team throughout the course preparations and during the course.

Course design

Every programme starts with a live virtual onboarding session taking place about two weeks prior to the live sessions. At the onboarding session the organizers will provide a brief course overview and introduce the course structure and pre-course work also referred to as self-paced study material. This material consists of pre-recorded lectures, scientific methodology protocols (text and video format), and introductions to computational analysis, tutorials for various tools and software, and exercises. During the self-paced study time the participants can contact trainers for individual support and requests via EMBL eCampus communication means.

The live part of the course is approximately twice two hours per day and focuses on interactive and engaging sessions. Every virtual course starts with an introductory session on the course logistics, including key elements of the code of conduct and setting the scene. This is followed by another key element: the ice breaking activity, where course organizers, trainers and participants introduce themselves, their work including the challenges they are facing, and the expectations for the course. This activity reinforces discussions and networking and illustrates the common participants′ challenges and expectations leading to an open and inclusive course culture. The live sessions of the course are structured in daily sub-topic specific outlines addressing the learning outcomes, participant time-zone adjusted agenda and course material.

Based on the course requirements for hands-on computational analysis sessions the participants receive cloud or virtual machine access with the requested software installations to guarantee a smooth completion of the self-paced and live learning exercises.

Self-paced study material

After the onboarding live session, the asynchronized course part starts, where each individual participant works through the self-paced study material based on their time convenience. This part focuses on the content delivery through pre-recorded lectures, protocol and methodology booklets and videos of the practical sessions. The complete content is provided through EMBL eCampus. Several trainers use this opportunity to align participants knowledge by providing exercises of different level of difficulty or pre-course assignments. One example is the pre-course work for computational practical sessions, where the participants acquire basic knowledge through exercises prior to the advanced live virtual sessions. Throughout the self-paced study time, participants can contact trainers and speakers via the forum or direct messaging on EMBL eCampus.

Live virtual sessions

The synchronized live virtual sessions focus on scientific exchange and active learning principles to achieve the long-term gains of the scientific content (Styers et al., 2018). The theoretical content of the self-paced period is addressed in either panel discussions or interactive sessions with the scientific experts. During the wet-lab practical live sessions, participants have the opportunity to follow selected critical steps of the methodologies streamed from the laboratory or scientific facility. The workflow always tries to answer real scientific problems, which is enhancing participants' engagement. Depending on the course, the illustrated technology and feasibility, we grant the participants a remote access to the scientific machines e.g. microscope systems for hands-on practice sessions.

Another interactive session type consists of case studies. The participants are grouped into teams either randomly or based on their scientific background. Each team receives a different scientific challenge which they need to solve by implementing the gained scientific knowledge. On the last course day, each team presents their work and receives feedback from the other course participants and the trainers. These collaborative activities foster their transferable skills like critical thinking and working in a team.

In either poster sessions or student presentation sessions, the participants have the unique opportunity to present their own scientific project to the scientific experts and their fellow participants. These sessions provide every participant with additional valuable and appreciated feedback. The lively discussions can also lead to new projects or initiate scientific collaborations.

Conclusions of the virtualization and outlook

To overcome the key challenges of the virtual transformation, we developed EMBL eCampus for the EMBL Heidelberg centred courses. EMBL eCampus is a customized platform combined with guidelines and templates to facilitate the virtual content delivery and course design for organizers and trainers. The virtual practical courses started in August 2020 and covered scientific topics like microbial metagenomics, *Drosophila* genetics and genomics, and the use of machine learning in image analysis. The very first virtual practical course on Cryo-Electron Microscopy in August 2020 received 333 completed applications for 24 participant slots. Thus far we delivered 12 virtual courses in the last 10 months. All together 1550 European and international scientists have applied for 244 participant slots, showing a clear need and interest for advanced training in cutting-edge research methodologies and technologies.

Each course, as well as the whole virtual course programme, benefits from the trainer and participant feedback and its implementation. The feedback survey is designed to collect anonymized quantitative and also qualitative (via open questions) data. We have so far analysed 10 virtual courses surveys. Overall, the virtual courses have a recommendation rate of 95.1%, which is comparable to the 2019 recommendation rate of the face-to-face delivered courses of 96.09%. We also asked the question "How did this virtual practical course compare to physical attendance at meetings?" to gain feedback for potential new course designs. Although 46.45% stated "not as good", 41.95% rated the virtual courses as "about the same" and 11.2% "better". Especially participants of computational analysis courses considered the virtual delivery format to be better. The open feedback often stated the reduced social interactions and networking opportunities despite our virtual course design efforts.

The digitalization of the EMBL Advanced Course Programme provides opportunities for the post-COVID time. Even though already prior to the pandemic we utilized social media and chat portals, we find that EMBL eCampus offers advantages and beneficial features that we plan to continue using once the face-to-face trainings are again possible. One opportunity is the self-paced study material that we aim to use during a pre-face-to-face course period to align the knowledge levels of our diverse audience. We are collecting further data to access this subject. Altogether, the pandemic has provided us the opportunity to digitalize our training programme, and this has opened up new formats and delivery modes for our advanced scientific courses.

References

EMBL (2021a). About – EMBL is Europe's leading life sciences laboratory. Retrieved from: https://www.embl.org/about/

EMBL (2021b). eCampus. Retrieved from https://ecampus.embl.de/

Laurillard, D. (2012). *Teaching as a Design Science: Building Pedagogical Patterns for Learning and Technologies.* Routledge.

Styers, M. S., van Zandt, P-A., & Hayden, K.L. (2018). Active Learning in Flipped Life Science Courses Promotes Development of Critical Thinking Skills. *CBE-Life Science Education, 17*(3), a39, 1-13. doi:10.1187/cbe.16-11-0332

Wilkinson, M. D., Dumontier, M., Aalbersberg, I. J., Appleton, G., Axton, M., Baak, A., Blomberg, N., Boiten, J. W., da Silva Santos, L. B., Bourne, P. E., Bouwman, J., Brookes, A. J., Clark, T., Crosas, M., Dillo, I., Dumon, O., Edmunds, S., Evelo, C. T., Finkers, R., Gonzalez-Beltran, A., Gray, A. J., Groth, P., Goble, C., Grethe, J. S., Heringa, J., 't Hoen, P. A., Hooft, R., Kuhn, T., Kok, R., Kok, J., Lusher, S. J., Martone, M. E., Mons, A., Packer, A.L., Persson, B., Rocca-Serra, P., Roos, M., van Schaik, R., Sansone ,S. A., Schultes, E., Sengstag, T., Slater, T., Strawn, G., Swertz, M. A., Thompson, M., van der Lei, J., van Mulligen, E., Velterop, J., Waagmeester, A., Wittenburg, P., Wolstencroft, K., Zhao, J., & Mons, B. (2016). The FAIR Guiding Principles for scientific data management and stewardship. *Scientific Data, 3*, a160018. doi: 10.1038/sdata.2016.18

Lessons from a Pandemic for the Future of Education
European Distance and E-Learning Network (EDEN) Proceedings
2021 Annual Conference | Madrid, 21-24 June, 2021
ISSN 2707-2819
doi: 10.38069/edenconf-2021-ac0047

USING VIRTUAL LABORATORY ENVIRONMENT FOR SCIENCE EDUCATION IN DIFFERENT EDUCATIONAL SETTINGS

Athanasios Sypsas, Evgenia Paxinou, Dimitris Kalles, Hellenic Open University, Greece

Abstract

Although hands-on laboratory experiments have been traditionally used in education, virtual laboratories have become popular in science courses due to their specific features. In this study, we asked for the students' opinion on using a 3D desktop-based virtual reality biology lab in two different educational settings, upper secondary education (Lyceum) and University. Our findings indicate that both Lyceum and University students found the use of the virtual laboratory interesting, when learning and practicing on the use of an optical microscope. According to the students' answers in a specially designed Likert-style questionnaire, this virtual reality-based learning experience was rather satisfactory, helped them easily understand the new topic of microscopy and filled them with confidence regarding their capability to conduct the specific microscopy experiment in a real biology lab. These results, combined with similar findings from other studies, suggest that virtual environments are viewed favourably by students and could be used supplementary to traditional teaching methods applied in hands-on laboratories in different educational settings.

Introduction

The rapid advances in ICT and the ever-increasing Internet access use provide new educational tools both for educators and students (de Jong & van Joolingen, 1998). The access to information is increased and the collaboration between educators and students is enhanced (Smetana & Bell, 2012) contributing significantly to a better understanding of the different scientific concepts (Allen Moore & Russell Smith, 2012).

Simulations in modern ICT educational applications, are often used in science education as they can support constructive learning, while they are very effective in dynamically engaging learners in the learning process (Makransky, Thisgaard, & Gadegaard, 2016). In the education field, simulations provide an educational environment for experiments, helping learners to comprehend and adopt real laboratory practices and skills (de Jong & van Joolingen, 1998). However, instructors in the Science, Technology, and Engineering field are sometimes reluctant to adopt the new technological approaches, particularly in distance education, since hands-on laboratory sessions are required (Potkonjak et al., 2016) and have always been the key pillar of science education (Hofstein & Lunetta, 2004). In order to achieve their educational purposes, laboratories must be fully equipped, concerning materials, facilities and training staff. When these requirements cannot be completely met, virtual laboratories (VLs) may offer a supplementary but essential solution, especially in distance education and when epidemiological situations (i.e., COVID-19 era) prevent students from on-campus laboratories. Having also in mind that positive attitudes toward science tend to decline with age, from primary through the secondary school years (Marginson et al., 2013), virtual environments can help students not to be deprived from their school labs, an environment that contributes to occurrence of meaningful learning. VLs are based on simulations of models used to abstractly describe a physical laboratory and the experiments taking place therein (Rossiter, 2016). Thus, while users perform their experiments in the VL, they get familiar with the laboratory environment and, consequently, can more actively participate in the educational process. Through virtual experimentation, learners familiarize themselves and become active learners (Paxinou et al., 2020a; 2020b), because decision-taking and learning by doing are promoted, when interacting with virtual environments (Martín-Gutiérrez et al., 2017). Furthermore, the use of technology-enhanced simulation leads to higher educational outcomes, compared to traditional educational methods (Paxinou et al., 2020a; 2020b), even if the target groups are learners that bring a zero to minimum prior knowledge on science topic. The vital benefits of VLs usage are identified in many studies, in various science domains (Heradio et al., 2016).

VLs are used in different educational settings as effective supplementary educational tool. However, the majority of applications are developed for the post-secondary educational settings, since computer laboratories needed for VLs are better organized and maintained at these settings. Additionally, post-secondary education students are familiar with the educational and ICT skills needed for experimentation in VL environment. Consequently, the most demanding applications of VLs are implemented in post-secondary education settings (Sypsas & Kalles, 2018).

The present study aims to investigate the students' opinion from different educational setting on using a 3D desktop-based virtual reality biology lab, called Onlabs, to be trained on the operation of a photonic microscope. In our research two target groups, a class from the upper secondary education (Lyceum) and a class from the higher education followed the same virtual reality-oriented teaching method regarding the microscopy experiment. Finally, the two groups expressed their opinion on satisfaction, interest, confidence, understanding and cognitive load items using a 5-point Likert scale (1 = *Strongly Disagree*, 5 = *Strongly Agree*), evaluating this way, their learning experience. Our study pointed out that the group of young students in the secondary education had similar attitude towards the usefulness and the effectiveness of embedding a virtual lab in the learning procedure of a science course, with the students in higher education.

The Participants and the Educational Materials

The Participants

The sample consisted of 47 students, 23 undergraduate students from the Department of Primary Education at the University of Patras in Greece, and 24 upper secondary education (Lyceum) students from the city of Preveza, also in Greece. The undergraduate students were enrolled in the Computers and Education course, a course where students are primarily practicing in the computer use, are informed about the new educational software for primary and secondary education and are educated on technology-assisted teaching and learning. The Lyceum students were enrolled in science course, a course where, among other tasks, they are practicing in Chemistry and Biology experiments. These two totally different groups were selected with the assumption that they both represent a novice audience that brings a zero to minimum prior knowledge on the operation of a photonic microscope.

The Virtual Reality Tool

The virtual laboratory environment used in the present study is the Onlabs software (https://sites.google.com/site/onlabseap/). It is developed by an interdisciplinary team at Hellenic Open University (HOU), a distance education institution that is mastering the distance learning education. HOU has always been trying to introduce in the learning procedure new ways to communicate laboratory skills to the distance learning students. Recently, it was the students' demand to use a software that would help them remotely gain the basic experimental skills before appearing to the university premises. The virtual laboratory environment is depicted in Figure 1.

Figure 1. A screenshot from the virtual environment of Onlabs

The Likert-Style Questionnaire

One of the most important roles, an educational application like Onlabs, must achieve is to maximize motivation. Motivation according to Keller (1983) is the goals you set, the efforts you spend to achieve them and your persistence trying to achieve them. The questionnaire used in this survey was based mostly on the Keller' work and especially on his ARCS Model. This model describes the students' motivation to learn in terms of four characteristics: Attention, Relevance, Confidence and Satisfaction. In our inquiry the Attention variable was replaced by the Interest variable, we omitted the Relevance variable and we added Understanding and Cognitive Load components. The current study tries to examine students' motivational response to VR technology and to better understand the reasons for this students' preference.

Methodology

The process of our study didn't harm or put the participants in a position of discomfort. The students were volunteers, taking part in the process of their own free will. They were given information on the methodology and the purpose of the research and they filled in the questionnaire by using as ID, a number, randomly selected, protecting this way their anonymity. Both undergraduate and secondary education students followed, the same teaching method presented in Table 1. The only difference in the followed procedure was in step 3, where the undergraduate students interacted with Onlabs and practice on the microscopy experiment in the premises of their Institution, whereas the Lyceum students interacted with Onlabs at home.

Table 1: Steps in the teaching scenario for undergraduate and secondary education students

Step/No	The Activities	
1	All students attended an hour face-to-face tutorial. The tutor used PowerPoint slides to introduce the principles of microscopy. The different parts of a photonic microscope, as well as their specific function, were also presented	
2	All participants entered the Computer Lab and the tutor performed a complete microscopy procedure in Onlabs environment	
3	(a) The undergraduate students used their own PC in the Computer Lab and performed the microscopy experiment once again, in Onlabs environment	(b) The Lyceum students went home, used their home PC and performed the microscopy experiment once again, in Onlabs environment
4	All students filled in the Likert style questionnaire in order to express their opinion on the specific learning experience, and handle it to the tutor	

Results

The SPSS 26 statistical analysis program was used to analyse the data. In order to compare means of the answers for the two groups of students, the independent samples t-test was used. Additionally, observation data and also some discussion with all students was taken into consideration to support the quantitative data. Table 2 presents the five questions of the questionnaire that aim at evaluating the students' interest in Onlabs.

Table 2: The interest questions

Question ID	The Question
I1	This educational method is not at all boring
I2	This educational method has some points that stimulate my curiosity
I3	The quality of the graphics, illustrations, etc., helped keep my attention on the lesson
I4	During the course I never felt irritated, although lots of new topics were introduced
I5	I would choose this educational method again for all my experimental exercises

Figure 2 presents the percentages of the students' answers in the questionnaire, regarding the interest questions (I1, I2, I3, I4 and I5), based on the 5-point Likert scale (1 = *Strongly Disagree*, 5 = *Strongly Agree*).

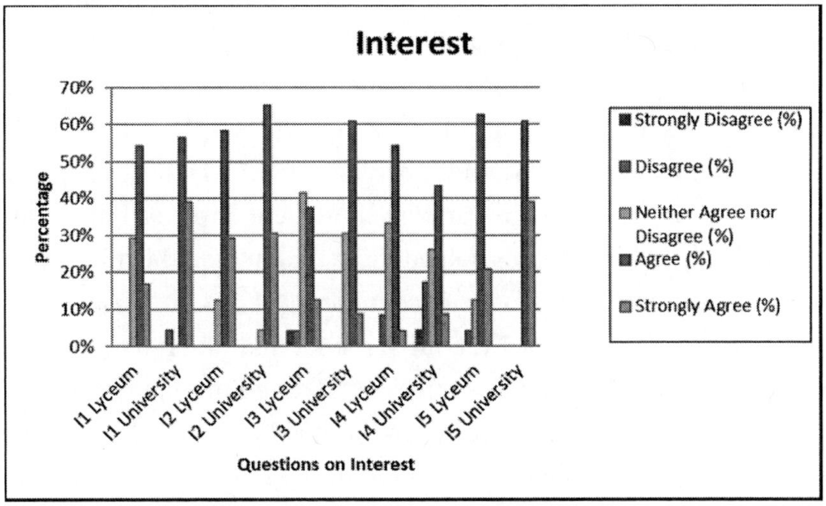

Figure 2. Percentages of the students' answers regarding the Interest questions

The visualization of the students' answers indicates that Lyceum and University students are almost equally interested in Onlabs as a new educational application. Table 3 demonstrates the rest of the question in our questionnaire were the Understanding (U) the Confidence (C), the Cognitive Load (CL) and the Satisfaction (S), after the students' interaction with Onlabs, is evaluated.

Table 3: The Understanding, Confidence, Cognitive Load and Satisfaction questions

Question ID	The Question
U1	This educational method helped me understand the microscopy procedure
C1	After following this educational method, I felt confident that I will do well in this course
C2	I believe that this educational method will help me use the microscope in the biology
CL1	All steps in the microscopy procedure seemed easy to me
CL2	This educational method helped me understand microscopy much better than my biology textbook
S1	I was really satisfied following this educational method

The percentages of the students' answers in Understanding, Confidence, Cognitive Load and Satisfaction questions, based on the 5-point Likert scale (1 = *Strongly Disagree*, 5 = *Strongly Agree*) are presented in Figure 3. The answers indicate that both Lyceum and University students felt confident that will do well in their laboratory courses. Moreover, students stated that Onlabs helped them understand the microscoping procedure and offered them satisfaction during its use. The two groups had almost identical averages concerning the scales and the questions. First, on the scale of Interest, Lyceum students' responses were ($M = 3.82$, $SD = .53$) and University's ($M = 4.02$, $SD = .47$). This indicates more than half of the Lyceum (70%) and University (82.5%) students agreed or strongly agreed that Onlabs stimulated their curiosity and kept their attention on the lesson. Second, on the question of how Onlabs helped them understand the microscopy procedure, the means were ($M = 4.00$, $SD = .72$) for Lyceum and ($M = 4.30$, $SD = .47$) for University students. This indicates that 84% of Lyceum students and all (100%) University students agree or strongly agree that Onlabs helped them towards comprehending the microscoping procedure. Regarding the confidence scale, Lyceum ($M = 4.38$, $SD = .58$) and University students ($M = 4.22$, $SD = .52$) had almost identical attitude. Conversely, concerning cognitive load, means for Lyceum were ($M = 3.94$, $SD = .54$) and for University ($M = 3.91$, $SD = .42$), indicating that (73%) of Lyceum and (73.9%) of University students felt that the educational procedure based on Onlabs was well organized and helped them understand all the new principles. Finally, on satisfaction question, students' responses were ($M = 3.92$, $SD = .65$) for Lyceum and ($M = 3.87$, $SD = .69$) for University. Approximately (83%) of Lyceum and (78%) of University students regarded that Onlabs educational approach offered them satisfaction.

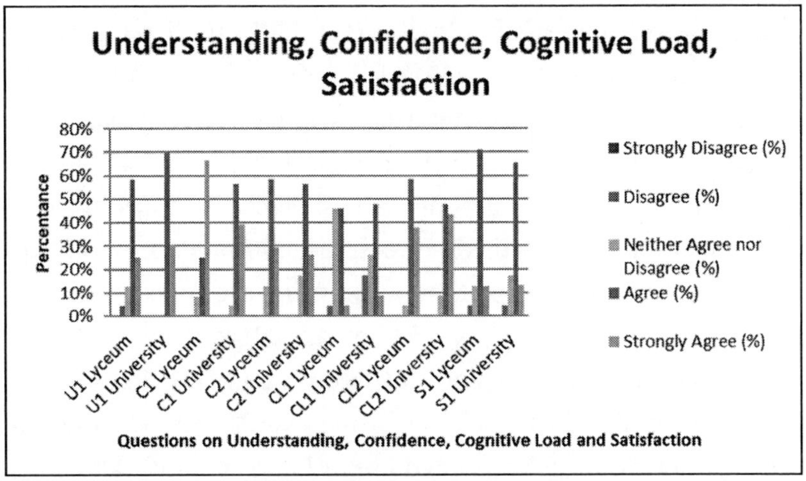

Figure 3. Percentages of the students' answers regarding Understanding, Confidence, Cognitive Load and Satisfaction questions

The results of independent samples t-test for the above means are presented in Table 4.

Table 4: t-test results

Scale/ Question	t-value	p-value	df	Result
Interest	1.37	.178	45	This difference is considered to be not statistically significant
Understanding	1.70	.095	45	This difference is considered to be not statistically significant
Confidence	0.99	.330	45	This difference is considered to be not statistically significant
Cognitive Load	0.17	.863	45	This difference is considered to be not statistically significant
Satisfaction	0.24	.812	45	This difference is considered to be not statistically significant

As results indicate, there is no significant difference between Lyceum and University students for all scales and questions of the questionnaire. Both Lyceum and University students agreed that Onlabs based educational approach irritated their interest, helped them concentrate on the lesson, understand the microscoping experiment, and all the new principles.

Discussion

In the present study, we investigated the results of the use of the Onlabs virtual laboratory environment for Lyceum and University students, concerning their interest, understanding, confidence, cognitive load and satisfaction during the specific educational approach. The results showed that the students were interested in the specific innovative approach, as the virtual environment encouraged their involvement. This finding is in consistence with the study of Parong and Mayer (2018), where is stated that Virtual Reality environments as a new popular technology is more motivating than conventional media.

Similarly, in other studies, the use of animations and VLs has been reported to challenge students, increase their intrinsic motivation to study and their interest towards lessons (Kollöffel & de Jong, 2013). Moreover, the use of Onlabs both for Lyceum and University students contributed in the increase of microscoping procedure understanding, as they played an active role during the experimentation. These findings are comparable with other studies, where students were using interactive computer animations with different scenarios and parameters, which helped them acquiring the concepts and making sense of them and also increase their knowledge (Akpınar, 2014; Polly et al., 2014). As far as cognitive load is concerned, students both in Lyceum and University agreed that Onlabs led them to positive cognitive outcomes. The same results were reported in other studies (Bonde et al., 2014). However, the combined use of hands-on and virtual experimentation could have led to higher cognitive learning outcomes and have helped students to learn better than doing either a physical or virtual experiment alone (Parong & Mayer, 2018). Data from the present study indicated that the students felt confident and satisfied when using virtual laboratory as part of the educational procedure, since they found Onlabs environment easy to use and stimulating. These findings are consistent with previous research that presents the virtual environments as tools that contribute to students' confidence and self-efficacy increase (Makransky et al., 2016).

Limitations and Future Research

Although our results presented that Undergraduate and Lyceum students showed a similar positive attitude towards Onlabs, it must be kept in mind that this study was carried out with a small sample of participants. Therefore, although our research gave us some promising hints about the potential educational character of Onlabs, we must emphasize the necessity for further investigations of the effects of VR on more numerous groups of students. Furthermore, since the main aim of this project was to find out the students' opinion about Onlabs, a questionnaire with more questions should be designed. By designing a brief questionnaire, our intention was to get sincere answers by not tiring the respondents.

Conclusion

This study revealed that both Lyceum and University students found interesting the use of the Onlabs VL, when studying and practicing on focusing on a specimen by using an optical microscope. The students were interested in this learning experience and claimed that they have easily understood the new topic of microscopy, a topic with a quite high intrinsic load. After their interaction with the virtual environment, the students were satisfied and were feeling very confident to repeat the real microscopy experiment, this time in a real biology lab. The students' answers in the given questionnaire showed that both Lyceum and University students had similar attitude towards the virtual reality lab, as the differences in their responses were considered to be not statistically significant.

References

Akpınar, E. (2014). The use of interactive computer animations based on POE as a presentation tool in primary science teaching. *Journal of Science Education and Technology, 23*(4), 527-537. https://doi.org/10.1007/s10956-013-9482-4

Allen Moore, W., & Russell Smith, A. (2012). Effects of video podcasting on psychomotor and cognitive performance, attitudes and study behaviour of student physical therapists. *Innovations in Education and Teaching International, 49*(4), 401-414. https://doi.org/10.1080/14703297.2012.728876

Bonde, M. T., Makransky, G., Wandall, J., Larsen, M. V, Morsing, M., Jarmer, H., & Sommer, M. O. A. (2014). Improving biotech education through gamified laboratory simulations. *Nature Biotechnology, 32*(7), 694-697. https://doi.org/10.1038/nbt.2955

Heradio, R., de la Torre, L., Galan, D., Cabrerizo, F. J., Herrera-Viedma, E., & Dormido, S. (2016). Virtual and remote labs in education: A bibliometric analysis. *Computers and Education, 98*, 14-38. https://doi.org/10.1016/j.compedu.2016.03.010

Hofstein, A., & Lunetta, V. N. (2004). The Laboratory in Science Education: Foundations for the Twenty-First Century. *Science Education, 88*(1), 28-54. https://doi.org/10.1002/sce.10106

de Jong, T., & van Joolingen, W. R. (1998). Scientific Discovery Learning with Computer Simulations of Conceptual Domains. *Review of Educational Research, 68*(2), 179-201. https://doi.org/10.3102/00346543068002179

Keller, J. M. (1983). *Development and use of the ARCS model of motivational design.* Enschede, Netherlands: Technische Hogeschool Twente.

Kollöffel, B., & de Jong, T. A. J. M. (2013). Conceptual understanding of electrical circuits in secondary vocational engineering education: Combining traditional instruction with inquiry learning in a virtual lab. *Journal of Engineering Education, 102*(3), 375-393. https://doi.org/10.1002/jee.20022

Makransky, G., Bonde, M. T., Wulff, J. S. G., Wandall, J., Hood, M., Creed, P. A., & Nørremølle, A. (2016). Simulation based virtual learning environment in medical genetics counseling: an example of bridging the gap between theory and practice in medical education. *BMC Medical Education, 16*(1), 98. https://doi.org/10.1186/s12909-016-0620-6

Makransky, G., Thisgaard, M. W., & Gadegaard, H. (2016). Virtual simulations as preparation for lab exercises: Assessing learning of key laboratory skills in microbiology and improvement of essential non-cognitive skills. *PLoS ONE, 11*(6), 1-11. https://doi.org/10.1371/journal.pone.0155895

Marginson, S., Tytler, R., Freeman, B., & Roberts, K. (2013). *STEM: country comparisons: international comparisons of science, technology, engineering and mathematics (STEM) education.* Melbourne, Vic.: Australian Council of Learned Academie. https://doi.org/10.1093/0195300912.003.0009

Martín-Gutiérrez, J., Mora, C. E., Añorbe-Díaz, B., & González-Marrero, A. (2017). Virtual technologies trends in education. *Eurasia Journal of Mathematics, Science and Technology Education, 13*(2), 469-486. https://doi.org/10.12973/eurasia.2017.00626a

Parong, J., & Mayer, R. E. (2018). Learning science in immersive virtual reality. *Journal of Educational Psychology, 110*(6), 785-797. https://doi.org/10.1037/edu0000241

Paxinou, E., Georgiou, M., Kakkos, V., Kalles, D., & Galani, L. (2020a). Achieving educational goals in microscopy education by adopting virtual reality labs on top of face-to-face tutorials. *Research in Science & Technological Education,* 1-20. https://doi.org/10.1080/02635143.2020.1790513

Paxinou, E., Panagiotakopoulos, C. T., Karatrantou, A., Kalles, D., & Sgourou, A. (2020b). Implementation and Evaluation of a Three-Dimensional Virtual Reality Biology Lab versus Conventional Didactic Practices in Lab Experimenting with the Photonic Microscope. *Biochemistry and Molecular Biology Education, 48*(1), 21-27. https://doi.org/10.1002/bmb.21307

Polly, P., Marcus, N., Maguire, D., Belinson, Z., & Velan, G. M. (2014). Evaluation of an adaptive virtual laboratory environment using Western Blotting for diagnosis of disease. *BMC Medical Education, 14*(1). https://doi.org/10.1186/1472-6920-14-222

Potkonjak, V., Gardner, M., Callaghan, V., Mattila, P., Guetl, C., Petrović, V. M., & Jovanović, K. (2016). Virtual laboratories for education in science, technology, and engineering: A review. *Computers and Education, 95*, 309-327. https://doi.org/10.1016/j.compedu.2016.02.002

Rossiter, J. A. (2016). Low production cost virtual modelling and control laboratories for chemical engineering students. *IFAC-PapersOnLine, 49*(6), 230-235. https://doi.org/10.1016/J.IFACOL.2016.07.182

Smetana, L. K., & Bell, R. L. (2012). Computer Simulations to Support Science Instruction and Learning: A critical review of the literature Computer Simulations to Support Science Instruction and Learning: A critical review of the literature. *International Journal of Science Education, 34*(9), 1337-1370. https://doi.org/10.1080/09500693.2011.605182

Sypsas, A., & Kalles, D. (2018). Virtual laboratories in biology, biotechnology and chemistry education: a literature review. In K. Nikitas & M. Basilis (Eds.), *Proceedings of the 22nd Pan-Hellenic Conference on Informatics* (pp. 70–75). Athens, Greece: ACM New York, NY, USA ©2018. https://doi.org/10.1145/3291533.3291560

Lessons from a Pandemic for the Future of Education
European Distance and E-Learning Network (EDEN) Proceedings
2021 Annual Conference | Madrid, 21-24 June, 2021
ISSN 2707-2819
doi: 10.38069/edenconf-2021-ac0048

HOW DOBA BUSINESS SCHOOL ADOPTED ITS BUSINESS MODEL DUE TO CORONAVIRUS PANDEMIC?

Marina Letonja, Živa Veingerl Čič, Anita Maček, Marko Divjak, Doba Business School, Slovenia

Abstract

The coronavirus pandemic (pandemic) is posing difficult and unpredictable challenges for Higher Education Institutions (HEIs). They have to adapt their business models (BMs), traditional working mechanisms and the way they transfer their knowledge to their students. The aim of this paper is to show how HEI of applied sciences overcame these challenges, and how they adapted its BM. The case study methodology was used. Based on the case of DOBA Business School Maribor, Slovenia, authors present how it reacted to the changed business and education circumstances. Discussion and concluding remarks stress out the lessons Doba Business School has learned from the pandemic so far and how these insights can help other HEIs to change their BMs in order to cope better in these challenging times.

Introduction

Knowledge management is essential to drive organizations through the various uncertain circumstances. The understanding of needed changes and adaptation of BMs is essential to manage the knowledge of HEIs to get through the pandemic. Capacity of creating, employing, and deploying knowledge is critical to protect the business and to guarantee that it can continuously contribute to the value creation dynamics. The pandemic has caused experimentation with online learning by HEIs, as many have so far used traditional teaching. It is safe to say that the pandemic will have an impact and has already affected education and we are convinced that much will change in this area even after the pandemic is over, especially if online learning proves successful. Therefore, we are interested in how to adapt the higher education BMs to ensure that students have access to quality higher education, despite the transformation of knowledge transfer from traditional to online teaching.

The multidisciplinary field of knowledge management can provide useful insights to help to think and rethink the BMs with a knowledge management capacity of effectively absorbing and reacting to the pandemic' impacts. Online teaching in HEIs requires additional support for teachers in the field of didactics for online learning, online assessment of knowledge, using technology to encourage interaction, cooperation between students, in short, transformation of study implementation (Dominko Baloh, 2020).

But pandemic is also an opportunity for improvement. Circumstances have shown that those organizations that have succeeded in adapting to change in a timely manner and dared to try new BMs were more successful. Many HEIs were faced with uncertainty, fear or lack of knowledge about the transition to fully online education. Many of questions were not responded quickly. We are currently conducting "trial and error" experiments and are learning from mistakes. Adaptation of both, professors, and students, is needed in the midst of teaching semesters. Revision of content of the courses, the new methods of assessment and examination is required.

As online learning universities and universities with blended or traditionally distinct BMs are studied, the primary goal of this paper is to present various adjustments to the BM of private universities due to the pandemic through a presentation of the experiences of Doba Business School. Although online education is a great time saver, it also requires the adaptation of professors, online mentors and students. Students and professors who met in classrooms a few weeks ago are now trying out alternative methods of collaboration and knowledge transfer.

As part of adapting to online education, Chinese universities have organized a series of educations for faculty members with emphasis on pedagogy, didactics of online teaching, and building relationships with students (Zhaohui, 2020). In the classroom, the professor can immediately detect if students are absorbing concepts and can change the pace of teaching accordingly. When teaching online it is necessary to choose different mechanisms for determining the appropriateness of acquired knowledge. The solution is certainly a continuous and repeated examination. Many professors are not trained at the moment to properly carry out the online learning process. A major problem of online education is also the isolation of students and the inability to establish a belonging to a group that in real life creates a sense of competition and motivates everyone to succeed (Govindarajan & Srivastava, 2020).

The aim of the study was to investigate and detect the lessons learned from the adaptations of BMs of Doba Business as private HEI due to learning methods in the situation of pandemic.

Methodology

In order to reach the main aim of the research authors used case study design. The case for research was private HEI in Slovenia, Doba Business School Maribor.

Doba Business School is the leading provider of online learning in the Slovenian higher education area. It has more than 20 years of tradition in online learning with more than 9000 graduates, development, scientific and research work, first-rate knowledge, use of modern and innovative pedagogical approaches, and internationalisation with international students position Doba Business School among the most ambitious HEIs in Southeast Europe.

Presentation of Doba Business School adaptation to the pandemic situation

In this section the researched case will be presented in detail. In the Table 1 adaptation of business model is presented.

Table 1: Adaptation of BMs of Doba Business School

BM blocks	Doba Business School
Value Proposition	Online study implementation model that functions in pandemic without adaptations. Webinars (within courses) opened to the public. Active response to the needs of education providers to share experiences with online learning. Proactive approach to the government educational institutions with the offer of sharing more than 20 years of online study experiences.
Customer Relationships	Supportive, motivational communication with students, academic and professional staff. Subtle pandemic communication with Croatian students (the earthquake in Croatia). Extending research and pedagogical to the consultancy role. Sharing experience in online learning with public (SIQ) Sharing online study experience with governmental institutions. (NAQHE). Flexibility of academic process.
Channels	Use existing online communication tools (MS Teams, Blackboard, Go To Webinars) for students and external publics From marketing focused communication to professional and pandemic communication.
Customer segments	Students Businesses Professional publics Governmental public
Revenue Stream	No short-term effects.

Key Activities	Study implementation – adaptation of pedagogic process regarding additional motivation, flexibility in deadlines for submitting assignments, pandemic communication. Informing students on current situation through website, video, and email communication. Use of new communication channel – MS Teams for all meetings of pedagogic and professional staff, with management.
Key Resources	Increased extent of workload of academic staff due to motivational activities, additional deepened communication with students and businesses and due to increased professional communication. Increased extent of workload for professional staff, online mentors.
Key partnerships	Deepening partnerships with businesses – inclusion of guest speakers from businesses into webinars for students about the current communication with employees on hold, laid off, on remote work and working in the company.
Cost structure	Program for potential defaulters.

As it can be seen from the Table 1 key activities within the adoption of the BM were concentrating on effective informing process of students; implementation of different online tools that enable home working and different measures implemented in order to encourage motivation. Regarding key resources block increased extent of workload of academic staff due to motivational activities, additional deepened communication with students and businesses and due to increased professional communication was recognized. On the revenue it did not have any short term effect. And regarding channels that were used, MS Teams, Blackboard, go to webinars were used the most.

Given the existing clear, modern and efficient organization of the Doba Business School, the adjustment of the BM was quick and efficient.

During the pandemic, Doba Business School also faced challenges of adaptation of the study implementation model. Below the process of adaptation is explained in detail.

Personnel and legal implementation

All employees were ordered to work from home in accordance with the applicable labour legislation and the existing rules. Employees were acquainted with key instructions and with tips for protecting personal data and business secrets while working from home. Legislative measures related to mitigating the consequences of the pandemic for employers were regularly monitored and Doba Business School acted in accordance with them. There were regular online meetings within departments to ensure that everything worked smoothly and with as few complications as possible.

Organizational implementation

Doba Business School adapted and upgraded the existing model of organization and cooperation among managers and employees, which took place entirely in the online environment (meetings, weekly coordination, reviewing key tasks, solving operational challenges etc.). Heads of organizational units communicated with their co-workers with a motivational-oriented letter several times a week, and the Director of the Doba Business School held weekly online meetings with all employees to inform them about the current events at the Doba Business School, the successes during that time and the organization and implementation of work. All employees were acquainted with the entire communication with students, Work tips, prepared by professors, were shared.

Technical implementation

Instead of many tools for online inter-personal communication, employees have started to use only one communication channel (MS Teams) uniformly. Considering the technical possibilities no major challenges were faced when introducing work from home, also due to effective technical assistance. Students and other stakeholders of the Doba Business School did not feel any consequences of our employees working from home.

Adjustments of the study implementation model

The existing online study model was adapted only in communication with students, which has become even more subtle and flexible (e.g. extension of assignments submission deadlines).

Implementation of the study process

The implementation of study activities continues in accordance with the existing model, without interruptions or changes, according to the plan of courses in a virtual learning environment. All assessment of knowledge is taking place in accordance with standards and protocols.

Social responsibility and information

Doba Business School is committed to the active co-creation of favourable social conditions in the environment in which it operates, which is why enhanced information during the pandemic was provided. Every 14 days, a letter was sent to all the stakeholders informing them about current events at the Doba Business School, papers written by professors and related to the current situation were shared. The students and the interested public were offered a free tour of a series of webinars, with tips on how to deal with constant change during this time. The Dean writes a letter to all stakeholders of the Doba Business School once a month, in which he writes about the current and future economic situation and measures. The webinars from the regular learning process, which we opened to the public, were attended en masse – for example, a webinar on communication and impact techniques was attended by more than 800 participants.

Discussion and proposals for further research

The aim of this paper was to demonstrate how Doba Business School Maribor responded to the introduced lockdown measures and adapted its BMs accordingly. The core element of the BMs of Doba Business School is reflected in the implementation of accredited study programs, which serve as the main source of revenues. It can be seen from the analysis that Doba Business School, which has been pursuing fully online implementation of study programs for more than 20 years, has not changed a lot. Online courses were implemented as scheduled without major interruptions. However, the professors did adjust their communication and assessment requirements, taking into account that most students were challenged with heavier burdens due to remote work, additional family obligations, even natural disaster etc. The professors did communicate with students more frequently, used more supportive messages and demonstrated more flexibility regarding the assignments' submission deadlines.

However, it needs to be emphasized that high quality online education is much more than just transferring the lectures into virtual environment. Online learning is not about using technology as such; it is about exploiting the benefits of technology for the purposes of pedagogy and to enhance the attainment of learning outcomes. Online learning is highly student-centred while traditional learning is highly professor centred. In other words, in online learning the courses should be designed in a substantially different way, which requires an efficient virtual learning platform as a basic precondition, course design experts, IT support and most importantly skilled professors. First, the professors should understand and accept the paradigmatic shift from traditional to online teaching, and second, they should possess specialized pedagogical skills to be able to adopt novel pedagogical approaches typical for online teaching, in order to effectively support the students in the process of attaining the learning outcomes. The relevance of proper pedagogical and didactical skills for high quality online teaching was emphasized by many experts (e.g. Dominko Baloh, 2020; Zhaohui, 2020).

It would certainly be interesting to analyse how the sudden shift to online teaching affected the students, their knowledge gains and the attainment of course-specific competences and learning outcomes, which serves as a viable suggestion for further research.

Also, it would be interesting to monitor if and how will HEIs proceed from mere immediate actions to introducing more advanced and proficient models of online learning in their business and study implementation strategies in the near future. As indicated by DeVaney et al. (2020; p.5): "As the emergency subsides but normal fails to return, HEIs need to do more. There's a good likelihood that virtual learning — in some capacity — will need to be a part of education for the foreseeable future. HEIs need a response framework that looks beyond the immediate actions. They have to prepare for an intermediate period of transition and begin futureproofing their institutions for the long term."

Apart from adapting the study implementation model, other shifts in the BMs were also identified as described in Table 1. Table 1 shows Doba Business School intensified and adapted the communication with external stakeholders (future students, business organizations, teaching experts and professional audience). With its long tradition of online learning, Doba Business School has taken the opportunity to position itself as an expert and a leading provider of high-quality online learning. This has been achieved by organizing a series of events and by providing advice on the implementation of online learning for different professional associations. Also, in times of pandemic, Doba Business School completely changed its promotional marketing communication to reach potential students with supportive, professional, and pandemic communication. Content-specific papers and webinars with hands-on advice on how to overcome the pandemic have been prepared and shared with the audience.

Conclusions

Although the adopted case study approach has limitations in transferring the key findings to a wider population, it still seems reasonable to speculate that traditional and online HEIs have experienced and responded to the pandemic in a substantially different way. While traditional HEIs were mostly struggling with the sudden switch to online teaching and learning, HEIs with prior experience with online learning implementation, on the other hand, had the opportunity to increase productivity, to search for and to respond to new business opportunities and to enhance their reputation as experts in online learning.

References

De Massis A., & Kotlar A. (2014). The case study method in family business research: Guidelines for qualitative scholarship. *Journal of Family Business Strategy, 5*(1), 15-29.

DeVaney, J., Shimshon, G., Rascoff, M., & Maggioncalda, J. (2020, May 5). Higher Ed Needs a Long-Term Plan for Virtual Learning. Harvard Business Review (online) [Blog post]. Retrieved from https://hbr.org/2020/05/higher-ed-needs-a-long-term-plan-for-virtual-learning

Dominko Baloh, J. (2020). Je prihodnost visokega šolstva v izobraževanju na daljavo, Finance. Retrieved from https://topjob.finance.si/8960495/Prihodnost-slovenskega-visokega-solstva-je-v-izobrazevanju-na-daljavo?cctest&

Govindarajan, V., & Srivastava, A. (2020, March 31). What the Shift to Virtual Learning Could Mean for the Future of Higher Ed, Harvard Business Review [Blog post]. Retrieved from https://hbr.org/2020/03/what-the-shift-to-virtual-learning-could-mean-for-the-future-of-higher-ed

Harrison, H., Birks, M., Franklin, R., & Mills, J. (2017). Case Study Research: Foundations and Methodological Orientations. *Forum Qualitative Sozialforschung / Forum: Qualitative Social Research, 18*(1), Art. 19. Retrieved from http://nbn-resolving.de/urn:nbn:de:0114-fqs1701195

Osterwalder, A., & Pigneur, Y. (2009). *Canvas BM Generation.* Self published.

Zhaohui. W. (2020, Mach 16). How Chinese university is responding to coronavirus. World Economic forum [Blog post]. Retrieved from https://www.weforum.org/agenda/2020/03/coronavirus-china-the-challenges-of-online-learning-for-universities/

Lessons from a Pandemic for the Future of Education
European Distance and E-Learning Network (EDEN) Proceedings
2021 Annual Conference | Madrid, 21-24 June, 2021
ISSN 2707-2819
doi: 10.38069/edenconf-2021-ac0049

CHANGE LIFE TO ONLINE: PEDAGOGICAL RELATIONSHIP IN PANDEMIC TIME

Ana Mouraz, Ana Nobre, Universidade Aberta, Portugal

Abstract

Suddenly, the distance education system, which had been created to reach audiences traditionally without access to on-site teaching offers, became the norm. Teachers and Schools had to face this important question from day to night: how to continue to educate, share knowledge, help students and motivate them in the construction of knowledge? The purpose of this communication is to reflect on the effects of the schools closure, due to pandemic, on the pedagogical practices of teachers, namely on the pedagogical relationship. 59 Portuguese teachers of basic and secondary education were questioned, in a casual sample, but diversified in terms of the subjects they teach.

The data obtained allow to conclude that despite all the constraints, the pedagogical relationship was maintained and even came out reinforced from the confinement experience.

Introduction

Today, in the pandemic situation, educational activity was forced to mobilize to respond to a huge social demand. Distance learning has been a resource to answer, not to the traditional intentions of this type of offer (increase the qualification of the workforce, find new audiences and market segments, etc.), (Mouraz & Nobre, forthcoming), but to a social demand that stems directly from the constraints imposed by the states. Such demand has been addressing the question: how to continue to educate, share knowledge, help students and motivate students in the construction of knowledge?

Peraya and Peltier (2020) recall how the pedagogical practices with digital technologies and the individual and collective practices of students and teachers were questioned many times during the first confinement due to the pandemic-COVID-19. In just a few days, developments and changes that seemed to take years have accelerated dramatically.

In the spring of 2020, all kindergartens, basic and secondary schools and higher education institutions, in Portugal and worldwide, had to change, in a few days, to distance education. The schools were closed, the face-to-face classes were cancelled. Surprisingly, most Portuguese, European and global institutions have gone from massive presence to massive detachment, in all senses of the word: geographical distance, physical distance, relational distance and cognitive distance from reality. (Nobre et al, 2021)

Finding out the dimensions and thinking about the scope of this drastic change has been the work of many researchers in the humanities and educational sciences this year that we have a pandemic situation.

Anthropological Effects

Teaching activity, at the forefront of our educational systems, currently faces an unprecedented social and anthropological dynamic, associated with technological acceleration, already well underway. This new dynamic will certainly lead to a long-awaited and expected paradigm shift in teaching and learning (Devinney & Dowling, 2020).

Philosopher Claire Marin (2020), an expert on individual and collective changes and disruptions, wrote that "in the face of a disaster, we feel reassured by considering it as a parenthesis rather than a warning ", the warning of 'an imbalance, a rupture, a transition or a transformation. For this philosopher, the experience of the pandemic and its implications (cataclysmic return of great fear) and massive (more than half of humanity confined for long months) is an experience with a very strong destructive potential in the psychic, moral, political, social dimensions and economic, because this experience deconstructs the imaginary constructions, habits, rules of operation and relationships that underlie our societies. Suddenly, all activities directly associated with what we call culture, started to have to exist digitally or to be suspended waiting for the epidemiological control of the pandemic. When they could continue to happen with new and tight rules, which in many cases, accentuated the digital experience of living collectively: could anyone be part of a choir or an orchestra? Could anyone participate in a conference or a political demonstration? Could anyone visit an exhibition or go to the theatre? Could anyone participate in a religious celebration or organize a family or friends party? The answer to the previous questions is, in almost all cases, "yes, one can", but only if this participation is mediated by digital communication technologies. The possibility of being physically with others has strict rules and the new social etiquette promotes the physical distance from others. Changing life online was the motto. What effects does this change have? Historian Françoise Hildesheimer (2020) emphasizes that epidemics play a fundamental role in social, political, economic and sociological development in history. However, their impacts are measured only at the moment of their cessation. Insofar as it is the latter that allows "a reversal of the economic situation in all areas" (Hildesheimer, 2020) and opens new way of living. How life can be lived when personal relations are distanced?

Pedagogical effects

Many schools and teachers developed, before the pandemic, pedagogical work processes in virtual environments (some digital platforms for quizzes, but also for videoconferencing, the virtual classroom, made available by school publishers, or others digital resources, with limited time). Those experiments were running quite well in some schools but were not generalized (Isaías et al, 2017). With the pandemic, these environments were appropriated by the teachers and allowed them to operate a rapid change, without many arrangements, in a very similar way to what they were doing in the classroom (Morgado et al, 2021).

The main concern of teachers and Portuguese schools was to maintain communication with all their students during the school closure (Nobre et al, in press). On the other hand, schools reported the effort to maintain contact with students from the most disadvantaged social groups, using other mechanisms and devices, such as traditional mail or the telephone. Having solved this access (Martins, 2020; OECD, 2020), the next concern was to adapt to the digital dimension what seemed to be the essence of teaching activity. There were many questions from teachers, at all levels of education, that highlighted this concern: What are the main elements of a distance learning course? How should I organize my discipline at a distance? What are the pedagogical practices that I can implement? How do I develop remote assessments? How do I set up remote group work? How to properly articulate the synchronous sessions of the virtual classroom and the asynchronous ones? etc. (Moreira et al, 2020). Through these questions asked everywhere at the same time, the educational community has also experienced its state of emergency.

A revision of the literature, meanwhile published on the effects of the pandemic on pedagogical issues, emphasizes the opportunity, returned by the digital, that education should be centred on the student that learn and less on the teacher that teaches (Doucet, et al, 2020; Pokhrel & Chhetri, 2021). On the other hand, this inventory also shows an evident difference between the potential of digital as an educational medium and what was put into practice by schools and teachers and was documented in these studies. Thus, some authors find that there has been a transposition from classroom to distance learning rather than a real transition, (Caron, 2020). Others put the change in terms of a reinforcement in the form of creative, handmade, intuitive use of ICT devices, instead of a massive exploration of knowledge and pedagogical practices available and widely studied and used for decades (Nobre, 2018).

One of the specific elements of this attempted transposition stems from the use of synchronous time and the balance between synchronous and asynchronous learning activities. At least in the first confinement, and as mentioned by Nobre et al. (forthcoming), schools sought to maintain schedules, often too busy for synchronous classes, as they had not yet realized the increased effort that distance learning carry on.

Three axes summarize the essentials of the pedagogical relationship (Postic, 1984) that are important to transposing to online: the contact time between teachers and each student; the modes of assessment and providing feedback that teachers give students and opportunities to collaborate with classmates. In the particular case of many of the students involved, it is also interesting to question the mediating role of parents and guardians as an element of achieving the pedagogical relationship. The third axis corresponds to opportunities for interaction with colleagues and the development of collaborative work between students, which teachers should encourage (Mendes et al., 2018).

The purpose of this communication is to reflect on the effects of the schools closure, due to pandemic, on the pedagogical practices of teachers, namely on the pedagogical relationship.

Methodology

From an operational point of view, the axes of analysis will be:

- The main ways of using synchronous time and the support required from parents and EE in the development of learning tasks.
- The mechanisms used by teachers to make formative assessment, and to give feedback to students.
- The opportunities created by teachers to promote collaborative work among students.

The research takes on a pilot character, since a "traditional" topic is being focused - the pedagogical relationship, but in a completely new circumstance, because the environment of this relationship is online (Moreira et al., 2020). Furthermore, the decision to pursue this online modality to accomplish pedagogical relationship was not a choice of teachers or students. The study follows a mixed methodology, which collected quantitative and qualitative data, from a semi-open questionnaire designed to collect information about the effects of the pandemic on the pedagogical practices of teachers and schools.

59 Portuguese teachers of basic and secondary education were questioned, in a casual sample, but diversified in terms of the subjects they teach.

In this paper we will present data from referred questionnaire, but only regarding the aspects of the pedagogical relationship, as explained above.

The data were collected through a questionnaire applied digitally via Google forms and were treated in the excel program. The coding of the open responses was done manually.

Results

Communication modes to assure pedagogical relationship

An analysis of the Figure 1 shows that the use of digital platforms was the way most frequently mentioned by teachers to maintain the pedagogical relationship with their students. Respondents balanced the synchronous and asynchronous sessions at similar levels. The phone, the WhatsApp network and the use of pre-recorded classes had less frequent or even null expressions.

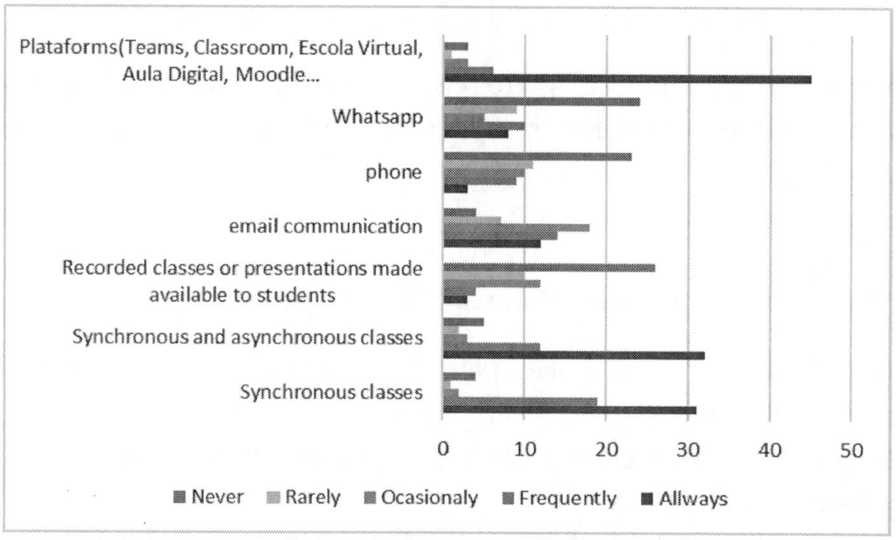

Figure 1. Communication modes to assure pedagogical relationship

The devices used by teachers to do formative assessment, and to give feedback to students

As shown in the Figure 2 and the support required from parents and EE in the development of learning tasks. The feedback given by the teachers happened, especially during synchronous classes. Then, the written forms, whether in the forums, in the mail or other associated forms, were the modalities referred to.

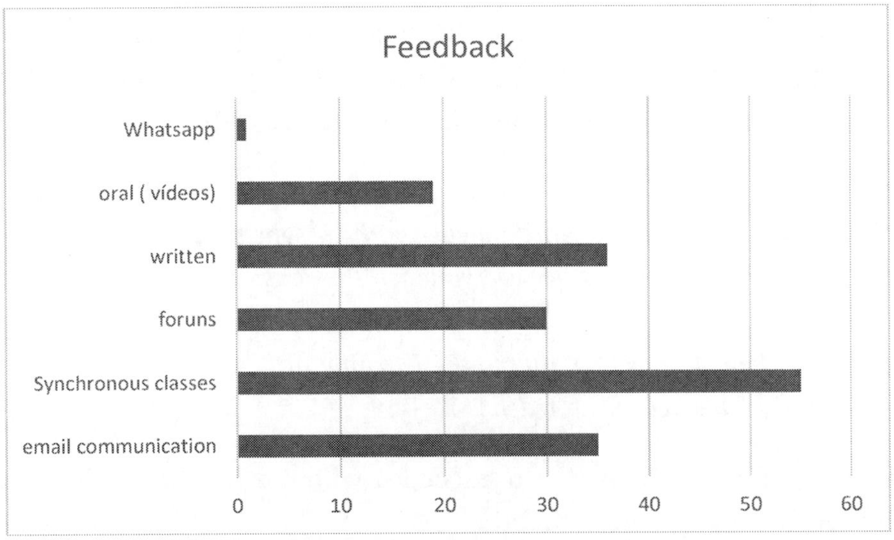

Figure 2. The devices used by teachers to do formative assessment, and to give feedback to students

The opportunities created by teachers to promote collaborative work among students

Thirty-seven respondents said they had requested group work from their students while twenty-two said they had not done so.

As for the quality of the work developed, it was considered by the teachers to be very good and good (Figure 3).

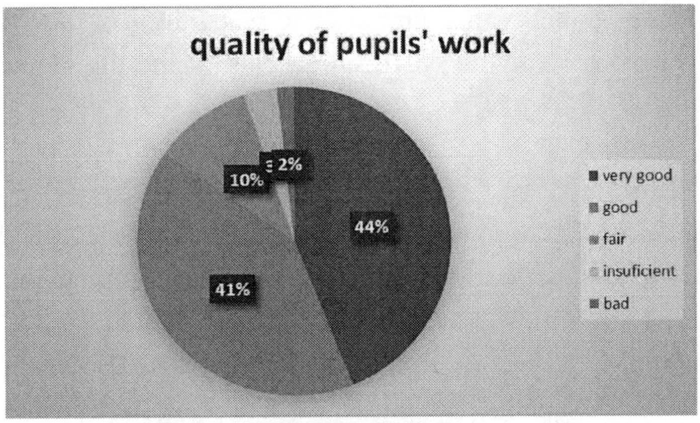

Figure 3. Quality of collaborative work

Most of the requested collaborative work had the primary intention of promoting discussion among students on the subjects researched and reaching various perspectives. On fewer occasions, group work was used to carry out research work and subsequent presentation of results, in order to encourage collaboration and mutual assistance between students, as well as to promote meaningful learning. Some teachers reported having continued with the work started before school closure.

When asked about the effects that distance education had on relations with students, there were some testimonies that emphasized distance. However, surprisingly, many teachers found a different proximity to the students, having established bonds that they had not yet developed.

> *"It allowed for a more open dialogue, both in synchronous sessions and through social networks, since everyone felt the constant need for attention from the teachers and someone who listened to them, listening to the problems they were feeling, due to the learning difficulties and the lack of contact with colleagues and teachers."*

At the same time, this proximity is also associated with the fact that students are in their own environment and are more authentic

> *"In the age group of 10 years there were students who, being in their environments dancing, became much more uninhibited! And with very positive results."*

Another effect of this proximity was the knowledge of the reality of each student, namely the family and socio-economic contexts, although it cannot be generalized, several testimonies were collected indicating that this proximity was also established with the families, either because there was more contact, or because more responsibilities were given to them in monitoring the children. Such a situation has occasionally resulted in relationships of greater empathy with families and recognition of the teachers' work, since the parents ended up observing the synchronous classes and the requested work to their children.

Conclusion

The data obtained show that despite all the constraints, the pedagogical relationship was maintained and even came out reinforced from the confinement experience. The interviewed teachers used mostly synchronous classes, which partially combined with asynchronous activities. It was in this way that they took care of the pedagogical relationship with their students. Despite this option of transposing the presence to synchronous models, the feedback on the tasks performed by the students took place mostly in written form, even though in some cases the forums were chosen to do so. Another idea, identified in the data collected, indicates some redistribution of pedagogical power by parents and EE, whose role and performance seems to have been valued by teachers. However, there is still little information on the long-term effects of these feedlots. A recent OECD study warns of the greater risk that this closure entails for students in situations of greater fragility. The hysteresis induced by school closures may be more prevalent among students from less privileged backgrounds. (OECD, 2020)

Baptiste Morizot (2020), reminds us of our interdependence with the world and with others: a learning device can be thought of as a living organism (composed of teachers, students, professionals, etc.) in permanent relationship with the world that the fence and with which the bonds are formed and renewed to feed each other. When the terms of that relationship change and it needs to be feed up in digital environments, it is important to see if that interactive and promoter requirement of the relationship fulfils its function.

References

Devinney, T., & Dowling, G. (2020, May 14). Is this the crisis higher education needs to have? Times Higher Education [Blog post]. Retrieved from https://www.timeshighereducation.com/features/crisis-higher-education-needs-have

Doucet, A., Netolicky, D., Timmers, K., & Tuscano, F. J. (2020). Thinking about pedagogy in an unfolding pandemic (An Independent Report on Approaches to Distance Learning during COVID-19 School Closure). Work of Education International and UNESCO. Retrieved from https://issuu.com/educationinternational/docs/2020_research_covid-19_eng

Hildesheimer, F. (2020, May 15). Cette mondialisation de masse des phénomènes épidémiques, c'est du jamais vu. Le Monde [Blog post]. Retrieved from https://www.lemonde.fr/idees/article/2020/05/15/on-ne-peut-plus-seulement-definir-l-epidemie-comme-grand-personnage-archaique-de-l-histoire-d-hier_6039718_3232.html

Isaias, P., Reis, F., Coutinho, C., & Lencastre, J. L. (2017). Empathic technologies for distance/mobile learning: an empirical research based on the Unified Theory of Acceptance and Use of Technology (UTAUT). *Interactive Technology and Smart Education, 14*(2), 159-180. Retrieved from http://www.emeraldinsight.com/doi/abs/10.1108/ITSE-02-2017-0014.

Martins, S. (2020). A educação e a covid-19: desigualdades, experiências e Impactos de uma pandemia não anunciada. In R. Carmo, I. Tavares, & A. Cândido (Eds.), *Um Olhar Sociológico sobre a Crise Covid-19 em Livro* (pp. 37-55). Lisboa: Observatório das Desigualdades, CIES-Iscte.

Mendes, A, Bastos, G, Amante, L, Aires, L., & Cardoso, T (2018). *Modelo Pedagógico Virtual.* Cenários de desenvolvimento. Lisboa: Universidade Aberta.

Moreira, J. A., Henriques, S., Barros, D., Goulão, M. F., & Caeiro, D. (2020). Educação Digital em Rede: Princípios para o Design Pedagógico em tempos de pandemia. Universidade Aberta, Educação a Distância e elearning, nº 10. Lisboa. ISBN978-972-674-881-6. doi 10.34627

Morgado, J. C., Lencastre, J. A., Freires, T., & Bento, M. (2021). Smart Education as Empowerment: Outlining Veteran Teachers' Training to Promote Digital Migration. *Technology, Knowledge and Learning.* https://doi.org/10.1007/s10758-021-09494-6

Morizot, B. (2020). *Manières d'être vivant. Enquêtes sur la vie à travers nous.* Arles : Actes Sud.

Mouraz, A., & Nobre, A. (forthcoming). Os efeitos da pandemia no desenho e realização de e-atividades no ensino superior. In Educação Superior: (Re)Configurações de um campo em Movimento. Revista Internacional De Educação Superior (RIESUp)"

Nobre, A. (2018). Multimedia technologies and online task-based foreign language teaching-learning. *Tuning Journal for Higher Education, 5,* 75-97. ISSN-e: 2386-3137.

Nobre, A., & Mouraz, A. (2020). Reflexões sobre os efeitos da pandemia na aprendizagem digital. In O (Re)inventar da Educação em Tempos de Pandemia. Dialogia. São Paulo, n. 36, p. 367-381, set./dez. 2020

Nobre, A., Mouraz, A., Goulão, M. F., Henriques, S., Barros, D., & Moreira, J. A. (2021). Docência para a Educação Digital em Rede: Comunicação e Colaboração em Ambientes Virtuais de Aprendizagem. In *Revista Praxis.*

OECD (2020). *The impact of COVID-19 on student equity and inclusion.*

Peraya, D., & Peltier, C. (2020). Ingénierie pédagogique : vingt fois sur le métier remettons notre ouvrage. *Distances et médiations des savoirs, 29.* Retrieved from http://journals.openedition.org/dms/4817

Pokhrel, S., & Chhetri, R (2021). A Literature Review on Impact of COVID-19 Pandemic on Teaching and Learning. *Higher Education for the Future, 8*(1), 133-141. https://doi.org/10.1177/2347631120983481

Postic, M. (1984). *Relação Pedagógica.* Coimbra: Coimbra Editora.

Lessons from a Pandemic for the Future of Education
European Distance and E-Learning Network (EDEN) Proceedings
2021 Annual Conference | Madrid, 21-24 June, 2021
ISSN 2707-2819
doi: 10.38069/edenconf-2021-ac0050

CREATIVE METHODOLOGIES: DESIGNING A FRAMEWORK FOR TEACHER REFLECTION AND AUTHORSHIP

Paula Carolei, Le@d (Uab-Pt), Unifesp, Portugal

Abstract

This research has as its main objective to create, test and improve methodologies and artefacts that help teachers to reflect to transform their practices, making them more creative. Actions are expected that go beyond envisioned planning, but that the teacher is able to concretize, evaluate and continuously improve his/her pedagogical actions. This paper describes the creation of a framework that aims to promote reflection on creative methodologies by teachers, helping them to make explicit the creative movements they already make highlighting their authorial moments, their limits, challenges and difficulties, as well as getting to know new creative possibilities.

The data used for the initial construction of this framework was collected in two online courses on Design of Pedagogical Strategies, in which the participating teachers had to describe their teaching practices. From the qualitative analysis of this data, we mapped the challenges and strains in the construction of pedagogical strategies, as well as the fashions and trends that appeared in the discourses. An analysis of formative needs was made and a categorization was created based on a theoretical reflection and critical analysis of the trends presented in the teachers' data, emphasizing the importance of teachers' authorial and creative stances in their methodological construction. In this article, we will describe the mapped data, the categorization and the theoretical foundations that supported the construction of this framework. We will also describe the categories and the first validation phase already carried out as well as the next steps for a large-scale application.

Introduction

This project is part of a post-doctoral research that addresses the contribution of Design methodologies for teacher education. The main aim of this research is to create, test and improve methodologies and artefacts that help teachers to design and transform their practices beyond a merely envisioned planning, but rather to deliver meaningful and transformative pedagogical actions. The artefacts created may facilitate diagnosis or contextual mapping, trigger reflection or support the recording, visualization and construction of processes and projects. They can also be experimental interfaces such as games and simulations, or mapping tools that help to build and evaluate pedagogical paths and trajectories.

Considering the complexity of the teacher training context, we cannot consider isolated resources, but rather devices that are the conjunction of actions involving human and non-human actors and the reverberations of these actions. If we intend to have a more authorial, emancipatory and creative action, it is necessary to build devices and rebuild them in an open and collective way that contemplates multiplicities. (Santos, 2014)

The purpose of our research project is to develop devices and artefacts that support the teacher's authorship, considering the complexity and potential of the Design, in order to promote a teachers' training not only in its instrumental aspects, but also in the creation of devices and formative ambiences.

Thus, we must overcome a logic of didactic planning that is limited to the actions to choose, to order, to adapt, and propose new perspectives in which the teacher has greater strategic authorship and is a designer of new possibilities of settings and formative paths. It is to go beyond prescription, normative or valorisation of instrumental logic, to assume an attitude in constant movement, plural, open, unfinished, dialogical (Ribeiro, 2019).

But what is it to be creative? What are creative methodologies?

They are movements in which the teacher has authorship of pedagogical strategies in a conscious way. It is not a simple instrumental process, but rather the creation of possibilities for conversations, dialogues, collective and collaborative authorship between all the educational actors.

The creative process is not spontaneous and can, and should, be supported by structures and models, and also by processes of thought recording and explicitation, as long as these are not just bureaucratic, mechanical and unconscious.

On creative learning, Resnick (2018) describes its dimensions as in four "Ps":

- Project: ideation, construction of models and value solutions.
- Peers: sharing ideas, principles and productions.
- Passion: new discoveries and interests in content, materials and methodologies.
- Play: learning through play, experimenting, testing, making mistakes, experimenting.

The four "P"s have been refined and deepened in the creative learning network and in this movement the importance of personal purpose and more social and collective dimensions have emerged with an emphasis on listening methodologies and constructions that consider the socio-cultural context. Passion, learning by playing and experimentation have been offered not only linked to concrete materials and places, but also to the work with the imaginary and the virtual. Creativity is always in the openness, movement and dialogue. It is not a complete and ready-to-use structure, but something that allows a constant networking construction.

Considering the premise of learning, how can we develop an artefact that helps teachers to reflect on their practices on the basis of these dimensions and enhance their authorship and their participation in networked constructions? How can a framework help in this matter?

Rollings and Morris (2004) describe the importance of producing frameworks as instruments of procedural change. Similarly, Salen and Zimmerman (2006) underline the importance of tools that help both the conceptual explicitness and the support of practical and concrete procedures, and frameworks are very useful to visualize either theoretical models or description of practices and procedures.

We understand that a framework is more than a set of standards or a model to be followed. It is a support or reference guide to support the explicitness of the intentionality elements of pedagogical planning, of the contextual elements, or of other pedagogical elements such as resources and activities to be developed.

The dimensions of the framework presented in this article are intended to provide a foundation for the construction of didactic actions, but also to encourage reflection. Much more than a model to be followed, a framework is a support structure in which important elements and paths are highlighted for the authorship, adaptation and contextualization not only of resources and activities, but of the practices as a personal transformation.

This framework aims to promote reflection on creative methodologies by teachers, helping to make explicit the movements they already make, to value practices unique to contexts and life trajectories, helping to build moments of authorship and autonomy, identifying and overcoming limits, and taking the risk of exploring new possibilities and taking emancipatory stances.

This framework was built from critical analysis of teachers' speeches about their practice, in a qualitative research that made explicit evidence in the contradictions that emerge from these speeches and inferences about their formative needs. From that, it was proposed a framework that explicits support paths both to the practice and to the reflection about more creative methodologies.

Research Methodology

Since the research is propositional, that is, it is expected to create solutions in the form of educational artefacts that transform practices, we chose the Design Science Research (DSR) approach, which considers the construction of devices as a possibility of research intervention (Dresch, 2015). In this case, the framework has this proposal to support research-training as a propositional action to transform practices.

The first stages of research involving DSR are complex mappings of a reality or context, in our case, it was an exercise of making explicit the controversies about pedagogical practices, from an invitation to describe and share practices made in a course on Design of Pedagogical Strategies; for this, we used the Cartography of Controversy as the principle of this analysis.

The Cartography of Controversy is presented by Venturini (2010) as a set of techniques to map tensions in complex situations in which the network of relationships is materialized in a discourse or in an interaction, for example in the recordings of an online course, in a social network, etc.

Venturini (2010) highlights that the research methodology of the cartography of controversies is very suitable for situations in which the community experience or discursive actions.

For this initial cartography that was the basis for the construction of the Framework, we used data from pedagogical practice obtained in two moments: a university extension course and a teacher training course, both offered online by a professor at the Federal University of São Paulo.

Results and framework construction

The first extension course on Design of Pedagogical Strategies took place in 2018, in the online modality, with a workload of 40 hours and offered to 200 teachers from the general public. We had 79 teachers who responded to all the activities and authorized the use of the data. In this course, we had the mapping of the controversies between planning and design; part of this mapping is described in the Master's dissertation (Ribeiro, 2019). The inputs came from detailed reflection questionnaires on pedagogical planning, resources used, proposed activities, and strategy construction.

Teachers were also invited to share their practices in discussion forums.

The other teacher training course, took place in 2020 with 200 university teachers within the public university training program, of whom 130 responded to all activities and authorized the use of data. In this course a commented visual planning was analysed, in which the participant presented his proposal of didactic action using a visual presentation methodology with icons and colours representing theories and educational elements, and commented on the methodologies and strategies chosen.

In the data from the first course, we mapped the controversies by considering two main data: the reflection questionnaires on their didactic planning and the discussion forum in which they explained, in detail, their practices and commented on those of their colleagues.

On the one hand, in the questionnaires there were multiple choice and open questions, but they were more targeted. Alternatively, in the forums, answers were expected to be more contextualized, as the aim was to describe the challenges of the practical actions and solutions found.

For the analysis of the results, especially the open questions and the answers given in the forum, software capable of analysing long texts (semantic analysis – fromtext – www.fromtext.net) was used, revealing terms of interest throughout a paragraph and the words in its periphery, detecting the relationships between them. This tool was fundamental to highlight the resources, the activity and the actions of the teachers, making explicit their relations within the context itself.

In this analysis we highlight the following mapped controversies and formative needs:

Table 1: Controversies and formative needs

Dimensions of Practice	Controversies	Identified Formative Needs
Planning References	Participants said they use official references in planning, but described the use of informal references from blogs and social networks without any critical qualification. Participants said they are inspired by references and produce their own materials, but in the description of practices there is neither a detailed description of the processes of curation, remixing, nor of the processes of creation.	Explain the planning processes. Identify the relevance of both normative and everyday sources and the cultural contexts in which didactic actions are carried out Exercise the processes of curating, remixing and authoring resources.
Planning of Collective actions	The participants highlight the importance of collective planning and interdisciplinary actions, but describe isolated and poorly planned actions in the short, medium and long term.	Experimentation with interdisciplinary, collective and collaborative projects.

Objectives and Competences	The participants recognize the importance of describing objectives and competences, but do not present the complexity of describing the acts of doing beyond technical and instrumental skills or specific examples only focused on conceptual content.	Knowing how to describe competences, going beyond specific objectives and procedures, but establishing complex connections with concrete reality and its transformation.
Educational Projects	Most teachers state the importance of working through projects, but highlight difficulties in working in this manner, as well as not having a clear idea of the more investigative methodologies and processes.	To know and experiment with project-based learning strategies or other investigative experiences and practices.
Resources and educational activities	Most of the resources and activities described are content resources to be consumed, few are presented in an open form or with a view of remixing and adaptation. Most activities are reactive such as questions and answers.	Teachers need to know other possibilities of activities that have a proposal for a more authorial action on the part of the student. They should be invited to create and be supported in the monitoring and evaluation of these activities.
About strategies or new methodologies design	Teachers declare to know some trends, such as active methodologies or flipped classroom, but they do not make explicit a personal construction of the practice in which they include these elements.	To reflect on how they construct their practice and how to go beyond prescription, towards something authorial in which the teacher constructs the acts of curriculum together with the student and with references from the educational context itself.

In the second course, the textual discourse of the group of teachers was not assessed. The visual representation of practice was analysed, which presented as icons: the most common types of resources, activities and strategies, teaching models, and what they present as a need to transform their practice.

Almost all the plans were lessons, with 87% predominance of expository-demonstrative lessons. There are some report production activities, some discussion activities and case studies, but these are at moments after the expository lecture. What was interesting in this data is that making their own visual construction helped the participant to reflect on their practice, as the colours highlighted the pedagogical approach and it became evident to the subjects themselves that there is an expository focus and a need to transform their practices.

Another point of analysis of the teachers' discourses was what they considered as trends for the transformation of their practices.

From the first group of teachers, the term with the highest occurrence was "Active Methodologies", which appeared in 67% of the teachers' discourses. This term was associated with the following elements: "active student", PBL, projects, gamification.

The phrases were generic, stating the importance of the student being at the centre of the process, but without explaining how. We verified only 5 occurrences (2.4%) of practices described in detail in the methodological process.

The second term with the highest occurrence was "flipped classroom", which appeared in the text of 45% of the respondents. In this case, they highlight the issue of time, the moments of demonstration/exhibition versus moments of exercise, the duality between theory and practice also appears, and in some cases, the difference between synchronous and asynchronous. In this case, the focus was on the class structure and its temporal models.

Other relevant occurrences were: gamification, STEAM, culture maker, hackthon.

In the second group of teachers, the same terms also appeared in the comments as formative needs or methodologies that they want to learn, but had no practice concretized in visual planning.

I present a table with the analysis of the educational trends cited, their description adapted from Bacich and Moran (2018), how these trends can be translated into practical actions and the controversies:

Table 2: Trends, design, practice and controversies

Trends	Pedagogical Design	Proposals and practical possibilities	Controversies encountered
Active Methodology	Active methodologies are all actions in which the student is the centre of the process.	Pedagogical strategies in which students are more active and are invited to solve problems or develop projects and processes. There are various levels of complexity and autonomy of student action from solving proposed problems,	The proposal is to have a rich set of strategies that promote student empowerment, but often a mix of approaches emerges that end up being reduced to prescriptive actions and do not value the student's process and their multiple ways of learning. Another challenge highlighted is the difficulty in acknowledging the need to hold the student accountable for his or her learning.

Flipped Classroom	Proposes to reverse the traditional logic of explanation in class and practice/exercise at home.	It proposes that the presentation of concepts can be recorded and that the student watches, and that the didactic moment with the presence of the teacher and the class should be more practical and with follow-up.	It values the practical and the interaction moment, but still maintains the separation between theory and practice and considers the hierarchy: presentation of concepts and application. There is also a cling to the "lecture" model.
Culture Maker /Hackthon /Steam	These three methodologies have a common proposal to practice first, valuing the idea of doing to learn and proposing that learning can be enhanced by recording and improving processes. It proposes a culture of sharing and open logic.	The focus of maker culture is on doing/making for learning. It brings the principles of digital making to learning, in which the "maker" must build solutions and prototypes. Hackthons are events of creation and project methodologies. STEM or STEAM emphasizes the interaction between science and art.	In the teachers' discourse the need for the student to do appears, but there is no deep description of the forms of registration, modelling and reflection. The main challenge of these approaches is to value the moments of reflection and theorization of the doing, which are sometimes neglected and not mapped, even when they are shared.
Gamification	Language of (physical) games and (digital) games applied in pedagogical strategy.	The language of games has many narrative and immersive elements that promote student action and can contribute both to motivation and engagement, and to more complex learning practices and problem-solving projection.	Gamification can be very deep and creative when it proposes complex and exploratory actions, but the forms of gamification cited by teachers still have a more behavioural and reactive logic, in which the student is only invited to react and not to build, to propose or to imagine.

Based on the mapped controversies and formative needs and considering the principles of creative learning, we designed the first prototype of the framework with the following concerns:

- To help to know the authorial movements and to make explicit the action of each actor.
- To know the diversities and complexities of the student's performance/creation and their strategic role in these authorial processes.
- Know the importance and possibilities of the collective and social dimension, both as a cultural context and in working with diversity, inclusion and social transformation.

- Support the construction of physical, digital or symbolic spaces and scenarios as spaces for experimentation, performance and experiences.

Based on these concerns we designed tracks with practical possibilities and reflective questioning. The tracks are not unique pathways that must be followed linearly, but are complex examples, of possible dimensions that can be adapted and deepened as the design of the devices and environments is concretized by the teachers.

The proposed tracks and their creative learning focuses were:

- Investigative – Projects;
- Immersive and playful – Learning through play;
- Practical and experimental – Learning through play as free experimentation;
- Collaborative and social intervention – Learning in pairs;
- Analytical and argumentative – Learning in pairs, with passion and project;
- Dramatic and expressive – Learning with passion.

The complete framework can be accessed here:
https://gamificacaocriativa.com/frameworks/

Evaluation and next steps

The framework was initially created as a prototype in a google form and validated by ten higher education teachers who intend to work with creative methodologies.

These teachers were asked to evaluate whether they agreed with the movements presented in each track and asked for suggestions of other dimensions they felt were missing. All the teachers surveyed recognized the potential for reflection of the artefact, but pointed out that, to support the process of authorship, it would be necessary to present more examples of projects, scenarios and devices contemplating the dimensions proposed in the framework, so that teachers could be inspired and take their first steps.

The next prototype will be built with visual spaces with examples of projects with the dimensions described.

It is understood that teacher training is not a simple process, much less instrumental, nor are there artefacts that, by themselves, solve such complex problems, but it is possible to support the reflection and action so that teachers have references in the tracks they decide to build.

The new version of the framework, expanded with the requested examples and with new visual representations, will be mass-tested in at least two courses for teacher training in Brazil and Portugal by the end of 2021.

In these courses, the framework will be evaluated as production support, so we will have as evidence the projects built by teachers using the framework as support.

References

Bacich, L., & Moran, J. (2018). *Metodologias ativas para uma educação inovadora: uma abordagem teórico-prática.* Porto Alegre: Penso.

Bordenave J. D., & Pereira, A. M. (2010). *Estratégias de ensino-aprendizagem* (28th ed.). Petrópolis: Vozes.

Dresch, A. (2015). *Design Science research: método de pesquisa para avanço da ciência e tecnologia.* Porto Alegre: Bookman.

Kessel, Z. (2017). Metodologias ativas e a formação de professores: O desafio de formar o educador do século XXI, conectado às demandas de uma geração cada vez mais digital. São Paulo. *Revista Educatrix, 7*(13), 70-73.

Latour, B. (2012). *Reagregando o social : uma introdução à teoria do ator-rede.* Salvador: Edufba; Bauru: Edusc.

Macedo, R. S. (2012). Atos de Currículo e Formação: o príncipe provocado. *Revista Teias, 13*(27), 67-74.

Ribeiro, N. C. R. (2019). *Design de estratégias pedagógicas como proposta de formação de professores.* (Dissertação de Mestrado). Universidade Federal de São Paulo, Diadema.

Rollings, A., & Morris, D. (2004). *Game Architecture and Design.* Indiana: New Rider.

Salen K., & Zimmermann, E. (eds.) (2006). *The game design models in The Game Design Reader: rules of play antology.* Cambridge: MIT Press.

Santos, E. (2014). *Pesquisa-formação na Cibercultura.* Santo Tirso, Portugal: White Books.

Venturini, T. (2010). Diving in magma: how to explore controversies with actor network theory. *Public Understanding of Science, 19*(3), 258-273.

Zabala, A., & Arnou, L. (2010). *Como aprender e ensinar competências.* Porto Alegre: Artmed.

Lessons from a Pandemic for the Future of Education
European Distance and E-Learning Network (EDEN) Proceedings
2021 Annual Conference | Madrid, 21-24 June, 2021
ISSN 2707-2819
doi: 10.38069/edenconf-2021-ac0051

EMERGENCY RESPONSES TO THE COVID-19 CRISIS IN EDUCATION: A SHIFT FROM CHAOS TO COMPLEXITY

Barbi Svetec, Blaženka Divjak, Faculty of Organization and Informatics, University of Zagreb, Croatia

Abstract

This paper presents a pilot research of approaches taken by European Union (EU) Member States (MSs) in the emergency response to the COVID-19 crisis in pre-tertiary education. It includes a multi-case study of four MSs, examining their education systems' digital readiness and "fitness for change", as well as decision-making practices. We use the Cynefin framework of decision contexts to explore different paths in shifting from chaos to complexity. The preliminary findings of this research indicate that a factor positively influencing education systems' response was not exclusively their digital readiness, but also "fitness" in terms of ongoing reforms and preparedness for change. The findings also suggest that MSs generally continued with their usual decision-making practices, with tendencies towards centralisation of crucial decisions, which is in line with the Cynefin framework, arguing for stronger leadership in chaotic contexts.

Introduction

Due to the COVID-19 pandemic, across the EU, from mid-March 2020 and for at least two months, school closures were nearly universal, affecting more than 95 million students at all educational levels (EC, 2020g; p.11). In the worldwide emergency, education leaders had to "adopt a proactive approach to contributing to the mitigation of the impact of the pandemic and to prevent learning loss" (Reimers & Schleicher, 2020; p.7). The shift to distance learning relied heavily on digital learning practices, though the switch to digital learning and teaching often had to be done with haste and without enough time for preparation (EC, 2020e; p.6). However, "emergency is not the time to put into effect complex institutional plans for distance learning that were meant to be implemented over months or years" (Daniel, 2020; p.93). Despite the substantial development of digital infrastructure of schools in the past decade, there are still significant disparities between MSs (EC, 2020g, p. 11), and while digital technologies enabled numerous students to continue learning in the crisis, there was also a barrier for those lacking access, equipment or skills (EC, 2020e; p.3). Even though all MSs resorted to predominantly digital learning and teaching, there were differences in their approaches. Some may be linked with the digital readiness of their education systems, others with national specificities and traditions, including those related to decision-making.

Theoretical foundation of research

To make a better understanding of the decision-making in the context of the COVID-19 crisis in pre-tertiary education, it may be useful to put it in the perspective of the Cynefin framework, as created by David Snowden. In Snowden's words (2002; p.104), "Cynefin creates four open spaces or domains of knowledge all of which have validity within different contexts". As pointed out by French (2015; p.1638), the Cynefin framework was introduced "to categorise contexts for inference and learning, knowledge management and decision making". Snowden and Boone (2007; p.2) emphasised that, in the Cynefin framework, contexts are "defined by the nature of the relationship between cause and effect". In the four contexts, *simple, complicated, complex,* and *chaotic,* leaders need to recognise the situation and act appropriately. *Simple* contexts include stability and clear relationships between cause and effect, apparent and uncontested answers, unquestioned decisions, and common understanding. *Complicated* contexts also contain clear relationships between cause and effect, but these are not evident to everyone; they can include several right answers and require looking into various options, which may call for expertise. In *complex* contexts, the right answer cannot be identified, and reasons behind events can be understood only in hindsight; in such contexts, leaders need to let patterns and possible solutions emerge and then identify the appropriate ones. In *chaotic* contexts, it is not possible to identify the relationships between cause and effect, as they are changing, and there are no patterns to identify; leaders need to act immediately to set up order, detect where there is stability, and then work to shift from *chaos* to *complexity*, where patterns can be identified, which may contribute to preventing further crises and recognising opportunities (Snowden & Boone, 2007). According to Kurtz and Snowden (2003; p.477), shifting from the *chaotic* to the *complex* is "a matter of creating multiple attractors, or swarming points, around which un-order can instantiate itself". McLeod and Childs (2013) pointed to a similar way of discussing management styles, in relation to *tame* and *wicked* problems, as distinguished by Rittel and Webber (1973). Namely, according to Grint (2005; p.1473), *tame* problems are *complicated* and *wicked* are *complex*; the third type, he identified as *critical*, was associated by McLeod and Childs with the *chaotic* domain (2013; p.123). From the perspective of behavioural strategy, Foss (2020; p.1324) stressed that decision-making in the COVID-19 emergency had been characterised by "novelty, complexity and open-endedness" (with reference to Mintzberg et al., 1976) and a "lack of clarity".

If put in the perspective of Cynefin, the onset of the pandemic in March 2020 has all characteristics to be identified as a *chaotic* context. It brought a severe emergency and concern about human safety, calling for an instant response and immediate decision-making, taking into account the constantly changing, completely unpredictable circumstances. Probing actions and decisions made in this context were the basis for a further shift to a *complex* context, with some patterns and solutions already emerging, some stability returned, and new opportunities revealed. In the *complex* context, some sort of an organised educational process has started, i.e. a majority of students have instruction on a regular daily basis and teachers have support in the delivery of teaching. Nevertheless, there are still many unknowns and incomplete solutions, such as those related to vulnerable groups of students and teachers left behind, as well as the social component of learning and good assessment practices missing on a broader level. In the next section, we are going to analyse the approaches taken by MSs in the first semester of 2020 to make the shift from *chaos* to *complexity*, using Cynefin as a theoretical framework.

Methodology

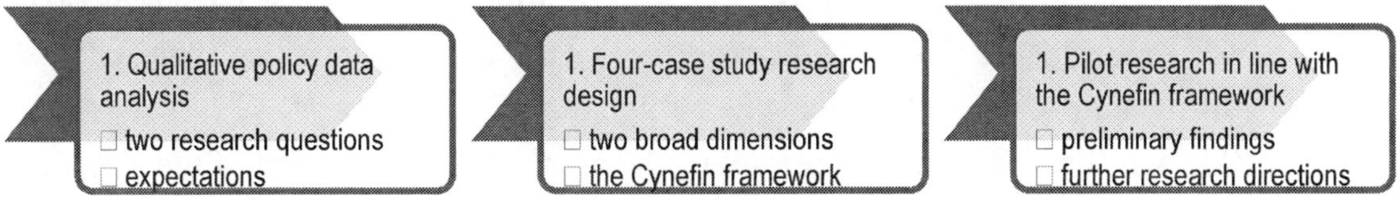

Figure 1. Research design of the pilot research

As presented in Figure 1, the first step in our research was a qualitative data analysis, which included primarily policy papers, national and official EU documents, as well as international organisations' research reports, related to the development of digital education and responses of MSs' education systems to the pandemic. Based on that, we recognised there had been significant differences between MSs' education systems before the pandemic, related to several factors. As the most prominent ones, we identified the state of reform processes in education and the level of digitalisation. Besides that, we recognised that the responses to the pandemic's threat to education included centralised support, digital repositories and training, but also decentralised, often school-level, organisation and responsibility for the continuation of educational processes.

In the second step, we used the multi-case study research method and placed MSs in a matrix based on two categories (Yin, 2018). The first category referred to the digital readiness of an MS's education system and its "fitness" for the emergency shift to predominantly digital learning and teaching. The European Framework for Digitally Competent Educational Organisations was consulted, which proposes seven key elements related to effective digital education: teaching and learning practices, professional development, assessment practices, content and curricula, collaboration and networking, infrastructure, and leadership and governance practices (EC, 2015). Based on that, we examined to what extent education systems had been modernised, in terms of e.g. availability of equipment, teachers' and students' digital skills, and curricula. The second category referred to the level of centralised versus decentralised decision-making in education. Here we examined e.g. at what levels crucial decisions were made and whether support and guidance were provided by education authorities. Based on the combination of the two categories, we grouped MSs into four clusters, as shown in Figure 2.

In the third step, we conducted a pilot research. We selected one distinguished representative from each of the clusters and researched its case in more detail, to demonstrate different national circumstances and approaches. Since, in the case study research design, sufficient access to data is needed and it is suggested that cases which are most likely to provide answers to research questions should be chosen (Yin, 2018), cluster representatives with the most adequate public data were selected. The aim of the pilot research was to answer two research questions.

- RQ1: What approaches did MSs take in their immediate response to the COVID-19 crisis, considering their digital readiness? Our expectation was that successful shifting did not depend exclusively on high digital readiness.
- RQ2: Was the level of decision-making during the COVID-19 crisis aligned with the regular orientation of an MS's education system in terms of (de)centralisation? Our expectation was that MSs stayed aligned with the regular level of (de)centralisation of decision-making and guidance.

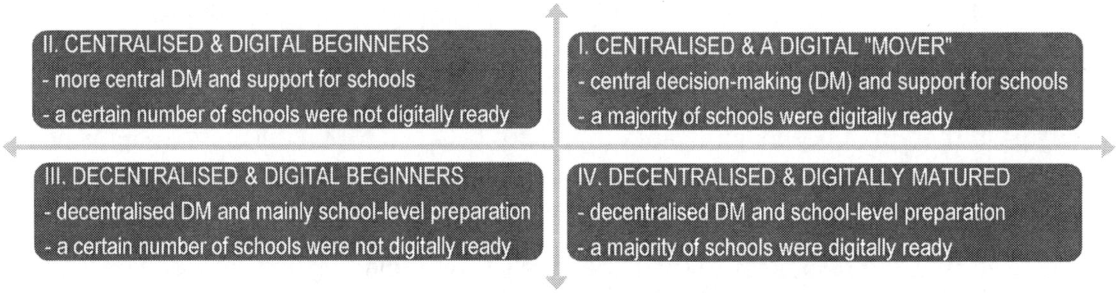

Figure 2. Clustering of MSs according to two categories

Results

Croatia as a representative of cluster I.

According to the Digital Economy and Society Index (DESI) 2020 (based on 2019 data), though positioned slightly below the EU average on the percentage of individuals with at least basic digital skills, Croatia was slightly above the EU average in above-basic digital skills (EC, 2020a; p.7). Croatia is the only MS with all 16–19 year-olds having at least basic digital skills. A Comprehensive Curricular Reform and the e-Schools project have been in full roll-out since 2019, enhancing the use of ICT in learning and teaching. Since 2018/2019, Informatics has been a compulsory subject in certain grades of primary and secondary schools and optional in others, and since 2019/2020 ICT included as a cross-curricular topic in all grades. (EC, 2020f; p.44) The Teaching and Learning International Survey (TALIS) 2018 showed that a below-average percentage of teachers felt (very) well prepared to use ICT in teaching and let students frequently/always use ICT for schoolwork. However, an above-average percentage had ICT for teaching included in recent professional development activities. (OECD, 2019; p.30) In 2019, more than 40 000 teachers underwent training within the curricular reform and the e-Schools project (EC, 2020f; p.44). Considering the infrastructure, although in 2017–2018 schools were less equipped and connected than the EU average (EC, 2019a; pp.39-40), since 2019, two large projects (e-Schools and Comprehensive Curricular Reform) have been providing all schools with the necessary equipment, and within the curricular reform, students have been provided with tablets. Croatia managed to respond well to the crisis, with current reforms and projects providing the basis for a rapid shift to distance education and effective provision of online classes (EC, 2020f; p.45). Considering decision-making, education governance is divided between the state level and municipalities. Decisions on closure and re-opening of schools were made at the central level, and national education authorities provided strong guidance and support (MSE, 2020b). As the crisis started, video lessons were provided centrally for both primary and secondary schools, available via television and online (EC, 2020f; p.49). Teachers were encouraged to prepare and deliver their own content and set up virtual classrooms. Various targeted documents were issued to support the transition, including instructions on the organisation of distance learning and teaching, and assessment and grading in virtual environments. (MSE, 2020b) An Action Plan for the Development of Distance Education was developed (MSE, 2020a).

Hungary as a representative of cluster II.

The DESI index 2020 suggested that in Hungary, the proportion of individuals with both at least basic and above-basic digital skills was below the EU average, with no progress made in recent years (EC, 2020c; p.7). An outline of the digital competence framework was adopted in 2019. A new core curriculum, introducing the subject "digital culture", was published to apply from September 2020 (EC, 2020f; p.154). TALIS 2018 suggested that an above-average percentage of teachers felt (very) well prepared to use ICT in teaching, but a below-average percentage let students frequently/always use ICT for school work (OECD, 2019; p.30). In 2017–2018, schools were far less digitally equipped and connected than the EU average (EC, 2019a; pp.39-40). Project funding in 2017-2020 provided equipment for state schools in less developed regions, and equipment and training for teachers (EC, 2020f; p.158). The transition to predominantly digital learning and teaching during the crisis pointed to differences in teachers' preparedness and students' access.

Yearly national competence testing suggested that about 20% of students had limited or no access to digital education (Hermann, 2020, as cited in EC, 2020f), which might have worsened the learning deficit of disadvantaged students. (EC, 2020f; p.154) Education governance is shared between the central government and municipal school districts, and recent reforms have centralised the system (OECD, 2015a; p.15). Decisions regarding closure and re-opening of schools and adaptation of teaching practices were orchestrated at a more central level (OECD, 2021; p.47). The education authority issued a recommendation for the organisation of digital education, and distance education was supported by a central platform, though other collaborative spaces were used as well (EC, 2020c; p.4) and each school could select a digital platform to work with (Molnar et al., 2020; p.606).

Slovakia as a representative of cluster III.

As reported in the DESI index 2020, the percentage of individuals with both at least basic and above-basic digital skills was below the EU average, with a decrease in numbers (EC, 2020d; p.7). Schools are autonomous to decide whether to include digital competences as a separate subject or integrated in other compulsory subjects (EC, 2019b; p.30). According to TALIS 2018, an around-average percentage of teachers felt (very) well prepared to use ICT in teaching, but a below-average percentage let students frequently/always use ICT for school work (OECD, 2019; p.30). In 2018 it was established that in lower secondary schools teachers used ICT mostly to present content, and rarely to enhance students' knowledge (State School Inspectorate, 2018, as referenced in EC, 2020f; p.280). In 2017–2018, schools were less digitally equipped and connected than the EU average (EC, 2019a; pp.39-40). Though digitally equipping schools and students has been a priority, the crisis highlighted the lack of adequate digital resources, the need for equal access to quality digital learning, as well as improving teachers' digital skills, learning management systems, and support to the disadvantaged (EC, 2020f). Decision-making usually involves the state, municipality/region, and school level, with schools granted relatively high autonomy (OECD, 2015b; p.15). While decisions on closure or re-opening of schools were made at the central level, schools had autonomy in deciding on learning resources, teaching requirements, and adapting teaching practices (OECD, 2021; p.47). Education authorities established a portal to support online learning and teaching and assessment (EC, 2020d; 2020f).

Finland as a representative of cluster IV.

According to the DESI index 2020, Finland ranked among the highest in the EU in both at least basic and above-basic digital skills (EC, 2020b; p.7). Digital competences are included in curricula; since 2016–2017 in primary and lower secondary education transversally, and in upper secondary education there are related optional courses. Digital skills of teachers are highly developed. (EC, 2020f, p. 103) According to TALIS 2018, a below-average percentage of teachers felt (very) well prepared to use ICT for teaching, but an around-average percentage frequently/always let students use ICT for school work (OECD, 2019; p.30). In 2017–2018, Finland was among the highest-ranking MSs in terms of digitally equipped and connected schools (EC, 2019a; pp.39-40). Well-developed digital education, with high-skilled teachers and good infrastructure, enabled successful dealing with the crisis. Though distance education worked well, there is also a fear that students in need of more support might have progressed less than their peers. (EC, 2020f) Finland's education system is highly decentralised, with most education-related decisions taken at a municipal and institutional level (OECD, 2020; p.18). Decisions on closure and re-opening of schools were made at the central level, on learning resources and teaching requirements at a local level, and on adapting teaching practices at multiple instances (OECD, 2021; p.47). Support and guidance were provided at the central level. Several main education platforms were used; there was an online hub with resources created to support teachers. (EC, 2020f; p.107) The fact that decisions regarding technical and practical aspects were left to municipalities and schools is "one example of the high level of trust in teachers and school leaders that defines much of what happens in Finnish schools" (Sahlberg, 2020; p.363).

Discussion

It could be argued that the onset of the pandemic in March 2020 had all elements to be characterised as a *chaotic* context. As pointed out by Foss, the situation was "deeply uncertain and ambiguous" and "sensemaking" was particularly important (2020; p.1324). Several months, or even weeks into the pandemic, when certain practices were established, a great majority of MSs were already in a *complex* context, able to analyse the situation, draw lessons and make more structured plans. They had different starting positions, national contexts, and traditions, both of which might have affected their approaches. We tried to shed light on these aspects to enable a better understanding of their responses.

If we look at the digital readiness, based on the limited number of cases, it could be argued that education systems that were better prepared in terms of digital skills, curricula, and infrastructure, also faced fewer challenges and negative effects in shifting to predominantly digital learning and teaching. On the one hand, there is Finland which, according to the DESI index 2020 (EC; 2020b), was placed the highest in the overall ranking, as well as in the human capital category, with digital skills well above the EU average. Finland has digital competences included in the curricula, highly skilled teachers, and adequate infrastructure. It does not surprise that, with such preconditions, Finland was able to successfully manage the crisis. On the other hand, there is Croatia, ranking below the EU average in the overall DESI 2020 index (EC; 2020a), and a bit below the average in the human capital category, but above-average in advanced digital skills. In

Croatia, digital competences have only recently been included in the curricula, and teachers' competences and infrastructure have advanced rapidly in the last several years. Croatia also managed to respond well to the crisis, which was largely enabled by recent projects and initiatives focused on the development of digital education, underway as the crisis struck. In this context, it can be noted that education systems "fit for change" were not necessarily and only those ranking the highest on various parameters related to digital capacity. What is also important is the "agility" of the system, its adaptiveness to change, reforms underway, and capacity to react in case of need. Moreover, based on the findings of the four cases, it could be concluded that, in cases of MSs which were less digitally prepared and possibly less "fit for change", this shift to large-scale digital education highlighted the existing gaps, primarily in infrastructure and access, as well as teachers' competences. Though learning inequalities are not linked only with MSs whose systems were less digitally ready, their scale may depend on the digital readiness. Finally, regarding our research questions, we could say that the pilot research supports our expectation that a successful response to the crisis was not predetermined by a high level of digital readiness. To answer the research question with higher confidence, more case studies should be considered.

As far as decision-making is concerned, it was connected to different levels of governance in different MSs. Although Snowden and Boone argue that, in *chaotic* contexts, "communication of the most direct top-down or broadcast kind is imperative" (2007; p.6), this should be put in the perspective of already established practices, not to worsen the chaos by introducing new ones amidst of it. If we look at the four analysed MSs, it can be concluded that decisions regarding the closure and re-opening of schools were made at more centralised levels – even in Finland, with its decentralised education system, which may be interpreted in support of the mentioned claim by Snowden and Boone. However, when it comes to decisions related to adapting teaching practices, the findings show different practices, including both centralised and decentralised decision-making. Across the EU (EC; 2020f), guidance and support were in some form (guidelines, platforms, repositories or other) provided at the centralised level. Considering the limitations of the available data, it is not really possible to draw conclusions about how strong, overarching or used these support and guidance were, though. However, regardless of that, it can be concluded that schools also had high levels of responsibility – in MSs such as Slovakia or Finland, they were supported but had broad autonomy, and in Croatia, they were firmly guided but the final implementation was also down to them. Nevertheless, if we return to our research question, we can conclude that the locus of decision-making during the crisis did reflect the regular organisation of education governance, but also that in some MSs the role of central-level decision-making might have been stronger than in regular contexts.

The last could be expected if we consider the Cynefin framework, where it is noted that, in a *chaotic* context, stronger leadership is needed to move to a less ambiguous situation.

We propose some preliminary findings, but with a wide range of limitations arising from the limited number of cases and methodological constraints. It can be argued that there was no universal approach in transitioning from *chaos* to *complexity* and that successful responses were achieved using different approaches. However, there are numerous other aspects (variables) in MSs' responses to the crisis, which could also be distinguished as important. For example, the quality of learning and teaching, acquired learning outcomes, and inclusiveness would be essential dimensions in determining the success of a response for all students at a satisfactory level. These aspects would be worth exploring in further research. Moreover, this paper focuses primarily on the initial responses in early 2020 (though some data refer to the entire year), so in further research, longitudinal data collection needs to be conducted. It would be worth exploring how MSs have been dealing later on, in *complex* contexts, and establish whether possibly, as patterns have emerged and the pandemic is being put under control, these may already be characterised as *complicated*. Finally, lessons learned from this crisis must be carefully noted and collected, to build education systems' resilience to similar threats in the future.

Conclusions

In this paper, we presented a pilot research focused on the emergency responses of EU MSs' education systems in the first months of the COVID-19 crisis. The research included a multi-case study of four MSs, in which their digital readiness before the crisis and "fitness for change", as well as the orchestration of decision-making in the crisis were examined. The decision-making process that enabled the shift from *chaos* to *complexity* was discussed from the perspective of the Cynefin framework. The results of the multi-case study suggest that high digital readiness before the crisis may not have been the necessary prerequisite for a successful shift to mostly digital learning and teaching and that even though MSs were inclined to keep their usual decision-making practices, there were tendencies towards more centralised country-level approaches, which is in line with the Cynefin framework, suggesting stronger leadership is needed in *chaotic* contexts. However, considering the limitations of this research and numerous other aspects which may be relevant when discussing education systems' responses, its role is primarily to open questions and call for further research, and not to elicit any final conclusions.

References

Daniel, S. J. (2020). Education and the COVID-19 pandemic. *Prospects, 49*(1-2), 91-96.

European Commission. (2019a). *2nd survey of schools: ICT in education: objective 1: benchmark progress in ICT in schools, final report.*

European Commission. (2019b). *Digital education at school in Europe* [Eurydice Report].

European Commission. (2020a). *Digital economy and society index (DESI) 2020, country profile—Croatia.*

European Commission. (2020b). *Digital economy and society index (DESI) 2020, country profile—Finland.*

European Commission. (2020c). *Digital economy and society index (DESI) 2020, country profile—Hungary.*

European Commission. (2020d). *Digital economy and society index (DESI) 2020, country profile—Slovakia.*

European Commission. (2020e). *Digital education action plan 2021–2027: Resetting education and training for the digital age.*

European Commission. (2020f). *Education and training monitor 2020: Country analysis.*

European Commission. (2020g). *Education and training monitor 2020: Teaching and learning in a digital age.*

European Commission. Joint Research Centre. (2015). *Promoting effective digital-age learning: A European framework for digitally competent educational organisations.*

Foss, N. J. (2020). Behavioral Strategy and the COVID-19 Disruption. *Journal of Management, 46*(8), 1322-1329.

French, S. (2015). Cynefin: Uncertainty, small worlds and scenarios. *Journal of the Operational Research Society, 66*(10), 1635-1645.

Grint, K. (2005). Problems, problems, problems: The social construction of 'leadership'. *Human Relations, 58*(11), 1467-1494.

Kurtz, C. F., & Snowden, D. J. (2003). The new dynamics of strategy: Sense-making in a complex and complicated world. *IBM Systems Journal, 42*(3), 462-483.

McLeod, J., & Childs, S. (2013). A strategic approach to making sense of the "wicked" problem of ERM. *Records Management Journal, 23*(2), 104-135.

Ministry of Science and Education. (2020a). *Action Plan for Development of Distance Education – Distance Education Model.* Retrieved from https://mzo.gov.hr/news/coronavirus-organisation-of-distance-teaching-and-learning-in-croatia/3634

Ministry of Science and Education. (2020b). Coronavirus – organisation. Retrieved 7 May, 2021, from https://mzo.gov.hr/news/coronavirus-organisation-of-distance-teaching-and-learning-in-croatia/3634

Molnar, G., Namesztovszki, Z., Glusac, D., Karuovic, D., & Major, L. (2020). Solutions, experiences in online education in Hungary and Serbia related to the situation caused by Covid-19. *Proceedings of the 2020 11th IEEE CogInfoCom*, 601-606.

OECD. (2015a). *Education Policy Outlook: Hungary.* Retrieved from https://www.oecd.org/education/policyoutlook.htm

OECD. (2015b). *Education Policy Outlook: Slovak Republic.* Retrieved from https://www.oecd.org/education/policyoutlook.htm

OECD. (2019). *TALIS 2018 Results (Volume I) Teachers and School Leaders as Lifelong Learners.* OECD Publishing.

OECD. (2020). *Education Policy Outlook: Finland.* Retrieved from https://www.oecd.org/education/policyoutlook.htm

OECD. (2021). *The state of school education: One year into the COVID pandemic.*

Reimers, F. M., & Schleicher, A. (2020). *A framework to guide an education response to the COVID-19 pandemic of 2020* [OECD Policy Responses to Coronavirus (COVID-19)]. OECD.

Rittel, H. W. J., & Webber, M. M. (1973). Dilemmas in a general theory of planning. *Policy Sciences, 4*(2), 155-169.

Sahlberg, P. (2020). Will the pandemic change schools? *Journal of Professional Capital and Community, 5*(3/4), 359-365.

Snowden, D. (2002). Complex acts of knowing: Paradox and descriptive self-awareness. *Journal of Knowledge Management, 6*(2), 100-111.

Snowden, D. J., & Boone, M. E. (2007). A Leader's Framework for Decision Making. *Harvard Business Review, 10.*

Yin, R. K. (2018). *Case study research and applications: Design and methods* (6th ed.). Los Angeles: SAGE.

Lessons from a Pandemic for the Future of Education
European Distance and E-Learning Network (EDEN) Proceedings
2021 Annual Conference | Madrid, 21-24 June, 2021
ISSN 2707-2819
doi: 10.38069/edenconf-2021-ac0052

THE PERCEPTIONS OF ENGLISH PREPARATORY SCHOOL INSTRUCTORS ON ONLINE EDUCATION THROUGH THE COMMUNITY OF INQUIRY IN THE COVID-19 PROCESS

Sabire Akay, Bahçeşehir University, Kürşat Gültekin, Yıldız Technical University, Eda Şafak, Bilgi University, Sueda Çakir, Biruni University, Ayşegül Liman Kaban, Bahçeşehir University, Turkey

Abstract

The purpose of this study is to investigate the perceptions and experiences of English preparatory school instructors from the perspective of the Community of Inquiry (CoI) framework in online education settings during the Covid-19 pandemic. The study employs a mixed-methods research design, specifically concurrent triangulation design. The quantitative phase of the study includes a survey completed by 140 prep school instructors using snowball sampling. The survey examines the perceptions of participants concerning the three elements of the community of inquiry, teaching presence, social presence and cognitive presence, as well as the challenges the participants faced during online education. The qualitative phase comprises semi-structured interviews with 6 of the participants who took the survey. The interview questions focus on the advantages and disadvantages of online education along with the participants' efforts to create interaction in their classes. Data from the survey were analysed using SPSS in the form of descriptive statistics with means, percentages and standard deviations. The interviews were recorded, transcribed and coded through thematic content analysis. The results of the survey indicate that while a slightly significant positive correlation was found between overall COI, teaching presence and social presence with online teaching experience, no significant correlation was found between online teaching experience and cognitive presence with an r score close to .0. Furthermore, prep school instructors create interaction during online teaching using collaborative tasks, Web 2.0 tools and personal information from students. The findings from the interviews suggest the following emerging themes: assessment and feedback, social interaction and getting to know students, convenience, technical problems, and attendance issues.

Introduction

Countries were faced with a challenging situation when Covid19 hit the world in May 2019. As of the beginning weeks of 2021, more than 100 million cases have been reported (WHO Coronavirus Disease (COVID-19) Dashboard, n.d.). People are losing their loved ones in different parts of the world, while at the same time trying to cope with the emotional side of being in lockdown. The education sector was affected as deeply as all other sectors. Because of the health risks, many schools closed and immediately switched to online education at the start of the crisis. Campuses and school grounds were left empty, and teachers had to speak to their students through a screen. As a result of such a big transition, problems followed: internet connection problems, motivation issues, anxiety, being at home with other members of the family all the time, etc. Many reports were published to offer solutions to the problems. For instance, Dorn et al., (2020) suggested differentiating education according to needs and context, designing systems unique to the online situation, and forming real relationships.

To be able to reach students more effectively during these hard times, the importance of collaboration and interaction has been emphasized. Scull et al., (2020) found participation and engagement to be important concepts during online education. Collaboration helps students enhance their learning process through many benefits. For example, Panitz (1997) reported 67 advantages of collaborative learning. Webb et al. (1997) expressed the benefits of collaborative learning for, especially low achievers. Liman Kaban (2021) reported that collaborative activities resulted in a satisfactory learning environment and that there must be an interaction between teachers, students and the content.

The *Community of Inquiry* model is a collaborative learning approach for the online environment and was created by Garrison et al. (2000). It features three main elements, which are social presence, teaching presence and cognitive presence. All these features interact with each other and are considered important for an effective online learning situation.

With the current Covid19 online education systems in mind, this article aims to examine teachers' perceptions of the online learning process through the lens of Community of Inquiry. In the literature review section, collaborative learning, online collaborative learning and the Community of Inquiry model will be explained. Subsequently, the data will be presented with the survey results regarding teachers' perceptions and interviews with six of the teachers, followed by a discussion of these findings.

Purpose of the Study

It has been known that the education system was affected due to the pandemic, and it has been a major concern. Due to the health threats, schools instantly transitioned to online classes. During these challenging times, to grasp students more successfully, it is important to promote a constructive and engaging atmosphere in the classroom, as it lets students learn and connect. Collaboration allows students to develop their academic experience by offering several advantages. The *Community of Inquiry* model is a collective learning method for the online atmosphere and was developed by Garrison et al. (2000). There are three main aspects which are social presence, teaching presence and cognitive presence. Each of these aspects are interdependent, and the framework requires to have all the features running together to be successful. With the features of CoI in mind, therefore, regarding the findings and the analysis, the purpose of the study is to provide insight about the overall perceptions and experiences of the instructors during the online learning process through the perspective of Community of Inquiry (CoI) during the Covid-19 pandemic.

Literature Review

Collaborative Learning

Although collaborative learning has received considerable attention in recent years, especially with the rise of online platforms, the concept is in fact not new. According to Gaillet (1994), collaborative learning has a long history. Working as a professor of logic and philosophy between 1774 and 1826, George Jardine invented a method for peer review to be used in writing classes. Jardine believed that when learners engaged in collaborative tasks, they would improve interpersonal skills which are important traits for both academic and work life. Jardine argues that a sense of community and learners' taking responsibility are important in the classroom. Bruffee (1984) explains that the term *collaborative* was coined in the 1950's by English middle school teachers and a biologist.

Collaboration is a concept which encompasses a wide range of approaches. For this reason, researchers do not seem to agree on a specific definition of collaborative learning (Dillenbourg, 1999). Roschelle and Teasley (1995, as cited in Dillenbourg, 1999) define collaboration as "a coordinated, synchronous activity that is the result of a continued attempt to construct and maintain a shared conception of a problem". Panitz (1999) states that "Collaboration is a philosophy of interaction and personal lifestyle where individuals are responsible for their actions, including learning and respect the abilities and contributions of their peers."

It may be better to view collaboration as more than just a classroom technique. The term implies a way of handling problems where learners share authority and responsibility, and they respect each other's contributions and together reach consensus (Panitz, 1999). In collaborative learning, there is a paradigm shift from teacher-centeredness to learner-centeredness (Smith & MacGregor, 1992). Emphasis is on learners' interactions where they may have to deal with intragroup conflicts as they improve their interpersonal skills.

Dillenbourg (1999) discusses the importance of interaction while collaborating. Because collaborative learning requires interaction among learners, this interaction results in different cognitive mechanisms than individual learning, such as reduced cognitive load and knowledge elicitation. However, the availability of conditions for interaction may not automatically mean that interaction will occur. A concern is how to raise the chances for interaction to take place. Four ways are suggested:

- setting up initial conditions;
- specifying roles based on a scenario;
- scaffolding interactions by specifying interaction rules;
- monitoring and regulating interactions as a facilitator, rather than a tutor.

Laal and Ghodsi (2001) list four major advantages of collaborative learning: social, psychological, academic benefits, along with innovative techniques for assessment. Panitz (1999) describes an increased understanding among learners as a possible major benefit of collaboration. Collaborative learning also adds to the range of activities in the classroom, and in doing so, does not necessitate complete abandoning of traditional techniques (Smith & MacGregor, 1992). The tasks resemble real-life tasks and prepare learners for business or governmental positions for later in their lives (Bruffe, 1984).

An issue is how to assess student learning at the end of a collaborative process. Dillenbourg (1999) maintains that assessment might be difficult because the collaborative process or product may be vague to assess. Whether to assess individual performance or group performance is another question. Perkins (1993, as cited in Dillenbourg, 1999) states that "assessing group work through individual performance would be as meaningless as assessing a painter without his brush."

Online Collaborative Learning

The emergence of the Internet has led to rapid developments in education and interaction. Harasim (2012) explains the formation of collaborative learning in the internet environment under the title of Online Collaborative Learning Theory as a model where students are reinforced and supported for studying together on a certain focus and as a result, learning is created by actively creating knowledge. In this context, OCL has a three-step system, which includes idea generation, idea organization and intellectual convergence respectively, and these steps together form the foundations of the knowledge community. (Figure 1) Studies in the field of OCL have also considered the participation and role of teachers and teacher candidates in the process and researched their perceptions and views. In a study, it has been revealed that online collaborative learning can be an incentive for teachers at points such as salary, certification, and personal goals (An et al., 2008). In a study conducted by Sansone et al. (2019) with pre-service teachers' on OCL perceptions, it was stated that working in online groups was a positive source of motivation not only individually but also in group integrity. Along with this, it was stated that there can be enrichment in knowledge and skills with OCL through metacognition and creativity.

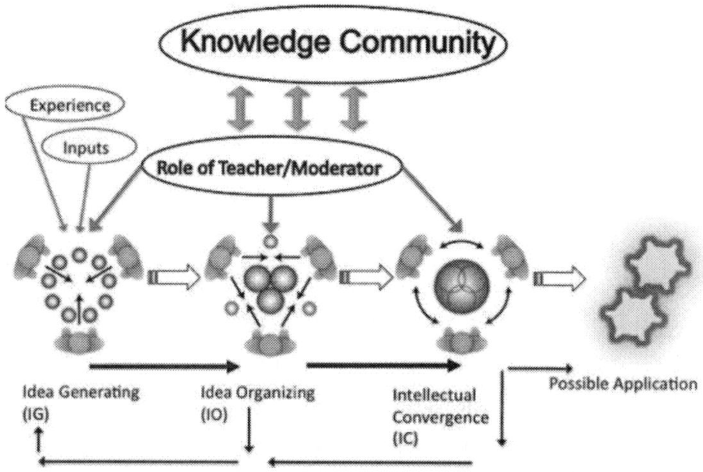

Figure 1. Online Collaborative Learning (from Harasim, 2012; p.95)

OCL has also created various perceptions and thoughts on students, another stakeholder in the education process, and numerous studies have been found in the literature for this. In the student community-oriented study conducted by Waugh et al. (2016), students emphasized a supportive and collaborative learning environment and stated that the amount of communication in the process gradually increased. In a study conducted in the United States, the OCL process of the students was evaluated with the Community of Inquiry model, and it was found that as the students better understood the assessment and instructions in the process, they cooperated better and enabled them to connect with their peers and learn better (Faja, 2013). In a study conducted with graduate students, the perceptions of students from diverse cultures on OCL were studied and the students stated that it offered a cross-cultural opportunity in the knowledge construction process and small group work (Kumi et al., 2017).

It can be stated that the relationship between OCL and various variables in social issues is also investigated in the literature. For example, in a study examining the connection between students' perception on technology and OCL, it was emphasized that collaborative studies influence students' intrinsic motivation and the development of social ties in this process (Magen Nagar et al., 2018). In the research on OCL, the stress state of the students has also become a subject of research. In the studies conducted by Jung et al. (2011), the importance of self-efficacy on OCL stress was emphasized and it was stated that Japanese students' collaboration process and use of technology can cause stress on OCL as well. Studies on the connection of OCL with 21st century skills can be found in the literature. In the study conducted by Simpson (2010), OCL and critical thinking were studied, and the study conducted over book rap, it was stated that OCL is a situation that supports the critical thinking process through student engagement. In the studies conducted in 2020, interactions between online collaboration and the Covid-19 process were also examined. In the study of Järvelä et al. (2020) on group interactions in the pandemic process, it was stated that a well-developed collaborative learning process can increase group performance and have an impact on metacognition. Demuyakor (2020) conducted research on online learning in pandemics in higher education institutions and revealed the difficulty of community building, social interaction, and collaboration in this study. In summary, in these studies in the literature, it can be stated that OCL has effects on teachers and students in cognitive, social, and other fields.

Community of Inquiry (CoI)

Garrison et al. (2000) extended and implemented the theories of Lipman (2013) and Dewey (1959) as a theoretical basis for online learning. The first premise was that preparation for higher learning is more incorporated into a student/teacher inquiry community (Lipman, 1991). Lipman (2003) proposed that analytical or reflective thought and curriculum methodologies ought to be built by a community of inquiry. This presumption also corresponded to the educational theory of Dewey (1959), which defined education as a mutual remodelling of background. The surroundings of the analysis were an experience of collaborative and constructional learning in a research environment.

Figure 2. Community of Inquiry Image (from Anderson & Koole, 2013)

Garrison (2011) defines a community of inquiry (CoI) as a community of individuals working collaboratively to build personal sense and shared understanding through intentional critical discourse and reflection. The CoI framework advocates deep methods instead of surface learning approaches and attempts to create the conditions needed for improved cognitive processing. Among various theories of online education, the CoI model concentrates on simple philosophical and epistemological concepts and theories of learning. In this way, the CoI system represents a mechanism to create a clear in-depth learning atmosphere by building up three components: social presence, cognitive presence, and teaching presence (see Figure 1). All three presences must be matched to have a successful investigative mechanism and to achieve better order learning.

Akyol and Garrison (2011) in more than 10 years of study, CoI theoretical framework has verified its tremendous ability to build, direct and analyse e-learning methods, tactics, and techniques – notwithstanding the fact that the dimensionality of the CoI theoretical framework components and dynamics are validated. The primary implication is that the CoI system has contributed to a rigorous analysis of how to use distance education to promote strategic thought and improved learning outcomes. The theoretical structure of the CoI is adopted to contribute a design of metacognitive knowledge, online discourse, and the control of reflection.

Considering the previous studies in the literature, this study aims to examine the perception of English preparatory school instructors' online education within the framework of Community of Inquiry (COI) and seek answers to the following research questions:

- What are the perceptions of teachers in online teaching environments from the perspectives of Community of Inquiry (COI)?
- How do university English preparatory school instructors create interaction during Covid-19 pandemic?
- What are instructors' experiences with online collaborative learning during Covid-19 pandemic?

Methodology

Research Design

This study employs mixed methods research design with a quantitative survey and qualitative interview phase. The mixed methods approach is preferred for several reasons. Creswell (2009) states that such an approach strengthens understanding and that results from one approach supports those from the other. In particular, the concurrent triangulation design is chosen for this study due to time constraints to collect data. As for the timing of data collection and analysis, qualitative and quantitative data will be collected concurrently, analysed separately, and findings will subsequently be compared. As Creswell (2009) indicates, concurrent data collection may be necessary when time limits impose a constraint. This also prevents revisiting the data collection site multiple times. Quantitative and qualitative data are regarded to have equal weight in this research, and thus contribute with equal importance. Findings from both types of data support each other and strengthen the findings. Morse (1991) also mentions that methodological triangulation, the use of more than one types of data, enhances the power of the findings, and helps address an issue more effectively.

A visual diagram which summarizes the process in this study can be found below. In this diagram, a mixed methods notation is used where capital letters for both qualitative and quantitative abbreviations imply equal importance, and arrows between the collection and analysis phases suggest a sequence.

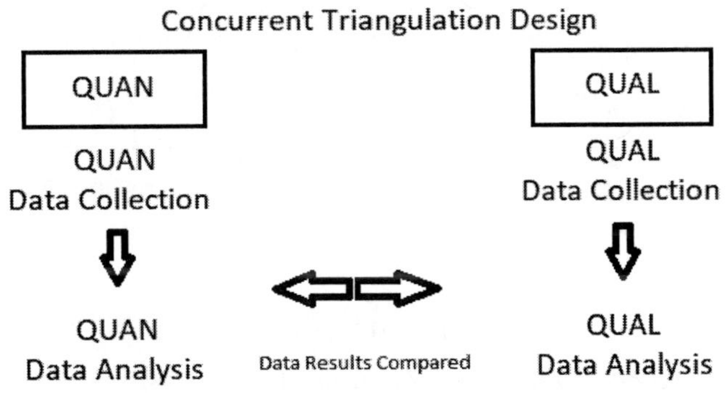

Figure 3. A Visual Diagram of the Research Design (Taken from Creswell, 2009)

Setting and Procedures

The present study aims to investigate the perceptions of prep teachers in online teaching environments from the perspective of CoI. In that sense, the context of this study is prep schools in Turkey. As the sampling method of the study is random, many instructors from various universities around Turkey participated to study. In general, the students in Turkey take a proficiency exam to establish whether they would start their departments immediately or a prep year is required. According to the results of the exam, the students are replaced to appropriate level classes to learn English. (A1, A2, B1, B2, C1). The levels are determined by CEFR. The general duration of the prep program lasts seven months and four modules which includes skills and main course classes. Some of the institutions provide an integrated approach, whereas some of them offer skill-based instruction. At the end of the program, students reach a level where they have common skills in English.

For this study, various prep schools from universities around Turkey are sampled, including public and foundational ones. Although there are slight differences in their program, one significant is common for this term; all schools offer online education. The general aim of all prep programs is to deliver quality English language education to students who are non-native speakers of English; and further, to equip them with the English language skills they will need to express themselves competently in the context of English medium instruction within their departments. Along with this the programs assure for the instructors an encouraging environment for professional development, critical thinking skills and digital skills. The students receive 20 hours of instruction on average. Each lesson lasts 45 minutes, and all the schools employ a communicative-based approach to teach a foreign language.

In prep schools, the instructors are graduates of ELT, ELL, or Linguistics. Many of them are graduates of MA, however, there are some who are current MA students. Their age ranges to 23 to 50. Their teaching experience ranges 1 to 20. All of them deliver online lessons currently. The schools are based in Turkey.

The data collection tool, which is a survey, will be sent to instructors online. The participation is voluntary. The participants will do the survey online and send it through Google Forms. Also, the interviews will be held online due to the current situation. The overall data will be collected once the optimum number of instructors are surveyed.

Participants

The population of this study is the EFL instructors in Turkey whereas the sample is the EFL instructors at English preparatory schools of universities. Certain generalizations about the population who are EFL instructors in Turkey can be made with the data which was collected from the narrowed target group sample as EFL teachers at preparatory schools of three foundation universities and one state university.

This study was carried out with 140 (109 females, 31 males) EFL instructors working at English preparatory schools of foundation and state universities located in Turkey. Among 140 participants, regarding the age groups, 5 of the instructors were under the age of 25. 31 instructors were between the ages of 25–29 years old, 67 instructors were between the ages of 30–39 while 29 instructors were between 40–49 years old. Lastly, 8 of the instructors were between 50–59 years old. With respect to the highest level of education, out of 80 participants, 49 instructors hold a bachelor's degree whereas 81 instructors have a master's degree. Lastly, 10 instructors hold a doctoral degree.

On behalf of years of teaching experience, among the 140 participants, 34 instructors had 1–5 years of experience, 39 instructors had 6–10 years of experience and teaching experience of 34 instructors was 11–15 years. In addition, 12 participants had 16–20 years of teaching experience. Finally, 21 participants had more than 20 years of teaching experience.

Regarding the online teaching experience, 32 instructors have been teaching online for 1 to 6 months whereas 81 instructors have been teaching online for 7 to 11 months. In addition, 20 instructors have been teaching online for 1 to 3 years while the 4 instructors had 4–5 years of online teaching experience. Finally, 3 instructors have been teaching online more than 5 years.

With respect to the language levels that instructors teach, out of 140 instructors, 19 instructors teach A1 level, 58 instructors teach A2, 34 instructors teach B1 level, 17 instructors teach B2 level, and 11 instructors teach C1 level. Finally, 1 instructor teaches C2 level.

Additionally, in terms of daily internet consumption, 72 teachers have been online 1 to 6 hours, 58 teachers have been online 7 to 12 hours and lastly 10 teachers have been online more than 13 hours in a day.

Furthermore, on behalf of the existing students, out of 140 participants, 6 instructors had 2 to 10 students, 52 instructors had 11 to 20 number of students, 63 instructors had 21 to 30 number of students and 9 of the instructors had 31 to 49 number of students. Finally, 10 of the instructors had 50 to 99 students.

Regarding the specific area instructors teach, out of 140 instructors, 84 of them teach language-based courses and 49 of the instructors teach skill-based courses. In addition, 2 of the instructors teach both language-based and skill- based courses. Regarding the other areas, one instructor teaches content-based courses, one teaches SAP health, the other one teaches integrated skills supported by grammar handout and finally one teacher gives teacher training courses.

For the sake of this study, participants will be selected randomly to apply random sampling. During the selection process, random sampling will be applied for both quantitative and qualitative data to gather in depth information about the phenomenon.

Data Collection

Table 1: COI Survey Instrument

Presence Categories	Sub-Categories	Item Number
Teaching Presence	Design & Organization	4 Items
	Facilitation	6 Items
	Direct Instruction	3 Items
Social Presence	Affective Expression	3 Items
	Open Communication	3 Items
	Group Cohesion	3 Items
Cognitive Presence	Triggering Event	3 Items
	Exploration	3 Items
	Integration	3 Items
	Resolution	3 Items
TOTAL		34 Items

In this mixed research study, data was collected in a single time with survey and semi-structured interview as qualitative and quantitative. The Community of Inquiry (COI) Survey (Arbaugh et al., 2008) instrument was used for quantitative data with minor adaptations to collect the data online via Google Forms. The original COI survey is a presence survey that consists of three parts and includes general evaluation of education through presences by students (Table 1).

Since this study includes the evaluation of teachers' online education process, the emphasis on teacher perspective and online education was added to the items with 5-points Likert scale from strongly disagree to strongly agree (Appendix A). In the first section of the survey, demographic information questions were included in the form of gender, age, educational status, and the institution of work. In the second section of the survey, items related to teacher presence were given under three headings. In the third section, questions about social presence were given under three headings. In the fourth section, cognitive presence questions were given under four headings. The use of surveys benefits researchers because of its economical and fast turnarounds (Creswell, 2009). The use of Google Forms facilitates the reporting of question-oriented and participant-oriented outputs, supports the electronic storage of information in the system and the security of participant information. To increase the reliability of the interview, the original survey and the adapted version was presented to the field expert and her opinion was taken. Besides, Cronbach's Alpha was used to calculate internal consistency due to adaptations made on the survey. In the qualitative part of the study, 10 participants were selected with purposeful sampling and semi-structured interviews were held with these participants to detail the opinions of the participants on the subject. It has been stated to the participants that the interviews were used for research purposes and will be recorded, and their consent has been obtained. According to Creswell (2009), interviews provide an advantage in increasing the in-depth explanation of the study by adding the thoughts and experiences of the participants. Furthermore, interviews can provide a multidisciplinary approach by creating a balance between empathetic engagement objective awareness with individuals' views and common points (Miles et al., 1994). For the participants to express their opinions more easily, the questions were given in Turkish, and the answers were collected in Turkish. These questions are:

- What are the advantages and disadvantages of the online education process?
- What are you doing to create classroom interaction in this process?

Data Analysis

All responses of the participants were exported via Google Forms for the quantitative part. Quantitative data items were analysed in the form of descriptive statistics with means, percentages, and standard deviation. The data obtained from Google Forms were transferred to SPSS and tables and trends will be given through demographics and presences. For qualitative data analysis, first interview audio recordings were written down. The analysis was done as thematic content analysis by hand. According to Miles et al., (1994), thematic content analysis enables researchers to create a systematic and organized cognitive map for the common themes and patterns. After the participants' responses were examined in general terms, codes were created in chunks, and categories and themes were created based on these codes. Interpretation of the created theme and important codes has been made in the further sections. For the reliability of the created themes and codes, a cross-check was made by the researchers and the results obtained were compared. The interpretation of all the information obtained from data analysis is available in the findings and discussion sections.

Findings

This section shows the findings based on the research questions. Findings are presented as both quantitative (COI Questionnaire) and Qualitative (Semi-structured interviews) data. While the first research question focuses on teachers' perceptions of online education by addressing Community of Inquiry elements and items, the second research question targets the findings of teachers' collaboration in online education. On the other hand, the third question aimed to reveal teachers' experiences of collaborative practices in online education.

Quantitative Findings

In this part of the study, the first research question focusing on quantitative data will be discussed. The data obtained with the COI Questionnaire was analysed using the Pearson Correlation Coefficient with the SPSS v26 tool. The findings of the quantitative analysis related to the research question are presented below with tables.

Findings related to the 1st research question

Descriptive statistics and Pearson correlation coefficient were applied to questionnaire data focusing on COI elements and online teaching duration data.

To determine the effect of the Community of Inquiry model on the online teaching experience of the instructors, descriptive statistics with means and standard deviation examined for overall COI and COI elements. Table 2 below shows the mean and SD of the overall COI and COI elements for the sample group. As shown in the table, the mean score of the overall questionnaire is 3.95 with a standard deviation of 0.89. For the sub-headings of the Community of Inquiry, the mean score of the teaching presence is 4.16 with a standard deviation of 0.82 while the mean score of social presence is 3.71 with 1 standard deviation. The last component of model, cognitive presence has 3.90 mean score with a standard deviation of 0.87.

Table 2: The Means of the COI Questionnaire

Group	M	SD	N
COI Overall Questionnaire	3.95	0.89	140
Teaching Presence	4.16	0.82	140
Social Presence	3.71	1.00	140
Cognitive Presence	3.9	0.87	140

To find out the item-based descriptive scores, mean and standard deviation for each element is calculated. The result of the item-based descriptive statistics is shown in Table 3 below. For the teaching presence, mean score of item 2 "I clearly communicate important course goals." is 4.39 with a 0.79 standard deviation as the strongest element, followed by item 11 "I help to focus discussion on relevant issues in a way that helps the students to learn." with 4.30 mean score and standard deviation of 0.88 and item 10 "My actions reinforce the development of a sense of community among the students." with a 4.28 mean score and a standard deviation of 0.87.

Table 3: The means of the Teaching Presence Items

Item	Mean	SD	N
T1	4.25	0.74	140
T2	4.39	0.79	140
T3	4.14	0.80	140
T4	4.26	0.81	140
T5	4.07	0.81	140
T6	4.09	0.82	140
T7	4.09	0.89	140
T8	4.00	0.89	140
T9	4.19	0.81	140
T10	4.28	0.87	140
T11	4.30	0.88	140
T12	4.08	0.81	140
T13	4.07	0.79	140
T14	4.12	0.80	140

For the category of social presence, item 7 "I feel comfortable disagreeing with my students while still maintaining a sense of trust." selected as the strongest element with 4.02 mean and standard deviation of 0.90 followed by item 1 "Getting to know my students gives me a sense of belonging in the course." with 3.98 mean score and a standard deviation of 0.86 and item 6 "I feel comfortable making my students interact with other students." With 3.96 mean score and a standard deviation of 0.95.

Table 4: The means of the Social Presence Items

Item	Mean	SD	N
S1	3.98	0.86	140
S2	2.94	1.20	140
S3	3.56	1.07	140
S4	3.8	0.99	140
S5	3.73	1.07	140
S6	3.96	0.95	140
S7	4.02	0.90	140
S8	3.66	1.02	140
S9	3.82	0.95	140

Table 5: The means of the Cognitive Presence Items

Item	Mean	SD	N
C1	3.71	0.91	140
C2	4.24	0.83	140
C3	3.91	0.98	140
C4	4.04	0.84	140
C5	3.86	0.94	140
C6	4.21	0.78	140
C7	4.07	0.76	140
C8	4.04	0.80	140
C9	3.65	0.92	140
C10	3.72	0.87	140
C11	3.67	0.94	140
C12	3.64	0.86	140

For the category of cognitive presence, item 2 "My course activities pique curiosity on students." is the strongest element with the mean score of 4.24 and a standard deviation of 0.83 followed by item 6 "I have my students use online discussions so that they can appreciate different perspectives." with 4.21 mean score and a standard deviation of 0.78 and item 4 "I make students use various sources of information to approach the problems that arise." with the mean score of 4.04 and a standard deviation of 0.84 and item 8 "I enable the students to create explanations and solutions with the learning activities." with the mean score of 4.04 and a standard deviation of 0.80.

To find out the correlation level and significance between the Community of Inquiry model elements and online teaching experience of the sample group, Pearson Correlation Coefficient was performed. The results of the Pearson Correlation Coefficient are shown in the Table 6. As illustrated in the table, there is a positive and slightly significant correlation between the online teaching experience of the sample group and overall COI model; $P > .05$. The correlation score of 0.069, which is near to 1, shows that between COI model and online teaching experience, there is a small strength of association.

Table 6: Pearson Correlation Coefficient

		Online Teaching Experience	COI Model
Online Teaching Experience	Pearson Correlation	1	0.069
	Sig. (2-tailed)		0.446
	N	140	140
COI Model	Pearson Correlation	0.069	1
	Sig. (2-tailed)	0.446	
	N	140	140

To make a more detailed interpretation about the sub-categories, correlation scores between sub-categories and online teaching experience calculated separately as well. The results of the correlation score of the teaching presence and online teaching experience is given in the Table 7. As shown in the table, there is a positive and slightly significant correlation between online teaching experience and teaching presence category; $P > 0.5$. The correlation found for online teaching experience and teaching presence as 0.097, which can be assumed as small strength of association with a close score to .1.

Table 7: Pearson Correlation Coefficient

		Online Teaching Experience	Teaching Presence
Online Teaching Experience	Pearson Correlation	1	0.097
	Sig. (2-tailed)		0.254
	N	140	140
Teaching Presence	Pearson Correlation	0.097	1
	Sig. (2-tailed)	0.254	
	N	140	140

Table 8 below shows the correlation level between social presence and online teaching experience. As shown in the table, the correlation between these two items indicates a slightly significant positive correlation with 0.086 correlation r score: $P > 0.5$. It means there is a small strength of association between social presence and online teaching experience with a score near to .1 r score.

Table 8: Pearson Correlation Coefficient

		Online Teaching Experience	Social Presence
Online Teaching Experience	Pearson Correlation	1	0.086
	Sig. (2-tailed)		0.311
	N	140	140
Social Presence	Pearson Correlation	0.086	1
	Sig. (2-tailed)	0.311	
	N	140	140

Lastly, for the category of cognitive presence, Table 9 shows the correlation level between cognitive presence and online teaching experience. As shown in the table, there is no correlation between online teaching experience and cognitive presence $P > 0.5$. The correlation found for online teaching experience and cognitive presence as 0.025, which can be assumed as no strength of association with a close score to 0.

Table 9: Pearson Correlation Coefficient

		Online Teaching Experience	Cognitive Presence
Online Teaching Experience	Pearson Correlation	1	0.025
	Sig. (2-tailed)		0.733
	N	140	140
Cognitive Presence	Pearson Correlation	0.025	1
	Sig. (2-tailed)	0.773	
	N	140	140

Overall, the results show that considering the online teaching experience and COI model, while a slightly significant positive correlation was found between overall COI, teaching presence and social presence with online teaching experience, no significant correlation was found between online teaching experience and cognitive presence with an r score close to .0.

Qualitative Findings

After completing the quantitative phase of the study with a questionnaire, qualitative study conducted with semi-structured interviews with 6 participants. Two main questions were asked as planned and clarification and verification questions were added with the sequence of the interviews. The data obtained with semi-structured interviews were coded by the researchers, and then categories and themes were created. The findings of the qualitative data analysis are given below in connection with the second and third research questions.

Findings related to the 2nd research question

In this part of the study, the second research question is focused on, and the distribution of interaction-oriented elements is included.

Table 10: Interaction-based Themes

Interaction	Use of Collaborative Tasks
	Use of Web 2.0 Tools
	Use of Personal Information

The themes that emerge from the interviews with teachers regarding interaction are use of collaborative tasks, use of Web 2.0 tools, and use of personal information themes. In the interviews, it was determined that the participants had problems with interaction at first, and then they tried to find solutions to these problems in the axis of the themes specified.

Use of Collaborative Tasks

Use of collaborative tasks has been determined as one of the methods frequently used by teachers to provide and strengthen interaction in online lessons. It was understood that this had positive outcomes in the lessons. For example, according to the 1st interviewee, it was stated that collaborative tools influence student-student interaction:

> *"...We had collaborative task days in face-to-face education. They were doing numerous studies in groups. We started doing this online as well, and thus, we created student-student interaction..."*

This view was supported by the 2nd interviewee as follows:

> *"And I started to use group work or pair work activity. There were some breakout rooms for the online tools. I mean, I changed the rooms between the students so that they can be pairs, or they can be in a group with the other team."*

It is also expressed by the 2nd interviewee that the collaborative studies provide interaction with students as well as engagement:

> *"...And I got into the room, and I was just very excited because I didn't expect my students to be so engaged as that."*

Moreover, interviewee 6 emphasized the importance of motivation and attention in interaction and collaborative tasks by adding.

> *"To motivate them, I try to spare at least one-third of the lesson to speaking to interactive activities. It is pair work or group work and speaking and playing games."*

In addition to all these, she explained the focus of the students in this process as follows:

> *"They really liked games with each other, but mostly they like interacting with each other in groups."*

Considering the findings on collaborative tasks and interaction, it can be stated that positive reflections are obtained from the teacher interviews.

Use of Web 2.0 Tools

The second point that teachers discuss interaction is to include various Web 2.0 tools in the process. Teachers explained how they used Web 2.0 tools for interaction in the process by giving examples from several tools. For example, interviewee 1 gave examples of Web 2.0 tools and explained that his interaction was positively affected as follows:

> *"...I started to use the web tools we used in the classroom, also online. I think the interaction within the lesson has increased with web tools such as Padlet, Voicethread, Nearpod."*

Interviewee 2 supported this idea by offering the following similar web 2.0 tools:

> *"...I use them online, online, different applications, like for instance: Google jamboard, popplet, padlet, I mean, they are very useful."*

Moreover, she reported that such tools are also good for engaging students and increasing their curiosity as follows:

> *"They want to see it more. for that reason, that was another effective way for me to keep up the interaction because they were asking questions, even if they do not understand they just ask "Oh, teacher, what does it mean?"*

Interviewee 3 expresses that Web 2.0 tools are beneficial in terms of interaction in groups and discussion questions as follows:

> *"I used Mentimeter and Jamboard a lot. I make them groups and ask them to discuss the questions on Mentimeter and Padlet."*

Furthermore, comments that Web 2.0 tools are also advantageous in terms of synchronous interaction have been made by interviewee 6:

> *"I use Google Documents, and make groups with the students. I ask them to use Google Documents to write jointly at the same time. They really liked it and found it really helpful, beneficial for each other because they interact, speak to each other and at the same time, they write it, they can make the changes."*

Considering the interview outputs, the participants achieved positive results in terms of the interaction of Web 2.0 tools.

Use of Personal Information

The last interaction method used jointly by the participants is the use of personal information. Positive and negative outcomes were obtained in this regard. For example, Interviewee 4 has stated that it has started this process quite well:

> *"I started the year by asking them to write to me, to send me an email telling me about themselves, telling me anything that they would like, personal or not, or just how many siblings they do have and things like that."*

He added that he categorized all this data in numerous ways to use it while creating interaction afterwards:

> *"...first of all, I made lists of students according to their likes and dislikes for example, which student does what, what kind of music he listens..."*

He stated that at the end of this process, which he progressed by transforming from small groups to large groups, he achieved positive outcomes:

> *"...they are talking to each other; they are interacting with each other all the time."*

It is possible to encounter similar outputs during the interview with Interviewee 6:

> *"...it's like you put students into groups and you can also change their groups, their pairs. In this way, they start to get to know each other better..."*

Interviewee 2 also stated that he used personal questions to learn more about students:

> *"So, it was like, you know, I was asking personal questions. I was asking, you know, more and more on individual questions."*

However, he stated that he could not get the outputs he expected in this regard:

> *"...but then I saw that it wasn't very well ... They did not, Even Some of them didn't listen to each other."*

In this context, it has been revealed that personal information has positive results in some groups as well as negative results in some groups.

Findings related to the 3rd research question

Six themes were created from the survey open ended questions and these themes are assessment and feedback, social interaction, convenience, technical problems, getting to know the students, and attendance issues.

Assessment & Feedback

Assessing and evaluating students' progress was another issue described by most of the participants. When their experiences were asked about the online teaching process, the difficulty of assessing students' improvement in online settings was mentioned by instructors. Some of them investigated this issue in terms of cheating and plagiarism. They mentioned the difficulty of determining if the students are doing their exams on their own or not. For instance, Interviewee 1 explained her experiences:

> *"...the school decided not to use locker applications during the tests. However, because of this, visible copying and plagiarism problems occurred in student works. To prevent this, we started sending the questions randomly from the pool system, but we still know that the students somehow continue this plagiarism".*

Even if many institutions started to take some precautions, the assessing issue was considered as an ambiguous process. Like Interviewee 1, Interviewee 2 shared her experiences and emphasized the difficulty of observing students' development. She stated:

> *"They might, you know, if you give them writing homework, they might just do it from Google Translate. And it was a problem for me because I was asking their own thoughts, their own ideas, and their own learning process."*

> *"So, I couldn't see their writing, how much actually, how developed the writings were at the end of the term."*

Interviewee 4 also dwelled on the same point but additionally argued that this is similar with traditional settings, and it is up to students who are willing to learn or not:

> *"We don't even know whether they do their exams on their own or not, so you just have to trust them, we'll let the one who wants to learn and let the others who don't, get away with it, and that's the same whether you're teaching at school or online."*

Some of them evaluated this issue from a distinct perspective rather than cheating, as Interviewee 1 suggested, the assessment process is challenging as you do not evaluate it on paper, but from a computer, which is tiring. Not all the experiences were negative in terms of assessment and evaluation. According to the answers given by the participants, assessment in online education has some advantages as it develops students' skills of technology and collaboration. Interviewee 1 shared her experiences as follows:

> *"A more reflective evaluation process was formed for the students in this process. The final and midterm exam decision of the school also affected us, and we updated our assessment mostly as individual and group projects. Students evolved both technologically and as 21st century skills by making a variety of presentations, videos, poster work, and discussion forums and they became more focused in their learning process."*

Assessing students' improvement via exams is not sufficient. Teachers need to evaluate their students' progress regularly by giving feedback to their work. When the participants shared their experiences, they also emphasized their problems and solutions they found about giving feedback. Different strategies were employed by different instructors. As Interviewee 1 explained her experiences about giving feedback to students' writings homework:

> *"At first, I was forgetting the beginning and end of the sentence while I was reading. Later, I started using audio feedback to solve this. I was able to create specific and overall feedback by recording my thoughts piece by piece."*

Other participants who experienced the same problems, produced different solutions. Interviewee 2 found diverse ways to overcome feedback problems such as utilizing peer feedback and online collaborative feedback tools:

> *"I use some online documents like I was giving them online feedback, I was writing something, and I was asking a question. I was asking a question. And then they were writing the answer question to the documents, and they were doing it simultaneously. So, I was able to give them feedback online*

> *while I am seeing them. They were while they were writing, I was seeing them. So, it was an effective way for me to give them more accurate, more fluent feedback. And sometimes I was using it for peer feedback. And it was also a good one because they were seeing each other online and they gave feedback to each other."*

Social interaction

Most of the teacher participants interviewed complained about the difficulty of creating social interaction in the online lessons. Some of them reported overcoming such difficulties by using some techniques. For instance, interviewee 1 stated that he had difficulty interaction in class in the beginning because the students had their cameras turned off, but he later found a solution and "the interaction within the lesson has increased with web tools such as Padlet, VoiceThread, Nearpod." Interviewee 2 had the same problem regarding turned-off cameras since she thought not seeing the students meant a lack of eye contact and body language. She believed that seeing them through cameras was necessary to understand their needs and added that using breakout rooms worked as a solution because.

> *"They were asking questions to each other, and they seemed more enthusiastic because they were joking and they were making fun of it."*

Interviewee 5 looked at the camera issue at a different angle: She considered seeing students' homes as something we did not have during face-to-face education because.

> *"You know more about their privacy, this is interesting because if they turn on their camera, you can see where they live, so you can see their room, their bedroom, their living room."*

Besides using cameras in class, another concern for the interviewed teachers was trying to get to know the students. They reported trying diverse ways to know their students on a personal level. For instance, interviewee 4 explained that she began every lesson with a song while the students waited for her to start the lesson. At the beginning of the semester, the same teacher asked her students to write personal emails to her and talk about themselves in the emails.

> *"[She tried] to memorize anything, any small information that they thought valuable to give to me."*

She added:

> *"... all I made lists of students according to their likes and dislikes for example, which student does what, what kind of music he listens, what kind of sports she has done, oh these two, they play tennis so I should talk about this, I should mention them and put them in a Breakout room together and things like that."*

Interviewee 6 mentioned that even they had the group work opportunities via breakout rooms, the class still lacked the cooperation, or the real atmosphere. It should be added that this teacher mostly had his camera turned off because of connection problems.

Attendance Issues

Most teachers interviewed reported issues related to attendance. For interviewee 1, being present as a student was something that she expected from her students mainly because student presence was necessary for her to understand their needs and interests, and to connect with them. She stated that she only saw some students.

> *"Maybe three or four times. Just that is it for the whole semester. They do not like it. And I needed it."*

Not all interviewees reported attendance as a disadvantage. Interviewee 2 explained that students were at home and had nothing else to do; therefore, they came back to online class immediately after the break. In contrast, during face-to-face education, she explained that she told.

> *"the ten minutes and then they come after 20 minutes. Some of them are not extremely strict about time even if I told them over and over, they didn't do it."*

However, she mentioned one drawback regarding this issue, as well.

> *"Some of my students didn't, you know, you don't always know what the problem of the students is not coming to the class. I mean, sometimes there is a technical problem. You might trust your students."*

As a result, interviewee 2 felt there could be a connection between a student being absent in class and technological problems; yet, she had doubts in her mind. In the situation with interviewee 5, she had attendance problems in the class with which she had communication problems. She had another class where everything seemed to run smoothly, but in this class which she could not find a common ground in terms of communication,

> *"The number of students who attend my classes and my partner's classes, I can say that, is like between 5 and 8. This is the number of students and when you have them, the thing is they don't laugh at your jokes, they are like robots."*

Interviewee 6 related attendance problems to the availability of the lesson recordings, because students knew they could watch the lessons later even if they were absent. The teacher reported that he

> *"Used to have full attendance, especially starting from the beginning. But now, most of the term went by fifty percent of attendance. And it dropped even by half so far, at the last four weeks, I must say. Just 6 or 6, between 7 to 10 students started to attend classes."*

He considered another factor for poor attendance, which was the long hours of classes. He explained that students might have found sitting for four full hours in front of the computer too long.

Convenience

The other theme elicited from the interviews is "Convenience". Most of the participants stated that their experience of the online education process is convenient, and they reported some personal advantages about the online education process. In addition, participants expressed their opinions that the process is time-saving and comfortable when they compare the online education process with face-to-face education. For example, interviewee 3 expressed his opinions on convenience as follows:

> *"First of all, regarding the advantages... I can say that it is convenient, easy to conduct, easy to follow both for me and for my students, no preparation is needed in terms of physical activities. So far everything has been good for me, there is a safe environment, and I haven't encountered any problems at all."*

Like interviewee 3, interviewee 4 felt the same in terms of the convenience of the online education process and shared her personal feelings about the process as advantages. Interviewee 4 reported her feelings as follows:

> *"Should I talk about personal advantages? OK... then setting up a lesson in the comforts of my own house makes everything easier and I feel less tired*

> *when I'm starting the first lesson in the morning for example, so as I am less tired, I am more relaxed, I am usually relaxed in the classroom."*

Furthermore, interviewee 4 gave an example about why she felt comfortable and convenient during the process as follows:

> *"For example I start every morning by playing a fun song so whenever I start the lesson whenever the students start coming into the Zoom, I greet them, I welcome them by dancing and playing a good song to them so it is much better than the classroom because in the classroom the only thing that I can do is just to say" good morning, how are you, are you awake yet", or things like that... so here it feels more personal."*

In analogy to the opinions of the interviewees above, participant 5 shared his feelings on personal advantages of the online education process as follows:

> *"Like most people, I can begin with, not having to get up at 6 in the morning, for example, because this was my usual time. Now almost I save 2 hours from the morning, and then, going to school and coming back home, this is like 3 hours, so I can say that I save almost 5 hours a day. You do not have to get up early, this is a big advantage. If you do not live so close to the campus, and this is the biggest advantage I can say. And of course, you teach from the comfort of your home. You see this is my armchair. I mean I am comfortable. Not like you're in the class."*

Besides the 4 interviews mentioned above, interviewee 6 shared the same opinions with the other participants that the process has physical advantages for teachers. In addition, participant 6 reported the burdens of going to school. According to his experience, he mentioned that not waking up early, getting dressed and stacking in traffic was quite relaxing.

Technical Problems

According to the interviews, the theme "Technical Problems" emerged as a disadvantage of the online education process. Most of the participants shared similar and common opinions on technical problems that they have been going through during the online education process.

According to interviewee 2, technical problems occurred during the process from time to time. He explained the issue as a disadvantage as follows:

> *"Well... for the technical problems, some of my students didn't, you know, you don't always know what the problem of the students is not coming to the class. I mean, sometimes there is a technical problem."*

Besides, he supported his opinions with an example as follows:

> *"I have to say open your camera; I want you to speak. But they do not want to do it because I do not know why. They say my microphone is broken, so I cannot open it right now. I have to create other solutions for them."*

Regarding the technical problems, interviewee 3 mentioned the technical problems as a disadvantage as follows:

> *"So... Well... there might be some external difficulties and problems such as internet connection, computer, not enough equipment and so on."*

Furthermore, interviewee 6 had similar opinions as participant 3 that internet connection is a disadvantage of the online process. Interviewee 6 supported his opinions on technical problems as follows:

> *"We cannot turn on the cameras; you know... because of the internet connection. At the beginning, I always stuck to turning on the camera, but later, there were connection problems with me or the students or on the system, but we started not to turn on the cameras."*

In analogy to the statements of the participants above, interviewee 1 reported the technical problems as a disadvantage as well. During interview 1, it was reported that to be unaware of technology in this century was the biggest problem and participant 1 explained his opinion with an example as follows:

> *"We also had some technological problems. When we switched to MS Teams, there were no breakout rooms at first. It was torture to have the group work done synchronously. Fortunately, the breakout room feature was also active for MS Teams. These were one of the biggest problems because they caused a lot of glitches in the classroom. Although we publish many guidelines, brochures, helpdesks, videos, it is very sad that that's happening still."*

Remote Education Tools

As shown below in Table 11, considering the findings of the interviews in terms of remote education tools, the following tools are utilized the most by the participants of the study.

Table 11: Remote Education Web Tools

Learning Management System	Video Conferencing Tools	Web 2.0 Tools	Communication Tools
Itslearning	Zoom MS Teams Adobe Connect	Nearpod Dice Rolling Jamboard Popplet Padlet Mentimeter Classroom Screen Kahoot Quizlet Google Docs	Whatsapp

Discussion

Discussion of findings of 1st Research Question

When the literature is examined, it is exceedingly difficult to come across COI-focused surveys in which the participants consist of teachers. In one of these studies, Knudsen (2019) discussed teachers' evaluation of the professional development process with the COI framework. As a result of this study, considering three presences, teaching presence got the highest result, while social presence got the lowest result. Considering the overall mean scores, there is a positive alignment between the current study and Knudsen (2019) study. There are some studies conducted with teacher candidates by considering COI survey, in the literature. For example, in the study conducted by Makri et al. (2014), the relationship between pre-service teachers' education and blended learning was examined with COI, and considering three presences in this study, teaching presence got the highest result, while social presence was the lowest. This result is in line with the current study as well. On the other hand, there are no previous studies involving the relationship between both online teaching experience and COI. In line with the correlation data obtained from this study, it can be considered as a pioneer study in future studies on online teaching experience and COI.

Discussion of findings of 2nd Research Question

The findings obtained in response to the second research question focused on interaction and at this point, collaborative tasks, Web 2.0 tools and personal information sub-findings were obtained. In this context, considering the COI, the findings mostly match under the title of social presence. First, Yamada and Goda (2018) focused on COI and collaborative tasks and stated that collaborative tasks have a positive effect on social presence as a result of supporting them with a good interface. Moreover, in the study conducted by So and Brush (2008), a link was found between collaborative learning and social presence, and a positive result was obtained by seeing that this link supports satisfaction. When the results of this study were examined, in-line results were obtained with these studies in the literature and a link was found between collaborative tasks and social presence. Secondly, when the literature is examined, it is possible to come across studies focused on interaction, Web 2.0 tools and social presence. For example, Cunningham (2015) focused on the effect of Voki on social presence and concluded that it is positively effective in creating a social presence in an online environment. Similarly, Holbeck and Hartman (2018) examined four Web 2.0 tools named Flipgrid, Breakout Edu, Loom and Remind on social presence and interaction, and it was determined that such Web 2.0 tools have positive effects on establishing a connection in the digital environment. This study proceeds in alignment with the studies in the literature and states that the Web 2.0 tools are positive for students' interaction. Finally, the importance of personal information regarding interaction is emphasized. At this point, Kear (2010) stated in his study that getting to know each other and creating personal profiles have a positive effect on online communication and increase social presence. Similarly, Yıldız (2009), in his study on social presence in a Web-based environment, stated that personal information sharing is a positive element for social presence and interaction by creating an affective impact. In this context, there are broadly similar results between this study and the literature, and it can be noted that it is an alignment for most parts. In short, it has been supported by the links between this study and past studies where collaboration and interaction elements are linked to social presence and create positive effects.

Discussion of findings of 3rd Research Question

The participants mentioned trying ways to increase collaboration between students and interaction between the teacher and the students. The necessity of improving collaboration and interaction has been reported in the literature. For example, Lowenthal and Dunlap (2018) found out that teachers could improve their social presence through three techniques. First, the teacher must provide individualized feedback to students. Second, the teacher must organize the lessons so that collaboration among students can take place. Third, the students must easily access the teacher when they need it. These three aspects were reported as important by the students for a positive connection to occur in class. Although the participants reported having difficulty at the beginning of the online education process regarding creating a social presence in class, they tried to overcome these difficulties by using different techniques, such as using breakout rooms to increase interaction. This goes in parallel to Richardson et al., (2010), who suggest that teachers should use activities at the beginning of lessons to increase feelings of trust, including charts or meeting with classmate sessions. The students should be able to respond to each other's discussions. There should also be collaborative group activities such as projects and small group discussions. The participants said that they tried to get to know the students better through personal emails or talking about themselves. Similarly, Tu and Mclsaac (2002) argue for the benefits of building informal and personal relationships with students. They explain that several features may help teachers enhance social presence, such as knowing the students personally, forming informal connections with students, and improving trust.

Our participants expressed that they had attendance issues, such that many students were absent most of the time. They provided several reasons, including internet connection problems, or the availability of the recorded videos. The participants also mentioned the effect of long class hours. Similar problems were reported in the literature. Nambiar (2020) examined the attendance of students during the Covid19 period and found that some students said they had connection problems or lacked the motivation to attend the classes. Another reason for poor attendance reported by Nambiar was that students felt bored during online education. Likewise, Arona and Srinivasan (2020) described that lower rate of attendance, along with less personal relationships in class and a lack of interaction were common problems faced in online classes.

One of the problems surrounding online education is the fast and evolving position of the instructor. (Berge & Collins, 1996; Coppola et al., 2001; Syverson & Slatin, 2010). From a distinct perspective, the roles of the instructors have changed positively and most of the participants in our study reported that they have been taking advantage of this transformation in terms of convenience. According to our results, we found that most of the participants stated that their experience of the online education process is convenient and reported some personal advantages. Besides, participants reported their opinions that the process is time-saving and comfortable when they compare the online education process with face-to-face education. We found that instructors' perceptions of convenience are linked to their personal advantage and satisfaction. In contrast to our findings, Capra (2011), Humphries (2012), Fein and Logan (2003) stated that one of the biggest problems confronting the teachers is their time requirement. Since preparation, organizing and teaching an online class requires some time.

The participants mentioned that technical problems have been occurring and it became a serious concern and disadvantage that affect social presence during the process of online education. Most of the participants reported similar and common opinions on technical problems that they have been going through during the online education process. A similar statement was stated in the literature. Lack of access to computers, greater demands for time, disparities in personal preferences, opposition by students and teachers to new techniques, and absence of support facilities for students and staff and the lack of sufficient curriculum and technological support are general issues for students and teachers. (Furst Bowe, 1996; Galusha, 1997; Morrison & Lauzon, 1992).

Some of the participants stated that camera issues occurred due to the lack of internet connection during the classes. A similar statement was shown in the literature. Communication problems involve the quality of faculty communication with language boundary structures (Limperos et al., 2015; Sherry, 1996; Sundar, 2008). The evolving position of faculty often influences teacher/student contact. Instructors take their hints in a classroom in person through the verbal and nonverbal experiences of students in the classroom (Coppola et al., 2001). These affective hints are impossible to take if the faculty cannot see the faces of its students (Crawley et al., 2009).

Assessment and feedback are among the key parts of any learning process and especially for online education they may present some drawbacks but at the same time, they can offer new learning and teaching techniques (Tallent Runnels et al., 2006; p.103). The findings of this study revealed that language instructors have been experiencing challenges such as cheating and plagiarism and opportunities as improving digital skills about feedback and assessment issues during the online education process. For many instructors, cheating and plagiarism were the most problematic point in terms of assessment. Although there is no study investigating teachers' experiences about assessment in online education to the authors' knowledge, the findings are well-matched with the assumptions from previous studies as Dick et al., (2003) suggested cheating is quite common in education and it is discussed by Rowe (2004) it is hard to determine who is answering the questions at a remote site.

The participants of the study also explained the ways that they try to improve their experiences about feedback and assessment. Some of them utilized online tools, audio feedback, peer feedback, and collaboration. These strategies for better feedback were also found in another study by Liang et al., (2004) where instructors expressed that they use peers as a resource in online classes. Also, the instructors are said to use this feedback challenge as an opportunity for teamwork and collaboration. It is suggested that through online teaching the instructors realized the significance of collaborative learning and peer feedback. In that sense, the findings of the present study and the previous ones are well-matched.

Furthermore, from the perspective of CoI, feedback and assessment issues cannot be placed only in one category. They could be enhanced in terms of cognitive, social and teacher presence. In a recent study conducted by Fiock (2020) there are several suggestions listed about the components of teaching and learning. As cited from the study, using peer evaluations in the form of feedback (Rovai, 2000; Stephens & Roberts, 2017), providing frequent opportunities for testing and feedback (Richardson et al., 2009) for enhancing cognitive presence; using audio-feedbacks (Lowenthal & Dunlap, 2018; Richardson et al., 2009) integrating Web 2.0 tools into feedback process (Peacock & Cowan, 2016; Richardson et al., 2009; Stephens & Roberts, 2017), using peer review for relationship building (Lowenthal & Dunlap, 2018) for enhancing social presence, and providing constructive and timely feedback to students (Watson et al., 2017) for enhancing teaching presence are suggested. It is clearly seen from the findings of the present study that the instructors consciously or unconsciously utilized techniques and strategies that support all three presences in their online teaching experience.

Limitations and Further Studies

Although this study offers some important insights in terms of collaboration with the instructors working in the English Preparatory School and the Community of Inquiry model, there are some limitations of this current study. First, one of the limitations is that it includes limited sample size and settings. Further studies can work with larger samples and multicultural groups. Also, the study data were collected in a relatively short time, and in further studies, more valid and reliable results can be obtained with longitudinal studies over a longer period and a specific treatment process. Lastly, this current study includes only instructors of English Preparatory School. A comparative study can be done by including the English Preparatory School students in future studies for a better insight into the Community of Inquiry model and online education experience.

Conclusion

The present study was conducted through the perspective of CoI Framework (Garrison et al., 2000). Although the study had several dimensions, the instructors' perceptions on their own social, cognitive, and teaching presence level indicated that even the online education had severe effects at the beginning, one of the most important stakeholders have now progressed more, especially in terms of CoI. The study also served as a self-reflection in which the instructors evaluated their own online teaching process, and the teaching presence subcategory was the highest among all implying that they perceive themselves as highly present or struggling to be during online education. Also, the English instructors now have sufficient self-confidence about their own teaching. As the results of the present study showed that in terms of CoI, the instructors' perceptions are relatively positive, their voices also revealed that this specific process cannot be considered without its drawbacks. The instructors commonly had to deal with assessment & feedback issues, technological/technical problems, less social interaction with students. What is implied from their voices is that many problems that were experienced seemed common and even without getting any help, the instructors found similar solutions to those problems. High perception levels in CoI, voices from the instructors and common issues that arose from the study about online education have several implications for further studies to explore more about the sub-themes obtained from the findings and their relations to other variables.

References

Akyol, Z., & Garrison, D. R. (2009). Community of Inquiry in Adult Online Learning: Collaborative-Constructivist Approaches. In T. T. Kidd (Ed.), *Adult Learning in the Digital Age: Perspectives on Online Technologies and Outcomes* (pp. 52-66). Hershey, PA: IGI Global.

Akyol, Z., & Garrison, D. R. (2011b). Assessing Metacognition in an Online Community of Inquiry. *Internet and Higher Education, 14*(3), 183-190.

Akyol, Z., Garrison, D. R., & Ozden, M. Y. (2009). Online and Blended Communities of Inquiry: Exploring the developmental and perceptual differences. *International Review of Research in Open and Distance Learning, 10*(6), 65-83.

An, H., Kim, S., & Kim, B. (2008). Teacher perspectives on online collaborative learning: Factors perceived as facilitating and impeding successful online group work. *Contemporary Issues in Technology and Teacher Education, 8*(1), 65-83.

Aragon, S. R. (2003). Creating social presence in online environments. *New Directions for Adult and Continuing Education, 2003*(100), 57-68.

Arbaugh, J. B., Cleveland-Innes, M., Diaz, S. R., Garrison, D. R., Ice, P., Richardson, & Swan, K. P. (2008). Developing a community of inquiry instrument: Testing a measure of the Community of Inquiry framework using a multi-institutional sample. *The Internet and higher Education, 11*(3-4), 133-136.

Arora, A. K., & Srinivasan, R. (2020). Impact of pandemic COVID-19 on the teaching–learning process: A study of higher education teachers. *Prabandhan: Indian journal of management, 13*(4), 43-56.

Berge, Z. L., & Collins, M. (1996). *Facilitating interaction in computer mediated online courses.* Background paper presented at the FSU/AECT Distance education conference, Tallahassee, FL.

Bruffee, K. A. (1984). Collaborative learning and the "conversation of mankind". *College English, 46*(7), 635-652.

Capra, T. (2011). Online education: Promise and problems. *Merlot Journal of Online Learning and Teaching, 7*, 288–293.

Coppola, N. W., Hiltz, S. R., & Rotter, N. (2001). Becoming a virtual professor: Pedagogical roles and ALN. *Proceedings of the 34th Annual Hawaii International Conference.* System Sciences, 2001.

Creswell, J. W. (2009). *Research design: Qualitative, quantitative, and mixed methods approaches* (3rd ed.). Sage Publications, Inc.

Cunningham, J. M. (2015). Mechanizing people and pedagogy: Establishing social presence in the online classroom. *Online Learning, 19*(3), 34-47.

Darabi, A., Arrastia, M. C., Nelson, D. W., Cornille, T., & Liang, X. (2011). Cognitive presence in asynchronous online learning: A comparison of four discussion strategies. *Journal of Computer Assisted Learning, 27*(3), 216-227.

Demuyakor, J. (2020). Coronavirus (COVID-19) and online learning in higher institutions of education: A survey of the perceptions of Ghanaian international students in China. *Online Journal of Communication and Media Technologies, 10*(3), e202018.

Dewey, J. (1959). My pedagogic creed. In J. Dewey (Ed.), *Dewey on Education* (pp. 19-32). New York: Teachers College, Columbia University. (Original work published 1897)

Dick, M., Sheard, J., Bareiss, C., Carter, J., Joyce, D., Harding, T., & Laxer, C. (2002). Addressing student cheating: definitions and solutions. *ACM SigCSE Bulletin, 35*(2), 172-184.

Dillenbourg, P. (1999). *What do you mean by collaborative learning?*

Faja, S. (2013). Collaborative learning in online courses: Exploring students' perceptions. *Information Systems Education Journal, 11*(3), 42.

Fein, A. D., & Logan, M. C. (2003). Preparing instructors for online instruction. *New Directions for Adult and Continuing Education, 100*, 45–55.

Fiock, H. (2020). Designing a community of inquiry in online courses. *The International Review of Research in Open and Distributed Learning, 21*(1), 135-153.

Gaillet, L. L. (1994). An historical perspective on collaborative learning. *Journal of Advanced Composition*, 93-110.

Galusha, J. M. (1997). Barriers to Learning in Distance Education. *Interpersonal Computing and Technology Journal, 5*(3), 6-14. Retrieved January 30, 2021 from https://www.learntechlib.org/p/85240/

Garrison, D. R. (2003). Cognitive presence for effective asynchronous online learning: The role of reflective inquiry, self-direction and metacognition. *Elements of Quality Online Education: Practice and Direction, 4*(1), 47-58.

Garrison, D. R. (2011). *E-Learning in the 21st Century: A Framework for Research and Practice* (2nd ed.). London: Routledge/Taylor and Francis.

Garrison, D. R., & Arbaugh, J. B. (2007). Researching the community of inquiry framework: Review, issues, and future directions. *Internet and Higher Education, 10*(3), 157-172.

Garrison, D. R., & Kanuka, H. (2004). Blended learning: Uncovering its transformative potential in higher education. *The Internet and Higher Education, 7*(2), 95-105.

Garrison, D. R., Anderson, T., & Archer, W. (2000). Critical inquiry in a text-based environment: Computer conferencing in higher education model. *The Internet and Higher Education, 2*(2-3), 87-105.

Garrison, D. R., Anderson, T., & Archer, W. (2001). Critical thinking, cognitive presence, and computer conferencing in distance education. *American Journal of Distance Education, 15*(1), 7-23.

Harasim, L. (2012). *Learning Theory and Online Technologies.* New York/London: Routledge.

Hiltz, S. R., & Turoff, M. (1993). *The network nation: Human communication via computer.* MIT Press.

Holbeck, R., & Hartman, J. (2018). Efficient strategies for maximizing online student satisfaction: Applying technologies to increase cognitive presence, social Presence, and teaching Presence. *Journal of Educators Online, 15*(3), n3.

Humphries, S. (2010). Five challenges for new online teachers. *Journal of Technology Integration, 2*, 15-24.

Järvelä, S., & Rosé, C. P. (2020). Advocating for group interaction in the age of COVID-19. *International Journal of Computer-Supported Collaborative Learning, 15*(2), 143-147.

Jonassen, D., Davidson, M., Collins, M., Campbell, J., & Haag, B. B. (1995). Constructivism and computer-mediated communication in distance education. *American Journal of Distance Education, 9*(2), 7-26. https://doi.org/10.1080/08923649509526885

Jung, I., Kudo, M., & Choi, S. K. (2012). Stress in Japanese learners engaged in online collaborative learning in English. *BJET – British Journal of Educational Technology, 43*(6), 1016-1029. https://doi.org/10.1111/j.1467-8535.2011.01271.x

Kirschner, P. A., Martens, R. L., & Strijbos, J. W. (2004). CSCL in higher education? In J. W. Strijbos, P. A. Kirschner & R. L. Martens (Eds.), *What we know about CSCL* (pp. 3-30). Springer, Dordrecht.

Klemm, W. R., & Snell, J. R. (1996, March). *Integrating the World Wide Web and Non-Web Information in Computer Conferences.* Paper presented at the 13th International Conference on Technology and Education. Proceedings. Louisiana. USA.

Knudsen, K. K. (2019). *Applying the Community of Inquiry Framework in Instructional Technology Blended Professional Development* (Doctoral dissertation). Widener University.

Kumi-Yeboah, A., Yuan, G., & Dogbey, J. (2017). Online collaborative learning activities: The perceptions of culturally diverse graduate students. *Online Learning, 21*(4), 5-28.

Kupczynski, L., Ice, P., Wiesenmayer, R., & McCluskey, F. (2010). Student perceptions of the relationship between indicators of teaching presence and success in online courses. *Journal of Interactive Online Learning, 9*(1).

Laal, M., & Ghodsi, S. M. (2012). Benefits of collaborative learning. *Procedia-Social and Behavioral Sciences, 31*, 486-490.

Leh, A. S. (2001). Computer-mediated communication and social presence in a distance learning environment. *International Journal of Educational Telecommunications, 7*(2), 109-128.

Liang, X., & Creasy, K. (2004). Classroom assessment in web-based instructional environment: Instructors' experience. *Practical Assessment, Research, and Evaluation, 9*(1), 7.

Liman Kaban, A. (2021). YAITS: The Design and Development of a Personalized E-Book Platform for EFL Learners. In Giannikas, C. N. (Ed.), *Teaching Practices and Equitable Learning in Children's Language Education* (pp. 171-190). IGI Global. http://doi:10.4018/978-1-7998-6487-5.ch009

Lipman, M. (1991). *Thinking in Education.* Cambridge: Cambridge University Press.

Lipman, M. (2003). *Thinking in Education* (2nd ed.). Cambridge: Cambridge University Press.

Lowenthal, P., & Dunlap, J. (2018). Investigating students' perceptions of instructional strategies to establish social presence. *Distance Education, 39*(3), 281-298. https://doi.org/10.1080/01587919.2018.1476844

Makri, K., Papanikolaou, K., Tsakiri, A., & Karkanis, S. (2014). Blending the Community of Inquiry Framework with Learning by Design: Towards a Synthesis for Blended Learning in Teacher Training. *Electronic Journal of e-Learning, 12*(2), 183-194.

Miles, M. B., & Huberman, A. M. (1994). *Qualitative data analysis: An expanded sourcebook.*

Morse, J. M. (1991). Approaches to Qualitative-Quantitative Methodological Triangulation. *Nursing Research, 40*(2). Retrieved from https://journals.lww.com/nursingresearchonline/Fulltext/1991/03000/Approaches_to_Qualitative_Quantitative.14.aspx

Nambiar, D. (2020). The impact of online learning during COVID-19: students' and teachers' perspective. *The International Journal of Indian Psychology, 8*(2), 783-793.

Paechter, M., Maier, B., & Macher, D. (2010). Students' expectations of, and experiences in e-learning: Their relation to learning achievements and course satisfaction. *Computers and Education, 54*(1), 222-229.

Palloff, R. M. & Pratt, K. (2007). *Building online learning communities: Effective Strategies for the Virtual Classroom* (2nd ed.). San Francisco: Jossey-Bass.

Panitz, T. (1999). *Collaborative versus Cooperative Learning: A Comparison of the Two Concepts Which Will Help Us Understand the Underlying Nature of Interactive Learning.*

Rafaeli, S. (1988). From new media to communication. *Sage Annual Review of Communication Research: Advancing Communication Science, 16*, 110-134.

Richardson, J. C., & Swan, K. (2003). Examining social presence in online courses in relation to students' perceived learning and satisfaction. *Journal of Asynchronous Learning Networks, 7*(1), 68-88.

Richardson, J. C., Ice, P., & Swan, K. (2009). *Tips and techniques for integrating social, teaching, & cognitive presence into your courses.* Poster session presented at the Conference on Distance Teaching & Learning, Madison, WI.

Richardson, J. C., Arbaugh, J. C. Cleveland-Innes, M., Ice, P., Swan, K., & Garrison, D. R. (2010). *Using the community of inquiry framework to inform effective instructional design.* Paper presented at the 2010 AECT Research Symposium: Bloomington, IN, 2010. https://doi.org/10.1007/978-1-4614-1785-9_

Rourke, L., Anderson, T., Garrison, D. R., & Archer, W. (1999). Assessing social presence in asynchronous text-based computer conferencing. *The Journal of Distance Education/Revue de l'ducation Distance, 14*(2), 50-71.

Rovai, A. P. (2000). Building and sustaining community in asynchronous learning networks. *Internet and Higher Education, 3*, 285–297. https://doi.org/10.1016/S1096-7516(01)00037-9

Rowe, N. C. (2004). Cheating in online student assessment: Beyond plagiarism. *Online Journal of Distance Learning Administration, 7*(2).

Sansone, N., Cesareni, D., Bortolotti, I., & Buglass, S. (2019). Teaching technology-mediated collaborative learning for trainee teachers. *Technology, Pedagogy and Education, 28*(3), 381-394.

Short, J., Williams, E., & Christie, B. (1976). *The social psychology of telecommunications.* John Wiley & Sons.

Smith, B. L., & MacGregor, J. T. (1992). *What is collaborative learning.*

So, H. J., & Brush, T. A. (2008). Student perceptions of collaborative learning, social presence and satisfaction in a blended learning environment: Relationships and critical factors. *Computers & Education, 51*(1), 318-336.

Stephens, G. E., & Roberts, K. L. (2017). Facilitating collaboration in online groups. *Journal of Educators Online, 14*(1), 1-16. Retrieved from https://eric.ed.gov/?id=EJ1133614

Svenning, L., & Ruchinskas, J. (1984). Organizational teleconferencing. In R. Rice (Ed.), *The new media: Communication, research, and technology* (pp. 217-248). Beverly Hills, CA: Sage.

Syverson, M. A., & Slatin, J. (2010). Evaluating learning in virtual environment. Retrieved from http://www.learningrecord.org/caeti.html

Tallent-Runnels, M. K., Thomas, J. A., Lan, W. Y., Cooper, S., Ahern, T. C., Shaw, S. M., & Liu, X. (2006). Teaching courses online: A review of the research. *Review of Educational Research, 76*(1), 93-135

Tu, C. H. (2000). On-line learning migration: from social learning theory to social presence theory in a CMC environment. *Journal of Network and Computer Applications, 23*(1), 27-37.

Tu, C-H., & McIsaac, M. (2002). The Relationship of Social Presence and Interaction in Online Classes. *The American Journal of Distance Education, 16*(3), 131-150. doi:10.1207/S15389286AJDE1603_2

Vaughan, N., & Garrison, D. R. (2005). Creating cognitive presence in a blended faculty development community. *The Internet and Higher Education, 8*(1), 1-12.

Walther, J. B. (1997). Group and interpersonal effects in international computer-mediated collaboration. *Human Communication Research, 23*(3), 342-369.

Walther, J. B., & Burgoon, J. K. (1992). Relational communication in computer-mediated interaction. *Human Communication Research, 19*(1), 50-88.

Watson, F. F., Bishop, M. C., & Ferdinand-James, D. (2017). Instructional strategies to help online students learn: Feedback from online students. *TechTrends, 61*, 420-427. https://doi.org/10.1007/s11528-017-0216-y

Waugh, M. L., & Su, J. (2016). Student perceptions of a successful online collaborative learning community. *Journal of Interactive Online Learning, 14*(1).

Whiteman, J. A. M. (2002). *Interpersonal Communication in Computer Mediated Learning.*

Yamada, M., & Goda, Y. (2018, March). The Effects of Social Presence Visualization based on a Community of Inquiry Framework. *Proceedings of the Society for Information Technology & Teacher Education International Conference*, 1014-1019. Association for the Advancement of Computing in Education (AACE).

Yoon, S. W. (2003). In search of meaningful online learning experiences. *New Directions for Adult and Continuing Education, 2003*(100), 19-30.

AUTHOR INDEX